Historical Thinking in South Asia
A Handbook of Sources from Colonial Times to the Present

Historical Thinking in South Asia

A Handbook of Sources from Colonial Times to the Present

Edited by
MICHAEL GOTTLOB

OXFORD
UNIVERSITY PRESS

OXFORD
UNIVERSITY PRESS

YMCA Library Building, Jai Singh Road, New Delhi 110 001

Oxford University Press is a department of the University of Oxford. It furthers the
University's objective of excellence in research, scholarship, and education
by publishing worldwide in

Oxford   New York

Auckland   Cape Town   Dar es Salaam   Hong Kong   Karachi   Kuala Lumpur
Madrid   Melbourne   Mexico City   Nairobi   New Delhi   Shanghai   Taipei   Toronto

With offices in
Argentina   Austria   Brazil   Chile   Czech Republic   France   Greece   Guatemala
Hungary   Italy   Japan   South Korea   Poland   Portugal   Singapore   Switzerland
Thailand   Turkey   Ukraine   Vietnam

Published in India by Oxford University Press, New Delhi

First published in 2003
Second Impression 2005

ISBN 019 566217 2

Typeset in Goudy 10.5/13
By Eleven Arts, Delhi 110 035
Printed in India by Roopak Printers, Delhi 110 032
Published by Manzar Khan, Oxford University Press
YMCA Library Building, Jai Singh Road, New Delhi 110 001

To Bianca
and
the friends at Dharwad

Contents

Preface

The glance across borders and the interest in comparison have become a matter of course in the age of globalization. This regards historical thinking as much as other phenomena of the political and social world. The fact that, along with the increasing contacts between states and societies, economic systems and cultures, and their progressive interdependence, the question about the peculiar ways of dealing with the past is raised, seems to require no specific explanation.

However, the interest in difference is inextricably interwoven with the interest in history itself. Not only in the sense that the present situation can be seen as a result of historical processes. The issues of cultural diversity and temporal change are interrelated in a fundamental way, both follow from the changeability and mouldability of human living conditions. Therefore, cultural comparison always includes a reflection on the foundations of history. And this is particularly the case if the subject of comparison is historical thinking itself.

Historical thinking was drawn to comparison from the very beginning. From time immemorial, collective subject agents, when trying to reassure themselves of their identity and continuity through memory, have had to cope with the phenomenon of difference: with the otherness of neighbouring societies, peoples and cultures as much as that of their own past. The internal structures of communication are affected by the contacts with the external world. By relating the actions of one's own people to those of other peoples, the early historiographers discovered the fundamental contingency of events. When Herodotus described the Greek confrontation with the Persians, he had to deal with facts and occurrences beyond the common sense horizon. And when he depicted the way of life of the Scythians, Egyptians, etc., it served the Greeks as a mirror of their own historically formed particularity.

In a new and profound way, western historiography has been drawn into comparison and confrontation with the Other since the age of European discoveries and expansions when contacts and mutual influences became frequent and durable, even between those societies and cultures which hitherto had existed in relative isolation. The increasing experience of contingency created a new quest for orientation and this contributed indirectly to the emergence of the modern concept of history with its basic assumptions of a universal nexus of causation and development. With the integration of the many histories into the master narrative of civilizational evolution, led to perfection by Europe, the Alien was included in the western horizon of interpretation. But only partially. What was not understood (or not accepted) remained all the more banned from it. What constituted the historicity of the Other, the openness and peculiarity of his development, was largely neglected by western historiography. A tendency towards singularization of history becomes apparent here which is in a tense relationship with the idea of a multiplicity of developments.

It was in this (practical and theoretical) context that the West came into close contact with the South Asian cultures and made these a preferred subject of its comparative study of civilizations. The stagnant character of Hindu society lent itself to demonstrating the historical dynamic of Europe. The Indians' apparent neglect of the past (also noticed by the Chinese and Muslims) was attributed to a fundamental ahistoricity of their culture. On this basis, colonial rule could be even legitimized as a mission of historicization. The South Asians, for their part, were confronted in a drastic way with the nexus between self-assertion and the capability for social change in the encounter with the West. Under the impression of the new historical dynamic the traditional modes of dealing with contingency were called into question and Indians became increasingly receptive, even though with some hesitation, to western forms of historical interpretation. The manifold attempts to retain one's equilibrium between the upholding of tradition and the urge to modernize are reflected in the texts of this volume.

Seen from the perspective of colonized South Asia, the experience of the Other which in the West contributes to the modernization of historical thinking, appears in a quite different light. What is expansion for the West, means limitation to the East, what for Europeans is a confirmation of their innovative powers, is experienced as a weakening of tradition in South Asia. If on the one side the confrontation and comparison of cultures illustrates civilizational progress, on the other it demonstrates one's own backwardness. While in the consciousness of modern Europe Self is developing through temporal change, in South Asia, so it appears to many, Self can be retained only in the assertion against change. Even those among Indian reformers, who regarded the adoption of western patterns of thought as a condition of political survival and as providing a chance for improvement, remained sceptical as to whether sovereignty is possible over processes of change which meant the connection to a dynamic originating externally. How can the insight into the processual character of society be reconciled with the claim to autonomy and self-assertion in the context of western-dominated history? This is a central issue in the modernization of historical thinking in colonial South Asia. The experience of alienation furthers essentializing strategies (the construction of origin of myths, forms of inclusivism, etc.), getting in the way of a self-confident referring to the Other and a constructive attitude to one's own changeability.

The impression of being exposed to processes steered from outside is confirmed by the form of their conceptualization in western historiography. In western theorizing about history, the specific experience of non-Europeans played hardly any role for a long time. History was an affair of the advanced peoples in which others participated, if at all, only in a peripheral or subordinate position. And even if the interest in non-European actors is increasing today, they are not yet fully recognized as equally competent interpreters of global historical processes. There is a fundamental asymmetry between the participants in the global discourse on history. While for the non-Europeans European history is always present as a point of reference, the western discipline has hardly taken notice of non-western perspectives on the world. A fixation on alien actors and interpreters on the one side corresponds to a disregard for others and their history on the opposite side.

This raises queries about the meaning of alterity and multiplicity in modern historical thinking. Does it necessarily follow from the integration of the many histories into a single world history that it banishes those cultural differences the experience of which once contributed to the idea of universal evolution? Does modern history itself embody a tendency to reduce the multiplicity of perspectives?

The issue regards inner alternatives, relating to the evolution of one's own society, as much as outer ones. The vanishing of the Old and the Habitual is part of the production of the New and the realization of the Possible. The modern historical discourse, interested in change for its own sake, is the place where in the light of past experience options for the future become visible. Here, too, the question about forms of alienation and mechanisms of colonization has to be asked, the question whether in the process of deciding about alternatives new forms of determinism might take effect which restrict the capacity for understanding and negotiating. The certainty regarding the new potential which is offered today by almost unlimited information (as also intercultural contacts and comparisons) is confronted with the uncertainty about whether openness and multiplicity will be augmented or reduced in the end. The optimization of social evolution and the diversity of options are in a relationship of tension.

Given the narrowing down of the many histories towards a single global history, the doubts about the openness of developments have gained increasing urgency and constitute a major challenge to historical thinking. Historical thinking anywhere in the world is caught between diverse pasts and a common future which is all too easily identified with that of western civilization or its dominant practices and technologies. Not only non-European societies like those of South Asia, even the West itself with its inclination towards accelerating development, is faced with the question about the possibilities to articulate alternatives and the chances to realize them. If the experience of multiplicity was a condition for the discovery of history as a process of evolution, today, in the non-Europeans's struggle for a self-determined dealing with temporal change, the very foundation of historical reflection is put up for discussion.

Acknowledgements

The collection of sources presented here was first published as part of a German project on historical thinking in intercultural comparison (8 vols, Frankfurt/M.: Humanities Online, 2002) initiated and supported by Jörn Rüsen. The discussions of the research group 'Making Sense of History' organized by Rüsen at the Centre for Interdisciplinary Research in Bielefeld (1994–5) established an ideal framework for drawing up a general catalogue of questions on historical thinking in different cultures. The talks with Achim Mittag, who was working on historical thinking in China at the time, were also conducive to the production of ideas and systematization of the material.

For useful suggestions and information, I would like to thank R. A. Abou-El Haj, George Berkemer, Stephan Conermann, Vasudha Dalmia, Tilman Frasch, Ferdinand Geister, Herbert Herring, Lila Hüttemann, Fritz Kramer, Barbara and Rainer Lotz, Jürgen Lütt, Jamal Malik, Klaus E. Müller, Dietmar Rothermund, Maria Schetelich, Anna Schmid, and Christiane Schnellenbach. In India, I had occasion to talk to Neeladri Bhattacharya, Ashis Nandy, K. Raghavendra Rao, Suresh Sharma, D. L. Sheth, and Romila Thapar. Most of all, I am indebted to B. D. Chattopadhyaya, who was generous with his time and his knowledge and who showed a continuous interest in the progress of the work. To Annakutty Findeis and Mariam Dossal I owe the opportunity of presenting parts of my findings at the University of Mumbai. In Dharwad, I found support with K. R. Basavaraja, R. Bhat, S. Ritti, A. Sundara, and C. Veerabasanna. Arya Acharya has been a constant source of encouragement. I would like to thank him for the many conversations and his generous friendship.

The librarians in Dharwad (Karnatak University), New Delhi (Nehru Museum and Library), London (School of Oriental and African Studies, India Office Library), Bielefeld (Universitätsbibliothek), Heidelberg (Südasien-Institut), and Berlin (Staatsbibliothek, Zentrum Moderner Orient) are also remembered with gratitude for their assistance.

I am grateful to Nalini Adinarayanan and Robert Leitch for their help in preparing the English manuscript. My thanks for their care over the production and editing of the book go to the editors at Oxford University Press.

Finally, I would like to thank the German Academic Exchange Service (DAAD) for a fellowship offered to me after the end of my work as Visiting Lecturer at Karnatak University Dharwad and the Centre for Interdisciplinary Research (ZiF) in Bielefeld for accepting me as a Research Fellow.

The volume is dedicated to my wife, Bianca, and the friends at Dharwad who, during the five years of our stay (1989–94), included us in their midst and made us participate in the reciprocal reference of cultures by which life in India is so much distinguished.

For permission to reproduce individual extracts, I would like to thank:

Peter J. Marshall and Cambridge University Press, Cambridge, for Jones, 'On the Hindus';

Advaita Ashrama, Calcutta, for Vivekananda, 'Modern India';

Sahitya Samsad, Calcutta, for Chatterjee, 'A Few Words About the History of Bengal';

Verinder Grover and Deep & Deep Publications, New Delhi, for Tilak, 'Karma Yoga and Swaraj';

B. R. Publishing Corporation, New Delhi for Majumdar, 'Ancient Indian Colonization in the Far East'; Devahuti, 'Problems of Indian Historiography';

Oxford University Press, New Delhi, for M. N. Roy, 'India in Transition'; Nilakanta Sastri, 'History of South India'; Nandy, 'Towards a Third World Utopia'; Ranajit Guha, 'On Some Aspects of the Historiography of Colonial India'; Gadgil and Ramachandra Guha, 'Cultures in Conflict';

Jawaharlal Nehru Memorial Fund, New Delhi, for Nehru, 'India's Growth Arrested';

Rupa & Co., Calcutta, for Tagore, 'Nationalism in India';

Sri Aurobindo Ashram, Pondicherry, for Aurobindo, 'The Advent and Progress of the Spiritual Age';

Sagar Publications, New Delhi, for Coomaraswamy, 'What has India Contributed to Human Welfare?';

HarperCollins Publishers, London, for Panikkar, 'Asia and Western Dominance';

Academy of Islamic Research and Publications, Lucknow, for Nadwi, 'India During Muslim Rule';

The Islamic Foundation, Markfield, Leicestershire, UK, for Qureshi, 'Lost Opportunities';

Vikas Publishing House, New Delhi, for Kosambi, 'The Difficulties Facing the Historian';

Embassy of the Federal Republic of Germany, New Delhi, for Verma, 'The Past: A Self-Contemplation';

as well as Romila Thapar, M. N. Srinivas, R. S. Sharma, S. Gopal, Nirmal Verma, Ashis Nandy, Uma Chakravarti, Ranajit Guha, Madhav Gadgil, and Ramachandra Guha for giving their consent.

The texts by Sayyid Ahmad Khan, Shibli Nu'mani, M. Iqbal, A.H. Ali Nadwi, and I.H. Qureshi have been selected and introduced by Jamal Malik.

Introduction

1. India and Europe: Forms of Approaching and Distancing in the Historicized World

Among the problematic legacies of colonial historical writing in and on South Asia are the patterns of periodization. A paradigm for this was James Mill's *History of British India* (1817) with its division of Indian history into a Hindu, an Islamic, and a British era. The convention of linking the major breaks in the Indian evolution with the influence of alien cultures has found its way even into the history of historical thinking. More than 'medieval' historical writing, with its coexistence of Hindu traditions and Muslim views of the past, it is the modern discourse of history in South Asia which is regarded as an import.[1]

Apart from pragmatical aspects (like that of setting the limits of a selection of sources), historical periodizations also include general assumptions about the significance and meaning of the developments which are reconstructed. And in the case of India even the far-reaching political consequences are visible. Mill's classification of Indian history has influenced the collective self-understanding of Hindus and Muslims, anticipating, in a way, the two-nation theory of the 1940s. However, the differentiation of 'Ancient', 'Medieval', and 'Modern India' that is predominant today is also based on a European model, and the same applies to the tradition–modernity dichotomy. Finally, even the classification into 'colonial', 'pre-colonial', and 'post-colonial' India does not provide any escape from the problem that the country's history is viewed from an external perspective.[2]

[1]For the question of the overlapping of Sanskrit tradition and Islamic historiography, see the concluding remarks in Romila Thapar's essay, 'The Search for a Historical Tradition: Early India' (Rüsen et al. forthcoming).

[2]For the nexus of periodization and identity formation in nineteenth-century India, see Brajadulal

The western forms of periodization have been largely assimilated by the Indian discipline of history as its own, and this makes them a part of historical thinking in India.[3] The Indian historical discipline, in its self-assessment, openly confesses to being rooted in the western intellectual tradition, a confession which is keeping alive certain doubts about its legitimacy. When speaking about the western impact on historical thinking in India, one has to distinguish between different levels, however. First is the experience of being challenged by a foreign reality, which always and everywhere stimulates historical reflection by creating a need for clarity about one's own identity. Second is the specific confrontation of (western) modernity with (Indian) tradition, which creates among Indians, a need for new forms of conceiving continuity and change. Finally, the modern discourse of history suggests a nexus between historical memory and purposeful action, which, after some time, begins to be regarded by some Indians as the key to regaining lost agency.

The 'historicization' of thinking can be generally described as a process in which the experience of change came to occupy a pivotal place in the cultural orientation of man, and the study of these changes (a study that combined theoretical reflection with empirical research), was established as a means of exerting an influence on the course of events (Küttler et al. 1997: 11).[4] This process began in European historiography from the late eighteenth century, that is, at the same time when western efforts to investigate the culture and society of India intensified. It was against the background of the recent innovations in the historical discipline of the West that the Indian way of dealing with the past appeared, more than ever, to be deficient. The early history of the country was especially shrouded in mystery; India seemed to have 'lapsed into a sort of amnesia about its ancient past (Kejariwal 1988: 221)'. Histories of modern Indian historiography often begin with statements like: 'Historiography was practically unknown to the Hindus at the beginning of the nineteenth century (Majumdar 1991: 7).'[5]

The pioneers of Indian historical research, notwithstanding their criticism of the ancestors' neglect of the past, had not denied Indians a sense of history altogether. According to Rajendralal Mitra, neither Ganesh (the god of knowledge) nor Sarasvati (the goddess of learning) have encouraged historical studies. 'Indian literature is almost void of all authentic historical records.' India's 'heroes and their mighty exploits, her greatness and her early civilization, where they live, live but in a song' (Mitra 1875: 1). And Ramkrishna Gopal Bhandarkar acknowledged: 'India has no written history'; but he also added: 'The historical curiosity of the people was satisfied by legends' (Bhandarkar 1985: 1). The old ways of recording the past, however, were increasingly left out of consideration. Pre-colonial texts were used as sources, but were not seen as

---

Chattopadhyaya 1998: 13ff. The dominance of the tradition–modernity dichotomy is criticized by Sumit Sarkar, 'Rammohun Roy and the Break with the Past', in Joshi, 1975: 46–68, here 47. For the difficult search for alternatives, see the remarks in Richard M. Eaton, '(Re)imag(in)ing Other[2]ness: A Postmortem for the Postmodern in India', Journal of World History 11 (2000), 57–78, here 69–70.

[3]For recent accounts of the history of Indian historiography, see Michael Gottlob, 'Writing the History of Modern Indian Historiography: A Review Article', Storia della Storiografia 27 (1995), 125–46.

[4]Cf. This does not mean, however, that there was no historical thinking before or outside this process.

[5]See also Romesh Chandra Majumdar, 'Nationalist Historians', in Philips 1961: 416–28, here 416.

documents of historical thinking.[6] Thus was consolidated the idea of a total affiliation of the Indian historical discipline to the European: 'We had to start from scratch.'[7]

This seems to reinforce the suspicion about the discourse of history on the part of those post-colonial critics who view it mainly or exclusively as a constituent of colonization (and not only as an alien way of thinking but also as an alienating one).[8] The western stereotype of an ahistorical India is given a positive meaning here and defended as an element of one's own particularity. However, the sweeping rejection of historical thinking in the name of a recovery of Self not only clouds the view of the inner controversies about continuity and change within Indian society, it also fails to appreciate its inherent potential as a critique of colonialism.[9] Among the strategies of colonization were also forms of dehistoricization. If the colonizers legitimized their interference in Indian reality by the device of historicizing the non-historical, they were engaged, at the same time, in obstructing the promised control over temporal change (Chatterjee 1993: 10). While the Indians were included in the new historical dynamic, they were increasingly deprived of their power to decide about their own way of life. Under these circumstances, the striving for regaining historical agency became a central component in the struggle for autonomy. The fact that colonial thinking imposed itself on that of the colonized, is a problem that must not be underestimated. But it is worth considering whether or not a discipline of history which reflects on its involvement in the process of colonization and takes seriously the experience of the victims may contribute to resisting the present tendencies of neo-colonialism.

1.1 The Western Construction of the Ahistorical Orient

The necessary critique of the role of history in the process of colonization should not mean that, in the confrontation of cultures, modes of thinking and ways of life, and their inner changeableness and malleability are overlooked. Such oversight could itself be a consequence of the colonial situation. The development of cultures is closely associated with the experience of the Other; both are interrelated. The conditions of colonial dependence, being an extreme form of the experience of otherness, have had a special impact on the interpretation of change, among the colonizers as well as the colonized. Before looking at the innovations of Indian

---

[6]Cf. Sumit Sarkar, 'Many Worlds: The Construction of History in Modern India', *Storia della storiografia* 19 (1991), 61–72, here 61. Of course, this can also be seen as an effect of the Anglicizing educational system, which contributed to the very impression of a *tabula rasa* as much as it interrupted older traditions: 'With the rapid disappearance of knowledge of Persian, our Westernized intelligentsia became entirely dependent on it for knowledge of their immediate past.' Sarkar, 'Rammohun Roy and the Break with the Past' (Joshi 1975: 59).

[7]Bimala Prosad Mukherji, 'History', in Gupta 1958: 360–85, here 361. It is only in more recent accounts that the forms of negotiation between traditional-Indian and modern-western modes in nineteenth century historiography are made visible. For details, see below.

[8]See, for instance, Nandy 1983. For the embedding of affirmative and denouncing attitudes to colonialism in the 'impact-response frameworks', see Sarkar 1998: 188.

[9]For the share of modern consciousness in the Indian resistance against foreign rule, see Suresh Sharma, 'Raja Rammohan Roy: The Inaugurator of the Modern Age', in Alok Bhalla and Sudhir Chandra 1993: 93–111, here 95.

historical thinking under the impression of western presence, one should briefly consider how, in the West itself, the encounter with alien cultures and the emergence of modern historical thinking were interlocked.

With the European discoveries and conquests, the notions of Self and Other, and of space and time, gradually changed. For a long period, tidings about the fabulous and rich Orient had remained a source of uncertainty to European self-confidence. As late as the seventeenth and eighteenth centuries, reports about the antiquity of Chinese culture relativized the belief in the outstanding importance of the Jewish-Christian tradition (Schulin 1958: 139). European expansion and the decline of the oriental powers diminished the threat associated with the Other; and the feeling of political supremacy also increased European confidence in their own intellectual capacities. If western science was confronted with unknown problems, the mastering of them confirmed its universal validity.[10] Simultaneously, the gradual opening up of the entire globe contributed to the historicization of thinking. If the unknown hitherto had often been linked with utopian expectations, now, after reaching the extreme spacial boundaries, the idea of transcending given horizons was temporalized, and utopia became associated with the future. It was only now that the notion of a linear, irreversible and global process of evolution became dominant in western thinking. The new conceptualization of time had its repercussions on the understanding of cultures distributed in space. Alien cultures could now be associated with the past and viewed as an earlier stage of universal evolution spearheaded by the progressive societies of Europe. The journey to distant lands then was, from the European perspective, also a journey into their own history. The stability and continuity of China, which had once been the object of admiration, were now criticized as stagnation.

In Voltaire (1694–1778), both tendencies are tangible: the universalization of the historical interest and the relating of the Other to the western perspectives of development. He replaced the Christian interpretation of history and its orientation towards spiritual salvation (*Heilsgeschichte*) with the idea of a universal process of civilization in which the Chinese and Indian cultures were recognized as equally important, even if their historical testimonies were not compatible with certain statements in the Bible.[11] History was conceived in a new manner as world history. According to Voltaire, the Indians were the oldest people, and their country was the cradle of civilization.[12] Measured by the progress of the West, however, it could not be

[10]Thanks to the regular working of the natural laws, the causal nexus of things could be studied anywhere: 'I have always thought with you that we possess at this time very great advantages towards the knowledge of human Nature. We need no longer go to History to trace it in all its stages and periods. History, from its comparative youth, is but a poor instructour .... But now the Great Map of Mankind is unrolled at once; and there is no state or Gradation of barbarism, and no mode of refinement which we have not at the same instant under our View. The very different Civility of Europe and of China; The barbarism of Tartary, and of Arabia. The Savage State of North America, and of New Zealand.' Edmund *Burke to William Robertson*, 9 June, 1777, in *The Correspondence of Edmund Burke*, III, ed. George H. Guttridge (Cambridge 1961), 350.

[11]Even in the English *Universal History from the earliest account of time to the present* (London 1736–65), the rivalry between Far Eastern and biblical peoples was visible. Cf. Grewal 1975: 4.

[12]Voltaire, however, in a strikingly uncritical manner, followed the statements of Hindu chronology. Cf. Marshall and Williams 1982: 118.

overlooked that they 'had sunk into the depths of superstitions from their cultural heights long ago' (quoted in Schulin 1958: 77) .

In the evolutionary theories of the Enlightenment, the diverse forms of society were inserted into the temporal framework of global development, with European civilization marching ahead and the others following suit. Just as western progress was reflected in the spacial variety of peoples and cultures, their achievements, in turn, were reduced to their share in evolution as defined by the Europeans.[13] The new time-orientation corresponded to a new form of political hierarchization, and the situating of alien societies at earlier stages of evolution became a way of subordinating them.[14]

It was under the influence of these overlapping tendencies to temporalize space and to spatialize history that the first steps towards the investigation into India's past were taken by western historians—with considerable differences in the stances adopted. In William Jones (1746–94), who was oriented towards the 'common origins' of cultures rather than the unity of human nature, the prevailing reductionism of the rationalists was confronted with a pronounced interest in the variety of things. With his assumption of a common root of Indian and European languages and mythologies, he suggested that the Indian past deserved an esteem similar to that of Greek antiquity. Jones mocked at the Europeans who, with their one-sided appreciation of western classical literature and their ignorance of eastern learning, appeared to him like 'savages, who thought that the sun rose and set for them alone, and could not imagine that the waves which surrounded their islands left coral and pearls upon any other shore'.[15] He thought that oriental literature, in case of its adequate reception by the Europeans, could play the role of rejuvenating people, as Greek literature had done during the Renaissance.[16]

Certainly, Jones was influenced by Enlightenment thought himself. He, too, spoke of the 'inferiority of most Asiatick nations, ancient and modern, to those in Europe' and explained this with the absence of the 'idea of political freedom'. The Indian territories, therefore, were a country 'which providence has thrown into the arms of *Britain* for their protection and welfare'.[17] But he also recognized that 'in some early age they [the Indians] were splendid in arts and arms, happy in government, wise in legislation and eminent in various knowledge'.[18] More than others, Jones emphasized the intrinsic value of the alien culture. Asia, in his eyes, had 'many

[13]'First rule when speaking about occurrences in Asia: we Europeanize them.' Schlözer 1797: p. IX.

[14]Whereas, in the wake of the European expansion, the alien societies were drawn closer to the western imagination in terms of space, they were distanced in terms of time. For the 'denial of coevalness' and the forms of temporal distancing in the discourse of Anthropology, see Fabian 1983: 25, 30–1 passim.

[15]William Jones, 'Grammar of the Persian Language', in *The Works of Sir William Jones*, ed. Anna Maria Jones, with life of the author by Lord Teignmouth (London 1807) (quoted hereafter: *Works* 1807), V, 163–446, here 166.

[16]Cf. also Friedrich Schlegel, 'Über die Sprache und Weisheit der Indier' [1808], in *Kritische Ausgabe seiner Werke*, ed. Ernst Behler, VIII (München 1975), 305.

[17]'On Asiatick History' (1793) (*Works* 1807, III: 205–28, here 215, 216).

[18]'On the Hindus' (Marshall 1970), 246–59, here 251.

beauties and some advantages peculiar to herself',[19] and the knowledge of Asiatic philosophy was necessary 'to complete the history of universal philosophy'.[20] Even though he believed in the advancement of contemporary European civilization and regretted that India had declined since the classical period, especially with regard to the knowledge of its own past,[21] he had considerable reservations about theories which tended to relate the differences to stages of rationalization in a way that the earlier and simpler forms were superseded by more complex ones. Jones took care that the engagement in the study of his own culture did not affect the perception of the other. Even where he aimed to see the chronology of the Old Testament confirmed by the history of the Asiatic peoples,[22] he was nevertheless concerned 'to omit nothing essential' that could aid in the discovery and understanding of the foreign civilizations.[23]

The sceptical position taken up against rationalism corresponded to the high value Jones placed on the imaginative. This, too, facilitated the acknowledgment of differences. If the Europeans were superior in terms of rationality, the great prerogative of Asia was in the sphere of poetry. To Jones, the Indians were people 'with a fertile and inventive genius' and in contrast to the West the poetical imagination appeared still alive in India—an idea that, later, was to arouse the fascination of the romantics.[24] Even if poetry had reached its heights earlier than reason, this did not mean that one had 'to identify "civilization" with the march of the mind' (Grewal 1975: 51).

Jones sought to mediate between the European perspective and the recognition of Indian culture in its uniqueness. It was an attempt 'both to understand cultures in their own terms, and to measure and define them according to some culturally neutral standards'.[25] He insisted that 'men will always differ in their ideas of civilization, each measuring it by the habits and prejudices of his own country' and that 'poetry and eloquence' as well as 'courtesy and urbanity' could be a 'juster measure of perfect society'.[26]

It was this openness to the multiplicity of civilizational processes which was criticized by James Mill (1773–1836), who denounced Jones' ideas on the subject as 'crude, vague and indeterminate' (Mill 1817 II: 138–9). For Mill, the yardstick of civilization was the realization of practical purposes according to the utilitarian principle of the greatest happiness of the

---

[19]'The Second Anniversary Discourse' (1785) (*Works* 1807 III: 10–23, here 12).

[20]'The Philosophy of the Asiaticks' (*Works* 1807 III: 229–52, here 233).

[21]Jones regretted that 'these people had since then substituted astrological calculations for a viable chronological scheme and had buried their history in "a cloud of fables".' 'On the Hindus' (Marshall 1970: 251).

[22]Jones was always interested in showing 'that all our historical researches have confirmed the *Mosaick* accounts of the primitive world'. But even in the case of differing statements he insisted that '*Truth is mighty, and, whatever be its consequences, must always prevail*'. 'On Asiatick History' (*Works* 1807: 208). Italics in original. For the relation between Bible studies and Indology in the eighteenth century, see Alun David, 'Sir William Jones, Biblical Orientalism and Indian Scholarship', MAS 30 (1996), 173–84.

[23]'On the Hindus' (Marshall 1970: 246).

[24]Ibid., 259.

[25]For the difficulties of this attempt 'both to respect the uniqueness of cultures, and to define a neutral idiom in which cultures could be compared and contrasted', see Majeed 1992: 43. Notwithstanding his influential role as an Orientalist, Jones' approach represented a minority position in dealing with foreign cultures. Inden 1990: 67.

[26]'On the Arabs' (*Works* 1807, III: 50).

greatest number: 'Exactly in proportion as Utility is the object of every pursuit, may we regard a nation as civilized.' (Mill 1817 II: 134; Grewal 1970: 73) And it was precisely in this respect that Indian society resembled the 'rudest and weakest states of the human mind' (Mill 1820 I: 461). Asia was an area to Mill where 'darkness had always prevailed'. This did not mean, however, that the differences between the 'most cultivated European and the wildest savage' were cemented once and for all; civilization was only a question of education (Mill 1931: 20). For Mill, in fact, Indian social and political life was 'not only an object of curiosity in the history of human nature' but also one 'of the highest practical importance' (Mill 1820 I: 456). The insight into the course of human nature which could be gained from the study of Indian history should also be to the advantage of the Indians themselves.

India's cultural heritage did not have any value of its own. On the contrary, Mill actually aimed at a 'programme to emancipate India from its own culture' (Majeed 1992: 127, 43).[27] Education, according to him, had to ensure that reason dominates feelings and passions and strengthens the natural tendencies towards progress. In India, this had been hitherto prevented by the influence of religion. Even the classical literature of India was an 'offspring of a wild and ungoverned imagination' and without 'genius and taste'. In this respect, too, the Indians had been 'stationary for many ages' (quoted in Grewal 1970: 83–4). If Jones believed in the utopian potential of classical culture, Mill saw the rational structuring of the future placed at risk precisely by this admiration for antiquity. The Orientalists perpetuated barbaric customs and despotism by giving the ancient period 'the aura of a mythical golden age.

Mill's polemic against the myth of classical civilization and his plea for radical reforms in India were always related to political controversies within Britain as well.[28] What was at stake was the fundamental problem of whether the law should be based on general principles or on accumulated experience. Mill favoured the introduction of a legal system in India that was suitable for social progress instead of simply transferring the English common law.[29] His way of relating the particular and the general to each other was totally different from that of Jones. It was not the common origin of races (about which nothing could be said, according to Mill) but the causal nexus of things (general laws ruling particular facts) which gave unity to human nature.[30] Thus he integrated the Otherness which fascinated Jones into the realm of the familiar. On the other hand, he distanced it in time and emphasized the Hindus' low stage of evolution: 'By conversing with the Hindus of the present day, we, in some measure, converse with the Chaldeans and Babylonians of the time of Cyrus; with the Persians and Egyptians of the time of Alexander.'

[27]There was a certain tension, however, between the active interference of reason with reality and the idea of a passive object to be moulded by education.

[28]This is a fact which may explain some of the harsh judgements about Indians; it also testifies to the importance of India in the debates in England at the end of the eighteenth century. The *HBI* cannot be viewed only as 'an attempt to apply utilitarianism to British India'. Majeed 1992: 128.

[29]If 'considerable progress towards improvement' was to be achieved in India, the British had to get rid of the deep-rooted prejudice 'that English law is the standard of perfection to which everything should be fitted'. Quoted in Majeed 1992: 132.

[30]Even according to John Stuart Mill, his father trusted too much in 'the intelligibleness of the abstract, when not embodied in the concrete'. *Autobiography*, 35, 27, quoted in Majeed 1992: 134.

(Mill 1817 II: 190, quoted in Grewal 1970: 85) Moreover (and what would hurt the Indians most), he placed the Islamic civilization at a higher level than Hinduism. Accordingly, the Muslim conquest of India was not the cause but the result of Indian backwardness. To relate India's downfall to the invasions was nothing but a 'saving hypothesis' in Mill's eyes (Mill 1820 I: 460). India seemed to be excluded from the process of civilization, and it could enter it only under the guidance of the West. If Jones had considered the Indians just as historical as the Europeans, in spite of the current decadence, according to Mill they had yet to be made historical.

Based on the accounts of British experts, such as Jones, Mill, and Colebrooke, the German philosopher G.W. F. Hegel (1770–1831) in his teachings gave the notion of ahistorical India a philosophical definition.[31] Hegel, who, with his theory of world history as the 'progressing from the imperfect to the perfect', had a lasting influence on western historical thinking, did not deny the achievements of Indian culture, but he criticized their romantic glorification. The unchangeability of India was described by him as follows: 'India [...] is as much an early as a present form, which has remained static and fixed and has completed itself in the full inward development' (174).[32] In India there was struggle, 'but without anything that was developed or enhanced by it' (206). Actual history occurred in India even less than in China, 'as the dreamy Indian spirit is not up to the prose of history and has never risen to a fixed political form' (quoted in Schulin 1958: 82).

The lack of historical writing in India was of particular significance, because Hegel credited historical consciousness and its manifestation through historiography with having a decisive relevance in the emergence of politics: 'As the Indians do not have any history in the sense of historiography, they do not have history as actions (res gestae), i.e. no development towards a truly political status' (204). To him it seemed self-evident: 'In the case of a people like this we should not look for what we call history in its double meaning' (202). India was 'historical' only 'in itself and for us', that is for the modern western observer. India's significance in world history was limited to being seen by the Europeans as their country of desire. Since India had not developed the necessary conceptual means of historical thinking, it had remained outside the world historical process, to which it could be connected only through European conquest. It was 'the necessary fate of the Asiatic empires to be subjugated by the Europeans' (179).

The nexus between the promise of universal progress and the practice of colonization was symptomatic of modern Europe's approach towards alien cultures. Even Karl Marx (1818–83), who criticized British rule in India in his articles for the *New-York Daily Tribune* (1853ff.), perceived the English, notwithstanding their destructive measures, as an 'unconscious tool of history'. According to Marx, 'the country which is more developed shows the less developed

---

[31]Hegel 1970: 78. It is to this edition that the page numbers in the text refer. In the development of the spirit, on its course from the East to the West—'because Europe is the end of world history, Asia the beginning' (134)—Asia has taken one important step: 'In Asia the light of the spirit has dawned and with it the history of the world' (130).

[32]Hegel refers explicitly to the discovery of the relatedness of Indo-European languages (82), but he situates the shared past outside history (83).

Marx

one only its own future' (Marx 1970, Preface: 12). He presumed the movement of India along the western path of development to be inevitable, and he was among those who contrasted the progressive West with stagnant nations, a view which determined the Europeans' assessment of the non-European world for a long time.

By examining the practice of colonial administration, one can trace the manner in which comparison of the Indian reality with the European past gradually led to the imagination of the British present as the Indian future. The initial strategy, to adapt to local realities and manage the modernization of India through its own institutions, was increasingly replaced by that of bringing India in line with the English pattern of evolution.[33] Indicative of the success of the 'Anglicists' over the 'Orientalists' in the realm of administration is the famous 'Minute on Education' (1835) by T. B. Macaulay. The British historian, who served in India as President of the Law Commission from 1834 to 1838, denied in his outline of a new educational policy any civilizational value of the Indian tradition. The inferiority of the Indian as against the European mind was evident, according to him, especially in the field of history: 'All the historical information which has been collected from all the books written in the Sanscrit language is less valuable than what may be found in the most paltry abridgments used at preparatory schools in England.'[34] A similar judgement had been presented by Mill against Jones and his esteem for eastern wisdom. But Macaulay went a step further and made England the only yardstick of civilization. Instead of expecting, like Jones, a revitalization of the European spirit by the study of Indian culture, now it was English literature that was to effect historical progress in India. This required the education of mediators among the native population, 'a class of persons, Indian in blood and colour, but English in taste, in opinions, in morals and in intellect'.[35]

This kind of political pedagogy had an effect of polarization in the relations between East and West and turned history itself into an element of essentializing strategies. The image of a static Indian culture led to the conviction that 'the East required one's presence there more or less for ever' (Said 1991: 215). The gradually arising 'illusion of permanence' among the British corresponded to the assumption that Indians were 'non-autonomous, passive, historically non-active, indeed for that very reason ahistorical, and therefore ever in need to be acted upon by others.' (Chatterjee 1996: 74) For Lord Curzon, the British Viceroy at the turn of the century, Oriental studies represented the 'necessary furniture of the empire'. In the heyday of colonialism and imperialism, the western concept of history and progress had become a means of downgrading. Ethnology and anthropology, too, were almost calculated to distance 'those who were 'observed from the Time of the observer' (Fabian 1983: 25).[36] The Underdeveloped and the Other were

[33]For this process, cf. Kopf 1969: 236ff. 'The plan of modernization changed from the orthogenetic transformation of the alien imports to the complete heterogenetic transformation of the indigenous tradition.' Ibid., 288.

[34]Thomas Babington Macaulay, 'Minute of the 2nd February, 1835', in Macaulay 1935: 345–61, here 349. In another frequently quoted remark, Macaulay compared the value of the entire Oriental literature with the content of a single shelf in a European library. Ibid.

[35]Macaulay, loc. cit., 359. For the nexus between English education and the establishment of colonial rule in India, see the excellent study by Viswanathan 1989.

[36]'Most importantly, by allowing Time to be resorbed by the tabular space of classification, nineteenth-century anthropology sanctioned an ideological process by which relations between the West and its Other,

now identical.[37] It was the temporal distance between the cultures which gave 'meaning [...] to the distribution of humanity in space'. In the evolutionary theory of the natural sciences the tendency towards essentialism came to its completion. 'Evolutionary anthropologists made difference "natural", the inevitable outcome of the operation of natural laws.'[38] Finally, the evolutionary differences became racial ones, which could no longer be bridged by historical change and which established an eternal relationship of subordination.[39]

In the typologies of races, the western capability for progress was sometimes considered a specific quality of the Aryans.[40] In the context of South Asia, however, this linkage was thwarted by the concept of Indo-European languages and peoples, which postulated common ethnic roots of Indians and Europeans. In pursuance of certain ideas of Jones, the seemingly alien was recognized as 'one of us'.[41] This meant that another explanation had to be found for Indian backwardness. In the work of Max Müller (1823–1900), it was precisely the racial aspect which led back to the historicization of the differences. The study of Sanskrit represented to him an expansion of the European collective memory: 'It has added a new period to our historical consciousness, and revived the recollections of our childhood, which seemed to have vanished for ever' (Müller 1883: 29); Just as the romantics had associated with the image of India's eternal childhood a utopia in the past, interest was once again focused on the lost potential of one's Self which could be recovered. Under the influence of advancing industrialization and with a sceptical attitude towards the belief in progress, Müller discovered the spiritual East as the opposite pole of the materialistic West. Nevertheless, the land of desire remained a merely internal residue as against the unavoidable external progress in which, it was generally assumed, India, too, would finally get involved.[42]

The historical significance of India was not reduced to that of a remote past.[43] Müller

---

between anthropology and its object, were conceived not only as difference, but as distance in space *and* Time.' Ibid., 147.

[37]'That which is past is remote, that which is remote is past: such is the tune to which figures of allochronic discourse are dancing.' Ibid., 127.

[38]Ibid., 25, 147.

[39]The lower grade of the alien was now determined by nature. Mill had never deduced social differences from racial causes.

[40]Higher intellect and historical progress were claimed for the Aryan race as opposed to the unchangeability of the Chinese and the East Asians. See Joan Leopold, 'British Applications of the Aryan Theory of Race to India, 1850–70', *English Historical Review* 89 (1974), 578–603.

[41]Friedrich Max Müller, 'The Last Results of the Sanskrit Researches in Comparative Philology', in Bunsen 1854, I: 129–30.

[42]'The romantic insists that India embodies a private realm of the imagination and the religious which modern, western man lacks but needs.' However, the romantic did not accept the values and institutions of the East as 'ready-made substitutes', but appropriated their experience in a compensatory perspective or as a corrective. Ronald Inden, 'Orientalist Construction of India', *MAS* 20 (1986), 401–46, here 433, 442.

[43]It was not only a question of 'relating the past and the Other to ourselves'. Hans G. Kippenberg, 'Die Relativierung der eigenen Kultur in der vergleichenden Religionswissenschaft', in Matthes 1992: 103–14, here 108.

stressed the relevance of contemporary India with regard to the challenges of modernity: 'You will find yourselves everywhere in India between an immense past and an immense future. [...] Take any burning questions of the day [...], India will supply you with a laboratory such as exists nowhere else'. (Müller 1883: 13) But the approximation of India to the European present meant its inclusion in the West-defined, yet universally imagined, perspective of development: 'India is not, as you may imagine, a distant, strange, or, at the very utmost, a curious country. India for the future belongs to Europe, it has its place in the Indo-European world, it has its place in our own history, and in what is the very life of history, the history of the human mind'. (Müller 1883: 14) This, of course, was at the cost of the very characteristics of India which were otherwise thought of with nostalgia. But even Müller had no doubt about western advancement and superiority. The childlike nature of India was ranking below the maturity of Kantian philosophy. 'While in the Veda we may study the childhood, we may study in Kant's *Critique* the perfect manhood of the Aryan mind.'[44] If, in the view of Mill and Hegel, India had never found its access to history, according to Müller, it had in any case, lost it again and the diagnosis of eternal childhood, too, could demonstrate the necessity of educational processes and legitimize benevolent interference from outside.[45]

From the perspective of the victims of colonialism, European research of the Indian past contributed to the country's occupation. What Johannes Fabian has said about the 'possessive past' of anthropology can also be said about the use of history: it was 'analogous to the exploitation of natural resources found in colonial countries'. (Fabian 1883: 95)[46] The work of the historians belonged to cultural domination and control; it was part of colonial knowledge which not only served to exercise power but, as Nicholas B. Dirks emphasizes, obeyed the same logic: 'Colonial knowledge both enabled colonial conquest and was produced by it.'[47] According to Edward Said, oriental (and historical) studies did not serve colonialism only in retrospect, but had conceived the Orient as an object of subjugation right from the beginning.[48]

1.2 The Self-Assurance of Indian Traditions

Equating historical research and political subjugation, however, thus excluding, even today, any possibility of agreement between East and West regarding shared history, would not only

[44]Müller, 'Introduction', in Kant, *Critique of Pure Reason*, quoted in Halbfass 1990: 133.

[45]Inden, 'Orientalist Construction of India', 442.

[46]For the link between colonialist history and economic exploitation, cf. also Guha 1988: 4, 13. Similarly, with regard to anthropology, Cohn 1987: 136ff.

[47]Nicholas B. Dirks, 'Introduction', in idem 1992, 1–25, here 3.

[48]'To say simply that Orientalism was a rationalization of colonial rule is to ignore the extent to which colonial rule was justified in advance by Orientalism, rather than after the fact.' Said 1991, 39. However, Said's position between essentialist and historicist forms of reasoning remains unclear. Cf. MacKenzie 1995: 6–7, 11, who shows that Said's occasionally surfacing anti-historicism is a historicism 'which is in itself essentially ahistorical'. See also the critical comments by Aijaz Ahmad, 'Between Orientalism and Historicism. Anthropological Knowledge of India', *Studies in History* 7 (1991), 135–63, here 138, 154; David Kopf, 'Hermeneutics versus History', *JAS* 39 (1980), 495–505.

underestimate the openness of modern history to the experience of the Other and the New, but would also overlook the autonomy and creativity of Indians in making use of it.[49] Certainly, the instrumental nexus between western research interests and the claim to rule the country is already evident in the work of early 'administrative historians',[50] a long time before history, under the catchword of 'civilizing mission', was explicitly made an element in the legitimation of colonialism.[51] On the other hand, in the second half of the nineteenth century, when the idea of progress began to be used in order to justify permanent subordination, it had taken on the form of classification and had been dehistoricized to such an extent that first tendencies to self-criticism began to surface (Maine 1875; Lyall 1910 [1893]).[52] As regards Indians, historicization did not automatically mean 'colonialism by consent'. Here, too, it is necessary to consider each particular context and the various individual interests.[53] The Brahmanic scholars, who served as linguistic and cultural experts and informants of the colonial administrators, played their own active role in the western reconstruction of the Indian past.[54] While interpreting and defending their culture, they were also interested in maintaining their control over tradition. Their monopoly of interpretation, however, was questioned by other representatives of the indigenous culture. In the intercultural encounter, forms of innercultural dissent were also blended in.

Nevertheless, while taking into account these nuances, it cannot be overlooked that the perspectives of mutual reference were not equal, and that the 'situation of the encounter and "dialogue" between India and Europe [was] an uneven, asymmetrical one' (Halbfass 1990: 173). Generally speaking, Indian curiosity about the West was not comparable to the western interest in India, which had continued for a long time in the past. In the temporalized self-consciousness of 'modern' Europeans vis-à-vis 'backward' Indians, such asymmetry acquired a specifically historical dimension, so that the establishment of British rule in India was ascribed to the reason of history itself. It was this link between western historical consciousness and colonial

---

[49]That there was a link between the domination of nature and political power was perceptible even on the other side: 'The intellectuals learnt less from Shakespeare and Mill and very much more of modern technology and science—and from the very beginning attempts were made to assimilate the latter into the language of the country.' Sarkar, 'Rammohun Roy and the break with the past' (Joshi: 1975), 67.

[50]The easy passage between research and the exertion of power is tangible in a remark by Alexander Dow: 'The success of Your Majesty's arms has laid open the East to the researches of the curious.' Dow, *History of Hindostan*, 1770–2, quoted in Dipesh Chakrabarty, 'Postcoloniality and the Artifice of History: Who Speaks for "Indian" Pasts?', *Representations* 37 (1992), 1–26, here 5.

[51]According to Barun De, the preconceptions of British historians in the late eighteenth century have to be distinguished 'from the nineteenth-century outlook [...] of either Indian elite nationalism or British officials who ascribed *herrenvolk* status to themselves.' Barun De, 'Problems of the Study of Indian History. With Particular Reference to Interpretations of the 18th Century', in *Proceedings of the IHC, 49th Session* (1988), 1989, 1–56, here 14.

[52]For a critical evaluation of these tendencies, see Metcalf 1995: 66ff; Stokes 1959: 313ff.

[53]Cf. K. N. Panikkar, 'The Intellectual History of Colonial India: Some Historiographical and Conceptual Questions', in Bhattacharya and Thapar 1986: 403–33, here 409.

[54]For the attitude of the pandits, see Marshall and Williams 1982: 77.

rule which has stimulated and, at the same time, hampered the emergence of modern historical thinking in South Asia.

The asymmetry discussed above is also reflected in the difference between the prevailing modes of explanation and interpretation. If Europeans attempted to understand the alien culture with the use of scientific methods, Indians reflected on the new experience primarily in the sphere of religion.[55] The confrontation of western science and eastern religion has dominated debates for a long time. Europeans as well as Indians have seen in it a decisive difference between the two cultures—with diverging assessments and implications, however. From the perspective of western Enlightenment, the religion of the Hindus stood for the backwardness of the East. Indian reformers, for their part, equated modern science with the progressiveness of the West,[56] but in India, unlike Europe, 'science was not perceived as possessing an alternative authority to religion' (Jones, K. 1989: 212). The utilitarians' secularizing critique denied the intrinsic value and future prospects of Indian culture. In this, it displayed a remarkable proximity to Christian missionary activities (notwithstanding the many ideological differences): India's connection to history by conquest was similar to the idea of spiritual salvation by conversion.[57]

In particular, the tracing of all social evils to Hinduism left a deep scar in the cultural self-esteem of Indians, and the inclination to contrast East and West as areas of stagnation and progress proved to be an obstacle for the historicization of thinking.[58] However, the tendencies to polarization were countered by equally persistent attempts at approaching. Jones and Müller were convinced that Indian imagination and spirituality could serve as a revitalization and correction of western rationality, while Indian reformers pinned their hopes on western science and technology as factors of social improvement. Rammohun Roy (1772–1833) was a mediator between East and West and, at the same time, personified 'the first grand affirmation of India's willingness and ability to break with the past in a modern direction'.[59] A contemporary of Mill and Hegel, Roy provided counter-evidence to the alleged ahistoricity of India, both theoretically and practically. He gave the Hindu tradition a worldly interpretation and made use of its basic

[55]'Religion seemed to form such an important part of the Indian heritage that one could scarcely deny it without seeming to deny the heritage itself.' Warren M. Gunderson, 'The Fate of Religion in Modern India: The Cases of Rammohan Ray and Debendranath Tagore', *Studies on Bengal* (East Lansing 1975), 125–42, here 125.

[56]For the building of barriers as a possibility to subscribe to scientific values without denying, religious truth, cf. Gunderson, ibid., 125.

[57]See Michael Gottlob, 'India's Connection to History: The Discipline and the Relation between Center and Periphery', in Fuchs and Stuchtey 2002: 75–97. For the similarity of Utilitarians and Evangelicals in their attitude to India, see Grewal 1975: 67–8. According to Charles Grant and William Wilberforce, the only way of improvement for the Indians was the conversion to Christianity. They described Hinduism as 'rotten to the core and incapable of any sort of restoration, reform, or renaissance'. Kopf 1969: 142.

[58]On the other hand, Indian religions in general represented a fruitful ground for the absorption of foreign ideas.

[59]Sharma, 'Raja Rammohan Roy' (Bhalla and Chandra 1993), 93.

principles to promote social reforms. Roy criticized the contemporary form of Hindu religion and questioned, in particular, the ritual practices of the priests which he exposed as pure inventions, stating that 'falsehood is common to all religions without distinction'.[60] Roy's critique had set in before he came into personal contact with the Europeans, but later he also assumed western views, which could be used to the advantage of the indigenous society. His openness towards the Other and interest in modernization were closely connected to each other. Indian reality and western experience were related in a way that was aimed at a conscious structuring of the future.[61]

Roy was ostracized by opponents in the orthodox[62] establishment, who reproached him with being an innovator, a modifier of Hindu tradition, an imitator of the British, and a friend of the Muslims. They branded the efforts to reform as an expression of the decadence of *kaliyuga*.[63] Roy, on his part, accused the orthodox themselves of falsifying tradition.[64] He held the Brahmans and the pandits responsible for passing on their knowledge only selectively and for hiding the holy tradition of the Upanishads behind the 'dark curtain of the Sungscrit language'.[65] According to Rammohun, original Hinduism was to be looked for in the texts, not in the rituals. Thus he attempted to deprive priestly authority and forms of superstition of their uncontrollable substantiation. In his recourse to tradition, he was less selective than his opponents (and some of his successors), taking into consideration not only the Vedanta but also later texts like the Puranas and the Tantras.[66] In view of the reformers' reference to the texts, which were made more easily accessible through printing and translations, Kenneth Jones has spoken of a 'Protestantization' of Hinduism (Jones, K. 1989: 213–4).[67] The proximity of Hindu reform to the concept of reformation in the Christian church is confirmed by Roy who is said to have stated once to the British missionary Alexander Duff: 'I begin to think that something similar might have taken place in India; and similar results might follow from a reformation of popular idolatry.' (Quoted in Halbfass 1990: 207)

[60]*Tuhfatul Muwahhiddin*, c. 1803, quoted in Sumit Sarkar, 'Rammohum Roy and the Break with the Past' (Joshi 1975), 49.

[61]'In an English translation of one of the *Upanishads*, made in 1816, Rammohun Roy was probably the first of the intelligentsia to divide Indian history into an age of god (the age of the Upanishads, 900–600 BC), an age of darkness (600 BC to AD 1800), and an age of future expectations, when India could again flow in the mainstream of world progress.' David Kopf et al. [Edward L. Farmer] 1977: 679. See also Roy's historical sketch (1822) in 'Brief Remarks Regarding Modern Encroachments on the Ancient Rights of Females', in Essential Writings 1999: 147–55, here 147–8.

[62]For the problematical use of the term 'orthodox' in the context of Hindu tradition, see Heinrich von Stietencron, 'Hinduism. On the Proper Use of a Deceptive Term', in Sontheimer and Kulke 1989: 11–27.

[63]It was especially foreign rule and the insubordination of women that were regarded as symptoms of kaliyuga.

[64]It was also, and in particular, the profane interest of the Brahmans in certain property rights that was criticized by Roy: 'in the rites, ceremonies, and festivals of idolatry, they find the source of their comforts and fortune' (1816). *The English Works of Rammohan Roy*, ed. Kalidas Nag and Debajyoti Burman (Calcutta 1946), II, 44.

[65]'Translation of an Abridgment of the *Vedant*', in Essential Writings 1999: 1–14, here 2.

[66]Cf. Roy's introductory remarks to his translation of the *Isa Upanishad*, in English Works 1946, II: 39–49, here 41. Gunderson, 'The Fate of Religion in Modern India', 131.

[67]The rising literacy among the people has also to be taken into account.

Roy referred to the authority of the scriptures not only to criticize the orthodox; it was also for the sake of tradition itself that he wished 'to restate and reaffirm ancient truths of the Upanishads'.[68] His efforts to re-establish the true faith aimed at the self-assertion of the indigenous culture, as against the claim to superiority and missionary zeal on the part of others.[69] Roy's interest in Christianity and its practical ethics was stimulated by his concern for the modernization of his own society.[70] However, he did not advocate the complete Anglicization of the education system, but differentiated between the 'useful mechanical arts' of the British, which should be taken up, and the field of 'science, literature, or religion', in which India could perhaps teach the others.[71] In accordance with the British 'reform-from-within technique,' he aimed to strengthen those Indian traditions which were in line with the universal tendencies of rationalization.[72]

Nevertheless, Roy's idea of social improvement was not exclusively oriented towards rationality either, which was conceded only a limited practical importance. Reason could serve as a guide when contradictions occurred in the traditions, but 'we soon find how incompetent it is, alone, to conduct us to the object of our pursuit',[73] for it creates a 'universal doubt, incompatible with principles on which our comfort and happiness mainly depend'. In advocating the simultaneous improvement of 'our intellectual and moral faculties, relying on the goodness of the Almighty Power',[74] one may see an early appeal to Indian spirituality, which was highlighted by later reformers.

Half a century after Roy, Swami Dayanand Sarasvati (1824–83) undertook another attempt to further social improvement by referring to the past. Dayanand, too, opposed certain manifestations of religion like idol worship, temple service, and pilgrimage; he demanded the abolition of caste restrictions in favour of universal fraternity among Hindus and fought against the discrimination of women and child marriage, and for the acknowledgment of rational principles of ethics.

[68]Sharma, 'Raja Rammohan Roy', 94. Apart from this, since Warren Hastings' decrees of 1772 and 1780, reference to the Shastras was indispensable in all issues of Hindu 'personal law'.

[69]'Never before had the tensions of intellectual choice in India involved such a cruel dilemma. The need for a break with the past was acutely felt. But a break with the past that would question the very specificity of India seemed unacceptable.' Sharma, 'Raja Rammohan Roy', 108.

[70]Referring to processes of secularization in the West helped counter the sweeping accusations against Hindu religion by Christian missionaries. 'Vice was thus turned into the simple result of ignorance'. John Morearty, 'The Two-Edged Word: The Treacherousness of Symbolic Transformation: Rammohan Roy, Debendranath, Vivekananda and "The Indian Golden Age"', in *Studies on Bengal* (East Lansing 1975), 85–105, here 89.

[71]Roy to Lord Amherst, 1823, quoted in Sarkar, 'Rammohum Roy and the Break with the Past, 48.

[72]As examples, cf. the argumentation against the custom of sati (see below) as well as Roy's tract on *The Universal Religion: Religious Instructions Founded on Sacred Authorities* (1829), which referred exclusively to Hinduism. Roy brought to bear a higher universality of Hinduism as against Christianity and an evolutionary advantage of the Indians over the Europeans. The 'first dawn of knowledge' had occurred in India and the rest of the world was indebted to the Indians in this respect. *English Works* (Allahabad 1906), 906ff. Cf. Halbfass 1990: 215.

[73]'Translation of the *Céna Upanishad*' [1816], in *The Essential Writings of Raja Rammohun Roy* 1999: 15–21, here 15.

[74]Ibid.

Dayanand, who founded the reformist organization Arya Samaj and, with this, exerted a considerable influence on the emerging Hindu nationalism, preached a dynamic attitude towards life. The world did not appear to him as *maya* but as a reality which could be scientifically perceived and purposefully structured. Action was related to this world, and not even the striving for *moksha* could be separated from it. Even the *sannyasi* had to make himself useful.

Dayanand's critique of tradition also borrowed ideas from Christianity and Islam, when replacing, for example, the primeval *rishis* with the idea of holy scriptures, in which God had revealed himself through the Word. The 'Luther of India', as Dayanand was called by his followers, was aware of his proximity to western ideas. He acknowledged the discipline, sense of duty, and patriotism of the British and attempted to rekindle these virtues in the Hindus. But he conceived 'the holy work of reform'[75] neither as emulation of the West nor as a real innovation. What was on his agenda was a return to the origins. Under the slogan 'Back to the Vedas!', he propagated the revival of the Golden Age. The call for a restoration of true faith made all later additions to the stock of tradition appear as deviations.[76] More than Roy, Dayanand played off the antiquity (and thereby the closeness to divine inspiration) of the selected scriptures against orthodox positions. The revelation (*shruti*) was reduced to a few texts only.[77] The writings, for which divine authority could be claimed were, according to Dayanand, the Vedas and the Upanishads, the Law of Manu, the Mahabharata and other texts. The Puranas, in contrast, were explicitly excluded.

Reference to the earliest tradition, however, not only served as justification against orthodox Hindus, but, increasingly, was intended to assert the superiority of Hinduism over other religions. Dayanand, therefore, tried to show that the admired qualities of the West had been common among ancient Hindus. Since he believed that the Veda contained complete human knowledge, he stated that even modern inventions, like the railway and the telegraph, had already been known to the Vedic poets (Lütt 1970: 100).[78] He explicitly moved away from Roy and the Brahmo Samaj, whom he accused of imitating the West: 'Copying is not a sign of wisdom.'[79]

[75]*Autobiography of Svami Dayananda Sarasvati*, quoted in Klimkeit, 1981: 173.

[76]He even postulated monotheism, relying on the fact 'that in the Veda only one god was mentioned. [...] He explained the various names of gods as being different names of one and the same god.' Lütt 1970: 100.

[77]While, for Dayanand, the divine revelation was definite, for others it was not fixed once and for all; it could be complemented by *Avatars* and by the experience of *bhakti*. Cf. J. T. F. Jordens, 'Dayanand Sarasvati's Concept of the Vedic Golden Age', in idem 1998: 64–76, here 73. That there was no general consensus on the timeless authority of the Vedic revelation has been shown recently by Roy W. Perrett, 'History, Time, and Knowledge in Ancient India', *History and Theory* 38 (1999), 307–21, here 314–15. See also Sheldon Pollock, 'Mimamsa and the Problem of History in Traditional India', *Journal of the American Oriental Society* 109 (1989), 603–10.

[78]William Jones had already pointed out that, for the Hindus, the confrontation with Christianity as such did not constitute any problem of consistency: 'The Hindus [...] would readily admit the truth of the Gospel; but they contend that it is perfectly consistent with their *sastras*.' William Jones, 'On the Gods of Greece, Italy, and India', in Marshall 1970: 196–245, here 245. Jones had tried to substantiate these assumptions. Even in the case of Newton, he thought it was possible 'that the whole of his theology and part of his philosophy may be found in the Vedas'. *Works* 1807, III, 246.

[79]Quoted in *Sources of Indian Tradition*, II: 61. Later, in the campaigns for cow protection and for Hindi as official language, he made himself a defender of the central values and symbols of the Hindus. With this he

The strict demarcation from the Other was enhanced by the identification of the Hindus as Aryans.[80] Thus, the restoration of the Golden Age was supposed to bring back Aryan power, too. Certainly, the Vedic religion was universal, its principles could be rationally realized; nevertheless, the Aryans, being the original receivers of the message, occupied a special place in it.[81] The congruence of ethnic and religious community had its geographical dimension in the equation of the land of the Aryans (aryavarta) with the land of dharma; its linguistic equivalent was the veneration of Sanskrit (the language of the Aryans: arya bhasha) as the medium of the holy revelation.

The effect was double-edged. If the reference to Aryanism was a gain in homogeneity, it became more difficult to deal with the inner diversity of Indian society.[82] It is precisely in its strict delineation, so argue contemporary critics of 'Syndicated Hinduism', that it follows a rather un-Indian model of religion, namely that of the Christians and Muslims.[83] Moreover, the nativistic recourse to origins not only meant a radical narrowing down of perspectives it also rendered the concept static and thus contradicted its intended creativity and agency. By making divine revelation a historical point of reference, Dayanand drew it into a close relation to the present. Correspondingly, the recovery of the original perfect order, which had always been beyond the real horizon of expectations, became a concrete political commitment.[84] With this, however, what had hitherto granted certain liberties precisely because of its distance, in, dealing with contingent experience became an element of restriction.[85] The occurrences of change were denied any temporal sense by Dayanand; the postulated productivity was not perceived as historical by him. In fact, the dehistoricizing elements in the traditional Brahmanic dealing with contingency were even radicalized.

Swami Vivekananda (1863–1902) was the last of the charismatic Hindu reformers of the nineteenth century, and, like his predecessors, he linked the intention of renewal with the recourse to the

---

sought to escape his precarious position with regard to orthodox Hinduism. The inner-Hindu conflict was thus transformed into a confrontation of the Hindus with the non-Hindus. This was first directed against proselytizing Christians, but then also led to conflicts with the Muslims.

[80]The self-definition as Aryans was preferred by Dayanand to that as Hindus, a designation going back to Muslim use. See below, Section 2.2.

[81]This established a primacy among Indian citizens for those who professed the 'Aryan form of Hinduism'. Cf. Kenneth Jones 1989: 97.

[82]That the Aryan-Theory could also be used against the Brahmans (Aryans as invaders), is shown by the arguments of the Dalits (for these motives in Jotirao Phule, cf. Thapar 1975: 15–16), as well as by the resentment of the Dravidians. See below, Section 2.2. Moreover, it could be used by the British as a legitimation of their 'civilizing mission' in the sense of a re-Aryanization of the Indians. Cf. Leopold, 'British Applications of the Aryan Theory of Race'. .

[83]Cf. Thapar 1992: 71; idem, 'Syndicated Moksha?', Seminar 313 (Sept. 1985), 14–22. Dayanand's exclusivism, of course, has also to be seen in the context of the British politics of Anglicization.

[84]Cf. Jordens, 'Dayanand Sarasvati's Concept of the Vedic Golden Age', in idem 1998: 71.

[85]Dayanand carefully took note of new results of research in the chronology of ancient India and referred to them in his calculations.

past. Trying to convey an activist attitude towards life to Hindus, he demanded a 'spirit of self-reliance', professed his 'thirst for improvement' and insisted on an 'extensive vision infinitely projected forward' (quoted in Kakar 1978: 163). As a reaction to foreign rule, which had turned into open imperialism in the meantime, Vivekananda's critique and reformulation of tradition were more radical (and in some instances also more self-contradictory) than those of Roy at the beginning of the century.

Vivekananda defended his concept of dynamic action even against the authority of the scriptures: 'Who cares what your scriptures say? I will go into a thousand hells cheerfully if I can rouse my countrymen, immersed in tamas (darkness), to stand on their own feet and be men inspired with the spirit of Karma yoga.' (Quoted in Kakar 1978: 175) According to him, religion was essentially linked with strength: 'The religion that does not bestow strength on the heart is no religion for me, whether it is that of the Upanishads, the Gita or the Bhagavatam.' (Quoted in Klimkeit 1981: 278) With an allusion to the western stereotype of the 'effeminate' Indian culture, he stated: 'It is a man-making religion that we want. It is man-making theories that we want.'[86]

Vivekananda's emphasis on Indian self-assertion and agency did not exclude the encounter with the Other. The 'cosmopolitan Swami'[87] explicitly repudiated the old purism and exclusivism of the Hindus.[88] It was precisely the disregard of the Other that he considered responsible for the 'degradation of the Indian mind'. Isolation from the external world had weakened India and made it a colony of the West in the end. But there was no justification in the Shastras for this attitude.[89] He confessed without further ado: 'We have indeed many things to learn from others, yes, that man who refuses to learn is already dead.'[90]

Instead of shutting off India hermetically against the West, he thought of a mutual give and take; India was to be seen mainly as a giver and, in any case, as an equal player.[91] India should try to advance the general spiritualization of mankind in the face of the materialistic tendencies of the West and, in this way, contribute 'to the progress and civilisation of the world'.[92] The renewal of Indian society involved going beyond its own boundaries: 'It is not only that we must revive our own country [...] my idea is the conquest of the whole world by India.'[93] By relating the peculiarities of East and West to universal tendencies of evolution, Vivekananda contributed

[86]'My Plan of Campaign', in *The Complete Works of Swami Vivekananda* (1989) (quoted hereafter: CW), III, 224.

[87]Agehananda Bharati, 'The Hindu Renaissance and its Apologetic Patterns', JAS 29 (1970), 267–87, here 282.

[88]This criticism was expressed in a sarcastic way: 'The paths of knowledge, devotion and Yoga—all have gone, and now there remains only that of Don't touch me: Don't touch me: The whole world is impure and I alone am pure.' Quoted in N. K. Devaraja 1975: 135.

[89]According to him, a 'broader conception of life' was expressed in the texts of antiquity, before the 'national vigour' disappeared. 'The Work before Us', CW III, 270, 271, 272.

[90]'The Common Bases of Hinduism', CW, III, 366–84, here 381. 'Religion for a long time has come to be static in India. What we want is to make it dynamic.' Ibid., 383.

[91]Indians had 'to teach a great lesson to the world'. 'The Work before us', CW, III, 272.

[92]'The Work before us', CW, III, 276.

[93]Ibid., 277.

towards the temporalization of the conflict situation. This opened up all-embracing perspectives, the expansion of Indian spirituality was to indicate the road to universal fraternity.[94]

Vivekananda's dealing with the past was also distinguished by an increased empirical basis and more differentiation. The openness towards the Other and the New corresponded to an unconditional acceptance of the variety and changeability of social organization and religious practices.[95] However, he strictly distinguished between the substance and the secondary elements of religion.[96] Based on this distinction, he sought to reconcile the quest for change with the adherence to tradition: 'This is my method—to show the Hindus that they have to give up nothing but only to move on in the line laid down by the sages and shake off their inertia, the result of centuries of servitude.'[97]

Vivekananda opposed the Arya Samaj and its rigidity as much as the more flexible Brahmo Samaj; both of them had produced only 'useless mixtures'.[98] He looked instead for a self-determined way of change: 'We must grow according to our nature. [...] We, with our traditions, with thousands of years of karma behind us, naturally can only follow our own bent. [...] If you find it is impossible for the European to throw off the few centuries of old culture which there is in the west, do you think it is possible for you to throw off the culture of shining scores of centuries? It cannot be.'[99]

Unlike Roy and Dayanand, Vivekananda has made an attempt to interpret the universal processes of change systematically, and with the use of Indian categories. Take, for instance, his essay 'Modern India':[100] on the basis of three fundamental forces (wisdom, passion, and gravity) and secondary factors like geography and personality, a dynamism unfolded, in which these powers were centralized successively in the hands of the four *varnas*, followed each time by processes of decentralizing. While the centralization always ended in stagnation, the decentralization again led to change. Thus the history of the entire world appears a succession of the eras of Brahmans, Kshatriyas, Vaishyas, and Shudras.

---

[94]A similar sketch of universal history is found in 'Raja Yoga': 'Different races take to different processes of controlling nature. [...] The externalists and the internalists are destined to meet at the same point, when both reach the extreme of their knowledge.' CW, I, 133.

[95]This included the caste system: 'Caste is a very good thing.' Interview with *The Hindu*, Feb. 1897, CW, V, 214. The caste system could even be made the pivotal point of a theory of social change: 'The plan in India is to make everybody a Brahman, the Brahman being the ideal of humanity. If you read the history of India, you will find that the attempts have always been made to raise the lower classes. Many are the classes that have been raised. Many more will follow till the whole will become Brahman. That is the plan.' Ibid. In a similar sense, a 'brahmanisation [...] of all classes and groups' is later referred to by Nehru. Cf. *An Autobiography* (New Delhi 1980), 432.

[96]Cf. Dietmar Rothermund, 'Traditionalism and National Solidarity in India', in Moore 1979: 191–7, here 192–3. 'It is the substance, the principle, that does not change. [...] The new method is—evolution of the old.' CW, V, 215.

[97]'A Plan of Work for India' (1895), CW, IV, 373.

[98]The Brahmo Samaj went too far with its readiness for adaptation: 'The test of truth for this Brahmo Samaj is "what our masters approve"; with us, what the Indian reasoning and experience approves.' CW, VIII, 477–8.

[99]'On India and her Problems', quoted in Varma 1967: 108–9. Cf. Klimkeit 1981: 276.

[100]See below, Sources, Section 1.2.

Indian and western patterns of historical interpretation are coming together here. If the sketch, on the one hand, reminds us of the traditional cyclical world-view, it is interspersed, on the other hand, with linear notions of development. The gradual emancipation of the Shudras is an example.[101] Another tendency of evolution, the growing dominance of consciousness over matter, corresponds to the expansion of spirituality propagated by Vivekananda (Someswarananda 1986: 17). At the end of the essay, however, particular emphasis is given to the virtues of the warrior (Kshatriya).[102] This is hardly compatible with India's spiritual mission.[103] But when it comes to political dynamism, even the vision of mutual give and take is suppressed by the demarcation between friend and foe: 'Zealous love for one's own people and country, showing itself in bitter hatred against another [...] is undoubtedly one of the main causes which lead to the advancement of one nation over another, by way of uniting itself in hostilities against one another.'[104]

The spiritual and the secular, the cyclical and the linear are often not reconciled with each other by Vivekananda.[105] The claim to historical agency tends to insert the spiritualization into the material context, which it is supposed to break through. On the other hand, the western dynamic, for its part, is encompassed by the timeless Indian existence, which includes any alien experience and anticipates all future developments. Thus Vivekananda infers with regard to the variety and changes of religion: 'Ours, as I have said, is the universal religion. It is inclusive enough, it is broad enough to include all the ideals. All the ideals of religion that already exist in the world can be immediately included, and we can patiently wait for all the ideals that are to come in the future to be taken in the same fashion, embraced in the infinite arms of the religion of the Vedanta.'[106]

In contrast to the early attempts of Hindus to reconcile their religious views and practices with the insights and demands of modernity, tendencies to modernization among the Indian Muslims can be observed only with a certain delay. Muslims found it difficult to adjust to English education and administration and gradually fell behind the Hindus. In 1837, Persian had been replaced

[101]The rule of the Shudras was traditionally seen as a symptom of kaliyuga.

[102]The essay concludes with a pathetic appeal to the manly vigour of India: 'O Thou Mother of Strength, take away my weakness, take away my unmanliness, and make me a Man!' ('Modern India', 480). Also: 'I want the strength, manhood, *kshatravirya* or the virility of a warrior.' *CW*, III, 224, quoted in Kakar 1978: 175.

[103]If Vivekananda emphasizes: 'Our religion is truer than any other religion, because it never conquered, because it never shed blood', in the same essay he also demands 'iron muscles and nerves of steel'. 'The Work before us', *CW*, III, 274, 278.

[104]'Modern India', *CW*, IV, 471. M. N. Roy has criticized Vivekananda's nationalism as 'spiritual imperialism'. Cf. Roy 1922: 193.

[105]The parallelism of the 'directional approach and circular path' is also noted by Someswarananda 1986: 9–10.

[106]Vivekananda, 'The Sages of India', *CW* III, 251–2. Vivekananda was convinced that 'Hinduism in principle already anticipates all future developments within itself'. Halbfass 1990: 238. And also the other way round: 'Regardless of the underlying postulate that the quiet transhistorical inclusiveness of the Vedanta is superior to the historical restlessness of European thought—the Vedanta is supposed to prove itself, to actualize its potential, in the current historical situation.' Ibid., 371.

with English as the official language, and after the failed revolt of 1857–8, which British authorities associated mainly with the Muslims, the end of Mughal rule was formally sealed. There were no prospects of regaining the dominance which had lasted for centuries. In this situation it was Sayyid Ahmad Khan (1817–98) who initiated a movement among the Muslims that should pave the way for modernization, just as Rammohun Roy had done among the Hindus. Impressed by the West's expansion and its scientific and technological advancement, Khan believed that only through inner reform and enlightenment could Indian Muslims regain control over their fate.

Khan sought to get his co-religionists interested in new scientific discoveries and he took care that European works became more accessible through translation into Urdu. Given the reservations of Muslims against western institutions, he founded the Muhammadan Anglo-Oriental College (Madrasat ul-ulum Musalmanan) in Aligarh in 1875,[107] which was to facilitate 'European education within a Muslim religious and moral environment'.[108] In fact, what was at stake was not just the acceptance of western education. It also had to be reconciled in a convincing manner with Islamic tradition. Khan, who, in his way of interpreting the Koran, reminds us very much of Roy's arguments regarding Hinduism, attempted to resolve the conflict between tradition and modern education by attributing the existing defects of the religious practice to later corruptions of what was originally a pure faith. The Koran itself was in no contradiction to natural laws, as the 'word of God' could not contradict the 'work of God'.

Of course, the Golden Age to which Muslim reformers referred lay outside the area of Indian culture. It was the historical expansion of Islam on which their hope for revitalizing tradition was ultimately based.[109] In general, it can be said about the religious reform movements of Hindus and Muslims that their adoption of modern western categories in the effort to provide their traditions with a new foundation did not always facilitate understanding *between* the communities, but rather hardened the lines of demarcation (Kenneth Jones 1989: 211). Syncretistic forms were now viewed with suspicion and were considered to have contributed to the degeneration from original purity. Moreover, there were instances of orthodox and traditionalist resistance within the communities, in the case of Khan as much as in the case of Roy earlier. In his attempt to demonstrate the compatibility of science with Islam, Khan was opposed in particular by the *madrasa* of Deoband (founded in 1867), whose theologians pronounced a *fatwa* against him.

Difficulties of this kind were characteristic of all movements of reform, revival, renaissance, etc. which attempted to merge the appropriation of the New and the defence of indigenous culture. Certainly, the religious traditions had their approved mechanisms of accommodating to social and political changes. In Hinduism, innovations could be interpreted, for example, as specific requirements of kaliyuga.[110] Great charismatic figures were worshipped as avatars, who

[107]In 1920 it became the Aligarh Muslim University.

[108]However, in the curriculum of Aligarh, the teaching of history had only a subordinate role. Cf. Lelyveld 1996: 245.

[109]This tendency can be observed even more in Shibli Nu'mani and in Muhammad Iqbal. See below.

[110]Cf. Jordens, 'Dayanand Sarasvati's Concept of the Vedic Golden Age' (in idem 1998), 67. The 'transitional movements' partly stayed in a century-old continuity of religious dissent. Cf. Kenneth Jones 1989: 210ff.

restated the moral order.[111] But worldly sense conceptions could not evolve independently against the dominance of transcendental interpretations—perhaps precisely because of the latter's flexibility in dealing with changing conditions.[112]

Under the circumstances of colonial rule, tensions between the New and the Old were intensified by increasing feelings of alienation. The challenge manifested itself particularly in the advancement of secularization. The western concept of progress did not only mean innovation and irreversible change, but also included the prevailing of science over religion.[113] The sweeping critique of India's religious traditions made it almost impossible to reconcile them with western modernity. If Roy came close to the concept of self-determined evolution guided by reason, Dayanand's attempt to renew Indian religion and society on the basis of the Vedas, in which all human knowledge had been laid down, amounted to its total dehistoricization. In Vivekananda, the emphasis on spirituality and the adoption of the material achievements of the West remained without reconciliation. The new and alien reality could be adopted only in the form of inclusion in or anticipation by the Self.[114]

The way in which Indian tradition is absorbed into concepts of universal history by the secular West, as shown above, gives expression to an asymmetric relation between West and East. This is countered by Neo-Hinduism with a different sort of asymmetry: inclusivism, according to which the Other and the New are always implicit in the Self. However, inclusivist dealing with the phenomenon of change contradicts a historical view of the relation between the cultures as much as does the western typology of progressive and static societies. The Hindu reform movements emphasize, it is true, the dynamic elements of Indian culture, but their tendencies towards essentialism render it difficult to conceive meaningful processes of change. The result is not historicization of the relation between the cultures, but a hierarchical subordination of the Other below the Self. Even the reformers' claim to the spiritual tradition is questioned. According to Agehananda Bharati, the insistence 'that things Indian had been "scientific", hence *really* modern, through the ages'[115] exhibits equally anti-Sanskritic as well as anti-historical elements.[116]

---

[111]Cf. Agehananda Bharati, 'The Hindu Renaissance and its Apologetic Patterns', *JAS* 29 (1970), 267–87, here 282. B. G. Gokhale, '"THUS IT HAS BEEN". The Indian View of History', in idem 1961: 1–23, here 14–15.

[112]Jan C. Heesterman has said, about the specifically Indian solution to the 'inner conflict of tradition', that in it the spheres of immanent power and transcendent spirituality formed a totality. Heesterman 1985.

[113]For the postulated reconciliation between science and religion, see Torkel Brekke, 'The Conceptual Foundation of Missionary Hinduism', *The Journal of Religious History* 23 (1999), 203–14, here 213.

[114]Inclusivism has been described by Paul Hacker as a specifically Indian form of the encounter with the Other and the integration of the experience of the Other into one's own horizon: 'Religiöse Toleranz und Intoleranz im Hinduismus', in idem, *Kleine Schriften*, ed. by Lambert Schmithausen (Wiesbaden 1978), 376–88.

[115]Bharati, 'The Hindu Renaissance', 274. Barun De, too, concludes: 'Indian liberal utopianism mistook its historical past.' De, 'A Historiographical Critique of Renaissance Analogues for Nineteenth-Century India', in idem 1977: 178–218, here 211.

[116]Bharati, 'The Hindu Renaissance' 123, 269. Bharati contrasts the modern English-speaking *sadhu* with the traditional agent of Sanskritization. Srinivas, on the one hand, regards the representatives of the new elite as continuing an indigenous tradition of self-critique going back to Vedic times; even bhakti and Vaishnavism were examples of it. On the other hand, he views the 'reinterpreted Hinduism' as the result of a concurrence of

2. THE AGENDA OF A MODERN INDIAN HISTORIOGRAPHY

In the religious reform movements, which were directed at social change and cultural self-assertion alike, the past became a subject of debate in a new way. Even if the reformers themselves made only sporadic reference to emerging empirical research, their efforts added in a decisive manner to the growing 'hunger for history'.[117] Viewing tradition as a problem and making its critical examination a basis for renewal, Roy, Dayanand, Vivekananda, Khan, and others defined, to some extent, the categorical framework that was to determine historical thinking in South Asia in the period of colonial rule and the freedom movement.

Orientalist and historical research in the West offered both support and challenge to the Indian search for a rational relationship to the past. It was not by adoption of a ready-made model,[118] but through a long process of reception, comparison, and modification or even rejection of methods, concepts, strategies, and basic assumptions that the Europeans' approach to the past (whether Indian or their own) made an impact on Indian thinking. We will trace, here, the European impact on forms of historical thinking in South Asia, with reference to three central features of the modern western concept of history: the consciousness of method, an explicit relation of the past to practical purposes, and the linear interpretation of change, that is the tendencies of empiricization, perspectivization and processualization.[119] The institutionalization of history as a specific research discipline was the clearest manifestation of these tendencies but not the only one. Innovations also entered the spheres of literature and politics, which were in manifold interaction with the emerging academic discourse. Moreover, as the indigenous roots of modernization are generally reconsidered today,[120] it should be noted that even historical thinking in South Asia did not exclusively follow western lines.[121]

The sectionwise arrangement of the sources presented in this volume, each section focusing on one of the features mentioned, does not intend to assign authors to academic schools or political positions, even if histories of historiography frequently put 'objectivists' against 'nationalists' or

---

westernization and the revival of Sanskrit culture. It was 'essentially a puritanical movement in which an attempt was made to distinguish the "essence" of Hinduism from its historical accretions.' Srinivas 1995: 131.

[117]Rabindranath Tagore, 'Aitihasik Citra', quoted in Kaviraj 1995: 124, 185.

[118]Much of what today appears as the western mode of history was formed in coping with non-western realities and the notion of 'Indian tradition' became fixed by way of its confrontation with the West. The reciprocal reference in the evolution of these concepts is emphasized in Peter van der Veer, 'History and Culture in Hindu Nationalism', in Ritual, State and History in South Asia: Essays in Honour of J. C. Heesterman, ed. A. W. van den Hoek, D. H. A. Kloff and M. S. Oort (Leiden: Brill, 1992), 717–32.

[119]For a systematic foundation of the 'disciplinary matrix' of the historical discipline, see Jörn Rüsen, Historische Vernunft [Grundzüge einer Historik I: Die Grundlagen der Geschichtswissenschaft] (Göttingen: Vandenhoeck and Ruprecht, 1983) 24ff. Rüsen here distinguishes five factors: interests (need of orientation), ideas (leading aspects), methods of research, forms of representation, and functions of existential orientation.

[120]The precolonial beginnings of the modernization of historical thinking in India have been pointed out by Barun De, 'A Preliminary Note on the Writing of the History of Modern India', Quarterly Review of Historical Studies 3 (1963–64), 39–46, here 41.

[121]For resistant traditions and alternatives to the dominant discourse, see below, Section 3.

'traditionalists' against 'modernists'.[122] Nor are the sections related to subsequent phases, although periods of methodization, nationalization and processualization can be distinguished and set off against each other according to the first occurrence of source critique, a clear political perspective and the idea of progress.[123] What is at stake, rather, is the various attempts at clarification of practical problems, which occur partly synchronically and partly in phase displacement and which are interlocked and related to each other. These attempts can be observed in exemplary manner in certain authors or texts and they are increasingly systematized in the new discipline of historical research.[124]

2.1 History as an Object of Research

In the massive resistance to Roy's efforts to print and translate some of the sacred texts, it becomes tangible that the mere rendering accessible of traditional knowledge hitherto monopolized by the Brahmans meant a deep break in Indian culture. On the other hand, a new empirical interest in the past manifested itself even among the traditonal elite. During the time of Roy's reform activities, the first history books printed in Bengali appeared from the pen of three pandits who were working as language teachers at the College of Fort William.[125] Ramram Basu's *Raja Pratapaditya Charita* (1801),[126] the biography of a king, Rajiblochan Mukhopadhyay's *Maharaj Krishnachandra Rayasya Charitram* (1805), and Mrityunjay Vidyalankar's *Rajabali* (1808),[127] chronicles of rulers, appear to Ranajit Guha as 'the site of a contest between very different, indeed mutually antagonistic ways of interpreting the past'. Mrityunjay Vidyalankar's integration of the mythical past and the most recent events up to the rise of the East India Company into one continuous narration was characterized by 'too easy a traffic between the secular and the supernatural, between fact and fancy'. Nevertheless, the very fact that the work 'should lend itself to be questioned at all on the ground of evidence and authenticity' testifies to the increasing relevance of empirical research (Guha 1988: 32).[128]

[122]K. N. Panikkar, 'The Intellectual History of Colonial India. Some Historiographical and Conceptual Questions', in Bhattacharya and Thapar 1986: 403–33, here 405, has shown how difficult it can be to relate intellectual movements to specific social conditions and political positions. Some approaches can serve almost antagonistic political purposes. For the need of a 'social history of historiography' that is still to be written, see Sumit Sarkar 1997: 1–49, here 1–2.

[123]Cf., for instance, Sabyasachi Bhattacharya, 'Paradigms lost: Notes on social history in India', *EPW* XVII (April 1982), 690–6; idem, 'History from Below', *Social Scientist* 119 (April 1983), 3–20, here 6–7; Satish Chandra, 'Main Trends in Historical Sciences in India: 1900–70', in idem 1996: 57–82.

[124]The interpretations suggested here should not undervalue other aspects in the author's thinking. The range of the respective historical interest is made evident in the Sources section through the indication of further source material.

[125]The College of Fort William had been set up in 1800 with the vocation of preparing young employees of the East India Company in the indigenous languages and cultures.

[126]According to William Carey, the Head of the Bengali section at Fort William, this was the first prose book in Bengali.

[127]According to Partha Chatterjee, this was 'the first history of India in the Bengali language that we have in print': Chatterjee 1993: 77. Mrityunjay Vidyalankar counted among the opponents of Roy. Cf. Halbfass 1990: 210–11.

[128]In 1840, the growing need for factual knowledge of the past was expressed by Krishna Mohun Banerjea,

The growing prestige of historical knowledge was enhanced by the inclusion of history in the syllabus of missionary schools and colleges. The use of examples from history (mostly from European antiquity) emphasized the link between historical memory and practical life. The disparaging comments of the utilitarians about the reliability of Indian records,[129] in their own way, also evoked rising attention to the 'real' facts of the past. The results of epigraphical, numismatic and archaeological research (with their partly sensational discoveries) not only demonstrated the success of western research methods; the foundation of a reliable chronology of early Indian history also bestowed a new stability and offered orientation amidst all the uncertainty of the present situation.[130]

The systematic research into and representation of ancient Indian history, in particular, produced, as Romesh Chunder Dutt summed up some decades later, a widespread interest in the past. Max Müller's Edition of the Rig Veda, at the latest, 'opened to Hindu students generally the great and ancient volume, which had hitherto remained sealed with seven seals to all but a very few scholars; and it awakened in them a historical interest in the past—a desire to inquire into their ancient history and ancient faith from original sources' (Dutt 1963: VIII).[131]

A mutual influence of historical research and literature can be observed in the beginnings of novel writing. The 'large-scale use of historical material for writing fiction'[132] correlated with the restructuring of empirical material through new narrative forms. At the same time, demand was raised to strictly separate history and fiction from each other, and, as a result, the term *itihasa* finally acquired its definite linkage to the factual.[133] The increasing appreciation of factual knowledge corresponded to a growing doubt about the reliability of the Puranas.[134] This intensified the call for the adoption of scientific methods.

---

who, in his 'Discourse on the Nature and Importance of Historical Studies', complained about the 'lamentable want of authentic records in [...] literature'. *Selection of Discourses Delivered at the Meetings of the Society for the Acquisition of General Knowledge* (Calcutta 1840), quoted in Nandy, 1995: 65.

[129]What was also criticized was Indians' incapability to use the sources properly. Mill related the defeat of Tipu Sultan in his struggle against the British at the end of the eighteenth century to the lack of organization and of generalization in dealing with tradition characteristic of a 'rude and early state of society'. Cf. Majeed 1992: 137.

[130]This tendency was supported by more empathetic accounts of Indian history, like the one written by Elphinstone (see below, Sources, Section 1.1).

[131]Dutt 1963. Dutt considered Rammohun Roy and Dayanand Sarasvati to be among the pioneering *Indian* scholars. For the confrontation between oral tradition and written culture in the late nineteenth century, see Sumit Sarkar, '"Kaliyuga," "Chakri", and "Bhakti": Ramakrishna and His Times', *EPW* (18 July 1992), 1543–66.

[132]This can also be seen as an indicator 'of an emerging, though still inchoate, feeling of selfhood for the people'. Meenakshi Mukherji, 'Rhetoric of Identity: History and Fiction in Nineteenth Century India', in Alok Bhalla and Sudhir Chandra 1993: 34–47, here 34. The historical interest reflects a totally new approach to life: 'Interest in the past is a necessary offshoot of man's active involvement in the present as something real and important (not *maya*).' Meenakshi Mukherjee 1985: 42.

[133]Cf. Meenakshi Mukherjee 1985: 42.

[134]Cf., for instance, Tarinicharan Chattopadhyay's remarks about the unreliability of Sanskrit sources: 'All Sanskrit sources that are now available are full of legends and fabulous tales; apart from the *Rajatarangini* there is not a single true historical account.' *Bharatbarsher itihas* (1878), quoted in Partha Chatterjee 1993: 95.

As regards the professionalization of research[135] in India, the systematic gathering of source materials, and the development of new ways to interpret them, British institutions for a long time represented the most important framework. The process of a gradual involvement of Indian researchers in this work is best personified by Rajendralal Mitra (1822–91), who was in the service of the Asiatic Society of Bengal for thirty-five years, first as a secretary and librarian and later as a member of the 'Council', before he became the Vice-President and was finally elected President of the society.[136] Outstanding among the historians working in colleges and universities was Ramkrishna Gopal Bhandarkar (1837–1925), a pioneer of both methodical source critique and research-based historiography. He sought to bring Indian historiography up to the level of western standards, hoping that Indians would one day assume their 'legitimate place among the investigators of the political, literary and religious history of our country and not allow the Germans, the French, and the English to monopolize the field'.[137] According to Bhandarkar, the Indian search for a glorious past had to be strictly tied to 'reliable evidence'. He urged the historian to document all versions in case of conflicting testimonies.

Even Bhandarkar, however, whose work is still regarded as a model of unbiased, objective research, was aware of the relationship between historical cognition and practical issues. Indian investigators, unlike the more detached foreigners, legitimately took 'a personal interest in the religious and social institutions that now prevail in the country, their past history and the efforts that are now made to modify and reform them'.[138] The adoption of the philological and historical method of source critique, in fact, meant more to Bhandarkar than just the acquisition of technical tools. It served to improve the general capabilities of theoretical analysis and practical judgement and offered orientation in the search for the good and the reasonable (Collected Works, I: 891). Just as the rational approach to tradition characterized the attitude of the reformers, the first professional historians, on their part, perceived historical research as a support of social reforms.

The new skills not only served the critical self-examination of Indian society; they also helped revise western assumptions and overcome prejudices about India.[139] Some of these had even entered textbooks of schools and colleges. As early as 1857, Nilmani Basak protested against conveying the impression to the students that 'the ancient Hindus were a stupid lot'.[140] Some

[135] According to O. P. Kejariwal, it began only after 1850: Kejariwal 1988: 153.

[136] Mitra supervised the publications of the Bibliotheca Indica, published the antiquarian section of the Journal of the Asiatic Society of Bengal, and was also involved in great editing projects. See below, Sources, Section 2.1.

[137] 'The Critical, Comparative, and Historical Method of Inquiry, as Applied to Sanskrit Scholarship and Philology and Indian Archaeology', in Collected Works of Sir R. G. Bhandarkar, ed. Narayana Bapuji Utgikar and Vasudev Gopal Paranjpe (Poona 1933) (quoted hereafter: Collected Works), I, 362–92, here 392.

[138] 'The Ideal of an Indian Scholar', in Collected Works, I, 476–9, here 478 (first published in The Times of India, 19 July 1893).

[139] Cf. Bhandarkar on the 'Aberrations of European Scholars' and 'Instances of uncritical methods' in his 'Presidential Address at the Opening Session of the First Oriental Conference of India, held at Poona on the 5th of November 1919', in Collected Works, I, 316–31, here 321ff.; see also: 'The Critical, Comparative, and Historical Method', 392.

[140] Nilmani Basak, Bharatbarsher itihas [History of India], 3 Vols. (1857–8), quoted in Guha 1988: 40–1.

time later, Rajanikanta Gupta (*Sipahi Juddher Itihas*, 1880) and Akshaykumar Maitreya (*Sirajuddowla*, 1898) took up the fight about memory more systematically. Based on their familiarity with the sources, they countered English interpretations and their bias with empirical evidence.[141] The wrong assessment by western experts of entire branches of literature with regard to their informational value was also criticized. Radha Kumud Mookherji opposed the sweeping devaluation of Indian tradition as being mere 'poetry and fiction'. Texts like the Brahmanas, and Sutras had not been written to cultivate the imagination, but had served 'actual purposes of life', which they reflected and documented (Radha Kumud Mookherji 1921: 71–2).

The methodical appropriation of Hindu tradition put increasing emphasis on early Indian history as against that of the Mughal epoch, which, because of its easier accessibility, hitherto had mainly attracted western research interest. Not without a critical comment on Hindu orthodoxy, R. C. Dutt demanded: 'For the Hindu student, the history of the Hindu period should not be a blank, nor a confused jumble of historic and legendary names, religious parables and Epic and Puranic myths.' By highlighting the educational value of history, Dutt pointed out its relevance for collective self-understanding: 'No study has so potent an influence in forming a nation's mind and a nation's character as a critical and careful study of its past history. And it is by such study alone that an unreasoning and superstitious worship of the past is replaced by a legitimate and manly admiration (Dutt 1963: XI)'.

The expectations about the role of history in the formation of identity certainly also produced dangers to the standards of critical research. This became particularly evident in the rising trends to communalize history according to regional, linguistic or religious aspects, as for instance in the description of the Marathas' struggle against Muslim rule, in which Shivaji was worshipped as a hero of Hindu resistance. Jadunath Sarkar (1870–1958) tried to give a more realistic and detached account of the events. He also acknowledged the Mughals' contribution to the modernization of India.[142] While Bhandarkar worked towards the demystification of early Indian history, Sarkar focused on a rational and objective approach to the history of the Mughal empire. 'The headlong decay of the age-old Muslim rule in India, and the utter failure of the last Hindu attempt at empire-building by the new-sprung Marathas [...] must be studied with an accuracy of details as to facts and penetrating analysis as to causes, if we wish to find out the true solutions of the problems of modern India and avoid pitfalls of the past.'[143] Convinced that the methodical investigation into the past should aid the capability to progress, Sarkar 'urged that an accurate understanding of the large-scale forces operating in the subcontinent in Mughal times and of the failures of both Mughals and Marathas would better serve the needs of modern Indians than

[141]Rabindranath Tagore viewed Maitreya's efforts as the beginning of a free Bengali historiography and a success 'in breaking our mental bonds'. Quoted in Guha 1988: 53. For the criticism in textbooks of Krishnachandra Ray and Kshirodchandra Raychaudhuri, cf. Partha Chatterjee 1988: 90.

[142]'It broke the isolation of the provinces and the barrier between India and the outer world, and thus took the first step necessary for the modernization of India and the growth of an Indian nationality in some distant future.' Jadunath Sarkar, 'Preface' in idem 1988, I: XV. However, even Sarkar himself contributed to the disparaging treatment of the Muslims. For these tendencies in his account of the history of Bengal, see Joya Chatterji 1995: 183ff.

[143]Ibid., XV.

a thoughtless patriotic broadside'.[144] Sarkar had to defend himself against both sides. Patriotic historians from Maharashtra were filled with indignation at the critical examination of Marathi sources; Muslim readers accused him of hurting the feelings of the followers of Islam with his depiction of Aurangzeb.

Nevertheless, even among Muslims, reformers like Sayyid Ahmad Khan and his student and collaborator Muhammad Shibli Nu'mani (1857–1915) attempted to reconcile the religious tradition with scientific and methodic principles. After Khan had demonstrated it in the Koran exegesis, Shibli attempted to substantiate scientific history out of the Islamic scholarly tradition, which had sunk temporarily into oblivion and had become corrupted.

Finally, the critical potential of historical research was also brought to bear against subliminal social and economic interests.[145] To the early Marxists, the Brahmanic monopoly of tradition appeared as an expression of class rule. S. A. Dange saw at work a conspiracy of Brahmans who continued to suppress other traditions in the interest of their moral incontestability; they hid behind the alleged fictionality of the literary testimonies of ancient India as soon as it contained negative details about Hindu culture (cf. Dange 1949: 20–1). The social reformer and Dalit leader B. R. Ambedkar also complained about the 'intolerance of the Brahmin scholar towards any attempt to expose the brahmanic literature' and the 'conspiracy of silence'.[146] He himself had suffered from it during his investigations into the origins of Shudras and Untouchables. The widening of the source base in a different direction was brought about by the emerging economic history. D. Naoroji and R. C. Dutt referred in particular to the 'blue books' of the government, not least for the sake of their reliability and their persuasive power with British readers.

If the examination of evidence helped unveil as ideology some widespread assumptions about Indian society, it was the research in early Indian history which, in Dutt's eyes, also helped remove 'the very common and very erroneous impression that Ancient India has no history worth studying, no connected and reliable chronicle of the past which would be interesting or instructive to the modern reader' (Dutt 1963: 2). The improving knowledge of ancient history made the Indian records appear even more valuable than those of other classical cultures. The texts of the Hindus, in spite of lacking many things available in the better documented traditions of the West, distinguished themselves in that 'they give us a full, connected and clear account of the advancement of civilization, of the progress of the human mind, such as we shall seek for in vain among the records of any other equally ancient nation' (Dutt 1963: 1).[147]

Methodical dealing with the records of the past turned out to be an element of Indian self-

---

[144]Frank Conlon, '(Sir) Jadunath Sarkar', in Boia 1991: 364–5.

[145]An early attempt to include the life of the common people in the account of history had been undertaken by the British historian William Hunter. Cf. Sabyasachi Bhattacharya, 'History from Below', Social Scientist 119 (April 1983), 3–20, here 5.

[146]Ambedkar 1948: p. III. Ambedkar appealed to the historian 'to use his imagination and intuition to bridge the gaps left in the chain of facts by links not yet discovered and to propound a working hypothesis suggesting how facts which cannot be connected by known facts might have been inter-connected' (p. VI). 'For without trained imagination, no scientific inquiry can be fruitful and hypothesis is the very soul of science.' Ibid., p. VII.

[147]For the primacy of the interest in the history of civilization, cf. Mill, HBI, I, 30.

confidence, for the simple reason that it was proof of the very rationality which was denied Indians by many observers from the West. Especially, the opening up of the civilizational dimension of Indian history was directed against western efforts to tie India down to a position of dependence, even at the intellectual level. Yet, in spite of the pervasive spirit of improvement, there was also a need for continuity, for linking the new with tradition. 'It is not enough that any particular reform that may be suggested is good in itself. The question that is of vital importance is whether it can be engrafted on the existing organism of Hindu Society, whose roots go back into prehistoric times and which contains vestiges of all that it has at any period of its life assimilated or had to struggle against.'[148]

Historical thinking at the turn of the century was confronted with the problem of how social progress and the self-assertion of tradition against colonialism were to be reconciled. Emerging forms of nativism, as will become evident in the next section, obscured the view of the Indian capacity for change as much as did western racism.

2.2 *In Quest of a Perspective*

R. G. Bhandarkar claimed the objectivity of historical research against western errors of judgement; he nevertheless also argued against Indian attempts to make the knowledge about the past too easily serve political purposes. He opposed, in particular, the 'angle of vision' of that sort of Indian whose 'tendency may be towards rejecting foreign influence on the development of his country's civilization and to claim high antiquity for some of the occurrences in its history'.[149] Bhandarkar complained that 'a false race-pride has sprung up and dominates the minds of a great many persons, old as well as young'.[150] With this, he took a stand on certain assumptions about the Indian past, underlying mainly the work of nationalist historians.

On the other hand, towards the end of the nineteenth century, it had become evident to some that only by relating to the current situation and by consciously directing the research interest towards the acquisition of political autonomy would that dimension of reality become accessible in which Indians could perceive themselves as historical actors. This occurred, initially, outside the academic discipline, and it was in particular the novelist Bankimchandra Chatterjee (1838–94) who made the fact of foreign rule a basic question of historical research: 'Why are we a subject nation?' 'Why have we remained subjugated for so long?' In his answer, which he hoped would contribute to throwing away the shackles of dependence, he emphasized the absence of a tradition of historiography in India: 'There is no Hindu history.' If heroism was lacking, this

[148]Bhandarkar, 'The Ideal of an Indian Scholar' (*Collected Works*, I), 478. This applies also to the mediation between old and new forms of erudition. For Bhandarkar's relation to the 'old school' of traditionally educated Pandits, see his 'Presidential Address' at the Oriental Conference in 1919 (*Collected Works*, I), 316–17.

[149]Bhandarkar, 'Presidential Address', 319–20. Cf. also idem, 'The Critical, Comparative, and Historical Method' (*Collected Works*, I), 392, 417ff.

[150]'The Ideal of an Indian Scholar', 471. Mitra, too, had rejected that sort of patriotism which, in the end, uncritically accepted anything that was of indigenous origin. Cf. Sisir Kumar Mitra, 'Raja Rajendralal Mitra', in Sen 1973: 1–14, here 13.

was mainly due to a lack of records: 'The Hindus have no such glorious qualities simply because there is no written evidence.'[151] The insight into the practical importance of historical memory led back to questions of political strategy: 'A nation with historical reminiscences of its past glory tries to retain its glory, and if this be lost, it tries to regain it. [...] Nowadays Bengalees want to be great, but alas! Where are the historical reminiscences of Bengalees?'[152]

In addition to the lack of indigenous historiography, there were distortions at the hands of foreign historians, who systematically suppressed the achievements and the physical prowess (*bahubol*) of the Hindus in their accounts.[153] None of the books on Bengal written by British authors 'contain a true history of Bengal'. The private life of Muslim rulers who were described in those works constituted 'not even a partial history of Bengal. It does not have any connection with Bengal's history.' The Bengalis, Bankimchandra concluded, had to write their history themselves, from their own viewpoint and relating to their own interests: 'We need a history of Bengal, otherwise there is no hope for Bengal. But who will write it? You will write it, I will write it, everyone will write this history. Whosoever is a Bengalee will write it.' It could not be left to a single individual but required the united endeavour of the entire community: 'It has to be done through collective effort.'[154] Through the authentic account of the common past political agency could be regained.[155]

In spite of his critical stand on the accounts of foreign historians, Bankimchandra did not recommend continuing the indigenous tradition of the Puranas either. Postulating a nexus between historical memory and political agency, he consciously adopted western notions of history.[156] He admitted candidly that the Bengalis had received the ideas of freedom and national solidarity from the British.[157] For the sake of improvement, even imitation was allowed to a certain extent.[158]

[151]*Bankim Rachanavali*, II, 236, quoted in T. W. Clark, 'The Role of Bankimchandra in the Development of Nationalism', in Philips 1961: 429–45, here 436.

[152]'*Bangalar itihas sambandhe kayekti katha*' ('A few words about the history of Bengal'), in *Bankim Rachanavali*, II, 336–40, here 336 (see below, Sources 2.2). This insight made some Bengali contemporaries believe that the lack of Hindu historiograpy was to be attributed to the ruling Muslims who had consciously destroyed the history books extant in earlier times. Cf. Chowdhury 1998: 52.

[153]'Because Indians are weak and effeminate.' Quoted in Clark, 'The Role of Bankimchandra', in Philips 1961: 435–6.

[154]'*Bangalar itihas sambandhe kayekti katha*' loc. cit.

[155]'In this mode of recalling the past, the power to represent oneself is nothing other than political power itself.' Partha Chatterjee 1993: 76.

[156]Bankimchandra could have referred, however, even to new tendencies in Bengali literature. According to Guha, already in Ramram Basu and Mrityunjay Vidyalankar (see above), the effort at demythologizing the past corresponded to a closer relation to the present. Guha 1988: 34, 36.

[157]'Of all the things we have learnt from the British, the concepts of independence and nationalism are to me the most important.' 'Bharater kalanka', in *Bankim Rachanavali*, II, 234–41, here 241, quoted in Meenakshi Mukherji, 'Rhetoric of Identity', 39.

[158]'One cannot learn except by imitation. Just as children learn to speak by imitating the speech of adults, to act by imitating the actions of adults, so do uncivilised and uneducated people learn by imitating the ways of the civilised and the educated. Thus it is reasonable and rational that Bengalis should imitate the English.'

Opposed to the tendency to trace back all modern achievements to Indian origins, Bankimchandra perceived the evolution of mankind as analogous to that of scientific progress: 'In worldly matters I accept the teachings of science in demonstrating that the world is evolving gradually from an incomplete and undeveloped state towards a complete and developed form.'[159] However, he held no brief for an Anglicizing reformism. He followed a different strategy of Indian modernization that, while adjusting to the standards set by the West, would reserve an inner space for the indigenous culture which gave expression to Indian identity and even established a certain level of superiority over the materialistic West (Partha Chatterjee 1993: 26). He referred in particular to the 'non-possessive, non-utilitarian concept of duty' of the Bhagavadgita which formed the core of dharma (Partha Chatterjee 1996: 66). The combination of western science and eastern spirituality, then, was supposed to produce the perfect human being: 'The day the European industries and sciences are united with Indian dharma, man will be god.'[160]

It was assumed that what appeared antagonistic to western eyes was implicit in Indian thinking: 'The philosophy of spirit is beyond the limits of Western science, not opposed to it.'[161] But Bankimchandra did not escape from the dilemma that became evident in Vivekananda, too (see above):[162] the notion of historical agency aiming at self-determined processes of development was confronted with the assumption of a timeless essence of Indian culture. Bankimchandra conceived the required collective consciousness as 'national religion' (anushilan). This had yet to be created by the intellectuals as protagonists.[163] Even the possibility of changes in the interpretation of the divine truth was not ruled out: 'As times change, it is necessary to reinterpret

'Anukaran', in *Bankim Rachanavali*, II, 201, quoted in Partha Chatterjee 1996: 65. After all, even the English sought to learn from others.

[159]'Krishnacarita', in *Bankim Rachanavali*, II, 434, quoted in Partha Chatterjee 1996: 62. Bankimchandra went as far as to concede that, with reference to social progress, British rule in India could be viewed as a welcome improvement. 'For one who is oppressed, it makes no difference whether the oppressor is one's compatriot or whether he is foreign.' *Bharatvarser svadhinata evam paradhinata*', quoted in Partha Chatterjee 1996: 64.

[160]'Dharmatattva', in *Bankim Rachanavali*, II, 633, quoted in Partha Chatterjee 1996: 66.

[161]'Shrimadbhagavadgita', in *Bankim Rachanavali*, II, 701, quoted in Partha Chatterjee, 1996: 69. The West was not able to understand the East. 'European scholars, like Professor Max Müller, have been very eloquent on the importance of the study of the Vedas, but their point of view is exclusively the European point of view, and fails to represent the vastly superior interest Vedic studies possess of us, natives of the country.' 'Vedic Literature: An Address', in *Bankim Rachanavali*, I (*English Works*) (Calcutta 1969), 150. In a dispute (1882) with William Hastie, Bankimchandra reproached certain Europeans with a 'monstrous claim to omniscience': 'No knowledge to them is true knowledge unless it has passed through the sieve of European criticism. All coin is false coin unless it bears the stamp of a Western mint'. 'The Intellectual Superiority of Europe', in *Bankim Rachanavali*, I, 210. A European 'will fail in arriving at a correct comprehension of Hinduism, as—I say it most emphatically—*as every other European who has made the attempt has failed.*' 'European Versions of Hindoo Doctrines', in *Bankim Rachanavali*, I, 205. Emphasis in original.

[162]It has not been ascertained how far Vivekananda, in his conception of Hinduism, had been influenced by Bankimchandra's ideas as expressed in his posthumously published essays on the philosophy of religion.

[163]'I do expect that if intellectuals accept this religion, a national character will finally be built.' 'Dharmatattva', in *Bankim Rachanavali*, II, 651, quoted in Partha Chatterjee 1996: 73.

the words of God in accordance with the new social conditions and the advances in social knowledge.'[164] But in view of the impending alienation, in the current confrontation with an oppressive Other, the New is perceived as a revival of something that has existed since time immemorial. In order to show that 'Hinduism is the greatest of all religions', one had only to 'sweep it clean of the dross that had accumulated over the centuries'.[165]

This attitude cannot be explained simply by referring to traditional Indian inclusivism. The positive attitude to change and the experience of the Other is too evident, despite the reference to the eternal and universal dharma. It may be rather the essentialist structure of Orientalism to which Bankimchandra remains bound in a way which Partha Chatterjee has described as follows: 'We have in Bankim a reversal of the Orientalist problematic, but within the same general thematic.' The western typology of historical and ahistorical cultures is countered by him in a manner which is itself typological instead of exposing the ahistorical character of the typology: he aims at 'a specific subjectivity for the nation, but within an essentialist typology of cultures in which this specificity can never be truly historical'.[166]

This ambivalence is symptomatic of the 'moment of departure' of Indian nationalism around 1885, and of the difficult reconciliation between the will to change and political self-assertion under the prevailing conditions of colonialism. The defence of the particular is in problematical relationship with the tendencies to temporalization and appears to favour essentialism. Even in European nationalism, which was taken up by Bankimchandra as a model, the implied eternity and unchangeability of tradition often ran counter to the postulated historicity and malleability of conditions. In this way, the characteristic and the permanent were invoked in the face of the levelling process of modernization. Under the circumstances of colonialism, the fear of impending alienation was intensified, since the indigenous culture appeared to the colonizer to be historically superseded, if it was not considered completely ahistorical and consequently a legitimate object for conquest. If the colonizer thought of the Indian future only in terms of emulating western progress, nationalist historians almost automatically assumed it to be their task to prove that the desired modern achievements were genuinely Indian and, basically, were always inherent in Indian reality.[167]

Bankimchandra did not translate his programmatic ideas into concrete historiography. His lasting impact on the historical views of the public was mainly due to his novels, in which he gave

[164]'Shrimadbhagavadgita', in *Bankim Rachanavali*, II, 695, quoted in Partha Chatterjee 1996: 74.

[165]'Dharmatattva', in *Bankim Rachanavali*, II, 668, quoted in Partha Chatterjee 1996: 74. In the posthumously published 'Letters on Hinduism' (*Bankim Rachanavali*, I, 227–69) it becomes evident that for Bankimchandra the principles of 'true Hinduism' were valid for 'all times and for all mankind'. Quoted in Klimkeit 1981: 105.

[166]Partha Chatterjee 1996: 73. For the concepts of 'thematic' and 'problematic', following Anwar Abdel Malek ('Orientalism in Crisis', *Diogenes* 44 [1963], 102–40), see Partha Chatterjee, 1996: 36ff.

[167]Moreover, the inner realm remains encompassed by conditions of colonialism as much as the inner realm of the romantics is by the modern state and society (see above). Cf. Gyan Prakash, 'Writing Post-Orientalist Histories of the Third World: Perspectives from Indian Historiography', *Comparative Studies in Society and History* 32 (1990), 383–408, here 388.

vivid descriptions of Hindu resistance against foreign invaders. With this Bankimchandra hoped to strengthen the feeling of solidarity and to create a sense of pride in the past, a basic requirement of political agency. The consciousness of national history that was taking shape in the literary imagination soon began to invade the political sphere and stimulate public agitation. In Maharashtra, another centre of national uprising besides Bengal, it was Bal Gangadhar Tilak (1856–1920) who systematically used the memory of former glory as a weapon in the fight against colonial rule. Tilak, like Bankimchandra and the religious reformers, rejected the image of the passive, other worldly Hindu and propagated an activist notion of the Indian tradition. His interpretation of the classical texts, especially the Bhagavadgita, gave emphasis to practical aspects and *karma yoga*. According to Tilak, the ancestors had 'never intended that the goal of life should be meditation alone. No one can expect Providence to protect one who sits with folded arms and throws his burden on others. God does not help the indolent.'[168]

In determining political objectives, Tilak went beyond most of his contemporaries. According to him, the Indian fight was directed not only at improving conditions within the existing institutional framework but at attaining self-rule: *swaraj*. By swaraj, though, he did not mean only external freedom but also a freedom perceived internally. There was a link between individual salvation (moksha) and the autonomy of the people. 'What is then this Swaraj? It is a life centred in Self and dependent upon Self.'[169] While the freedom struggle was anchored in the religious sphere, religious salvation depended on political preconditions: 'It is my conviction, it is my thesis, that Swaraj in the life to come cannot be the reward of a people who have not enjoyed it in this world.'[170]

Tilak's way of thinking also contained elements of western modernity, as becomes evident, for instance, in his postulate that 'swaraj is my birthright'.[171] But he projected the modern concepts like that of the Indian nation back to the remote past: 'During Vedic times India was a self-contained country. It was united as a great nation. That unity has disappeared bringing on us great degradation and it becomes the duty of the leaders to revive that union.'[172] Tilak did not intend to legitimize internal reforms but to demonstrate the superiority of the Indian tradition over that of others. With his own investigations, he entered into competition for the earliest possible dating of the Hindu culture. The assumption was that the Vedas represented the oldest tradition of mankind from which all knowledge originated.[173] On the one hand, this freed Indians from being impelled to see themselves as backward and established, to a certain extent, even a primacy with regard to evolution. Tilak stressed, as a special quality of Hinduism, its compatibility with the discoveries of modern science. On the other hand, he pointed out the eternal quality of Hindu dharma and contrasted it with the time-bound nature of Christianity.

Unlike the reformist approaches of Dayanand and Bankimchandra, Tilak's interest in the

[168]'Karma Yoga and Swaraj', in Grover 1990: 215–6.
[169]Ibid. For similar ideas of Gandhi, see below.
[170]Ibid.
[171]The principle of natural equality contradicted orthodox principles. Cf. Klimkeit 1981: 230.
[172]B. G. Tilak, 'The Bharata Dharma Mahamandala', in Tilak 1922: 36.
[173]Thus the origin of the Vedas was dated to the time of c. 4000 BC. Cf. Tilak 1893 and 1903.

past was linked with social conservatism. He demanded strict adherence to tradition, which was an intrinsic value and, therefore, should not be perceived selectively: 'A true nationalist desires to build on old foundations. Reform based on utter disrespect for the old does not appeal to him as constructive work. [...] We do not want to anglicize our institutions and so denationalize them in the name of social and political reforms.'[174] Even though Tilak factually borrowed from western concepts, he insisted on the divine sanction of traditional Hindu values and opposed their revision or modernist reformulation.

Tilak also discovered religious feelings to be an important force in the fight for independence. Instead of relying on intellectual constructs, he appealed to the living tradition and made efforts to revive old festivals and regional loyalties. The processions in honour of Lord Ganesha, for instance, provided the national movement with a religious aura. In this manner, practical efficiency joined hands with adherence to old institutions. If 'we give a more or less new turn to the old institutions, they will in all probability become popular and soon they will be permanent' (quoted in Embree 1988: 32). The activation of and control over emotions required strict contrasts between the Self and the Other: 'If you forget your grievances by hearing words of sympathy, then the cause is lost. You must make a permanent cause of grievance.'[175]

Vinayak Damodar Savarkar (1883–1966), too, utilized the memory of the past in order to unleash forces of resistance against foreign rule when, on the occasion of the fiftieth anniversary of the Mutiny of 1857, he presented the historical events as *The Indian War of Independence*.[176] Savarkar was the most radical among those who rejected the western stereotype of Indian passivity and sought to prove the contrary.[177] Collective memory was consistently directed towards the realization of practical purposes. Savarkar was not only convinced in a general sense that 'the nation that has no consciousness of its past has no future', he also aimed to make this consciousness a concrete factor in the nation's development. India should become an autonomous historical agent: 'The nation ought to be the master and not the slave of its own history.' (Savarkar 1947: XXIII) Unlike other nationalists, Savarkar did not attempt to deduce political activism from religious tradition, as, according to his convictions, only violence could help under conditions of foreign rule. Purely religious ideals were to be realized later.

[174]Tilak's Letters to the *Mahratta*, 13 December 1919, quoted in Varma 1967: 213.

[175]Tilak 1919: 46, quoted in Bipan Chandra, 'Nationalist Historians' Interpretations of the Indian National Movement', in Bhattacharya and Thapar 1986: 194–238, here 196. The 'sense of a common grievance and the inspiration of a common resolve' were also appealed to by other politicians, such as Surendranath Banerjea, for the sake of nation building. Cf. Chandra, ibid., 212–13.

[176]For the making of this text, see Surjit Hans, 'The Metaphysics of Militant Nationalism', in Alok Bhalla and Sudhir Chandra (eds), 1993: 190–231.

[177]His radical activism made him one of Gandhi's major opponents. The arguments in *Hind Swaraj* were partly directed against Savarkar. It was a follower of Savarkar, Nathuram Godse, who in 1948 became the murderer of Gandhi. For a reflection on the hidden complicity between the assassin and his victim, see Ashis Nandy, 'Final Encounter. The Politics of the Assassination of Gandhi', in idem 1980: 70–98.

This did not mean renouncing the aura of sacredness, however.[178] Savarkar, who criticized earlier representations of the Mutiny in the name of objective research, insisted on the meticulous distinction between the essential and the accidental. The essential motives and aims of the rebels, according to him, had been *swadharma* and swaraj. Both were connected in such a way that the fight for freedom was the prerequisite for the worship of God: 'True religion cannot exist where slavery [...] is rampant.' This meant, conversely: 'He who does not attempt to acquire Swaraj, he who sits silent in slavery, he is an atheist and hater of Religion.' In his own way, Savarkar, too, pointed to the combination of politics and spirituality as a decisive element of Indian history: 'In the East all revolutions take a religious form'. (Savarkar 1947: 9–11)

The appeal to religious feelings also penetrated the concept of Hindutva, in which Savarkar sought to systematically respond to the question of the nation as a subject of historical agency. He evaded the dogmatism of the orthodox and their exclusivist claim to tradition. Being aware that a convincing definition of Hindudom had not been achieved so far and, in view of inherent contradictions and disintegrating instances in the religious and social life of Hindus, Savarkar conceived homogeneousness as a goal rather than as a given fact. He realized that collective identity was based on constructions and depended on political will.

Referring to space and people appeared insufficient to him, since the Indian territory could be perceived as their country even by Muslims and Christians, and it could not be denied that the converts among them had the same blood in their veins as the Hindus. Moreover, Hindustan was not the Aryans' 'original home', it was only an 'adopted home' (8) [Note: Page numbers in brackets refer to Savarkar 1989.] Even in ethnic terms, instead of insisting on a purely Aryan origin, Savarkar only postulated a common racial heritage, which had been brought about through a process of fusions.[179] The decisive factor of cohesion, according to him, was common civilization (Sanskriti). It was through civilization, a 'miniature secondary creation of man' (92), that different national units in the world were formed. The adherence to a particular community always included elements of explicit consent. A Hindu, thus, was not simply one who was born a Hindu, but who *wanted* to be a Hindu: 'who [...] has inherited and claims as his own the Hindu Sanskriti, the Hindu civilization, as represented in a common history, common heroes, a common literature, common art, a common law' (100).

Nevertheless, the declared association was also bound to soil and race in some way. Once the territory had been taken in possession, it became a factor of durability: it is the land 'that connects the remotest past to the remotest future'. The grown attachment to the territory has the advantage that it 'enlists nature on our side' (31). By referring to ties of blood, too, Savarkar assumed a higher necessity for the declared adherence. 'We are not only a nation but a Jati, a born brotherhood. Nothing else counts, it is after all a question of heart. [...] We feel we are a

---

[178]Actually, Savarkar sought to convince the Hindus that 'they had to systematically de-paganize their faith'. Cf. Nandy et al. 1995: 68.

[179]Savarkar explicitly welcomed the commingling of races. The caste system was seen as secondary and also as an element of separation.

JATI, a race bound together by the dearest ties of blood and therefore it must be so' (89–90).[180] The reference to racial ties and territory secured the fiction of continuity, vital for the imagined community.[181] However, Savarkar went yet a step further and distinguished between the fatherland (*pitribhu*) of all inhabitants of the subcontinent and what India meant to Hindus, namely *punyabhu*, the country of salvation. Muslims and Christians residing here, if they took their belief seriously, had their spiritual home elsewhere, and, therefore, their loyalty towards India was divided. The Hindus were at home here, they lived in their 'Holyland' (116).[182]

Along with the idea of territory, which became the 'Holyland', Savarkar sought to make other historically established ties more durable and more efficient with the help of religion. Faith came into play, at first, from a purely functional point of view.[183] Religious feelings were used for contrasting friend and foe, they 'consolidated' the community and mobilized the political will.[184] But in the course of argumentation, nation and religion moved closer and closer to each other and almost conflated so that, on the one hand, faith determined the boundaries of the political community and, on the other, the nation itself became an object of religious veneration. Hindutva had primacy over Hinduism but, since the latter's aura was needed, this point was generally left undecided. The territory 'from Sindhu to Sindhu' was seen as that of the seers and of revelation and, at the same time, was recalled as the land of sacrifices offered by people in the fight against the enemy (112).

Even history and myth were merged in a way that made it possible to utilize their respective advantages alternately without taking into account their differences. Savarkar, then, could reject the allegation 'that the Hindus have no history' (93), stating that the Hindus were probably 'the only people who have succeeded in preserving their history' (93). The great epics were seen by him as historiography; the Ramayana and the Mahabharata, so he was convinced, 'would bring us together and weld us into a race' (94). Conversely, in the present fight for freedom, too, the interpretation of the past was stylized as the 'holy work of the historian',[185] who laid bare the sense of the nation's history which was always inherent in it.[186] Ultimately, Savarkar's insight into the subjective and constructive character of history gets lost again; the

[180]For the use of the concept of *jati* in the discourses of the nationalists, cf. Partha Chatterjee 1993: 220ff.

[181]Cf. (following Maurice Halbwachs) Assmann 1999: 88, 274.

[182]For the origin of this notion in the *Vishnu Purana*, cf. Nandy et al. 1995: 67.

[183]Regarding the quest for political agency, Savarkar observed: 'The ideal conditions, therefore, under which a nation can attain perfect solidarity and cohesion would, other things being equal, be found in the case of those people who inhabit the land they adore, the land of whose forefathers is also the land of their Gods and Angels, of Seers and Prophets; the scenes of whose history are also the scenes of their mythology.' (Savarkar 1989: 136). 'No people in the world can more justly claim to get recognized as a racial unit than the Hindus and perhaps the Jews.' (Savarkar 1989: 90).

[184]For the dominance of modernism in Savarkar, cf. Suresh Sharma, 'Savarkar's Quest for a Modern Hindu Consolidation', *Studies in Humanities and Social Sciences* 2 (1995), 189–215.

[185]Savarkar 1947: 1. For the closeness of the idea of the nation to 'religious modes of thought', cf. Anderson 1991, 11 passim.

[186]Other nationalists, too, imagined the re-awakening of something already existing, e.g. 'the sleeping consciousness of the great Hindu Nation'. Prakash, 1938: 22, quoted in Bipan Chandra 1984: 224.

interest in a timeless-religious sanction of the postulated homogeneity of people, territory, and culture gains the upperhand.

While patriotic writers and politicians increasingly referred to former Indian greatness and glory and sought to make historical memory a factor of practice, the academic discipline also fell into the spell of nationalism in the end. The idea of the nation can be seen as both cause and effect of the growing interest in history. If the discovery and imagination of a great past contributed to creating a national consciousness, the nation, for its part, became the focal point of historical research. In many of the historians of the 1920s, such as H. C. Raichaudhury, K. P. Jayaswal, R. C. Majumdar, R. K. Mookerji, and H. C. Ohja, the idea of ancient India as a political unit belonged to the underlying assumptions of research (Thapar 1978: 11–12). What had partly had an auto-suggestive effect in the historical imagination of Bankimchandra now had to be established empirically. After the ancient Hindus or Aryans had been identified as historical subjects, a search began for signs of nationality and statehood in the earliest records. Radha Kumud Mookerji, for example, traced the consciousness of a 'fundamental unity' in Indian history back to the days of the great empires, which became the preferred topics of research. He opposed the insinuation that India lacked a tradition of politics, and that concepts like sovereignty and central rule were unknown to the ancient Hindus and were brought to India by foreigners, either the Persians or the Greeks.[187]

Frequently, criticism was directed against the sweeping judgements of western researchers of Indian politics and history, which could be used to legitimize colonial rule. Kashi Prasad Jayaswal (1881–1937) made efforts to correct those accounts which tended to contrast western democracy and Oriental despotism.[188] By furnishing proof of republican forms of government (ganas and samghas) and other political institutions in ancient India, he claimed, in Hindu Polity (1924), the institutions of a parliament and constitutional monarchy for Hindus. He rejected widespread western speculations about the Greek influence on early India as grossly exaggerated.[189]

In his basic ideas about history in general, Jayaswal was largely oriented towards the new dynamic: 'The test of a polity is its capacity to live and develop.' Since modern elements could be observed at many stages in the course of Indian history—'Vaishnavism preached the equality of all men'—there were good reasons for a confident outlook on the time to come: 'The Golden Age of his [the Hindu's] polity lies not in the Past but in the Future.' The confrontation with the Europeans, 'the greatest constitutional polity of modern times', represented an existential challenge to Indian capacities: 'The contact is electrifying: it can either kill or rejuvenate the Race.' (Jayaswal 1936: 366–7) On the other hand, the emergence of the modern Indian nation

[187]Radhakumud Mookerji 1921: 70. Nevertheless, the 'composite system', according to Mookerji, was typical of India and in general also better. See also idem 1914.

[188]'Jayaswal's main concern was to show the totally unacceptable character of all foreign rule and its calculated policy to denationalise the enslaved nation.' B. P. Sinha, 'Kashi Prasad Jayaswal', in Sen 1973: 81–94, here 88.

[189]This was directed against historians like Vincent Smith and W. W. Tarn. Cf. Thapar 1978: 13. Similar arguments were used by A. K. Coomaraswami with regard to Indian arts. See below, Section 3.

was regarded as the mere revival of an ancient political entity, which was undermined time and again by conquerors and foreign rulers: 'The Shakan rule aimed at denationalising the Hindus and destroying their national system.'[190] Interpretations like this were readily adopted by politicians and were confirmed or extended by their own research. Lala Lajpat Rai (1865–1928), for example, assumed that 'fundamentally India has been a nation for the last 2000 years, in spite of the fact that at times it has been divided into several kingdoms and principalities, sometimes under a common empire and at others independent of each other'.[191]

New archaeological discoveries complied with the desired image. The discovery of the Indus Valley civilization in the 1920s emphasized in an impressive manner the antiquity of Indian culture. With the excavations of Harappa and Mohenjo Daro, its origins could be dated to a time earlier than hitherto believed. The rediscovery of Kautilya's *Arthashastra* (1905),[192] with its model of a sovereign state, seemed to finally disprove the western prejudice about the lack of political consciousness among the early Hindus. Accounts of the persistent Indian influence on the peoples of South East Asia also strengthened national self-confidence. Memories of the cultural impact on other nations compensated for the humiliating experience of colonial subjugation.[193] According to Romesh Chandra Majumdar (1888–1975), the Hindus' attitude to South East Asia was different from the behaviour of the modern British in India; it rather resembled the civilizing influence of ancient Greece and Rome within the European sphere. The imagining of a Greater India, therefore, not only strengthened the belief in former Indian glory, but also confirmed India's spiritual mission. In contrast to modern colonialism, the Indian expansion did not include, according to Majumdar, the exploitation of the natives but was, on the contrary, to their advantage (1979: 34–5).[194] Majumdar did not completely reject the utility of foreign influences for the modern period, either.[195] However, in view of the distancing connotations in the western ideology of a civilizing mission, he emphasized the tendencies of rapprochement in the case of Indian colonization.[196]

The underlying assumption of a primordial political unity of Hindus not only hampered the insight into the meaning of historical change; the quest for national homogeneity also had the

---

[190]Jayaswal 1990: 48. The fight of the Bharasivas against the Kushanas was yet another episode in the eternal struggle for existence of the Indian nation and set an inspiring example for modern freedom fighters. Cf. Sinha, 'Kashi Prasad Jayaswal', 89.

[191]*Young India* (reprint, Delhi 1965), 38, quoted in Bipan Chandra, 'Nationalist Historians' Interpretations', in Bhattacharya and Thapar 1986: 214.

[192]The *Kautilya-Arthashastra*, which was compared to the political writings of Machiavelli, was edited by R. Sastri (1909), who also published an English translation (1915). It is open to debate whether the text is really that of Kautliya, the chancellor of Chandragupta Maurya in the fourth century BC.

[193]Apart from Majumdar's multi-volumed *Ancient Indian Colonies in the Far East* (1927), see Radha Kumud Mookerji 1912.

[194]Vivekananda, in his programme of a spiritual conquest of the world, had also invoked 'the forgotten glory of this cultural empire'. Cf. Halbfass 1990: 190–1.

[195]Thus he also welcomed historiography as a British import. See below, Section 4.1.

[196]Nevertheless, Majumdar also displays a sense of superiority with regard to the 'primitive' colonized.

effect of driving a wedge between religious communities. The increasing quest for cohesion among Hindus led to the exteriorization of non-Hindus.[197] The multi-layered and complex forms of coexistence which had grown over the centuries were devalued against the unifying tendencies of nationalism. At the centre of the problem was the relationship between Hindus and Muslims. If, for Hindus, the memory of the suppression of centuries strengthened anti-colonial resistance, the Muslims based their self-confidence on the memory of their own rule in India.

Muslims had their own tradition of historical thinking, and the interpretation of history, in the sense of the dissemination of Islam, did not allow putting up with the present conditions under colonialism. Even in better times, some Muslim chroniclers had criticized rulers who had not taken seriously their Islamic mission. Now, with the rise of the East India Company, Muslims saw themselves displaced to an alien country. After Shah Wali Ullah (1703–62) had attempted to unite all Muslims in a common loyalty to their faith, his son Shah Abdul Aziz (1746–1824), faced with the decline of the Mughal empire, felt that India, once a homeland of Islam (dar ul-Islam), had been transformed into a land of unbelief (dar ul-harb). More and more, Muslims felt themselves provoked to wage a jihad.

Western historiography of India contributed, directly or indirectly, to hardening the confrontation between Muslims and Hindus. 'Before Jones, Indian history had been almost synonymous with Indo-Muslim history, after Jones, it became almost synonymous with Hindu history. The Muslims were moved from the centre to the periphery of the history of the subcontinent.'[198] Despite his high regard for Arabic-Islamic culture, Jones viewed the Muslim conquest as having caused the decline of Hindu civilization.[199] Mill, too, with his periodization of Indian history into the Hindu, Mohammedan, and in phases, British contributed to a stricter demarcation of the religious communities; and Henry M. Elliot, in order to make British domination appear to the Hindus almost like a liberation, emphasized the despotic nature of Muslim rule.[200]

This was in line with the view of the Hindus, insofar as the pre-Islamic period seemed all the more to have been the Golden Age of India, which should be restored. The Muslims, in contrast, turned their gaze back to the period of Islamic rule, the memory of which was also kept alive by the formal continuation of the Mughal empire till 1857. Among Muslims, too, there was a leaning towards Puritanism and a return to spiritual origins, and this movement was as ambivalent as that among the Hindus; it could serve both conservative and progressive goals, traditionalism and modernization.[201] However, even the reformers subscribed to the separateness of the religious communities and kept their distance from the Indian National Congress. Sayyid Ahmad Khan preferred British rule to the idea of a democratic India with a Hindu majority

---

[197]For the concept of 'exteriorization', cf. Joachim Matthes, 'The Operation called "Vergleichen"', in idem 1992: 75–99, here 92–3. See also the remarks on the 'process of ethnification' in Oommen 1997: 41, note 9.

[198]Grewal 1975: 32. Jones 'used the term "Indian" interchangeably with the "Hindus".' Ibid., 43.

[199]According to Mill, however, this assumption was apt to conceal the intrinsic backwardness of the Hindus. Cf. Mill, HBI, II, 146, n. 2.

[200]Cf. Elliot, 'Original Preface' (1849), in idem and Dowson 1867: XV-XXVII. Chandra 1984: 212–13.

[201]See, for instance, Sayyid Ahmad Barelwi (1786–1831) and the Wahhabi conspiracies of the 1860s and 1870s.

(Embree 1988: 35). The prospect of independent statehood worried many Muslims, and the fears were yet to grow with the increasing tendencies of communalization.

The demand for a separate Muslim nation state followed a similar logic to the conception of Hindu India. When Muhammad Iqbal (1877–1938) tried to outline the principles of Islamic communalism in his 'Pakistan speech' (1930), he, too, referred to the spiritual superiority of the Orient to the materialistic West: 'Islam does not divide the single entity of mankind into incompatible duality of spirit and matter.' In Islam, 'spirit and matter, Church and State were organically bound with each other'. On the one hand, the traditional unity of people and religion was emphasized; this unity, on the other, served to support the modern demand for a separate Islamic nation. 'The truth is that Islam is not a church. It is a state.' What had to be kept in mind was: 'The principle of European democracy cannot be applied to India without recognising the fact of communal groups.' The postulated Islamic nation state was legitimized as a defender of higher values and, therefore, ultimately of the interests of India and Asia. Communalism thus could even be presented as serving political harmony: 'Communalism, in its higher aspect, then, is indispensable for the formation of a harmonious whole in a country like India.' Iqbal linked the demand for a separate centralized Muslim state with the view that, in the long run, it would 'solve the problem of India as well as of Asia'.[202]

Similar to the struggle for self-assertion among the Hindus, where direct threads led from religious reform movements to forms of communalism, for many Muslims, too, religion had a higher cohesive force than the new idea of the Indian nation. Nevertheless, the two-nation theory and the struggle for Pakistan were not only and not primarily based on religion. For the leader of the Muslim League, Mohammad Ali Jinnah (1875–1948), it was mainly political and historical experience which confirmed that the differences between Hindus and Muslims were irreconcilable: 'The history of the last twelve hundred years has failed to achieve unity and has witnessed, during the ages, India always divided into Hindu India and Muslim India.'[203]

It was not only Muslims and Christians (fewer in number, but also considered outsiders) who had difficulties with their self-understanding in the emerging national movement. Other subnational groups experienced the problem in the reverse and were in danger of being swallowed by the new political feelings of community of the Hindus. Religious communities which had emerged on Indian soil, such as the Sikhs, Jains, and Buddhists, and also ethnic minorities and social pariahs, as were regarded as Hindus by the nationalists, when it came to establishing their majority status.[204] This was the other side of the dialectic of nationalization and communalization, integration and fragmentation. The tendencies to exteriorize the Other stood in correlation with

[202]Muhammad Iqbal, 'Presidential Address at the Annual Session of the Muslim League, held at Allahabad, 1930' (Pakistan speech), quoted in Ahmad and von Grunebaum 1970: 148–51.

[203]Jamil-ud-Din Ahmad 1960, I: 161.

[204]Cf. Rao 1979. That forms of inclusion could also lead to communalism is shown by the example of the Sikhs. For sources and further reading on the historical consciousness of the Sikhs, see below in the Sources section.

the striving for inner uniformity. This, too, was opposed to traditional ways of handling the inner diversity of Indian society.

However, since Indian history was being reinterpreted from an anti-colonial perspective and the regaining of lost or suppressed agency had become a topic of political discourse, regional, social, or linguistic identities could also be reconstructed in a new way and thus compete with the nationalism of the INC.[205] It was especially in the Dravidian South, which, at all times, had differed from the North culturally, linguistically, and ethnically, that a separate form of traditionalism emerged,[206] and after the poets' academy (Sangam) of the Tamil kingdoms had been brought back to memory by Dravidological research, the idea to revive an undistorted Tamil culture gained momentum. In 1910, advocates of South Indian particularity founded the Dravidian Association.[207] The critical impulses against the existing hierarchies, however, were hardly strong enough to overcome the essentialism inherent in the prevailing forms of identity as such.

Some of the social movements, with their striving for emancipation, came into conflict with ethnic and religious nationalism too. Political Hinduism, worried about mass conversions of Untouchables, began to discover the outcasts, who were marginalized in an extreme manner, as part of the Hindu nation. Bhimrao Ramji Ambedkar (1891–1956), the leader of the Dalits ('broken men'),[208] as they now called themselves, rejected this suggestion, pointing out that Hindu society, as such, was dominated by a logic of exclusion: how could integration be based on Hindu religion and its Dharmashastras if dharma itself was the criterion for demarcation between caste Hindus and outcasts?[209] From the perspective of caste Hindus, the Dalits had always been *mlecchas*, that is impure, and, therefore, stayed outside the religious community. Suspicious about the INC establishment, which was not ready for real social changes, Ambedkar asked on behalf of the Dalits: 'Is there any human tie that binds them to the rest of the Hindus?' (Ambedkar 1945: 184)

The claim to historicity and autonomy, articulated by the nationalists as against the colonial regime, could be used by the Dalits to question, on their part, a social system which, by referring to an eternal cosmological order, reduced them to the role of the passive and mute.[210] The

[205]Cf. N. C. Saxena, 'Historiography of Communalism in India', in Hasan 1981: 302–25, here 314.

[206]'All structural elements which we observe in the process of decolonization of the developing countries and their breaking away from western dominance are anticipated in South India in the opposition against the Aryan North.' Klimkeit 1971: 41.

[207]Eugene F. Irschick shows that the new Dravidian self-awareness, in which the image of an ancient indigenous culture serves the orientation towards the future, was itself the result of a dialogic process between the local population and the colonial administration: Irschick 1994: 67ff. See also idem 1986; Nasir Tyabji, 'Dravidian Notions of History', *Seminar* 364 (Dec. 1989), 19–23. For the emergence of regional historiography, see below, Section 4.2.1.

[208]For the definition of the social category of Dalit as well as the self-representation of social movements in India, see Fuchs 1999: 170ff.

[209]The outcasts were viewed as *adharma*, staying outside dharma. Ambedkar also rejected the claim of the moral or spiritual superiority of Indians as pure ideology. For nothing was in his eyes as amoral as the treatment of the Untouchables.

[210]For other silenced voices of historical actors, like those of women, for instance, see below, Section 4.5.

conceptual self-representation within Hindu society had always been denied to the outcasts. 'It is the alienation of Untouchables from the symbolic processes of Indian society, the lack of ability to represent themselves in their own terms in the arenas of meaning where the significance of central symbols is determined, that constitutes the real essence of their oppressed status.'[211] Communities like the Mahars in the neighbourhood of Bombay had their own origin myths in which they described themselves as descendants of higher ranks who had lost their status under contingent circumstances, and these narratives competed with the dominant Brahmanic doctrine. The endeavour to revive these traditions (and record them in the written word), which was initiated by Jotirao Phule (1826–90) in the nineteenth century, presented a challenge to the representatives of the great tradition, both practically and theoretically.[212] It not only questioned the Brahmans' monopoly of interpretation, but also exposed a strategy of dehistoricization in their dealing with the past.[213]

Ambedkar, too, explained Untouchability, socially and politically, as a manifestation of oppression. He not only rejected the institution as such, but also opposed the way it was legitimized in the Shastras. While placing historical interpretation against myth, Ambedkar established the claim of the Dalits to autonomous agency in the face of its denial by Brahmanic teaching.[214] At the political level, this seemed to be possible only by conceiving and organizing the Dalits as a community separate from Hindu society (Ambedkar 1945: 198).[215] Ambedkar demanded exclusive constituencies and specific safeguards for Dalits, similar to those afforded to other minorities. On the other hand, he rejected the tracing back of social contradictions to ethnic rivalries and rather referred to the old conflict between Brahmans and Buddhists (Ambedkar 1948: IV–V). Despite all separating factors, Dalits and caste Hindus remained connected through a system of mutual reference in Ambedkar's conception.

Partha Chatterjee has described strategies of the outcasts which enabled them to evade the existing social hierarchy and yet share a wider context with the other sections of society: 'What we have is a desire for a structure of community in which the opposite tendencies of mutual separateness and mutual dependence are united by a force that has a greater universal moral

[211]Michael B. Schwartz, 'Indian Untouchable Texts of Resistance: Symbolic Domination and Historical Knowledge', Social Analysis 25 (1989), 131–41, here 139.

[212]Even with regard to Redfield's concept of the 'great tradition' (see below), the Mahars are cited as an example of those who questioned its normativity instead of trying to get integrated to it: Robert J. Miller, 'Button, Button ... Great Tradition, Little Tradition, Whose Tradition?', Anthropological Quarterly 39 (1966), 26–42.

[213]'The most significant ideological effect of Manu and the Shastras is the dehistorization and naturalization of cultural practice.' Schwartz, 'Indian Untouchable Texts of Resistance', 135.

[214]Cf. Srinivasan, 'Dr. Ambedkar's Search for Roots', New Quest 116 (March-April 1996), 81–90, here 89. There was a public burning in Mahad (1927) of the manusmriti, the oldest scriptural authority of the caste system. See Omvedt 1995: 44. Ambedkar also questioned the idea of the particular capacity of Hindus for synthesis, an idea which was cherished in the nationalism of the elite. For a similar critique by Phule, cf. Omvedt 1995: 23.

[215]See Partha Chatterjee, 'Caste and Subaltern Consciousness', Subaltern Studies VI (1989), 169–209. Ambedkar insisted on a separate identity of the Dalits even in the face of the reconciling strategy of Gandhi, before an agreement on their fair representation within the INC and a systematic support of the 'Scheduled Castes' was arrived at. That the same problematic existed even in the reaction of orthodox caste Hindus, who were not prepared to abolish the traditional demarcations.

actuality than the given forms of the dominant dharma.'[216] Looking at Ambedkar from this angle, his appeal to the modern principle of equality aimed at replacing the hierarchical social order while he was at least aware—this is shown by the simultaneous reference to the traditional demarcations—that certain forms of caste discrimination would continue even within a new constitutional framework. Ambedkar distrusted the supposed democratization of upper-class Hindus who, not only for the sake of inherited cultural values but also because of substantial economic advantages, would not give up the orientation towards the caste system. The Dalits, in their claim to historicity, still had to take into account the continuing Brahmanic strategy of dehistoricization. This resulted in a paradoxical situation: Ambedkar condemned caste more radically than others, who still conceded some temporary positive function to this institution or regarded it as no more than a superstructural phenomenon; and yet he adhered, to a certain extent, to traditional forms of negotiating 'mutual separateness and mutual dependence'. A reason for this may lie in the intention not to deny one's own cultural roots in the simultaneous fight for social change and national self-assertion.[217]

This leads back to the contradictions between claims to historicity and the prevailing essentialism in the discourse of the nationalists. Their postulate of a primordial Indian nation can be read as an answer to the ideology of the colonizer and his construction of an ahistorical Orient. However, it also corresponds to older strategies of dehistoricization in Indian society. The Brahmanic mode of coping with contingency by referring to the eternal cosmic order, evident also in their dealings with outcasts and Dalit narrative traditions, has probably had its impact on the arguments of nationalists against foreign rule. It was no coincidence that precisely those currents which aimed at replacing the caste system with the solidarity of the Aryans or Hindus (Arya Samaj, Hindutva)[218] led to perspectivizations of India's eternal 'struggle for existence and power', which went far beyond the area of Indian culture, including the idea that Hindus 'could dictate terms to the whole world' (Savarkar 1989: 141). Here, the inner-cultural hierarchy is turned to the outer world and transformed in a global ranking of cultures.[219]

[216]Chatterjee, 1993: 197. Chatterjee views this also as an indigenous expression of 'a desire for *democratization*'. Ibid.

[217]For the alternative of Sanskritization or westernization, see Philip Constable, 'Early Dalit Literature and Culture in Late Nineteenth- and Early Twentieth-Century Western India', MAS 31 (1997), 317–38, here 337. In fact, some Dalit communities still pinned their hope mainly upon the possibilities of raising their status within the caste system. For the case of the Yadava movement, see Saxena, 'Historiography of Communalism' (in Hasan 1981), 314. For the anthropological concept of Sanskritization and westernization, see below, Section 4.3.

[218]For the reciprocal referring of Hindu nationalism and Dalit self-consciousness, see Shalini Randeria, 'Hindu-Nationalismus: Aspekte eines Mehrheits-Ethnizismus', in: Reinhart Kößler and Tilman Schiel (eds), *Nationalstaat und Ethnizität* (Frankfurt/M. 1994), 75–110.

[219]For the inclusion of alien cultures and their gradation, see above, Section 1.2. The Hindu-Muslim relationship, too, can be considered as being under the ambivalent impression of Hindu inclusivism, which makes the religion tolerant to those outside its fold, but intolerant to those within its fold. Cf. Javeed Alam, 'Tradition in India under Interpretive Stress: Interrogating its Claims', *Thesis Eleven* 39 (1994), 19–38, here 28; Michael Gottlob, 'Inklusionen und Exklusionen in der Begegnung zwischen Indien und Europa', in Rolf Kloepfer and Burckhard Dücker (eds), *Kritik und Geschichte der Intoleranz* (Heidelberg 2000), 93–100.

There emerged, however, other strategies of self-assertion. Some reformist and revolutionary movements began to relate Self and social change to each other instead of holding on to old traditions, against inner obstacles as much as external ones. Beyond the essentialist confrontations of East and West, the processual character of reality became visible.

2.3 *Conceptualizations of Temporal Change*

If some of the reformers were criticized for being imitators of the British, Bhandarkar reminded his countrymen that learning from others did not contradict Indian traditions. The ancient Hindus, so venerated by the revivalists, had not hesitated to make the knowledge of the Greek astronomers their own and revere them as *rishis*.[220] Bankimchandra, too, had made it clear that imitation under certain circumstances could help regain the ability to act and could be a means of improvement. In historical writing, in any case, he did not want to return to the Puranas, which he found to be unsuitable for creating agency. Bankimchandra, in his belief in scientific progress, was close to the notion of processuality, even if, due to the colonial situation and the contrast between Self and Other, it did not turn into a dominant principle of interpretation.

As early as the beginning of the nineteenth century, Rammohun Roy had attempted to measure how far the appropriation of western experience was possible within the framework of Indian culture. He, on his part, continued precolonial efforts to modernize, the sources of which did not dry up even under conditions of colonialism. Even later, in the case of 'traditional modernizers' like Vidyasagar, indigenous elements in the strategies of reform often turned out to be the most effective and promising.[221] The traditional 'Xenology'[222] of the Hindus, allowed the assimilation of the knowledge of others, for the sake of improvement, and even accommodation to changing political conditions was possible.[223] The increasing European influence initially signified, to many, a desirable development: 'Conscious of the anomie that had preceded the colonial conquest and faced with a well-established state system based on liberal principles, most of them accepted and even welcomed British rule as divine dispensation.'[224] As a restoration of the moral order (dharma), the experience of change could be harmonized with traditional concepts of time and sense.

[220]Bhandarkar, 'The Critical, Comparative, and Historical Method' (see below, Sources, Section 2.1), 393.

[221]See Tripathi 1974; idem, 'The Role of Traditional Modernizers: Bengal's Experience in the 19th Century', *Calcutta Historical Journal* 8 (1983–4), 1–16, 116–22.

[222]For this concept, see M. Duala-M'bedy, *Xenologie: Die Wissenschaft vom Fremden und die Verdrängung der Humanität in der Anthropologie* (Freiburg (1977); Halbfass 1990, 173, 507.

[223]See above, Section 1.2. Thus, newly introduced religious restrictions or duties were presented under the category of *Kalivarjya* ('something that should be avoided in *kaliyuga*'). Even new political institutions, such as kingship, could be explained with reference to the deterioration of conditions. For these mechanisms of accommodation to occurrences of change, cf. Jordens, 1998, 67. Jordens also points to the dialogue between Yudhisthira and Bhishma in the Mahabharata on the issue of 'whether the king makes the age or the age makes the king'. Ibid., 68. For the texts in which the necessary innovations of kaliyuga are discussed, see P. V. Kane, *History of Dharmashastra*, III (Pune 1930–62), 926–68.

[224]K. N. Panikkar, 'The Intellectual History of Colonial India', 421. The contrasting of the present situation with that of Muslim rule, and viewing the British as guarantors of Indian improvement, was supported by the British themselves, for instance by Mill and Elliot. Cf. Barun De, 'Problems of the Study of Indian History', 13, 14.

The belief in the fundamental unchangeability of dharma itself, however, conflicted with a general processualization in the perception of the flow of events. Therefore, when the reform policies widened the horizon of expectations, including significant and lasting innovation, the roads parted. For radical reformers like the group around the young writer Henry Derozio (1809–31),[225] real modernization required a definite break with tradition. For the orthodox, who felt that reform activities were a threat to their very existence, the New now appeared to be an indication of the decadence of kaliyuga rather than a step towards averting it.

If the negotiation between the Old and the New (or indigenous customs and external influences), in the traditional mode, oscillated between generous inclusivism and strict demarcation, it was mainly the enforced policy of Anglicization since the 1830s that overtaxed the capacity to accommodate and activated the mechanism of exclusion. It increased the difficulties of the mediators, who always had to fight on two fronts: conscious of their own tradition, they defended Indian culture against the patronizing colonial power; as agents of progress, they opposed orthodox forces within the indigenous society.[226]

The creative potential of the vernacular languages and the ability acquired by their speakers to balance little and great traditions came to their aid. The vernaculars were increasingly used as a medium of reflection and education, besides the 'holy' language Sanskrit and the administrative languages (Persian, English),[227] and it was in these languages that the first works of modern Indian historiography were written. A new way of dealing with phenomena of temporal change had already become evident in the Bengali textbooks of Fort William College mentioned above (Section 2.1). Here, the practical and future-oriented time of modern history surfaced beside the sacred time and absolute past of the myths, so that Ramram Basu, according to the judgement of Guha, 'set out consciously to produce a history rather than yet another Puranic tale'.[228] Besides the tendencies towards empiricization and perspectivization in approaching the past, there were also those towards a linearization of time, in contrast to the traditional cyclic forms of interpretation prevailing in the Puranas. Even if the 'struggle for historicization was to continue for a while yet', the 'indigenous, rationalist historiography' gained ground and, 'by the middle of the century, it felt strong enough to make decisive inroads into the Puranic past' (Guha 1988: 35–6). Nilmani Basak, in *Bharatvarsher Itihas* (1857–8), switched over to Mill's periodizing pattern (without taking up the latter's value judgements, though) after just mentioning the *yuga* cycles.[229] And

---

[225]Derozio taught English and History at the Hindu College (founded in 1817) in Calcutta.

[226]In defence against the former, they had to reconstruct tradition in modern language, whereas for the latter, they had to formulate the New in traditional language.

[227]Cf. Partha Chatterjee 1993: 7, who relates this development to the strategy of reserving an 'inner domain of cultural identity' against foreign rule (see above). Roy's translations into Bengali also belong to this context.

[228]Guha 1988: 34. The new mode of structuring the occurrences from one's own present had a desacralizing effect. For Partha Chatterjee, however, the puranic character of the text is still dominant. While contemporary events could be represented by Hindus in the form of Purana, Muslims like Munshi Alimaddin (*Dillir rajadir nam*, Barisal 1875) could interpret them in view of God's final intervention in favour of Islam. Cf. Partha Chatterjee 1993: 84, 86–7.

[229]Sarkar, 'Many worlds: The construction of history in modern India' (as in note 10), 66. Basak, in his biographical stories *Nanabari* (Nine Women, 1852), recast even the mythic time of the Ramayana 'into a linear discourse, situated, like a novel, in homogeneous time'. Guha 1988: 39.

if Bankimchandra postulated a 'true history' to be one which was written in order to enhance national agency, this also implied the orientation towards improvement. However, as Vidyasagar observed, the easy inclusion of modern knowledge into the traditional could impede the actual modernization of thought. 'Lately a feeling is manifesting itself among the learned of this part of India [...] that when they hear of a Scientific truth, the germs of which may be traced out in their Shastras, instead of shewing any regard for that truth, they triumph and the superstitious regard for their own Shastras is redoubled.' By promoting the vernacular education system, he aimed instead at the production of 'a useful class of men' who, with a new self-confidence, would avoid the wrong alternatives of either Anglicization or remaining in a state of backwardness.[230]

Outside of Bengal, too, new forms of historiography developed in the vernaculars,[231] in which the cycles of Puranic cosmology contrasted with linear conceptions of time. In the Hindi-belt, it was Shiva Prasad (1823–90) above all who contributed to the reception of the 'Whig idea of history', first by translating English historical works, and later by presenting his own account of Indian history: *Itihasa Timirnasak* (1864).[232] Influenced by ideas of European Enlightenment, Prasad wanted to show his countrymen 'that, notwithstanding their very strong antipathy to "change", they *have* changed, and *will* change'.[233] Like Bankimchandra, he intended to modernize Indian society by way of the introduction of western concepts (progress, patriotism, etc.) (Sudhir Chandra 1992: 38). In the case of Prasad, however, expectations of progress were still linked with the presence of the English.[234] The new national consciousness of the 1870s and 1880s led to the critique that Prasad's work 'spoke about Indian institutions in a way similar to that of the Christian missionaries' (Lütt 1970: 62).

The transition from expectations of progress associated with British rule to the disillusionment of these expectations is personified in Prasad's disciple Harishchandra of Benares (1850–85). Even in his eulogies of the British, in which he affirmed his loyalty, he criticized colonial economic policies. The English, according to him, were basically the originators of progress in India, but they also hindered it in some aspects. He deplored the 'flow of wealth to a foreign land',[235] and long before the swadeshi agitation of the early twentieth century, he requested that Indians buy only goods manufactured in their own country. In fact, the British appeared to be worse than

---

[230]Vidyasagar to F. I. Mouat, 7 September 1853, quoted in Sumit Sarkar 1998: 246.

[231]For new forms of historiography in Maharashtra and Kerala, see K. N. Panikkar, 'In Defence of "Old" History', *EPW* (1 October 1994), 2595–7, here 2596.

[232]The literal meaning of the title is 'history as the destroyer of darkness'. The work served as a textbook in the North-West Provinces.

[233]Prasad, 'Preface' (1873) Italics in original.

[234]When he mentioned foreign rule as a cause of India's decline, he referred exclusively to the Muslim period. Cf. Lütt 1970: 59. Prasad's notion of progress is given an additional accent by his critique of the ancient Aryans (the origin of all social evil) and the contemporary Brahmans.

[235]*Bharat Durdasha*, 1880, quoted in Sudhir Chandra 1992: 31. 'People here have been beguiled by the power and trickeries of the machine. They are daily losing their wealth and gaining in distress. Unable to do without foreign cloth, they have become the slaves of foreign weavers.' Quoted ibid.

the Muslim conquerors, who had not been ardent reformers but had remained in the country and had not taken away its riches.[236]

History was conceived by Harishchandra as a process of enlightenment and modernization, but the idea of progress now served to support the demand for Indian autonomy.[237] Towards the end of the century, with the spread of national consciousness and increasing insights into structures of colonial exploitation, the dilemma of being caught between the will to change and the defence of tradition intensified, leading to an open dispute about the primacy of social reform or political independence.[238] Moreover, the experience of the present misery fitted into the traditional notion of inevitable decline which was revived in those years.[239] Thus even a reformer like Harishchandra could join in the complaint about the evils of kaliyuga, usually described as a period of foreign rule.[240] In his play *Bharatdurdasha* (The Misery of India, 1880), however, Harishchandra also invoked the messianic hope for 'a new, good age when this period of Kaliyuga ends and Kalki, the tenth incarnation of Vishnu, will appear on a white horse, with a weapon in his hand in order to punish the wicked and to reward the righteous, to create the world anew and to initiate a new "age of truth" (*satyayuga*)' (Klimkeit 1981: 153).

This vision of a new satyayuga can hardly be seen as an indigenization of the concept of progress. Both remained apart from each other. Harishchandra, like Dayanand, sought to prove the existence of things in ancient India which 'today are considered to be modern and about which the foreigners boasted, calling them their own'.[241] Nevertheless, he did not give up completely the idea of rationally planned development in favour of inclusivism.[242] He made, instead, a distinction between the unchangeable religious essence of dharma and the temporal, social characteristics of *samaj dharma*.[243] In this way, he could describe the current

[236]A similar critique had been formulated by Bhaskar Pandurang Tarkadkar as early as 1841, in a series of contributions to the *Bombay Gazette*, published under the pseudonym 'A Hindoo'. Cf. Panikkar, 'The Intellectual History of Colonial India' (as in note 53), 423, 425, 411. If Prasad had contrasted the 'reactionary' Muslims with the 'progressive' British, the 'levelling effect of colonial exploitation' made Muslims fellow sufferers. Sudhir Chandra 1992: 127. Harishchandra displayed a striking interest in the social situation of the Muslims. Ibid.: 117.

[237]'To Shiva Prasad, British rule was necessary for the reform of India; to Harishchandra reform was needed for the abolition of foreign rule.' Lütt 1970: 77.

[238]For the alternative: through reform to Independence or through Independence to reform, see Appadorai 1973.

[239]For the revival of the kaliyuga motif in the late nineteenth century, see Sumit Sarkar, 'Renaissance and Kaliyuga: Time, Myth and History in Colonial Bengal', in idem 1998: 186–215.

[240]For the coexistence of 'Kaliyug theory and the belief in progress', see Lütt 1970: 78–84.

[241]'Vaishnavism and India', quoted in Lütt 1970: 90. The entitlement to exclusivity, typical of the revival movements, is asserted here: 'Our Aryan forefathers have created the oldest culture and are therefore the mentors of the entire world both in matters that concern the behavior of the individual and in matters that concern the government of the nation.' Ibid. Harishchandra, however, did not refer to the Vedas but to the Ramayana.

[242]This is also due, perhaps, to the specifically Vaishnava cult of bhakti. In Harishchandra's understanding of the love of God as something common to all religions, *rajabhakti* and *deshabhakti*, love for the government and love for the country, could co-exist. Cf. Klimkeit 1970: 155.

[243]For the 'double-sided concept of dharma' in Harishchandra, see Lütt 1970: 84ff.; Dalmia 1997: 25.

state of India as a symptom of kaliyuga and, at the same time, consider pragmatically the possibilities of social improvement.[244]

It was the separation of concrete strategies of social improvement from the religious sense concepts which seems to have contributed in a decisive manner to the perception of history as a linear process. With his complaint about the drain of wealth, Harishchandra referred to a discussion of material developments which was less exposed to acid tests in the attempts to combine western modernity and Indian tradition.[245] The issue of the economic repercussions of British rule was first raised in public and systematically analysed by Dadabhai Naoroji (1825–1917). Naoroji investigated the links between poverty in India and the draining away of huge sums of money by the British since the second half of the eighteenth century. He denounced the transfer of Indian resources to England, calculated to the amount of 30 or 40 million pounds annually and, with this, denied the liberals their good conscience (Naoroji 1901: VIII). About a quarter of the 'national debt' attributed to India by the British was actually an 'English debt to India!'[246]

Naoroji's arguments were basically still very pro-British and he acknowledged the advantages of western rule in India. While linking the devastating experience of Indian poverty with British policies in India and exposing the interest in power and possession behind the ideology of a civilizing mission, he was confident about the positive course of history in general, which he thought should be stimulated in combined efforts. He reminded the British of their promises and duties and affirmed expectations that redemption of the promises would lead to 'a great and glorious future for Britain and India'. Referring to western observers like John Bright—'The good of England must come through the channels of the good of India'—, he appealed to enlightened British self-interest: 'The present system of government is destructive and despotic to the Indians and un-British and suicidal to Britain'.[247] Naoroji's arguments were not only based on economics. He also examined the effects of colonialism on the political culture of the motherland due to the brutalization of those involved in colonial administration.

The Marathi lawyer, economist, historian and social reformer Mahadev Govind Ranade (1842–1901), too, examined the current tendencies of evolution in Indian society and criticized colonialism for obstructing real modernization and advancement. Similar to Naoroji, he analysed the drain in economic terms, and also reflected on the political context.[248] He opposed, in particular, the emerging international division of labour between industrial countries and suppliers of raw material, because, in his view, it was the dominance of the agrarian sector

[244]With reference to the latter aspect, religion itself could largely be reduced to its social elements. This becomes evident in some remarks of the Ballia speech. At the same time, the English example taught that only a close connection between religion and politics led to enduring progress. See below, Sources section.

[245]But it was exposed, of course, to the tensions within Indian society. Cf. Sumit Sarkar 1983: 87.

[246]Cf. Naoroji's homonymous essay in Naoroji 1887: 26–50.

[247]Naoroji 1901: VIII, II. 'The early nationalists were claiming that they were more loyal to the true goals of the Indian empire than were their English rulers.' Bernard S. Cohn, 'Representing Authority in Victorian India', in Hobsbawm and Ranger 1983: 165–209, here 209.

[248]For the controversy regarding Ranade's attitude to the drain theory, cf. Bipan Chandra 1991: 673–4.

that caused continuing poverty in India. Ranade proposed to build up an Indian industry and to strengthen already existing structures, a task which could not be left to economic forces alone. He took a critical stand on the free-trade ideology and believed that the state should play an active role in the process of industrialization. The Government should promote modern methods of production in agriculture and industry, as well as foreign trade and migration. Influenced by the German economist Friedrich List and the historical school of economics, Ranade conceived development as an 'organic growth of society'. Modernization and cultural heritage were to be reconciled by means of the 'method of tradition'.[249] He strongly argued against a mode of thinking in nativist categories and asked the advocates of revivalism to which origin they wanted to return. For, he argued, each so-called original state of things had itself resulted from a process of development and was thus conditioned by history.[250]

Ranade and Naoroji conceived the indigenous society as changeable and susceptible to intervention. For both of them, the question was no longer whether changes occurred, but why they occurred and how they could be influenced. Based on their findings, and elaborating on them, Romesh Chunder Dutt (1845–1909), at the turn of the century, presented the first comprehensive *Economic History of India* (1902–4). He described in it the gradual integration of the country into the world market, which was organized according to British interests. Here, Indians appeared mainly as suppliers of raw material and as consumers of English products. Dutt showed how these changes destroyed the self-sufficiency of home industries and handicrafts, which had determined the materialistic life of India till then.

Despite his insight into the exploitative character of colonial economy, Dutt did not deny the blessings of British rule. He explicitly welcomed western education, liberal ideas, modern science, efficient administration, and political stability and unity, and thus confirmed, to a certain extent, the self-understanding of the British, according to which they had freed India from anarchy and chaos. But he accused them of furnishing Indians with advantages only in small doses. The British had brought 'peace but not prosperity' to India.[251] The process of industrialization was hindered rather than promoted in the end.

The achievements of modern times were occasionally described by Dutt as a mere restoration of previous conditions: 'All that we wish to indicate is that the Hindu mind in the modern age has, under the influence of new light and progress, travelled once more in the same direction, though with feeble effort, as it did in the days of its ancient vigour.'[252] Even in other passages of his historiographical work, Dutt tended to view current development as a revitalization of the ancient dynamism of Bengal and India. But despite the obvious elements of essentialism in his thought, Dutt was aware of the ideological implications of the concept of development, with the

[249]Ranade 1915: 90, 111–13, 125–7, 132, 158.

[250]Cf. Sudhir Chandra, who views the inclusion of modernity in the origins to be counterproductive: 'Revivalism constitutes the most irretrievable mode of self-forgetting.' Chandra, '"The Language of Modern Ideas": Reflections on an Ethnological Parable', *Thesis Eleven* 39 (1994), 39–51, here 41.

[251]R.C. Dutt 1960, II: XIII. For Dutt's reformist ideas and his belief in progress, see also his *England and India* (1897).

[252]Quoted in L. A. Gordon 1974: 54.

effect that the Indian claim to self-determination was also inserted by him into a temporal horizon. Based on the assumption of an inherent Indian potential for industrial growth which had been prevented from developing, the idea of progress, which hitherto had been used to legitimize British rule, now served to establish the Indian claim to autonomy. In this mode of argumentation, national self-assertion and the historical interpretation of change tended to coincide.

Economic Nationalism became an important ideological component of the freedom movement, and the 'drain of wealth' was adopted as a political catchword.[253] The new relevance given to economic issues in the discourse of national self-assertion not only lowered inner tensions as described above, it also had a universalizing effect. The insight that 'economic laws are everywhere the same',[254] presented by Dutt to counter discriminating stereotypes about India, undermined the prevailing essentialism and opened up the perception to the global contexts in which the processes of development were unavoidably entangled. This made it possible to conceive the relation between tradition and change in a more extroverted way. Instead of invoking the restoration of original greatness, universalists like Rabindranath Tagore and Jawaharlal Nehru as well as a rising number of critical intellectuals aimed to stimulate the creative or revolutionary dynamics.[255] They looked beyond the realization of independence and anticipated the question of how Indian society, after liberation from colonialism, should be organized.

After the success of the Russian October Revolution, discussion about social change in South Asia was also influenced by Marxism. Manabendra Nath Roy (1887–1954), who, within the international communist movement, made himself a spokesman of the repressed in the colonized countries, conceived the various national freedom struggles as elements of global revolutionary processes. With reference to a completely new vision of life, he criticized revivalist movements as an expression of the conservative or reactionary interests of certain groups whose advocates were concerned mainly with preserving the supremacy of the traditional elite.[256]

[253]The *swadeshi* movement of 1905 based its protest, to a large extent, on Naoroji's and Dutt's arguments. Aurobindo was convinced that without Dutt's *Economic History*, the boycott campaign would hardly have been successful. Cf. Nilmani Mukherjee, 'Romesh Chunder Dutt (1848–1909)', *Quarterly Review of Historical Studies* 3 (1963–4), 183–8, here 187. According to Bipan Chandra, the dynamic of the national movement was perhaps ahead of the historical consciousness formulated by members of the discipline. In his view, the nationalist historiography was '*not as advanced* as the movement itself'. Chandra, 'Nationalist Historians' Interpretations', 197. Emphasis in original; cf. also idem 1991: 749–50.

[254]Quoted in Chakrabarti, 'Romesh Chunder Dutt', in A. Kumar 1971: 128.

[255]In a critical turn against nationalism, Tagore postulated the primacy of the social over the political and of change over persistence. Cf. Sachin Sen 1947: 204–5. To Tagore, society was the 'civilizing agent'. Ibid., 305. See below, Section 3.

[256]M. N. Roy 1922: 180–1. Tagore, too, reproached the nationalists with being 'in their social attitude the most conservative': *Nationalism in India*, 94. Even against Naoroji, anti-Brahmanical movements in South India formulated (in 1893) the suspicion that he only intended to stabilize social conditions through the attainment of political freedom: 'While the British were working for "truth, justice and impartiality" in the interest of the underprivileged masses in India, the brahmin-dominated INC was demanding Swaraj in order to re-introduce the brahmin supremacy.' Quoted in Anand 1991: 80.

With the work of Roy and other Marxists, the explanatory and interpretive potential of materialistic thinking, which had become evident in Economic Nationalism, unfolded further. The rising interest in social and economic issues implied a critique of the cultural tradition cherished by the nationalists. Essentialist notions dissolved before the awareness of universal historical progress. In Roy's concept of history, the specifically Indian experience was hardly taken into account. Further, he reduced the value of spirituality which others had seen as a fundamental characteristic of the Indian way of life. 'The claim that the Indian people as a whole are morally less corrupt, emotionally purer, idealistically less worldly, in short, spiritually more elevated, than the bulk of the western society, is based upon a wanton disregard for reality.'[257] Roy considered Gandhi's 'moralizing mysticism' an expression of this wrong idea of India's global mission.

The trust in the course of history not merely replaced the religious sense claimed by others but opposed it. History took on the meaning of a material evolutionary process, which spiritual traditions were hampering at the ideological level and, therefore, had to be fought against.[258] For the sake of a clear perspective more 'theoretical foundation' was required than that offered by the nationalists, according to Roy.[259] Disillusionment with the expectations nurtured by the British should lead to a clear analysis of the historical situation instead of nostalgia for mythical origins. Indian history had to be written according to insight into the laws of material change.[260] Only with this insight was it possible to act appropriately, that is in a way that was directed towards emancipation and progress.

Referring to the universality of the laws of historical evolution, Roy also criticized the exclusion of India from the mainstream of history prevailing in large parts of Marxist theory. India, according to him, was in the capitalistic stage of development after feudalism had disappeared in the wake of the Mutiny of 1857. At the political level, he vehemently opposed Lenin, who gave priority to national liberation over socialist revolution in the colonial countries. According to Roy, there was no prospect of actual freedom without the revolutionary vigour of farmers and workers.

Roy's historical determinism and his disregard for India's cultural heritage provoked counter-criticism not only from nationalists but also from some of the modernizers.[261] However, the notion of the historical process as a reality that could be scientifically analysed was further consolidated in the anti-colonial movement, due to the influence of Marxism. It was Tagore's tradition-conscious universalism and the idea of socialism that influenced the historical thinking of Jawaharlal Nehru (1889–1964), with whom modernization in the political sphere of India is

[257]M. N. Roy, 'India's Message', quoted in *Sources of Indian Tradition*, II, 300.

[258]Taking up certain insights of anthropology (see, for instance, E. B. Tylor, *Primitive Culture* 1913), Roy assumed the existence of an early age without religion in India, thus questioning others' attempts to go back to religious origins.

[259]'India in Transition', in *Selected Works* 1987: 185–8, here 188.

[260]'India in Transition', 186.

[261]See Sudipta Kaviraj, 'The Heteronomous Radicalism of M. N. Roy', in Pantham and Deutsch 1986: 209–35.

generally associated. Nehru sought to reconcile cultural heritage and social progress. He believed in the 'capacity of the Indian people to change and adapt themselves to the modern world without giving up the basic values they had imbibed in their prolonged existence as a people and a civilization'.[262] Explicitly rejecting the essentialist contrasting of Orient and Occident, he sought to explain their difference in historical terms: 'I do not understand the words Orient and Occident, except in the sense that Europe and America are highly industrialized and Asia is backward in this respect.' Industrialization, however, was the outcome of recent historical developments; it was 'something new in the world's history'.[263]

Historical circumstances had been causes of colonial rule and the course of history would also lead to its end.[264] Nehru assumed a link between external dependence and inner stagnation.[265] The 'social culture' of a country could become a barrier to progress. In fact, the decline of Indian civilization had begun long before the invasion of the Muslims. And general conditions, even under the rule of the great Akbar, had not improved substantially.[266] At the time of the European conquest, Asia really had been without 'vigour and vitality', while Europe, at the same time, experienced its heyday. The lesson from this was that the current struggle against imperialism had to be closely connected with the fight for internal reform: India had to become dynamic in order to achieve independence. And of course, it should be independent to let its forces unfold without hindrance. The contrast between East and West assumed a temporal meaning in Nehru's thinking; it was embedded in universal processes, judging by which colonial rule itself could be denounced as being opposed to progress.[267] If Nehru hoped for a regaining of India's 'dynamic outlook and spirit of adventure', this did not mean the revival of former greatness but an alignment with the general course of world history.[268] The search of the ancients for an

[262]Bipan Chandra, 'Nehru's Sense of History', in idem 1993: 159–65, here 164.

[263]Nehru 1989: 151. Followers of the stereotypical view of India as 'religious, philosophical, speculative, metaphysical, unconcerned with this world, and lost in dreams of the beyond', it was Nehru's suspicion, perhaps had second thoughts and hoped India would 'remain plunged in thought and tangled in speculation, so that they might possess this world and the fullness thereof, unhindered by these thinkers, and take their joy of it'. Ibid., 152.

[264]India had seen phases of political and cultural heights in the past, before the situation changed completely in the sixteenth century: 'While Europe was taking advantage of and exploiting the powers of nature, Asia, static and dormant, still carried on in the old traditional way, relying on man's toil and labour.' Ibid., 263.

[265]'A civilization decays much more from inner failure than from an external attack.' Ibid. 263.

[266]'Not even Akbar made any basic difference to that social context of India, and after him the air of change and mental adventure which he had introduced subsided, and India resumed her static and unchanging life.' Ibid., 264.

[267]'And so we come back to the Orientalist thematic. Only now is the difference between East and West reduced from the essential to the conjunctural.' Partha Chatterjee 1996: 136–7. According to Nehru, one could distinguish two Englands. If the one represented cultivation and modernity, the other was brutal and reactionary (1989: 287). But both were inseparable. The 'Plunder of Bengal' only made possible the industrial revolution in England. Cf. David C. Gordon 1971: 48.

[268]'This was an object which had been globally determined by the inexorable logic of universal history.' Partha Chatterjee 1996: 158. Change now appeared as something normal, to which one had to adapt. The violent revolutions in the past had resulted from the refusal to accept change. And the terror of the French Revolution

'ultimate reality' and the mysticism of medieval times should be replaced by an orientation towards the spirit of the times (*yugadharma*), about which Nehru said: 'Humanity is its god and social service its religion.' (Nehru 1989: 557)

The Indian freedom fight thus could be seen as a constituent of global tendencies: 'Was not the world marching rapidly towards the desired consummation? [...] Our national struggle became a stage in the longer journey [...] Time was in our favour.' (Nehru 1995: 363) The course of events at large was promising for the future, for 'history teaches of growth and progress and of the possibility of an infinite advance for man.'[269] This confidence in universal history was enforced by Nehru's adoption, however selective, of Marxism. As 'the general character of social, political and intellectual life in a society is governed by its productive resources',[270] the historical process appeared as a reality which could be rationally planned and kept under control.[271] In the eyes of later critics, Nehru's historical optimism was not justified. It seems that in Nehru's conception the general course of development remained outside the range of Indian politics. 'The universal principle and the world standards had been already set by history; there was no room for choice on those matters.'[272]

Not all Indians regarded the processes of change as being reconcilable with the values of tradition. Advocates of more radical modifications criticized not only the concessions to the old elite but the subordination of social emancipation to the fight for independent statehood in general. Ambedkar, who took into account that traditional forms of discrimination would survive (see above), nevertheless emphasized the necessity of fundamental changes if social reforms were to be realized: 'For Untouchability to vanish, it is the Hindu who must change.' (Ambedkar 1945: 197)[273] Even if Ambedkar did not regard the solution of the Dalit problem to be contained in

had been 'a flea-bite compared to the chronic evils of poverty and unemployment'. Nehru, *Glimpses of World History*, quoted in Chandra, 'Nehru's Sense of History', 161.

[269]'The last letter', in *Glimpses of World History*; 2 Vols. (Allahabad: Kitabistan, 1934–5).

[270]'The Basic Approach', in *Jawaharlal Nehru's Speeches*, IV (New Delhi 1954–68), 121, quoted in Partha Chatterjee 1996: 160.

[271]The confidence in science and the manoeuvrability of social and economic processes is reflected in the foundation of the National Planning Committee (1938–9) of the INC. Nehru, like others before him (Bankimchandra and Tilak), attempted to show that science and tradition were not opposed to each other and that they harmonized in India better than in the West (Nehru 1989: 514–5). Therefore, instead of oscillating between 'blind adherence to her old customs and a slavish imitation of foreign ways', India could refer to the future with self-confidence and orient herself towards universal progress. Ibid., 564.

[272]Partha Chatterjee 1996: 159. 'World History resides Elsewhere' and India searches for a 'place within that universal scheme of things'. Ibid., 161–2. According to Chatterjee, the Indian bourgeoisie had no hegemony over the indigenous society and limited itself to 'passive Revolution' (Gramsci). 'Nationalist discourse at its moment of arrival is passive revolution uttering its own life-history.' Ibid., 51. The same applies, according to Chatterjee, to the belief in scientific progress: 'The progression of Time in the domain of science was also something which took place Elsewhere.' Ibid., 144.

[273]According to Ambedkar, the evolution of Hindu society, after having passed through the phases of Brahmanism of the Vedic period and the 'revolutionary' phase of Buddhism during the time of the Mauryas,

the general tendencies of historical progress, this did not stop him from making reference to them. In Gandhi he saw the Pangloss, who admired anything that belonged to Hinduism and who, in the end, only gave a new philosophical justification to the existing social order instead of altering it. By defending institutions like the caste system, Gandhi presented himself as a 'social reactionary' (Ambedkar: 1945: 307–8).[274]

The Marxists relied on the belief that universal historical processes would unfold, in disregard of cultural peculiarities and, in their course, would dissolve the caste system, too. On the threshold of Independence, Rajani Palme Dutt (1896–1974) presented his *India Today* (1940, 1947), a comprehensive account of recent Indian history on the basis of Marxist teaching. In it he reconstructed the emergence of a New India which, after many centuries of being repeatedly conquered, was finally to become the subject of its own history. Dutt placed Indian attainment of sovereignty in the wider context of the defeat of British imperialism altogether, which in its turn was only a step in the struggle against the general system of economic exploitation. He made it clear that there was another conflict underlying the fight for national freedom: 'The basic problem of India is not only national but social.' The result, therefore, could not consist in Nehru's neutralized modernity, but in a new confrontation. 'This is a situation packed at every turn with social dynamite.' (R. P. Dutt 1989: 15)

The Marxists, with their concept of history as a dialectical process of class struggles, went beyond the historical perspective of nationalism and located the fundamental conflicts within Indian society itself.[275] The nationalists had viewed historical consciousness to be an important factor in the fight against foreign rule and, even to the modern-minded among them, inner change was mainly a means of national self-assertion. To those who conceived independence as a stage on the way to social emancipation, the rewriting of Indian history had produced mainly 'counter-mythology' against 'conventional imperialist mythology' so far. With it, the nationalists turned 'their gaze backwards, not forwards' (R. P. Dutt 1989: 16) .

According to S. A. Dange,[276] too, bourgeois historiography in India failed to understand the epochal changes when it tried to take examples from the Indian past in order to find orientation in the present. The political and social circumstances of the present 'were something *totally new in history*, which past experience could not explain' (Dange 1949: 10). The industrial revolution had transformed the whole world into one unit, new forces and classes had emerged, and to understand this, 'the science of history of the bourgeois historians, Indian and foreign, could provide no laws'. (Ibid.: 10–11) For Dange, too, nationalist historiography was only a defence of the Indian bourgeoisie against the ideological use of history by the English. The facts were 'laid out in a way to battle with the enemy'. (Ibid.: 4) And if historical interest had shifted

---

had come to an early standstill with the 'counter-revolutionary' Hinduism and its caste system. 'Revolution and Counter-Revolution in Ancient India', in *Dr. Babasaheb Ambedkar: Writings and Speeches*, III (Bombay: Education Department, Government of Maharashtra, 1987), 316–7.

[274]M. N. Roy, too, attacked Gandhi and viewed Hindu mysticism as being near to fascism. Cf. M. N. Roy [1983], quoted in Klimkeit 1971: 56.

[275] Sabyasachi Bhattacharya, 'History from Below', *Social Scientist* 119 (April 1983), 3–20, here 7.

[276]Shripat Amrit Dange (1899–1994) for many years was the leader of the Communist Party of India (CPI).

from political issues to social history, this was only to draw the masses into the national freedom fight. 'But obviously it was a false picture of nationhood and of the freedom movement'. (Ibid.: 12) And a false image of history. The middle class used distortion of history in order to disorientate the workers.

The Marxist critique of bourgeois ideology shows how much the interpretation of history has itself become a factor of politics.[277] With the investigation into society's capability for progress, a new dimension came into play, which had repercussions on the formation of identity, on perspectives and on demarcations. Instead of imagining an unchangeable Indian Self opposed to an eternally threatening Other, ever evolving communities and cultures, systems and structures came into sight, including their manifold (internal and external) interactions.

3. Resistant Traditions, Alternative Histories, Idiosyncrasies

The impact of western historical thinking on Indian dealings with past experience and temporal change is reflected not only in its systematization through methodical research; subliminally, it penetrated almost all areas of life and thought. The entire practice of colonial administration, with its basic assumptions and categories, the semantics of the enquiries, statistical surveys, census reports, etc.—all of this disseminated a historicized world-view which the colonized had to deal with.[278] Even defensive positions could hardly escape contagion from the new thinking.[279] Resistance against colonial rule made extensive use of the modern political idiom of the West.[280] The historical knowledge and categories of the Europeans had become a 'hegemonic force in Indian self-perception', and nationalist historiography was determined 'to discover European virtues and institutions in India's past'.[281] The trust in scientific methods, the search for national identity and the anticipation of progress not only determined the new discipline of history, it also became important instances of Indian self-understanding in general.

There were areas, however, in which the resistance of tradition was more persistent and occasionally stood up to western influences, referring consciously to the non-modern character of indigenous thought. Certainly, even the world of the priests and pandits experienced changes and was affected partially by modernization. This is reflected in the example of the cosmopolitan

[277]Cf. D. L. Sheth, 'Politics of Historical Sense Generation. The Case of India', in Rüsen et al. forthcoming.

[278]Cf. Panikkar, 'In Defence of "Old" History', 2595; idem, 'Search for Alternatives: Meaning of the Past in Colonial India', in idem 1995: 108–22. It has been shown, however, that historical categories could also be used for quite unhistorical forms of classification. See above, Section 1.1.

[279]Even 'the traditionalist, who cognitively resists modernity, includes elements of the latter inevitably in his own resistance'. Peter L. Berger et al. 1975: 142, 144. Cf. also Javeed Alam, 'Tradition in India under Interpretive Stress: Interrogating its Claims', Thesis Eleven 39 (1994), 19–38, here 25.

[280]'Nationalist historiographers accepted the patterns set for them by British scholarship. They accepted the periodization of Indian history into the Hindu, Muslim, and British periods, later addressed as the ancient, medieval, and modern eras; relegated caste to sections on "Society", that is, to the history of society with politics left out; and reiterated the long and unchanging existence of a Sanskritic Indic civilization.' Prakash, 'Writing Post-Orientalist Histories of the Third World', 388.

[281]Panikkar, 'In Defence of "Old" History', 2596.

swamis and modern rishis like Vivekananda and others (see above). In contrast, the preaching of Sri Ramakrishna (1836–86) testifies to the continuation of tradition without its modern reformulation. The teacher of Vivekananda almost represented the counter-programme of the latter's striving towards historical agency. All central elements of the modern concept of history were negated by him. Orality was opposed to the written word, contemplation to political perspectives, kaliyuga to progress. Among the evils of kaliyuga were precisely those features which were associated with historicity. 'There was a partial turning away from forward-looking male activism towards a series of logically-distinct but often intermingled "Others": past as contrasted to present, country vs. city, a deliberate feminisation as opposed to active masculinity, the attractive playfulness and irresponsibility of the child and the pagal as against the goal-oriented instrumental rationality of the adult male.'[282] Ramakrishna's teachings attracted, in particular, those members of the Anglicized middle class whose expectations of modernization had been disillusioned and who experienced certain phenomena of modern life as a daily humiliation. The forcible ushering in of mechanized time discipline, for example, contrasted with the conventional rhythm of life and exacted a high degree of adjustment from the people involved. The same applies to the spatial concentration of bureaucratic work (chakri): 'Chakri thus became a "chronotype" of alienated time and space, late 19th century Kaliyuga's heart of darkness, the principal format through which awareness of subjection spread among colonial middle-class males.'[283]

Among the Muslims, too, there were some who saw western influence at work in the very concepts in which anti-colonial resistance was generally articulated. They consequently rejected the aspiration to develop a separate state which, with its secular principles was, in their view, an adulteration of Islamic tradition. Sayyid Ab'l-ala-Maududi (1903–79), in contrast to many western-educated Muslim intellectuals, adhered to Islamic ways and views, which he held to be superior to western civilization, even in the fields of economics, politics, and education. Maududi did conceive South Asian Muslims as a separate community, but not in the sense of a nation. He emphasized the universal mission of Islam, which was hindered by the boundaries between nation states.[284] With a critical look at the history of Muslims in India, he showed how exceeding

---

[282]Sumit Sarkar, '"Kaliyuga," "Chakri", and "Bhakti": Ramkrishna and His Times', EPW (18 July 1992), 1543–66, here 1548. Also 'Brahmans corrupted by too much rational argument' and 'rationalistic criticism of traditional verities' counted among the symptoms of kaliyuga. Ibid., 1549. Some of the disjunctions which were supposed to characterize the relationship between western and indigenous cultures, like that of written vs oral, were age-old parts of Indian reality itself. Indian culture 'has had a literate elite for well over two thousand years, but [...] still tried till the late 18th century to keep its most sacred texts in purely oral form'. Ibid., 1552.

[283]Sarkar, '"Kaliyuga," "Chakri", and "Bhakti"', 1550. Ramakrishna Paramahansa's talks in Calcutta were recorded by his disciple Mahendranath Gupta and appeared in five volumes: Sri Sri Ramakrishna Kathamrita, 1897–1932. English version: The Gospel of Sri Ramakrishna, originally recorded in Bengali by M., a disciple of the Master, translated into English with an Introduction by Swami Nikhilananda (Madras: Sri Ramakrishna Math, 1981). Particularly illuminating is Ramakrishna's account of his visit to the house of the reformer Vidyasagar. Further reading: Friedrich Max Müller, Ramakrishna, His Life and Sayings (New York 1899); Romain Rolland, Essai sur la mystique et l'action de l'Inde vivante, 2nd ed. (Paris 1966).

[284]Even Iqbal, however, had expressed the fear that 'the national idea is racializing the outlook of Muslims and thus materially counteracting the humanizing work of Islam'. Quoted in Anand 1991: 184.

involvement in worldly interests had damaged the spread of Islam and its ideas. Neither Muslim immigrants nor Indian converts had produced a way of life in the subcontinent which was in accordance with Islam. The tendency to mix with followers of other religions was especially to be blamed for this. Only Aurangzeb had fulfilled the duties of Islam in his politics.[285] Maududi pleaded for the Islamization of practical life under the existing conditions. After the founding of Pakistan was accomplished, however, he moved there and attempted to bring to bear his ideas against the secular tendencies within the new state.

Resistance against orientation towards the West could also be offered, as shown by Maududi, in the form of an alternative claim to universality, which questioned the sense of historical evolution defined by the West and mostly identified with the triumph of western civilization. Even the insistence on cultural superiority, however, did not always ensure protection against the infiltration of western ideas. This is exemplified by Muhammad Iqbal (in the case of the Muslims) as much as by Swami Vivekananda (in the case of the Hindus). Some who countered western concepts of universal history with specifically eastern sense assumptions and associated a claim to supremacy with them appeared to commit themselves to a dynamism which was in a problematic relationship with the spiritual character of tradition.[286] In contrast to this, there were also attempts to relate western and eastern civilizations by referring to a universalism of a higher order. Here, indigenous traditions were brought to bear in a new manner. Some leading figures in literature, religion, art, and politics, while reflecting on problems of temporal change in East and West, consciously kept their distance from the modern concept of history—and with exactly this challenged the innovative potential of historical thinking.

To Rabindranath Tagore (1861–1941), who had initially sympathized with the nationalists, it increasingly appeared that these were themselves agents of westernization. They based their striving for a powerful Indian state on a historical experience which was not their own.[287] The determination of India was not political but social, directed towards association rather than demarcation.[288] India, since time immemorial, had been confronted with the race problem and it aimed at a kind of unity which, in contrast to the political monotony of Europe, did not suppress

[285]Aurangzeb was particularly hated among Hindu communalists because of his intransigence. Maududi, in contrast, emphasized the spiritual characteristics and negated the worldliness and aggressivity of Islam often associated with the concept of jihad. See Maududi 1946; idem 1955.

[286]Thus Vivekananda's activism, for instance, contrasted with traditional spirituality, his missionary zeal with the Hindus' aversion to proselytizing.

[287]'The educated Indian at present is trying to absorb some lessons from history contrary to the lessons of our ancestors.' Indians should not 'borrow other people's history', as did the Japanese. 'Nationalism in India', in Tagore 1992: 83, 84. The subsequent page numbers in brackets refer to this edition.

[288]This relates to the internal situation at first: 'India never recognizes differences as differences; to her the alien is not an enemy.' Herein is symbolized the 'unity of the many countries of India, of the many epochs, and of the many hearts'. *Rabindra Rachanavali* (Calcutta: Vishva Bharati, 1939–65), III, 550–1 and XXIV, 368, quoted in Arabinda Poddar, 'Rabindranath Tagore: Beyond Nationalism', in idem 1977: 168–95, here 185–6. With the overcoming of the internal boundaries, however, India also exerted an influence on other countries because this was a 'problem of the world in miniature' (88).

diversity. The issue was 'to make an adjustment of races, to acknowledge the real differences between them where these exist, and yet seek for some basis of unity' (78).[289] The realization of unity in diversity constituted India's identity and was at the same time its contribution to the history of the world.[290]

With reference to the inner sphere of spirituality, claimed but often betrayed by the nationalists, it had to be candidly admitted 'that it is providential that the West has come to India' (85). The work for understanding between races and classes in India had come to a standstill due to the rigid caste system. It was blocked by an 'authority of traditions that are incongruous anachronisms in the present age' (88). The failure to grasp the changeability and temporality of conditions, the 'mutability which is the law of life' (90), had made the life drain out of the social system.[291] By acquiring western culture and humanity, it was possible, according to Tagore, 'to impart to our life a movement and to our ideals a vitality that shall give them the impulse to produce new flower and fruit'.[292] Instead of expecting the revival of an imagined original greatness, he aimed at strengthening the creativity of the mind. In view of the universal connectedness of things, however, the West should concede 'that the East has her contribution to make to the history of civilization' (85). Not on the basis of a typological classification, but in a comprehensive perspective of dialectic interaction in which nothing was exclusively western or eastern any more,[293] Tagore called up both sides: 'Let us have a deep association.' (85)

Tagore advocated a close relationship not only because it was in accordance with traditional Indian striving for understanding, but also in view of a truly historical concept of change. His critique of western materialism had to be seen from this perspective: 'European civilization is perhaps building up underneath a vast desert of matter.'[294] The West had missed its own historicizing mission, as it had brought slavery instead of the envisaged freedom (86). In spite of all its dynamism, it had escaped the 'rule of things' no more than the static Indians. The West, on its way to a 'commercial civilization', was in danger of 'killing time and space' (98).[295]

---

[289]Even earlier, Tagore had confronted the Indian tradition with that of the West in cultural rather than political terms. For the *samaj/rashtra*, society/state and culture/politics dichotomies, cf. Sumit Sarkar 1998: 22ff.

[290]Tagore's interest in 'Greater India' can also be seen from this perspective. To Tagore, the country (*desh*) was 'not a mere geographical expression, but a continent of human characters and human aspirations'. Tagore, 'Greater India' (1927), quoted in Poddar, 'Rabindranath Tagore: Beyond Nationalism', 185.

[291]Around 1900, Tagore had defended the existing Brahmanical world-view against western ideas of modernization. At the same time, in an attempt to reconcile the traditional family system and social order with India's orientation towards progress, Satish Mukherji and the Dawn Society invoked the Brahmanical hegemony as a stabilizing factor. Cf. Sumit Sarkar 1998: 27ff. Later, however, referring to the erstwhile cultural impact of the Hindus on South-East Asia, Tagore complained about India that had increasingly retired 'into a miserly pride of exclusiveness, into a poverty of mind [...] that has lost its light and has no message to the pilgrims of the future'. Tagore in the Preface in *Journal of the Greater India Society* (1926), quoted in Halbfass 1990: 191.

[292]Quoted in Sachin Sen 1947: 297.

[293]'There is only one history—the history of man. All national histories are merely chapters in the larger one. And we are content in India to suffer for such a great cause.' (78)

[294]'The East and the West' (1891), quoted in Poddar, 'Rabindranath Tagore: Beyond Nationalism', 171.

[295]Not only political but also economic nationalism is unmasked as an alienation of Indian tradition.

The future, instead, 'is waiting for those who are rich in moral ideals and not in mere things' (85). By being determinded 'to guide our history to its perfect end' (99), India ensured that the force of inner life was realized and the outer world was kept under its dominance. With this, India contributed to the sense of history in the new era of universalization, 'when man shall discover his soul in the spiritual unity of all human beings' (81). In the global issue of racial unity, India was spearheading the process of civilization.[296] In its reflection on the challenges of modernity, it became the promoter of historical creativity. Thus it was precisely for the sake of historicity that India should remain true to its own character.

While Tagore based his critique of western practice on the experience and potentialities of historical life itself, Aurobindo Ghose (1872–1950) sought to incorporate the realities of East and West in a comprehensive, ultimately transhistorical dynamic. Aurobindo, who was deeply acquainted with the western way of life and politics, had first associated himself with the movement of Bengali and Indian nationalism. In the development of Bengali literature, the aesthetic renewal of which was represented by Bankimchandra and Tagore, he saw the paradigm of the rebirth of India.

Later, Aurobindo sought to transcend the East–West dichotomy by integrating both sides in a comprehensive concept of change that was based on a divine plan of salvation and in which nationalism represented only a phase.[297] Nevertheless, religion remained closely tied to the fate of the nation, as in the case of Bankimchandra and Vivekananda. And the spiritual mission also served Indian expansion. Indians could claim superiority here, since they had privileged access to 'divine laws' by means of the 'divine languages' of Bengali and Sanskrit and of their philosophy, which was at the root of the wisdom of mankind. The universal process of evolution had an eastern foundation.[298]

While Aurobindo maintained that the Vedas and the Upanishads represented the first glorious period of mankind, he moved on to the idea of a world community (*The Ideal of Human Unity*, 1919), towards which he strove as a 'spiritual anarchist'. In the concept of integral Yoga, the realization of practical purposes (*sadhana*) was not recognized as having any significance on its own any more.[299] In contrast to the radical activism of the early period, Aurobindo remarked: 'We thought once, when we worked, that the perfection of the day would come by "action" and

---

Tagore denounces the exploitation through colonial economy but, at the same time, warns against the deadly path of industrial development. Here the universality of the economic laws postulated by R. C. Dutt (see above, Section 2.3), was associated with new compulsions in the age of industrialization.

[296]'What India has been, the whole World is now.' (78)

[297]'The West is not inferior in its spiritual search and, even if not to such an extent, has its saints, wise men and mystics, and the East has had its materialistic tendencies.' *Messages of Sri Aurobindo and the Mother* (Pondicherry 1952), II, 19–20, quoted in Wolff 1957: 11.

[298]'Finally, the devotion to "Mother India" took on the form of a message to the entire world, based on the spiritual heritage of India.' Kurt Dockhorn, *Tradition und Evolution* (Gütersloh: Mohn, n. d. [1969]), 27, quoted in Klimkeit 1990: 136–7.

[299]Cf. Sri Aurobindo, *The Life Divine*, last chapter.

we found out that it was not possible. We had to give up acting in that sense. [...] The limit is to ensure that the work is never allowed to disturb Yoga.' (Purani 1959, II: 160–1)

In *The Human Cycle*, Aurobindo integrated the variety of historical experience into a concept of cosmic evolution. Like Johann Gottfried Herder (1744–1803), he saw each nation as a specific expression of the history of mankind. Just as the Greeks had cultivated the idea of beauty and the Romans that of ethics, the Indians had cultivated the idea of spirituality. This also included instances of innovation: 'By stating that God cannot do what has not been done before, you are denying the possibility of change and thereby of evolution, the realization of what has not been realized, the action of the divine force, the divine grace.' The evolutionary sense, however, was not derivable from human activity itself. Instead it was said: 'Evolution is the omnipotence of grace in action.'[300] What was at stake in the advancement of the subjective, the individual, and the rational age was the 'evolution of consciousness from a mythic stage through rationality to a suprarational integration'.[301] It was only through spiritual evolution that the worldly process could harmonize with cosmic truth. According to Aurobindo, 'historical time is a moving spectrum of manifesting consciousness'. Whatever else could be said about the processes of change, their sense lay in the 'revelation and manifestation of the absolute spirit in and through Time'; it was not a product of human creativity.[302]

Unlike Tagore, who had based Indian self-assertion as against the modern West on an appropriation and critical examination of historical thinking, Aurobindo sought refuge in the trans- or super-historical. The highest stage of evolution could be achieved by man only as an individual, not as a social being (a part of collective life); the individual transcended the outer reality without altering it. Eliade spoke of the 'ritual internalization' of the cosmic process in Aurobindo, Henry Schwarz of a 'humanized cosmology'. The notion of acting here remains in an unclear position between the creative process and a quasi-natural determinism.

The art historian Ananda K. Coomaraswamy (1877–1947) argued explicitly against the modern concept of history and the increasing dominance of scientific thinking in approaching the past. In a review of Sarvepalli Radhakrishnan's *Eastern Religions and Western Thought* (1939), he distanced himself from the efforts at 'pacification' in the relationship between East and West and stated the incompatibility of the Hindu tradition with western thinking. Radhakrishnan, according to Coomaraswamy was an 'Orientalist' and had already abandoned striving towards spiritual freedom.[303]

Coomaraswamy rejected the idea of India's adjustment to the historical actuality of the West and countered western modernity with Oriental or Indian traditionality (Halbfass 1990: 371). Echoing the allegations of Bankimchandra, who had declared the western Indologists to be incompetent with regard to the religious traditions of India, he referred to the incapability of

[300]Sri Aurobindo, *The Human Cycle*, quoted in Wolff 1957: 113.

[301]Peter Heehs, 'Myth, History, and Theory', *History and Theory* 33 (1994), 1–19, here 17.

[302]Reddy 1984: 19. 'The leading principle in history is the Divine Will working, but not necessarily through the will of man and human reason.' Ibid., 3.

[303]'Eastern Religions and Western Thought', *The Review of Religion* 6 (1941–2), 129–45, here 136, 140–1.

modern intellectuals 'to entertain at one and the same time empirical and transcendental "explanations" of experience.'[304] While Bankimchandra had nevertheless attempted to reconcile western modernity with Indian tradition, Coomaraswamy insisted on the peculiar value of the latter. 'Tradition', according to him, was 'in no way "opposed" to science, although independent of science, and severely critical of the accumulation of facts without a relation of these facts to any unifying principle.'[305] This was quite different from Bankimchandra's attempt to incorporate western knowledge in the eastern tradition. The mysteries could not be explained in scientific language and the revelation of the 'Vedic incantations' was not accessible to historical interpretation. 'The East [...] has still preserved and is still conscious of the metaphysical bases of its life, while the modern West is almost completely ignorant of traditional metaphysics [...] and is at the same time actively and consciously anti-traditional.'[306] Coomaraswamy emphasized (like Bankimchandra) the Indian ability to accept the Other as being a superior principle of the East, in contrast to the western concept of linear progress which was conflicting with it (and yet found favour in Bankimchandra's eyes).

India, therefore, instead of striving for a connection to western modernity, should insist on traditionality—not only for its own sake, but also in the interest of the West.[307] This did not mean simply defending things as they were. The preservation of tradition rose above ancient values themselves: 'Tradition can give modern people the wish to seek a new quality in their own lives without giving the impression that the details of past solutions are currently valid.' The study of tradition in its metaphysical meaning, according to Coomaraswamy, did not exhaust itself in internalizing certain ideas of the past, but was 'an invitation to a life-long search' (Lipsey 1977: 267, 275). Opposed to the inclusion of Indian art, culture and society in a supposedly universal process of civilization, he insisted on a sense of human existence that lies beyond the concept of development.[308]

Among the leaders of the freedom movement, it was, above all, Mohandas Karamchand Gandhi (1869–1948) who not only questioned the colonizer's view of history, but also formulated the peculiarity of Indian tradition in radical opposition to what constituted history in western thinking. He countered western civilization, so admired by many Indian nationalists, with an alternative social order, which was directed towards self-restraint instead of expansion, understanding instead of domination.

[304]Coomaraswamy, 'Eastern Religions and Western Thought', 138. Cf. K. R. Stunkel, 'The Meeting of East and West in Coomaraswamy and Radhakrishnan', *Philosophy East and West* 23 (1973), 517–24, here 520.

[305]Coomaraswamy, 'Eastern Religions and Western Thought', 138.

[306]Ibid., 144.

[307]'That the East did not find the way to modernity on its own appears as a fundamental strength.' Halbfass 1990: 371.

[308]Thus, even the benevolent interference in Indian affairs was seen by Coomaraswamy as ambivalent. According to him, it was not only the compassion for the discriminated against, but also the hostility of the industrial societies towards pre-industrial forms of society which found expression in the western criticism of the caste system. Cf. Nandy, 'Evaluating Utopias', in idem 1992: 1–19, here 8.

Gandhi's disapproval of the historical mode of the West manifested itself most obviously in his critique of modern industrial society, which destroyed morals and religion. In clear contrast to the view of historicizers like Bankimchandra, Vivekananda, or Nehru, Gandhi deduced the dependence of India not from a lack of modernity but from an excess of it (Partha Chatterjee 1996: 86). For Gandhi, who consistently stood by the primacy of the spiritual, it was evident that India's modernization destroyed the very autonomy which it was supposed to defend.[309] His criticism was also directed against the notion of a historical development that was accomplished by physical strength. Only when moving away from the conventional concept of history, when looking beyond wars and revolutions, did the spiritual dimension of events become visible. Thus Gandhi was convinced that 'a nation is happy that has no history. It is my pet theory that our Hindu ancestors solved the question for us by ignoring history as it is understood today and by building on slight events their philosophical structure. Such is the *Mahabharata*. And I look upon Gibbon and Motley as inferior editions of the *Mahabharata*.'[310]

Gandhi's concept of agency was characterized by 'soul force' instead of 'physical strength' or 'body force' and it even included suffering as a meaningful element. Concerned about the rehabilitation of the victims of history, Gandhi did not conceive of a counter-history which was just a reversal of the victor's history. The specific quality of the experience of suffering had to be preserved in it.[311] Suffering was not to be equated with idleness. In passive resistance, it could be purposefully brought into action as the readiness to sacrifice oneself, and this was done in a way which included the adversary in the process of reflection. By no means did Gandhi accept the western stereotype about Indian unchangeability. He realized that 'nothing in this world is static, everything is kinetic. If there is no progression, then there is inevitable retrogression.'[312] Therefore, the recourse to origins or the simple holding on to the *status quo* was no solution. In opposition to conservative interests, Gandhi insisted on profound changes in Indian society. Revealing more historical consciousness than revivalists and admirers of ancient Indian greatness, he stated: 'If we are to make progress, we must not repeat history but make new history. We must add to the inheritance left by our ancestors.'[313]

Even teleological notions and forms of processuality can be found in Gandhi. Regarding signs of increasing *ahimsa*, he said: 'If we believe that mankind has steadily progressed towards ahimsa, it follows that it has to progress towards it still further.'[314] Gandhi frequently expressed

[309]Thus, even in the case of successful industrialization, liberty would not be achieved in India. Modernization and industrialization alienated even (and above all) the English themselves.

[310]*The Collected Works of Mahatma Gandhi* (New Delhi 1958–84) (cited hereafter: CWMG), Vol. 25, 128 [*Young India*, 11 September 1924].

[311]With this he contrasted the power-related concept of politics with a 'Hindu concept of courage'. Kantowsky 1986: 142.

[312]CWMG, Vol. 72 [*Harijan*, 11 August 1940], 351.

[313]Quoted in Balkrishna Govind Gokhale, 'Gandhi and History', *History and Theory* 11 (1972), 214–25, here 222. Cf. also the remark in *Hind Swaraj*: 'To believe that what has not occurred in history will not occur at all is to argue disbelief in the dignity of man.' CWMG, Vol. 10, 40.

[314]CWMG, Vol. 72 [*Harijan*, 11 August 1940], 351.

his confidence in the perfectibility of human nature and in the beneficial course of time: 'Human history is a meaningful process, a significant development. [...] Below in the depths is to be found the truly majestic drama, the tension between the limited effort of man and the sovereign purpose of the universe. Man cannot rest in an unresolved discord. His progress is marked by a series of integrations, by the formation of more and more comprehensive harmonies.'[315] But Gandhi made it clear once again that meaningful elements can be found only on a deeper level than that of historical events: 'That which is permanent and therefore necessary eludes the historian of events. Truth transcends history.'[316]

Ultimately, sense (truth) could not be derived from the observation of superficial changes, but only by dedicating oneself to the eternal. Even the struggle for swaraj, according to Gandhi, had a religious as well as a political meaning, it was aimed at *inner* freedom, too: 'God was always present in history', and 'unqualified non-violence was the only means of coming to terms with His historical destiny for man'.[317] With this, an eschatological element was introduced into the reflection on history. Man cannot find peace with himself 'till he has become like unto God'.[318] Therefore, besides the victims of history, at the centre of consideration was 'a small body of determined spirits fired by an unquenchable faith in their mission', the avatars, the incarnations of the divine spirit, who could discover new meanings for human action and 'alter the course of history'.[319] The relationship between religion and politics escapes any simplifying formula in Gandhi. On the one hand, the spheres were explicitly separated by him.[320] It was possible to strive for swaraj for purely worldly motives. On the other hand, Gandhi, for himself, sought to closely connect them. The practice of *satyagraha* was directed towards political independence and personal salvation (moksha) alike. However, even the transcendent truth sometimes revealed itself in actual life: 'No good comes fully fashioned out of God's hands, but has to be carved out through repeated experiments and repeated failures by ourselves.'[321]

Gandhi's epoch-making achievement has been seen by some precisely in the realization of

---

[315]Quoted in M.G. Gupta 1991: 86.

[316]CWMG, Vol. 25 [*Young India*, 11 September 1924], 129. 'I do dimly perceive that whilst everything around me is ever changing, ever dying, there is underlying all a living power that is changeless, that holds together, that creates, dissolves and recreates.' Quoted in Gokhale, 'Gandhi and History', 217.

[317]Gokhale, ibid., 216.

[318]Mahadev Desai, The Gospel of Selfless Action (Ahmedabad 1956), quoted in Gokhale, ibid., 218.

[319]Gandhi, Young India, 28 February 1929, quoted in Gokhale, ibid., 222.

[320]This corresponded largely to the traditional Indian way of dealing with change and eternity: 'While Hindus may, in ritual or in meditative states, experience a timeless "pure present", it is clear that in other contexts they do not.' Schwartz, 'Indian Untouchable Texts of Resistance', 138. Gandhi's satyagraha campaigns aim, as has been shown by Richard Lannoy, to attain an 'ideal state of equilibrium' instead of leading to processes of development. Lannoy 1971: 398ff. Nandy, too, criticizes the destruction of 'cultural elasticities' and of the 'capacity of cultures to return to something like their original state after going through a calamity'. Nandy, 'History's Forgotten Doubles', 55.

[321]Quoted in Gokhale, 'Gandhi and History', 219.

this relationship between religious and social or political objectives.[322] Non-violence and the readiness to suffer were related to the transcendent truth but, by practising compassion, also served to improve the human capabilitiy of mutual understanding.[323] If the divine destiny of man was realized in the processes of reconciliation, these processes could also be interpreted as this-worldly tendencies of humanization. It is open to debate, however, whether this should be viewed as historical thinking or rather an alternative to history. According to Balkrishna Govind Gokhale, the difference between history and mythology is effaced in Gandhi,[324] and Ashis Nandy insists on the anti-historical character of Gandhi's way of thinking.[325] In any case, the steadfast articulation of the experience of suffering, which too often has been justified by the progress of history, challenges the capability of modern historical thinking to become aware of its possibly repressive effects. This kind of self-scrutiny could also contribute to proceeding beyond the contrasting of 'historical' and 'non-historical', 'developed' and 'underdeveloped' societies or cultures.

4. AFTER COLONIALISM: HISTORICAL THINKING IN CONTEMPORARY SOUTH ASIA

The end of colonial rule in South Asia was a turning point in the history of the subcontinent, and that applies to historical thinking, too. With the independent states of India (1947), Pakistan (1947) and Sri Lanka (1948), not only did the circumstances of action change but also those of perception and cognition.[326] Foreign rule had always been regarded by nationalist historians as an obstacle to research and a distorting element.[327] The formerly passive objects of Orientalism had turned into active subjects reflecting autonomously on their historical perspectives. Given the new political agency, the processes of change could be assumed, with good reason, as proceeding in the right direction or, in any case, as susceptible to intervention. Thus it could be concluded, with regard to the economy, for instance: 'Once the political or state power was taken away from the foreign rulers and the full weight of the new power was thrown behind the indigenous economic effort, the colonial content of the economy would gradually disappear.'[328] The attainment

---

[322]According to Kantowsky, Gandhi's achievement was that he transformed the Hindus' 'classical interpretation of existence and related it to their environment and tradition, so that Hindu narcissistic striving for self-realization and a social life in the service of others were not incompatible any more, but depended on each other'. Kantowsky 1986: 135.

[323]All depended on the harmony between religious values and worldly means: 'The means used are pure in moral terms, and for Gandhi means and ends are convertible terms. Man's inner history as well as the true history of mankind should reveal this interplay of forces in the Gandhian manner.' Gokhale, 'Gandhi and History', 222.

[324]'For Gandhi, history is, then, the saga of man's striving to discover his own humanity, which is but a reflection of the Supreme.' Ibid., 225.

[325]For Nandy's approach to history, see below, Section 4.4.

[326]For the 'historical watershed', cf. Sudipta Kaviraj, 'Kolonialismus, Moderne und politische Kultur: die Krise Indiens', in Matthes 1992: 219–38, here 229.

[327]According to Sudhir Chandra, the liberation from an oppressive present could help 'to move more from the past to the present rather than the other way around'. Chandra 1992: 159.

[328]Bipan Chandra, 'Presidential Address' ['Colonialism and Modernization'], in Proceedings of the 32nd Session of the Indian History Congress (Jabalpur 1970), II, 1–31, here 19.

of independence, as was the common conviction, meant sovereignty with regard to collective memory as well as actual history. It comprised the ability to make, know and represent history in a 'post-colonial' manner.[329]

4.1 Objectivity, Prejudice, and the Call for Indian Frameworks of Interpretation

Nevertheless, whoever had expected that an undistorted image of history would emerge without conflicts after the attainment of Independence was to be disappointed very soon. An advocate of Rankean standards of objectivity like R. C. Majumdar stated after some years that 'the end of British rule has led to a steady deterioration in that critical method of historical studies which we Indians learnt from our contact with the West'. The decline of historical research was caused, according to Majumdar, not only by the constant interference of the Government in the business of historiography, but also by the attitude of many historians themselves: 'Certain new trends are growing among a section of Indian historians which violate the high ideals of truth.'[330]

Other historians approached the problem of a post-colonial foundation of historiography with more insight into the constitutive relatedness of historical knowledge to specific standpoints and perspectives. In 1972, Romila Thapar, in a series of radio lectures, concerned herself with 'Past and Prejudice' and confronted some of the assumptions which were at the centre of the nationalist as well as the western-colonialist view of Indian history with new results of research. As for the idea of an Aryan race, for instance, which had invaded India and conquered the natives settled there, archaeological and linguistic findings only indicated that groups of Aryan speaking peoples migrated into northern India and mixed with the indigenous population. Vedic culture, for the most part, has to be perceived as the result of this interaction.[331]

Besides the politically explosive issue of the Aryan origin of Indian culture and nation, some other stereotypes were questioned. These include the idea, fostered in the West, of a stagnant Indian society or that of its commitment to spirituality. Historical research has revealed that the social structure identified with the caste system was in no way as inflexible as had been assumed for a long time and that the otherworldly interest of Indians had not prevented an activist ethics of economy. Marx's concept of the Asiatic Mode of Production and Wittfogel's theory of Oriental Despotism were partly based on assumptions now empirically disproved. While examining conventional concepts in the light of new evidence, Thapar also occupied herself with widespread ideas about the lack of historical thinking in India and demanded a more self-

[329]Thus, the rewriting of Indian history was soon put on the agenda. Cf. Nandalal Chatterjee, 'Rewriting of Indian history', Indian Review 53 (Dec. 1952), 529–31. H. Mukherjee in 1959 specifically 16–24, postulates a post-colonial, critical treatment of Indian contemporary history based also on non-official sources and refers explicitly to Tagore's demand for a 'rewriting' from an Indian standpoint. See Kenneth Ballhatchet, 'The Rewriting of South Asian History by South Asian Historians after 1947', Asian Affairs (London, 15 Feb. 1984), 27–38.

[330]R. C. Majumdar, 'Indian Historiography: Some Recent Trends' (Presidential Address at the Sixth Annual Conference of the Institute of Historical Studies, Srinagar 1968), in S. P. Sen 1973, pp. XIX, XXI. For Majumdar's objectivism, cf. Sugam Anand, 'R. C. Majumdar: 1888–1975', in Ramesh Chandra Sharma et al., 1991: 155–67.

[331]Thapar, 'The Past and Prejudice', 25ff. In fact, the concept of an Aryan race had not existed in precolonial India.

confident appropriation of the Indian tradition of dealing with the past as against the exclusivist claims evinced by the western historical discipline.

Thapar did not question, however, the universality of the methodological standards. The enlightening potential of the scientific approach to history should rather be used in the interest of Indian self-determination. In contrast to this, in the late 1970s a group of historians, who sought to bring to the fore the specifically Indian features of history, questioned the suitability of western categories and even of comparative approaches for the interpretation of the Indian past. The Indian History and Culture Society (IHCS) focused attention of scholars on questions of value judgements, national identity, etc., and also criticized the use of non-Indian concepts like 'slave-owning society' and 'Asiatic Mode of Production'. The new association of historians, according to its president Devahuti, ultimately aimed at 'Indian frameworks of interpretation' for the Indian past; for 'the general becomes intelligible only through the specific, the universal through the unique.' The general concepts were to be gained from one's own experience. Historians with an orientation towards progress, in particular the Marxists, were countered by Devahuti: 'We have to be our own "messiahs", to feel, to understand, to interpret our own history.' (Devahuti 1979: X)

However, discussion of the problem of how, concretely, to mediate between the objectivity of research and the Indian perspective did not proceed beyond a few programmatic statements. In an attempt to bring to bear the judging subjectivity of the actors as against the flow of events, it was maintained that history, ultimately, was not about what happened, but about what people thought and said about it. Therefore, the Indian historian's interest should be directed towards 'what the Indian people, ordinary or special, thought and said about events and ideas', even if this meant the conversion of history into myths and symbols. It was 'by understanding the process of how they made history, the philosophers, the kings, the social reformers, the artists, etc.', that we shall 'be able to discern their attitude to history. This will supply us with Indian frameworks'. (Devahuti 1979: X–XI) It was recommended that only indigenous and ancient concepts and categories should be used. Thus even the 'Puranic approach to Indian history' was reconsidered.[332]

The assumption that Indian history, as a unique phenomenon, eludes the comparative approach altogether is related to the more general fear that there may occur a kind of alienation from one's cultural roots in the very categories which are used.[333] To base the understanding of the self on western concepts and principles is seen as a continuation of colonialism and imperialism. The subjugation of the non-Europeans could come as an attempt 'to "understand" their past and present in terms of categories which are imposed upon their society and make them mould their future in terms dictated by an alien culture'. Western science, with its claim to universality, is questioned as a threat to the multiplicity of the ways of life: 'By claiming that there can be

[332]The restriction on the use of categories for reasons of authenticity can result, however, in suppressing the capacities of historical reflection to transcend the given reality. This became evident during the nineteenth century, in some of the more fundamental attacks against western accounts of Indian history. To some critics, the future was not open since the past was always given. Cf. K. N. Panikkar, 'Conceptualizing communalism', *Seminar* 394 (June 1992), 26–8, here 27.

[333]For similar tendencies in Africa and Australia, see Helen Tiffin, 'Introduction', in Adam and Tiffin 1991: p. XII.

only one Man, it hits at the root of cultural specificity, i.e. the plurality of cultural reality.'[334] The cultural enslavement, it is concluded, should be opposed by a *counter-culture*.

4.2 Unity and Diversity, Particularity and Universality

The debate on objectivity and prejudice, scientific method and authenticity is closely associated with the question about the legitimacy of a political perspective in historical research. The demonstrative claim to the scientific status of history can also serve to provide a greater validity for one's own standpoint without making it explicit as such. In contrast, Barun De, during the 1988 session of the Indian History Congress, demanded to acknowledge the presence of practical interests and purposes in research and to make them better visible. After 1947, one had lost sight of the necessity 'of relating history to quotidian social events'. Till then historiography had helped 'to create a sense of nationality' and the political and social reality had been perceived as 'history in the making'. It is a theoretical as well as a didactical necessity to make history interesting, that is 'to relate it to the events, lives, or thought of actual people'.[335]

The issue of perspective, however, did not become any simpler after Independence, although (or better, because) one could perceive oneself now as an actor rather than a victim of history. The self-confidence emanating from the successful resistance movement conflicted with the British interpretation of a 'transfer of power'.[336] Even within Indian society itself, ideas about post-colonial agency moved in divergent directions. For a modernizer like Nehru, the end of colonial rule made it possible to freely combine Indian tradition and western technology (as pointed out by Bankimchandra), and he was convinced that this would unchain the forces of progress. For others, the preservation of tradition had higher importance. Introducing one of the co-operative projects on the rewriting of Indian history, it was said: 'India stands today three hundred and fifty million strong, with a new apparatus of state, determined not to be untrue to its ancient self, and yet to be equal to the highest demands of modern life'. Accordingly, it was seen as the task of the historian to provide strong support from tradition to efforts for the modernization of society; he had 'to investigate and unfold the values which age after age have inspired the inhabitants of a country to develop their collective will and to express it through the manifold activities of their life'.[337]

The newly-won sovereignty was supposed to fulfil itself in a self-confident formulation of India's role in the world as well as in an easy profession of inner diversity. If Nehru had attempted, in his historical and political reflections, to outline India's position in global affairs as that of an

[334]S. G. Kulkarni, 'Imperialism of Categories: Colonial Man in Search of a Cultural Identity', 36, 40. See also Alvares 1991.

[335]Barun De, 'Problems of the Study of Indian History' 51, 8, 7.

[336]Cf. Gita Dharampal-Frick, 'Das Endspiel des British Raj. Indiens Aufbruch in die Unabhängigkeit', *Geschichte in Wissenschaft und Unterricht* 48 (1997), 3–22, here 4–5.

[337]K. M. Munshi, 'Introduction', in *History and Culture of the Indian People*, I (Bombay: Bharatiya Vidya Bhavan, 1951), 12, 8.

active participant, K. M. Panikkar (1895–1963) depicted in his work the course of world history from an Asian or Indian perspective, in clear contrast to western viewpoints (Pannikar 1953). This involved the geopolitical and strategic interpretation of the dominance of European sea powers over the landmasses of Asia as well as the description of the irreversible enforcement of a 'commercial economy' of the western type on the societies of India, China, etc., which were quite differently structured. It was the cultural resistance of the Asians which had prevented total Europeanization. At the same time, a new feeling of solidarity among the peoples of the East emerged, and thus the end of the 'Vasco-da-Gama era' could well prove to be the beginning of an Asian era.

The waning importance of India's confrontation with British power was conducive to a regionalization in historical research,[338] particularly since regional diversity was acknowledged, at the political level, by a federal structure of the Union. Moreover, new theoretical approaches in anthropology rediscovered the 'little traditions' which had been overshadowed for a long time by the 'great' Brahmanic tradition.[339] This approach, developed by Robert Redfield in order to capture the heterogeneous and dynamic elements of a specific civilization, found a positive response in South Asia and contributed to the overcoming of essentialist concepts of Indian culture. The increasing readiness to differentiate also led to a better recognition of the regional cultures, which had always sought to integrate local and all-India realities[340] and which had become 'the actual carriers of the cultural development of India'.[341] The new interest in the regional peculiarities of Indian history has to be distinguished from the forms of political regionalism which had been articulated long before Independence, especially among South Indian Tamils.[342] In contrast to this, practicioners of regional history like Nilakanta Sastri (1892–1975) tried to avoid the extreme opposition of centralism and separatism.[343]

---

[338]Of course, the antagonism that dominated the colonial period did not disappear after 1947, but it lost some of its pervasiveness. Cf. Dietmar Rothermund, 'Nationale und regionale Geschichtsschreibung in Indien', *Periplus* 3 (1993), 75–82.

[339]Cf. the report of the States Reorganisation Commission (1955) as well as the studies of the Linguistic Survey of India. Basic: Redfield 1960.

[340]For the danger of falling back into that exclusivism again, which the differentiation was supposed to break, cf. Miller, 'Button, Button', 27. See also Kunal Chakrabarti, 'Anthropological Models of Cultural Interaction and the Study of Religious Process', *Studies in History* 8:1, n.s. (1992), 123–49, here 134–5. As in the case of Bengal with its Durga cult, there could also emerge regional 'great traditions'. State, region, land, and village can represent 'intermediary stages of tradition'. Chakrabarti, ibid., 145.

[341]Hermann Kulke, 'Regionen und Regionalkulturen in der indischen Geschichte', in C. Mallebrein (ed.), *Die anderen Götter* (Köln 1993). For an introduction to regional studies, see Hermann Kulke and Dietmar Rothermund (eds), *Regionale Tradition in Südasien* (Wiesbaden: Steiner, 1985), IXff.

[342] Here it had also developed into separatist movements seeking confirmation and legitimation from history. See above, Section 2.2.

[343]Another instructive example of regional identity between the national and the local is that of the Punjab with its religious, ethnic and linguistic plurality. See L. M. Khubchandani, 'Self-Images and Identities of the Punjabi People: Ethnic and Linguistic Realities', in P. C. Chatterji 1989: 165–77. The foundation of collective identity in the Punjab, with its multiple historical elements, is discussed (with methodological reflections on

In attempts to define the collective Self and the historical subject-agent, national, regional, and local traditions had to be reconciled. The fact that basic questions about the Self and the Other had not become any simpler after Independence was also reflected in the continuing conflict between religious communities. Certainly, the country was no longer in the grip of a foreign power which could play off one group or community against the other, but there was no longer a common enemy either, the combined fight against whom required the settling of differences. Due to the establishment of two separate states, what had been interior quarrels before now became international disputes, and many elements of the former confrontation between India and the West were now transferred to the antagonism between Hindus and Muslims. More than ever, the Muslims appeared as the quintessential Other to the Hindus, against whom Indian society was to be welded into a nation.[344]

Both experiences, the liberation from foreign rule and the partition of India, were linked in an intricate manner. If Independence stood for the regained autonomy of acting, the simultaneous foundation of Pakistan meant the ultimate experience of being victimized and humiliated. For many Indians, the partition of the country, in the course of which more than eight million people fled across the borders, accompanied by the most fierce outbreaks of violence, was nothing short of a 'vivisection of the motherland'.[345] And those who, even before, had based national identity on Hindutva felt all the more determined to define India as a Hindu state after the proclamation of the Islamic Republic of Pakistan (1956).

The general framework of communalist politics had changed. If, during the struggle for Independence, the communalism of the Muslims had been perceived mainly as a form of particularism as against nationalism, the communalism of the Hindus now posed as the latter's true realization. Hindu nationalism laid claim to the traditions and values of the majority as against the 'privileges' of the minorities. In contrast, the leadership of the Indian state, dominated by the Congress Party, explicitly professed the country's multicultural tradition and presented itself as the guarantor of tolerance and social modernization. Secularism and the protection of the minorities were safeguarded by the Constitution. The formula 'unity in diversity' became an often-pronounced maxim of Government politics.[346]

These principles also had to prevail, according to the view of the Nehru administration, in the public representation of the past. The writing and teaching of history, as far as they were

Merleau-Ponty and his idea of a 'lateral universal') by Dhillon 1994. For the striving for autonomy of the tribal population (Adivasi), see the remarks in Section 4.5 (Environmental History).

[344]The similarity to ontological conceptualizations of the quintessential Other is shown by Peter Heehs, 'Indian Communalism: A Survey of Historical and Social-Scientific Approaches', in idem 1998: 124–42, here 131.

[345]Not only for Hindu nationalists like Savarkar, India as the field of dharma (*dharma kshetra*) had a divine vocation. Cf. Savarkar, *Indian War of Independence*, 10.

[346]Nehru, according to whom nationalism followed from modernization, viewed particularist movements as reactionary: 'Communalism is one of the obvious examples of backward looking people trying to hold on to something that is wholly out of place in the modern world and is essentially opposed to the concept of nationalism.' Quoted in N. C. Saxena, 'Historiography of Communalism in India', 303–4.

under the control of the state, were expected to emphasize 'communal harmony' in the life of the Indian people, which was required in the interest of national integration and uninterrupted social and economic progress. Pluralistic society was thus provided with a dimension of historical depth, and modernization appeared as an authentic continuation of the cultural heritage.

The semi-official *History of the Freedom Movement in India*, written by the journalist and historian Tara Chand, testifies to this attitude (see below, Sources: Section 4.2.2). Initially, R. C. Majumdar had been chosen to write the book. But his draft, which deviated in some essential points from the Government line, was passed over. According to Majumdar, 'composite culture' was a politically motivated construct and the notion of Hindu-Muslim fraternity was not in accordance with the facts. An account based on this assumption would be 'not only a great historical error, but also a political blunder'. In Majumdar's eyes, foreign rule had begun with the Delhi Sultanate and not only with the victory of Robert Clive: 'The major part of India lost independence about five centuries before, and merely changed masters in the eighteenth century' (Majumdar 1971: XIX, XII). Of course, the underlying distinction between invaders and indigenous population depended, for its part, on political presuppositions,[347] which steered investigations and entered the historian's principles of selection. While Tara Chand laid stress upon evidence of communal harmony, Majumdar emphasized the evidence of Hindu-Muslim conflict as being a constant feature of Indian history.

Majumdar's position found favour with those for whom the achievement of Independence was but a first step towards national revival and who made the Golden Age of the Hindus the central point of reference of their historical orientation. Organizations like the Rashtriya Svayamsevak Sangh (RSS), and the opposition party Jana Sangh, demanded the Hinduization of historical consciousness.[348] The close linking, by communalists, of historiography to political purposes was increasingly opposed by well-known representatives of the academic guild.[349] In the ongoing dispute over the social function of historical knowledge, the standards of scientific research are upheld on one side, while, on the other, a religious aura is created, occasionally connected with resentments against non-Indian rationalism. Nevertheless, the confrontation cannot simply be reduced to one between modernity and tradition, science and faith; for the Hindutva school of history makes claims to the prestige of modern science, too.

[347]Thus the coming of the Aryans was seen in a completely different manner from that of the Muslims, namely as a civilizing mission (if not, as in recent times, the Aryans are declared to represent the indigenous population). Even the British subjection of India could be partly accepted as contributing to the weakening of the previous Muslim invaders. Cf. B. D. Chattopadhyaya, 'Cultural Plurality, Contending Memories and Concerns of Comparative History: Historiography and Pedagogy in Contemporary India', in Rüsen et al. forthcoming.

[348]The RSS platform of 1949 aimed to 'overcome the diverging tendencies among the Hindus which result from the difference of sects, faiths, castes and dogmas' and to show them 'the greatness of their past'. Quoted in Klimkeit 1971: 259. For Jana Sangh's 'Resolution on Indianisation' (1952), see Madhok 1971, 98–9.

[349]At a seminar organized by All India Radio in October 1968, Romila Thapar, Harbans Mukhia and Bipan Chandra presented a comprehensive survey of the communalist interpretation of Indian history, which later appeared as a book: *Communalism and the Writing of Indian History* (1969). Directed against the attempt to indigenize history, the authors also pointed out the colonial origin of some of the interpretive concepts presented as genuinely Indian. See also Romila Thapar, 'The Past and Prejudice', and Devahuti's remarks about the 'civil war' in Indian historiography (see above).

This became evident in the campaign about the alleged birthplace of the god Rama (*Ramjanmabhumi*) in Ayodhya. With the destruction of the Babri mosque in December 1992, the communalization of history reached heights hitherto unknown.[350] It was not only the 'correction' of memory which was at stake but the undoing of historical wrong. The rewriting of history turned into a manifest attempt to take one's revenge.[351] However, the communalists, irrespective of all tendencies to mythification, were eager to give their assertions the appearance of empirical validity. The Vishva Hindu Parishad (VHP) presented extensive documentation and 'evidence', and made claims to historical truth.[352] What prevails is a kind of double strategy: if, on the one hand, the sacredness of the issue is conjured up, on the other, one's own position should appear as having a scientific foundation.[353]

It is in the inadmissible mixing of myth and history that secularist critics see the core of communalist dealing with the past. They insist on a 'demarcation between the limits of belief and historical evidence' and underline the competence of the modern discipline (see below, Sources). To others, the growing intolerance appears to be partly a byproduct of modernization itself. Sudipta Kaviraj, for instance, confronts the European model of the nation state and its clear-cut mode of identifying its members with the 'fuzziness of boundaries' in the traditional communities.[354] Ashis Nandy views the virulent 'ethnocidal, colonial theories of history' in particular as helping 'to subvert and discredit the traditional concepts of interreligious tolerance that had allowed the thousands of communities living in the subcontinent to co-survive in neighbourliness'.[355] The language of the Hindu communalists themselves is dominated by western and modern categories and does not belong to the tradition which they claim.[356] On the other hand, a secularism which bases tolerance mainly on the expected fading away of religious ties has to explain how exactly it relates to those traditions which constitute the very difference

[350]It was architectural monuments and religious sites in particular which became, in the course of time, symbols of national identity. The reconstruction of the Somnath temple served, above all, the consolidation of the new self-esteem after Independence. For the significance of architecture in the representation of the past, see Metcalf 1995: 152ff. The same can be observed with regard to the Dalada Maligawa (Tooth Temple) as a symbol of Buddhist identity in Sri Lanka. Cf. Juergensmeyer 1993: 38.

[351]'History is rewritten through reversal of history.' B.D. Chattopadhyaya, 'Cultural Plurality', loc. cit.

[352]Cf. Heehs, 'Myth, History and Theory'.

[353]The VHP openly confesses this double strategy, leaving no doubt, however, that even without empirical evidence there would be sufficient legitimation for their position: 'The ground relating to faith would in any case continue to be operative.' V. H. Dalmia, quoted in Parthasarathy, 'Soft Hindutva and Nationalism', 21.

[354]Kaviraj 1995: 113. That the attempt of the Government 'to secularise what it took to be religious institutions' was all but a 'benign process' is discussed in Vivek Dhareshwar, '"Our Time". History, Sovereignty and Politics', *EPW* (11 February 1995), 317–24, here 319. According to Partha Chatterjee, the intensity of the conflict corresponds to a fixity which has more to do with western classificatory rigorism than with the more flexible traditional concept of jati: Chatterjee 1993: 223. For the distinction between lived and reflected tradition, see Javeed Alam, 'Tradition in India under Interpretive Stress: Interrogating its Claims', *Thesis Eleven* 39 (1994), 19–38, specifically 32ff.

[355]Nandy, 'Secularism', *Seminar* 394 (June 1992), 29–30, here 29.

[356]Ashis Nandy, 'Three propositions', *Seminar* 402 (Feb. 1993), 15–17, here 17. The reproach against academic history of using non-Indian concepts thus reflects on the 'Sanghs, Parishads, and Samajs' themselves.

that is to be tolerated. It also threatens to neutralize values which have been conducive to non-secular forms of tolerance.[357] The efforts of Gandhi, for instance, to base national unity and inter-religious understanding on indigenous social and political institutions conflicted with the urge to modernize and have hardly been conceived, so far, as an alternative in historical writing.[358]

The other countries of South Asia find themselves in a similar predicament, trying to maintain an equilibrium between national unity and cultural or ethnic diversity.[365] In Pakistan, the question as to how the vision of a Muslim state was to be translated into actual constitutional arrangements remained controversial. If Maududi had been sceptical about the concept of a Muslim nation in the beginning, he nevertheless migrated to Pakistan after Partition and worked towards the realization of a truly Islamic order.[360] In contrast, the historian Ishtiaq Hussain Qureshi (1903–81), an early supporter of the idea of Pakistan, tried to mediate between tradition and modernity, religion and scientific progress. 'The real service to Islam today lies in bringing up children [...] not only as true Muslims but simultaneously as brillant experts in all walks of life, capable of thinking for themselves and holding their own against their counterparts in other lands.'[361] Irrespective of Pakistan's birth from the spirit of religious tradition, Qureshi constructed a secular identity which could be traced back to the 5000-year-old Indus civilization.[362] The secession of

[357]Cf. T. N. Madan, 'Secularism in Its Place', *Journal of Asian Studies* 46 (1987), 747–59, here 754. Interestingly, Indian emigration and the processes of globalization have contributed to boosting communalization. Cf. Sudhir Kakar, 'Religious group identity', *Seminar* 402 (Feb. 1993), 50–5, here 52. It is particularly expatriate Hindus, with their distance from the native country and their vicinity to western modernity, who turn out to be the preferred clients of Hindutva organizations such as the VHP.

[358]The insistence on Hindu *agency* alone represented a break with tradition and also worked as a sort of amnesia. Cf. Nandy 1983: 24–5. The negligence of the sometimes considerable differences between the numerous sects in favour of a unitary Hinduism was in striking contrast to the emphasis on the differences between Hindus and Muslims. For the entire context of communalism and history, see Michael Gottlob, 'Communalism, Nationalism, Secularism. Historical Thinking in India before the Problem of Cultural Diversity', forthcoming in Rüsen et al.

[359]For Bangladesh, see S. R. Chakravarty and V. Narain (eds), *Bangladesh, Vol. I: History and Culture* (New Delhi 1986); Rafiuddin Ahmed, *Religion, Nationalism and Politics in Bangladesh* (New Delhi: South Asian Publishers, 1990); Tazeen M. Murshid, 'State, Nation, Identity: The Quest for Legitimacy in Bangladesh', *South Asia*, 20: 2 (1997), 1–34. For Sri Lanka, see John D. Rogers, 'Post-Orientalism, Orientalism and the Interpretation of Premodern and Modern Political Identities: The Case of Sri Lanka', *JAS* 53 (1994), 10–23; Dagmar Hellman-Rajanayagam, 'Tamils and the meaning of history', *Contemporary South Asia* 1 (1994), 3–23; Gunawardana 1995; Jeganathan and Ismail 1995.

[360]An Islamic state was legitimized, according to Maududi, only by implementing the principles of the Koran in practical life. Cf. Maududi 1969: 158–9. 'As a Muslim, I don't believe in the idea of a government of the people, through the people and for the people', but I believe in the sovereignty of God.' Quoted in Syed 1984: 35.

[361]Ishtiaq Hussain Qureshi, 'Lost Opportunities: The Musing of a Student of History', in Khurshid Ahmad and Zafar Ishaq Ansari 1979: 57–73, here 73.

[362]Here, the entire past from the earliest settlement is reconstructed as the prehistory of Pakistan. Javeed Alam, 'Composite Culture and Communal Consciousness: The Ittehadul Muslimeen in Hyderabad', in Dalmia and von Stietencron 1995: 338–57, here 341.

Eastern Pakistan (1971), however, could hardly be prevented, due to the ethnic and linguistic differences between the two parts of the country.[363] For the new state of Bangladesh, then, even Buddhism in pre-Islamic Bengal could become an element of identity formation.

The specifically South Asian component of Islamic history was expressed mainly in the self-consciousness of the Muslims who had stayed on in India after Partition. Abul Hasan Ali Nadwi (1914–2000) attempted in his works to make the experience of the Indian Muslims accessible to their non-Indian coreligionists and to show that that experience was a contribution towards the civilization of Islam. At the same time, he sought to convince the Hindu majority in India that the Muslims' close relatedness to the Arabic culture was a great benefit to the country.[364] While emphasizing the merging of the conquerers with the indigenous population, he compared the positive impact of the Muslim presence in India with the negative effects of British colonial rule.[365]

4.3 Tradition and Modernity, Continuity and Change

The phenomena of fragmentation in the self-understanding of the nation are caused not only by the variety of ethnic, linguistic, or religious affiliations, but also by the dynamic of social and economic change.[366] Essentialist ideas about cultural heritage contrast with uninterrupted efforts at modernization after 1947, which, in spite of their colonial prehistory, were hardly disputed initially. The concept of '"development", the modern theodicy', which was 'accepted by the westernized Indian elite and their scientific advisors',[367] found support even among Hindu nationalists, despite their strong commitment to tradition.

The Indian Constitution, proclaimed in 1950, was drafted by a political elite that was oriented towards progress. Although, during its deliberation, there had been a dispute once again over the issue of social emancipation and the preservation of traditional forms of community (especially in the villages),[368] the state became a driving force of change and the most important 'modernising agent'. More than the Directive Principles of the Constitution, it is the institutions of economic planning which express the belief in the feasibility of progress and the general historicizing of thinking. The Five-Year Plans of the Indian Government are documents of

[363]Problems of collective self-understanding in Pakistan also become evident with the presence of Muslim immigrants from the Indian dispersion who, even today, are not yet fully integrated. Cf. Aziz 1969.

[364]Cf. Muhammad Qasim Zaman, 'Arabic, the Arab Middle East, and the Definition of Muslim Identity in Twentieth Century India', Journal of the Royal Asiatic Society, Series 3, 8, 1 (1998), 59–81.

[365]Cf. Nadwi, 'Introduction', in Maulana Hakim Syed Abdul Hai 1977: 2–3.

[366]The different factors can reinforce each other. For the connection between ethnic conflicts and the results of development planning, see Amedeo Maiello, 'Ethnic Conflict in Post-Colonial India', in Chambers and Curti 1996: 99–114.

[367]Detlef Kantowsky 1986: 182. For the link between developmentalism and the nation state and for the continuities with the colonial period, cf. David Ludden, 'India's Development Regime', in Dirks 1992: 247–87.

[368]For the debates between Ambedkar, the chairman of the Drafting Committee, and the followers of Gandhi, see the extracts in Sources of Indian Tradition, II, 340ff.; also David Ludden, 'Orientalist Empiricism: Transformations of Colonial Knowledge', in Breckenridge and van der Veer 1993: 250–78, here 271–2.

developmentalism.[369] The socialist elements of the economy were supposed to ensure that liberation from foreign rule had an effect on internal relations, and that Indian society was protected from the symptoms of disintegration typical of western capitalism.

The fact that the idea of progress would assert itself smoothly in opposition to that of tradition was not to be taken for granted, in view of Gandhi's influence on the freedom movement.[370] But the hegemony of western thought (whether of the capitalist or the socialist variant) in the post-colonial world worked to the advantage of Indian modernizers: 'The victorious side enjoys the crucial advantage of affiliation with a "world consciousness", thus having access to vastly superior ideological resources for running the machineries of a "modern" state. In this it can [...] even mobilize for purely nationalist purposes the "economic" slogans of a socialist ideology.'[371] Nehru's urge for the integration of India into universal economic and social dynamics was supported by his belief in the compatibility of Indian tradition and scientific progress.

For the Indian modernizers, the biggest external obstacle had vanished with the removal of foreign rule, so that they could now concentrate on solving internal problems. Many did not take into account, however, the dilemma between the demand for consistent decolonization and the fact of westernization, which continued in the attempt to catch up with global development. The repeated falling short of planning goals was frequently explained by allusions to the hindering elements of tradition. For foreign experts of development, who intended to unleash a 'revolution of expectations', the issue was still, like at the times of James Mills, to emancipate India from its cultural heritage.[372] Western social scientists in their Area Studies often held on to essentialist notions of an alien and ahistorical India, which was represented mainly by the caste system.[373] Thus, traditional society was considered to be a set of conditions, the overcoming of which was the prerequisite of development. On the basis of the tradition-modernity dichotomy, even Indian experts sometimes viewed the contrast to the West as unbridgeable.[374] Preserving tradition and intentions for social change were often juxtaposed without being reconciled.

[369]Cf. Prakash, 'Writing Post-Orientalist Histories', 393. In the theoretical introduction to the first Five-Year Plan, reference is made to a change of the 'socio-economic framework'; in the second Five-Year Plan (1956), a 'socialist pattern of development' is introduced. The Five-Year Plans, of course, have their own dynamics. The horizon of expectations is continually enlarged, and actual development can hardly keep pace with it.

[370]'Paradoxically, while this strategy won the political battle for India's independence, the cultural vision it represented was defeated. At the moment of Independence, the historical mode emerged as triumphant.' Sheth, 'Politics of Historical Sense Generation', 374.

[371]Partha Chatterjee 1996: 169. 'We now tend to think of the period of colonialism as something we have managed to put behind us, whereas the progress of modernity is a project in which we are all, albeit with varying degrees of enthusiasm, still deeply implicated.' Partha Chatterjee 1993: 14.

[372]For the 'revolution of the rising expectations', cf. Kantowsky 1986: 175.

[373]For explanatory models of social change in anthropological research, see Cohn 1987: 168, 195 passim.

[374]A. K. Saran, reflecting on 'Hinduism and Economic Development in India', pointed out the incompatibility of Indian tradition and western rationality: 'Between two systems claiming to seek the truth, there can be no synthesis except on the basis of agreement on basic truths and postulates. Hinduism and modern science are as opposed as truth and error.' Quoted in Maria Mies, 'Das indische Dilemma. Neo-Hinduismus, Modernismus und die Probleme der wirtschaftlichen Entwicklung', 174.

According to anthropologist M. N. Srinivas (1916–99), Indian social scientists had to adjust to the fact that 'developing countries are today arenas for conflict between the old and the new'. A return to the precolonial state of India was not possible as, under the existing conditions, a reestablishment of 'the old order would only mean starvation and misery for millions'.[375] Independent India appeared to be forced, for her very survival, 'to commit herself to a policy of quick elimination of traditional and hereditary inequalities, and in particular, of Untouchability'.[376] Srinivas analysed indigenous mechanisms of social change and linked the politics of modernization to the capability inherent in Indian tradition to synthesize and adjust. If he accepted caste as a distinctive feature of Indian society, he countered the allegedly static character of the latter by uncovering its specific forms of mobility. In his work about the Coorgs in Southern Karnataka (M. N. Srinivas 1952), he described how lower castes sought to climb up the social hierarchy by adopting certain rites and habits like vegetarianism, for instance. 'Sanskritization', as he called this upward movement was based on the principle of emulation of allegedly higher ways of life especially that of Brahmans. According to the same logic, even contemporary processes of westernization could be explained. Here, modern-minded Brahmans who were oriented towards western ideas and values acted as mediators for the whole of society. With his investigations, Srinivas revealed an ability to change in Indian society, which had been obscured for long by the contrasting of static tradition with dynamic modernity.

Some critics considered Srinivas' concept of Sanskritization yet to be too rigid and urged historicizing the Brahmanic tradition itself: 'The brahminical tradition is never a static entity, but a dynamic reality with many intermediate layers.'[377] Moreover, besides the Brahmans, there were other groups which sought to find acceptance across the country.[378] Similar to the plea to distinguish between different forms of great tradition (which was not simply to be identified with Sanskrit tradition), different forms and strategies of social mobility had to be taken into account. The manifold criticism, however, makes it all the more clear how much the new approach has contributed to historicizing the notion of Indian culture.[379]

[375]M. N. Srinivas 1972: 166. 'Sociologists from developing countries are therefore forced to take a positive attitude toward social change.' Ibid., 168.

[376]Ibid., 88. For the historical self-understanding of the Dalits, see above, Section 2.2.

[377]Kunal Chakrabarti, 'Anthropological Models', 143.

[378]Cf. Bhattacharya, 'Paradigms Lost', 695. According to Milton Singer, *The Social Organization of Indian Civilization*, there actually existed four forms of Sanskritization. Cf. Chakrabarti, 'Anthropological Models', 131. For more instances contradicting the evidence of Srinivas' concept, cf. ibid., 133.

[379]There were also some insights into the media of tradition. The Puranas, which were neglected by some revivalists, are ascribed a decisive role in the process of Sanskritization and of assimilation between the great and little traditions. Especially, the Upapuranas, 'which were "more exclusively adapted to suit the purposes of local cults and the religious needs of different sects than the Mahapuranas"' have preserved the traces of regional cults. Chakrabarti, 'Anthropological Models', 139. In the conceptual framework of the great tradition, the Brahmans' efforts to repress rivalling traditions once again become tangible: 'the Brahman was engaged in a gigantic "cut-and-paste" job, attempting to continually revise and propagate an orthodox version of *the* Great Tradition.' Miller, 'Button, Button', 27. Emphasis in original. Sanskritization therefore functioned as both a confirmation of Brahmanical dominance and its potential threat.

Other studies on phenomena of change in India have been criticized for isolating specific aspects from the general context of development. Thus H. S. Oberoi demanded, in this case with regard to certain psycho-historic studies about the religious reform movements of the nineteenth century, that a precise reference be made to the concrete historical occurrences of change in India which were all too easily identified with those of the western world. With the underlying assumption that social change is universal and quasi-natural, the implicit tendencies of continuing colonization were often overlooked.[380] In fact, even the more dynamic models of anthropological research are partially in line with early Orientalism. If the western knowledge of the Orient had once enabled the Europeans to conquer India, 'now it authorizes the area-studies specialist and his colleagues in government and business to aid and advise, develop and modernize, arm and stabilize the countries of the so-called Third World'.[381] Ronald Inden complains that India's historical self-understanding is still determined by western discourse: 'Despite India's acquisition of formal political independence, it has still not regained the power to know its own past and present apart from that discourse.'[382]

If the theorem of Sanskritization was a step towards historicization for the sociologist and anthropologist, it appeared only as a 'commonplace to the historian'. From the perspective of the historian, 'Sanskritization' served to label the phenomena of social change, without connecting this with a hypothesis.[383] The changes were not clearly classified according to exogenous or endogenous causes, nor were they specified with reference to conflicts, class antagonisms, power structures, etc. It was above all the Marxist historians who criticized the quasi-neutral description of modernization processes without identifying their inherent contradictions. The crucial questions of 'why and where a caste chooses to Sanskritise itself'[384] were not answered, and the inequalities and conflict structures within Indian society were ignored. The Marxists also insisted on an analysis of the specifically colonial character of modernization in India.[385] In a way, the dispute initiated by Naoroji and others, as to whether backwardness had to be seen as a sign of Indian stagnation or the result of colonial intervention, was revived under modified circumstances. But it was also a question about the primacy of politics or economy in the process of development.

[380]Cf. Harjot Singh Oberoi, 'The "New" Old Trope. The Application of Psychohistory in the Study of Socio-religious Movements in Colonial India', *Studies in History* 2 n.s. (1986), 255–73, here 269–70. Sudhir Kakar, in contrast, has shown, with reference to the 'mutual reinforcement of psyche and culture', how change manifests itself also in the alteration of childhood patterns, which is not simply an adaptation to western 'normality' but produces unforeseeable situations of conflict. Kakar 1978: 182.

[381]Inden, 'Orientalist Construction of India', 408.

[382]What was at stake was 'to produce a knowledge of India that helps restore that power, that focuses on the problematic of formulating and using a theory of human agency which avoids the pitfalls of the representational theory of knowledge.' Inden, 403.

[383]Bhattacharya, 'Paradigms Lost', 695.

[384]Hetukar Jha, 'Lower Caste Peasants and Upper Caste Zamindars in Bihar, 1921–5', *IESHR* 14 (1978), 4, quoted in Bhattacharya, 'Paradigms Lost', 695.

[385]Chandra, 'Presidential Address', 2.

If, from a liberal point of view, the problem of imperialism had been solved with the transfer of power in 1947,[386] Bipan Chandra called for identifying the persisting structure of capitalist world market forces as factors of the continuing backwardness.[387]

The Marxists, on the other hand, still had problems reconciling the universality of the laws of historical evolution with the particularity of the Indian experience. Marx's own statements about India and the Asiatic Mode of Production were a problematic point of departure in this regard.[388] In order not to consider India ahistorical or regard its past as historically irrelevant, some rejected the concept of the Asiatic Mode of Production and sought to reconstruct the history of the subcontinent more in accordance with the 'normal course' of social evolution.[389] Only a few went as far as S. A. Dange, who had tried to prove even the existence of a slave-owning society in early India.[390] However, there seemed to be enough evidence for an Indian form of feudalism. D. D. Kosambi distinguished between a 'feudalism from above' during the post-Gupta period and a 'feudalism from below' in the period since the Delhi Sultanate. (Kosambi 1956: 295ff., 358ff.) Later, it was, above all, R. S. Sharma who applied the concept of feudalism to the conditions in the period between the fourth and the thirteenth centuries. Sharma defined feudalism broadly as a social arrangement, 'in which the possessing class appropriated the surplus produce of the peasants by exercising superior rights over their land and persons'.[391] On another occasion, he described the 'lord-servile-peasant relationship' as a condition of feudalism.[392]

There was a lively controversy in India over feudalism and the Asiatic Mode of Production. Critics of Sharma's thesis[393] not only pointed to the differences between Indian and European conditions, for example the institution of feudal law, but also to the 'highly divergent periods in which supporters of the view have located that discovery'. The term 'semi-feudalism' also testifies

[386]'Since the essence of colonialism was seen as colonial state policy, colonialism was considered to be already dead on 15 August 1947.' Chandra, 'Presidential Address', 20.

[387]Cf. ibid. A similar criticism was expressed during the 1970s in some studies on Rammohun Roy and the Bengal Renaissance, questioning the dominant interpretation of the modernizing effect of the western presence in India. See the contributions of Ray, Sarkar, and others in Joshi 1975; Asok Sen 1977; Barun De, 'Renaissance Analogues'.

[388]Irfan Habib sought to show that Marx and Engels had later given up their initial views on India: 'Problems of Marxist Historical Analysis', in Kurian 1975. For similar difficulties in Wittfogel's concept of 'Oriental Despotism', cf. O'Leary, 1989: 235ff. For the dealing of Indian historians with Marxist theorems, cf. ibid., 324.

[389]For this change of roles between Marxist and liberal historians with regard to the conceptualization of identity and history, cf. R. S. Sharma, 'Methods and Problems of the Study of Feudalism in Early Medieval India', IHR 1 (1974), 81–4, here 81.

[390]For Dange's book (1949) and Kosambi's critique of the same, see below, Sources, Section 4.3.

[391]R. S. Sharma 1965: 272, quoted in O'Leary 1989: 325.

[392]Cf. O'Leary, ibid., 328.

[393]Cf. the contributions in Sircar 1966; also Dietmar Rothermund, 'Feudalism in India', in idem, 1970, 165–78. The objections relate to empirical questions (had there been castles, Vassals, etc.?), to questions of regional differentiation (cf. Burton Stein) or to the methodological question of whether and how the European and Indian social systems can be compared at all. Cf. O'Leary 1989: 326–7. Sharma's answers to the objections are found (for example) in 'How Feudal was Indian Feudalism?', *Peasant Studies* 12 (1985), 19–43.

to conceptual problems.[394] The attempt to get around Marx's ethnocentrism by assuming a European pattern of evolution in the history of India itself[395] was seen by some as a further neglect of the latter's particularity. To perceive the Indian social order as a form of feudalism seemed, to Ashok Rudra, like trying to explain European society by referring to the Indian caste system (Rudra 1988: 88). The Marxist theorems which aim at a general explanation of the dynamics of history, like that of class struggle[396] and that of the relationship between base and superstructure, found wider acceptance than the schematic evolutionary model of Historical Materialism. But those, too, had to be applied in a differentiated manner. Kosambi always sought to recognize the cultural and spiritual factors of history. According to Rudra, Max Weber, rather than Marx, should be followed in acknowledging that 'the stability of the Indian social order has been very largely due to the Hindu dharma' (Rudra 1988: 55–6).

From Marx's statement that the history of India is nothing but a series of conquests it is not very far to the doubt as to whether Indians are capable of making their own history or of governing themselves—a supposition which had been vehemently opposed by nationalist historians like Jayaswal (see above). For M. N. Roy and his followers it had been a matter of course to use patterns of historical explanation which were based on European experience;[397] now, however, the search for a non-Eurocentric Marxism was on the agenda, raising questions like: 'Why was it possible for European imperialism to stop the process of development in India? Why was it not possible for the Indian society to resist the imperialist onslaught? Why was it not possible for Indian imperialism (or, say, Chinese imperialism) to stop the process of capitalist development in Europe?' (Rudra 1988: 47)

Bipan Chandra rejected the question of western researchers as to why a capitalist economy had not emerged in India and pointed out the absence of capitalist development under British rule, which was supposed to further Indian modernization.[398] Historical thinking as such did not yet come in for criticism in these debates, but it became evident that 'one can question the basic assumption that the course of western society is the natural course of social evolution. Cannot other societies have their own dynamics?'[399] In a more fundamental manner, Dipesh Chakrabarty, too, approaches the problem of whether the recognition of cultural difference in the framework of Marxism as a 'master narrative of history' is possible or if the Indian working class are condemned 'forever to a state of "low classness" unless they develop some kind of

[394]Harbans Mukhia, during the 1979 Session of the Indian History Congress, answered the question formulated in the title of his lecture 'Was There Feudalism in Indian History?' simply with 'No': *Journal of Peasant Studies* 8 (1981), 273–310. Marx's categories were not suitable for the interpretation of the Indian past.

[395]Rudra 1988: 87. Sharma's theses and the 'implications of the debate over Indian feudalism are devastating for "Asiatic" readings of Indian history'. O'Leary 1989: 329.

[396]Cf. Kosambi, who, in the chapter 'The underlying philosophy' (1956: 8–14), outlines the conception of history as a sequence of class struggles.

[397]Cf. Kaviraj's criticism of the Eurocentrism of M. N. Roy: 'The Heteronomous Radicalism of M. N. Roy', in Pantham and Deutsch 1986: 233–4.

[398]Chandra, 'Presidential Address' ['Colonialism and Modernization'], 3.

[399]Kulkarni, 'Imperialism of Categories', 41.

cultural resemblance to the English'.[400] The basic issue, ultimately, remains: How can the 'Third World' write its own history?

4.4 Critique of the Western Concept of History and Development: The Dignity of Non-Modern Peoples

Theoretical debates like those among Marxist historians revealed a new level of self-scrutiny in Indian historical thinking. If, for a long time, the reflection was dominated by interest in development and progress, this has itself become an object of criticism in the meantime. Post-colonial resistance against continuing tendencies of westernization associated itself with western post-modern scepticism about the concept of history as such.

Frequently, the starting point was the disillusionment of former Marxists, whose attempts at a better articulation of specifically Indian experiences led to doubt as to whether these could be grasped at all within the historical mode of interpretation. Nirmal Verma goes far beyond the historians' critique of certain western concepts and opposes the entire project of historicizing Indian thinking. Taking as a basis the European concept of history, it can only be stated that 'India has no history'. In spite of all external changes, 'no fundamental difference has come about the basic flow of Indian life'. Certainly, one had 'to compromise in practical life on the constantly changing historical reality', but 'the dark myth-roots of our consciousness allowed the water of history to flow over them, without getting hurt themselves'. This was in accordance with the traditional Indian way of dealing with change: 'to accept history at the practical level and totally ignore its pressure at the intellectual level.'[401]

British rule forced Indian intellectuals to decide 'whether the path of progress and development was identical to that which had been presented to them as an ideal by the English masters' (12–13). Verma expresses an uneasiness similar to that of Marxist historians about the vicinity of the Bengal Renaissance to the ideology of colonialism. But according to him, the crucial problem lies in the endeavour 'that we become a "historical" people'. The acceptance of the alternative 'historical vs non-historical' was already a mistake. Actually, it was a struggle between two 'ways of life'. Western civilization wanted to impose the 'ideal of man, history and future on a way of life that did not require these "ideals" at all' (13). The idea of 'history' placed before the Indians the question of 'future', which, until then, 'had no great significance in their emotional world' (17). The belief in the future conceals 'a deep contempt for the present' (18) in that it demands unjustified sacrifices from it. Gandhi alone had been capable of linking the future with our past (19) and of reconciling the processes of change with the dynamics of our country (20).

[400]Dipesh Chakrabarty 1989: 222. For the issue of a teleological construction of history between universalism and exceptionalism, cf. also idem, 'Class Consciousness and the Indian Working Class: Dilemmas of Marxist Historiography', *Journal of Asian and African Studies* 23 (1988), 21–31.
[401]Nirmal Verma, 'Die Vergangenheit: Eine Selbstbesinnung', in Lutze 1980: 15–21, here 10–11. Page numbers that follow refer to this edition.

Ashis Nandy, too, refers to Gandhi while criticizing the historicization of Indian thinking. For Nandy, it is a form of intellectual alienation, a 'second colonization' which legitimizes the first (Nandy 1983: XI). Nandy opposes the incorporation of Indian culture and society into a pattern of evolution, which appears, to him, deterministic. With its assumption of universal stages of development, modern historical thinking brings about a suppression of 'alternative worldviews, alternative utopias and even alternative self-concepts.' It is not only a question of marginalization: 'The peripheries of the world often feel that they are victimized not merely by partial, biased or ethnocentric history, but by the idea of history itself.'[402] The hegemony of historical thinking contributes to the persistence of colonialism beyond the end of foreign rule. Instead of incorporating Indian society as pre-modern into western models of evolution or reconstructing it nativistically as having always been modern, Nandy demands that it be acknowledged as non-modern and non-historical. He counters modernity and progress with the 'dignity and autonomy of non-modern peoples' (Nandy 1983: 59). What is at stake is not alternative history but an alternative to history.[403]

In reality, it was not by assimilation into the modern world of history but by the 'authentic innocence' of Gandhi that the Indians had overcome colonialism—'however much the modern mind might like to give the credit to world historical forces'.[404] Gandhi, by his adherence to myth, had succeeded in eluding the 'unilinear' development concept used by the West to justify its rule over 'immature' or 'primitive' societies. 'He rejected history and affirmed the primacy of myths over historical chronicles' (55). What in other societies is called the 'dynamic of history' is the 'dynamic of the here-and-the-now' in India. 'The diachronic relationships of history are mirrored in the synchronic relationship of myths' (57). In contrast to the western notion of history as a linear process, traditional Indian society had conceived the past as a means to either confirm the present or to change it. If, in western culture, oriented towards an open future, memory is used to break the power of the past over the present (Habermas), in India the future was open only to the extent that it was a rediscovery or revival of the past. If, for the West (Freud, Marx), the evil came from the past and salvation lay in the future, for India both evil and salvation came from the past. 'Myths are the essence of a culture', while history is 'at best superfluous and at worst misleading'. (59)

Nandy's critique of history goes beyond the mere defence of Indian ways of thinking against those of the West; it has a universal and epistemological dimension. The concept of history, according to him, has a colonizing impact even on the life of the colonizer, in particular since the time when history was established as a scientific discipline. The discipline of history 'now exhausts the idea of the past.' The 'imperialism of history' hardly allows any other access to the past except the scientific one, so that we are 'willing to hand over central components of ourselves to the historians for engineering purposes'.[405] The lost security, once imparted by legends, myths,

---

[402]Ashis Nandy, 'Towards a Third World Utopia', in idem 1992: 20–55, here 46.

[403]Nandy, 'History's Forgotten Doubles' 53. As instances of the demand for 'alternative histories', Nandy cites the historiographical works of Vinay Lal and Dipesh Chakrabarty.

[404]Nandy: 1983: XIII. Page numbers that follow refer to this text.

[405]Nandy, 'History's Forgotten Doubles', 54, 56. However, according to Partha Chatterjee 1993: 168, it is

and epics, is supposed to be provided today by institutionalized historical research.[406] However, modernization and industrialization themselves are leading to that uprooting and exiling which bring about the search for roots and traditions, the call for nationality and ethnicity and other 'pseudo-solidarities'—and also the demand to take revenge on history.[407]

The experience of colonized peoples has been revealing with regard to a more general issue. Victims were expected to put up with present sufferings in view of a better future. Even Marxists had pointed out that, as a reward for suppression, 'the ahistorical primitives would one day [...] learn to see themselves as masters of nature and, hence, as masters of their own fate'. Today, however, even in the West, there are doubts about a world-view 'which believes in the absolute superiority of the human over the nonhuman and the subhuman, the masculine over the feminine, the adult over the child, the historical over the ahistorical, and the modern or progressive over the traditional or the savage'. (Nandy 1983: IX, X)

The anti-historicism of Verma and Nandy and their critique of the Indian movements of modernization as being part of colonization come close to Edward Said's verdict on Orientalism.[408] Orientalist research served the self-identification of the European, not that of the Oriental. According to Nandy, one has to insist that 'India is not non-West; it is India.' (Nandy 1983: 73) Said's notion of an eternal, insurmountable antagonism, however, met with counter-criticism even in the Orient[409] and provoked the query: 'Was the relationship between cultures only spatial (European/non-European) or also temporal (past/present), and: did a present have the right to criticise its own past?'[410] If the western concept of universal history is lamented for its

---

the fundamental task of historians to wrest a 'temporary state of suspension' from the universal categories of the social sciences or rather acknowledge 'a state of unresolved tension'.

[406]Nandy, 'History's Forgotten Doubles', 56.

[407]'The Hindu nationalists systematically began to use the newly discovered discipline, history.' The 'key words of political modernism in India' show 'constant emphasis on nationalism, secularism, national security, history, and scientific temper'. Nandy et al. 1995: 60–1, 78. The Hindu nationalists themselves opt for modernization and, at the same time, seek to gain the support of its victims through the construction of simple traditions.

[408]For Said's conclusion that imperialism and critiques of imperialism belong to the same cultural practice (cf. his essay 'Orientalism Reconsidered', 1984), see Aijaz Ahmad, 'Between Orientalism and Historicism. Anthropological Knowledge of India', Studies in History 7 (1991), 135–63, here 154. For the continuation and refinement of Said's critique of western historicism by post-colonial theoreticians from South Asia such as Homi Bhabha and Gayatri Chakravorty Spivak, see Young 1990.

[409]See, for instance, Sadek Jalal [Sadiq Galal] al-Azm, 'Orientalism and Orientalism in Reverse', Khamsin 8 (1981), 5–26. Cf. Ahmad, 'Between Orientalism and Historicism', 163.

[410]Ahmad, 'Between Orientalism and Historicism', 153. Ronald Inden, who claims to achieve for India the same as Said had achieved for the Arabic Orient, i.e. 'recentering the Indian world', also assumed, notwithstanding his distancing from essentialism, a 'unitary civilization' and an 'unchanging nature of this civilization'. Here, too, according to Ahmad, there remains the task for the Indian critic to 'bring our past and our present in some kind of centred and focused relation'. Ahmad, ibid., 162, 156, 157. For epistemological problems of Said's relativistic approach, see Dietrich Harth, 'Relativism in comparative literature: A short reconsideration with special reference to Edward Said's "Culture and Imperialism"', Rivista di Letterature moderne e comparate 48 (1995), 403–12.

inherent ethnocentrism, one should not overlook the fact that the post-modern critique of history, which is often welcomed as an ally, is also centred in the West and continues a tradition of the metropolis's cultural and intellectual hegemony over the periphery. The 'silent worlds of tradition' are not easily regained by a discourse which for its part belongs to the western elite culture with its constructs, imaginations, and inventions.[411] The post-modern critique itself is suspected of being 'a way of depriving the formerly colonized of "voice"', of weakening the very process of decolonization which it claims to strengthen.[412]

4.5 Subalternity and Agency, Fragmentation and Globalization

The practice of (internal and external) colonization comprises forms of dehistoricization. Thus the self-assertion of the colonized can also consist in the fight for recovery of denied or suppressed historicity. While Nandy views the colonized as 'victims of history' and attempts to rehabilitate them by questioning the very categories of historical thinking, the *Subaltern Studies*, founded by Ranajit Guha in 1982, stood, in principle, by the concept of a historically oriented agency and pursued the 'project of restoring this agency to the historical subject by writing about it'.[413] The *Subaltern Studies*, too, oppose both the western imperialist and the Indian nationalist schools of historical writing, which preferred certain interests and forms of agency to others. The anti-colonial (but elitist) nationalist historiography remained largely in the settings of British colonial history, having taken over its basic theoretic assumptions and lines of interpretation and having only moved other actors to the foreground: Indian idealists in place of British administrators.

The *Subaltern Studies*, in a sense, continue the tradition of a 'history from below' which, in the context of anti-imperialist impulses, attempts to give a voice to the non-organized and the socially and politically marginalized.[414] Guha mistrusts the universalizing, modernizing, and liberating role of capitalism and confronts the bourgeoisie, dominant but not hegemonic in India, with the experience of colonialism as an expression of its own historical limitations.[415] In contrast to earlier Marxist approaches, however, one of the outstanding features of the project is its avoidance of concepts of totality, which expropriate the Subaltern of his specific experience in the name of the evolution of the whole. The project emphasizes the 'local and transitory

[411]Javeed Alam, 'Tradition in India under Interpretive Stress: Interrogating its Claims', *Thesis Eleven* 39 (1994), 19–38, here 27.

[412]Barbara Christian, 'The Race for Theory', *Cultural Critique* 6 (1987), 51–64, quoted in Tiffin, 'Introduction' in Adam and Tiffin 1991, p. VIII. For the critique of the attempts to play off eastern myth against western history, see T. N. Dhar, 'History, Myth and the Post-colonial', in Trivedi and Mukherjee 1996: 141–52. As Dipesh Chakrabarty states: 'The question of colonialism itself remains an absent problem in much post-structuralist/post-modernist writing.' Chakrabarty, 'Marx after Marxism: A Subaltern Historian's Perspective', *EPW* (29 May 1993), 1094–6, here 1094.

[413]Ahmad, 'Between Orientalism and Historicism', 158.

[414]See Bhattacharya, 'History from Below', 3–20.

[415]See Ranajit Guha, 'Dominance without Hegemony and Its Historiography', *Subaltern Studies* 6 (1989), 210–309.

character of this agency, its lack of totalisation [...] which has neither origin nor stable contour'.[416] Freed from the issues of a universal teleology, in which Indians remain in the shadow of western actors and interpreters of historical change, the 'strategy for recovery' aims at the 'recuperation of a non-western subject-agent'.[417] By consciously limiting itself to the fragmentary, it also resists the nationalists' exclusive claim to the image of a homogeneous 'Indic Civilization', in which internal issues of dominance are left out of consideration.[418]

In the eyes of some critics, however, the conception of the Subaltern as an original 'constitutive subject-agent',[419] with a distinctive consciousness and a specific tradition, itself implies essentialism and brings about forms of 'ethnicised history'.[420] Ultimately, the Subalterns, whose 'consciousness of resurgency' had been neglected in all previous historiography, appear to be a construct of 'history's Other' (Schwarz 1997: 140). The uncertainties addressed in the criticism and discussion of the *Subaltern Studies* project throw some light on the duality of the post-colonial discourse, which, on the one hand, is interested in the post-modern deconstruction of forms of legitimizing colonial power (to which western historiography also belongs) and, on the other hand, claims for the mobilization of resistance the very notion of historical agency which post-modernism denies. The Subaltern, then, is too much of an historical subject to come up to the level of post-modern critique and does not have enough class-consciousness and orientation towards the state, in the eyes of others, to give expression to successful political strategies. In an effort to unite both aspects, there is always the threat of the one or the other intention fading away. The approach of coming to the aid of the 'dispossessed' as *historien engagé*, of constituting their agency 'by making sense of them', would remain incomplete without insight into the conditions of power. Unlike the post-modern critique of history, post-colonial discourse is characterized by interest in actual political achievements.[421] Guha, in any case, always relates the 'insurgent subjectivity' to material structures of suppression.[422]

In the wake of the *Subaltern Studies* project, historical research in India has (re)discovered

[416]Ahmad, 'Between Orientalism and Historicism', 158. Even Marxists, of course, had differentiated between beneficiaries and victims in the process of development and had replaced national essences and identities with phenomena of rule, rebellion, etc. Cf. Prakash, 'Writing Post-Orientalist Histories', 395.

[417]Rosalind O'Hanlon, 'Recovering the Subject: Subaltern Studies and Histories of Resistance in Colonial South Asia', *Modern Asian Studies* 22 (1988), 189–224, here 208.

[418]Chakrabarty, 'Postcoloniality and the Artifice of History', 21. The *Subaltern Studies* make use, often in an eclectic way, of the innovations in social and cultural theories (in anthropology, linguistics, psychology, etc.). With this, they also defend, by the way, the interest in inner plurality of the 'occidentalized' West. See the case studies in Carrier 1995.

[419]O'Hanlon, 'Recovering the Subject', 210.

[420]Dipankar Gupta, 'On Altering the Ego in Peasant History: Paradoxes of the Ethnic Option', *Peasant Studies* 13 (1985), 5–24, here 8–9. See also the critical remarks in Adam and Tiffin 1991, XI–XII.

[421]Chakrabarty points to questions of power behind textual criticism: 'This Europe, like "the West", is demonstrably an imaginary entity, but the demonstration as such does not lessen its appeal or power.' Chakrabarty, 'Postcoloniality and the Artifice of History' (as in note 50), 21.

[422]O'Hanlon, 'Recovering the Subject', 206.

other remote areas: regional and local traditions, the self-consciousness of the Dalits, tribal identities, gender roles, etc. Suppressed voices are made out and subject-agents are named that hitherto had been absorbed by encompassing concepts—in the nationalist as well as in the colonialist discourse. Occasionally, retaining the idea of an autonomous agency has been questioned as a product of western bourgeois Enlightenment, and the masculine heroism in the representation of anti-colonial resistance has been rejected, because both reproduce those power structures which should be abolished.[423] Nevertheless, it has been summarized: 'That the rhetoric and the claims of (bourgeois) equality, of citizen's rights [...] have in many circumstances empowered marginal social groups in their struggles is undeniable—this recognition is indispensable to the project of the *Subaltern Studies*.'[424]

The opening up of new perspectives is evident, particularly in women's history. Its foundation included a stocktaking of modern historical thinking in South Asia. From the outset, the attempt to modernize India had been associated with the plea for women's emancipation. A considerable part of the criticism of Roy and other reformers (Vidyasagar, Ranade) was directed against 'man's inhumanity to women'. The improvement of their situation was supposed to be both effect and means of historicizing: 'The conclusion was obviously that only by freeing women and by treating them as human beings could Indian society free itself from social stagnation.'[425] Not only reformers but even traditionalists felt urged by western critique to discover the dignity of women in the Indian tradition. In this way, the 'counter myth' of the high status of women in the Vedic era arose.[426]

Nevertheless, history remained the domain of men. Women, whether as researchers or actors, were only indirectly involved. And the way in which they appeared in the accounts of historians shows that greater participation by them was hardly thought of, even under different conditions.[427] As to the issue of the agency of women, who appeared to be victims of both colonial rule and patriarchal society, the problem of denied self-determination was redoubled. Thanks to modern thinking, new options for articulation opened up, but new boundaries were also set. According to the ideology of colonialism, which occasionally (especially in the racist variant) described the antagonism of the rulers and the ruled as analogous to the gender roles, Indians were considered as effeminate and, for this very reason, ahistorical (see Sinha 1995; Chowdhury, 1998). This resulted, on the part of the nationalists, in strategies of masculinization, which is evident even in the case of a reformer like Vivekananda.[428] The situation of early nationalism

[423]At the same time, other forms of resistance, among which even that through indifference with regard to the political sphere, are overlooked. Cf. ibid., 196–7, 223.

[424]Chakrabarty, 'Postcoloniality and the Artifice of History', 21.

[425]David Kopf, 'Rammohun Roy and the Bengal Renaissance. An Historiographical Essay', in Joshi 1975: 21–45, here 37.

[426]See, in particular, Altekar 1987.

[427]Cf. Meenakshi Mukherjee, 'Story, history and her story', *Studies in History* 9 (1993), 71–85.

[428]Cf. Rosalind O'Hanlon, 'Cultures of Rule, Communities of Resistance: Gender, discourse and tradition in recent South Asian historiographies', *Social Analysis* 25 (1989), 94–114, here 106–7. For Bankimchandra's

was still ambiguous in this aspect, in that the intended historicization was accompanied by a revival of the traditional mother cult. In the later stage of nationalism and especially in the Hindu chauvinistic movements of the present, the inherent femininity is completely absorbed by a new cult of masculinity.[429]

This way of appropriating the experience of women is being rejected by feminist historians today.[430] The revision of established historiographical constructs, however, is more than an Indian version of feminist theories in the West. Feminist historiography in India, it is true, has been stimulated by the international debate. But it is also interested in identifying the structures of colonial dependence[431]—structures which are recalled, occasionally, even in the tutelary attitude of western feminist and solidarity groups.[432] The new formulation of female agency in the history of South Asia is limited neither to the analysis of pre-colonial patriarchy nor to the post-colonial critique of the virile project of European power politics and its Indian adepts.[433] Women in South Asia can be defenders of traditional forms of self-confidence as well as advocates of modern rights.[434]

From feminist historiography and its queries regarding the dominant concept of history, one can build bridges to other neglected dimensions of historical research and imagination.[435] The increasing concern for ecological issues, too, leads to new insights into the processes of

---

rejection of the western stereotype, see above, Section 2.2. Gandhi, too, referred to the alleged 'effeminacy', tracing it back, however, to the modern 'doctors' and their interventions, which are weakening the forces of nature. *Hind Swaraj* (as in note 317), 35f. For the use of gender metaphors, cf. also Nandy 1983: 10–11.

[429]Vandana Shiva, who analyses the tendencies of masculinization in the mother cult of the nationalists, distinguishes between Aurobindo's image of the mother and that of today's chauvinists. If Aurobindo referred to the strong, protecting mother, today it is the virile sons of India who fight for the honour to protect a helpless motherland. 'Masculinization of the Motherland', in Mies and Shiva 1993: 108–15. For tendencies of masculinization, cf. also Nandy et al. 1995: 68. For psycho-historical interpretations, cf. Kakar 1978: 140ff.

[430]Even in the struggle against sati, what was at stake was not so much the status of women but that of 'scriptural sanction' and tradition. Cf. Lata Mani, 'Contentious Traditions: The Debate on *Sati* in Colonial India', in Sangari and Vaid 1989: 88–126, here 118. For this thesis, see Sumit Sarkar, 1998: 261.

[431]See the survey of Nancy Falk, 'Gender and the Contest over the Indian Past', *Religion: An International Journal* 28 (1998), 309–18.

[432]Cf. Gayatri Chakravorty Spivak, 'Three Women's Texts and a Critique of Imperialism', *Critical Inquiry* 12:1 (1985), 243–61. For the necessary 'decolonization of feminism', see Gayatri Chakravorty Spivak's discussion with Jean François Chevrier and Françoise Joly: 'Vom Politischen und Poetischen', in *Politics-Poetics. Das Buch zur Documenta X* (Ostfildern: Cantz Verlag, 1997), 760–9, here 764.

[433]Cf. Tiffin, 'Introduction' in Adam and Tiffin 1991, pp. X-XI.

[434]For the contradictions which rule out a simple construction of 'emancipatory narratives', see Chakrabarty, 'Postcoloniality and the Artifice of History', 11–16. That the feminine voice in Indian history had been articulated even in old myths, was overlooked in the wake of the orientation towards the western mode. See Ajit Mookerjee 1988.

[435]Vandana Shiva, the eco-feminist who has been awarded the alternative Nobel prize, combines her criticism of the 'Masculinization of the Motherland' (see above) with that of the modern concept of development

modernization and colonization. Studies in environmental history reveal the link between social conflicts (during colonial times and after) and the replacement of traditional methods of natural cultivation by industrial forms of production. Thus, the destruction of ancient 'systems of conservation and resource management' produces migrants who prove to be 'invisible refugees of development'.[436]

The vanishing of 'traditional man-nature systems'[437] is accompanied by changes in mental attitudes, and vice versa. The appropriation and utilization of natural resources, increasing to forms of ruinous exploitation, are in line with what has been conceived in modern historical thinking as progress. Just as Europe's colonial grip on the non-European world could be seen, from a rationalist point of view, as extending the domination of nature, the new market-oriented attitudes to nature within the former colonies mark the worldwide assertion of the developmental logic of the West.

The processes of economic expansion and the inclusion into the world market even of remote areas can hardly be undone. There are efforts at rehabilitation of traditional ways of living and producing, which partly coincide with the critical ecological consciousness in the West. However, instead of simply converting the self-criticism of the West into Indian self-assertion and playing off pre-industrial traditions against modernity, Indian environmentalists attempt to strengthen their own perspectives. In view of an alternative concept of development, one has to consider that the ecological debate in India 'has taken an altogether different track from its Western counterpart'. Here, it is not situated in a post-materialist context, but it 'is firmly rooted in questions of production and use' (Gadgil and Guha 1993: 245). The ecological issues are connected with there of material survival and of political and cultural self-assertion. Once again, the post-colonial historical interest rules over the post-modern critique of history. Autonomous agency is also being defended against an ecology that is defined one-sidedly from western needs.

With insight into the consequences of the 'dynamics of growth in a finite world' (Meadows), however, the non-modern ways of life and those close to nature today can be brought to bear more convincingly than before on the economic system of the West, which is linked with the historical experience of colonial expansion and industrialization. Their protagonists can mix self-consciously in the discourse about the common future and global developmental perspectives. As for the fear of imbalances in the relationship between past, present, and future, it can be concluded that, from an ecological point of view, determinism today is connected not so much with visions of the future to which the present is sacrificed, but with the compulsions and needs created by current practices, which debase the living conditions of future generations. These are affected by the lavish use of resources in the present, similar to the way in which the peripheries are by the greed of the centres. With necessary consideration for the future, the time concepts of non-modern societies can no longer be simply put up with as obsolete.

---

and the new approach to nature. Cf. Shiva, 'Masculinization of the Motherland', 111–12; idem, *Staying alive: Women, Ecology, and Survival in India* (New Delhi: Kali for Women, 1988).

[436]Nandy, 'History's Forgotten Doubles', 55.

[437] Nandy, 'The Traditions of Technology', in idem 1992: 77–94, here 87.

Recent developments of historical thinking in South Asia testify in manifold ways to the simultaneous trends of fragmentation and globalization. While subnational identity formations continue on the basis of regional, religious, and linguistic ties, there is an increasing involvement in global processes, as is reflected in the debates on ecology and economy, demographic change and migration, information networks and media, etc.[438] They develop, on the one hand, under the impact of a universalism—defined in the West—that calls into question cultural diversity. On the other hand, the dominant tendencies, as against the marginalized, cannot be claimed any more to represent *the* sense of history. Dipesh Chakrabarty has shown how, in all approaches to comparative history hitherto, the European historical experience always served as the *tertium comparationis*; western concepts are used even in the appropriation of the Indian past by Indians themselves. The non-European has to make himself understood by the Europeans in their language, if his histories should not be considered irrelevant and outdated. Even to understand of his own history, reference to the master narratives of the European past is needed, because it was there that the modern concept of history was evolved. A reverse reference does not occur and has not even seemed necessary till recently.

This 'asymmetric ignorance' cannot be overcome by retreat to particularistic positions. It is rather a question of making evident the indissoluble tension between the postulated unity of history and its persistent heterogeneities.[439] Chakrabarty proposes the project of 'provincializing Europe', which aims at a clarification of the modern concept of history with regard to the restraining elements in its expansion—a project which also can rely on Europe's own interest in plurality. In the non-European debate on the colonial heritage, of which modern historical thinking is a part, a kind of self-reflection on the foundations of history is taking place, which has hardly been recognized as yet by the discipline's European branches. It is, as David Washbrook has stated, 'perhaps only in the light of reflections from South Asia, Africa and other parts of the non-European world that Europe itself can come to appreciate the nature and significance of its own history'.[440] Just as, in the post-colonial world literature, stories are being narrated which assume the western reader's acquaintance with a world that has hitherto been unknown to him, non-European historiography, too, could bring to light experiences which are not included in or anticipated by European history.

---

[438]Even in reflections on the Indian position in Cyberspace, the notions of space and time, nation and history are set in motion. Cf. Ravi Sundaram, 'Indischer Cyberspace. Über "realen" und "virtuellen" Nationalismus' (Indian Cyberspace. On 'real' and 'virtual' nationalism), *Blätter des Informationszentrums Dritte Welt* 228 (March 98), 26–9.

[439]Chakrabarty, 'Postcoloniality and the Artifice of History' 2, 20–1. See Michael Gottlob, 'Auf der anderen Seite der Globalisierung. Indische Rückfragen an die westliche Geschichte', in Blanke, Jaeger, and Sandkühler 1998: 287–300, here 297ff..

[440]D. A. Washbrook, 'Progress and Problems: South Asian Economic and Social History, c. 1720–1860', in Metcalf 1990: 199–239, here 235 (first in *MAS* 22 [1988], 57–96).

Sources

India and Europe: Forms of Approaching and Distancing in the Historicized World

1.1 WESTERN INDOLOGY AND THE CONSTRUCTION OF THE AHISTORICAL ORIENT: ORIENTALISM, UTILITARIANISM, COMPARATIVE HISTORY OF CULTURE

The confrontation between western interpretations of India in a historical perspective and Indian efforts at reformulating indigenous traditions represented the basic framework of historical thinking in South Asia during the nineteenth century.[1] It is exemplified here by three European authors and four Indian religious reformers.

Other authors who are of particular importance for the western approach to Indian history are: Charles Grant, *Observations on the State of Society among the Asiatic Subjects of Great Britain*, 1797–1813, representative of the evangelical missionaries' image of India; Henry Thomas Colebrooke, 'On the Philosophy of the Hindus',[2] who sought to include India in the universal history of philosophy; Mountstuart Elphinstone, who, in his *History of India: The Hindu and*

---

[1]The general cognitive approach of the West to Indian past and present is expressed not only in historiography, but also in ethnography, cartography, census reports, etc. All the disciplines were most closely related to the practical requirements of colonial administration. For the work of the 'administrative historians', see E. T. Stokes, 'The Administrators and Historical Writing on India', in Philips 1961: 385–403. For the connection between the establishment of political power and the interest in Indian tradition, see Cohn, 1988, especially: 'Notes on the History of the Study of Indian Society and Culture', 136–71; David Ludden, 'Orientalist empiricism: Transformations of Colonial Knowledge', in Breckenridge and van der Veer 1993: 250–78; Crook 1996. For the evaluation of western research on India from an Indian perspective, see Datta 1954; Mittal 1995–98; Chakrabarti 1997. For a survey of the dealing with Indian history in the West and for hints at a better representation of Asian cultures in textbooks, see Embree and Gluck 1997.

[2]*Transactions of the Royal Asiatic Society* (1826), 439–61.

Mahometan Periods (1841), gave a more sympathetic treatment of India after Mill's pejorative account (it became a standard textbook in Indian colleges); Henry M. Elliot, 'Original Preface' (1849) in idem and John Dowson (eds.), *The History of India as Told by its Own Historians*, I (1867), pp. XV–XXVII, reveals the advantages of British rule in India by comparing it with the despotism of the Muslim era.[3]

(Sir) William Jones (1746–94) is one of the founders of Oriental Studies and Indology.[4] His assessment of Sanskrit as the 'sweet sister' of Greek and Latin[5] and his works on ancient Indian literature and history not only contributed to the blossoming of western interest in India but also offered, to Indians themselves, images of their culture that helped establish a new historical self-understanding.

> *Jones was born in London and was the son of a mathematician father. He took an interest in Persian and Arabic during his years of study at Oxford. In the early 1770s, he wrote his first essays on Oriental literature. Versatile and active as a poet, literary critic, linguist and historian, he finally turned to the Bar. It was his career as a judge that brought him to India. He arrived at Calcutta in 1783 in order to take office at the Bengali Supreme Court of Judicature. In India, Jones wished to give his knowledge of the Orient the finishing touch, and soon he was busy as a researcher, translator, compiler, and organizer, supported by the Governor General Warren Hastings.[6] In 1784, he founded, along with Charles Wilkins (1749–1836), the Asiatic Society of Bengal and its periodical Asiatic Researches, thus contributing, even on the institutional level, to the establishment of philological and historical research in India.[7]*

Following the French *Encyclopédie*, Jones classified all human knowledge into 'History, Arts and Sciences', associating them with the three 'most considerable powers of the human mind', that is 'memory, imagination, and reason'.[8] History was based, however, not exclusively on memory, but belonged also to the two other spheres. The historian should also resort to 'antecedent

[3]See Robert Eric Frykenberg, 'The emergence of modern "Hinduism" as a concept and as an institution: A reappraisal with special reference to South India', in Sontheimer and Kulke 1991: 29–49. The representation of India in the various sketches of universal history, philosophy of history, theories of social change, etc., has also had its impact on the western imagination. See the works of Hegel and Marx, Johann Gottfried Herder, Leopold von Ranke, Henry Thomas Buckle, Oswald Spengler, Arnold Toynbee, etc. These, however, are themselves based on Indological research, which has been given preference here. For the reception and controversial discussion of Max Weber and Louis Dumont, see below, Section 4.3.

[4]Cf. Ronald Inden, 'Orientalist Constructions of India', *MAS* 20 (1986), 401–46, here 416; Grewal 1975: 8.

[5]Jones, with his assumption, found himself in a 'well-established tradition of enquiry' which he elaborated and disseminated further. Cf. Marshall 1970: 15. A more precise definition of the family of the Indo-European languages was put forward by Franz Bopp and others as late as the 1830s.

[6]'It is my ambition to know India better than any other European ever knew it', Jones wrote to Lord Althorp in 1787. Quoted in Grewal 1975: 35. Kalidasa's *Shakuntala* (1789) and the Laws of Manu: *Institutes of Hindu Law* (1796) were among his translations.

[7]See Kejariwal 1988.

[8]'The Philosophy of the Asiaticks' ('Eleventh Anniversary Discourse', 1794), in *Works* 1807, III, 229.

reasoning' and activate his imagination in order to produce works which were of more than mere antiquarian interest. With respect not only to 'Asiatic history' but to history in general, Jones stated that 'in the *details of history*, truth and fiction are so blended as to be scarce distinguishable'.[9] He postulated the strict distinction between truth and fable, in order that we do not end up with a 'phantom of our imagination instead of reality'.[10] Nevertheless, imagination was a constituent of history. Jones acknowledged the scientific standards, but he pronounced himself against the suppression of experience by excessive theory. To him 'accumulated experience and wisdom of all ages and all nations'[11] counted more than general teachings through historical examples: 'The practical use of history, in affording particular *examples* of civil and military wisdom, has been greatly exaggerated.'[12]

Among Jones' numerous contributions to orientalist research, the most relevant to the historian are the investigations into mythology ('On the Gods of Greece, Italy and India') and chronology ('On the Chronology of the Hindus').[13] Based on Chinese accounts as well as the descriptions in the Puranas, he refuted exaggerated assumptions regarding the antiquity of Indian civilization, common among Indians but also accepted uncritically by many Europeans (for example Voltaire and Raynal). Speaking about the investigations into the Indian past, Jones regretted that 'no *Hindu* nation, but the *Cashmirians*, have left us regular histories in their ancient language'. However, in view of what was available in the Puranas and Itihasas, narratives, dramas, and other works of literature as well as the accounts of the Mughal period, there was hope that 'from all these materials, and from these alone, a perfect history of *India* [...] might be collected by any studious man, who had a competent knowledge of Sanscrit, Persian and Arabick'.[14]

The following extract is taken from the 'Third Anniversary Discourse', presented by Jones on 2 February 1786, to the Asiatic Society of Bengal in Calcutta. It was designed to be the first of a series of lectures on the five most important cultures of Asia.[15] Jones offered a survey on the investigations into the complete Hindu civilization and the multiple achievements, starting from the 'earliest authentick records' up to the 'Mohammedan conquests', frequently referring to its similarity or comparability with those of ancient Europe.

[9]'On Asiatick History, Civil and Natural' ('Tenth Anniversary Discourse', 1793), *Works* 1807, III, 205–28, here 214. Emphasis in the original.

[10]Jones, *Histoire de Nader Chah* (1770); *Works* 1807, XII, 311–95, quoted in Majeed 1992: 35. In the introduction to this work, Jones speaks at large about the duties of the historian, referring to models from ancient and medieval European historiography.

[11]Quoted in Grewal 1975: 41. For Jones' description of the common law as 'collected wisdom of many centuries, having been used and approved by successive generations', cf. Majeed 1992: 44.

[12]'On Asiatick History', 214. Emphasis in original.

[13]Marshall, 1970, 196–245, 262–89. The linguistic findings, which pointed out common characteristics of Europeans and Asians, were confirmed by similarities in mythology. The idea of a common origin of peoples, languages and religions is dealt with in the Ninth Anniversary Discourse: 'On the Origin and Families of Nations' (*Works* 1807, III, 185–204).

[14]'On Asiatick History', 211, 214.

[15]These were, apart from India, the Chinese, the Tartarian, the Arabic, and the Persian cultures.

On the Hindus (1786)

By India, in short, I mean that whole extent of country, in which the primitive religion and languages of the Hindus prevail at this day with more or less of their ancient purity, and in which the *Nagari* letters are still used with more or less deviation from their original form.

The Hindus themselves believe their own country, to which they give the vain epithets of *Medhyama* or Central, and *Punyabhumi*, or the Land of Virtues, to have been the portion of Bharat, one of nine brothers, whose father had the dominion of the whole earth; and they represent the mountains of Himalaya as lying to the north, and, to the west, those of Vindhya, called also Vindian by the Greeks; beyond which the Sindhu[16] runs in several branches to the sea, and meets it nearly opposite to the point of Dwaraca, the celebrated seat of their Shepherd God,[17] in the south-east they place the great river Saravatya; by which they probably mean that of Ava, called also Airavati[18] in part of its course, and giving perhaps its ancient name to the gulf of Sabara.[19] [...]

Their sources of wealth are still abundant even after so many revolutions and conquests; in their manufactures of cotton they still surpass all the world; and their features have, most probably, remained unaltered since the time of Dionysius; nor can we reasonably doubt, how degenerate and abased so ever the Hindus may now appear, that in some early age they were splendid in arts and arms, happy in government, wise in legislation, and eminent in various knowledge: but, since their civil history beyond the middle of the nineteenth century from the present time, is involved in a cloud of fables, we seem to possess only four general media of satisfying our curiosity concerning it; namely, first, their languages and letters; secondly, their philosophy and religion; thirdly, the actual remains of their old sculpture and architecture; and fourthly, the written memorials of their sciences and arts.

I. [...] The Sanscrit language, whatever be its antiquity, is of a wonderful structure; more perfect than the Greek, more copious than the Latin, and more exquisitely refined than either, yet bearing to both of them a stronger affinity, both in the roots of verbs and in the forms of grammar, than could possibly have been produced by accident; so strong indeed, that no philologer could examine them all three, without believing them to have sprung from some common source, which, perhaps, no longer exists: there is a similar reason, though not quite so forcible, for supposing that both the Gothick and the Celtick, though blended with a very different idiom, had the same origin with the Sanscrit; and the old Persian might be added to the same family, if this were the place for discussing any question concerning the antiquities of Persia.[20] [...]

II. Of the Indian religion and philosophy, I shall here say but little; because a full account of each would require a separate volume: it will be sufficient in this dissertation to assume, what might be proved beyond controversy, that we now live among the adorers of those very deities, who were worshipped under different names in old Greece and Italy, and among the professors

[16]The Indus. (PJM)

[17]Dvaraka, the town of Krishna. (PJM)

[18]Presumably the Irrawaddy. (PJM)

[19]Ptolemy refers to the Gulf of Martaban as 'sinus Sabaracus'. (PJM)

[20]In his essay 'On the Persians' delivered in 1789 Jones was to argue that strong similarities existed between 'Parsi' and (on the evidence of a 'zend glossary' in Duperron's *Zend-Avesta*) Avestan and Sanskrit (Jones, *Works*, I, 79–87). (PJM)

of those philosophical tenets, which the Ionick and Attick writers illustrated with all the beauties of their melodious language. On one hand we see the trident of Neptune, the eagle of Jupiter, the satyrs of Bacchus, the bow of Cupid, and the chariot of the Sun, on another we hear the cymbals of Rhea, the songs of the Muses, and the pastoral tales of Apollo Nomius. In more retired scenes, in groves, and in seminaries of learning, we may perceive the Brahmans and the Sarmanes, mentioned by Clemens,[21] disputing in the forms of logick, or discoursing on the vanity of human enjoyments, on the immortality of the soul, her emanation from the eternal mind, her debasement, wanderings, and final union with her source. The six philosophical schools, whose principles are explained in the *Dersana Sastra*, comprise all the metaphysicks of the old Academy, the Stoa, the Lyceum; nor is it possible to read the *Vedanta*, or the many fine compositions in illustration of it without believing, that Pythagoras and Plato derived their sublime theories from the same fountain with the sages of India. [...]

III. The remains of architecture and sculpture in India, which I mention here as mere monuments of antiquity, not as specimens of ancient art, seem to prove an early connection between this country and Africa: the pyramids of Egypt, the colossal statues described by Pausanias and others, the sphinx, and the Hermes *Canis*,[22] which last bears a great resemblance to the *Varahavatar*, or the incarnation of Vishnu in the form of a Boar, indicate the style and mythology of the same indefatigable workmen, who formed the vast excavations of Canarah,[23] the various temples and images of Buddha, and the idols, which are continually dug up at Gaya, or in its vicinity. The letters on many of those monuments appear, as I have before intimated, partly of Indian, and partly of Abyssinian or Ethiopick, origin; and all these indubitable facts may induce no ill-grounded opinion, that Ethiopia and Hindustan were peopled or colonized by the same extraordinary race; [...]

IV. It is unfortunate, that the *Silpi Sastra*, or collection of treatises on arts and manufactures, which must have contained a treasure of useful information on dying, painting, and metallurgy has been so long neglected, that few, if any, traces of it are to be found; but the labours of the Indian loom and needle have been universally celebrated; and fine linen is not improbably supposed to have been called Sindon, from the name of the river near which it was wrought in the highest perfection.[24] [...] That the Hindus were in early ages a commercial people, we have many reasons to believe; and in the first of their sacred law-tracts, which they suppose to have been revealed by Menu many millions of years ago, we find a curious passage on the legal interest of money, and the limited rate of it in different cases, with an exception in regard to adventures at sea;[25] an exception, which the sense of mankind approves, and which commerce absolutely requires, though it was not before the reign of Charles I that our own jurisprudence fully admitted it in respect of maritime contracts.

[21]Clemens Alexandrinus, who wrote early in the third century AD, mentioned both Brahmins and 'Sarmans' in his *Stromata* (McCrindle, *Ancient India in Classical Literature*, 183–4). (PJM)

[22]Greek interpretations of the Egyptian god Hermanubis assumed a connexion with Hermes. The god was often represented with a jackal's head. (PJM)

[23]Kanheri, on the island of Salsette near Bombay. (PJM)

[24]The Indus. (PJM)

[25]Laws of Manu, VIII, 157; Jones, *Works*, III, 297. (PJM)

We are told by the Grecian writers, that the Indians were the wisest of nations; and in moral wisdom, they were certainly eminent: their *Niti Sastra*, or System of Ethicks, is yet preserved, and the fables of Vishnuserman, whom we ridiculously call *Pilpay*, are the most beautiful, if not the most ancient, collection of apologues in the world. [...]

The Hindus are said to have boasted of three inventions, all of which, indeed, are admirable, the method of instructing by apologues, the decimal scale adopted now by all civilized nations, and the game of chess, on which they have some curious treatises; but, if their numerous works on grammar, logick, rhetorick, musick, all which are extant and accessible, were explained in some language generally known, it would be found, that they had yet higher pretentions to the praise of a fertile and inventive genius. Their lighter poems are lively and elegant; their epick, magnificent and sublime in the highest degree; their *Puranas* comprise a series of mythological histories in blank verse from the Creation to the supposed incarnation of Buddha; and their *Vedas*, as far as we can judge from that compendium of them, which is called *Upanishat*,[26] abound with noble speculations in metaphysicks, and fine discourses on the being and attributes of God. Their most ancient medical book, entitled *Chereca*,[27] is believed to be the work of Siva; for each of the divinities in their Triad has at least one sacred composition ascribed to him; but, as to mere human works on history and geography, though they are said to be extant in Cashmir, it has not been yet in my power to procure them. What their astronomical and mathematical writings contain, will not, I trust, remain long a secret: they are easily procured, and their importance cannot be doubted. The philosopher, whose works are said to include a system of the universe founded on the principle of attraction and the central position of the sun, is named Yavan Acharya, because he had travelled, we are told, into Ionia: if this be true, he might have been one of those, who conversed with Pythagoras; this at least is undeniable, that a book on astronomy in Sanscrit bears the title of *Yavana Jatica* which may signify the Ionick Sect;[28] nor is it improbable, that the names of the planets and Zodiacal stars, which the Arabs borrowed from the Greeks, but which we find in the oldest Indian records, were originally devised by the same ingenious and enterprizing race, from whom both Greece and India were peopled.[29]

[From: Jones, 'On the Hindus', in *The British Discovery of Hinduism in the Eighteenth Century*, ed. by Peter J. Marshall (Cambridge: Cambridge UP, 1970), 246–61, here 249, 251–4, 257–60.][30]

[26]Jones' knowledge of the *Upanishads* seems to have been confined to Daru Sukoh's Persian translation. (PJM)

[27]A treatise named after the semi-legendary Charaka, probably a court physician of the second century AD. (PJM)

[28]It seems to be generally accepted that Indian astronomy owed much to the Greeks. *Yavanacharya* means 'Greek teacher' and the treatise *Yavan-Jataka* was probably of Greek origin (PJM). With reference to this, R. G. Bhandarkar later demonstrated the ability of the early Indians to learn from others and improve. See below, Section 2.3.

[29]In a 'Discourse on the Antiquity of the Indian Zodiac' Jones elaborated on his view that the Indian version could not have been borrowed from the Greeks (as is now believed to have been the case), but that both Indians and Greeks must have 'received it from an older nation' (Jones, *Works*, I, 334) (PJM).

[30]First edition: *Asiatic Researches*, I (1789), 414–32. Reprinted in: *Works* 1807, III, 24–46; *Sir William*

JAMES MILL (1773–1836) is, in clear contrast to William Jones, the exponent of the utilitarian image of India. If Jones was interested in the recognition and understanding of the Other in its particularity, Mill's *History of British India* embodied the rationalist's interest in the general. Mill sought to utilize the detailed knowledge of the Orient, accumulated by Jones and others, for insight into the process of civilization. If Jones emphasized the closeness of the alien culture, Mill highlighted the evolutionary gap between contemporary Indian society and the progressive West.[31]

> *Mill was the son of a shoe maker in North Water Bridge (Scotland) and was educated in the spirit of enlightenment and common-sense philosophy at the University of Edinburgh. After completing his studies and working for a short period as a private tutor, he went to London in order to become a journalist. In London he came into close contact with Jeremy Bentham, in collaboration with whom he elaborated the theory of utilitarianism. From 1806 onwards, Mill worked on the* History of British India. *After its publication, he took office (in 1819) as Assistant Examiner of Correspondence in the East India Company and was later promoted to Chief Examiner, a position that gave him a great influence on the British administration in India and enabled him 'to carry into practice the principle of utility as he had expounded it in his* History of British India' *(Stokes 1959: 48).*

Mill's idea of history evolved within the framework of a comprehensive research programme, including general epistemological questions as well as investigations into various fields of applied science, especially politics and economics.[32] Everything was centred around the idea of education, of which 'the whole science of human nature is [...] but a branch'.[33] Knowledge, according to Mill, had to serve the improvement of society.

History was conceived by Mill as a process of civilization, and its study was thought to be a reinforcing factor. Since the generalization of experience allowed for the 'anticipation of the future from the past'[34] the 'laws of human nature' were 'the end, as well as instrument, of every thing'.[35] Correspondingly, Mill sought to discover the causes of events and 'to refer particular

---

Jones: A Reader, ed. Satya S. Pachori (Delhi: Oxford University Press, 1993), 172–8. The complete *Discourses Delivered at the Asiatick Society 1785–1792* have been reprinted recently as a facsimile by Routledge/Toemmes (London 1993). A brief survey of Jones' vast research interests is given in Garland Cannon, 'Sir William Jones' Indian Studies', *Journal of the American Oriental Society* 91 (1971), 418–25. Further reading: Garland Cannon, *Sir William Jones: A Bibliography of Primary and Secondary Sources* (Amsterdam 1979); S. N. Mukherjee 1968.

[31]Mill's criticism was directed not only against Jones, but also against William Robertson ('An *historical disquisition concerning the knowledge which the ancients had of India*', 1791). Both exerted a considerable influence on conservative politics in Britain. Cf. Inden, 'Orientalist Construction of India', 417.

[32]*Analysis of the Phenomena of the Human Mind* (1828); *The Elements of Political Economy* (1821); *The Principles of Toleration* (1837). Mill also wrote the articles 'On Education' and 'On Colony' for the supplementary volume of the *Encyclopaedia Britannica*.

[33]'On Education', quoted in Majeed 1992: 142.

[34]*The Human Mind*, I, 130, quoted in Majeed 1992: 136.

[35]*The History of British India* 1820, I, 10 (quoted hereafter: *HBI*).

facts to general laws'. The aim was a science of civilization with 'comprehensive maxims for judging the future by the past'.[36]

The *History of British India* was intended to be a 'critical history', that is a 'judging history'. What Mill lacked in authentic experience of India and linguistic competence was supposed to be more than counterbalanced by the 'superiority of the comprehensive student over the partial observer'.[37] His account soon gained the reputation of a model of theory-based historiography. Macaulay appreciated Mill's book as 'the greatest historical work which has appeared in our language since that of Gibbon' (qtd. in Grewal 1975: 68). In a short time, the *History of British India* became a standard work, and over decades it continued to be a 'hegemonic textbook of Indian history',[38] which was used in the preparatory courses of British colonial officers. It became a part of that 'refined knowledge of the orient' which, according to Edward Said, supported the 'supervisory imperial authority' and was a 'cornerstone of the whole system'.[39] Mill represents the dilemma of a 'liberal' approach to colonial rule: while Jones could be taken up by the conservatives, Mill was later referred to by Anglicists and imperialists.[40] As to Mill's impact on the historical thinking of the Indians, it provoked them, through his harsh judgements, to prove the contrary.[41]

The *History of British India* offers an account and analysis of modern Indian history and the establishment of British rule. After a survey of the chronology and ancient history of the Hindus, Mill gives an introduction to their form of government, social conditions and culture. This is

---

[36]'James Mill's Review of Charles Viller's Essay on the Spirit and Influence of the Reformation', *The Literary Journal* (Jan. 1805), 81–2, quoted in Grewal 1975: 71.

[37]*HBI*, I, 20 (note 6). Jones was convinced that 'no man ever became a historian in his closet'; he emphasized the importance of 'personal observation' and 'local knowledge' as well as 'primary sources', quoted in Majeed 1992: 139; Mill, on the other hand, believed that: 'A man who is duly qualified may obtain more knowledge of India in one year, in his closet in England, than he could obtain during the course of longest life, by the use of his eyes and his ears in India.' *HBI*, I, 7. He dismissed the interest in the Other as a product of mere fashion. One generation later, Elphinstone, in his *History of India* (1841), would again bring up the lack of personal acquaintance with India against Mill. Cf. Nicholas B. Dirks, 'Colonial Histories and Native Informants: Biography of an Archive', in Breckenridge and van der Veer 1993: 279–313, here 281.

[38]Inden, 'Orientalist Constructions', 417–8. In Inden's view the *HBI* is the 'model explanatory text'. Ibid., 415.

[39]Said 1991: 215. William Bentinck, who, as Governor-General from 1829 to 1835, introduced new guidelines for the colonial administration, is said to have stated before his departure for India: 'I am going to British India, but I shall not be Governor-General. It is you that will be Governor-General.' It is debatable whether Bentinck's statement referred to Mill or to Bentham. Cf. Stokes 1959: 51.

[40]However, while Mill preferred the Indian languages as the medium of education, it was only Macaulay who stated some time later: 'We have to educate a people who cannot at present be educated by means of their mother tongue.' Macaulay, 'Minute of the 2nd February, 1835', in 1935: 345–61, here 349. For Macaulay's educational policy in India, see Elmer H. Cutts, 'The Background of Macaulay's Minute', *American Historical Review* 58 (1952–3), 824–53; R. K. Das Gupta, 'Macaulay's Writings on India', in Philips 1961: 230–40.

[41]'For the first nationalist historians of India it represented precisely what they had to fight against.' Partha Chatterjee 1993: 99. The consequences of this can still be observed, a century later, in K. P. Jayaswal's quarrel with Vincent Smith. See below, Section 2.2. Of course, this encouraged a way of thinking in terms of contrasts and antagonisms rather than tracing processes of change and development.

followed by 'General Reflections', in which Mill arrives at comprehensive judgements about the Hindus and their 'progress toward the high attainments of civilized life'.[42] There is also an account of the Muslim invasions. It is followed by a comparison of the two civilizations showing that the epoch of Muslim rule did not altogether mean a period of decay for the Hindus, but had brought progress to a certain degree.

The History of British India (1817)

GENERAL REFLECTIONS: To ascertain the true state of the Hindus in the scale of civilization, is not only an object of curiosity in the history of human nature; but to the people of Great Britain, charged as they are with the government of that great portion of the human species, it is an object of the highest practical importance. No scheme of government can happily conduce to the ends of government, unless it is adapted to the state of the people for whose use it is intended. In those diversities in the state of civilization, which approach the extremes, this truth is universally acknowledged. Should any one propose, for a band of roving Tartars, the regulations adapted to the happiness of a regular and polished society, he would meet with neglect or derision. The inconveniences are only more concealed and more or less diminished, when the error relates to states of society which more nearly resemble one another. If the mistake in regard to Hindu society, committed by the British nation, and the British government, be very great, if they have conceived the Hindus to be a people of high civilization, while they have in reality made but a few of the earliest steps in the progress to civilization, it is impossible that in many of the measures pursued for the government of that people, the mark aimed at should not have been wrong.

The preceding induction of particulars, embracing the religion, the laws, the government, the manners, the arts, the sciences, and literature, of the Hindus, affords, it is presumed, the materials from which a correct judgment may, at last, be formed of their progress toward the high attainments of civilized life. That induction, and the comparisons to which it led, have occupied us long, but not longer, it is hoped, than the importance of the subject demanded, and the obstinacy of the mistakes which it was the object of it to remove.

The reports of a high state of civilization in the East were common even among the civilized nations of ancient Europe. But the acquaintance of the Greeks and Romans with any of the nations of Asia, except the Persians alone, was so imperfect, and among the circumstances which they state so many are incredible and ridiculous, that in the information we receive from them on this subject, no confidence can be reposed. [...]

It was unfortunate that a mind so pure, so warm in the pursuit of truth, and so devoted to oriental learning, as that of Sir William Jones, should have adopted the hypothesis of a high state of civilization in the principal countries of Asia. This he supported with all the advantages

---

[42]HBI, I, 456. Even if a critical evaluation of the sources concerning the early period showed that Indians 'are perfectly destitute of historical records' and the accounts were limited to 'incredible fictions', it was possible, according to Mill, thanks to new research on 'the institutions, the laws, the manners, the arts, occupations and maxims of this old people', to gain some idea of Indian society. And this was, in contrast to the knowledge about the life of kings and the circumstances of battles, 'by far the most useful and important part of history'. HBI, I, 28, 30.

of an imposing manner, and a brilliant reputation; and gained for it so great a credit, that for a time it would have been very difficult to obtain a hearing against it.

Beside the illusions with which the fancy magnifies the importance of a favourite pursuit, Sir William was actuated by the virtuous design of exalting the Hindus in the eyes of their European masters; and thence ameliorating the temper of the government; while his mind had scope for error in the vague and indeterminate notions which it still retained of the signs of social improvement. The term civilization was by him, as by most men, attached to no fixed and definite assemblage of ideas. With the exception of some of the lowest states of society in which human beings have been found, it was applied to nations in all the stages of social advancement.[43]

It is not easy to describe the characteristics of the different stages of social progress. It is not from one feature, or from two, that a just conclusion can be drawn. In these it sometimes happens that nations resemble which are placed at stages considerably remote. It is from a joint view of all the great circumstances taken together, that their progress can be ascertained; and it is from an accurate comparison, grounded on these general views, that a scale of civilization can be formed, on which the relative position of nations may be accurately marked.

Notwithstanding all that modern philosophy had performed for the elucidation of history, very little had been attempted in this great department, at that time when the notions of Sir William Jones were formed,[44] and so crude were his ideas on the subject, that the rhapsodies of Rousseau on the virtue and happiness of the savage life surpass not the panegyrics of Sir William on the wild, comfortless, predatory, and ferocious state of the wandering Arabs. 'Except,' says he, 'when their tribes are engaged in war, they spend their days in watching their flocks and camels, or in repeating their native songs, which they pour out almost extempore, professing a contempt for the stately pillars and solemn buildings of the cities, compared with the natural charms of the country, and the coolness of their tents: thus they pass their lives in the highest pleasure of which they have any conception, in the contemplation of the most delightful objects, and in the enjoyment of perpetual spring.'[45] 'If courtesy,' he observes, 'and urbanity, a love of poetry and eloquence, and the practice of exalted virtues, be a just measure of perfect society, we have certain proof that the people of Arabia, both on plains and in cities, in republican and monarchical states, were eminently civilized for many ages before their conquest of Persia.'

We need not wonder if the man, who wrote and delivered this, found the Hindus arrived at the highest civilization. Yet the very same author, in the very same discourse, and speaking of the same people, declared, 'I find no trace among them till their emigration of any philosophy but ethics;' and even of this he says, 'The distinguishing virtues which they boasted of inculcating,

[43]One of the chief circumstances from which Sir William Jones drew conclusions respecting the high civilization of the Hindus was the supposition that they never went abroad, a supposition which is now well known to have been erroneous. See *Asiatic Researches*, VI, 531, and I, 271. (JM)

[44]The writings of Mr. Miller of Glasgow, of which but a small part was then published, and into which it is probable Sir William had never looked, contained the earliest elucidations of the subject. [...] (JM) See John Miller of Glasgow, *Observations Concerning the Distinction of Ranks in Society*, 1771.

[45]*Essay on the Poetry of Eastern Nations*. Voltaire exclaimed, on reading Rousseau's panegyrics, 'Jamais n'avais-je tant d'envie de marcher a quatre pattes.' (JM)

were a contempt of riches and even of death; but in the age of the seven poets, their liberality had deviated into mad profusion, their courage into ferocity, and their patience into an obstinate spirit of encountering fruitless dangers.' He adds: 'The only *arts* in which they pretended to excellence (I except horsemanship and military accomplishments) were poetry and rhetoric.' It can hardly be affirmed that these facts are less than wonderful as regarding a people 'eminently civilized;' a people exhibiting 'a just measure of perfect society.'[46]

Among the causes which excited to the tone of eulogy adopted with regard to the Hindus, one undoubtedly was, the affectation of candour. Of rude and uncultivated nations, and also of rude and uncultivated individuals, it is a characteristic, to admire only the system of manners, of ideas, and of institutions to which they have been accustomed, despising others. The most cultivated nations of Europe had but recently discovered the weakness of this propensity: Novelty rendered exemption from it a source of distinction: To prove his superiority to the prejudices of home, by admiring and applauding the manners and institutions of Asia, became, therefore, in the breast of the traveller, a motive of no inconsiderable power. [...]

MAHOMEDAN AND HINDU CIVILIZATION: After this display of the transactions to which the Mahomedan nations have given birth in Hindustan, it is necessary to ascertain, as exactly as possible, the particular stage of civilization at which these nations had arrived. Beside the importance of this inquiry, as a portion of the history of the human mind, and a leading fact in the history of India; it is requisite for the purpose of ascertaining whether the civilization of the Hindus received advancement or depression, from the ascendancy over them which the Mahomedans acquired. [...]

Under Muhammad of Ghazni,[47] the great sovereign of Persia, who combined in his service all the finest spirits that Persian civilization could produce, the Hindus could not be said to be over-run, or held in subjection by a people less civilized than themselves. As little could this be said under the descendants of Muhammad, who, though inferior to him in personal qualities, were themselves formed, and served by men who were formed, under the full influence of Persian arts and knowledge. The same was undoubtedly the case with the princes of the Ghurian dynasty.[48] They, and the leaders by whom they were principally served, were, in respect of training and knowledge, in reality Persians. It will not be denied, that the Moghuls the last of the Mahomedan dynasties of Hindustan, had remained a sufficient time in Transoxiana and Persia, to have acquired all the civilization of these two countries, long before they attempted to perform conquests in India. The Persian language was the language they used; the Persian laws, and the Persian religion, were the laws and religion they had espoused; it was the Persian literature to which they were devoted; and they carried along with them the full benefit of the Persian arts and knowledge, when they established themselves in Hindustan.

[46]'The Fourth Anniversary Discourse', in *Asiatic Researches*, II: 3, 9, 14. (JM).
[47]Mahmud of Ghazni, AD 998–1030.
[48]The Ghurids put an end, in 1186, to the rule of the Ghaznavids in the Punjab and founded the Delhi Sultanate in AD 1206.

The question, therefore, is, whether by a government, moulded and conducted agreeably to the properties of Persian civilization, instead of a government moulded and conducted agreeably to the properties of Hindu civilization, the Hindu population of India lost or gained. For the aversion to a government, because in the hands of foreigners; that is, of men who are called by one rather than some other name, without regard to the qualities of the government, whether better or worse; is a prejudice which reason disclaims. As India was not governed by the Moghuls, in the character of a detached province, valued only as it could be rendered useful to another state, which is the proper idea of foreign conquest; but became the sole residence and sole dominion of the Moghul government, which thereby found its interest as closely united to that of India, as it is possible for the interest of a despotical government to be united with that of its people, the Moghul government was, to all the effects of interest, and thence of behaviour, not a foreign, but a native government. With these considerations before the inquirer, it will not admit of any long dispute, that human nature in India gained, and gained very considerably, by passing from a Hindu to a Mahomedan government. [...]

Compare the *Mahabharata*, the great narrative poem of the Hindus, with the *Shah Nama*, the great narrative poem of the Persians; the departure from nature and probability is less wild and extravagant; the incidents are less foolish; the fictions are more ingenious; all to a great degree, in the work of the Mahomedan author, than in that of the Hindu. But the grand article in which the superiority of the Mahomedans appears is history. As all our knowledge is built upon experience, the recordation of the past for the guidance of the future is one of the effects in which the utility of the art of writing principally consists. Of this most important branch of literature the Hindus were totally destitute. Among the Mahomedans of India the art of composing history has been carried to greater perfection than in any other part of Asia.

[From: Mill, *The History of British India*, 2nd ed. (London: Baldwin, Cradock and Joy, 1820), I, 456–9, 697, 699–700, 723–4.][49]

Taking up the romantic interest in India, FRIEDRICH MAX MÜLLER (1823–1900) elaborated on the idea of Indian culture as representing the stage of childhood in the evolution of mankind. He formed the image of the passive, spiritual India as a necessary corrective to the active, materialistic West.

[49]The *History of British India* was published in three volumes by Baldwin, Cradock, and Joy in London, 1817. Many reprints and re-editions, the most recent of which by University of Chicago Press (abridged version by William Thomas, 1975) and by Routledge (1997). A critically commented edition was presented by H. H. Wilson, who extended the work from 1805 to 1834: Wilson 1840 (quoted: *HBI*, 4th ed.). Further reading: Duncan Forbes, 'James Mill and India', *The Cambridge Journal* 5 (Oct. 1951–Sept. 1952), 19–33; Cyril Henry Philips, 'James Mill, Mountstuart Elphinstone and the History of India', in Philips (1961), 217–29; J. S. Grewal, 'James Mill and Hinduism', *Bengal Past and Present* LXXV n. 159 (1966), 57–68; Surendra Gopal, *James Mill*, Ph.D. Thesis, University of Mysore, 1972; Javed Majeed, 'James Mill's "The History of British India" and Utilitarianism as a Rhetoric of Reform', *MAS* 24 (1990), 209–24.

Max Müller[50] was born in Dessau (Germany), the son of the romantic poet Wilhelm Müller, whose enthusiasm for the Greek freedom fight was conducive also to the emerging interest in the ancient civilization of India. Müller studied Classical Philology and Sanskrit in Leipzig and Berlin, where Franz Bopp (1791–1867) was one of his teachers. In 1846, he went to London in order to elaborate, under the guidance of Horace Hayman Wilson, an edition of the Rigveda.[51] *Two years later, Müller settled down in England and in 1854 he became Professor for European Languages, later for Comparative Mythology, in Oxford. After his retirement in 1875, Müller dedicated himself mainly to the editing and translating of classical texts.*

Müller, who was one of the pioneers not only in Sanskrit philology but also in the comparative study of language, mythology and religion (Müller 1864, 1873, 1909), used, in the beginning, findings about the relationship between 'Indo-European' languages as a basis for assuming a common racial heritage of the peoples. The idea of an Aryan race was rejected later by him, but its repercussions are still evident and its implications discussed.[52]

The study of Indian languages and literatures was of particular relevance in the context of historical education, according to Müller. The knowledge of universal history and the evolution of the human intellect would remain incomplete without taking into account our 'nearest intellectual relatives, the Aryans of India' (15). If the study of history, in its essence, aimed 'to know how we have come to be what we are' (16), knowledge of Indian culture provided Europeans with 'missing links in our intellectual ancestry' (21), 'added a new period to our historical consciousness, and revived the recollections of our childhood' (29–30). With it, the 'concept of the European man' (29) itself changed.[53]

Müller, who had never been to India but who, through his edition of the *Sacred Books of the East* (50 Vols., 1879–1900), contributed substantially to the dissemination of knowledge about Indian and Asian cultures in Europe, was (and is) welcomed by many Indians as a sympathetic interpreter of their ways of life and thought.[54] Proponents of a more militant Indian self-understanding, such as Bankimchandra Chatterjee, Dayanand Sarasvati and Bipin Chandra Pal,

[50]Posthumously appeared his *My autobiography: A fragment*, 1901. Müller's wife Georgia edited *The Life and Letters* (1902). See also Nirad C. Chaudhuri 1974.

[51]*Rig-veda-sanhita: the sacred hymns of the Brahmans*, together with the commentary of Sayanacharya, 6 Vols. (1849–74).

[52]For a critique of the 'Aryan Invasion Theory' and Müller's alleged political motives in disseminating it, see Rajaram 1995: 85ff.

[53]The page numbers in brackets refer to Max Müller, *India—What can it teach us?* (London 1883). In a letter to B. Malabari (1882), Müller warned against viewing the past as something absolute and pleaded for relating it historically to the present and the future. Georgia Müller 1902: II, 110–11.

[54]'To modern Hinduism, Müller has become the Western Indologist par excellence.' Halbfass 1990: 134. According to Romesh Chunder Dutt, Müller had 'done more than any living scholar to elucidate ancient Hindu literature and history'. Dutt 1963 IX. Müller had warned the students in Cambridge against Mill's 'History of British India', which was part of their syllabus. He described it as 'most mischievous' and he held it 'responsible for some of the greatest misfortunes that have happened to India'. Müller 1883: 42.

were critical of Müller.[55] According to some post-colonial theorists, Müller displayed all the ambivalence of that care and solicitude which rendered the effect of colonialism even more pervasive: 'To him, the India that was living was not the true India and the India that was true had to be but dead' (Nandy 1983: 17).

The following extracts are taken from a series of lectures delivered by Müller at the invitation of the Board of Historical Studies at Cambridge University for future members of the Indian Civil Service. In striking contrast to the emphasis, typical of the British colonial administration, on maintaining a certain distance from the country and its inhabitants, Müller hoped that the study of Sanskrit literature enabled officials to feel at home among the Indians (Müller 1883: 5).

India—What Can It Teach Us? (1883)

After some preliminary remarks about his initial doubts regarding the utility of the lectures for the listeners who, perhaps, had their own doubts regarding the importance of Sanskrit literature compared with that of classical Greece, Müller returns to the question formulated in the title:

You will now understand why I have chosen as the title of my lectures, *What can India teach us?* True, there are many things which India has to learn from us; but there are other things, and, in one sense, very important things, which we too may learn from India. If I were to look over the whole world to find out the country most richly endowed with all the wealth, power, and beauty that nature can bestow—in some parts a very paradise on earth—I should point to India. If I were asked under what sky the human mind has most fully developed some of its choicest gifts, has most deeply pondered on the greatest problems of life, and has found solutions of some of them which well deserve the attention even of those who have studied Plato and Kant—I should point to India. And if I were to ask myself from what literature we, here in Europe, we who have been nurtured almost exclusively on the thoughts of Greeks and Romans, and of one Semitic race, the Jewish, may draw that corrective which is most wanted in order to make our inner life more perfect, more comprehensive, more universal, in fact more truly human, a life, not for this life only, but a transfigured and eternal life—again I should point to India.

I know you will be surprised to hear me say this. I know that more particularly those who have spent many years of active life in Calcutta, or Bombay, or Madras, will be horror-struck at the idea that the humanity they meet with there, whether in the bazaars or in the courts of justice, or in so-called native society, should be able to teach *us* any lessons. Let me therefore explain at once to my friends who may have lived in India for years, as civil servants, or officers, or missionaries, or merchants, and who ought to know a great deal more of that country than one who has never set foot on the soil of Aryavarta, that we are speaking of two very different Indias. I am thinking chiefly of India, such as it was a thousand, two thousand, it may be three thousand years ago; they think of the India of to-day. And again, when thinking of the India of to-day, they remember chiefly the India of Calcutta, Bombay, or Madras, the India of the towns. I look to the India of the village communities, the true India of the Indians. What I wish to show to you, I mean more

---

[55]See below, Sections 1.2 and 2.2. For the history of research in the religious systems of ancient India, see N. N. Bhattacharyya 1996.

especially the candidates for the Indian Civil Service, is that this India of a thousand, or two thousand, or three thousand years ago, aye the India of to-day also, if only you know where to look for it, is full of problems the solution of which concerns all of us, even us in this Europe of the nineteenth century. [...]

All I wish to impress on you by way of introduction is that the results of the Science of Language, which, without the aid of Sanskrit, would never have been obtained, form an essential element of what we call a liberal, that is an historical education,—an education which will enable a man to do what the French call s'orienter, that is, 'to find his East', 'his true East', and thus to determine his real place in the world; to know, in fact, the port whence man started, the course he has followed, and the port towards which he has to steer. We all come from the East—all that we value most has come to us from the East, and in going to the East [...] everybody ought to feel that he is going to his 'old home', full of memories, if only he can read them. [...]

What then, you may ask, do we find in that ancient Sanskrit literature and cannot find anywhere else? My answer is, We find there the Aryan man, whom we know in his various characters, as Greek, Roman, German, Celt, and Slave, in an entirely new character. Whereas in his migrations northward his active and political energies are called out and brought to their highest perfection, we find the other side of the human character, the passive and meditative, carried to its fullest growth in India [...].

At first sight we may feel inclined to call this quiet enjoyment of life, this mere looking on, a degeneracy rather than a growth. It seems so different from what we think life ought to be. Yet, from a higher point of view it may appear that those Southern Aryans have chosen the good part, or at least the part good for them, while we, Northern Aryans, have been careful and troubled about many things. It is at all events a problem worth considering whether, as there is in nature a South and a North, there are not two hemispheres also in human nature, both worth developing—the active, combative, and politcal on one side, the passive, meditative, and philosophical on the other; and for the solution of that problem no literature furnishes such ample materials as that of the Veda, beginning with the Hymns and ending with the Upanishads. We enter into a new world—not always an attractive one, least of all to us; but it possesses one charm, it is real, it is of natural growth, and like everything of natural growth, I believe it had a hidden purpose, and was intended to teach us some kind of lesson that is worth learning, and that certainly we could learn nowhere else. We are not called upon either to admire or to despise that ancient Vedic literature; we have simply to study and to try to understand it.

There have been silly persons who have represented the development of the Indian mind as superior to any other, nay, who would make us go back to the Veda or to the sacred writings of the Buddhists in order to find there a truer religion, a purer morality, and a more sublime philosophy than our own. I shall not even mention the names of these writers or the titles of their works. But I feel equally impatient when I see other scholars criticising the ancient literature of India as if it were the work of the nineteenth century, as if it represented an enemy that must be defeated, and that can claim no mercy at our hands. That the Veda is full of childish, silly, even to our minds monstrous conceptions, who would deny? But even these monstrosities are interesting and instructive; nay, many of them, if we can but make allowance for different ways of thought and language, contain germs of truth and rays of light, all the more striking, because breaking upon us through the veil of the darkest night. Here lies the general, the truly human interest which the ancient literature of India possesses, and which gives it a claim on the attention, not only of Oriental scholars or of students of ancient history, but of every educated man and woman.

There are problems which we may put aside for a time, aye, which we must put aside while engaged each in our own hard struggle for life, but which will recur for all that, and which, whenever they do recur, will stir us more deeply than we like to confess to others, or even to ourselves. It is true that with us one day only out of seven is set apart for rest and meditation, and for the consideration of what the Greeks called *Ta megista* 'the greatest things'. It is true that that seventh day also is passed by many of us either in mere church-going routine or in thoughtless rest. But whether on week-days or on Sundays, whether in youth or in old age, there are moments, rare though they be, yet for all that the most critical moments of our life, when the old simple questions of humanity return to us in all their intensity, and we ask ourselves, What are we? What is this life on earth meant for? Are we to have no rest here, but to be always toiling and building up our own happiness out of the ruins of the happiness of our neighbours? And when we have made our home on earth as comfortable as it can be made with steam and gas and electricity, are we really so much happier than the Hindu in his primitive homestead? [...]

We imagine we have made life on earth quite perfect; in some cases so perfect that we are almost sorry to leave it again. But the lesson which both Brahmans and Buddhists are never tired of teaching is that this life is but a journey from one village to another, and not a resting-place. Thus we read: 'As a man journeying to another village may enjoy night's rest in the open air, but, after leaving his resting-place, proceeds again on his journey the next day, thus father, mother, wife, and wealth are all but like a night's rest to us—wise people do not cling to them for ever.'[56] Instead of simply despising this Indian view of life, might we not pause for a moment and consider whether their philosophy of life is entirely wrong, and ours entirely right; whether this earth was really meant for work only (for with us pleasure also has been changed into work), for constant hurry and flurry; or whether we, sturdy Northern Aryans, might not have been satisfied with a little less of work, and a little less of so-called pleasure, but with a little more of thought, and a little more of rest. For, short as our life is, we are not mere Mayflies that are born in the morning to die at night. We have a past to look back to and a future to look forward to, and it may be that some of the riddles of the future find their solution in the wisdom of the past.

[From: Müller, *India—What Can It Teach Us? A Course of Lectures*, delivered before the University of Cambridge (London: Longmans, Green & Co., 1883), 6–7, 31–2, 96–100.][57]

[56]Boehtlingk, *Sprüche*, 5101. (FMM)

[57]The extracts are from the first and third lectures. Also in *Collected Works*, 20 Vols. (London: Longmans, Green, 1898–1903), Vol. 13. Further reading: Dietmar Rothermund, 'Max Müller and India's Quest for a National Past', in *Friedrich Max Müller: 150th Birth Anniversary*, ed. Heimo Rau (Bangalore 1973), 53–62; J. M. Kitagawa and J. S. Strong, 'Friedrich Max Müller and the Comparative Study of Religion', in N. Smart (ed.), *Nineteenth Century Religious Thought in the West*, III (Cambridge 1985), 179–213.

1.2 THE SELF-ASSURANCE OF INDIAN TRADITIONS: REFORM, RENAISSANCE, REVIVAL

Just as Jones, Mill, and Müller stand for certain European interpretations of Indian culture in a historical perspective, Rammohun Roy, Dayanand Sarasvati, Swami Vivekananda, and Sayyid Ahmad Khan represent the attempts of Indians to renew and reassert their traditions in confrontation with the modern West. Their attempts, in various ways, either adopt, modify or reject[58] the categories of Jones, Mill, and Müller. Common to them all is the intention to prove the historicity of their own society. This is put into practice by the various reform movements either founded or inspired by them, such as the Brahmo Samaj, Arya Samaj, Prarthana Samaj, Ramakrishna Mission, and Aligarh movement.[59]

Roy's ideas and reform initiatives were continued by Iswar Chandra Vidyasagar (1820–91), who not only, like the former, worked with a 'skilful use of tradition as a sanction for social reform' in his campaigns, but also contributed to the introduction of modern historiography.[60] The Arya Samaj has produced its school of historiography, too. Ramadeva (*Vedic India*, 1911) and Raghuvir Sharan Dubli (*The True History of India*, 1913), both writing in Hindi, aimed first and foremost to arouse patriotism.[61]

The reform movements have become objects of general reflections on modernization, colonialism, and history in postcolonial South Asia, especially among Marxists, postmodern critics and in the context of *Subaltern Studies* (see below). The emphasis on the tradition-modernity dichotomy in historical research is said to have obscured the retarding effects of colonialism and imperialism on economic development.[62] It is also open to debate whether the religious reform movements can be viewed as being representative of contemporary Indian self-perception at all.[63]

---

[58] According to Wilhelm Halbfass, the 'historical and hermeneutical situation' at the beginning and at the end of the nineteenth century was reflected in an exemplary manner by Roy and Vivekananda. This does not mean only the assimilation of western influence in India, but includes the presentation of Indian traditions to the West. It was also a means of self-understanding, an effort at '"actualization" of the original teachings of Hinduism'. Halbfass 1990: 221.

[59] See Kenneth Jones 1989.

[60] Amales Tripathi, 'The role of traditional modernizers: Bengal's experience in the 19th century', *Calcutta Historical Journal* 8 (1983–4), 1–16, 116–22, here 15. See also idem 1973; A. R. H. Copley, 'Ram Mohun Roy and Vidyasagar: Dynamics and Constraints in their Role as Moralists', *Calcutta Historical Journal* 11 (1986–7), 25–41. For Vidyasagar's achievement as a historiographer, see Vidyasagar 1848.

[61] Cf. H. L. Singh, 'Modern Historical Writing in Hindi', in Philips 1961: 461–72, here 463, 466. Sometimes this even contradicted the earlier critical intentions of the reformers. In 1951, the Arya Samajist Bhagavaddatta criticized R. C. Majumdar and K. M. Munshi 'for what he considers to be a distortion of Indian history. To call our great men mythical personalities [...] is to abuse our ancient Rishis'. Ibid., 470. The fact that Dayanand himself had taken a critical stance on the rishis is overlooked here. For a philosophic reflection on contemporary Hinduism and history in the intellectual context of the Ramakrishna Mission, see Swami Adiswarananda in his essay 'Philosophy of History: The Hindu View', in Mahadevan and Cairns 1977: 23–58.

[62] Sarkar, 'Rammohum Roy and the Break with the Past' in Joshi 1975: 46–68, here 66.

[63] Cf. Rajat K. Ray's critique of the mythography of the Bengal Renaissance in the 'Introduction' in Joshi 1975: 1–20, here 2; Harjot Singh Oberoi and his sceptical inquiry about the 'Identity Crisis': The "New" Old

RAJA RAMMOHUN ROY (1772–1833)[64] is venerated as the 'father of modern India'. His critique and reformulation of tradition and his systematic analysis of social reality from the aspect of its possible improvement made him one of the pioneers of a new historical consciousness in India.

> Roy's biography reflects the situation of the Bengali upper class in the period of transition from the decline of the Mughal empire to the political establishment of the British East India Company. The family of Kulin Brahmans and worshippers of Chaitanya[65] belonged to the Persian-educated elite. His father had served the Maharani Bishnukumari of Burdwan as a finance officer and, after the Permanent Settlement Act (1793), participated in the rise of the 'new Gentry' under British dominance. Rammohun received his basic education in the house of his father. He learnt Arabic, Persian, and Sanskrit, and acquired a good knowledge of Islamic theology and of classical Hindu philosophy. It was his involvement in the bank business which brought him into contact with the English administrators. After nine years of collaboration with the East India Company, he retired from this activity in 1814 in order to dedicate himself to social reforms and ethical-religious questions. In 1823, he opposed the founding of a Sanskrit College in Calcutta because he favoured English as a medium of education, which he believed to be more conducive to the dissemination of scientific knowledge.[66] In 1831, Roy went on a voyage to England. He died during his stay in Bristol.[67]

Roy's critique of contemporary religious practice is already evident in his early work titled *Tuhfatul Muwahhidin* (ca. 1803–4),[68] in which he sought to reduce faith to the assumption of a creator, a soul and a transcendent world. The belief, common to all religions, in a single supreme essence was the result of reasoning and in accordance with the natural tendency of man, according to Roy.

Even if he has not worked out a comprehensive theory of social progress, Roy's writings are consistently related to practical utility and moral improvement.[69] In the introduction to an English

---

Trope. The Application of Psychohistory in the Study of Socio-religious Movements in Colonial India', *Studies in History* 2 n.s. (1986), 255–73, here 266.

[64]The date of birth is controversial. Cf. Halbfass 1990: 518.

[65]Chaitanya (1485–1533): Influential *bhakti* preacher and founder of a Krishna sect in Bengal.

[66]Instead of teaching 'metaphysical distinctions of little or no practicable use', he demanded 'to develop and regulate all the powers of the mind, the emotions and the workings of conscience'. Quoted in Tripathi, 'The Role of Traditional Modernizers', 10.

[67]The voyage to England would have been unthinkable for an orthodox Brahman. Roy's brief curriculum vitae in a letter to his friend Mr. Gordon in Calcutta ('The autobiographical letter, 1832', in *The Life and Letters of Raja Rammohun Roy*, ed. Sophia Dobson Collet [Calcutta: Sadharan Brahmo Samaj, 1962]) is said to be the first autobiography written by an Indian in English. See Sinha 1978, 46–7, 85–9.

[68]The brief work, written in Persian, was published in an English translation (*Gift to Deists*) by Maulavi Obaidullah El Obaide of the Adi Brahmo Samaj in 1884; *English Works* 1906: 941–58. Sumit Sarkar points to the Islamic components and other eighteenth-century tendencies taken up by Roy before becoming acquainted with western thinking. Sarkar, 'Rammohun Roy and the Break with the Past', loc. cit., 52. The 'indigenous mechanisms of change in traditional Indian society' are referred to by Rajat K. Ray, 'Introduction' in Joshi 1975: 6, 7–8.

[69]This also becomes evident in his correspondence with politicians and in petitions to the British authorities. For the political context of his writings, see J. K. Majumdar 1983 [1941].

version of the *Kena Upanishad,* he expressed his hope 'that the translation of the Vedas will tend to discriminate those parts of the Vedas which are to be interpreted in an allegorical sense, and consequently to correct those exceptionable practices, which not only deprive Hindoos in general of the common comforts of society, but also lead them frequently to self-destruction'.[70] In a letter of 1828, Roy wrote: 'It is, I think, necessary that some change should take place in (the Hindu) religion, at least for the sake of their political advantage and social comfort.'[71]

Roy's translation work was part of the critique of tradition as well as of cultural self-assertion.[72] Even his interest in *The Precepts of Jesus: The Guide to Peace and Happiness* (1820) was mainly directed towards a model in which the combination of faith and social utility could be exemplified. The principles of Christianity, according to Roy, were 'more conducive to moral principles, and better adapted for the use of rational beings'.[73]

Notwithstanding resistance mainly from orthodox Hindus, Roy's impact was considerable.[74] He had sought to institutionalize his ideas of reform by founding, in 1815, the Atmiya Sabha (Society of Friends), which existed only for a few years. The Brahmo Sabha, founded in 1828 for the veneration 'of the one true God', was also close to dissolution at the time of Roy's death, but was revived by Debendranath Tagore under the name of Brahmo Samaj and grew to be an influential reform organization.[75] In the course of time, inner tensions arose between the orientation towards the 'tide of progress' and the preservation of the transmitted faith, a universalist perspective and the national character of religion.[76] While Debendranath was more interested in the dissemination of the teachings of the Vedanta, Keshub Sen supported, above all, social reformist tendencies. Later, when the national movement began to emerge, Ramananda Chatterji tried to reconcile the social reformist impulse with 'creative nationalism'.[77]

The following extract is taken from Roy's introduction to the English translation of an

[70]Quoted in Morearty 1975: 87.

[71]Quoted ibid.

[72]The bilingual or multilingual character of the emerging western-educated elite enabled it to oscillate between the inner and the outer realms. Halbfass 1990: 241.

[73]*English Works* 1947, IV, 94–5, quoted in *Sources of Indian Tradition,* II, 16.

[74]For the 'shifting image' of Roy with the subsequent generations, see David Kopf, 'Rammohun Roy and the Bengal Renaissance. An Historiographical Essay', in Joshi 1975: 21–45. The debate on how to reconcile modernization with the self-assertion of Indian tradition refers to him even today. According to Sumit Sarkar, Roy's achievements were 'both limited and extremely ambivalent', even if the gradual withdrawal from the original positions is ascribed more to the limitations of the times than to the person. The 'indigenously born rationalism' has been hampered rather than promoted by western influence. Sarkar, 'Rammohum Roy and the Break with the Past', 53, 63. According to Ashis Nandy, Roy personified the latent ambivalence of society with regard to customs like sati, and it was precisely this which made him a symbol of the reform movements. Nandy, 'Sati: A Nineteenth Century Tale of Women, Violence, and Protest', in idem, 1990: 1–31, here 25. Still, Roy did not ignore the fact of political dependence, as becomes evident in some sceptic remark about the future of India.

[75]For the significance of this reform movement, see David Kopf, 'The Brahmo Samaj Intelligentsia and the Bengal Renaissance: A Study of Revitalization and Modernization in Nineteenth Century Bengal', in Crane 1970: 7–48; idem 1979.

[76]Kopf, 'Rammohun Roy and the Bengal Renaissance loc. cit., 38ff.

[77]Cf. Kopf, 'Rammohun Roy and the Bengal Renaissance', 44.

abridged version of the Vedanta. It was the first in a series of translations from Sanskrit into English. The Vedanta, with its monotheistic ideas, was to become the most important body of texts for the religious reform movements in the nineteenth century. To orthodox Hindus, the very act of translation of these writings, whether into English or Bengali, was sacrilege.

To the Believers of the Only True God (1816)

The greater part of Brahmans, as well as of other sects of Hindus, are quite incapable of justifying that idolatry which they continue to practise. When questioned on the subject, in place of adducing reasonable arguments in support of their conduct, they conceive it fully sufficient to quote their ancestors as positive authorities! And some of them are become very ill-disposed towards me, because I have forsaken idolatry for the worship of the true and eternal God! In order, therefore, to vindicate my own faith and that of our early forefathers, I have been endeavouring, for some time past, to convince my countrymen of the true meaning of our sacred books; and to prove, that my aberration deserves not the opprobrium which some unreflecting persons have been so ready to throw upon me.

The whole body of the Hindu Theology, Law and Literature, is contained in the *Vedas*, which are affirmed to be coeval with the creation! These works are extremely voluminous; and being written in the most elevated and metaphorical style, are, as may be well supposed, in many passages seemingly confused and contradictory. Upwards of two thousand years ago, the great Vyasa, reflecting on the perpetual difficulty arising from these sources, composed with great discrimination a complete and compendious abstract of the whole, and also reconciled those texts which appeared to stand at variance. This work he termed *The Vedanta*, which, compounded of two Sanskrit words, signifies 'The Resolution of All the Vedas'. It has continued to be most highly revered by all Hindus, and in place of the more diffuse arguments of the *Vedas*, is always referred to as equal authority. But from its being concealed within the dark curtain of the Sanskrit language, and the Brahmans permitting themselves alone to interpret, or even to touch any book of the kind, the *Vedanta*, although perpetually quoted, is little known to the public; and the practice of few Hindus indeed bears the least accordance with its precepts!

In pursuance of my vindication, I have to the best of my abilities translated this hitherto unknown work, as well as an abridgment thereof, into the Hindustani and Bengali languages, and distributed them, free of cost, among my own countrymen, as widely as circumstances have possibly allowed. The present is an endeavour to render an abridgment of the same into English, by which I expect to prove to my European friends, that the superstitious practices which deform the Hindu religion have nothing to do with the pure spirit of its dictates!

I have observed, that both in their writings and conversation, many Europeans feel a wish to palliate and soften the features of Hindu idolatry; and are inclined to inculcate, that all objects of worship are considered by their votaries as emblematical representations of the Supreme Divinity! If this were indeed the case, I might perhaps be led into some examination of the subject: but the truth is, the Hindus of the present day have no such views of the subject, but firmly believe in the real existence of innumerable gods and goddesses, who possess, in their own departments, full and independent power; and to propitiate them, and not the true God, are temples erected and ceremonies performed. There can be no doubt, however, and it is my whole design to prove, that every rite has its derivation from the allegorical adoration of the true Deity; but at the present day all this is forgotten, and among many it is even heresy to mention it!

I hope it will not be presumed that I intend to establish the preference of my faith over that of other men. The result of controversy on such a subject, however multiplied, must be ever unsatisfactory; for the reasoning faculty, which leads men to certainty in things within its reach, produces no effect on questions beyond its comprehension. I do no more than assert, that if correct reasoning and the dictates of common sense induce the belief of a wise, uncreated Being, who is the Supporter and Ruler of the boundless universe, we should also consider him the most powerful and supreme Existence, far surpassing our powers of comprehension or description. And, although men of uncultivated minds, and even some learned individuals, (but in this one point blinded by prejudice), readily choose, as the object of their adoration, anything which they can always see, and which they pretend to feel; the absurdity of such conduct is not thereby in the least degree diminished.

My constant reflections on the inconvenient, or rather injurious rites introduced by the peculiar practice of Hindu idolatry which, more than any other pagan worship, destroys the texture of society, together with compassion for my countrymen, have compelled me to use every possible effort to awaken them from their dream of error: and by making them acquainted with their scriptures, enable them to contemplate with true devotion the unity and omnipresence of Nature's God.

By taking the path which conscience and sincerity direct, I, born a Brahman, have exposed myself to the complainings and reproaches even of some of my relations, whose prejudices are strong, and whose temporal advantage depends upon the present system. But these, however, accumulated, I can tranquilly bear, trusting that a day will arrive when my humble endeavours will be viewed with justice—perhaps acknowledged with gratitude. At any rate, whatever men may say, I cannot be deprived of this consolation: my motives are acceptable to that Being who beholds in secret and compensates openly!

[From: Roy, 'Abridgment of the Vedanta', *Selected Works of Raja Rammohun Roy* (Classics of Indian Politics), (New Delhi: Publications Division, Government of India, 1977), 261–74, here 261–3.][78]

The following text deals with the custom of burning widows along with the corpse of their husband on the funeral pyre, practised among high-caste Hindus. Faced with its revival at the end of the eigtheenth century, Roy, by quoting the ancient texts, disputed its foundation. With this and other writings, he urged the British authorities, reluctant to interfere into religious matters, to ban the custom.[79]

---

[78]The complete title is: *Translation of an Abridgment of the Vedant or Resolution of all the Veds, the most celebrated and revered work of Brahmunical theology, establishing the unity of the Supreme Being, and that He alone is the object of propitiation and worship*. The work appeared in Calcutta in 1816. *English Works* 1947, II, 57–72. Also in *Essential Writings* 1999: 1–14; Grover 1992.

[79]Even after the custom had been prohibited in 1829, it remained open to debate whether British authorities were entitled to do so. Not only Indians, but also British observers like H. H. Wilson expressed their criticism. Cf.

Suttee as a Religious Rite (1830)

Several essays, tracts, and letters, written in defence of or against the practice of burning Hindu widows alive, have for some years past attracted the attention of the public. The arguments therein adduced by the parties being necessarily scattered, a complete view of the question cannot be easily attained by such readers as are precluded by their immediate avocations from bestowing much labour in acquiring information on the subject. Although the practice itself has now happily ceased to exist under the Government of Bengal, nevertheless, it seems still desirable that the substance of those publications should be condensed in a concise but comprehensive manner, so that enquirers may, with little difficulty, be able to form a just conclusion, as to the true light in which this practice is viewed in the religion of Hindus. I have, therefore, made an attempt to accomplish this object, hoping that the plan pursued may be found to answer this end.

The first point to be ascertained is, whether or not the practice of burning widows alive on the pile and with the corpse of their husbands, is imperatively enjoined by the Hindu religion. To this question, even the staunch advocates for concremation must reluctantly give a negative reply, and unavoidably concede the practice to the option of widows. This admission on their part is owing to principal considerations, which it is now too late for them to feign to overlook. First, because Manu in plain terms enjoins a widow to 'continue till death forgiving all injuries, performing austere duties, avoiding every sensual pleasure, and cheerfully practising the incomparable rules of virtue which have been followed by such women as were devoted to one only husband'.[80] So Yajnavalkya inculcates the same doctrine: 'A widow shall live under care of her father, mother, son, brother, mother-in-law, father-in-law, or uncle; since, on the contrary, she shall be liable to reproach.'[81] Secondly, because an attempt on the part of the advocates for Concremation to hold out the act as an incumbent duty on widows, would necessarily bring a stigma upon the character of the living widows, who have preferred a virtuous life to concremation, as charging them with a violation of the duty said to be indispensable. [...]

The second point is, that in case the alternative be admitted, that a widow may either live a virtuous life, or burn herself on the pile of her husband; it should next be determined, whether both practices are esteemed equally meritorious, or one be declared preferable to the other. To satisfy ourselves on this question, we should first refer to the *Vedas*, whose authority is considered paramount; and we find in them a passage most pointed and decisive against concremation, declaring that 'from a desire during life, of future fruition, life ought not to be destroyed'.[82]

Majeed 1992: 141. Of course, the very fact of codification and interpretation of Hindu law by British judges like William Jones was a challenge to the indigenous tradition. But even among the Indians themselves, it was the principal issue of the control over tradition which was at stake in the reform projects. Nandy describes Roy's struggle against sati as exemplary of the conflict between the Old and the New, the Indigenous and the Imported, and relates it to Roy's personal family background. Nandy, 'Sati: A Nineteenth-Century Tale of Women, Violence, and Protest', loc. cit. For the British dealing with sati as an attempt to Anglicize Indian tradition, see Lata Mani, 'Contentious Traditions: The Debate on *Sati* in Colonial India' in Sangari and Vaid 1989: 88–126.

[80]Ch. V. Ver. 158. (RMR)

[81]Vide *Mitakshura*, Ch. i. (RMR)

[82]Ibid. (RMR)

While the advocates of concremation quote a passage from the *Vedas*, of a very abstruse nature, in support of their position, which is as follows: 'Oh fire, let these women, with bodies anointed with clarified butter, eyes coloured with collyrium[83] and void of tears, enter thee, the parent of water,[84] that they may not be separated from their husbands, themselves sinless, and jewels amongst women.' This passage (if genuine) does not, in the first place, enjoin widows to offer themselves as sacrifices. Secondly, no allusion whatever is made in it to voluntary death by a widow with the corpse of her husband. Thirdly, the phrase 'these women' in the passage literally implies women then present. Fourthly, some commentators consider the passage as conveying an allegorical allusion to the constellations of the moon's path, which are invariably spoken of in Sanskrit in the feminine gender:—butter implying the milky path; collyrium meaning unoccupied space between one star and another; husbands signifying the more splendid of the heavenly bodies; and entering the fire or, properly speaking, ascending it, indicating the rise of the constellations through the south-east horizon, considered as the abode of fire. Whatever may be the real purport of this passage, no one ever ventured to give it an interpretation as commanding widows to burn themselves on the pile and with the corpse of their husbands. [...][85]

The third and the last point to be ascertained is, whether or not the mode of concremation prescribed by Harita and others was ever duly observed? The passages recommending concremation, as quoted by these expounders of law, require that a widow, resolving to die after the demise of her husband, should voluntarily ascend and enter the flames to destroy her existence; allowing her, at the same time an opportunity of retracting her resolution, should her courage fail from the alarming sight or effect of the flames, and of returning to her relatives, performing a penance for abandoning the sacrifice, or bestowing the value of a cow on a Brahman.

---

[83]collyrium: black paste for cosmetic and medical use.

[84]In Sungskrit writings, water is represented as originating in fire. (RMR)

[85]Hindoos are persuaded to believe that Vyas, considered as an inspired writer among the ancients, composed and left behind him numerous and voluminous works under different titles [...], to an extent that no man, during the ordinary course of life, could prepare. These, however, with a few exceptions, exist merely in name, and those that are genuine bear the Commentaries of celebrated authors. So the Tuntrus, or works ascribed to Shivu as their author, are esteemed as consisting of innumerable millions of volumes, though only a very few, comparatively, are to be found. Debased characters among this unhappy people, taking advantage of this circumstance, have secretly composed forged works and passages, and published them as if they were genuine, with the view of introducing new doctrines, new rites, or new prescripts of secular law. Although they have frequently succeeded by these means in working on the minds of the ignorant, yet the learned have never admitted the authority of any passage of work alleged to be sacred, unless it has been quoted or expounded by one of the acknowledged and authoritative commentators. It is now unhappily reported, that some advocates for the destruction of widows, finding their cause unsupported by the passages cited by the author of the *Mitakshura*, by the Smarttu Rughoonundun or by other expounders of Hindoo law, have disgracefully adopted the trick of coining passages in the name of the *Poorans* or *Tuntrus*; conveying doctrines not only directly opposed to the decisive expositions of these celebrated teachers of law, but also evidently at variance with the purport of the genuine sacred passages which they have quoted. The passages thus forged are said to be calculated to give a preference to Concremation over virtuous life. I regret to understand that some persons belonging to the party opposing this practice, are reported to have had recourse to the same unworthy artifice, under the erroneous plea that stratagem justifies stratagem. (RMR)

Hence, as voluntarily ascending upon and entering into the flames, are described as indispensably necessary for a widow in the performance of this rite, the violation of one of these provisions renders the act mere suicide, and implicates, in the guilt of female murder, those that assist in its perpetration, even according to the above quoted authorities, which are themselves of an inferior order. But no one will venture to assert that the provisions, prescribed in the passages adduced, have ever been observed; that is, no widow ever voluntarily ascended on and entered into the flames in the fulfilment of this rite. The advocates for concremation have been consequently driven to the necessity of taking refuge in usage, as justifying both suicide and female murder, the most heinous of crimes.

We should not omit the present opportunity of offering up thanks to Heaven, whose protecting arm has rescued our weaker sex from cruel murder, under the cloak of religion; and our character, as a people, from the contempt and pity with which it has been regarded, on account of this custom, by all civilized nations on the surface of the globe.

[From: Roy, 'Suttee as a Religious Rite', in *Selected Works of Raja Rammohun Roy* (Classics of Indian Politics) (New Delhi: Publications Division, Government of India, 1977), 158–63.][86]

SWAMI DAYANAND SARASVATI (1824–83) sought to reconstruct the religious tradition of the Hindus as a modern doctrine and make it a force of renewal and self-assertion. He demanded the return to the origins and the undoing of all alienating change that had occurred in the course of time. The goal was the restoration of Hinduism which was, in principle, unchangeable.

> Dayanand Sarasvati (originally Mul Shankar)[87] belonged to a wealthy Brahman family in Kathiawar, a princely state in Gujarat. He was brought up in his parents' house and was prepared, through the study of Sanskrit, for a life as an orthodox Shaivite. He rebelled against the expectations of the family and, in 1846, began to live as a wandering sannyasi. As a member of a group of monks, he assumed the name Dayanand from his teacher Purnanananda Sarasvati. In 1860, he came to Mathura, a centre of Vaishnavism, where he remained for three years and was introduced to the study of the Vedas and the early Sanskrit scriptures by the aged Swami Virajananda. Subsequently, Dayanand preached in various places against Vaishnavism and, in 1869, challenged the renowned Pandits of Benares to a shastrarth (dispute). In this confrontation, he could not assert himself with his conviction that the Puranas were not to be

[86]First published under the title 'Abstract of Arguments Regarding the Burning of Widows, Considered as a Religious Rite', Calcutta 1830. *English Works* 1947: II, 130–6. Also in *Essential Writings*, 1999: 156–60. An 'Anti-Suttee Petition', presumably formulated by Roy, was presented to the House of Commons in London (*English Works* 1947: III 137–8). For commentaries and further reading on Roy, see Grover 1992; therein: Rabindranath Tagore, 'Inaugurator of the Modern Age', 537–9.

[87]Dayanand has given a description of his life the original Hindi version of which is newly edited in *Paropkari* 17, No. 5 (March 1975); the English translation is reprinted in K. C. Yadav (ed.), *The Autobiography of Swami Dayanand Sarasvati* (Delhi 1976). 'The very fact that a sannyasi writes about his life is a step against the established code of conduct that enjoins him not to talk, much less to write, about his pre-monastic life. It is understood that a sannyasi, who renounces this world takes a new birth and the door on his past life is completely shut.' Sinha 1978: 94–5.

considered as shruti *(revelation).*[88] *At a meeting with the Brahmo Samaj leaders Debendranath Tagore and Keshav Chandra Sen in Calcutta, he was encouraged in his reformist intentions. The Arya Samaj, founded by him, soon developed into one of the most influential movements of Hindu revivalism.*

As in the case of Roy, Dayanand's interest in the past was rooted in the endeavour to show that the existing forms of superstition were not sanctioned by tradition. Like Roy, his impulse was articulated before the first direct contact with Europeans.[89] His way of thinking assumed its specific form through a particular combination of the traditional and the modern, of mythic and scientific ideas.

The exact definition of what did or did not constitute the original essence of religion was formed by Dayanand only in steps. In the end, he confined the revelation to the Vedas, whose correct interpretation he sought to define in a commentary.[90] The shift in emphasis, from the personal search for moksha to the interest in establishing Hindu religiousness as an expression of group identity, was accompanied by a growing politicization in his thinking (Jordens 1978: 278, 290). Dayanand's vision was now directed towards the return of the Vedic Golden Age.

It is in this phase that his main work, *Satyarth Prakash* (Light of Truth), was conceived. In 1874, Dayanand began to dictate the text and, a year later, it appeared in its first version. The work is written in Hindi, which Dayanand preferred more and more over Sanskrit, as it ensured better dissemination of his teachings. In collaboration with a Hindi secretary, the book was revised for a second edition (Allahabad 1884). Linguistically and in its contents, the new version deviated considerably from the first one.[91]

Even without the background of English education, Dayanand found a great number of followers among the members of the rising middle class, for whom his teachings embodied the right combination of modernity and tradition.[92] *Satyarth Prakash* became the 'Bible' of the Arya

[88]The dispute ended with a victory for the Pandits, who referred to the authority of the Vedas. Even the reformer Harishchandra of Benares (see below), in his 'Dushanmalika' ('The Chain of Errors'), supported the arguments of the Pandits. Cf. Lütt, 1970: 107–9, 112–3.

[89]For the sometimes difficult distinction between western influences and indigenous traditions, see J. T. F. Jordens, 'Dayanand Sarasvati's Concept of the Vedic Golden Age', in idem, 1998: 64–76.

[90]*Rigvedadi Bhashyabhamika* (1877–8), ed. Y. Mimamshak (Amritsar 1967). It was his Guru Virajananda in Mathura who taught Dayanand to believe in the Vedic *dharma* as the only true and eternal religion.

[91]For the differences between the original edition (Benares 1875) and the revised edition (Allahabad 1884), to which refer the numerous later editions and the translations, see J. T. F. Jordens, 'Dayananda Saraswati and Vedanta: A comparison of the first and second editions of his *Satyarth Prakash*', IESHR 9 (1972), 367–79. See also H. B. Sarda, *Works of Maharshi Dayanand and Paropkarini Sabha* (Ajmer 1942).

[92]Cf. Lütt 1970: 104. The attractiveness of Dayanand's teachings for the western-educated and modern-minded Indians is demonstrated for instance in the support from the side of the young M. G. Ranade, who later became one of the leading liberal and Anglophile reformers (see below, Section 2.3). Cf. Klimkeit 1981: 183. Gandhi, in contrast, remarked: 'I have profound respect for Dayanand. I think that he has rendered great service to Hinduism. His bravery was unquestioned. But he made Hinduism narrow. I have read *Satyarth Prakash*, the Arya Samaj Bible. I have not read a more disappointing book from a reformer so great.' *Collected Works of Mahatma Gandhi*, Vol. 24 (1967), 145.

Samaj, the 'Community of Aryans', which was founded in Bombay in 1875,[93] but spread particularly in the Punjab and the United Provinces.[94] It was conceived as the core of a future brotherhood of all Hindus. After Dayanand's death, however, quarrels arose about the right interpretation of his teachings, regarding not only the correct understanding of the Vedas but also practical problems. What became particularly controversial was the importance of birth for rank within the community, which was seen by Dayanand as a hierarchy graded according to education and merit. Missionary activities among non-Hindus and converts (Christians and Muslims of low-caste origin) were intended to counteract the continuous loss to the Hindu fold. This practice of reconversions, along with spectacular purification ceremonies (*shuddhi*), provoked sharp criticism from orthodox Hindus.[95]

Light of Truth (1884)

Dayanand presents his teachings mainly in the form of questions and answers. After having dealt with non-Indian religions (Christian and Jewish, Ch. XIII; Islam, Ch. XIV), he turns to the various directions of Hinduism. He compares the conservative and irrational attitudes of the 'Indian Popes' with the resistance of the Roman Pope and the church against the progress of scientific knowledge (p. 295). But even with regard to competing reform movements, there are but few concessions made. As to the question of whether the principles of the Brahmo Samaj and the Prarthna Samaj were good, he says:

The principles are not entirely good, for how can the superstition of personal destitute of the knowledge of the Vedas be entirely true? Their good traits are that they have saved a few persons from being converted to Christianity, repudiated idolatry, and kept some people from being misled by false scriptures, and so forth. But the members have very little devotion to the interest of their country, have adopted the Christian manners and customs to a great extent, and have changed the rules of eating and drinking and marriage and ceremonies.

Thus to their heart's content they cry down the glory of their country and the greatness of its ancients, much less to mention their good, extol the English Christians etc. in their lectures, never mention even the names of Brahma and other sages; on the contrary, they assert that there have been no learned people in the world unto this day except the English, that the people of India have always been ignorant and they never made any progress before.

[93]The principles of the Arya Samaj of Bombay (28 theses) are reprinted in Jordens, 1978: 335–7.

[94]The ten principles of the Arya Samaj at Lahore are reproduced in K. Jones 1976: 321.

[95]Corresponding to the inner tension between the religious and the social-reformist interests in the Arya Samaj, one can perceive a traditionalist group following Lala Munshi Ram (Swami Shraddhananda) and the circle of modernists with Lala Lajpat Rai (1865–1928) as their leader. In 1892, a partition into two groups occurred, known, according to the respective spiritual centres, as the Gurukula-Party (or Mahatma-Party) and the College-Party (or Cultured Party). At Kangri (Hardwar) a high school (Gurukula Kangri Vishvavidyalaya) was founded in 1900 which gave emphasis to the study of Sanskrit. After Dayanand's death, a Dayanand Anglo-Vedic School was set up in Lahore (1884). Here English and natural sciences formed a central part of the curriculum, besides Hindu literature. This was the beginning of a movement which even today is of particular importance for the Indian educational system.

Q. The Europeans wear boots, coats, pantaloons, and eat in hotels with all persons; so they are progressive.

A. It is your mistake. For, all the Mahomedans and slum population eat food at one another's hands. Why don't they improve? The Europeans are advanced and enlightened from their merit and good deeds. They educate and train their boys and girls well, and marry after choosing a consort. [...]

Q. Are the Brahmacharis and Sannyasis good?

A. These orders are right in principle, but they are much corrupted now-a-days. Many persons assume the name of Brahmacharis and keeping long matted hair set up themselves hypocritically as holy men. They are ever engaged in muttering their god's name, and doing other rituals. They never do so much as to think of acquiring knowledge, which originally gave them the name of Brahmachari. They never take the least pains to study the Vedas or Brahma. These Brahmacharis are useless like the goitre. Those Sannyasis are also useless who are destitute of knowledge, and wander begging with a staff and bowl in the hand, who do not promote the cause of Vedic religion. [...] They think they have done their duty when they put on a coloured garment and got a staff in the hand. Thinking themselves to be superior to all others, they do no good work. Such monks are a burden to the earth. But those who do good to all the world, are all right, and praiseworthy. [...]

There was but Vedic Religion in the whole world 5000 years ago, when the great war, called the Mahabharat, was fought between the Kurus and the Pandus, in which almost all the great men perished and which led the Indian Empire to its downfall. Prior to that war the Indian civilisation was a wonder to the world and attracted the people of the world to come to India to learn science and art (as now they do by going to Europe, the seat of modern civilisation). Manu, II, 20 that India was the queen of the world, is borne out by a passage in the Matri Upanishat, which enumerates 17 Emperors that ruled over all the then known world. Of them, the last was Bharat, after whom India is still called Bharatkhand or Bharatvarsha or the land of Bharat.

The ancient Indians developed the military art to a wonderful stage rivalling its modern state, as there were fire-arms, called *shataghni* (cannon), *bhushundi* (musket), &c. The progress in philosophy, medicine, mathematics, poetry, and other branches of knowledge is attested by some of the books now extant and well known to scholars. It was from ancient India that knowledge travelled westward. It went first to Egypt, thence to Greece, thence to Rome and, spreading over all Europe, passed on to America. [...] But all this great progress was dashed to pieces by the great civil war, which ushered the age of ignorance.

Since then the Brahmins have given up their old austere training and ceased to teach the other classes of society. The people becoming ignorant, priest-craft was instituted in its most horrible form. The ignorant Brahmins taught that what they said was as true as the commandments of God, and all the best things of the world were intended for them. When the people who were barbarised most shamefully, believed all that they preached; the Brahmins virtually became the popes of India, and they acted, strange to say, on similar lines. The European popes used to write drafts on heaven in the name of Lord Jesus Christ. The Indian popes played the like tricks in a thousand forms. They are still misleading the people. The reason is on the surface: when the preachers are ignorant, the congregation goes to the devil. [...]

Some 140 years after Bhoja Vaishnavism came to be believed by the people. It was first taught by Shatkopa, a low caste and then by Yavanacharya, a Greek or Mahomedan. The only learned teacher was Ramanuja, who gave it a great impetus. [...]

The belief that God incarnated in Rama, Krishna, etc., is also false. The Vedas declare that God never takes on flesh, for being present everywhere, He has no necessity to incarnate.

Some people wrongly imagine that God comes down in an image on invocation by means of the Vedic verses. The falsity of this belief will be apparent when it is known that the invocating texts are not the Vedic verses. They are forged by popes to cheat the vulgar of money. The Yajurveda plainly says XXXII.3 that there is no image of God. The Kena Upanishat says, Know and adore Him as the Supreme Being who is not expressed by speech, which He stimulates by His presence.

Idolatry has begotten many evils in India. It makes the mind restless, as it soon graps an image and then it runs wild. It costs millions of money, which produce quarrel etc. Idolaters neglect their duties and become engaged in frivolities. The father, mother, teacher, guest, are the living images to whom service is due. [...]

The true religion is found in the Vedas and Upanishats, which enjoin that learned persons should teach and preach truth to the people, and show them the necessity of abandoning falsehood and of doing good at all. The knowledge of the Vedas, good company, belief in virtue, self-control, and pure character result in the obtainment of heaven.

[From: Dayanand Sarasvati, *Satyarth Prakash* (Light of Truth), English Translation by Durga Prasad (Lahore 1908), 376, 377, 385–6, 391–2, 395.][96]

SWAMI VIVEKANANDA (1863–1902) countered the alleged passivity and static nature of the Hindus by mobilizing their thirst for action. He tried to open up Indian society to the universal processes of improvement and to make Hindus believe in their own mission of spirituality.

Vivekananda was born in a family of the Kayasta caste.[97] His father was a lawyer with a modern outlook. Narendranath Datta (his original name) received his school education at the Mission College in Calcutta. As a student, he adhered to the Sadharan Brahmo Samaj. In 1882, he came under the influence of the mystic preacher Ramakrishna Paramahamsa (1836–

[96]First edition: Benares: Star Press, 1875. As the most reliable English edition is regarded the one by Yudhisthira Mimamsaka, Sonipat 1972. Other English translations by G. P. Upadhyaya (Allahabad 1956) and Vandematharam Ramachandra Rao (*Spot-Light on Truth*, Hyderabad 1988). Further reading: M. M. Deshpande and P. E. Hook (eds), *Aryan and Non-Aryan in India* (Michigan 1979); Jadunath Sarkar, 'Swami Dayanand Sarasvati. His Place in India's Life-History'; C. Rajgopalachari, 'Harmonising Hinduism with Modern Knowledge'; Radhakumud Mukerji, 'The Rishis of India'; all in *Dayanand Commemoration Volume. A Homage to Maharishi Dayanand Sarasvati From India and the World: In Celebration of the Dayanand Nirvana Ardha Shatabdi*, ed. Har Bilas Sarda (Ajmer 1933).

[97]Faced with the allegation of being a Shudra, Vivekananda reacted with the assertion of his pure Kshatriya descent. Cf. *The Complete Works of Swami Vivekananda* (quoted hereafter CW), 1989, III: 211.

86), whom he followed only after some initial reluctance. As a sannyasi, he assumed the name Vivekananda. In 1893, he travelled to Chicago, where he participated in the world parliament of religions and aroused great interest with his speeches on Hinduism. After his stay in the US and in England, he returned to India (1897), where, in the meantime, he had become famous as a hero of the spiritual rebirth of the Hindus.

While disseminating the message of the potential divinity of man, Vivekananda gave religion a practical, this-worldly meaning, 'converting Ramakrishna's message of inner devotion into a passionate plea for moral action in the world'.[98] The concept of *karma* was freed from its determination by caste and birth and closely related to a person's actions. The striving for salvation was tied to worldly reality, and this, in turn, was conveyed a spiritual dimension. It was this mutual relation which characterized Vivekananda's view of history.

Vivekananda's reformist efforts were provoked, above all, by the lack of autonomy of women and the situation of the lower castes.[99] Like Rammohun Roy, Vivekananda did not hesitate to demonstrate the postulated link between religion and the improvement of society with the example of other religions: 'Mohammed was the prophet of equality, of the brotherhood of man, the brotherhood of all Mussulmans.'[100] The neo-Vedantist teaching of the vitality of the *atman* made Vivekananda believe in the central importance of will-power. 'The Will is stronger than anything else. Everything must go down before the will, for that comes from God and God Himself. A pure and a strong will is omnipotent.'[101] The rhetorical force of his speech, with its accentuating formulations, made Vivekananda a charismatic leader among his contemporaries, and even today his writings capture the interest of the readers. The tension between traditionalism and

[98]Partha Chatterjee, 'A Religion of Urban Domesticity. Sri Ramakrishna and the Calcutta Middle Class', *Subaltern Studies* 7 (1992), 40–68, here 63–4. For the incompatibility of these positions, see Paul Hacker, 'Aspects of Neo-Hinduism as Contrasted with Surviving Traditional Hinduism', in idem, *Kleine Schriften*, ed. by Lambert Schmithausen (1978), 580–608, here 593–4. Vivekananda's social commitment, the striving for equality and the hope for universal brotherhood have been related to the idea of socialism, by Vivekananda himself as well as by others. Cf. Dietmar Rothermund, 'Traditionalism and Socialism in Vivekananda's Thought', in idem 1970: 57–64. India's global mission was conceived only as a temporary factor in the evolution to universal brotherhood. However, the quest for inner solidarity of the Hindus could also serve the fight for expansion.

[99]'Do you think our religion is worth the name? Ours is only "Don't touchism"'. Quoted in Sumit Sarkar, '"Kaliyuga," "Chakri", and "Bhakti": Ramkrishna and His Times', *EPW* (18 July 1992), 1543–66, here 1560. The critique of Hinduism related specifically to the lack of social commitment among the believers. 'No religion on earth preaches the dignity of humanity in such a lofty strain as Hinduism, and no religion on earth treads upon the necks of the poor and the low in such a fashion as Hinduism. The Lord has shown me that religion is not in fault, but it is the Pharisees and Sadducees in Hinduism, hypocrites, who invent all sorts of engines of tyranny in the shape of doctrines of Paramarthika and Vyavaharika.' *CW*, V (Epistles), 15.

[100]*CW*, IV, 133. In contrast to later nationalists, Vivekananda had no fear in this regard; he was 'firmly persuaded that without the help of practical Islam, theories of Vedantism, however fine and wonderful they may be, are entirely valueless to the vast mass of mankind.' *CW*, VI, 415–6.

[101]'My Plan of Campaign', *CW*, III, 224. Cf. also the poem 'To the awakened India', *CW*, IV, 387–9.

the intention to modernize is evident.[102] Vivekananda defined, for many of his contemporaries, the notion of the spirit of India; he provided politics with its 'saintly idiom'.[103]

Numerous lectures and essays, and even the poems, bear witness to Vivekananda's continuous search for historical orientation.[104] Self-doubts, suppressed in his public speeches, occasionally surface in his letters, and he returned to the introverted piety of Ramakrishna in his last years: 'This is the world, hideous, beastly corpse. Who thinks of helping is a fool. [...] I come, a spectator, no more an actor. Oh, it is so calm!'[105] The fame gained by Vivekananda through his performance at the world parliament of religions greatly helped popularize his cause of a strong, expansive India. With the help of the Ramakrishna Mission founded by him, he aimed to put into practice his teachings, which were directed towards 're-orientating the outlook of his brother disciples from ideas of personal salvation to a sympathetic comprehension of the needs of the world'.[106]

In his essay 'Modern India', Vivekananda undertook an attempt to reflect on the solidarity and strength of Indian society within a perspective on universal history. In the succession of castes, which rise to power one after another, the hope of India should be seen in the rise of the shudras.

Modern India (1899)

Vivekananda begins with an overview of Indian history from Vedic times as a continuous fight between priestly and monarchic power. The Vedic priest was not only in possession of the mantras, but also figured as the administrator of the king's fame: 'He is the historian.' Without him the king's 'worth and usefulness deserving of universal approbation are lost in the great womb of time' (439). Over the centuries, there occurred shifts in this power sharing, but not its abolition. Later than in other nations, kingly power succeeded over that of the priests. And even then, the priests managed to regain power before the Muslim rulers arrived in India and renewed the Kshatriya might. This observation is taken up again in the following excerpt.

[102] According to Agehananda Bharati, who has investigated the linguistic medium of Hindu Renaissance, Vivekananda is the best example of its ambivalent patterns: 'It was Vivekananda and his latter-day imitators, [...] who really created the diction and the style of the apologetic.' Bharati 1970: 278. Sudhir Kakar, too, views Vivekananda as both a 'proponent of the traditional Hindu world-image' and a 'prophet of change', an 'introspective yogi and activist monk', as 'striving for moksha' and 'pledge of service to the Indian masses'. Kakar 1978: 161. According to Kakar, in Vivekananda there are contending—'more than most other youths, Narendra's identity was a fragmented one' (179)—traditional and modern motives, good and bad mother, etc., until he believes to have found in Ramakrishna the desired synthesis. Kakar, however, concludes: 'Vivekananda's vision of a modern Indian identity that would integrate a rational, scientific model of inquiry and the aims of technological modernization with the essentials of the traditional Hindu world image, remains an unrealized ideal.' Ibid., 182.

[103] Bharati 1970: 274. For the 'saintly idiom', see W. H. Morris-Jones, 'India's Political Idioms', in Metcalf 1990: 402–23. Even a process of 'sadhuization' (Philip Singer) has been identified.

[104] See, e.g., 'Historical Evolution of India', *CW*, VI, 157–67.

[105] *Letters*, 422–3, quoted in Sarkar, '"Kaliyuga," "Chakri", and "Bhakti"', loc. cit., 1562.

[106] Swami Gambhirananda, *History of the Ramakrishna Math and Mission* (Calcutta 1957), 117–18, quoted in Sarkar, '"Kaliyuga," "Chakri", and "Bhakti"', 1559.

In the Vedic and the adjoining periods, the royal power could not manifest itself on account of the grinding pressure of the priestly power. We have seen how, during the Buddhistic revolution, resulting in the fall of the Brahminical supremacy, the royal power in India reached its culminating point. In the interval between the fall of the Buddhistic and the establishment of the Mohammedan empire, we have seen how the royal power was trying to raise its head through the Rajputs in India, and how it failed in its attempt. At the root of this failure, too, could be traced the same old endeavours of the Vedic priestly class to bring back and revive with a new life their original (ritualistic) days.

Crushing the Brahminical supremacy under his feet, the Mussulman king was able to restore to a considerable extent the lost glories of such dynasties of emperors as the Maurya, the Gupta, the Andhra, and the Kshatrapa.[107] Thus the priestly power [...] was under Mohammedan rule laid to sleep for ever, knowing no awakening. [...] But at the end of this Mohammedan period, another entirely new power made its appearance on the arena and slowly began to assert its prowess in the affairs of the Indian world. This power is so new, its nature and workings are so foreign to the Indian mind, its rise so inconceivable, and its vigour so insuperable that though it wields the suzerain power up till now, only a handful of Indians understand what this power is. We are talking of the occupation of India by England.

From very ancient times, the fame of India's vast wealth and her rich granaries has enkindled in many powerful foreign nations the desire for conquering her. She has been, in fact, again and again conquered by foreign nations. Then why should we say that the occupation of India by England was something new and foreign to the Indian mind? From time immemorial Indians have seen the mightiest royal power tremble before the frown of the ascetic priest, devoid of worldly desire, armed with spiritual strength—the power of Mantras (sacred formulas) and religious lore—and the weapon of curses. They have also seen the subject people silently obey the commands of their heroic all-powerful suzerains, backed by their arms and armies, like a flock of sheep before a lion. But that a handful of Vaishyas (traders) who, despite their great wealth, have ever crouched awe-stricken not only before the king but also before any member of the royal family, would unite, cross for purposes of business rivers and seas, would, solely by virtue of their intelligence and wealth, by degrees make puppets of the long-established Hindu and Mohammedan dynasties; not only so, but that they would buy as well the services of the ruling powers of their own country and use their valour and learning as powerful instruments for the influx of their own riches—this is a spectacle entirely novel to the Indians [...].

According to the prevalence, in greater or lesser degree, of the three qualities of Sattva, Rajas, and Tamas[108] in man, the four castes, the Brahmin, Kashatriya, Vaishya, and Shudra, are everywhere present at all times, in all civilised societies. By the mighty hand of time, their number and power also vary at different times in regard to different countries. In some countries the numerical strength or influence of one of these castes may preponderate over another; at some period, one of the classes may be more powerful than the rest. But from a careful study of the

---

[107]The Persian governors of Aryavarta and Gujarat. (SV)
[108]Truth or goodness, rule or passion, darkness or gravity.

history of the world, it appears that in conformity to the law of nature the four castes, the Brahmin, Kshatriya, Vaishya, and Shudra do, in every society, one after another in succession, govern the world. Among the Chinese, the Sumerians, the Babylonians, the Egyptians, the Chaldeans, the Aryas, the Iranians, the Jews, the Arabs—among all these ancient nations, the supreme power of guiding society is, in the first period of their history, in the hands of the Brahmin or the priest. In the second period, the ruling power is the Kshatriya, that is, either absolute monarchy or oligarchical government by a chosen body of men. Among the modern Western nations, with England at their head, this power of controlling society has been, for the first time, in the hands of the Vaishyas or mercantile communities, made rich through the carrying on of commerce. [...]

Therefore the conquest of India by England is not a conquest by Jesus or the Bible as we are often asked to believe. Neither is it like the conquest of India by the Moguls and the Pathans. But behind the name of the Lord Jesus, the Bible, the magnificent palaces, the heavy tramp of the feet of armies consisting of elephants, chariots, cavalry, and infantry, shaking the earth, the sounds of war trumpets, bugles, and drums, and the splendid display of the royal throne, behind all these, there is always the virtual presence of England — that England whose war flag is the factory chimney, whose troops are the merchant men, whose battlefields are the market-places of the world, and whose Empress is the shining Goddess of Fortune herself! It is on this account I have said before that it is indeed an unseen novelty, this conquest of India by England. What new revolution will be effected in India by her clash with the new giant power, and as the result of that revolution what new transformation is in store for future India, cannot be inferred from her past history.

I have stated previously that the four castes, Brahmin, Kshatriya, Vaishya, and Shudra do, in succession, rule the world. During the period of supreme authority exercised by each of these castes, some acts are accomplished which conduce to the welfare of the people, while others are injurious to them. [...] The Brahmin said, 'Learning is the power of all powers; that learning is dependent upon me, I possess that learning, so the society must follow my bidding.' For some days such was the case. The Kshatriya said, 'But for the power of my sword, where would you be, O Brahmin, with all your power of lore? You would in no time be wiped off the face of the earth. It is I alone that am the superior.' Out flew the flaming sword from the jingling scabbard—society humbly recognised it with bended head. Even the worshipper of learning was the first to turn into the worshipper of the king. The Vaishya is saying, 'You, madmen! what you call the effulgent all-pervading deity is here, in my hand, the ever-shining gold, the almighty sovereign. Behold, through its grace, I am also equally all-powerful. O Brahmin! even now, I shall buy through its grace all your wisdom, learning, prayers, and meditation. And, O great king! your sword, arms, valour, and prowess will soon be employed, through the grace of this, my gold, in carrying out my desired objects. Do you see those lofty and extensive mills? Those are my hives. See, how, swarms of millions of bees, the Shudras, are incessantly gathering honey for those hives. Do you know for whom? For me, this me, who, in due course of time will squeeze out every drop of it for my own use and profit.'

As during the supremacy of the Brahmin and the Kshatriya, there is a centralisation of learning and advancement of civilisation, so the result of the supremacy of the Vaishya is accumulation of wealth. The power of the Vaishya lies in the possession of that coin, the charm of whose clinking sound works with an irresistible fascination on the minds of the four castes. The Vaishya is always in fear lest the Brahmin swindles him out of this, his only possession, and lest the Kshatriya usurps it by virtue of his superior strength of arms. For self-preservation, the Vaishyas as a body are, therefore, of one mind. The Vaishya commands the money; the exorbitant interest that he can exact for its use by others, as with a lash in his hand, is his powerful weapon which strikes terror in the heart of all. By the power of his money, he is always busy curbing the royal power. That the royal power may not anyhow stand in the way of the inflow of his riches, the merchant is ever watchful. But, for all that, he has never the least wish that the power should pass on from the kingly to the Shudra class.

To what country does not the merchant go? Though himself ignorant, he carries on his trade and transplants the learning, wisdom, art, and science of one country to another. The wisdom, civilisation, and arts that accumulated in the heart of the social body during the Brahmin and the Kshatriya supremacies are being diffused in all directions by the arteries of commerce to the different market-places of the Vaishya. But for the rising of this Vaishya power, who would have carried today the culture, learning, acquirements, and articles of food and luxury of one end of the world to the other?

And where are they through whose physical labour only are possible the influence of the Brahmin, the prowess of the Kshatriya, and the fortune of the Vaishya? What is their history, who, being the real body of society, are designated at all times in all countries as 'base born'?—for whom kind India prescribed the mild punishments, 'Cut out his tongue, chop off his flesh', and others of like nature, for such a grave offence as any attempt on their part to gain a share of the knowledge and wisdom monopolised by her higher classes—those 'moving corpses' of India and the 'beasts of burden' of other countries—the Shudras, what is their lot in life? What shall I say of India? Let alone her Shudra class, her Brahmins to whom belonged the acquisition of scriptural knowledge are now the foreign professors, her Kshatriyas the ruling Englishmen, and Vaishyas, too, the English in whose bone and marrow is the instinct of trade, so that, only the Shudra-ness—the-beast-of-burdenness—is now left with the Indians themselves. [...]

But there is hope. In the mighty course of time, the Brahmin and the other higher castes, too, are being brought down to the lower status of the Shudras, and the Shudras are being raised to higher ranks. Europe, once the land of Shudras enslaved by Rome, is now filled with Kshatriya valour. Even before our eyes, powerful China with fast strides, is going down to Shudra-hood, while insignificant Japan, rising with the sudden start of a rocket is throwing off her Shudra nature and is invading by degrees the rights of the higher castes. The attaining of modern Greece and Italy to Kshatriya-hood and the decline of Turkey, Spain, and other countries, also, deserve consideration here.

Yet, a time will come when there will be the rising of the Shudra class, *with their Shudra-hood*; that is to say, not like that as at present when the Shudras are becoming great by acquiring the characteristic qualities of the Vaishya or the Kshatriya, but a time will come when the Shudras of every country, with their inborn Shudra nature and habits—not becoming in essence Vaishya or Kshatriya, but remaining as Shudras—will gain absolute supremacy in every society. The first glow of the dawn of this new power has already begun to break slowly upon the Western world, and the thoughtful are at their wits' end to reflect upon the final issue of this fresh phenomenon.

Socialism, Anarchism, Nihilism,[109] and other like sects are the vanguard of the social revolution that is to follow.

> [From: Vivekananda, 'Modern India', in *The Complete Works of Swami Vivekananda* (Mayavati Memorial Edition), IV (Calcutta: Advaita Ashrama, 1989), 438–80, here 447–50, 452, 465–7, 468.][110]

(Sir) SAYYID AHMAD KHAN (1817–98) attempted to demonstrate the compatibility of European education and rationalistic thinking with the tradition of Islam. He is also regarded as one of the founders of historiography in modern Urdu.

> *Sayyid Ahmad Khan was born in a notable family of Delhi and entered the services of the East India Company in 1839. He was one of the Indian loyalists during the rebellion in 1857. After the rebellion he was involved primarily in the problems of education among Muslims, to whom he wanted to impart European culture. This was the purpose of his visit to England during 1869–70. In 1870 he founded the Committee for the Better Diffusion and Advancement of Learning amongst the Muhammadans of India in Benares. When he retired in 1876, he began to institutionalize his ideas, by founding the Muhammadan Anglo-Oriental College at Aligarh with the help of the British and became its first chairman. He used his magazine* Tahdhib al-Akhlaq *to promote Urdu as a scientific language, especially when the Hindu members of a scientific society wanted to replace Urdu with Hindi for reasons of publication (1870). This helped Khan to build up a Muslim identity later, which was discriminated against by the Hindu dominated Indian National Congress. In spite of his commitment for Muslims and the division on the basis of religious aspects, he supported the integration of Indians in the Legislative Council. He argued pragmatically that the exclusion of Indians would not only disturb the stability of the nation but even threaten it. This speaks of his loyalty.*

Khan's reception of the European enlightenment is supposed to have made him aware of the principle of change and movement in history. In 1847 he published his *Athar al-Sanadid*, which points out the important monuments in Delhi, their assets, decorations, and inscriptions.

In 1855 he published the administrative Handbook of the Moguls, *A'in-e Akbari*, and explained the technical terms and loaned words used in it. This edition served then as a draft for the English translation of Blochman. 'Around 1870 he began to apply the Western methodology on the history of Arabia from the time of the Birth of Islam and on certain aspects of the prophet's biography (*sîra*) or the traditional biography of the prophet in a partly scientific manner and partly speculatively, apologetically. To do this work, which was the beginning of modern Indian historiography of Islam, published as *Essays on the Life of Mohammed* (1870) in

---

[109]Socialism took its birth in AD 1835. The initiator of Anarchism was Bakunin, who was born in AD 1814. Nihilism was first inaugurated in Russia in 1862. (SV)

[110]The original Bengali version of the essay appeared in 1899 under the title 'Bartaman Bharat' in the magazine *Udbodhana*. Further reading: A. V. Rathna Reddy, *The Political Philosophy of Swami Vivekananda* (New Delhi: Sterling, 1984), specifically 27–46 ('The Concept of History').

English and as *Khutubât-i Ahmadiyya* (1870) in Urdu, he consulted hand-written sources in the British Museum and the India Office Library in London; he also collected, in addition to Arabic works on *sîra* that were published in the Near East, rare Latin commentaries. He undertook this work to disprove the scientific but very controversial work of William Muir's *Life of Mahomet* (1858). It was an inspired work and met with public approval among the Western academics, who were sympathetically disposed towards Islam [...]. In its negative form it also set the example for modern Muslim apologetics. [...]. He remained, however, indebted to the theoretical concept of an accurate and scientific methodology' (Aziz Ahmad 1967: 39–40).

As early as in the introduction of his work about the unrest of 1857 (*History of the Bijnor Rebellion*, Urdu 1858), Khan expressed the view: 'May God grant me his guidance so that this history may be full and accurate. One-sidedness in historical writing is such a dishonest action, that its effect remains forever, so that the burden of the sin rests on the writer's neck until the Day of Judgement.' The account has been written 'after the most thorough investigation (*nihayat tahqiqat se*) and is completely true (*sahih*) and accurate (*sach*).' He responds to the colonialist complaint that as a Muslim and Indian he is biased and therefore not reliable: 'I feel persuaded that all rational men and friends of justice, will acknowledge that in recording the facts herein collected [in the book *Loyal Muhammedans*, part I, p. 9] I have in no instance been blinded by prejudice, or shown a wilful disregard of the claims of strict impartiality, since my statements will invariably be found to be supported by unimpeachable documentary evidence consisting of official reports and private testimonials ... and this will, I trust, silence all who may feel inclined to cavil at my facts.' (Quoted in Troll 1978–9: 103, 104)

Moreover, Khan saw himself as the promoter of enlightenment in the Muslim community and used his historiographical approach to reform the traditional Koran exegesis and to make it compatible with the discoveries of modern science. He had the greatest regard for the category Ratio (*'aql*) and often referred to early Muslim philosophers like Ibn Rushd (d. 1198), who played an important role in the self-understanding and the thought of the Islamic reform movement of the nineteenth century (*salafiyya* movement).[111]

Against the background of the growing secession from religion, which had risen due to the spreading of scientific discoveries, but also due to the supposed intellectual stagnation of the religious scholars, Khan was forced to deliver a new interpretation of religion, in that he often attacked the scholars who had gathered together for the purpose of learning at the seminary in Deoband after the defeat of the fight in 1857. His response to their lament, that he accepted the results of modern science and ideas of contemporary European naturalists uncritically, is given in his famous fifteen 'Principles of Exegesis'.[112]

[111]Ibn Rushd's concept of rationality denied any contradiction between revealed truth and the truth of reason. Leading Salafîs like Jamâl al-Dîn al-Afghânî and Muhammad 'Abduh utilized Ibn Rushd's ideas for their political-theological purposes and for the development of a new *'ilm al-kalâm*, besides his appreciation of reason (*'aql*) also his critique of mystics who misguide the people with their allegorical interpretations of the Koran and with the cult of saintly men.

[112]For the fifteen principles, see Troll, 1978–9: 276–8; Muhammad Daud Rahbar, 'Sir Sayyid Ahmad Khân's Principles of Exegesis Translated from his Tahrîr fî Usûl al-Tafsîr: First twelve principles', *Muslim World* 46 (1956), 104–12; (thirteenth–fifteenth principles), ibid., 324–35.

Principles of Exegesis (1880–95)

The principles explain the position of God as the Creator (Principles 1, 6, 7), the legation of the prophets and the mission of the Koran (Principles 2, 3, 4), the divine characteristics and the truthfulness of nature and the revelation (Principles 8, 14), the miracles (Principle 9) and the characteristics of Koran (Principles 5, 10, 11, 12, 13). In the fifteenth principle Khan puts forward eight main ideas, which are necessary to interpret a text correctly: the first six emphasize the necessity of establishing the exact original meaning of the word philologically or of revealing the hidden or implicit meanings or a special association. In the seventh main idea he discusses philological and rationalistic methods and in the eighth he arrives at the hermeneutic resolution of what has been said:

We believe that the glorious Koran in its actual words (*bi-lughati-hi*) is the speech of God. But when it is sent down in Arabic and in human language, i.e. in language understood by men, its meaning will be derived exactly as the meanings of (the speech of) an extremely eloquent speaker in Arabic. And just as men use trope, metaphor, allusions, similes, allegory, syllogistic argument, dialectical argument (*dalil iqna'i*), rhetorical argument, inductive argument and reductio ad absurdum (*ilzami*) in the same way we find these in the Koran. Besides we have to ponder on those verbal and procedural (*'amali*) promises which God has laid down and have to look into that style of speech and manner of the use of words peculiar to the Koran, and for which we have to seek the help of one verse to explain another. In determining the meanings of any speech, whether of God or man, the ascertainment of the following things is necessary:

(1) We must know that the word whose meanings we have determined was coined to yield the same meanings.

(2) We must determine whether that word is used in the sense for which it was originally coined or not.

(3) If that word has more than one meaning, then we must determine in which of the alternative senses it is used. Pronouns with interchangeable references too belong to this category of words.

(4) It is necessary to determine whether the word is used in its original sense which inheres in it, or in a metaphorical sense.

(5) It is to be determined if there is something hidden (or implicit) in the speech.

(6) It is necessary to determine if there is any particularisation (*takhsis*) in the meanings which the word indicates.

(7) It is necessary to see if there is any rational contradiction of the meanings determined in the light of reason. If there is, then the meanings are not correct. And there is nothing new in this. In fact all the doctors of Islam have followed this (principle) on hundreds of occasions, for example in the matter of God's sitting on the throne, of His having hands and legs, and many other words of this kind whose original meanings have not been adopted, because the rational argument was opposed to them. So there is no reason why we should not adopt some meanings of the words other than those which are impossible in the light of rational argument or are opposed to that law of nature which God Himself has declared or are opposed to (our) experience. [...] No doubt we have no choice but to turn to the existing lexical and literary

works when determining the meanings of the Koran. But supposing it is firmly proved that a certain word in the Koran is used in a way or in a sense not registered in lexical works or literature, we find no reason for hesitation in adopting that (usage or meaning). [...]

(8) In determining the meanings of the Koran another question also must be settled, namely, whether the speech upon which we found our argumentation is the real end of what is said (*kalam maqsud*) or just the means of the speech (*ghair maqsud*). For if it is the latter then argumentation cannot be based upon it. 'Not end' speech (*kalam ghair maqsud*) is found in the Koran in many places. [...] Involved in this is the large question of *ta'wil*. [...]

The Koran is in accordance with the reality of affairs. For it is the *vurd af Gad* (word of God) and is perfectly in agreement with the *vurk af Gad* (work of God). But the great miracle in it is that at every level of knowledge of ours, it guides uniformly and effectively in matters for which it (the Koran) is sent down. Its words have come down in a miraculous manner so that as the sciences continue to advance and as we ponder over it with regard to these advanced sciences, it will become known that its words are in agreement with reality in the light of these (newer sciences too), and it will be proved to us that the meanings we determined earlier, and which were proved wrong now, were a fault of our knowledge, and not of the words of the Koran. Hence if in the future, sciences advance to a point where the things ascertained today are disproved, then we shall turn to the Koran again and will certainly find it in agreement with reality. It will become known to us that the meanings we had determined earlier were a shortcoming of our knowledge, and that the Koran was free of all shortcomings.

[From: Sayyid Ahmad Khan, Principles of Exegesis, in *Muslim Self-Statements in India and Pakistan 1857–1968*, ed. by Aziz Ahmad and G. E. von Grunebaum (Wiesbaden: Harrassowitz, 1970), 34–6, 39.]

The Agenda of a Modern
Indian Historiography

2.1 HISTORY AS AN OBJECT OF RESEARCH

The western complaint about the lack of a sense of history in India (which sometimes revealed only the limitations of the underlying European concept) has nowhere been as justified as in view of the Indian disregard for historical source material. Apparently, there was little interest in the preservation of annalistic records and chronicles or temple lists of pilgrims, which got lost as much as many old coins did. As regards the architectural remains, the local population sometimes entertained fanciful ideas (Kejariwal 1998: 8–9).

Early western researchers and administrators met their need for information about the past mostly by recourse to the historiography of the Muslims. Nevertheless, if the texts (or oral traditions) of the Hindus were regarded as unreliable or insufficient, the example of Colin Mackenzie (1754–1821) and the Great Mysore Survey shows the variety of sources which could satisfy the historical curiosity around 1800.[1] In some of the Mahakavyas of the seventeenth century, for instance, increasing attention had been paid to the details of space and time.[2]

The first steps towards professionalization and methodization of historical research were taken within the organizational framework of British institutions, such as the Asiatic Society (founded in 1784) and the Archaeological Survey (founded in 1861). Historians were also recruited and employed at the colleges and the universities (Calcutta, Bombay, and Madras, founded in 1857).

[1]Considering the arbitrary handling of the material by the colonial authorities, however, N. B. Dirks speaks of 'erasing colonized histories'. Nicholas B. Dirks, 'Colonial Histories and Native Informants: Biography of an Archive,' in Breckenridge and Van der Veer 1993: 279–313, here 280.

[2]See Velcheru Narayana Rao and David Shulman, 'History, Biography and Poetry at the Tanjavur Court', in Seneviratne 1989: 115–30.

Indian initiatives to promote historical research were soon introduced by the new educational societies and organs of publication, first at the local and regional, then at the national level. In Bengal, where British rule had first been established, the question of tradition and continuity became particularly urgent in the agitation over the partition of the province in 1905. The periodical of the Calcutta Historical Society, *Bengal Past and Present. A Journal of Modern Indian and Asian History*, was founded in 1907. The Varendra Research Society at Rajshahi, established in 1910, aimed to encourage the systematic investigation into the past. Besides Bengal, it was Maharashtra which could boast of important centres of historical learning, such as the Oriental Research Institute in Pune (founded in 1917). Other regional magazines were the *Journal of the Bihar and Orissa Research Society* (1915ff.),[3] the *Journal of the Andhra Historical Research Society* (Rajahmundry 1926ff.), and the *Karnataka Historical Review* (Dharwad 1931ff.). Among the early all-India organs and institutions were the *Journal of Indian History* (Allahabad 1921, later Trivandrum) and the Indian History Congress with its *Proceedings of the Indian History Congress* (New Delhi 1935ff.).

Among the first Indian historians who reflected on problems of methodology and who based their accounts on their own research are Rajendralal Mitra, especially for the history of Orissa,[4] Ramkrishna Gopal Bhandarkar for the area of ancient Indian history, Jadunath Sarkar[5] for the period of the Mughal empire, Romesh Chunder Dutt[6] for modern Indian history, and Shibli Nu'mani for the history of the Muslims. Methodological reflections in a systematical framework are rare during this early period.[7] There are mainly statements in prefaces and ad hoc scattered remarks. This changes after Independence (see below, Section 4.1).

(Sir) RAMKRISHNA GOPAL BHANDARKAR (1837–1925) has gone down in the history of the Indian historical discipline as one of the first great researchers from original sources.[8] His writings are seen as paradigmatic achievements of modern Indian historiography.

> *Bhandarkar was born at Malwan (Ratnagiri district, Maharashtra), the son of a secretary in the Revenue Department. He was educated at Elphinstone College in Bombay, where he later*

[3]Founded by K. P. Jayaswal (see below, Section 2.2), since 1935 published separately for Bihar and Orissa.

[4]Mitra 1875–80. Mitra edited parts of the Vedas and Upanishads as well as the Yoga Sutras of Patanjali. For Mitra, see Gunderson 1970; K. K. Dasgupta 1976. Other Indian researchers, who were mainly involved in the editing of sources, were Bhagwanlal Indraji and Bhau Daji. Cf. A. L. Basham, 'Modern Historians of Ancient India', in Philips 1961: 260–93, here 280.

[5]The main works of Sir Jadunath Sarkar (1870–1958) are: *Fall of the Mughal Empire*, 4 Vols. (1932ff.), and *Shivaji and his Times* (1919). Both fields of research, Mughal and Maratha history, represented a special challenge to the historian's impartiality. Sarkar formulated his advice to the new generation of historians in 'A Word to Research Workers in Indian History', *Bengal: Past and Present* 76 (1957), 1–5. For Sarkar, see Tikekar 1964; Pawar 1985; Srivastava 1989.

[6]For Dutt and his *Economic History of India* (1902–4), see below, Section 2.3.

[7]See for instance Mohini Mohan Chatterjee 1927; K. V. Subrahmanya Aiyar 1941, 'Methods of Historical Research', in *Three Lectures* (Kannada Research Lectures Series No. 2, Dharwar), 1–38.

[8]Basham called him 'the earliest important indigenous historian of ancient India'. 'Modern Historians of Ancient India', in Philips 1961: 280.

(1867–72) taught Oriental Languages. In 1879, he was appointed professor at Deccan College in Pune, and in 1893 he took office as Vice-Chancellor of Bombay University. Besides his academic work, Bhandarkar was an active member of the All-India Social Conference and of the Prarthana Samaj. His reputation as a scholar is evident in awards given to him by the universities of Calcutta, Bombay, and Göttingen and in his honorary membership of the Royal Asiatic Society, the Deutsche Morgenländische Gesellschaft, the American Oriental Society, and the Institut Français. In 1903 he was appointed a member of the Legislative Council of the Viceroy, and in 1917 he was knighted.

Bhandarkar had gained a reputation as a Sanskrit scholar before his interest in history was awakened when he studied copper plate inscriptions. In 1884, he published his *Early History of the Dekkan*, which marks the beginning of the investigation into the Central and South Indian regional empires and has seen numerous editions and reprints. Apart from political and dynastic history, from earliest times to the Muslim conquest, the book also deals with the economic and social conditions and with religion, literature, and the arts. The account is based on a critical analysis of the sources, including the inscriptions. It was followed, in 1900, by *A Peep into the Early History of India*,[9] a brief account of Indian history from the foundation of the Maurya dynasty to the end of the Gupta empire. In the introductory remarks, Bhandarkar instructs the historian to approach the sources not like an advocate but like a judge and to present in his account nothing but 'dry truths'.[10]

Notwithstanding his demand for detachment, Bhandarkar conceived history as moral and practical teaching. As a reformer, he used his scholarship 'to show that many of the orthodox customs of this day had no foundation in the ancient Hindu religion'.[11] His book *Vaishnavism, Shaivism, and Minor Religious Systems*[12] still counts among the important works in this field.

Bhandarkar's main scientific effort was directed towards early Indian chronology, and his lasting influence consisted in having brought order to the confusing dates and in transforming the knowledge of ancient Indian history from a domain of legends to one of facts. As he summarized when looking back on his professional life, Indian historical studies had taken a decisive step in the direction of methodization: 'I close the active years of my life with an assured belief that sound critical scholarship has grown up among us, and that it will maintain

---

[9]First published in the *Journal of the Bombay Branch of the Royal Asiatic Society*, later as a monograph (Bombay 1920) as well as in the *Collected Works of Sir R. G. Bhandarkar* (Poona 1933), I, 1–61.

[10]James Mill had also compared the attitude of the historian with that of the judge in the law-court. See Mill 1820: I, 9.

[11]A. D. Pusalker, 'R. G. Bhandarkar', in: Sen 1973: 27–48, here 29. Bhandarkar intervened, for instance, in the debate on child marriage. Rejecting the position of Tilak, he pointed to ancient texts which argued against it. Bhandarkar advocated a moderate policy and believed that at first the 'sense of public duty' or 'corporate consciousness' had to be practised, before Independence could be envisaged. Cf. *Collected Works*, I, 479. British rule, according to him, offered chances of improvement to the Indians which had not existed under their own monarchs and, after all, also liberties which even some European peoples like the Germans and the Austrians did not enjoy.

[12]*Collected Works*, IV. First published in *Grundriß der indo-arischen Philologie*, III, 6 (Straßburg 1913).

its own against aspersions and attacks.'[13] Bhandarkar lives on, not only in his writings, but also in the work of the Oriental Research Institute at Pune, founded by him and later renamed after him. The *Annals of the Bhandarkar Oriental Research Institute* (1920ff.) still find a place among the most renowned periodicals in India.

The following extracts are taken from a lecture delivered by Bhandarkar on 31 March, 1888, during a public assembly of the Free Church College Literary Society in Bombay. Here, he demonstrates the methods of historical source critique and outlines the practical importance of scientific research for the orientation between tradition and modernity.

The Critical, Comparative, and Historical Method of Inquiry (1888)

A critical inquirer is one who does not accept an account of an occurrence just as it is presented to him, whether orally or in writing. He subjects it to certain tests calculated to prove its truth or otherwise. He takes care, for instance, to ascertain whether the person giving the account was an eye-witness to the occurrence, and if so, whether he was an unprejudiced and at the same time an intelligent observer. If his information is based on other sources, the critic endeavours to ascertain the credibility or otherwise of those sources. When it is a thing or a verified occurrence that he has to deal with, he does not satisfy himself with that view of its nature and relations that appears plausible at first sight. He seeks for extraneous assistance to enable himself to arrive at a correct view. One of the most efficacious means employed by him is comparison of like things or occurrences. This comparison enables him to separate the accidents of the thing or occurrence from its essential nature, and sometimes to arrive at a law which includes the thing or occurrence as a particular case and explains it. Though comparison may thus be considered one of the means of a critical examination, still its own proper results are so important that it deserves to be considered an independent method of inquiry. [...]

Criticism and comparison are of use not only in enabling us to arrive at a knowledge of what is true, but also of what is good and rational. A man born in a certain country with certain social and religious customs and institutions, and in a certain range of ideas, thinks those customs, institutions, and that range of ideas to be perfectly good and rational, and sees nothing objectionable in them, unless he is a man of genius. When, however, he comes to know of other customs, other institutions, and other ideas, and compares them with those to which he has become accustomed, he is able to find out any evil that there may be in the latter, and to see what is better and more rational. The comparison of the jurisprudence of different countries is calculated to afford valuable hints to the legislator for the improvement of the laws of his own country. Similarly, the critical observation and comparison of the social institutions of other countries and even of other religions will afford guidance to the social and religious reformer. Critical comparison is also of use in giving us juster notions of the beautiful. [...]

[13]'Presidential Address at the Opening Session of the First Oriental Conference of India, held at Poona on 5 November 1919', in *Collected Works*, I, 331, 320. On this occasion, Bhandarkar once again told the researchers: 'A critical scholar should consider his function to be just like that of a judge in a law-court.' Ibid. This admonition has become an often quoted obligation to Indian historians.

Before admitting the narrative contained in an ancient work to be historical, one ought to ask oneself whether the object of the author was to please and instruct the reader and excite the feeling of wonder, or to record events as they occurred. If the former, the narrative cannot be accepted as historical, but legendary. Our obvious and almost axiomatic notions of ordinary probability should also be brought to bear on the question. If a king, for instance, in such a narrative is represented to have reigned a thousand, or even two or three hundred years, one ought to understand that the author wants to excite the feeling of wonder and admiration in his reader, and was in all likelihood under the influence of that feeling himself. If we apply these tests to our existing Sanskrit literature, we must declare the *Ramayana*, the *Mahabharata*, and the Puranas to be not historical works. Of course, it is possible that they may have a historical basis, and some of the persons mentioned in them may have really existed; but we cannot assert that they did exist, without corroborative evidence such as is to be derived from contemporary inscriptions and the historical writings of foreigners. Now, if the object of the author be the latter, and the narrative answers to our tests of ordinary probability, the work must be accepted as historical. But we have very few such works in Sanskrit literature now extant. Probably, there were many more, but they are lost to us. The *Vikramankacarita*, the *Harsacarita*, the *Gaudavadha*, and the *Rajatarangini*[14] are works of this nature. I will also include deeds of grants inscribed on metallic plates, stone inscriptions, and coins among the historical documents now available to us. It appears to have been the custom in ancient times, as it is even now, to preserve genealogies of royal families. We find some given in the Puranas. These have a historical value as they are confirmed by inscriptions. But as the readings have in the course of time become corrupt, and the genealogies of different royal families seem to have been confused together, they are not to be relied on implicitly, without check and comparison. Now as to the contemporary caritras or the deeds of kings spoken of above, it ought to be remembered that the writers, being dependents or servants of the princes whose account is given therein, cannot be expected to be impartial historians of their patrons and masters; and must be regarded as open to the temptation of bestowing extravagant praise on them and their ancestors. [...]

Now, the point to be considered with reference to such a book as the *Rajatarangini* is that though the author is to be considered a contemporary historian so far as the period in which he lived is concerned, what were his authorities for the history of previous times? He does mention previous writers and speaks of having consulted eight historical works. But he begins his history with Gonarda I, who was the contemporary of Yudhisthira, and gives three names after him. The next 35 princes are, he says, unknown by name; and then mentions 13 more. This is the period for which, he says, he did not find full authorities, and mentions the books from which he got the 17 names given by him. The next period begins in 1184 BC, when a prince of the name of Gonarda III ascended the throne. The history is then carried on by Kalhana without a break up to his own times. One of the princes, however, is represented by him to have reigned for 300 years; and the

[14]The reference is to Bilhana's *Vikramankadevacarita* (eleventh century), a biography of the Chalukya king of the Dekkhan, Bana's *Harshacarita* (seventh century), an account of the early life of Harsavardhana of Kannauj, Vakpatiraja's *Gaüdavaha* (eighth century), a description of the deeds of king Yasovarman of Kanauj, and Kalhana's Kashmir chronicle *Rajatarangini* (twelfth century).

average duration of the reigns of the princes in the different groups is sometimes 48 years, sometimes 38. When it is remembered that this varies from 18 to 22 only, the chronology of Kalhana in the older portion of his history must be considered as not reliable. Though it appears very probable that he himself did not put on paper anything for which he found no authority, the works he consulted cannot be considered to be quite reliable themselves. And looking generally to the manner in which the text of old works gets corrupt in the course of time, this is perfectly intelligible. Still, since Kalhana mentions his having used inscriptions, and edicts or proclamations of kings, and states with what public works in Kashmir the names of some of the princes are connected and makes specific statements about them of another nature, the narrative portion of his history should, I think, be considered generally reliable, and also the chronology of the period nearer to his own time. [...]

In the same manner, the ideas and modes of thinking which from our acquaintance with the period we have seen to be prevalent should be referred to for help in interpreting a passage. If, instead of resorting to these methods, we take an isolated passage and interpret it according to modern usage, modern ideas, and fanciful or even true etymology, we may make it mean anything; and we shall thus find in the Vedas not only pure theism, but even railways and electric telegraphs. [...]

And now, gentlemen, and my Hindu friends in particular, a word as to my object in taking up this subject for to-night's discourse. It is no use ignoring the fact that Europe is far ahead of us in all that constitutes civilization. And knowledge is one of the elements of civilization. Experimental sciences and the sciences that depend on the critical, comparative, and historical method have made very great progress in Europe, and what deserves our earnest attention is that they are every day making further and further progress. The Europeans have derived much greater advantage from our connection with them than we have from their connection with us. [...] All this will show the activity of the European intellect, and convince us that the principle of progress is very strong in their civilization. But what advantages have we derived from them? A great deal of what they have got from us has but very indirectly been given to them by us; while they have placed before us a whole civilization, which undoubtedly is far superior to ours in a great many points.

The impulse to be communicated to us by it ought to be a hundred-fold stronger than that which we have communicated to them. Just as they have used the critical and comparative faculty with energy and produced the results I have just noted, we should use it and direct it not only to find what is true in science, but what is good and rational in social and religious institutions. But have we received the impulse, have we been using the faculty? Who can say we have, while our new literature is scanty and barren of any original idea and we are still quarrelling about female education, caste, and religion? Why should we not move on, side by side with Europeans, in the great fields of thought? Why should discoveries be made in France, Germany, and England, and not in India? If you say that in most of the branches there are facilities in Europe for making fresh additions to the existing stock of knowledge, while we have none in India, surely no costly laboratories are required to enable us to study the ancient literature of our country and its architectural remains and inscriptions, and to throw light on its political and literary history and its philology. This is a field in which we may successfully compete with Europeans, and in which we enjoy certain peculiar advantages. But these advantages can be turned to account only if we follow their critical, comparative, and historical method. My object, therefore, has been to call your attention to the nature and requisites of this method, in order that by its successful application to the branch of study I am speaking of, we may take our legitimate place among the investigators of the political, literary, and religious history of our country, and not allow the Germans, the French, and the English to monopolize the field.

And here I feel myself in duty bound, even at the risk of displeasing some of you, to make a passing allusion to the most uncritical spirit that has come over us of praising ourselves and our ancestors indiscriminately, seeing nothing but good in our institutions and in our ancient literature, asserting that the ancient Hindus had made very great progress in all the sciences, physical, moral, and social, and the arts,—greater even by far than Europe has made hitherto—and denying even the most obvious deficiencies in our literature, such as the absence of satisfactory historical records, and our most obvious defects. As long as this spirit exists in us, we can never hope to be able to throw light on our ancient history, and on the excellencies and defects of our race, and never hope to rise. While, if we shake ourselves free of such a bias, and critically and impartially examine our old records and institutions, we shall do very great service to our country; we shall be able to check the conclusions of some European scholars who are swayed by an opposite bias; and at the same time that by a clear perception of our great national defects we prepare the ground for healthy progress in the future we shall, I promise you, find a great deal in the past of which we may honestly be proud.

[From: Bhandarkar, 'The Critical, Comparative, and Historical Method of Inquiry, as Applied to Sanskrit Scholarship and Philology and Indian Archeology', in *Collected Works of Sir R. G. Bhandarkar*, ed. by Narayana Bapuji Utgikar and Vasudev Gopal Paranjpe (Poona: Bhandarkar Oriental Research Institute, 1933), I, 362–92, here 362–7, 373–4, 390–2.][15]

SHIBLI NU'MANI (1857–1915) is regarded as the founder and the pioneering practitioner of the critical Islamic historiography in Urdu.

> *Shibli Nu'mani, one of the leading Muslim intellectuals that Aligarh College produced, was born in a Qasbah in the district of Azamgarh in the United Provinces as the son of a lawyer. After studying British law he spent some time from 1882 onwards at Aligarh College, where he was influenced by Sir Sayyid Ahmad Khan and his liberal ideas on religion as well as by the philosophy professor Thomas Arnold (d. 1930), who introduced him to western literary criticism. Himself an autodidact and not a traditional 'âlim, Shibli received from him stimulus for important reforms. Many journeys to the Middle East,[16] as well as his studies of Arabic, Persian, and Urdu, made him famous beyond the local borders. Soon he established active relations with the Egyptian reformist group of Muhammad 'Abduh.*

At the centre of the efforts of Shibli was the introduction of English in the traditional teaching canon as well as the working out of a new philosophical theology ('*ilm al-kalâm*) following Ibn

[15]The text appeared first in Bombay, 1888.

[16]See the travelogue *Safarnâmah-ye Rûm, Misr o Shâm* (Agra: Mufîd-e 'Amm 1894), ed. Muhammad Riyâd (Lahore: Maqbûl Akademî 1988).

Rushd who, during his time, had rejected any contradiction between the revealed truth and the truth of rationality and who played an important role in the case of *salafiyya* reformers (Troll 1982: 169f, 199). Moreover, he wanted to reform Muslim historical writing.

His first important historiographical article was a stock taking of the Islamic educational system. As he was constantly in the shadow of the Aligarh management under Sayyid Ahmad Khan, Shibli looked out for new opportunities to carry out his innovative ideas. Various palaces and mainly the young Nadwat al-Ulama (founded 1893 in Kanpur) offered their patronage for his efforts for a while, till he had to leave the council due to personal differences. Shortly before his death he founded the Dâr al-Musannifîn in Azamgarh. One of his big projects was the critical history of Persian poetry in five volumes (*Shi'r al-'Ajam*), which is considered to be a standard work today. Besides this, he planned an encyclopaedia of Islamic history, in which he wanted to link secular and Islamic approaches.

Similar to the Salafis in Egypt, the reconstruction of the Golden Age of the prophets and the four Caliphs was of central importance to him, since it was only by imitating these role models that contemporary Muslims, who had moved away from the right path, could attain a new and better life. History for him therefore served as a moral lesson and a means to social progress.

Inspired by the series 'Heros of the Nations' in contemporary England, he started the series 'Heros in Islam' and wrote, besides *al-Kalam* (Cawnpore 1313 H.) and '*Ilm al-Kalam* (Agra 1902), some biographies of Muslim kings and thinkers, such as a study on the second Caliph al-Fârûq (1898), about al-Ghazzali (1902; reprint, Lahore 1952) and Mawlawi Rumi (Lahore 1909), as well as a prophet biography (*Sirat al-Nabi*) (Lahore, n.d.) that appeared posthumously. He admitted the intellectual superiority of the contemporary European humanities.

Shibli's view of history is influenced by the idea that Muslims had moved away from the right path, a view that was later shared by Maududi. The historical methodology, according to him, consisted of a synthesis of traditional Islamic sciences like chronicles and hagiographies on the one hand and western objective analysis on the other. In the introduction of *al-Fârûq* Shibli defined his own ideas of writing history as follows:

The Element of History (1898)

Most of the arts and sciences which spring up during the course of Civilization are evolved from crude pre-existing material. During the progress of Civilization these materials assume a definite form and, developing themselves into a systematic whole, acquire a particular name or title. For instance, methods of ratiocination and argumentation have existed in all ages, but it was only when Aristotle arranged these particulars in a definite order that they became known by the name of Logic and thus culminated into a positive science. The same may be said of History and Biography. Wherever there was a group of individuals on the globe, there were, to be sure, History and Biography to be met, for, in challenging and defying their rivals, men were wont to speak in terms of flowing pride of the glorious records of their ancestors; battles fought and engagements contested in the days of yore necessarily lent an additional charm to their gatherings and conversations, while old customs and usages were instinctively maintained as relics of their pristine progenitors, and these are the sources from which the treasures of History and Chronicle are replenished. Resting their claims on this basis, [...] all the nations of the world can affirm that in historical acquisition and legendary lore none of them falls short of the other.

Arabia, however, could boast of a peculiar idiosyncrasy in this general connection. The Arabs had precedence over other nations in the possession of certain characteristics which tended to contribute towards the solidarity of the chain of History. Thus genealogy was their passion. Even a child learnt by rote the genealogical table of his house and forefathers up to the tenth or twelfth degree, and his relish for preserving their lineage was so intense that they took to keeping the pedigrees even of their horses and camels. [...]

Thus it was that when Civilization dawned on Arabia, the books that were first written were historical works. Long before the advent of Islam the kings of the Hirah dynasty caused historical events to be committed to writing, which thus escaped the ravages of time. Ibn Hisham in his book *Al-Tijan*, speaks of having utilized these works. The spread of Islam was early marked by accumulation of a store of legends and traditions, but as it was long afterwards that the people took to writing books, no work on History appeared at this particular period; yet when the field of literary composition was once open, the first book that appeared was a historical one.

During the reign of Amir Mu'awiyah, who died in the year 60 H., there lived one 'Ubaid b. Sharyah by name who had seen the Days of Ignorance, and who knew the events connected with most of the battles fought between Arabia and Persia. This man was living at Sana when Amir Mu'awiyah sent for him and appointed certain writers and amanuenses to take down everything that he chose to dictate. The learned Ya'qub al-Nadim, in his book, *Fihrist* (Index) has referred to a number of treatises dictated by 'Ubaid. One of these is named *Kitab-ul-Muluk wa Akhbar-ul Madiyin* (the Book of Kings and the Story of the Ancients). This is presumably identical with the book the manuscript of which was prepared by the order of Amir Mu'awiyah. Next to 'Ubaid ranks 'Awatah b. al-Hakam (d. 147 H.) who was skilled in legendary lore as well as in the intricacies of genealogy. Besides contributing to historical topics of general interest, he wrote a book containing the history of the times of the Caliphs of Omayyad dynasty and of the reign of Amir Mu'awiyah. By the command of Hisham b. 'Abd-ul-Malik, in 117 H., the most detailed and exhaustive history of Persia was translated from the Pahlevi language into Arabic. This was the first book that was translated into Arabic from a foreign language. In the year 143 H., when commentaries on the Qur'an, the Traditions of the Prophet, and Islamic Jurisprudence began to be systematized and compiled, standard works on History and Biography also appeared. [...]

With the opening of the fifth century H. commences what may be called the Secondary Period which marks the first retrogressive step in the march of the science of History. Although quite a host of historians flourished in the latter period [...], it is a matter for regret that they rendered no service to History as a science. They lacked the characteristics of their predecessor and produced nothing that was new and original. Thus though it was a distinguishing feature of the writers of the Classical Period that every book written by them contained new and useful information hitherto undisclosed, their successors, on the contrary, adopted a totally different course. All they did was to take up some old work and modify, abridge and transform it without contributing any new matter to it. The learned Ibn Khallikan has pronounced the history written by Ibn al-Athir to be unsurpassed in point of excellence, and there can be no doubt that its universal popularity eclipsed the earlier historical works. [...]

It was one of the idiosyncrasies of the writers of the Classical Period that the events they narrated were substantiated by an unbroken chain of positive testimony, exactly in the same manner in which the sayings of the Prophet were traced through the medium of closely transmitted authority. The writers of the Secondary Period entirely gave up this plan. [...] The name of Ibn Khaldun, however, escapes this general censure. He laid the foundations of the philosophy of history of which not only the historians of the Secondary Period but the entire Muslim world might well be proud. [...]

An eminent author has thus defined History: 'The changes wrought by the course of nature in the condition of man, and the influence exerted by man over his natural environments, together constitute history.' Another writer gives the following definition: 'History is the tracing of those events and conditions which show the manner in which the Present sprang from the Past as an effect.' As the civilization and social systems, the ideas and impressions, and the religious orders which exist in the world at present, are the natural effects of the past events, History is the investigation of those past events and their arrangement in such an order as will admit of a delineation of the manner in which each present event resulted from the chain of past events.

According to the above definitions, two things follow which are absolutely necessary for history. Firstly, the account of a particular period should comprehend events and incidents of every description—cultural, social, ethical, and religious. Secondly, the chain of cause and effect must be traced in recounting all events.

The old historical works are lacking in both the above-mentioned requisites. They hardly touch upon the morals and manners, culture, and social conditions of the people. Only the events of the life of the ruler of the day are described, but even these events are nothing more than an account of conquests and civil wars. This defect is not limited to Islamic histories alone. All Asiatic histories run in the same style, which is justified by the fact that Asia had, from time immemorial, been the seat of absolute monarchies, and the grandeur and dogmatic authority of the ruler of the day used to overrule every other consideration. This necessarily meant that the pages of the history should contain nothing but accounts of the royal grandeur and glory, and, as in that age laws and statutes were nothing more than arbitrary mandates and unrestrained commands of the sovereign, it was deemed futile to attempt to record even the principles of Government and the system of Administration.

The main cause that led to the disregard of the chain of causality in the analysis of events was that, as a rule, writers of History were ignorant of Philosophy and the rational sciences, and they could not, therefore, think of the principles of the Philosophy of History and their working. Hence it is that in works of Biography and Hadith tradition had always the better of ratiocination throughout; in fact, the employment of the ratiocinative method was nominal. Toward the close of the Secondary Period Ibn Khaldun laid the foundation-stone of the Philosophy of history and formulated its principles and canons, but he had no time to make use of them in his own History. After this began a long period of literary decay for the Muslims and no one ever troubled about these matters. [...]

There are only two methods of testing the accuracy of an event, *i.e.* Tradition and Ratiocination. Tradition means that the account of an event is conveyed through the medium of the individual who was a personal witness of that event, that the chain of tradition can be closely traced down from this individual to the last narrator, and that the trustworthiness and veracity of the several narrators have been minutely inquired into, tested, and established.

Ratiocination signifies the rational criticism of an event. The Muslims might well feel proud of the fact that they have surpassed every other nation of the world in bringing the traditional lore to a high pitch of perfection. With a view to verifying traditions of every description, they left no stone unturned in their efforts to trace the transmitted and uninterrupted chain of authority, and after careful sifting and investigation of details as to the life and character of the narrators, they resolved it into a separate and permanent art which is known by the name of *Rijal* (Biography of the Authorities). This care and labour was at first brought into use in the collection and systematization of the sayings of the Prophet; but history also benefited by it. [...] European historians have brought history to a high degree of perfection at the present day, but they are far behind Muslim historians in this respect. They are perfectly indifferent to the veracity and trustworthiness or otherwise of an annalist which betrays complete ignorance of the art of criticism.

The laws of ratiocination were not unknown [...] but the fact is that this science did not make the progress which it should have; while it was hardly applied to history. The learned Ibn Khaldun, who flourished in the eighth century H., however, formulated the laws of ratiocination in a masterly manner when laying the foundations of the Philosophy of History. [...] He has further explained that in order to discover the truth of an event it is not expedient to trouble oneself at the very outset with the veracity and trusthwortiness or otherwise of the narrator. On the contrary, it should at first be ascertained whether the event itself lies within the pale of possibility, for, if the event is not possible, the veracity of the narrator is useless. Ibn Khaldun has also pointed out that possibility in such instances does not signify logical possibility but that which is possible in accordance with the laws of Nature and Society. [...]

The rules of ratiocination are of great help in investigating and sifting the truth of events. These rules have now been systematically formulated and the following are those which we can best utilize:

(1) Whether the event in question is possible according to the laws of Nature?

(2) Whether the general tendency of the people in the period in which the event occurred was in harmony or incompatible with its occurrence?

(3) Whether the strength of the testimony in support of the event is proportionate to the abnormality of the said event, if it happens to be extraordinary?

(4) How far the narrator has had recourse to conjecture and presumption in his description of the incident which he gives as a matter of fact?

(5) Whether the form in which the narrator has related the event is a perfect impression of it, or whether the presumption is that he has not been able to show both the sides of the picture and has failed to delineate all the features of the event?

(6) To calculate the degree and nature of the changes wrought in the tradition by the lapse of time and the different systems of rehearsal adopted by different narrators?

No one can question the accuracy or correctness of these rules and many a hidden secret might be disclosed through their medium. [...] Thus all the books of History extant today contain Omar's very strict laws regarding the non-Muslim nationalities. But when it is remembered that these histories were written during a period when fanaticism had taken strong hold of the Muslim world, and when, along with this, we go through the writings of the Classical Period in which we do not find any incident of this kind, or, when we do find them, they are extremely rare, we are driven to the conclusion that with the march of the forces of fanaticism the version of traditions grew spontaneously distorted. [...]

Moreover, those traditions which, in addition to their historical importance, also possess religious significance, clearly show that the more carefully they were analysed, the more were the doubtful and equivocal elements eliminated.

[From: Shibli Nu'mani, *Omar the Great* (*The Second Caliph of Islam*) (Lahore 1939), 1–27, here 1–5, 9–11, 20, 21, 25–6.)[17]

2.2 IN QUEST OF A PERSPECTIVE: PATRIOTISM, NATIONALISM, COMMUNALISM

The inner connection between historical consciousness and political agency was drastically demonstrated to the colonized when T. B. Macaulay introduced a new system of education for them, which aimed at comprehensive Anglicization of the indigenous elite. Macaulay did not attribute any practical value to the Indian tradition. This clear affront by the colonial authorities to the 'ahistorical' Indian culture now created an urgent need among Indians for clarification about the subjects and the perspectives of collective action.

Certainly, Indian accounts of the past had earlier been, implicitly or explicitly, related to practical issues, too. The seventeenth-century Mahakavyas mentioned above (Section 2.1), notwithstanding their tendency to Sanskritize and idealize, do include detailed descriptions of social and political innovations in contemporary life.[18] In the eighteenth century, the Oriya poet Brajanatha Bodajena wrote a realistic account of the Marathas' recent campaigns and ravages of war in Orissa.[19] The *Diaries* of Ananda Ranga Pillai (1709–61), too, are regarded as an early document of a modern interest in contemporary history.[20]

The growing public interest in history towards the middle of the nineteenth century was fulfilled, first and foremost, by literary magazines like *Bangadarshan* or *Harishchandra's Magazine*.

[17]Original: Muhammad Shibli Nu'mani, *al-Faruq*, A'zamgarh: Matba 'Ma'ârif, 1898 (Urdu). Further reading: Aziz Ahmad, *Islamic Modernism in India and Pakistan* (Oxford: Oxford University Press 1967), 77–86; Z. H. Faruqi, 'Sir Sayyid and Maulana Shibli', in Mohibbul Hasan (ed.), *Historians of Medieval India* (Meerut: Meenakshi Prakashan, 1969); Mehr Afroz Murad, *Intellectual Modernism of Shibli Nu'mani* (Lahore: Institute of Islamic Culture, 1976); Chr. W. Troll, 'The Fundamental Nature of Prophethood and Miracle: A Chapter from Shibli Nu'mani's Al-Kalam', in idem (ed.), *Islam in India; Studies and Commentaries*, I (Delhi: Vikas 1982), 86–115.

[18]See, for instance, the Mahakavya *Raghunathabhyudaya* by Ramabhadramba of seventeenth-century Tanjavur. Cf. Narayana Rao and D. Shulman, 'History, Biography, and Poetry at the Tanjavur Court', in Seneviratne 1989: 115–30. The new Mahakavyas as well as the historical folk epic have in common a new interest in individual facts: 'The past, in its particulars, mattered to their authors, and was endowed with meaning.' Ibid., 115.

[19]Cf. George D. Bearce, 'Intellectual and Cultural Characteristics of India in a Changing Era, 1740–1800', JAS 25 (1965), 3–17, here 6.

[20]*The Private Diary of Ananda Ranga Pillai: A Record of Matters Political, Historical, Social and Personal from 1736–1761*, 12 Vols., translated from the Tamil, ed. J. Frederick Price and K. Rangachari (reprint, New Delhi: Asian Educational Services, 1985). Pillai served as Chief Dubash of the French Governor of Pondicherry, Joseph François Dupleix. See M. Gobalakichenane, 'Ananda Rangappillai's Extended Diary', *Historical Review of Pondicherry* 17 (1991), 35–7.

Specific emphasis on history was laid in the periodical *Kavyetihas Samgraha*, published in Maharashtra since 1878. Here, as well as in the Bengali magazine *Aitihasik Chitra*,[21] the British interpretations of the Indian past were countered with Indian views (Meenakshi Mukherjee 1985: 43).

Just as in Europe, it was the historical novel and the historical drama which contributed to the popularization of the interest in the past. The emergence of the vernacular languages as media of literature and education (and consequently of collective self-awareness) was closely linked to the use of historical material and themes.[22] It was in literature that ethnic and cultural differences were first articulated, which were later used by communalist politicians to define national demarcations. The negative characteristics which were described in Bankimchandra's novels as typical of the Muslims could be associated with the Christians in Urdu literature.[23] The novels and narratives of Abdul Halim Sharar (1860–1926) depicted the glorious past of Islam and its superiority over western civilization.[24] The Muslims' role in the history of the Indian nation is at the centre of Abdul Karim (1863–1943), *Bharatbarshe musalman rajatver itibrtta* (Calcutta: Sanskrit Press Depository, 1898), and of Ismail Husain Siraj (1880–1931), author of the ballade *Anal prabaha*.[25] Representative of communalist tendencies among the Sikhs are the novels of Bhai Vir Singh.[26] However, there were also other approaches to cultural difference: Bhudev Chandra Mukhopadhyay (1827–94), in *Swapnalabdha Bharatbarsher Itihas* (The History of India as Revealed in a Dream, 1876), described the Hindu-Muslim relations in the language of kinship.[27]

BANKIMCHANDRA CHATTERJEE (1838–94) was one of the leading intellectuals in nineteenth-century Bengal. As a writer of historical novels, he stimulated the patriotic sentiment of his readers, 'dreaming up the icon of the nation' (Kaviraj 1995: 137). In his essays, he was not only one of

[21]*Aitihasik Chitra* was edited by Akshaykumar Maitreya (author of *Sirajuddaula*, 1897) and appeared, with interruptions, from 1899 until 1913.

[22]Cf. Ranajit Guha:1988: 28ff. For the blend of fiction and history in Oriya literature, with special reference to kavyas of Radhanath Roy, see Subhakanta Behera, 'Recreating History in Literature', *EPW* (3 June, 2000), 1901–3.

[23]Mukherjee 1985: 62–3. For Bankimchandra Chatterji, see below.

[24]See for instance Abdul Halim Sharar, *Lucknow: the last phase of an oriental culture*, a collection of essays originally published under the title 'Hinduism Men Mashriqi Tamaddun ka Akhri Namuna' in the magazine *Dil Gudaz* in (Lucknow 1913ff.).

[25]Cf. Partha Chatterjee 1995: 108. See also Rafiuddin Ahmed 1981.

[26]Cf. Oberoi 1981. For the historical tradition of the Sikhs, see Fauja Singh 1978. For the emergence of group identities in colonial and postcolonial South Asia, see Dietrich Reetz, 'In Search of the Collective Self: How Ethnic Group Concepts were Cast through Conflict in Colonial India', *MAS* 31 (1997), 285–315; Mitra and Lewis 1996.

[27]*Bhudev Racana Sambhar*, ed. Pramathanath Bisi (Calcutta: Mitra and Ghosh, 1969), 341–74. Cf. Partha Chatterjee 1995: 110ff., 222–3. For the history of mutual perceptions of Hindus and Muslims, see N. K. Wagle, 'Hindu-Muslim Interactions in Medieval Maharashtra', in Kulke and Sontheimer 1989: 51–66. For the recovery of non-modern forms of community, see the works of Kaviraj, Chatterjee, Nandy, etc., Section 4.2.

the first 'systematic expounders in India of the principles of nationalism' (Partha Chatterjee 1986: 54), but he also laid down the programmatic foundation of a modern, politically minded historiography.[28]

> Bankimchandra Chatterjee (Chattopadhyaya) was born in Kanthalpara near Calcutta. His father was a wealthy Kulin Brahman, serving the British authorities as a customs officer. Bankimchandra attended the University of Calcutta and was one of its first graduates. From 1869 to 1891, he worked as Deputy Magistrate in the colonial administrative service. As editor of the magazine Bangadarshan, he aimed to improve Bengali as a literary idiom. With his narratives, treatises and essays on social, philosophical and religious questions, he exerted a considerable influence on the literally and politically interested public.

Bankimchandra's historical interest first manifested itself in his dealing with European history, society, and literature. He felt particularly influenced by positivism and utilitarianism, and he tried to reconcile modern approaches to society with Indian traditions of thinking. He viewed the Italian Renaissance as an experience of exemplary importance for the present situation of Bengal.[29]

In a series of essays on the history and historiography of Bengal, Bankimchandra criticized the misinterpretations of the past in western accounts and outlined alternatives of a true Bengali history.[30] The following extract is taken from one of these articles.

[28]The importance of Bankimchandra for the historical consciousness in modern India is reflected in the fact that various studies on the subject focus on his work. Partha Chatterjee interprets Bankimchandra's thinking as being representative of the 'moment of departure' of Indian nationalism and shows the ambivalence between his approach to the 'problematic' and the unconscious surrender to the 'thematic' of Orientalism. The Self is conceived as the Other of the European (and according to the latter's categories). There is no attempt here to define the 'boundaries of the Indian nation *from within.*' Partha Chatterjee 1986: 55 For suppressed alternative approaches, of Bankimchandra himself as well as other contemporary authors, cf. Partha Chatterjee 1993: 113ff. Ranajit Guha, too, views Bankimchandra's manner of redemption of the claim to historicity as being in a problematic relation to his anticolonial intentions. The admiration of the modernity and physical strength of the British does not allow their colonizing character to become visible. Guha 1988: 3, 65. Sudipta Kaviraj speaks, in view of the dilemma between (desired) modernity and (accepted) subordination, of the 'unhappy consciousness' of Bankimchandra. Kaviraj 1995: 168.

[29]Before the term 'Bengal Renaissance' came into use to denote the epoch of early modernization, the analogy between the rediscovery of ancient Indian civilization and that of classical antiquity in Europe had been stressed by William Jones and Max Müller. Bankimchandra himself referred mainly to the period of Hindu resistance against the Muslims in the sixteenth and seventeenth centuries. The European pattern of periodization (classical Antiquity, dark Middle Ages, and Renaissance) offered many Hindus a plausible way of how to make modernization compatible with the pride in their own culture and, at the same time, give justification to the existing anti-Muslim feelings. The British self-representation as liberators from Muslim despotism also conformed to European anti-Islamism. Cf. Partha Chatterjee 1993: 102. For the use of Renaissance analogues in modern Indian history, see Barun De, 'A Historiographical Critique of Renaissance Analogues for Nineteenth Century India' in idem 1977, 178–218. A discussion of the concept of Renaissance is also found in Aurobindo, 'The Renaissance in India', Arya (Aug.–Nov. 1918).

[30]Bankimchandra's investigations into the works of contemporary historians are generally seen as a directive

A Few Words about the History of Bengal (1882–3)

A nation with historical reminiscences of its past glory tries to retain its glory, and if this be lost, it tries to regain it. The reminiscences of Crecy and Agincourt resulted in Blenheim and Waterloo—after its downfall, Italy rebuilt itself.[31] Nowadays Bengalees want to be great, but alas! Where are the historical reminiscences of Bengalees?

A history of Bengal is needed, otherwise Bengalees would not become complete beings. A person who keeps thinking that his ancestors have not achieved anything of value will not achieve anything himself. He thinks that this defect in his blood has been inherited. The seeds of the bitter 'Neem' (Magosa) germinate into bitter 'Neem' saplings. The seed of 'Makal' (a fruit which looks attractive but is inedible) yields only 'Makal' fruits. Bengalees who think their ancestors were weak, had no worth, did not achieve anything, had no greatness, they do not expect themselves to be anything but weak, of no worth and have no glory. They do not hope or strive to achieve much else, and without effort you do not achieve anything. But have the Bengalees indeed been always worth nothing, been weak and inglorious? The conquest of Ganesha, Chaitanya's Religion, Raghunatha's, Gadadhara's and Jagadisha's systems of logic, the verses of Mukundadasa, Joydeva and Vidyapati—where did these originate from?[32] There are also many more weak, worthless, inglorious nations upon this earth. But which of them has left us such great and permanent achievement as these works mentioned here? Don't you think that there must be some true substance in the history of Bengal?

But from where can we get the true substance? Is there any history of Bengal? The British wrote plenty of books on the history of Bengal—Mr Stewart's book is so voluminous and heavy that a strong, young man might be killed if it is thrown at him! Marshman and Lothbridge even earned a lot of money by writing the history of Bengal in a 'gossipy' style.[33] But do these books contain any historical facts about Bengal? In our opinion, none of these books written by British authors contain a true history of Bengal. These books contain only the history of those Muslims who gave themselves worthless titles such as 'Bengali Badshah', 'Subedar of Bengal', etc. They spent most of their time without any worries, in bed! This history of Bengal chronicles their births, deaths, family feuds, and food habits. But this is not the true history of Bengal—it is not even a partial history of Bengal. It does not have any connection with Bengal's history and it does not contain any history of Bengal. A Bengalee who accepts this account as being Bengal's history is not a true Bengalee. A Bengalee who is ready to accept without question the validity

---

for modern historical thought in India and, in particular, as a 'landmark in the growth of modern historical research and writing in Bengal'. Partha Chatterjee 1993: 247. According to A. R. Mallick, they were the great force encouraging the Bengali 'to undertake the research for an authentic history of his country'. 'Modern Historical Writing in Bengali', in Philips 1961: 446–60, here 449.

[31]English victories over the French in the Hundred Years' War (1346 resp. 1415), in the Spanish Succession War (Blindheim, Höchstädt, 1704) and in the war against Napoleon (1815).

[32]Chaitanya (1485–1533), founder of a Krishna sect in Bengal; Raghunatha Siromani (c. 1477–1547), Ganghadhara Batthacarya, Jagadisha Batthacarya: philosophers of the systems of Nyaya and Vaisheshika; Jayadeva's Gitagovinda (twelfth century) celebrates Krishna's love for Radha.

[33]Stewart 1813; Marshman 1844.

of facts laid down by Muslims, who are not only blinded by self-pride, but are also liars and full of hatred for the Hindus, is himself not a Bengalee. [...]

There is no history of Bengal. What goes by the name of it—that is no history. It is fiction—partly the account of the lives of a few worthless oppressors who were foreigners and belonged to a different religion. We need a history of Bengal otherwise there is no hope for Bengal. But who will write it? You will write it, I will write it, everyone will write this history. Whosoever is a Bengalee will write it. When the mother dies, there is so much joy in reminiscing about her! And this Bengal—the mother of all, the land of our birth—don't we find pleasure in talking about her?

Come, let us search for the history of Bengal. Whatever little is possible, let every individual do it—a small insect can build an island which stretches over miles. This is not to be done by one individual—it has to be done through collective effort. Many people might not know where to look for it. I am giving you a few examples. Where did the Bengalees originate from? Some say superficially that Bengalees are Aryans. But are all Bengalees Aryans? The Brahmins are indeed Aryans, but the members of the lower castes such as the 'Hari', 'Dom', 'Muchi' [cobbler], 'Karoa', are they also Aryans? If not, then where did they come from? To which family of non-Aryans do they belong? When did their forefathers come to Bengal? Who came first—the Aryans or indeed the non-Aryans? [...] How long has Europe been civilised? 400 years back in the fifteenth century Europe was even more uncivilised than us. By stroke of one incident Europe became civilised. All of a sudden Europe got back the perished, forgotten own Greek literature. Like a thin stream gets swelled by the rain water and inundate its banks, or a dying patient gets back his youthful strength after taking a miraculous medicine Europe suddenly flourished. [...] The Mughals after conquering Bengal tightened their rule, but how far was their rule extended? They expanded their kingdom, but how far did they come? [...] When did the Zamindari system come into being and how? What kind of position did they have during the Mughal empire? [...] When did the half of the indigenous population become Muslims? Why did they leave their religion? Why did they convert to Islam? Which castes converted to Islam? This is the most important information in the history of Bengal.

[From: Chatterjee, 'Bangalar Itihas Sambandhe Kayekti Katha,' in *Bankim Rachanavali*, ed. by Jogesh Chandra Bagal, II (Calcutta: Sahitya Samsad, 1965), 336–40. English translation by Sunanda Basu and Subhoranjan Das Gupta.][34]

Bankimchandra's own project of a history of Bengal was not realized. So it was mainly through his epic literature that he worked for the desired national and historical consciousness.[35] After he

[34]The text was originally published in *Bangadarshan* (1882–3). The other essays of Bankimchandra in *Bangadarshan* dealing with history are: 'Bharat-kalamka', 'Bangalar Itihas', 'Bangalar Itihaser Bhagnangsha', 'Bangalar Kalamka', all in *Bankim Rachanavali*, II.

[35]Dealing with the past in fiction rather than historiography also preserved the author, who was in the services of the colonial administration, from exposing himself politically. But even if the past always has to be 'invented' to a certain degree, the 'imaginary histories of resistance' suffered due to an indistinct relationship between fictionality and the illusion of the factual. On the one hand Bankimchandra was convinced of the

had written a novel in English (*Raj Mohan's Wife*) during his school days, he gained literary fame as a Bengali author with *Durgeshnandini* (1864).[36] This was followed by a long series of other novels, eight of which had a historical thematic, often dealing with Hindu resistance against foreign rule. Through the medium of 'imaginary history' (Kaviraj), Bankimchandra sought to create a new political self-confidence, 'to explore the potential forces and the new values dormant in the present.'[37] Novels like *Anandamath* and *Devi Chaudhurani* were designed to promote what empirical research and historiography had not achieved so far.[38]

Anandamath is the best-known and most powerful of Bankimchandra's novels—a key text for the first generation of Indian nationalists. The following extract gives an idea of how the narration creates a feeling of national solidarity and patriotic enthusiasm. The background is the uprising of an order of sannyasis fighting against Muslim troops under British leadership during the period of the declining power of the Nawab of Bengal and the emerging East India Company.[39] In chapter XI, it is narrated how Mahendra, who, along with his family, has left his village because of a famine, is introduced to the cult of the 'children' in the 'Abbey of Bliss'.[40]

Anandamath (1882)

The next day dawned. The desolate woods, so long dark and still, resounded gleefully with the joyous notes of birds. In that blissful morn and in that happy wood, Satyananda was sitting on

power of the imaginative, on the other hand heroism and national agency were assumed to be already existing. For the 'Discourse of Factual History', see Kaviraj, 1995, 117, 124ff.

[36]*Durgeshnandini* has been called 'the first Bengali novel in the modern European style, and the first work of creative imagination in Bengali prose'. J. C. Ghosh 1948: 152.

[37]Shantinath K. Desai, 'History as Setting', in Bhabatosh Chatterjee 1994: 508–11, here 509.

[38]'In his novels he provides alternative narratives through the construction of imaginary forces of resistance.' Meenakshi Mukherji, 'Rhetoric of Identity: History and Fiction in Nineteenth Century India', in Bhalla and Chandra 1993: 34–47, here 38. Bankimchandra was praised for his handling of historical material in his works even by renowned researchers like Jadunath Sarkar who, with reference to *Sitaram* (1887), emphasized that the events 'as delineated by the author are in the main accurate' and 'the backdrop of the novel is historically authentic'. Sarkar, 'Sitaram', in: Bhabatosh Chatterjee 1994: 89–99, here 89. Sarkar wrote an introduction for the Sahitya Parisad edition of *Anandamath*.

[39]There are contemporary references as well as historical ones: in 1879, Wamdeo (Vasudev) Balwant Phadke had been arrested and banned because of insurgent activities against the British, partly in collaboration with a group of sannyasis. The historical point of reference is a sannyasi rebellion during the famine of 1772–3. Just as in his other historical novels, Bankimchandra followed a historiographical account of the events, in this case Hunter 1868. Cf. A. K. Ray, 'History and the Romantic Imagination', in Bhabatosh Chatterjee 1994: 512–17, here 512–13.

[40]Problems for a political interpretation of the novel have been created by the way it ends, because after the defeat of the foreigners, during an appearance of God, the leader of the rebels, Satyananda, is advised to suspend the struggle instead of establishing immediately the desired Hindu empire. Maybe, British rule is thus accepted as a necessary step on the way to regaining strength—an interpretation that is suggested also by other texts of Bankimchandra. Nor do the critics agree on whether or not the emotions stirred up against the Muslims were actually directed towards the British. According to S. K. Desai, 'he prophesies the ultimate liberation of Mother India from the shackles of British imperialism.' 'History as setting', loc. cit., 511. Kaviraj sees in the

his deer-skin seat in the Abbey of Bliss for saying his morning prayer. Near him sat Jivananda. At this time Bhavananda came there with Mahendra. The monk silently went on with his worship and no one ventured to speak. When his prayers were done, Bhavananda and Jivananda both saluted him and took the dust of his feet before humbly taking their seats. Satyananda then beckoned to Bhavananda and took him out. We do not know what they talked about, but they shortly came back and the monk feelingly spoke to Mahendra with a smiling face: 'My child, I am very much distressed at your troubles. By the grace of the Lord alone could I save your wife and child last night. He then told him the story of Kalyani's rescue and said, 'Come. I will take you where they are.' So saying the monk led the way and Mahendra followed him into the temple. On entering it he found it to be a very high and spacious chamber. Even in the glorious morn smiling with the infant sun, when the woods were glistening as if decked with diamonds, this vast room was very dark. Mahendra could not at first see what there was in the room, but gazing and gazing on, he presently found a huge four-handed image, bearing in its four hands, the Conch, the Disc, the Club, and the Lotus; the Kaustubha shining in its breast and the Sudarsan Chakra before it looking as if it turned.[41] Two huge decapitated forms stood before it, painted as if drenched in blood, representing Madhu and Kaitabha.[42] To the left stood Lakshmi, the goddess of wealth, as though shaking with fear, with her ample locks flowing at ease and a garland of lilies on. To the right was Saraswati, the goddess of learning, surrounded with books and instruments of music and embodied symphonies. On the lap of Vishnu sat a charming figure, fairer far than Lakshmi or Saraswati and richer far than both. Super-human beings like the *Gandharvas, Kinnaras, Yakshas,* and *Rakshitas,* its were engaged in worshipping her.

The ascetic asked Mahendra in a deep and resounding tone if he saw everything there. 'Yes' answered Mahendra. 'Have you seen what is there on Vishnu's lap?' 'Aye, but who is *she?*' 'The Mother.' 'Who is the Mother?' 'She whose children we are.' 'Who is *she?*' 'You will know by and by; now say, "Hail Mother" and come to see more.'[43]

Then the ascetic led Mahendra to another chamber where he found a complete image of Jagaddhatri,[44] perfect and luxuriously decorated. Mahendra asked, 'Who is this?' 'The Mother,' said the celebate, 'as she *was.*' 'What do you mean by that?' 'In the past, she trampled under her feet the lion, the tusker and other beasts, and built her own beauteous palace over their homes.

'double endings' of the novels a conscious handling of the fact that the narration has an end, whereas history is open-ended. Kaviraj 1995: 150ff.

[41]*gadha:* club; *kaustubha:* jewel; *sudarsan chakra:* a wheel-shaped weapon. All of them are symbols of Vishnu.

[42]Madhu, Kaitabha: demons killed by Vishnu.

[43]The hymn 'Bande Mataram' ('I bow before thee, mother') sung by the 'children' became a battle-cry of the freedom movement during the agitation against the partition of Bengal (1905) and a sort of national anthem which was sung on the occasion of INC-sessions. This, however, met with the protest of the Muslims, who felt excluded. To venerate the homeland as the mother was 'highly non-standard in Hindu mythology', nor followed the pictorial representation of the 'mother' in the novel a practised cult. Cf. Kaviraj 1995: 137–8 It may be seen, however, as an allusion to the traditional Durga-Puja in Bengal. The western stereotype of the Indian character as effeminate is given a self-assertive turn by Bankim: the feminine is used by him as 'his constant symbol of power.' Ibid., 116.

[44]Jagaddhatri: mother goddess holding the earth.

She was adorned in a full suit of ornaments and was ever smiling and fair. She was like the young sun of the morning and is here painted in its hue. Make your obeisance to her.'

After Mahendra had bowed before the image of his mother-country which stood in the shape of the protectress of the world, the anchorite showed him a narrow tunnel and bade him come by it. He himself went before and Mahendra followed him apprehensively to a dark underground chamber where a streak of light had straggled in somehow. In that dim light he saw the figure of Kali.[45]

The celebate observed. 'Look what the mother has *now* become.' Mahendra cried with horror, 'Oh, Kali!' 'Yes, Kali, covered with the blackest gloom, despoiled of all wealth, and without a cloth to wear. The whole of the country is a land of death and so the Mother has no better ornament than a garland of skulls. Her own Good she cruelly tramples under her foot! Alas Mother!'

Tears rolled down the cheeks of the monk. Mahendra asked, 'Why are there arms in her hand?' 'We are her *children*, we have only just given her the arms. Say, "Hail, Mother".' Mahendra said, 'Hail, Mother' and made his bow to Kali. Then the monk showed him the way through another tunnel, bid Mahendra follow him, and himself began to climb up. Suddenly the rays of the morning sun flashed before their eyes and sweet warblers poured forth their delicious songs. In a large marble temple to which the alley led, Mahendra saw a golden image of the ten-handed goddess smiling brightly in the morning sun.

Bowing to this goddess, the monk observed: 'This is the mother as she *would be*:—her ten hands spreading on all sides and her varied powers appearing in them in the form of so many arms:—the enemy trampled under her feet and the lion at her feet engaged in killing her foes. Her hands,' he said, and tears rose to his eyes,—'point to all sides; the wielder of many arms and chastiser of her foes she stands—with luck-giving Lakshmi to her right and Vani, the spring of knowledge and science, to her left. With her stand Kartik, the emblem of strength, and Ganesa, the god of success.[46] Come, let us join in saluting her.' So saying, they joined their palms and looking upwards sang in harmony: *Sarva-mangal-mangalye sive sarvatha-sadhike saranye, tryambake gouri narayani namostute.*[47] They both bowed with deepest reverence, and when they rose, Mahendra inquired with a choking voice: 'When shall we look at this form of the mother?' 'When,' said the monk, 'all the children of the mother learn to call her so, then will she be propitiated.'

Mahendra abruptly asked, 'Where are my wife and daughter?' 'Come and you will see them.' 'Yes! I will see them but once, and then bid them adieu.' 'Why?' 'I want to take your noble vow.' 'Where would you send them,' asked the monk. Mahendra mused and then said, 'There is nobody in my house, I have no other place of refuge. And, in truth, where else would I find an

---

[45]In the appearance of the goddess Kali, symbolizing India as female divine force (*shakti*), religious pathos and politics are combined in a way typical of Bankimchandra and other Indian nationalists. The appeal to dark sentiment is seen by some as a regressive element. Cf. *Sources of Indian Tradition*, II, 131. How near this is to European forms of sacralizing national sentiment shows a comparison of the scene presented here with Giacomo Leopardi's poem 'All'Italia' (1818).

[46]Vani: Sarasvati; Kartik: son of Shiva.

[47]'She, who turns everything to the good and brings it to a success, she is to be hailed; salutations to Gauri and Narayani'.

asylum in these dire days?' 'Go out of the temple by the way you came by. At the door you will find your wife and daughter. Kalyani has not yet taken any food. You will find food where they are sitting. Give her some and then take what you like yourself; now you will not meet any of us. If your mind, however, remains unchanged, I shall come to you in proper time.'

Then suddenly the monk vanished by some strange passage. Coming out by the way shown to him, Mahendra saw Kalyani seated with her daughter within the pavilion on the yard.

[From: Chatterjee, *The Abbey of Bliss*, English translation by Nares Chandra Sen-Gupta (Calcutta: P. M. Neogi, 1906), 38–43.][48]

With nationalism on the rise, it was frequently the politicians who, in autobiographical reflections or through their own research, attempted to gain and offer historical orientation. Tilak and Savarkar are only two instances of a large number of activists in the freedom struggle who used history for political purposes.[49] The Arya Samaj leader Lajpat Rai (1865–1928) declared imperialism to be his 'sole object in referring to the past history of India'.[50] The RSS ideologue Madhav Sadashiv Golwalkar (1906–73), in his book *We, or our Nationhood Defined* (Nagpur 1939), based his definition of national solidarity on the strict opposition of Hindus and Muslims.[51] Both the communalist interpretations of history and those of the declared secularists were closely connected with political strategies.[52] The nationalist leader Subhas Chandra Bose (1897–1945) invoked the unity of all Indians in the resistance to British rule (Bipan Chandra 1986: 215, 234). Among the Muslim politicians it was the INC leader Maulana Abul Kalam Azad (1888–1958) who deduced an all-Indian perspective from the experience of a shared history.[53]

[48]Bengali text in: *Bankim Rachanavali* (Calcutta: Sahitya Samsad, 1958), I, 715–88 (11th ed. 1992, 581–644). The novel appeared first (1881) in serialized form in Bankimchandra's magazine *Bangadarshan* and one year later as a book. Before the end of the century, there were four new editions. It was translated into the major Indian languages and, in 1906, for the first time into English (by N. C. Sengupta). A second English translation was done by Aurobindo and his brother Barindrakumar Ghosh (1909). A translation by Basanta Coomar Roy with alterations of the text in the last part appeared under the title *Dawn over India* (New York 1941). For the second edition (1884), Bankimchandra wrote a Preface, in which he also specified his sources. Further reading: T. W. Clark, 'The Role of Bankimchandra in the Development of Nationalism', in Philips 1961: 429–45.

[49]For the social and political context of the emerging national consciousness, see A. R. Desai 1946.

[50]Lala Lajpat Rai, *Young India* (Delhi 1965), 32, quoted in Bipan Chandra, 'Nationalist Historians' Interpretations of the Indian National Movement', in Bhattacharya and Thapar 1986: 194–238, here 214. For a survey of historical research on the national movement in India, see S. P. Sen 1977; selected sources of Indian nationalism are found in Kedourie 1970.

[51]For the sake of the unity of people and territory, Golwalkar rejected the assumption of an Aryan invasion or migration to India. Cf. Bipan Chandra 1984: 217–18, 228. See also S. P. Udayakumar, 'Mapping the "Hindu" Re-Making of India', *Gandhi Marg* (Jan.-March 1998), 443–60. Even popular genres and oral traditions played an important role in the context of identity formation. Cf. Chandra, ibid., 211.

[52]Often it was in a political context that the premises were formulated which then guided the work of researchers. For the impact of the two-nation theory on historiography, see Satish Chandra, 'History Writing in Pakistan and the Two-Nation Theory', in idem. 1997: 43–56.

[53]See Azad's speech during the INC session at Ramgarh (1940): Ramachandrasekhara Rao 1969: 73–5.

BAL GANGADHAR TILAK (1856–1920) was one of those nationalist politicians who used Hindu traditions, customs, and sentiments as a powerful motive in the freedom fight. In his historical studies, he sought to establish the high antiquity of the Vedic culture and make it an element of national self-confidence.

> Tilak descended from a family of land owning Chitpavan Brahmans in Maharashtra; his father was a school-teacher. After studying law at Deccan College (Pune), Tilak became a committed educator and participated in establishing the Deccan Education Society and Fergusson College. As editor of the magazines Kesari and Mahratta, he wielded considerable influence on public opinion. Increasingly, he distanced himself from the moderate reformist politics of Ranade and Gokhale. He was imprisoned for sedition in 1897. The agitation over the partition of Bengal (1905) brought him into close contact with the extremists in the INC, and he finally became their leader. The British authorities reacted to his public instistence on swaraj and swadeshi by banning him to Mandalay in Burma (1908–14). Tilak's followers gave him the title Lokamanya ('honoured by the people'); for the British he became known as the 'father of Indian unrest'.

Fired with enthusiasm for Maratha history since his early years when he listened to the accounts of his grandfather, Tilak was influenced in his way of thinking and acting by the image of a glorious Indian past. In his book The Orion: Researches into the Antiquity of the Vedas (Bombay 1893), he tried to derive the superiority of the Indo-Aryans from early testimonies of their culture ('not later than 4000 BC'). In The Arctic Home in the Vedas. Being Also a New Key to the Interpretation of Many Vedic Texts and Legends (Pune 1903), he sought to prove the origin of the Aryans from the North.[54] During his imprisonment at Mandalay, Tilak wrote a two-volume commentary on the Bhagavadgita (Gita Rahasya: The Secret Meaning of the Gita, 1911), again with the intention of orientating political action by referring to cultural heritage.[55]

Just like Bankimchandra, Tilak relied to a large extent on the psychology of hero-worship. In search of 'inspiration and vitality', he made the Maratha prince Shivaji (1627–80), who had fought against Mughal rule, into a swadeshi hero. Tilak's conclusion about the success of Shivaji was: 'His life clearly shows that Indian races do not so soon lose the vitality which gives them able leaders at critical times.'[56] Shivaji's grave became a pilgrimage centre and his birthdays and his coronation anniversaries were celebrated as national holidays. National revivalist movements in Europe, such as the Italian Risorgimento, were used as a model. In the Bombay Ganesh processions, portraits of Garibaldi and Mazzini were shown (Borsa and Beonio-Brocchieri 1984).

(Included in this selection of testimonies are other important texts on political, economic and cultural aspects of modern India). For the faceting of standpoints also among the Muslims (anti-imperialist, anti-Hindu, pan-Islamic), see Bipan Chandra 1984: 233.

[54]Both texts in: Samagra Lokmanya Tilak, II (Poona: Kosari Prakashan, 1975).

[55]An unfinished 'Vedic Chronology and Vedanta Jyotisha' was published posthumously (1925).

[56]'Is Shivaji not a National Hero?' [1906], in Tilak 1922: 28–32, here 30–1. Tilak here defends the worship of Shivaji and the use of religious symbols in the freedom struggle against the criticism on the part of the moderates.

Karma Yoga and Swaraj (c. 1917)

The Karma Yoga which I preach is not a new theory; neither was the discovery of the Law of Karma made as recently as today. The knowledge of the Law is so ancient that not even Shri Krishna was the great Teacher who first propounded it. It must be remembered that Karma Yoga has been our sacred heritage from times immemorial when we Indians were seated on the high pedestal of wealth and lore. Karma Yoga or to put it in another way, the law of duty is the combination of all that is best in spiritual science, in actual action and in an unselfish meditative life. Compliance with this universal Law leads to the realization of the most cherished ideals of Man. Swaraj is the natural consequence of diligent performance of duty. The Karma Yoga strives for Swaraj, and the Gnyanin or spiritualist yearns for it. What is then this Swaraj? It is a life centred in Self and dependent upon Self. There is Swaraj in this world as well as in the world hereafter. The Rishis who laid down the Law of Duty betook themselves to forests, because the people were already enjoying Swaraj or People's Dominion, which was administered and defended in the first instance by the Kshatriya kings. It is my conviction, it is my thesis, that Swaraj in the life to come cannot be the reward of a people who have not enjoyed it in this world. Such was the doctrine taught by our forefathers who never intended that the goal of life should be meditation alone. No one can expect Providence to protect one who sits with folded arms and throws his burden on others. God does not help the indolent. You must be doing all that you can to lift yourself up, and then only you may rely on the Almighty to help you. You should not, however, presume that you have to toil that you yourself might reap the fruit of your labours. That cannot always be the case. Let us then try our utmost and leave the generations to come to enjoy that fruit. Remember, it is not you who had planted the mango-trees the fruit whereof you have tasted. Let the advantage now go to our children and their descendants. It is only given to us to toil and work. And so, there ought to be no relaxation in our efforts, lest we incur the curse of those that come after us. Action alone must be our guiding principle, action disinterested and well-thought-out. It does not matter who the Sovereign is. It is enough if we have full liberty to elevate ourselves in the best possible manner. This is called immutable Dharma, and Karma Yoga is nothing but the method which leads to the attainment of Dharma or material and spiritual glory. We demand Swaraj, as it is the foundation and not the height of our future prosperity. Swaraj does not at all imply a denial of British Sovereignty or British aegis. It means only that we Indians should be reckoned among the patriotic and self-respecting people of the Empire. We must refuse to be treated like the 'dumb driven cattle.' If poor Indians starve in famine days it is other people who take care of them. This is not an enviable position. It is neither creditable nor beneficial if other people have to do everything for us. God has declared His will. He has willed that Self can be exalted only through its own efforts. Everything lies in your hands. Karma Yoga does not look upon this world as nothing; it requires only that your motives should be untainted by selfish interest and passion. This is the true view of practical Vedanta the key to which is apt to be lost in sophistry.

In practical politics some futile objections are raised to oppose our desire for Swaraj. Illiteracy of the bulk of our people is one of such objections; but to my mind it ought not to be allowed to stand in our way. It would be sufficient for our purpose even if the illiterate in our country have only a vague conception of Swaraj, just as it all goes well with them if they have simply a hazy idea about God. Those who can efficiently manage their own affairs may be illiterate; but they are not therefore idiots. They are as intelligent as any educated man and if they could understand their village concerns they should not find any difficulty in grasping the principle of Swaraj. If illiteracy is not a disqualification in Civil Law, there is no reason why it should not be so in Nature's Law also. The illiterate are our brethren; they have the same rights and are actuated by the same aspiration. It is therefore our bounden duty to awaken the masses. Circumstances are changed, nay, they are favourable. The voice has gone forth 'Now or never'. Rectitude and constitutional agitation is alone what is expected of you. Turn not back, and confidently leave the ultimate issue to the benevolence of the Almighty.

[From: Tilak, 'Karma Yoga and Swaraj', in B. G. Tilak (*Political Thinkers of Modern India, IV*), ed. by Verinder Grover (New Delhi: Deep & Deep Publications, 1990), 215–7.][57]

VINAYAK DAMODAR SAVARKAR (1883–1966) made the awareness of a common history a central component in the formation of national identity. By narrowing the perspective to the fight for Hindu survival and laying emphasis on the antagonism between Hindus and Muslims, he prepared the ground for the communalist interpretation of Indian history.

> *Savarkar was born at Nasik in Maharashtra; he belonged to a family of Chitpavan Brahmans who set great store by traditional Indian and western education alike. Personal experience in his early youth made him hostile to anything alien. As a student at Fergusson College (Pune), he founded a 'Patriotic Society' in order to inspire his co-students with the glorious Indian past and to motivate them to fight actively for freedom. With the help of Tilak, he obtained a scholarship to study in England. As a law student in London (1906 to 1910), Savarkar was an activist of the Abhinav Bharat (Young India) group, which also planned terrorist actions (on the agenda was the assassination of the Viceroy, Lord Curzon). When a member of the group killed an official of the India Office, Savarkar was arrested (1911) and deported to the Andaman Islands, where he stayed till 1924. In 1937, Savarkar was elected president of the Hindu Mahasabha. After Independence, he remained politically active and supported the RSS in its agitation against the secular state.*

Savarkar's early historical interest is reflected in a history of the Sikhs (1907) and an account of Shivaji and the Marathas (Savarkar 1925). The Italian Risorgimento was used by him as a model for regaining past greatness. He compared Shivaji to Garibaldi and he translated Mazzini's autobiography into Marathi.[58]

Savarkar's account of the Indian uprising of 1857–8, written during the stay in London, is

[57]Reprint with kind permission by Deep & Deep Publications, New Delhi. First published in *Poona Sarvajanik Sabha Quarterly*. Further reading: S. M. Garge, 'Tilak's Standpoint regarding History', in Inamdar 1983: 155–9; S. S. Barlingay, 'L'historie, l'être historique et l'historiographie', in: *Histoire et diversité des cultures* (1984), 193–213, here 206ff.

[58]Savarkar 1946. Gandhi, in one of his essays (*CW*, V, 27–8) and in *Hind Swaraj* (see below, Section 3), rejected Savarkar's appreciation of Mazzini as a violent revolutionary.

an early attempt to rewrite Indian history. By interpreting the events as the 'First Indian War of Independence', that is as a warlike action instead of a mere 'Mutiny', Savarkar hoped once more 'to inspire the people to rise and wage a war to liberate their motherland'.[59] In fact, this 'Bible of the Indian revolutionaries' was later held responsible for the rising of another armed resistance, that of Subhas Chandra Bose's Indian National Army in the 1940s: 'Thanks to Savarkar's book [the] Indian sense of a "Mutiny" has been itself revolutionised.'[60] Even after 1947, the work was hailed as a 'major breakthrough in the mutiny studies' because Savarkar was the first to perceive an Indian standpoint and 'to hold very firm views on the popular character of the movement'.[61]

The Indian War of Independence (1909)

What, then, were the real causes and motives of this Revolution? What were they that they could make thousands of heroes unsheath their swords and flash them on the battlefield? What were they that they had the power to brighten up pale and rusty crowns and raise from the dust abased flags? What were they that for them men by the thousand willingly poured their blood year after year? What were they that Moulvies[62] preached them, learned Brahmins blessed them, that for their success prayers went up to Heaven from the mosques of Delhi and the temples of Benares?

These great principles were Swadharma and Swaraj.[63] The thundering roar of 'Din, Din', which rose to protect religion, when there were evident signs of a cunning, dangerous, and destructive attack on religion dearer than life,[64] and in the terrific blows dealt at the chain of slavery with the holy desire of acquiring Swaraj, when it was evident that chains of political slavery had been put round them and their God-given liberty wrested away by subtle tricks—in these two, lies the root-principle of the Revolutionary War. In what other history is the principle of love of one's religion and love of one's country manifested more nobly than in ours? However much foreign and partial historians might have tried to paint our glorious land in dark colours, so long as the name of Chitore has not been erased from the pages of our history, so long as the names of Pratapaditya and Guru Govind Singh are there, so long the principles of Swadharma

[59]See G. M. Joshi in his preface, 'The Story of this History', IX. Nevertheless, without making reference to Savarkar's work, the Institute of Marxism-Leninism of the C.C., C.P.S.U., too, has published Marx's and Engels's newspaper articles on the 'Revolt in India' under the title *The First Indian War of Independence 1857–9* (Moscow 1959).

[60]S. Subbarao, quoted in Joshi's preface, p. XIX. R. C. Majumdar later described the Independence movement of the twentieth century as the second Indian war of liberation, even if he, in his own account of the Mutiny, explicitly contested its interpretation as a national uprising: R.C. Majumdar 1963 [1957]. See below.

[61]Sashi B. Chaudhuri 1965: 23–4. The historical experience of the Mutiny became an important element of national self-assertion in the independence movement. Even for historical research in post-Independence India, the Mutiny represents a central issue. For a survey, see S. N. Sen, 'Writings on the Mutiny', in Philips 1961: 373–84; S. B. Chaudhury 1979; Snigdha Sen 1992 (on Savarkar: 157–73). From a different perspective: Darshan Perusek, 'Subaltern Consciousness and Historiography of Indian Rebellion of 1857', *EPW* (11 September 1993), 1931–6.

[62]moulvies: Islamic scholars.

[63]swadharma and swaraj: indigenous morals and self-rule.

[64]The rebellion broke out on the rumour that, for the lubrication of guns, animal grease had been used.

and Swaraj will be embedded in the bone and marrow of all the sons of Hindusthan![65] They might be darkened for a time by the mist of slavery—even the sun has its clouds—but very soon the strong light of these self-same principles pierces through the mist and chases it away.

Never before were there such a number of causes for the universal spreading of these traditional and noble principles as there were in 1857. These particular reasons revived most wonderfully the slightly unconscious feelings of Hindusthan, and the people began to prepare for the fight for Swadharma and Swaraj. In his Proclamation of the establishment of Swaraj, the Emperor of Delhi says, 'Oh, you sons of Hindusthan, if we make up our mind we can destroy the enemy in no time! We will destroy the enemy and will release from dread our religion and our country, dearer to us than life itself.' What is holier in this world than such a Revolutionary War, a war for the noble principles propounded in this sentence, 'release from dread our religion and our country, dearer to us than life itself?' The seed of the Revolution of 1857 is in this holy and inspiring idea, clear and explicit, propounded from the throne of Delhi, the protection of religion and country.

[From: Savarkar, *The Indian War of Independence 1857* (Bombay: B. G. Dhawale, 1947), 7–8.][66]

If the depiction of the Mutiny was directed to stimulate active Indian resistance, in *Hindutva*, Savarkar aimed at a precise definition of the political subject. He was aware of the contrast between the postulated homogeneity and the factual inner diversity of Indian society, being composed of Hindus, Jainas, Sikhs, Brahmos, Arya-Samajists, etc. The definition of the subject-agent could not simply be taken from tradition; this was evident since the efforts of Tilak and Dayanand Sarasvati.

Bankimchandra had taken a decisive step forward when he had related past events to present purposes and thus made historical knowledge a factor of politics. According to Savarkar, it was the anticipation of agency which constituted the identity of the nation. Everything depended on a common perspective. While Bankimchandra had still been oscillating between a Bengali and an Indian nation,[67] Harishchandra of Benares was already referring to an all-encompassing Hindustan. His wide definition 'he who inhabits Hindustan is a Hindu',[68] stood in contrast to

[65]Chitor: a big fort of the Rajput empire; Rana Pratap Singh: ruler of Chitor and fighter against the Mughal armies (sixteenth century); Guru Govind Singh: tenth Guru of the Sikhs (starting from Guru Nanak) who, in the seventeenth century, organized militant resistance against the Mughal emperor Aurangzeb.

[66]About the writing, printing, secret distribution, and subversive influence of the book, which was banned even before its publication, has emerged a separate story, adequate to its content. The book had first (1909) been written in Marathi, but attempts to print it in India or Germany failed. Finally, it was translated into English, printed in the Netherlands, and smuggled from there in hundreds of copies to India. While the ban against the book lasted almost till the end of colonial rule, several new editions appeared in the USA and in India; it was translated into various Indian languages. The first authorised and public edition appeared in Bombay in 1947, a new edition in New Delhi (Rajdhani Granthalaya) in 1970. Further reading: Surjit Hans, 'The Metaphysics of Militant Nationalism', in Bhalla and Chandra 1993: 190–231.

[67]Bankimchandra pointed to the presence of different nationalities in the country. Cf. Partha Chatterjee 1996: 55.

[68]See below, Section 2.3. Included were even the Muslims. In his *Indian War of Independence*, Savarkar had

Pratapnarayan Misra's narrow homogenizing formula 'Hindu-Hindi-Hindustan'.[69] Savarkar, too, insisted on the self-identification of the Indians as Hindus.[70] But the congruence of religion, territory, and people, which was underlying Dayanand's concept of the Aryan as a given reality, had still to be created. Even the religious heritage could be claimed only by those who had gained political agency.[71]

Hindutva was written during imprisonment and appeared anonymously in 1923. Characteristic of the claim to both rationality and a religious aura, the pamphlet was welcomed, on the one hand, as a scientific achievement and was, on the other hand, perceived as a *mantra*.[72]

Hindutva (1923)

The entire first half of the book is dedicated to the history of the terms 'Hindu' and 'Hindustan'. Savarkar seeks to show their early use and their mobilizing power which makes them preferable to alternatives such as Aryan, Aryavarsha, Bharat, etc. Moreover he distinguishes the political meaning of 'Hindutva' from the religious contents of the term 'Hinduism'. This is followed by reflections on the essence of Hindutva.

Throughout our inquiry we have been concerning ourselves more with what would have been or what should be. Not that to paint what should be is not a legitimate pursuit; nay, it is as necessary and at times more stimulating; but even that could be better done by first getting a firm hold of what actually is. We must try, therefore, to be on our guard so that in our attempt to determine the essentials of Hindutva we be guided entirely by the actual contents of the word as it stands at present. So although the root-meaning of the word Hindu like the sister epithet Hindi may mean only an Indian, yet as it is we would be straining the usage of words too much—we fear, to the point of breaking—if we call a Mohammedan a Hindu because of his

also counted the Muslims among the Indian freedom fighters. See also Gyanendra Pandey, 'Which of Us are Hindus?', in idem 1993: 238–72, here 245.

[69]Quoted in Meenakshi Mukherjee 1985: 57. In Pratapnarayan, the connection between people and country is inverted: 'We are the Hindus and the country is our land.' Or: 'Hindustan is ours because we are Hindus', quoted in Sudhir Chandra 1992: 119, 124, 125.

[70]If Savarkar thus neglected Dayanand's arguments in favour of the concept of the Aryan, he nevertheless gave a detailed account of the pre-Islamic use of the name 'Hindu'. Cf. D. N. Dhanagare, 'Three Constructs of Hinduism', *Seminar* 411 (Nov. 1993), 23–6, here 25. Dayanand Sarasvati had avoided the term 'Hindu' because of its non-Indian origins (see above, Section 1.2). Irrespective of the concept preferred, whether that of Hindu or that of Aryan: both religious revivalists and the national movement aimed at clear demarcations, thus rejecting or questioning the concept and practice of syncretism.

[71]Savarkar distinguished clearly between Hindutva and Hinduism. In a similar way to Vivekananda, who failed to reconcile spirituality and the material requirements of Indian historical agency, Savarkar regretted, in a letter to his brother, the Indians of the day were 'all Shudras and cannot claim access to the *Vedas* and Vedanta'. In contrast, England and America were already developed 'to that fullness, richness, and manliness—to Kshatriyahood and so stand on the threshold of that Brahminhood' which alone gave access to the 'sublime thoughts' of Vedanta philosophy. Savarkar, *Echo from the Andamans* (Nagpur n.d.), 24–5.

[72]Cf. the quotation from Swami Shraddhanand in the Preface of the 2nd ed., p. VII.

being a resident of India. It may be that at some future time the word Hindu may come to indicate a citizen of Hindusthan and nothing else; that day can only rise when all cultural and religious bigotry has disbanded its forces pledged to aggressive egoism, and religions cease to be 'isms' and become merely the common fund of eternal principles that lie at the root of all that are a common foundation on which the Human State majestically and firmly rests. But as even the first streaks of this consummation, so devoutly to be wished for, are scarcely discernible on the horizon, it would be folly for us to ignore stern realities. [...]

No word can give full expression to this racial unity of our people as the epithet, Hindu, does. Some of us were Aryans and some Anaryans; but Ayars and Nayars—we were all Hindus and own a common blood. Some of us are Brahmans and some Namashudras or Panchamas; but Brahmans or Chandalas—we are all Hindus and own a common blood.[73] [...] Some of us are monists, some pantheists; some theists and some atheists. But monotheists or atheists—we are all Hindus and own a common blood. We are not only a nation but a Jati, a born brotherhood. Nothing else counts, it is after all a question of heart. We *feel* that the same ancient blood that coursed through the veins of Ram and Krishna, Buddha and Mahavir, Nanak and Chaitanya, Basava and Madhava, of Rohidas and Tiruvelluvar courses throughout Hindudom from vein to vein, pulsates from heart to heart.[74] We *feel* we are a JATI, a race bound together by the dearest ties of blood and therefore it must be so. [...]

Paradoxical as it may sound to those who have fallen victims to the interested or ignorant cry that has secured the ear of the present world that the Hindus have no history, it nevertheless remains true that Hindus are about the only people who have succeeded in preserving their history—riding through earthquakes, bridging over deluges. It begins with their Vedas which are the first extant chapter of the story of our race. The first cradle songs that every Hindu girl listens to are the songs of Sita, the good. Some of us worship Rama as an incarnation, some admire him as a hero and a warrior, and all love him as the most illustrious representative monarch of our race. [...] What more shall we say? The stories of Ramayan and Mahabharat alone would bring us together and weld us into a race even if we be scattered to all the four winds like a handful of sand. I read the life of a Mazzini and I exclaim, 'How patriotic *they* are!' I read the life of a Madhavacharya and exclaim, 'How patriotic *we* are!' [...]

But what about the internecine wars amongst Hindus? We answer, what about the Wars of Roses amongst the English? What of the internecine struggle, of state against state, sect against sect, class against class, each invoking foreign help against his own countrymen, in Italy, in Germany, in France, in America? Are they still a people, a nation and do they possess a common history? If they do, the Hindus do. If the Hindus do not possess a common history, then none in the world does. [...]

A Hindu, therefore, to sum up the conclusions arrived at, is he who looks upon the land

[73]Nayar: warrior caste in Kerala; Namashudra: 'the respectable Shudra', Bengali term for Dalit (Untouchable); Chandalas: Untouchables, cremators.

[74]Mahavira: founder of Jainism, sixth century BC; Guru Nanak (1469–1539): poet and Sikh leader; Chaitanya (1486–1533): founder of a Krishna sect in Bengal; Basava: founder of the Lingayat sect, twelfth century; Madhava: vaishnavite theologian in South India, thirteenth century.

that extends from Sindu to Sindu[75]—from the Indus to the Seas,—as the land of his forefathers—his Fatherland (Pitribhu), who inherits the blood of that race whose first discernible source could be traced to the Vedic Saptasindhus[76] and which on its onward march, assimilating much that was incorporated and ennobling much that was assimilated, has come to be known as the Hindu people, who has inherited and claims as his own the culture of that race as expressed chiefly in their common classical language Sanskrit and represented by a common history, a common literature, art and architecture, law and jurisprudence, rites and rituals, ceremonies and sacraments, fairs and festivals; and who above all, addresses this land, this Sindhusthan as his Holyland (Punyabhu), as the land of his prophets and seers, of his godmen and gurus, the land of piety and pilgrimage. These are the essentials of Hindutva—a common nation (Rashtra), a common race (Jati), and a common civilization (Sanskriti). All these essentials could best be summed up by stating in brief that he is a Hindu to whom Sindhusthan is not only a Pitribhu but also a Punyabhu. For the first two essentials of Hindutva—nation and Jati—are clearly denoted and, connoted by the word Pitribhu while the third essential of Sanskriti is pre-eminently implied by the word Punyabhu, as it is precisely Sanskriti including sanskaras i.e. rites and rituals, ceremonies and sacraments, that makes a land a Holyland.

[From: Savarkar, *Hindutva. Who is a Hindu?*, 6th ed. (Delhi: Bharti Sahitya Sadan, 1989), 83, 89–90, 93–5, 115–6.][77]

Professional historians began to be influenced by nationalism in a significant way only after the beginning of the twentieth century, often against a self-understanding as detached, if not pro-British, researchers. See, for instance Radha Kumud Mookerji, *The Fundamental Unity of India* (1914);[78] H. C. Raichaudhury, *The Political History of Ancient India* (1923); and R. D. Bannerji, *The Age of Imperial Guptas* (1933). Hindu-Muslim relations could be handled either in a conciliatory manner, as in the case of Muhammad Habib, *Mahmud of Ghaznin* (1927), or in an intransigent way, as in the case of Muhammad Nazim, *The Life and Times of Sultan Mahmud of Ghazna* (1931).[79]

[75]Sindu: in other sites the writing is 'Sindhu' (Sanskrit: river). The terms 'Indus' and 'Hind', which derived from it, were Persian names for the land and were used later also for the population. It was only with the arrival of the Muslims that 'Hindu' came to denote the adherents of non-Islamic religions in India.

[76]Saptasindhus: seven rivers. Savarkar refers to the name (used in the *Rigveda*) of the land where the Aryans settled, a 'network of waterways'.

[77]Further reading: Vidya Sagar Anand, *Savarkar: A Study in the Evolution of Indian Nationalism* (London: Woolf, 1967); Jyoti Trehan, *Veer Savarkar: Thought and Action* (Delhi: Deep & Deep, 1991); Suresh Sharma, 'Savarkar's Quest for a Modern Hindu Consolidation', *Studies in Humanities and Social Sciences* 2 (1995), 189–215; Amalendu Misra, 'Savarkar and the Discourse on Islam in Pre-Independence India', *Journal of Asian History* 33 (1999), 142–84. Writings of and on Savarkar: Grover 1993.

[78]By the same author: *Local Government in Ancient India* (1919); *Nationalism in Hindu Culture* (1921); *Harsha* (1926); *Hindu Civilization* (1936).

[79]Cf. Peter Hardy, 'Modern Muslim Historical Writing on Medieval Muslim India', in: Philips 1961: 294–309, here 297.

In contrast to the (sometimes unconscious) communalist currents that flowed among the specialists of ancient and medieval India, some researchers of modern history emphasized the syncretistic tendencies, like, for instance, Pandit Sundarlal, *British Rule in India* (1929).[80] The first meeting of the All-India Modern History Congress in Pune (1935) also highlighted the shared historical experience of both communities. Thus Sir Shafa'at Ahmad Khan in his Presidential Address remarked about Hindu-Muslim relations: 'It seems at first, that contact is impossible. [...] Gradually, however, we find emerging a feeling of appreciation, crystallizing ultimately into a synthesis of Hindu and Moslem cultures.' This was said to be a result of the politics of Akbar. 'The two cultures, as well as the two races coalesced, for all practical purposes, so far as the interests of the State were concerned and we attained a conception of a common nationality which worked with irresistible force in the palmy days of the Mughal Empire.'[81]

In the case of KASHI PRASAD JAYASWAL (1881–1937), historical research was closely connected with the struggle for national self-assertion as against the European claim to superiority. The patronizing attitude to the colonized was to be rejected by producing evidence of early forms of political culture in India.

> *Born into the family of a rich merchant of the Kayasta caste, Jayaswal received his school education in Mirzapur and Benares. Subsequently, he went to England and studied history at Oxford. In London, where he qualified as Barrister-at-law, he came into contact with revolutionary-minded Indians such as Savarkar. Back in India (1909), Jayaswal could not start a university career because of his reputation as a dangerous revolutionary. He became a lawyer at the High Court in Calcutta, later in Patna. Nevertheless, he continued to dedicate himself to historical studies and was invited by the University of Calcutta to deliver lectures on constitution and law in ancient India. In 1924, Jayaswal was a member of the Bodh Gaya Temple Enquiry Committee set up by the INC and the Hindu Mahasabha. He played an active role in the foundation of the Patna Museum and the Bihar and Orissa Research Society (1914). The Jayaswal Research Institute in Patna is named after him.*

Jayaswal's field of research was the ancient history of India. Besides his *History of India, c. AD 150 to AD 350* (1933), he wrote important articles on topics of chronology, epigraphy and numismatics. Moreover, Jayaswal edited a Buddhist chronicle (*Arya-Manjusri-Mulakalpa*) of the ninth century AD under the title *An Imperial History of India*. He also published the *Journal of the Bihar and Orissa Research Society*, which today counts among the important historical periodicals.

The disparaging account of the Indian past and the judgement of political immaturity, as given in Vincent Smith's *Early History of India* (1904) and his *Oxford History of India* (1919), motivated Jayaswal to do his research on the political institutions in ancient India. The results of this work are presented in the book *Hindu Polity: A Constitutional History of India in Hindu Times*

---

[80]Among Sundarlal's heroes, there are also Muslim rulers, such as Sirajuddaula, Mir Kasim, Haidar Ali, and Tipu Sultan. Cf. H. L. Singh, 'Modern Historical Writing in Hindi', in Philips 1961: 461–72, here 467.

[81]Shafa'at Ahmad Khan, 'Presidential Address', in *Proceedings of the All-India Modern History Congress, First Session*, 1938, 1–63, here 7.

(1924).[82] Referring to early Buddhist sources, to Kautilya's *Arthasastra*, the Mahabharata, the *Allahabad Pillar Inscription* of Samudra Gupta as well as Greek sources, Jayaswal tried to prove the existence of a republican tradition in India from the sixth century BC to the fifth century AD. He maintained that the principle of representation had been known as early as Vedic times. Often those who were identified by western scholars as tribes in ancient India, in reality, mere republics.

In the second part of the book, Jayaswal dealt with the early Indian monarchy in order to prove 'that the Hindu kingship was contractual in nature'.[83] The Hindu kings, instead of claiming divine appointment, understood themselves as servants of the people and had to respond to legislating institutions. *Paura* and *Janapada* were viewed by Jayaswal as sovereign assemblies of the people and the coronation ceremony was presented as evidence of the constitutional nature of the Hindu monarchy.

Jayaswal's *Hindu Polity* is often cited as a negative instance of politically motivated historiography, in which he uses sources more like a pleading lawyer than an impartial judge as recommended by Bhandarkar. Others regard it as a book which 'revolutionised the study of Indian history'.[84] Undisputed is the great influence of Jayaswal's theses on the contemporary political consciousness. For the Indian nationalists, his work meant 'a much needed moral booster. [...] He established once and for all that forms of democracy were indigenous growth and left their imperishable impress on our lives. In fact the *Hindu Polity* became a second Gita for the Indian Nationality.'[85]

The following extracts from *Hindu Polity* deal with the republics and with the position of the king in the system of government. In the original, numerous Sanskrit passages are quoted in the notes.

Hindu Polity (1924)

RISE OF HINDU REPUBLICS AND HINDU TERMS FOR REPUBLICS: Hindu Republics are another illustration of the communal self-governing habits of the post-Vedic age, referred to in our last paragraph. The early Vedas know only monarchy. Departure from this normal constitution was made in post-Vedic times, and, as Megasthenes also records the tradition, 'sovereignty (*kingship*) *was dissolved and democratic governments set up*'[86] in various places. The Mahabharata, similarly, as we shall see in our discussion on Hindu Monarchy, considers monarchy alone as the Vedic form of government. [...]

---

[82]For the early evolution of this branch of research, see Ram Sharan Sharma, 'Historiography of Ancient Indian Polity up to 1930', in idem 1996: 1–13. According to Sharma, Indology owes to Jayaswal 'its greatest work on ancient Indian polity'. *Hindu Polity* 'became the Bible of the Indian nationalists'. Ibid., 4–5.

[83]B. P. Sinha, 'Kashi Prasad Jayaswal', in Sen 1973: 81–94, here 91.

[84]C. R. P. Sinha, 'Kashi Prasad Jayaswal—Career and Contributions', in Jayaswal 1988: 6.

[85]Sinha, ibid., 7. Following Jayaswal, Jayachandra Vidyalankar in *Bharatiya Itihasa Ki Ruparekha* (Outline of Indian History, 1933), also argued against Vincent Smith and the *Cambridge History of India*. He was specially interested in proving that ancient Indian history was the 'history of a virile and living nation' evident 'in the spread of Indian civilization in distant lands'. H. L. Singh, 'Modern Historical Writing in Hindi', in Philips (1961), 466. Vidyalankar combines this criticism with a plea for the indigenous languages as the proper medium for representing Indian history.

[86]*Epitomé of Megasthenes*, Diod. II. 38; McCrindle, *Megasthenes*, 38, 40. (KPJ)

The account of Hindu States of non-kingly forms of government presents a great chapter in the constitutional history of the race. We will therefore pay particular attention to it in these studies. Prof. Rhys Davids, in his *Buddhist India*, showed that republican form of government obtained in the country of the Buddha and his neighbours. But it had not been pointed out that our literature preserves technical names for Hindu Republics. One of these terms which first attracted my attention was the word *Gana*. In the *Acharanga-Sutra* of the Jaina branch of Hindu literature, I came across the terms *Do-rajjani* and *Gana-rayani* (II. 3. 1. 10) which struck me as defining constitutions. *Do-rajjani* were states ruled by two rulers; similarly, *Gana-rayani* would be states where *Gana* or 'numbers' ruled. In other places, I found the word *Gana* alone standing for a *Gana*-state. Further enquiry supplied evidence to confirm my belief that *Gana* denoted a republic and that its interpretation as then current ('tribe,' by Fleet and others; 'corporation of tradesmen or workmen,' by Bühler) was wrong. I further noticed that *Samgha* was another term in the same sense. [...]

It is necessary to ascertain what was exactly meant by *gana*. It means 'numbers': *gana-rajya* will therefore mean the rule of 'numbers', 'the rule by many'. Here the Buddhist Canon comes to our assistance. The Buddha was asked as to how the number of the monks was to be made out: 'At that time the people asked the Bhikkhus[87] who went about for alms: "How many Bhikkhus are there, Reverend Sirs?" The Bhikkhus replied, "We do not know, friends!" The people were annoyed .... They told this thing to the Blessed One.' The Buddha prescribed that the brethren should be counted on the *Uposatha* day by the system employed in a *gana* or by collecting voting tickets: 'I prescribe, O Bhikkhus, that you count (the Bhikkhus) on the day of *Uposatha* by the method of *ganas* (*ganamaggena ganetum*) or that you take the voting tickets (*salaka*).'

The Bhikkhus were to be counted in an assembly by the method of counting votes as done in a *gana*, or by the method of ballot-voting where tickets were collected. In this connection, let us also take the term *gana-puraka* of the Pali Canon. The *gana-puraka* was an officer who saw whether the lawful quorum of the assembly was formed before it transacted official business. It literally means 'the Completer of the Gana'. *Gana* thus was the assembly or parliament, so called because of the 'number' or 'numbering' of the members present. *Gana-rajya*, consequently, denoted government by assembly or parliament. The secondary meaning of *gana* came to be 'parliament' or 'senate', and as republics were governed by them, *gana* came to mean a republic itself. [...]

COUNCIL OF MINISTERS: Was the Hindu king a personal ruler? To answer this let us examine the position of the Hindu Council of Ministers. [...] The Council of Ministers is called the *Parishad*, in the *Artha-Shastra* and *Parisa*, in the *Jatakas*, the *Mahavastu* and Asoka's inscriptions. [...]

It is a law and principle of Hindu Constitution that the king cannot act without the approval and co-operation of the Council of Ministers. The law sutras, the law books and the political treatises are all unanimous on the point. Manu calls a king foolish who would attempt to carry on the administration by himself. He regards such a king as unfit. He lays down that the king must have 'colleagues', i.e. ministers; and that in their midst and along with them he has to consider ordinary and extraordinary matters of state; even ordinary business ought not to be

[87]Bhikkhus: holy mendicants.

done by one man, not to speak of the conduct of a kingdom. Yajnavalkya is of the same opinion and so are the other law givers. Katyayana ordains that the king should not decide even a law-suit by himself and that he should do it along with the Council. Even Kautilya, the greatest advocate of monarchy, has to say that matters of state should be discussed by the Council of Ministers and whatever the majority decides the king should carry out. It should be noted that this rule is enjoined even when there is a body of Mantrins[88] or cabinet separate from the Mantri-Parishad. The Artha Sastra says: 'When there is an extraordinary matter the Mantrins and the Mantri-Parishad should be called together and informed. In the meeting whatever the majority decide to be done, should be done (by the king).' It is remarkable that the king is not given even the power of vetoing. The Kautiliya in emphasising the importance of the Parishad says that Indra was called 'thousand-eyed', although he had only two eyes, because he had thousand wise members in his Mantri-Parishad or Council of State who are regarded as his eyes. [...] Ashoka in his Rock Series inscriptions, Section VI, says that when he has passed an order with regard to a gift or a proclamation, should a discussion arise in the Parishad (Council of Ministers) and they (the ministers) shelve it, he should be informed of it—if there was a division of opinion with regard to his proposal in the Parishad or a total rejection, he should at once be informed of it. That shows that the ministers had been for some time opposing the rulings of the Emperor.

Rudradaman was similarly opposed by his Ministers with regard to his proposal to repair the Sudarshana Lake. Opinion of Rudradaman's Ministers was against the king's proposal for repairing the Sudarshana water-works. They refused to pay for the repairs and the king had to pay from his private purse. Fortunately for Indian History the evidence of Rudradaman's inscription is as clear as any could be. It proves that the constitutional laws were not mere pious wishes, but they were as real as ordinary municipal laws of the law-books. Thanks to the Buddhist works which have preserved the great constitutional datum on the reign of Ashoka in their pathetic lament that the Emperor of the whole of India was deprived of his sovereign authority by the ministers of state. The Gatha quoted by the Divyavadana is more ancient than the compilation of the Divyavadana, and the former could not have been composed many centuries after the event. The monks were to gain nothing by an invention of such a story which threw discredit on a great personage of their religious history. They would not have invented a story which would have been a bad precedent in case other monarchs wanting to imitate the munificence of the Maurya Emperor.

[From: Jayaswal, Hindu Polity: A Constitutional History of India in Hindu Times, 2nd ed. (Patna: Eastern Book House, 1936 [Reprint 1988]), 23–5, 286–91.][89]

[88]Mantrins: ministers.

[89]The basic ideas of Hindu Polity had been formulated by Jayaswal as early as in his article 'An Introduction to Hindu Polity' The Modern Review (Calcutta), XIII (Jan.-June 1913), 535–41, XIV (July-Dec. 1913), 77–83, 201–6, 288–91, a contribution to the Third Hindi Literary Conference in Calcutta (1912). On that occasion already, Jayaswal had announced a treatise titled The Hindu Political Science. Further reading: B. P. Sinha, 'Kashi Prasad Jayaswal', in Sen 1973: 81–94; A. L. Basham, 'Modern Historians of Ancient India', in Philips 1961: 260–93; Aonshuman 1992.

ROMESH CHANDRA MAJUMDAR (1888–1975), during his long career as a teacher and researcher, rose to become one of India's most renowned historians.[90] His depiction of the early Indian colonization in Southeast Asia was an important stimulus to the national movement.

> *After his education at various colleges and the university in Calcutta, Majumdar went to Dacca in order to work at the Teachers' Training College. Soon he was appointed Professor of History at the University of Dacca (1921) where in 1937 he took office as Vice-Chancellor. Later he taught as Guest Professor at Benares Hindu University, Nagpur University and the universities of Pennsylvania and Chicago. He was an active member of the All-India Oriental Conference and the Asiatic Society of Bengal and also played a leading role in the Bharatiya Vidya Bhavan.*[91]

Soon after having presented his doctoral dissertation on *Corporate Life in Ancient India* (Calcutta 1919). Majumdar began to deal with the Indian influence in Southeast Asia. In 1927, he presented the first volume of *Ancient Indian Colonies in the Far East* (Lahore 1927), followed in 1938 by a second volume and in 1944 by a work titled *Hindu Colonies in the Far East*.[92]

After Independence, Majumdar turned to modern Indian history, with studies on the Mutiny (R.C. Majumdar 1963), on nineteenth-century Bengal (R.C. Majumdar 1960), and on the history of the freedom movement.[93] Majumdar also served as general editor of the multi-volumed *History and Culture of the Indian People* (1951–77), to which he himself contributed in considerable measure. In his account of the nineteenth century in Volume IX (*British Paramountcy and Indian Renaissance*, 1963), he applied a critical standard to British colonial politics. Nevertheless, in his survey of the evolution of the historical discipline he completely adopted the thesis that modern Indian historiography was a gift from the West.[94] Majumdar strongly advocated the impartiality of historical research. However, in the controversies about his interpretations, in particular the later ones, which sometimes deviated considerably from the established views, he did not always practise his advocated detachment.[95]

[90]He has been characterized as 'India's most prolific and influential practitioner of the historian's craft'. Frank F. Conlon, 'Romesh Chandra Majumdar', in Boia 1991: 357.

[91]The Bharatiya Vidya Bhavan was founded in 1938, with a vocation for promoting education, arts and culture.

[92]Majumdar, in his account, rejected the widespread western view of India's 'character of isolation and detachment'. One should remember, however, that as early as a hundred years before, John Crawford had reported in the Asiatic Society about the 'Existence of the Hindu Religion in the Island of Bali' (1816). Cf. Kejawiral 1988: 119ff.

[93]R. C. Majumdar 1961–2. For the controversy over Majumdar's draft for a Government sponsored account of the freedom struggle, see below, Section 4.2.2.

[94]R. C. Majumdar 1970. See also his contributions on 'Ideas of History in Sanskrit Literature' and 'Nationalist Historians', in Philips 1961: 13–28, 416–28, respectively.

[95]The main controversy was that about the interpretation of communal tensions between Hindus and Muslims. Majumdar considered them as a constant feature of Indian history, very much in the sense of the two-nation theory. According to Majumdar, the Muslims were 'in India but not of India': *Struggle for Freedom*, XI, 319. For Bipan Chandra, Majumdar's nationalism was 'permeated with chauvinism and communalism'. Chandra, 'Nationalist Historians' Interpretations', 213. See below, Section 4.2.2.

Majumdar's accounts of the Indian impact on Southeast Asia made a deep impression at the time of their publication. The image of the Indian spirit of enterprise revealed in them stimulated the national awakening. Nehru later confessed: 'I remember when I first read, about fifteen years ago, some kind of a detailed account of the history of South-East Asia, how amazed I was and how excited I became. New panoramas opened out before me, new perspectives of history, new conceptions of India's past' (Nehru 1989: 201) . In 1926, the Greater India Society was founded in Calcutta.[96]

The following extracts are taken from Majumdar's *Sain Dass Foundation Lectures* under the title *Greater India*, which summarize the material presented in earlier works.

Ancient Indian Colonization in the Far East (1940)

Having described the intercourse between India and the regions lying to its west, north and north-east, I shall now proceed to discuss in some details the part played by India in moulding the life and civilization of the people living to the east and south-east. As in the other case intercourse in this region also first began by way of trade, both by land and sea. But soon it developed into regular colonization, and Indians established political authority in various parts of the vast Asiatic continent that lay to the south of China proper and to the east and south-east of India. Numerous Hindu states rose and flourished during a period of more than thousand years both on the mainland and in the islands of the Malay Archipelago. Even when the Hindu rule became a thing of the past in India itself, powerful kings bearing Hindu names were ruling over mighty empires in these far-off domains. The Hindu colonists brought with them the whole framework of their culture and civilization and this was transplanted in its entirety among the people who had not yet emerged from their primitive barbarism.

This fascinating tale of the rise of a New India far away from the motherland has an epic grandeur of its own. But it is not possible to deal with that aspect, or even to go into details of the different states within a short space. I would, therefore, confine myself to a general account of the growth of Indian kingdoms in this region, and a somewhat detailed account of one or two important or typical examples. [...]

The Sailendra empire[97] differs in a striking degree from the conception of colonial empire in modern times. The Hindus did not regard their colonies as mainly an outlet for their excessive population and an exclusive market for their growing trade. These characteristics of modern colonization were perhaps not altogether absent, but they were not the dominant notes of the colonial policy in ancient India. In any case the colonies did not serve as a means of extending

[96]In the preface of the *Journal of the Greater India Society*, Rabindranath Tagore recalled the times when the Indian mind 'transcended her physical boundaries'. He also invoked the regaining of the erstwhile spiritual openness as against the present limitations and exclusiveness. Cf. Halbfass1990: 190–1. To Tagore, the discovery represented an enlargement of perspective and a loosening of the narrow linkage of people, culture, and country.

[97]The Sailendra dynasty ruled for several centuries over an empire founded in the eighth century on the Malayan peninsula; the cultural and civilizational influence (the Sailendras were Mahayana-Buddhists) was extended also to Java and Sumatra.

the political power of India, nor were they valued chiefly as a source of wealth which could be drained at will, without limit, to enrich the homeland of the colonists.

In short, the colonies were not regarded as a source of exploitation for the benefit of the conquering race. Whatever might have been the cause or nature of the original settlement of the Hindus in the various overseas possessions, ultimately it tended to be a cultural mission for the uplift of the conquered. Wherever they settled they introduced, to the fullest extent, the elements of culture and civilization of the motherland. Their religious and social institutions, and their language, art and letters, almost completely superseded those of the people among [whom] they lived. They themselves became children of the soil and made the colonies their only home. They never kept aloof from the native population and merged themselves into the indigenous society. They did not seek to extirpate the natives, in order to preserve their purity of blood, but they intermarried with them and formed a new but homogeneous population and society. By virtue of its inherent superiority the Hindu culture no doubt formed the dominant element in this fusion, but it was also influenced considerably by the impact of new ideas. The Hindu social institutions were adapted to the needs and habits of the people, and both religion and literature were transformed to a certain extent by the influence of the indigenous elements. The gradual effects of such fusion can be clearly studied in the domains of palaeography and art. The earliest inscriptions of the Hindu settlers in Malayasia are written in alphabets which can be hardly distinguished from Indian, so much so that it would not have been a matter of surprise at all if these records were discovered in some parts of India itself. But slowly local characteristics make their influence felt. The gradual changes in the development of the alphabets takes them farther and farther away from the Indian prototype, and ultimately an entirely distinct type of alphabet is evolved. Similarly the early products of art are distinctly Indian in conception, technique, and execution, and almost every phase of the mediaeval art of India is represented in Malayasia. From about the eleventh and twelfth centuries AD distinctive indigenous characteristics make their appearance. From the thirteenth century AD the transition becomes more rapid till the art of Malayasia becomes purely indigenous and entirely distinct in course of the next two or three centuries.

The Indians who settled in Malayasia readily merged themselves in the vast elements of native population and the result was a fusion of culture. But there was the great risk that even the inherent superiority of the Hindu culture might not counterbalance the sheer weight of numbers on the other side. This risk was minimized by the constant stream of colonization which flowed from the motherland bringing fresh vigour and life. But the moment this perennial spring ceased to flow the fountains fed by them also dried up. Thus the degree and extent of colonial enterprise in India set the pace of Indianization of the colonial culture and civilization. And when this spirit of colonization died away in India, the Indian element was rapidly submerged beneath the rising tide of the local and national spirit of the land to which the fusion beween a primitive people and a virile race had given birth. The Indian colonists would perhaps have been wiser in worldly sense, if they followed the examples of some modern colonists who practically extirpated the native population or held quite aloof from them by reducing them to abject wholesale slavery. This exclusiveness might have enabled the colonists to lord it over the people of the soil who would never be civilized enough to aspire after anything great and remain content with their lot as hewers of wood and drawers of water. But the Indian tradition was altogether different. They put more value on cultural conquest and no price was reckoned too high so long as this great mission was fulfilled. They aimed at the uplift of the people and not selfish gain by means of their exploitation; and instead of wielding the rod of masters they extended the hand of fellowship to the people among whom they found themselves.

[From: Majumdar, 'Ancient Indian Colonization in the Far East' (Sain Dass Foundation Lectures, 1940), in *India and South East Asia* (Delhi: B. R. Publishing Corporation, 1979), 16–35, here 16, 33–5].[98]

A specific case of nationalist historiography is that of the Indian Muslims. The effort at a renewal of the cultural traditions gave rise to the idea of an Islamic 'Pakistan'. (Sir) MUHAMMAD IQBAL (1877–1938) contrasted, in a similar way to some of the Hindu revivalists, the materialistic West with Eastern spirituality.

> *Iqbal was born in the historic city of Sialkot in the Punjab. After attending the local primary school he studied English and Arabic with Thomas Arnold in Lahore and successfully completed his studies in philosophy in 1899. When he arrived in Europe to study in 1905, he was a nationalist and a pantheist at the same time. He returned in 1909 as Pan-Islamist and almost a puritan, after he had written his dissertation 'Development of Metaphysics in Persia'. Very early in his life he assumed the Oriental studies and the western critique of civilization and he reached the conclusion that both the materialism of Europe and the esotericism of the Orient were reprehensible. In his numerous poems, written at different periods, the changes in his ideas can be easily traced. If the poems were at first influenced by Muslim powerlessness in a world dominated by colonials and Hindus (for example 'Shikwa', 1915) soon he was arguing for independence and emancipation of the Muslims ('Jawab-e Shikwa', 1912, 'Asrar-e Khudi', 1915). In 1918 Rumuz-e bekhudi was published, in which he pointed out the development of the national spirit against colonial rule.*

Iqbal's view of history was characterized by evolutionary ideas, constant dynamics, and movement, which he interpreted ethically. The universe and life were altogether in a continuous process of things coming into existence. Decline was due to the lack of dynamics, to stagnation. Human action leads to movement, which implies the appropriation of nature. The movement in history is therefore necessarily a move ahead (influences of Nietzsche, Bergson, etc.). Only the *élan vital* as the ontological reality of change and the movement, as well as the *Ijtihad* led to the perfect human being or the Muhamadan reality. Besides his numerous poetry collections, his prose text *Reconstruction of Religious Thought in Islam* (London 1934) gives further theoretical explanations. In it one can also find the oriental reception of oriental studies, where explanations are offered as to how Islamic history lost the dynamic element of its civilization, namely since the Mongol invasions.

[98]Further reading: Tarasankar Banerjee, 'Ramesh Chandra Majumdar: The Historian of Indian Nationalism', *Journal of Indian History* 59 (1981), 347–60; Himansu Bhusan Sarkar, 'R. C. Majumdar and his Work on South and Southeast Asia: A Panoramic Review (1888–1980)', *Journal of Indian History* 60 (1982), 306–29. Sugam Anand, 'R. C. Majumdar: 1888–1975', in Ramesh Chandra Sharma et al. 1991: 155–67.

In view of the increasing Muslim decline and the growing tension between Muslims and Hindus, Iqbal began to politicize the principle of ontological dynamics, by pointing out the necessity of a Muslim autonomy in South Asia, which reached its first peak in 1930 in the famous speech given on 29 December 1930, on the occasion of the annual meeting of the All India Muslim League in Allahabad. In it the poet-philosopher expressed the idea of a 'consolidated North-Western Muslim State' for the first time, that is, a separate nation for the Muslims in the North-West of the subcontinent. Rahmat Ali (d. 1951) was inspired by Iqbal's suggestion and concretized it in 1933, by giving a name to the nation so conceived: Pakistan, which means 'Land of the pure', and is, at the same time, an anagram of the Muslim regions (Panjab, Afghania [NWFP], Kashmir, Iran, Sind and Baluchistan). Rahmat Ali's creative idea of a sovereign nation ignored, however, the Muslims in the minority provinces and also those in Bengal.

Shortly before his death Iqbal had advocated, in a debate with a leading Deobandi, the territorial nationalism for Muslims. The Deobandi, in contrast, insisted on a 'united Nationalism' (*mutahhida qaumayat*), that is, Muslims would constitute a religious union in a territory among many others (the *millat* concept).

Pakistan Speech (1930)

It cannot be denied that Islam, regarded as an ethical ideal plus a certain kind of polity—by which expression I mean a social structure regulated by a legal system and animated by a specific ethical ideal—has been the chief formative factor in the life-history of the Muslims of India. It has furnished those basic emotions and loyalties which gradually unify scattered individuals and groups and finally transform them into a well-defined people. Indeed it is no exaggeration to say that India is perhaps the only country in the world where Islam, as a people-building force, has worked at its best. In India, as elsewhere, the structure of Islam as a society is almost entirely due to the working of Islam as a culture inspired by a specific ethical ideal. What I mean to say is that Muslim society, with its remarkable homogeneity and inner unity, has grown to be what it is under the pressure of the laws and institutions associated with the culture of Islam. The ideas set free by European thinking, however, are now rapidly changing the outlook of the present generation of Muslims both in India and outside India. Our younger men, inspired by these ideas, are anxious to see them as living forces in their own countries without any critical appreciation of the facts which have determined their evolution in Europe. [...]

The conclusion to which Europe is [...] driven is that religion is a private affair of the individual and has nothing to do with what is called man's temporal life. Islam does not bifurcate the unity of man into an irreconcilable duality of spirit and matter. In Islam, God and the universe, spirit and matter, church and state, are organic to each other. Man is not the citizen of a profane world to be renounced in the interest of a world of spirit situated elsewhere. To Islam matter is spirit realising itself in space and time. [...] In the world of Islam we have a universal polity whose fundamentals are believed to have been revealed, but whose structure, owing to our legists' want of contact with [the] modern world, stands today in need of renewed power by fresh adjustments. I do not know what will be the final fate of the national idea in the world of Islam. Whether Islam will assimilate and transform it, as it has assimilated and transformed before many ideas expressive of different spirits, or allow a radical transformation of its own structure by the force of this idea, is hard to predict. [...]

What, then, is the problem and its implications? Is religion a private affair? Would you like to see Islam, as a moral and political ideal, meeting the same fate in the world of Islam as Christianity has already met in Europe? Is it possible to retain Islam as an ethical ideal and to reject it as a polity in favour of national politics, in which a religious attitude is not permitted to play any part? This question becomes of special importance in India where the Muslims happen to be in a minority. The proposition that religion is a private individual experience is not surprising on the lips of a European. In Europe the conception of Christianity as a monastic order, renouncing the world of matter and fixing its gaze entirely on the world of spirit led, by a logical process of thought, to the view embodied in this proposition. The nature of the Prophet's religious experience, as disclosed in the Qur'an, however, is wholly different. It is not mere experience in the sense of a purely biological event, happening inside the experient and necessitating no reactions on his social environment. It is individual experience creative of a social order. Its immediate outcome is the fundamentals of a polity with implicit legal concepts whose civic significance cannot be belittled merely because their origin is revelational. The religious ideal of Islam, therefore, is organically related to the social order which it has created. The rejection of the one will eventually involve the rejection of the other. Therefore the construction of a polity on national lines, if it means a displacement of the Islamic principle of solidarity, is simply unthinkable to a Muslim. This is a matter which at the present moment directly concerns the Muslims of India. [...] The unity of an Indian nation, therefore, must be sought, not in the negation but in the mutual harmony and cooperation of the many. True statesmanship cannot ignore facts, however unpleasant they may be. The only practical course is not to assume the existence of a state of things which does not exist, but to recognize facts as they are, and to exploit them to our greatest advantage. [...]

Events seem to be tending in the direction of some sort of internal harmony. And as far as I have been able to read the Muslim mind, I have no hesitation in declaring that if the principle that the Indian Muslim is entitled to full and free development on the lines of his own culture and tradition in his own Indian home-lands is recognised as the basis of a permanent communal settlement, he will be ready to stake his all for the freedom of India. The principle that each group is entitled to free development on its own lines is not inspired by any feeling of narrow communalism. There are communalisms and communalisms. A community which is inspired by feelings of ill-will toward other communities is low and ignoble. I entertain the highest respect for the customs, laws, religions, and social institutions of other communities. Nay, it is my duty according to the teaching of the Qur'an, even to defend their places of worship, if need be. Yet I love the communal group which is the source of my life and behavior and which has formed me what I am by giving me its religion, its literature, its thought, its culture and thereby recreating its whole past as a living factor in my present consciousness. [...]

Communalism in its higher aspect, then, is indispensable to the formation of a harmonious whole in a country like India. The units of Indian society are not territorial as in European countries. India is a continent of human groups belonging to different races, speaking different languages and professing different religions. Their behavior is not at all determined by a common race-consciousness. Even the Hindus do not form a homogeneous group. The principle of European democracy cannot be applied to India without recognizing the fact of communal groups. The Muslim demand for the creation of a Muslim India within India is, therefore, perfectly justified. The [1929] resolution of the All-Parties Muslim Conference at Delhi, is, to my mind, wholly inspired by this noble ideal of a harmonious whole which, instead of stifling the respective individualities of its component wholes, affords them chances of fully working out the possibilities that may be latent in them. And I have no doubt that this House will emphatically endorse the Muslim demands embodied in this resolution. Personally, I would go further than the demands embodied in it. I would like to see the Punjab, North-West Frontier Province, Sind and Baluchistan amalgamated into a single State. Self-government within the British empire or without the British empire, the formation of a consolidated North-West Indian Muslim State appears to me to be the final destiny of the Muslims, at least of North-West India. [...]

The idea need not alarm the Hindus or the British. India is the greatest Muslim country in the world. The life of Islam, as a cultural force, in this country very largely depends on its centralisation in a specified territory. This centralisation of the most living portion of the Muslims of India, whose military and police service has, notwithstanding unfair treatment from the British, made the British rule possible in this country, will eventually solve the problem of India as well as of Asia. It will intensify their sense of responsibility and deepen their patriotic feeling. Thus possessing full opportunity of development within the body politic of India, the North-West India Muslims will prove the best defenders of India against a foreign invasion, be the invasion one of ideas or of bayonets. [...]

I therefore demand the formation of a consolidated Muslim State in the best interests of India and Islam. For India it means security and peace resulting from an internal balance of power; for Islam an opportunity to rid itself of the stamp that Arabian imperialism was forced to give it, to mobilize its law, its education, its culture, and to bring them into closer contact with its own original spirit and with the spirit of modern times. Thus it is clear that in view of India's infinite variety in climates, races, languages, creeds, and social systems, the creation of autonomous States based on the unity of language, race, history, religion, and identity of economic interests, is the only possible way to secure a stable constitutional structure in India. [...]

In conclusion I cannot but impress upon you that the present crisis in the history of India demands complete organization and unity of will and purpose in the Muslim community, both in your own interest as a community, and in the interest of India as a whole. [...] Our disorganized condition has already confused political issues vital to the life of the community. I am not hopeless of an intercommunal understanding, but I cannot conceal from you the feeling that in the near future our community may be called upon to adopt an independent line of action to cope with the present crisis. And an independent line of political action in such a crisis, is possible only to a determined people, possessing a will focalized by a single purpose. Is it possible for you to achieve the organic wholeness of a unified will? Yes, it is. Rise above sectional interests and private ambitions, and learn to determine the value of your individual and collective action, however directed on material ends, in the light of the ideal which you are supposed to represent. Pass from matter to spirit. Matter is diversity; spirit is light, life and unity. One lesson I have learnt from the history of Muslims. At critical moments in their history it is Islam that has saved Muslims and not vice versa. If today you focus your vision on Islam and see inspiration from the ever-vitalizing idea embodied in it, you will be only reassembling your scattered forces, regaining your lost integrity, and thereby saving yourself from total destruction. One of the profoundest verses in the Holy Qur'an teaches us that the birth and rebirth of the whole of humanity is like the birth of a single individual. Why cannot you who, as a people, can well claim to be the first practical exponents of this superb conception of humanity, live and move and have your being as a single individual? [...] In the words of the Qur'an: 'Hold fast to yourself; no one who erreth can hurt you, provided you are well guided.'

[From: Iqbal, 'Presidential Address', in *Sources of Indian Tradition*, II, 218–22].[99]

A special issue in the debate on Indian tradition and change was that of the emancipation of the Untouchables or Dalits. A new historical self-consciousness of the Dalits was first formulated by Jotirao Phule[100] and Gopal Baba Valangkar (1988). In a critical turn against the Puranic tradition with its reference to the eternal cosmic order, Phule tried to relate Untouchability to specific historical circumstances. According to Phule, the Dalits were the descendents of the most enduring Dravidian defenders against the invading Aryans. Moreover, the identity of the Dalits was related to certain religious cults with an anti-hierarchical appeal, such as bhakti. From this perspective, the Varna system appeared to Phule and Valangkar to be an addition of later theologians rather than an essential part of Hinduism.[101]

Studies on the emergence of caste classification from a Dalit perspective are continued today by researchers like H. L. Kosare, *Vidhabhartil Dalit Chalvalicha Itihas* (Nagpur 1984); Vasant Moon, *Madhyaprant-Varhadatil Dr. Ambedkarpurva Dalit Chalval* (Poona 1987); Saurabh Dube, *Untouchable Pasts: Religion, Identity, and Power among a Central Indian Community, 1780–1950* (Albany 1998). Ambedkar's idea of the struggle between Buddhists and Brahmans has been developed further by T. H. P. Chentharassery. He, too, accuses the 'Caste Hindu Historians' of having 'purposefully suppressed the History of the Indigenous Indians and picturised it in a distorted form'.[102] In different ways, both the fictional and autobiographical literature of the 'Dalit Sahitya' (beginning in the late 1960s) gives expression to the memory of the marginalized.

[99]*Speeches and Statements of Iqbal*, 2nd ed. (Lahore: Al-Manar Academy, 1948), 3–6, 8, 13, 15, 34–36. For Iqbal's idea of history, see also his poem 'The Importance of History', in *Sources of Indian Tradition*, II, 212. Further reading: D. R. Abdallah, 'Tahrik ki ahmiyyat Iqbal ki nazr men', *Journal of the Pakistan Historical Society* 20 (1977), part IV, Special Issue Allamah Iqbal Centenary, 1–21.

[100]See the texts (available till recently only in Marathi) of Jotirao Phule, *Samagra Vanmaya, Gulamagiri* (Bombay 1969 [1873]), now in *Collected Works of Mahatma Jotirao Phule*, II, Selections translated by P. G. Patil (Bombay: Government of Maharashtra, 1991). For Phule, see O'Hanlon 1985; *Jotiba Phule: An Incomplete Renaissance, Seminar Papers* (Surat: Centre for Social Studies, 1991).

[101]Cf. Philip Constable, 'Early Dalit Literature and Culture in Late Nineteenth- and Early Twentieth-Century Western India', MAS 31 (1997), 317–38, here 322.

[102]*History of the Indigenous Indians* (New Delhi: APH Publ. Corp., 1998), Preface. For the connection of Dalit historiography with the work of the *Subaltern Studies* group (chapter 4.5) see Kancha Ilaih, 'Productive Labour,

BHIMRAO RAMJI AMBEDKAR (1891–1956), the political leader of the Dalits, outlined their identity and political perspective, breaking away completely from Hindu tradition. He viewed Hinduism as a restriction on the potential for development, not only of the marginalized but of Indian society altogether.

> *Ambedkar belonged to the Mahar community in Maharashtra. His education at prestigious institutions, such as Elphinstone College in Bombay, Columbia University in New York (as a student of Economics, Anthropology and Sociology) and the London School of Economics, as well as his professional qualities (legal practice in Bombay, member of the Bombay Legislative Council) enabled him to rise to high offices of the State. After he had agreed to cooperate with the INC, he was assumed, in 1947, into Nehru's first cabinet as minister of justice and appointed president of the Drafting Committee for the Constitution. He could not assert with his demand for separate constituencies and villages for the Dalits, but the abolition of Untouchability was fixed in the Constitution. The retardation of the reforms[103] made him step down from office in 1951. Shortly before his death, he drew his conclusions from his critique of the Hindu social system and converted to Buddhism, followed by more than four million Indians, mainly from Maharashtra.[104] Whereas the political parties founded by him (the Independent Labour Party, the Republican Party) did not come up to expectations in the elections, his endeavours to improve educational standards among the Dalit population met with more success.*

The urge to explain the conditions of those who were suppressed by Hindu society was at the core of Ambedkar's lifelong involvement with history. During his days as a student in the USA, he began to deal with the historical roots of the caste system (*Caste in India*, 1924). And as late as the 1940s, when he was at the apex of his political career, he investigated the history of the Shudras and their gradual displacement by the Brahmans to the lowest grade in the hierarchy (*Who were the Shudras?*, 1946). Ambedkar argued against the idea (favoured by Phule and by the Dravidian movement) of an ethnic basis of the caste system and the identification of the outcasts with the pre-Aryan population of India.

Apart from Ambedkar's research on the origin of the caste system, it is in his speeches and

---

Consciousness and History: The Dalitbahujan Alternative', *Subaltern Studies* 9 (1996), 165–200. For the historical consciousness among the tribal population (Adivasi), see the hints for further reading in chapter 4.5 (Environmental History).

[103]What was at stake was above all the Hindu Code Bill, which was intended to reform the traditional Hindu personal law.

[104]As early as 1935, in an assembly of 10,000 followers near Nasik, where for many years access to the famous Kalaram Temple had been contested, Ambedkar had announced that, even if he was born a Hindu, he would not die a Hindu. Cf. Ambedkar, 'Mukti kon pathe' (Which Path to Liberation?), in *Sources of Indian Tradition*, II, 326–7. In this way, egalitarian norms and anti-Brahmanic tendencies were reconciled with indigenous religion and the esteem for the Indian past. Cf. Michael B. Schwartz, 'Indian Untouchable Texts of Resistance: Symbolic Domination and Historical Knowledge', in Seneviratne 1989: 131–41, here 136. Interested in a revival of Buddhism and its traditions were also intellectuals like Dharmanand Kosambi, P. Lakshmi Narasu and the Tagore family. Cf. Zelliot 1996: 190.

political manifestos that attempts at a historical understanding of Indian society and the Dalits can be found.[105] In his reckoning with the INC establishment, Ambedkar expressed a deep mistrust of the willingness to change on the part of Hindus and he reproached even Gandhi with fighting against foreign rule but not against class domination within India.[106] In the following extract, Ambedkar outlines his ideas regarding the separate identity of the Untouchables and the demand for a corporative representation of the Dalits.[107] Prefaced to the book as a motto is the phrase (uttered by the Melians in rejection of an offer to collaborate with the Athenians) from Thucydides' *History of the Peloponnesian War*: 'It may be your interest to be our masters, but how can it be ours to be your slaves?'

Aren't the Untouchables a Separate Element? (1945)

The grounds advanced by the Untouchables that they are separate from the Hindus are not difficult to comprehend. Nor do they require a long and an elaborate statement. The statement of their case can be fully covered by a simple question. In what sense are they Hindus? In the first place, the word 'Hindu' is used in various senses and one must know in what sense it is used before one can give a proper answer to the question. It is used in a territorial sense. Everyone who is an inhabitant of Hindustan is a Hindu. In that sense it can certainly be claimed that the Untouchables are Hindus. But so are the Muslims, Christians, Sikhs, Jews, Parsis, etc. The second sense in which the word 'Hindu' is used is a religious one. Before one can draw any conclusion, it is necessary to separate the dogmas of Hinduism from the cults of Hinduism. Whether the Untouchables are Hindus in the religious sense of the word depends upon what tests one adopts, the dogmas or the cults. If the tests of Hinduism are the dogmas of Caste and Untouchability then every Untouchable would repudiate Hinduism and the assertion that he is a Hindu. If the test applied is the acceptance of a cult such as the worship of Rama, Krishna, Vishnu, and Shiva and other Gods and Goddesses recognized by Hinduism the Untouchables may be claimed to be Hindus. [...]

One more point must be stressed. On the foregoing analysis, an Untouchable may be classed as a Hindu, only if the word Hindu is used in the religious but in the limited sense of a follower of a recognized cult. Even here, there is a necessity for giving a warning against concluding that the Hindu and the Untouchable have a common religion. The fact is that even as followers of recognized cults they cannot be said to have a common religion. The exact and appropriate expression would be to say that they have a similar religion. A common religion means a common cycle of participation. Now, in the observances of the cults there is no such common cycle of participation. The Hindus and the Untouchables practise their cults in segregation so that notwithstanding the similarity of their cults they remain as separate as two aliens do. Neither of these two senses of the word 'Hindu' can yield any result which can be of help in determining the political question, which alone can justify the discussion.

The only test which can be of use is its social sense as indicating a member of the Hindu

---

[105]See *Dr. Babasaheb Ambedkar: Writings and Speeches* (1987).

[106]Ambedkar 1945: 302. Cf. the suppressed speech which Ambedkar had intended to deliver on the occasion of the Annual Conference of the Jat Pat Todak Mandal of Lahore in 1936: Ambedkar 1990.

[107]Cf. N. C. Saxena, 'Historiography of Communalism in India', in Hasan 1981: 302–25, here 314.

society. Can an Untouchable be held to be part of the Hindu Society? Is there any human tie that binds them to the rest of the Hindus? There is none. There is no *connubium*. There is no *commensalism*. There is not even the right to touch, much less to associate. Instead, the mere touch is enough to cause pollution to a Hindu. The whole tradition of the Hindus is to recognize the Untouchable as a separate element and insist upon it as a fact. [...]

The first fallacy of the Congress lies in its failure to realize that the fundamental issue for settling the question whether to grant or not to grant constitutional safeguards is union versus separation of a social group in the population. Religion is only a circumstance from which unity or separation may be inferred. The Congress does not seem to have understood that the Musalmans and the Indian Christians have been given separate political recognition not because they are Musalmans or Christians but fundamentally because they form in fact separate elements from the Hindus.

The second fallacy of the Congress lies in its attempt to prove that where there is a common religion, social union must be presumed. It is on the basis of this reasoning that the Congress hopes to win. Unfortunately for the Congress, it cannot. For the facts are strongly against making a conclusive inference. If religion was a circumstance from which social union was made the only permissible inference, then the fact that the Italians, French, Germans and Slavs in Europe, the Negroes and the Whites in the U.S.A. and the Indian Christians, Europeans, and Anglo-Indians in India do not form a single community although they all profess the same religion, is enough to negative such a contention. The pity of the matter is that the Congress is so completely enamoured of its argument based on religion as an unifying factor, that it has failed to realize that there is no concomitance between the two and that there are cases where there is no separation although religions are separate, that there are cases where separation exists in spite of a common religion and what is worst, separation exists because religion prescribes it. [...]

If any conclusion is to be drawn from the hypothesis that the Untouchables are Hindus, it is that Hinduism has always insisted both in principle and in practice that the Untouchables are not to be recognized as a chip of the Hindu block but are to be treated as a separate element and segregated from the Hindus. [...]

Most people believe that Untouchability is a religious system. That is true. But it is a mistake to suppose that it is only a religious system. Untouchability is more than a religious system. It is also an economic system which is worse than slavery. In slavery the master at any rate had the responsibility to feed, clothe, and house the slave and keep him in good condition lest the market value of the slave should decrease. But in the system of Untouchability the Hindu takes no responsibility for the maintenance of the Untouchable. As an economic system it permits exploitation without obligation. Untouchability is not only a system of unmitigated economic exploitation, but it is also a system of uncontrolled economic exploitation. That is because there is no independent public opinion to condemn it and there is no impartial machinery of administration to restrain it. There is no appeal to public opinion, for whatever public opinion there is it is the opinion of the Hindus who belong to the exploiting class and as such favour exploitation. There is no check from the police or the judiciary for the simple reason that they are all drawn from the Hindus, and take the side of the Exploiters.

Those who believe that Untouchability will soon vanish do not seem to have paid attention to the economic advantages which it gives to the Hindus. An Untouchable cannot do anything to get rid of his untouchability. It does not arise out of any personal fault on his part. Untouchability is an attitude of the Hindu. For Untouchability to vanish, it is the Hindu who must change. Will he change?

Has a Hindu any conscience? Is he ever known to have been fired with a righteous indignation against a moral wrong? Assuming he does change so much as to regard Untouchability a moral wrong, assuming he is awakened to the sense of putting himself right with God and Man, will he agree to give up the economic and social advantages which Untouchability gives? History, I am afraid, will not justify the conclusion that a Hindu has a quick conscience or if he has it is so active as to charge him with moral indignation and drive him to undertake a crusade to eradicate the wrong. History shows that where ethics and economics come in conflict, victory is always with economics. Vested interests have never been known to have willingly divested themselves unless there was sufficient force to compel them. The Untouchables cannot hope to generate any compelling force. They are poor and they are scattered. They can be easily suppressed should they raise their head.

On this analysis, Swaraj would make Hindus more powerful and Untouchables more helpless and it is quite possible that having regard to the economic advantages which it gives to the Hindus, Swaraj, instead of putting an end to Untouchability, may extend its life. That Untouchability is vanishing is therefore only wishful thinking and a calculated untruth. It would be most stupid—if not criminal—to take it into account in considering the demands of the Untouchables for constitutional safeguards and ignore the hard facts of the present and their certainty to continue in the indefinite future.

[From: Ambedkar, *What Congress and Gandhi have done to the Untouchables* (Bombay: Thacker & Co., 1945), 183, 185–7, 196–8.][108]

2.3 CONCEPTUALIZATIONS OF TEMPORAL CHANGE: KALIYUGA, PROGRESS, REVOLUTION

Bengali textbooks written for the students of Fort William College in Calcutta (see Introduction, Sections 2.1 and 2.3) have been described as an interface between Indian and western ideas of history. With regard to the conceptualization of temporal change, too, remarkable innovations can be identified in these texts. Mrityunjay Vidyalankar (*Rajabali*) described current events according to the rules of the Puranas, interpreting them as phenomena of kaliyuga. Besides the traditional cyclical mode, there also appeared notions of linear processes.[109]

The first Indian accounts that explicitly followed the modern concept of progress were adaptations and translations of British texts, such as Ishwar Chandra Vidyasagar's *Bangalar Itihasa*, 1848 (after John C. Marshman, *History of Bengal*).[110] Shiva Prasad, too, was renowned

---

[108]The extract is taken from the eighth chapter: *The Real Issue*. Further reading: Rudolph and Rudolph 1967: 132–54; Partha Chatterjee 1995: 173–99; R. Srinivasan, 'Dr. Ambedkar's Search for Roots', *New Quest* 116 (March-April 1996), 81–90.

[109]See also the other texts mentioned in the Introduction (Section 2.3).

[110]Another book by Marshman (1867), had also been translated into Bengali.

as a translator before he presented his own history of India, *Itihasa Timirnasak* (1864), the first history of India in Hindi.[111]

The temporalization of thinking and its orientation towards change and future is reflected in a striking way in the semantics of the young, new, and dynamic, for instance in the names of reform movements (such as the Young Bengal of the 1830s) and in the titles of the works on contemporary history like *Indian National Evolution* (1917) by A. C. Majumdar and C. Y. Chintamani, *Young India, an interpretation and history of the National Movement from within* (1917) by Lajpat Rai, and *India in Transition* (1922) by M. N. Roy. The same applies to the titles of periodicals: Gandhi (*Young India*) followed the common trend as much as did the Marxists (*The New Age; The Vanguard of Indian Independence*). A close look, however, sometimes reveals ontologized concepts behind titles like *A Nation in the Making* (1925) by S. Banerjea. In fact, the invocation of the young and the new is sometimes in striking contrast to the simultaneous interest in the great antiquity of Indian culture. Innovation, then, is presented as an awakening after a long sleep.[112]

The early Marxist theorists and historians in India, who were faced with the problem of how to reconcile the bourgeois concept of national liberation with that of social emancipation, generally laid the emphasis on inner change. But this was not always in line with the international debate. While the latter increasingly opened itself to the issues of national freedom struggles in colonized countries, Indian communists moved 'in the opposite direction—*from* nationalism to Marxism'.[113] S. A. Dange, in his *Gandhi vs Lenin* (1921),[114] had reflected on the mutual support of national liberation and social emancipation on the basis of moral imperatives (Sanjay Seth 1995: 114). While it became increasingly evident that only the inclusion of the masses and the taking up of their social demands would ensure the success of the freedom fight, the question remained whether the preservation of traditional culture had to be regarded as an element of liberation.[115]

HARISHCHANDRA OF BENARES (1850–85) was a committed modernizer[116] and, increasingly, evolved as a critic of British colonial politics. His writings give an idea of the difficulties of the reformers who tried to reconcile traditional and modern western time concepts, kaliyuga, and the belief in progress.

[111]For Shiva Prasad, see Lütt 1970: 37–63. *Itihasa Timirnasak* was translated into English by M. Kempson, the director of the public education board: *A History of Hindustan* (1871).

[112]For the metaphor of the 'awakening' in European nationalism, cf. Anderson 1991: 195.

[113]Sanjay Seth 1995: 108. For the influence of Marxism in India and for the early communist movement, see Joshi and Damodaran, 1975; d'Encausse and Schramm 1989. In one of the first Indian texts on Marx (written in March 1912), Har Dayal viewed Marx as a modern *rishi*. Cf. Sharma, 'Savarkar's Quest for a Modern Hindu Consolidation', 207.

[114]S. A. Dange, 'Gandhi vs. Lenin', in idem, 1974, Vol. I.

[115]For the continuing debate on how past experience and the cultural peculiarities of India were to be integrated into the master narrative of Historical Materialism, see below. See also Dipesh Chakrabarty 1989: 223ff. Other early works written by Marxists on Indian history are: Hiren Mukherji 1946; D. P. Mukherji 1945 and 1948.

[116]'I have always taken pleasure in the enlightenment of my fellow countrymen.' Quoted in Lütt 1970: 98.

Harishchandra (his admirers called him Bharatendu) hailed from a wealthy family of the Agrawal caste (Vaishya). His father belonged to the Anglophile, progress-minded personalities of Benares. Harishchandra followed in his footsteps and was also influenced by his teacher Shiva Prasad and the social reformer Ishwar Chandra Vidyasagar. He was associated with the Hindu National Improvement Society, founded in 1872, and edited, from 1873, Harishchandra's Magazine (later titled Harishchandra Chandrika).

Harishchandra played a similar role in the Hindi-language area of the North Western Provinces as Bankimchandra Chatterjee did in Bengal. He tried to establish Hindi as a literary language by translating texts from Sanskrit.[117] With his works, especially his patriotic poems, he is counted among the pioneers of Indian national consciousness.

Like Bankimchandra, Harishchandra deplored the lack of a historiographical tradition in India: 'In the pure sky of India no moon of history can be seen!' (qtd. in Lütt 1970: 80). His interest in history is reflected in a number of scholarly investigations[118] as well as in making use of historical material in his literary creations. As a genre, Harishchandra preferred drama. Characterized by political and historical interest are the plays *Bharat Janani* (Mother India) and *Bharat Durdasha* (The Misery of India), in which the present time is described as an epoch of decadence due to the defeat at the hands of foreigners.

If Harishchandra's work, on the whole, represents the tensions between modernization and the self-assertion of tradition, in the following text the emphasis is on the quest for social progress.[119] Harishchandra had been invited to Ballia (near Benares) by the Arya Desopakarini Sabha and the Ballia Institute, in order to address an assembly on the occasion of the annual Dadri-mela and 'to say something about how to make India's progress possible'.

How can India be Reformed? (1884)

The reform should be such that there is progress in everything. In religion, in the work at home, in the work outside, in profession, in etiquette, in conduct, in the strength of body and mind, in society, in the child, in youth, in the old, in women, in men, in rich, in poor, in all parts of India, in all castes, in the whole country, there should be improvement. Give up all such things that may be a hindrance in this path, even if people call you worthless, call you naked, a Christian or a fallen-one. Just look at the plight of your country, and don't listen to their talk. [...]

Those who consider themselves well-wishers of the country, should sacrifice their comforts, riches, and prestige, and gird up their loins. Others will emulate them and in a short time everything will be done. Search for the root causes of our faults. Some are hidden under the cover of religion, some in the ways of the country, some in the comforts of the people. Get all of them out of their places. Tie them up and arrest them. What else can we say? Like, when some

[117]He also arranged for the translation of some of the historical novels of Bankimchandra Chatterjee and R. C. Dutt into Hindi.

[118]See the essays 'Akbar and Aurangzeb', 'Kasmir Kusum' (on Kalhana's *Rajatarangini*), 'Kaalchakra' (on problems of chronology, 1884) as well as biographies and historical accounts of various castes.

[119]The often quoted 'Ballia speech' is a key text in the search for national identity. See above, Section 2.2. For the controversial debate on Harishchandra as a traditionalist or a reformist, cf. Dalmia 1997: 42ff.

man comes to your house with the intention to rape (your women), the same ferocity with which you catch and beat him and with all your strength destroy him you should direct to whatever are the thorns in your path of progress; dig out their roots and throw them away. Don't be afraid. Until a hundred or two hundred persons are disgraced, thrown out of the caste, turned poor, imprisoned, and even get killed, no country will be reformed.

Now the question may be asked: 'Brother, we don't know the real meaning of the words "Progress" and "Reform". What can we consider as good? What shall we take, what shall we leave?' Well, some thoughts are immediately coming to my mind. I present them to you, listen: The base of all progress is *dharma*. Therefore, it is *dharma* that must be improved before anything else. See how religion and politics of the English are mutually joined; with this, they are progressing every day. If you look instead at our own country: our country is filled with various kinds of conventions, social organizations, medicinal practices, etc., all under the cover of religion.

Why is there your *mela* in Ballia, and the common bathing? So that the people who otherwise wouldn't meet each other, people from distances of five or ten *kos*[120] come to a common place and meet each other once a year, get to know each other's pain and joy, and buy those household things that are not available in the village. Why is there the holy fasting of Ekadashi?[121] So that by one or two fastings in a month the body is purified. When one takes a bath in the Ganga, first one sprinkles some water on the head and then one puts the feet in the river. Why is this custom? So that the heat doesn't climb up from the feet to the head and generate bad effects. Diwali[122] is celebrated for the reason that the houses may be cleaned at least once in a year. This festival is like your municipality.

Similarly, in all festivals, pilgrimages, religious observances, there is some strategy [reason]. Religious principles and social customs [needs] have been mixed like milk and water. The fault that has happened in the meantime is that people don't understand any more the meaning of what had been written down by the ancestors, and they consider only these [superficial] things as the true religion. Brothers, devoted singing at the feet of the supreme God is the only true religion. All the rest is social custom which can be chosen and changed according to place and time.

The second fault that happened is this, that the very descendants of the Mahatmas, sages, and *rishis*, not understanding the intentions of their fathers and grandfathers, created new religious rituals and inserted them into the Shastras. Thus, all days, all religious observations, all places became [indiscriminately] holy. So, you must understand once and for all why those wise *rishis* introduced particular things, and accept those things which are suited and helpful according to place and time.

There are many things that are considered today as contradicting the social order, but that are sanctioned in the Dharmashastras: these practices should be allowed. For instance, travel by ship, widow marriage, etc. Don't decrease the strength, potency, age, etc. of your children by marrying them off at a young age. Are you their mothers and fathers or their enemies? Let the strength in their body grow, let them learn a bit, let them first learn to worry about salt, oil,

---

[120]*kos*: two miles.

[121]Ekadashi: the eleventh day of each fortnight of the lunar month.

[122]Diwali: the festival of lights, for the celebration of Rama's and Sita's return to Ayodhya.

wood [livelihood], later their feet can get tied [bogged down in family life]. Bring to an end the practice of polygamy, a habit of aristocracy.

Educate the girls also, but not in the way teaching is done today, in which harm is done instead of helping them. Give them education in such a way that they learn about their country and their family customs, devotion to their husbands, and how to teach their own children in a natural way. The people of various faiths, like Vaishnavas, Shaktas, etc. should give up their mutual hostility. The present time is not for such quarrels. Hindus, Jains, Musalmans must all get together. Respect all, whether they may be of high or of low caste, and treat them according to their merit. Do not hurt the hearts of the people of low caste by insulting them. All people must join together.

The Muslim brothers, who have settled in Hindustan, should also stop considering the Hindus as inferior. They should treat the Hindus like true brothers and give up what would hurt their hearts. When a house catches fire the elder and younger sisters-in-law must forget their jealousy and together extinguish the fire. There are things that Hindus cannot have while the Muslims get them easily due to the influence of their religion. There are no caste divisions among them, no taboos in eating and drinking, no restrictions about travelling to England or other countries. Nevertheless, the Muslims have not yet improved their situation. Even now, many of them think that the Muslim Emporers are still on their thrones in Delhi and Lucknow. [...]

Brother Hindus! You, too, should not insist any more on all details of religious faith and practice. Increase mutual love and chant this *mahamantra*. Who lives in Hindustan, whatever his colour and whatever his caste, he is a Hindu. Help the Hindus. Bengalis, Marathas, Panjabis, Madrasis, Vaidiks,[123] Jains, Brahmos, Musalmans, all should join hands. Do all that which will increase the skills and help to keep your wealth within the country. Just as the Ganga turns into a thousand streams and then joins the sea, similarly, your money goes to England, France, Germany, America by a thousand routes. Even trivial things like a match-box are imported from there. [...]

Brothers, now wake up from sleep and contribute with all you can do to the progress of your country. Read only such books, play only such games, have only such conversations which are in your [country's] interest. Don't use foreign goods and foreign language. Contribute to the progress of your country, in your own language.

> [From: Harishchandra, 'Bharatvars ki unnati kaise ho sakti hai', in *Bharatendu Granthavali* (Bharatendu's Works), ed. by Shivaprasad Misra 'Rudra', III (Varanasi: Nagari Pracharini Sabha, 1953), 895–903. Translation by Arya Acharya.][124]

DADABHAI NAOROJI DORDI (1825–1917) was among the first Indians to systematically and empirically confront the actual situation of the country with the expectations of social progress

---

[123]Brahman caste.

[124]The original text in Hindi appeared in *Harishchandra's Journal* (3 Dec. 1884). The essay has been repeatedly reprinted and is also found in Hemant Sharma, ed., *Bharatendu Samagra* (Varanasi 1987), 1010–13. A free English translation is in Madan Gopal, *The Bharatendu. His Life and Times* (New Delhi 1972), 197–208. Hindi text and English translation are added as an appendix to Gyanendra Pandey, *The Construction of Communalism in Colonial North India* (Delhi: Oxford University Press, 1990), 267–78. Further reading: Lütt 1970, specifically 65–98; Sudhir Chandra 1992, specifically 25–34; for the Balia speech, see Dalmia 1997, 21–7.

nurtured by the British. The 'high priest of the drain theory' viewed the poverty of India as a consequence of colonial exploitation and, with this, became one of the most influential thinkers of Indian nationalism.

> *Naoroji belonged to a Parsee family in Bombay. The minority of Zoroastrians had left Persia after the advent of Islam and had settled mainly along the Indian Malabar coast. The Parsees had few religious reservations about western ideas and values. Naoroji attended Elphinstone College in Bombay and later taught in that institution as a professor of Mathematics. In 1855, he went to London as a businessman and lived there for most of his life. Nevertheless, he continued to play a role in India, where he was prime minister of the princely state of Baroda in 1872–3. In 1892, he was elected to the House of Commons as a candidate of the British Liberals from a London constituency. Here, he pleaded for more political rights for the Indians. Thrice (1886, 1893, 1906) he presided over sessions of the Indian National Congress.*

Naoroji was influenced by the writings of the Physiocrats and of John Stuart Mill. In his theory of the 'drain of wealth', he followed, for the most part, the economic principles prevailing in Europe. As early as the *Ninth Report of the Select Committee* (1783), a 'drain' from India to Great Britain had been mentioned. James Mill, too, in his *History of British India*, admitted the negative consequences of colonialism for the economy of the colonized countries: 'It is an exhausting drain upon the resources of the country, the issue of which is replaced by no reflex; it is an extraction of the life blood from the veins of national industry which no subsequent introduction of nourishment is furnished to restore.'[125] Rammohun Roy had also criticized the uneven distribution of the advantages of the Permanent Settlement Act (1793),[126] calling it a tribute to England. Naoroji himself mentioned 'England's Debt to India' for the first time on the occasion of a speech to the East India Association of London in 1867 (Naoroji 1887: 26–50).

The book *Poverty and Un-British Rule in India* contains a collection of dispersed texts dealing with particular aspects of the subject: letters, memorandums, parliamentary interventions, and speeches held on various occasions. Naoroji, who based his allegations mainly on official British source material (Blue Books), also expressed his opinion on the method of compiling statistics and of making proper use of them. Moreover, he always kept in mind the connection between material and spiritual wealth.

Poverty and Un-British Rule in India (1901)

The title of the book is *Poverty and Un-British Rule in India*, that is, the present system of government is destructive and despotic to the Indians and un-British and suicidal to Britain. On the other hand, a truly British course can and will certainly be vastly beneficent both to Britain and India.

Before dealing with the above evil qualities of the present system of government I would first give a very brief sketch of the benefits which India has derived from the British connection

---

[125]Mill, *History of British India*, Vol. VI, 671, quoted in Naoroji, *Poverty and Un-British Rule in India*, p. IV. On another occasion, Mill wrote, it was 'as if Yorkshire were to be drained and oppressed for the benefit of Middlesex'. James Mill, *On Colonies*, 22, quoted in Majeed 1992:138.

[126]See Rammohun Roy, 'Paper on the Revenue System of India', in *The Essential Writings of Raja Rammohun Roy*, 182–9.

and of the immense importance of India to Britain for Britan's own greatness and prosperity. The present advanced humanitarian civilisation of Britain could not but exercise its humane influence to abolish the customs of *sati* and infanticide, earning the everlasting blessings of the thousands who have been and will be saved thereby.

The introduction of English education, with its great noble elevating, and civilising literature and advanced science, will for ever remain a monument of good work done in India and a claim to gratitude upon the Indian people. This education has taught the highest political ideal of British citizenship and raised in the hearts of the educated Indians the hope and aspiration to be able to raise their countrymen to the same ideal citizenship. This hope and aspiration as their greatest good are at the bottom of all their present sincere and earnest loyalty, in spite of the disappointments, discouragements, and despotism of a century and half. I need not dwell upon several consequential social and civilising benefits. But the greatest and the most valued of all the benefits are the most solemn pledges of the Act of 1833, and the Queen's Proclamations of 1858, 1877, and 1887, which if 'faithfully and consciously fulfilled' will be Britain's highest gain and glory and India's greatest blessing and benefit. Britain may well claim credit for law and order which, however, is as much necessary for the existence of British rule in India as for the good of the Indian people; for freedom of speech and press and for other benefits flowing therefrom. [...]

I now come to the faults of the present un-British system of government, which unfotunately 'more than counter-balances the benefits'. The Court of Directors, among various expressions of the same character, said, in their letters of 17–5–1766 and others about the same time: 'Every Englishman throughout the country ... exercising his power to the oppression of the helpless Natives ... We have the strongest sense of the deplorable state ... from the corruption and rapacity of our servants ... by a scene of the most tyrannic and oppressive conduct that ever was known in any age or country.' Such unfortunately was the beginning of the connection between Britain and India—based on greed and oppression. And to our great misfortune and destruction, the same has remained in subtle and ingenious forms and subterfuges up to the present day with ever increasing impoverishment. [...]

These evils have ever since gone on increasing, and more and more counterbalancing the increased produce of the country, making now the evil of the 'bleeding' and impoverishing drain by the foreign dominion nearly or above £30,000,000 in a variety of subtle ways and shapes; while about the beginning of the last century the drain was declared to be £3,000,000 a year— and with private remittances, was supposed to be near £5,000,000—or one-sixth of what it is at present. If the profits of exports and freight and insurance, which are not accounted for in the official statistics, be considered, the present drain will be nearer forty than thirty millions. [...]

True British rule will vastly benefit both Britain and India. My whole object in all my writings is to impress upon the British people, that instead of a disastrous explosion of the British Indian Empire, as must be the result of the present dishonourable un-British system of government, there is a great and glorious future for Britain and India to an extent unconceivable at present, if the British people will awaken to their duty, will be true to their British instincts of fair play and justice, and will insist upon the 'faithful and conscientious fulfilment' of all their great and solemn promises and pledges. [...]

With the material wealth go also the wisdom and experience of the country. Europeans occupy almost all the higher places in every department of Government, directly or indirectly under its control. While in India they acquire India's money, experience, and wisdom, and when they go, they carry both away with them, leaving India so much poorer in material and moral wealth. Thus India is left without, and cannot have, those elders in wisdom and experience, who in every country are the natural guides of the rising generations in their national and social conduct, and of the destinies of their country—and a sad, sad loss this is! [...]

After having a glorious history of heroic struggles for constitutional government, England is now rearing up a body of Englishmen in India, trained up and accustomed to despotism, with all the feelings of impatience, pride, and high-handedness of the despot becoming gradually ingrained in them and with the additional training of the dissimulation of constitutionalism. Is it possible that such habits and training of despotism, with which Indian officials return from India, should not, in the course of time, influence the English character and institutions? The English in India, instead of raising India, are hitherto themselves descending and degenerating to the lower level of Asiatic despotism. Is this a Nemesis that will in fullness of time show to them what fruit their conduct in India produced? [...]

It is useless for the British to compare themselves with the past Native rulers. If the British do not show themselves to be vastly superior in proportion to their superior enlightenment and civilisation, if India does not prosper and progress under them far more largely, there will be no justification for their existence in India. The thoughtless past drain we may consider as our misfortune, but a similar future will, in plain English, be deliberate plunder and destruction.

[From: Naoroji, *Poverty and Un-British Rule in India* (Classics of Indian History and Economics) (Delhi: Publications Division, Ministry of Information and Broadcasting, Government of India, n. d.), II-IX; 'On Moral Poverty of India', in *Voices of Indian Freedom Movement*, Vol. I, ed. by J. C. Johari (New Delhi: Akashdeep Publishing House, 1993), 85–104, here 86, 98, 103.][127]

The social reformer MAHADEV GOVIND RANADE (1842–1901), by conceiving change as organic growth, sought to make it appear compatible with Indian tradition.

> Born in Niphad in the Nasik district of Maharashtra, Ranade belonged to an orthodox family of Chitpavan Brahmans. After completing his education at Elphinstone College and the newly founded university of Bombay, he taught economics, and, later, history and literature. Next, he progressed in a law career and finally became a judge at the Bombay High Court (1893). Throughout his working life, Ranade sought to contribute to the improvement of society. He was one of the first members of the Prarthana Samaj (Prayer Society) founded in 1867 on the model of the Brahmo Samaj. From 1878 to 1896, he edited the Anglo-Marathi daily paper Induprakash. In 1887, he started the Indian National Social Conference, during the annual meetings of which the advancement of the reform projects was discussed.

[127]First edition: *Poverty and Un-British Rule in India* (London: Swan Sonnenschein & Co., 1901). The 'Memorandum No. 2' ('The Moral Poverty of India and Native Thoughts on the Present British Indian Policy') was presented on 16 November 1880. Further reading: B. N. Ganguly 1965. For the wider historical context, see Bipan Chandra 1966. As a contemporary testimony, see Sri Aurobindo, 'The Man of the Past and the Man of the Future (Tilak & Naoroji)', in Grover 1993.

In his critical reception of contemporary economic theory, Ranade arrived at the conviction that the empirical approach would be preferable to universalistic theories: 'The subject must be studied historically and inductively'. Like Spencer, List, and Sismondi, he related economic grievances to specific political and social defects, which could be removed by purposeful intervention. The example of retarded industrial development in some countries of continental Europe showed that, by cautious guidance, a process could be initiated that led to growth and prosperity. History also told of the interfering hand of God, according to Ranade.[128]

In numerous essays, Ranade commented on problems of economic development and social reform, including famine, industrialization, drain, demography, and migration.[129] Ranade's interest in the past has found expression in his *Rise of Maratha Power* (1900),[130] which describes the achievement of the Maratha prince Shivaji. The improvement of conditions during the seventeenth century is related, also, to the inspiring influence of bhakti. Even Muslim rule was seen by Ranade as an important contribution to Indian unity and progress. Akbar's syncretic religion of *Din-I-ilahi* was viewed by him as a paradigm for secular politics. Instead of deploring their humiliation and regarding the Islamic invasions as the cause of Indian weakness which made possible the advent of colonial rule, Hindus should unite with Muslims and accept the present situation as a challenge to modernize: 'If the lessons of the past have any value, one thing is quite clear, that in this vast country no progress is possible unless both Hindus and Mohammedans join hands together and are determined to follow the lead of the men who flourished in Akbar's time.'[131] In Ranade's thinking, the conflict between religions and cultures was subordinate to the interest in progress. And he was convinced that the British, too, had contributed to the prosperity of India. Their presence meant a strengthening for the future.

The following extract is from one of Ranade's speeches before the Indian National Social Conference.

Revival and Reform (1897)

While the new religious sects condemn us for being too orthodox, the extreme orthodox sections denounce us for being too revolutionary in our methods. According to these last, our efforts should be directed to revive, and not to reform. [...] They advocate a return to the old ways, and appeal to the old authorities and the old sanction. Here, people speak without realizing the full significance of their own words. When we are asked to revive our institutions and customs, people seem to be very much at sea as to what it is they seem to revive. What particular period of our history is to be taken as the old? Whether the period of the Vedas, of the Smritis, of the Puranas or of the Mahomedan or modern Hindu times? Our usages have been changed from time to time by a slow process of growth, and in some cases of decay and corruption, and we cannot stop at a particular period without breaking the continuity of the whole. When my revivalist friend presses his argument upon me, he has to seek recourse in some subterfuge which really furnishes no reply to the question—what shall we revive? Shall we revive the old

---

[128]Quoted in Mukhopadhyay, *Evolution of Historiography in Modern India*, 82, 85.

[129]The essays are reprinted in Grover 1990a.

[130]Reprint, New Delhi 1961. Also in Grover 1990a: 147–267.

[131]'The Key to Progress' (1900), in Grover 1990a: 268–79, here 277.

habits of our people when the most sacred of our caste indulged in all the abominations as we now understand them of animal food and drink which exhausted every section of our country's zoology and botany? The men and the gods of those old days ate and drank forbidden things to excess in a way no revivalist will now venture to recommend. [...]

Shall we revive the internecine wars of the Brahmins and Kshatriyas, or the cruel persecution and degradation of the aboriginal population? Shall we revive the custom of many husbands to one wife or of many wives to one husband? Shall we require our Brahmins to cease to be landlords and gentlemen, and turn into beggars and dependants upon the king as in olden times? These instances will suffice to show that the plan of reviving the ancient usages and customs will not work our salvation, and is not practicable. If these usages were good and beneficial, why were they altered by our wise ancestors? If they were bad and injurious, how can any claim be put forward for their restoration after so many ages? Besides, it seems to be forgotten that in a living organism, as society is, no revival is possible. The dead and the buried or burnt are dead, buried, and burnt once for all, and the dead past cannot therefore be revived except by a reformation of the old materials into new organized beings. If revival is impossible, reformation is the only alternative open to sensible people, and now it may be asked what is the principle on which this reformation must be based? People have very hazy ideas on this subject. It seems to many that it is the outward form which has to be changed, and if this change can be made, they think that all the difficulties in our way will vanish. If we change our outward manners and customs, sit in a particular way, or walk in a particular fashion, our work according to them is accomplished. I cannot but think that much of the prejudice against the reformers is due to this misunderstanding. It is not the outward form, but the inward form, the thought and the idea which determine the outward form, that has to be changed if real reformation is desired. [...]

The new mould of thought on this head must be cast on the lines of fraternity, a capacity to expand outwards, and to make more cohesive inwards the bonds of fellowship. Increase the circle of your friends and associates, slowly and cautiously if you will, but the tendency must be towards a general recognition of the essential equality between man and man. It will beget sympathy and power. It will strengthen your own hands, by the sense that you have numbers with you, and not against you, or as you foolishly imagine, below you.

The next idea which lies at the root of our helplessness is the sense that we are always intended to remain children, to be subject to outside control and never to rise to the dignity of self-control by making our conscience and our reason the supreme, if not the sole, guide to our conduct. All past history has been a terrible witness to the havoc committed by this misconception. We are children no doubt but the children of God, and not of man, and the voice of God is the only voice [to] which we are bound to listen. Of course, all of us cannot listen to this voice when we desire it, because from long neglect and dependence upon outside help, we have benumbed this faculty of conscience in us. With too many of us, a thing is true or false, righteous or sinful, simply because somebody in the past has said that it is so. [...]

Similarly there is no doubt that men differ from men in natural capacities, and aptitudes, and that heredity and birth are factors of considerable importance in our development. But it is at the same time true they are not the only factors that determine the whole course of our life for good or for evil, under a law of necessity. Heredity and birth explain many things, but this Law of Karma does not explain all things! What is worse, it does not explain the mystery that makes man and woman what they really are, the reflection and the image of God. Our passions and our feelings, our pride and our ambition, lend strength to these agencies, and with their help the Law of Karma completes our conquest, and in too many cases enforces our surrender. The new idea that should come in here is that this Law of Karma can be controlled and set back by a properly trained will, when it is made subservient to a higher will than ours. This we see in our everyday life, and Necessity, or the Fates are, as our own texts tell us, faint obstacles in the way of our advancement if we devote ourselves to the Law of Duty. I admit that this misconception is very hard to remove, perhaps the hardest of the old ideas. But removed it must be, if not in this life or generation, in many lives and generations, if we are ever to rise to our full stature.

[From: Ranade, 'Revival and Reform. Address at the Eleventh Indian National Social Conference', Appendix in K. P. Karunakaran, *Religion and Awakening in India* (Meerut: Meenakshi Prakashan, 2nd ed., 1969), 145–57, here 151–5.][132]

ROMESH CHUNDER DUTT (1848–1909) was the pioneer of economic history in India. In his account and analysis of the structure of colonial economy, he exposed its exploitative nature, and, at the same time, described the intrinsic Indian potential of development that was hindered in its realization under the conditions of foreign rule.

> *Dutt belonged to a reputed Bengali family with an Anglophile outlook. Brought up and educated in Calcutta, he went to England at the age of 20, in order to take the examination for the Indian Civil Service and to prepare for the Bar. In London, he came into contact with the liberal ideas of William Gladstone, John Stuart Mill, Charles Dickens, etc. After his return, Dutt worked in the Indian Civil Service in Bengal from 1871 to 1897. In 1889, he presided over the session of the Indian National Congress in Lucknow. After retirement from the administrative service, he went to England again and worked for some time as a lecturer in Indian history at the University College in London. From 1904 on, Dutt served the Maharaja of Baroda as minister of finance, trying to put his political ideas into practice.*

Dutt's interest in history was aroused by literature,[133] and the first of his own writings were works of fiction too. Stimulated by the novels of Sir Walter Scott and personally encouraged

---

[132]Ranade's 'Annual Addresses' at the National Social Conference are collected in C. Y. Chintamani (ed.), *Indian Social Reform*, Part II (Madras: Thompson, 1901). Other texts by Ranade on economy and society: 1898, 1902, 1915. Further reading: Tucker 1977; Sugam Anand, 'MG Ranade', in idem, *Modern Indian Historiography*, 100–6.

[133]This could also be explained according to Dutt, by the peculiarity of Indian tradition: 'Although no work of a purely historical character has been left behind by the people of Ancient India, it is possible to gain from their works on literature and religion a fairly accurate idea of their civilization and the progress of their intellect and social institutions.' Dutt, *The Literature of Bengal* (1877), quoted in Nilmani Mukherjee, 'Romesh Chunder Dutt (1848–1909)', *Quarterly Review of Historical Studies* 3 (1963–4), 183–8, here 183.

by Bankimchandra Chatterjee, he wrote, six novels with a historical background; one of them, *The Lake of Palms* (1902), is regarded as 'perhaps the most sustained attempt to translate indigenous traditions into the language of "modern" ideas'.[134]

After writing history books for children during the 1870s,[135] Dutt turned to early Indian history and culture in the 1880s. He translated the *Rigveda* into Bengali (1885–7) and, later, parts of the Mahabharata and the Ramayana into English.[136] In 1889–90, he published his *History of Civilization in Ancient India* (three volumes), which highlighted the greatness of ancient Indian culture and which established Dutt's reputation as a patriotic historian. A *Brief History of Ancient and Modern Bengal* followed in 1892.

Since his years as a government officer in rural Bengal, Dutt was interested in issues of economic history. At a time when this discipline was hardly established even in the West, he published *The Peasantry of Bengal under Hindu, Muslim, and British Rule* (1874). It was, in particular, his impression of the repeated famines towards the end of the nineteenth century that made him write the *Economic History of India*, aiming 'to understand the condition of the Indian people—the sources of their wealth and the causes of their poverty'.[137] In this work, which deals with Indian economy since the battle of Plassey (1757), Dutt relies largely on parliamentary papers, official reports, letters, protocols, statistics, etc., which he quotes in long extracts, not only for the sake of thorough documentation, but also taking into account the English readers he was addressing.

The Economic History of India counts among the most influential works of historiography in India during colonial rule. Its reception was ambivalent, however. The revivalists felt confirmed in their view that the 'poverty and economic backwardness of India were due not to anything inherent in Indian society, but to the foreign intrusion' (Embree 1988: 45). Dutt also contributed to the widespread image of the idyllic Indian village community. Gandhi, who wept after reading Dutt's account of the destruction of traditional handicraft, made him a chief witness to his critique of modernity. Dutt, indeed, was sceptical about Manchester capitalism[138] and made it clear that 'every true Indian hopes that the small cultivation of India will not be replaced by landlordism, and that something of the home industries will survive the assaults of capitalism'.[139] The description

[134]Sudhir Chandra 1992: 69. The novel appeared first in Bengali under the title *Sansar* (1886) and then in English translation: *The Lake of Palms*. The historical background of Dutt's novels is mostly the period of Mughal rule, sixteenth and seventeenth centuries. Cf. Sudhir Chandra, 'The Cultural Component of Economic Nationalism: R. C. Dutt's *The Lake of Palms*', *IHR* XII (1985–6), 106–20.

[135]See *A Brief History of Ancient and Modern India*; and *History of India*. Written in 1879 in Bengali, the latter book aimed 'to encourage a sense of unity and past glory in the minds of the Bengali boys and to help them to remedy the errors and to encourage them to take to the path of progress'. Quoted in Mukherjee, 'Romesh Chunder Dutt', 185.

[136]Condensed into English verse (1910).

[137]'Introduction', p. V. For the same thematic, see also Dutt, *Famines in India* (1900); *Open Letters to Lord Curzon on Famines and Land Assessments in India* (1900).

[138]Cf. Jyoti Prakash Chakrabarti, 'Romesh Chunder Dutt: A Critic of the Economics of Colonialism', in Amal Kumar 1979: 126–47, here 142.

[139]*The Economic History of India*, quoted in Sunil Sen, 'Romesh Chandra Dutt', in Sen 1973: 320–8, here 326.

of the arrested economic development under colonialism can be seen, in a way, as an anticipation of the late twentieth century debate on 'de-industrialization' and the 'development of underdevelopment'.[140]

The Economic History of India (1902–4)

Excellent works on the military and political transactions of the British in India have been written by eminent historians. No history of the people of India, of their trades, industries, and agriculture, and of their economic condition under British administration, has yet been compiled. Recent famines in India have attracted attention to this very important subject, and there is a general and widespread desire to understand the condition of the Indian people—the sources of their wealth and the causes of their poverty. A brief Economic History of British India is therefore needed at the present time.

Englishmen can look back on their work in India, if not with unalloyed satisfaction, at least with some legitimate pride. They have conferred on the people of India what is the greatest human blessing—Peace. They have introduced Western Education, bringing an ancient and civilised nation in touch with modern thought, modern sciences, modern institutions and life. They have built up an administration which, though it requires reform with the progress of the times, is yet strong and efficacious. They have framed wise laws, and have established Courts of Justice, the purity of which is as absolute as in any country on the face of the earth. These are results which no honest critic of British work in India regards without high admiration.

On the other hand, no open-minded Englishman contemplates the material condition of the people of India under British rule with equal satisfaction. The poverty of the Indian population at the present day is unparalleled in any civilised country; the famines which have desolated India within the last quarter of the nineteenth century are unexampled in their extent and intensity in the history of ancient or modern times. By a moderate calculation, the famines of 1877 and 1878, of 1889 and 1892, of 1897 and 1900, have carried off fifteen millions of people. The population of a fair-sized European country has been swept away from India within twenty-five years. A population equal to half of that of England has perished in India within a period which men and women, still in middle age, can remember.

What are the causes of this intense poverty and these repeated famines in India? Superficial explanations have been offered one after another, and have been rejected on close examination.

---

[140]Another early contribution to economic history in India is Gadgil, 1924. An article by Morris David Morris ('Towards a Reinterpretation of Nineteenth-Century Indian Economic History', *Journal of Economic History* 23 (1963), 606–18), taking up the issue of the economic impact of colonialism, led to a debate in the 1960s which is documented in Morris 1969; the volume contains contributions by Morris, Toru Matsui, Bipan Chandra, and Tapan Raychaudhuri. For the ongoing Indian debate on deindustrialization, see Amiya Kumar Bagchi, 'De-industrialization in India in the Nineteenth Century: Some Theoretical Implications', *Journal of Development Studies* 12 (1976), 135–64; Marika Vicziany, 'The Deindustrialization of India in the Nineteenth Century: A Methodological Critique of Amiya Kumar Bagchi', *IESHR* 16 (1979), 105–46. For the global dimension of the issue, see André Gunder-Frank, 'The World Economic System in Asia before European Hegemony', *The Historian* 56 (1994), 259–76. For the political issue of development and underdevelopment in the 1970s and 1980s, see below, Section 4.3.

It was said that the population increased rapidly in India and that such increase must necessarily lead to famines; it is found on inquiry that the population has never increased in India at the rate of England, and that during the last ten years it has altogether ceased to increase. It was said that the Indian cultivators were careless and improvident, and that those who did not know how to save when there was plenty, must perish when there was want; but it is known to men who have lived all their lives among these cultivators, that there is not a more abstemious, a more thrifty, a more frugal race of peasantry on earth. It was said that the Indian money-lender was the bane of India, and by his fraud and extortion kept the tillers of the soil in a chronic state of indebtedness; but the inquiries of the latest Famine Commission have revealed that the cultivators of India are forced under the thraldom of money-lenders by the rigidity of the Government revenue demand. It was said that in a country where the people depended almost entirely on their crops, they must starve when the crops failed in years of drought; but the crops in India, as a whole, have never failed, there has never been a single year when the food supply of the country was insufficient for the people, and there must be something wrong, when failure in a single province brings on a famine, and the people are unable to buy their supplies from neighbouring provinces rich in harvests.

Deep down under all these superficial explanations we must seek for the true causes of Indian poverty and Indian famines. The economic laws which operate in India are the same in other countries of the world; the causes which lead to wealth among other nations lead to prosperity in India; the causes which impoverish other nations impoverish the people of India. Therefore, the line of inquiry which the economist will pursue in respect of India is the same which he adopts in inquiring into the wealth or poverty of other nations. Does agriculture flourish? Are industries and manufactures in a prosperous condition? Are the finances properly administered so as to bring back to the people an adequate return for the taxes paid by them? Are the sources of national wealth widened by a Government anxious for the material welfare of the people? These are questions which the average Englishman asks himself when inquiring into the economic condition of any country in the world; these are questions which he will ask himself in order to ascertain the truth about India.

It is, unfortunately, a fact which no well-informed Indian official will ignore, that, in many ways, the sources of national wealth in India have been narrowed under British rule. India in the eighteenth century was a great manufacturing as well as a great agricultural country, and the products of the Indian loom supplied the markets of Asia and of Europe. It is, unfortunately, true that the East Indian Company and the British Parliament, following the selfish commercial policy of a hundred years ago, discouraged Indian manufactures in the early years of British rule in order to encourage the rising manufactures of England. Their fixed policy, pursued during the last decades of the eighteenth century and the first decades of the nineteenth, was to make India subservient to the industries of Great Britain, and to make the Indian people grow raw produce only, in order to supply material for the looms and manufactories of Great Britain. This policy was pursued with unwavering resolution and with fatal success; orders were sent out, to force Indian artisans to work in the Company's factories; commercial residents were legally vested with extensive powers over villages and communities of Indian weavers; prohibitive tariffs excluded Indian silk and cotton goods from England; English goods were admitted into India free of duty or on payment of a nominal duty. [...]

Six years ago, there was a celebration in London which was like a scenic representation of the Unity of the British Empire. Men from all British Colonies and Dependencies came together to take part in the Diamond Jubilee of a Great Queen's reign. Indian Princes stood by the side of loyal Canadians and hardy Australians. The demonstration called forth an outburst of enthusiasm seldom witnessed in these islands. And to thoughtful minds it recalled a long history of bold enterprises, arduous struggles, and a wise conciliation, which had cemented a world-wide Empire. Nations, living in different latitudes and under different skies, joined in a celebration worthy of the occasion.

One painful thought, however, disturbed the minds of the people. Amidst signs of progress and prosperity from all parts of the Empire, India alone presented a scene of poverty and distress. A famine, the most intense and the most widely extended yet known, desolated the country in 1897. The most populous portion of the Empire had not shared its prosperity. Increasing wealth, prospering industries and flourishing agriculture had not followed the flag of England in her greatest dependency. [...]

The Indian Empire will be judged by History as the most superb of human institutions in modern times. But it would be a sad story for future historians to tell that the Empire gave the people of India peace but not prosperity; that the manufacturers lost their industries; that the cultivators were ground down by a heavy and variable taxation which precluded any saving; that the revenues of the country were to a large extent diverted to England; and that recurring and desolating famines swept away millions of the population. On the other hand, it would be a grateful story for Englishmen to tell that England in the twentieth century undid her past mistakes in India as in Ireland; that she lightened land taxes, revived industries, introduced representation, and ruled India for the good of her people; and that the people of India felt in their hearts that they were citizens of a great and United Empire.

[From: R. C. Dutt, *The Economic History of India* (Classics of Indian History and Economics) (New Delhi: Government of India, Publications Division, Ministry of Information and Broadcasting, 1960), Preface to the first edition, Vol. I and Vol. II.][141]

The initial impact of Marxism on Indian historical thinking is tangible, first and foremost, in the person and work of MANABENDRA NATH ROY (1887–1954). Roy rejected the assumption of a special Indian path in history, against European Marxists as well as Indian nationalists. He insisted on a consistent interpretation of the history of India according to the model of Historical Materialism.

---

[141]*The Economic History of India* appeared first in two separate volumes: *Economic History of India—Under Early British Rule* (London 1902); *Economic History of India in the Victorian Age* (London 1904). The book has seen numerous re-editions and reprints. Further reading: Sunil Sen, 'Romesh Chandra Dutt', in Sen 1973: 320–8; Rule, 1977.

Manabendra Nath Roy (originally Narendra Nath Bhattacharya) was born in Urbalia and belonged to a family of Bengali Brahmans. He got his school education in Calcutta. After participating, during the First World War, in an unsuccessful attempt to smuggle German weapons to India, he had to go abroad. In the U.S.A., Roy came into contact with socialist ideas; in Mexico he worked for the foundation of a Communist Party. He attended the second congress of the Communist International in Moscow as a delegate. Within the Secretariate of the Comintern, Roy was in charge of the communist movements in Asia. An unsuccessful mission in China (1927) led to his exclusion. In 1930, after two years in Berlin, he returned to India, where he was soon arrested and imprisoned for six years. Later, he tried to form a radical group (League of National Congressmen) within the INC, and in 1940 he founded the Radical Democratic Party. Finally, he turned away from Marxism and began to propagate 'radical humanism'. In Dehra Dun (at the foot of the Himalayas) he set up the Indian Renaissance Institute the vocation of which was to study the problems of political transformation in India. Since 1937, he edited the magazine Independent India, *which, in 1949, was renamed the* Radical Humanist.

Roy was first attracted by the ideas of Vivekananda and Bankimchandra. His impression of *Anandamath* inspired him to participate in the revolutionary activities of an extremist group (Indian National Congress Party) against foreign rule.

While in Mexico, he wrote the short work *India: Her Past, Present, and Future* (1918), in which he tried to explain to an alien public the Indian claim to independence and to correct the false idea of his country as conveyed by imperialists.[142] Roy laid claim to a tradition of tolerance and peacefulness for India, which he related to the Dravidian element (as different from the 'wild' Aryan one): 'India has never possessed the insane idea of wanting to be master of the world.'[143]

At the second congress of the Comintern (1920), Roy argued with Lenin over the role of the national bourgeoisie in the colonized countries. While Lenin recommended a limited cooperation with the national independence movements, Roy pleaded for keeping the struggle of the masses apart from that of the bourgeoisie and for strengthening class consciousness. [144] Even after renouncing Marxism, Roy continued to believe in the idea of history as a process of social improvement and rationalization. In *Reason, Romanticism, and Revolution* (Calcutta 1955), he distanced himself from Hegel and Marx, but took up some ideas of Engels regarding the link between natural and social processes.[145]

India in Transition is based on a 'report about the structure of the national economy and the class relations of contemporary India', in which Roy sought to clarify his position with regard to that of Lenin. Lenin himself had encouraged him to elaborate the report into a book 'which

---

[142]'Our history has been misinterpreted and badly written by imperialist authors causing the world to believe that before the so-called British conquest India did not exist as a nation and that the conquest meant progress for India.' *Selected Works* 1987: 87.

[143]Ibid., 90.

[144]Cf. Roy, 'An Indian Communist Manifesto', in Adhikary 1971: 151–5.

[145]Cf. Klimkeit: 1971: 52. Roy's conception of Radical Humanism is summarized in a lecture delivered in 1949: *The Philosophy and Practice of Radical Humanism* (New Delhi: 1970). His attitude remained materialistic in principle and was characterized by a deep mistrust of religion.

would give a realistic picture of the contemporary Indian society and open up the perspective of the Indian revolution'.[146] The work was praised, in the preface of its Russian version, as the 'first Marxist research work on India'. Later, however, Roy was blamed by Soviet historians for 'unscientific and artificial' constructions, because he had overestimated the progressive aspects of British politics in India compared to its deindustrializing effects.[147]

India in Transition (1922)

Roy begins by distinguishing three schools of thought offering orientation in the contemporary situation of transition. The accounts, written from an imperialist perspective and presenting the New India as a product of British educational efforts, are confronted with those of the moderate nationalists, who emphasize the autonomous vigour of renovation of the indigenous elite (and politically minded Indians) by way of constitutional reforms. Roy then proceeds:

There is a third school which also takes notice and talks about this transition. They are the extreme nationalists who have been dominating the stage for the last several years. Their socio-political philosophy is the hardest to comprehend, being hopelessly confused. The reason for this confusion is that they hold an entirely wrong conception of this transition, in spite of being the most rudely tossed and toppled by this great wave of popular upheaval. To them it is not so much a transition, but a revivalist period, through which India is passing. Because they think that the Indian people are struggling to liberate themselves from the political and economic bondage which obstructed their progress for centuries, not to begin a new life with a new vision, but to revive the old. But the past is doomed by history, one of whose most important chapters is the present transition.

All these diverse definitions and interpretations, nevertheless, do not alter the fact that India is changing and changing fast. Her people are out, consciously or unconsciously, to change their life. This is the fundamental phenomenon in all that is happening in India today. Neither the anxiety of the British Imperialists, nor the desire of the constitutional patriots, nor the fanaticism of the orthodox nationalists will be able to lead the rising Indian nation astray from the path marked out by those historical forces which determine human progress. Jointly or severally they may retard, confuse the forward march of the Indian people; but they cannot stop it forever. The real significance of the period of transition through which India is passing, is that after long and long years of forced stagnation, the progressive forces latent in the Indian society are asserting themselves. The future of the Indian nation is going to be shaped by the inexorable evolution of these forces.

The following chapters are written with a view to analyse the present situation and the prospective developments. In this analysis nothing has been taken for granted; realities, cold facts, have been examined in order to determine which way the wind is blowing. An attempt has been made to investigate the past, analyse the present and visualize the future, from the

---

[146]M. N. Roy Memoirs (1964): 551, 552, quoted in Seth 1995: 78, 104.

[147]Cf. O'Leary 1989: 319, 316. Sudipta Kaviraj reproaches Roy with 'a mistaking of Asia for Europe': 'The Heteronomous Radicalism of M. N. Roy', in Pantham and Deutsch 1986: 209–35, here 235.

point of view of Historical Materialism. To rewrite Indian history is a tremendous, although much needed task. No such pretension entered into the writing of these pages. They are written with an eye to problems much more immediate. The object of this work is first, to point out the material forces that are pushing the various classes of the Indian people in the present struggle; second, to point out the deep-rooted social character of the present unrest; third, to analyse the social tendencies embodied by the two principal schools of nationalism; and fourth, to indicate the revolutionary trend of the growing mass movement and to impress upon those concerned the necessity of conforming their programme and tactics according to it. [...]

With the help of the materials available, the real character of the transition through which the Indian society is passing, has been shown. Taking this analysis of the economic development of one section of the population and the corresponding exploitation of the rest, the future life and struggle of the rising Indian nation are to be judged. Neither a 'New India' nor a 'Young India' is going to be born from this transition, which will simply result in ushering the people of India into a more advanced stage of socio-economic development. India is not only struggling to free herself from the political domination of a foreign power, but she is moving ahead in the path of human progress and in doing so finds many cherished traditions of old prejudicial to this movement forward. Therefore her entire store of popular energy is in a state of revolt against everything which has so far kept her backward and still conspires to do so. This revolt, this great social upheaval, is the essence of the present transition, which marks the disappearance of the old, bankrupt socio-economic structure in order to be replaced by one which will afford the people greater facilities for progress. [...]

The most outstanding feature of the Indian national movement has been its lack of theoretical foundation. A modern political movement involving a sweeping mass-action, cannot go on for ever with antiquated religious ideology. On the other hand, the impotent constitutionalism of the Moderates falls miserably short of the mark although it serves the purpose of the bourgeoisie. The Indian people is engaged in a social struggle of historic and to a certain extent of unprecedented character. There must be a socio-political philosophy behind this great movement. This much-needed ideological background of our struggle is not to be invented from the imagination of great men; it will be evolved out of the material forces making the birth, growth and success of such a struggle possible. To study our social conditions, actual as well as of the past, and to watch the evolution of the economic forces is indispensable for those who desire to understand that the people of India are progressing along a course common to the entire human race. We have our peculiar problems to solve; there are peculiar obstacles to be overcome on our way. But the fact remains that we are involved in a great struggle which calls for profound understanding of the socio-economic forces making for the progress of the Indian people.

[From: Roy, 'India in Transition', in *Selected Works of M. N. Roy*, ed. by Sibnarayan Ray (Delhi: Oxford UP, 1987), 185–8.][148]

[148]The English edition of the book, written in collaboration with Abani Mukherji, appeared in 1922 in Berlin with the fictive publisher J. B. Target, Geneva. A Russian version had been published in 1921. A new edition has been brought out by the Indian Renaissance Institute: *India in Transition* (Bombay: Nachiketa, 1971). Further reading: B. S. Sharma 1965.

JAWAHARLAL NEHRU (1889–1964) stands for the political realization of the concepts of independent statehood, national integration and social modernization. In contrast to Gandhi, he attempted to convey to the Indians confidence in the course of history and in the possibilities of progress.

> Nehru was born at Allahabad in a Kashmiri Brahman family. His father, Motilal Nehru, had a liberal orientation and was a successful lawyer. At the age of fifteen, Jawaharlal was sent to England in order to complete his school education at Harrow and to study Natural Sciences and Law at Cambridge University. After seven years in England, Nehru returned to India in 1912 and entered his father's office. He became a member of the Indian National Congress and, after some time, rose to the position of General Secretary (1923). During the years of the freedom fight, Nehru was imprisoned several times. After the British withdrawal from India and the death of Gandhi, he became the dominating figure in Indian politics. From 1947 to 1964, he acted as India's first Prime Minister.

Nehru belonged to those western-educated intellectuals who 'discovered' their Indian roots only in a later process of acculturation. Before this, he had criticized his countrymen's inclination to tradition as an anachronism and an obstacle in the way to modernity. It was the experience of the fight against foreign rule and the need for a better understanding of the present situation which led Nehru to history and made him aware 'that I belonged to the past' and 'that the whole of the past belonged to me in the present. Past history merged into contemporary history.' (Nehru 1989: 23)

Nehru used his time spent in prison to formulate his ideas about Indian politics and history. From the jail he wrote letters to his daughter Indira, published later as a book: Glimpses of World History (1934–5). Again during imprisonment, he wrote his autobiography titled Towards Freedom (1936).[149] Here he took a critical stance on some of the ideas of Gandhi.[150] Nehru's declared purpose in writing the Discovery of India was to grasp the 'spirit of India' and to thus have a 'key to the understanding of my country and people', 'some guidance to thought and action'. Or, as he wrote in the chapter on 'the burden of the past': 'There is a special heritage for those of us of India, [...] something that is in our flesh and blood and bones, that has gone to make us what we are and what we are likely to be. It is the thought of this particular heritage and its application to the present that has long filled my mind' (Nehru 1989: 59, 36–7).

D. C. Gordon[151] views Nehru, in his attempt to reconcile Indian tradition with the challenges of modernity, as a typical 'reconstructionalist'. Notwithstanding the struggle against colonial rule, the antagonism of 'we' and 'they' is dissolved in the orientation towards universal progress. The reference was not to the Golden Age of India anymore but to the process of change.[152]

The Discovery of India, written while Nehru was in Ahmadnagar Fort prison, from April to

[149]See S. N. Mukherjee, 'My Discovery of Nehru: Autobiography as History', in idem., 1996: 138–48.

[150]Nevertheless, Nehru was also influenced by Gandhi's historical scepticism, to a certain degree. His modernism was qualified by the experience of the 'unpleasantness of history'. Asthana 1992: 159–60.

[151]Gordon 1971, specifically 45–52.

[152]Accordingly, Nehru based the idea of a unified nation on the will to synthesize rather than a static entity. The Indian National Congress, in fact, had to play 'a great role in fixing the idea of Indian unity in the minds of our masses.' 'The Unity of India' [1938], quoted in Seth 1995: 202.

September 1944, has become a classic among the many testimonies of Indian freedom fighters. It is viewed as one of the best accounts 'of the impact of colonialism on India and of the rise of the anti-imperialist national movement'.[153] According to Partha Chatterjee, it is the 'writings of this principal political architect of the new Indian state', in which 'one can find, more clearly than anywhere else, the key ideological elements and relations of nationalist thought at its moment of arrival' (Chatterjee 1996: 132). *The Discovery of India* has also been praised for its literary quality: as a brilliant piece of 'Renaissance historical writing'.[154]

India's Growth Arrested (1946)

A nation, like an individual, has many personalities, many approaches to life. If there is a sufficiently strong organic bond between these different personalities, it is well; otherwise those personalities split up and lead to disintegration and trouble. Normally, there is a continuous process of adjustment going on and some kind of an equilibrium is established. If normal development is arrested, or sometimes if there is some rapid change which is not easily assimilated, then conflict arises between those different personalities. In the mind and spirit of India, below the surface of our superficial conflicts and divisions, there has been this fundamental conflict due to a long period of arrested growth. A society, if it is to be both stable and progressive, must have a certain more or less fixed foundation of principles as well as a dynamic outlook. Both appear to be necessary. Without the dynamic outlook there is stagnation and decay, without some fixed basis of principle there is likely to be disintegration and destruction. [...]

Indian civilization achieved much that it was aiming at, but, in that very achievement, life began to fade away, for it is too dynamic to exist for long in a rigid, unchanging environment. Even those basic principles, which are said to be unchanging, lose their freshness and reality when they are taken for granted and the search for them ceases. Ideas of truth, beauty, and freedom decay, and we become prisoners following a deadening routine.

The very thing India lacked, the modern West possessed and possessed to excess. It had the dynamic outlook. It was engrossed in the changing world, caring little for ultimate principles, the unchanging, the universal. It paid little attention to duties and obligations and emphasized rights. It was active, aggressive, acquisitive, seeking power and domination, living in the present and ignoring the future consequences of its actions. Because it was dynamic, it was progressive and full of life, but that life was a fevered one and the temperature kept on rising progressively.

If Indian civilization went to seed because it became static, self-absorbed and inclined to narcissism, the civilization of the modern West, with all its great and manifold achievements does not appear to have been a conspicuous success or to have thus far solved the basic problems of life. Conflict is inherent in it and periodically it indulges in self-destruction on a colossal scale. It seems to lack something to give it stability, some basic principles to give meaning to life though what these are I cannot say. Yet because it is dynamic and full of life and curiosity, there

[153]Bipan Chandra, 'Nehru's Sense of History', in idem, 1993: 159–65, here 164.

[154]David Kopf, 'Hermeneutics versus History', *JAS* 39 (1980), 495–505, here 496. According to Kopf, it is 'perhaps the best account of India's past written by a nationalist in the twentieth century'. Kopf et al. 1977: 751–2.

is hope for it. India, as well as China, must learn from the West, for the modern West has much to teach, and the spirit of the age is represented by the West. But the West is also obviously in need of learning much and its advances in technology will bring it little comfort if it does not learn some of the deeper lessons of life, which have absorbed the minds of thinkers in all ages and in all countries.

India has become static and yet it would be utterly wrong to imagine that she was unchanging. No change at all means death. Her very survival as a highly evolved nation shows that there was some process of continuous adaptation going on. When the British came to India, though technologically somewhat backward, she was still among the advanced commercial nations of the world. Technical changes would undoubtedly have come and changed India as they have changed some western countries. But her normal development was arrested by the British power. Industrial growth was checked and as a consequence social growth was also arrested. The normal power-relationships of society could not adjust themselves and find an equilibrium as all power was concentrated in the alien authority, which based itself on force and encouraged groups and classes which had ceased to have any real significance. Indian life thus progressively became more artificial, for many of the individuals and groups who seemed to play an important role in it had no vital functions left and were there only because of the importance given to them by the alien power. They had long ago finished their role in history and would have been pushed aside by new forces if they had not been given foreign protection. They became straw-stuffed symbols of protégés of foreign authority, thereby cutting themselves still further away from the living currents of the nation. Normally, they would have been weeded out or diverted to some more appropriate function by revolution or democratic process. But so long as foreign authoritarian rule continued, no such development could take place. And so India was cluttered up with these emblems of the past and the real changes that were taking place were hidden behind an artificial facade. [...]

Within the framework of a sterile alien rule no effective solutions are possible, and national problems, unable to find solution, become even more acute. We have arrived in India at a stage when no half measures can solve our problems, no advance on one sector is enough. There has to be a big jump and advance all along the line, or the alternative may be overwhelming catastrophe.

As in the world as a whole, so in India, it is a race between the forces of peaceful progress and construction and those of disruption and disaster, with each succeeding disaster on a bigger scale than the previous one. We can view this prospect as optimists or as pessimists, according to our predilections and mental make-up. Those who have faith in a moral ordering of the universe and of the ultimate triumph of virtue can, fortunately for them, function as lookers on or as helpers, and cast the burden on God; others will have to carry that burden on their own weak shoulders, hoping for the best and preparing for the worst.

India must break with much of her past and not allow it to dominate the present. Our lives are encumbered with the dead wood of this past; all that is dead and has served its purpose has to go. But that does not mean a break with, or a forgetting of, the vital and life-giving in that past. We can never forget the ideals that have moved our race, the dreams of the Indian people through the ages, the wisdom of the ancients, the buoyant energy and love of life and nature of our forefathers, their spirit of curiosity and mental adventure, the daring of their thought, their splendid achievements in literature, art and culture, their love of truth and beauty and freedom, the basic values that they set up, their understanding of life's mysterious ways, their toleration of other ways than theirs, their capacity to absorb other peoples and their cultural accomplishments, to synthesize them and develop a varied and mixed culture; nor can we forget the myriad experiences which have built up our ancient race and lie embedded in our subconscious minds. We will never forget them or cease to take pride in that noble heritage of ours. If India forgets them she will no longer remain India and much that has made her our joy and pride will cease to be. [...]

The modern mind, that is to say the better type of the modern mind, is practical and pragmatic, ethical and social, altruistic and humanitarian. It is governed by a practical idealism for social betterment. The ideals which move it represent the spirit of the age, the Zeitgeist,[155] the Yugadharma. It has discarded to a large extent the philosophic approach of the ancients, their search for ultimate reality, as well as the devotionalism and mysticism of the medieval period. Humanity is its god and social service its religion. This conception may be incomplete, as the mind of every age has been limited by its environment, and every age has considered some partial truth as the key to all truth. Every generation and every people suffer from the illusion that their way of looking at things is the only right way, or is, at any rate, the nearest approach to it. Every culture has certain values attached to it, limited and conditioned by that culture. The people governed by that culture take these values for granted and attribute a permanent validity to them. So the values of our present-day culture may not be permanent and final; nevertheless they have an essential importance for us for they represent the thought and spirit of the age we live in. A few seers and geniuses, looking into the future, may have a completer vision of humanity and the universe; they are of the vital stuff out of which all real advance comes. The vast majority of people do not even catch up to the present-day values, though they may talk about them in the jargon of the day, and they live imprisoned in the past.

We have therefore to function in line with the highest ideals of the age we live in, though we may add to them or seek to mould them in accordance with our national genius. Those ideals may be classed under two heads: humanism and the scientific spirit. Between these two there has been an apparent conflict but the great upheaval of thought to-day, with its questioning of all values, is removing the old boundaries between these two approaches, as well as between the external world of science and the internal world of introspection. There is a growing synthesis between humanism and the scientific spirit, resulting in a kind of scientific humanism.

[From: Nehru, *The Discovery of India* (New Delhi: Jawaharlal Nehru Memorial Fund, 1989), 505–9, 557–8.][156]

[155]Zeitgeist (German): spirit of the times.

[156]*The Discovery of India* appeared first in 1946 at The Signet Press, Calcutta. A selection of Nehru's writings has been edited by Norma 1965. Further reading: Amiya Chakravarty 1952; Ravindran 1980; David Kopf, 'A Look at Nehru's World History from the Dark Side of Modernity', *Journal of World History* 2 (1991), 47–63; Satish Chandra, 'Nehru the Historian', in idem, 1997: 89–94.

RAJANI PALME DUTT (1896–1974) presented one of the first comprehensive analyses, based on Marxist principles, of Indian society under colonial rule. In his writings, Dutt made it clear that behind the political quest for independent statehood there was the social quest for emancipation from all types of exploitation.

> Dutt was born in Cambridge, the son of an Indian doctor and his Swedish wife. He was descended from the Rambagan Dutt family of Calcutta, to which also belonged the economic historian R. C. Dutt (R.P.D.'s grand-uncle). Dutt took up his studies at Oxford University, but had to withdraw after organizing, shortly before the outbreak of the Russian Revolution, a solidarity assembly for the Bolshevists. While he worked as a school-teacher for a living, he was among the founders and activists of the Communist Party of Great Britain. For a long time, he belonged to its Executive Committee and set up its Colonial Bureau.

Dutt was also a member of the Politbureau of the Communist Party of India (CPI, founded in 1925). As the editor of the papers *Daily Worker* and *Labour Monthly*, he regularly wrote columns about Indian politics. In 1936, Dutt and Ben Bradley published an article recommending a strategy to the Indian left that accepted the priority of the achievement of national independence (Dutt–Bradley Thesis).[157]

India Today was written in the years 1936 to 1939 and appeared in London (Left Book Club, 1940), not without censoring interventions from the publisher, Victor Gollancz. Immediately banned by the British authorities, the book was smuggled chapterwise to India, where it exercised great influence in leftist circles.

The Awakening of India (1940)

India is awakening. India, for thousands of years the prey of successive waves of conquerors, is awakening to independent existence as a free people with their own role to play in the world. This awakening has leapt forward in our lifetime. In the last 25 years a new India has emerged. Today India's advance to freedom, whatever the obstacles still to be overcome, is universally recognised as approaching victory in the near future. But the freeing of India removes the main base of modern imperialist domination of subject peoples. [...]

The rising contradictions, rooted in the social and economic, no less than the political conditions of India under imperialist rule, again and again defeat the attempts at harmony. The two levels, of the most advanced and elaborate finance capitalist exploitation and domination above, and of the lowest levels of social misery and backwardness below, are closely intertwined in a network of cause and effect. In between these two levels—between the two opposing extremes of the imperialist exploiters at the apex of the pyramid and the destitute producing masses at the base—exist a host of transitional forms, intermediary parasitism, subordinate mechanisms of exploitation, old decomposing forces and new advancing forces. Through it all, extending every year, develop the rising national consciousness of the Indian people and the rising economic demands of the hungry Indian masses. This is a situation packed at every turn with social dynamite.

The basic problem of India is not only national but social. The challenge of the Indian people

---

[157]'The Anti-Imperialist People's Front in India', *Labour Monthly* 18: 3, March 1936.

to imperialism is in its simplest sense a claim of one-fifth of humanity to freedom from foreign domination. But this demand for freedom inevitably strikes deeper than a claim for political independence in which it finds its political expression. It is at root a challenge to a deeply entrenched system of exploitation which has its seat in the City of London, but which is closely bound with a subordinate system of privilege and exploitation within India. The one cannot be touched without the other.

In this sense the Indian question is in the last analysis a social question. The basic problem of India is a problem of four hundred million human beings who are living under conditions of extreme poverty and semi-starvation for the overwhelming majority and are at the same time living under a foreign rule which holds complete control over their lives and maintains by force the social system leading to these terrible conditions. These hundreds of millions are struggling for life, for the means of life, for elementary freedom. The problem of their struggle and of how they can realise the aims is the problem of India.

The immediate aim of the struggle of the Indian people is national liberation, the conquest of national independence and the democratic right of self-government. But this aim represents the first stage of a deeper social struggle, of a moving social revolution within India. The national and social issues are closely intertwined, and the understanding of this interconnection is the key to the understanding of the Indian situation.

Social conservatism is still deeply rooted in India and profoundly affects the problems and character of the national movement. The effects of such social conservatism and reactionary tendencies weaken and disorganise the advance of the national movement. Just as imperialism has produced its mythology to cover up its real predatory record with the conventional picture of its 'civilising mission' so we need to be on guard against corresponding presuppositions and conventional mythologies in the opposite direction.

For, in opposition to the conventional imperialist mythology some backward looking sections in India have endeavoured to build up a counter-mythology. In reaction against the evils of imperialist domination, they have endeavoured to paint a picture of a golden age of India in the past before British rule. They seek to slur over the evils of the rotting social system which went down before the British onset. They seek, not only to explain historically, but to idealise and glorify just those reactionary survivals of India's past which hamper progress, weigh down the consciousness of the people and prevent unity. On the basis of these reactionary survivals they seek to build up national consciousness. In this way they have sought to turn the fight against imperialism into a fight against 'Western civilisation' in general. They turn their gaze backwards, not forwards. This is not to strengthen the national front, but to weaken it.

[From: R. P. Dutt, *India Today* (Calcutta: Manisha Grantalaya, 1989), 14–16.][158]

---

[158]The book appeared for the first time in India, in a revised and enlarged form, in 1947; it was newly edited in 1970, including the passages which had been censored before. Among Dutt's other publications are: *Modern India* (Bombay 1926), *The Crisis of Britain and the British Empire* (London 1953). Further reading: Sudipta Kaviraj, 'Marxian Theory and Analysis of Indian Politics', in *A Survey of Research in Political Science, IV: Political Thought*, 1986.

Resistant Traditions, Alternative
Histories, Idiosyncrasies

The defence against foreign rule and cultural colonization found its organizational expression mainly in nationalist and neo-Hindu movements, which, for their part, adopted western forms of historical thinking. But there were other ways of resistance to western influence. The holding on to indigenous intellectual traditions is exemplified, for instance, by the defence of the 'status quo in orthopraxy against Christians, Brahmos, and "atheists and rationalists"',[1] and by apologetic Sanskrit tracts which continued earlier inner-Hindu debates over religious change and plurality.[2] Treatises written by pandits, such as Vasudeva Sastrin Abhyankara, *Dharmatattvanirnaya* (Poona 1929), or Anantakrisna Sastrin, Sitarama Sastrin, and Srijiva Bhattacarya, *Dharmapradipa* (Calcutta n.d. [1937]), who refer to themselves as followers of the eternal *sanatana dharma*, discuss the impact of the presence of European mlecchas (Halbfass 1990: 260–1).

Traditional forms of scholarship persisted beside the new historical research methods and institutions.[3] Traditional calendars also continued to be in use, mainly for religious purposes but

[1] Sumit Sarkar, '"Kaliyuga," "Chakri", and "Bhakti": Ramkrishna and His Times', *EPW* (18 July 1992), 1543–66 (also in idem, *Writing Social History*, 282–357), here 1554.

[2] Richard Fox Young examines some of these texts in Young 1981. Vasudha Dalmia points to the gaps in research regarding the 'Dharma Sabhas' which emerged in the 1830s and their endeavour to defend *sanatana dharma*. Even though they were supposed to defend orthodoxy and tradition, they nevertheless were 'in fact, accommodating and articulating wide-reaching changes'. Dalmia criticizes the fact that 'these movements, often summarily denoted as "revivalist", have yet to be charted in any comprehensive fashion.' Dalmia 1997: 2–3

[3] The coexistence of modern and traditional scholarship is referred to by Bhandarkar in his 'Presidential Address' on the occasion of the Oriental Conference in 1919, *Collected Works*, I, 316–17. See also the Introduction, Section 2.1. For the persisting importance of indigenous forms of knowledge and the role of their representatives as members of autonomous networks of social communication in the face of the information systems of the state, see Bayly 1996.

also in secular contexts. The Shaka era (beginning in the year AD 78, when it is supposed to have been introduced by a Shaka king) and the Muslim Hijra era (beginning with AD 622, the year of Muhammad's flight from Mecca to Medina) continued to exist beside the Christian era of the West (BC, AD, today read as Common Era: BCE, CE).[4] An example of the resuscitated interpretation of time according to the yuga cycles is Aghorechandra Kabyatirtha's play *Kalir Abasan, ba Kalki-avatar Geetabhinoy* (The End of Kali, or the Coming of the Kalki Avatar, 1902) (Sumit Sarkar 1998: 207).

RABINDRANATH TAGORE (1861–1941), like other writers before him, viewed the spiritual East as the necessary complement of the materialistic West. East and West were not contrasted, however, in an essentialist manner, but embedded in universal processes of social change and creative work which had to be protected from impending tendencies of reification, in both hemispheres alike.

> *Tagore grew up in Calcutta in the special atmosphere of his family—Brahmans who had gained wealth and landed property through trade and cooperation with the British—and was influenced by modern thinking in his early youth. His grandfather Dwarkanath was the first Indian member of the Asiatic Society of Bengal; his father, Debendranath, reorganized the Brahmo Samaj. However, traditional Indian values were also transmitted to the children. Rabindranath left school at the age of 13 and later was sent for some years to England (1878–80). Back in Calcutta, he had his first success with poems and dramas. His comprehensive work, created over the next few decades, contributed to the evolution of Bengali as a literary idiom; in 1913, he was awarded the Nobel Prize for the English prose version of his* Gitanjali *(Song Offerings). His numerous journeys abroad made him the ambassador of Indian culture in the world. On the political level, Tagore participated in the agitation over the partition of Bengal (1905); later, while propagating a mutual understanding between East and West, he got into conflict with the nationalists. With Gandhi he disputed over non-cooperation and the proper way to autonomy. He returned the patent of nobility in protest against the massacre of Jallianwala Bagh (Amritsar, 1919). With the foundation of a school in Shantiniketan (1901), which later became a university (Vishva-Bharati), Tagore continued the tradition of the great Indian reformers.*

On the basis of the new historical and national consciousness in Bengal, prepared by Bankimchandra, Vivekananda and others, Tagore dealt with the problem of cultural identity and social change under various aspects. His great novels[5] reflect his endeavour to open

[4]This has to be clearly distinguished from Savarkar's demand for a new national calendar named 'Yudhishtar Samvat'. Cf. D Keer, Veer Savarkar, (Bombay 1966): 437–9; Suresh Sharma, 'Savarkar's Quest', 213. In *Hindutva*, Savarkar refers to the traditional concept of periodization: 'The Hindu counts his years not by centuries but by cycles—the Yuga and the Kalpa—and amazed asks: "O Lord of the line of Raghu [Rama], where has the kingdom of Ayodhya gone? O Lord of the line of Yadu [Krishna], where has Mathura gone!"' However, the *yuga* and the *kalpa* here are not associated with traditional sense concepts. Rather, the reference to myth is designed to reinforce secular expectations: 'If a people that had no past has no future, then a people that had produced an unending galaxy of heroes [...] have in their history a guarantee of their future greatness more assuring than any other people on earth yet possess.' *Hindutva*, loc. cit., 135

[5]See in particular the novel *Gora*, first published in serialized form, 1907–9.

up India to modernity, viewing internal change as necessary for survival and as a chance to develop.[6]

Tagore expressed his thoughts about history in a more discursive form in an essay about the historical novel (1898). This genre, according to him, made visible the wider horizon of life, the 'chariot of time', and represented the 'true aesthetic experience of history'. He described the past as the temporal dimension of the Self, which had to be added to that of space: 'Just as we want Bombay, Madras and Punjab to be near us, similarly we want a direct knowledge of the past of India. Fully aware of ourselves, we want to understand our identity both in space and time, as a unified great nation.'[7]

Tagore explicitly welcomed, in 1899, the appearance of the Bengali periodical *Aitihasik Chitra* (Images of History), which he hoped would contribute to the dissemination of historical knowledge and lead 'a crusade to free Indian history'. He contributed to this journal, 'a swadeshi factory of Indian history' designed 'to rescue our history from the hands of the foreigners', from the first edition.[8] In *Bharatvarsher Itihas* (The History of India, 1902), Tagore distinguished between two ways of dealing with the Other, 'by which one's society and civilisation can be safeguarded; either by killing and evicting the aliens or by bringing the aliens under its well ordered discipline and law. Europe, by adopting the first principle, kept open its conflict with the whole world; India, by adopting the second principle, tried to absorb all and everything gradually.'[9] In 'My Interpretation of Indian History',[10] Tagore depicted India's past against the background of the conflict between Brahmans and Kshatriyas. Increasingly sceptical about the expectations of modernization as cherished by the nationalists, Tagore saw the desired intellectual autonomy represented by the creativity of the artist rather than the deeds of the politician. This

[6]Tagore's poems also testify to this endeavour. See for instance *Bharat-Tirtha* (*Indian Pilgrimage*, 1910):

No one knows whence and at whose call
came pouring endless waves of men
rushing wilding alone—
to lose themselves in its sea;
Aryans and non-Aryans, Dravidians and Chinese
Scythians, Huns, Pathans and Moghuls—
all have merged and lost themselves in one body. [...]
Awake my mind, in the holy place of pilgrimage
on the shore of vast humanity
that is India.

[7]*Rabindra Rachanavali* (Calcutta 1961), XIII, 477, quoted in Meenakshi Mukherjee 1995: 57, 58. Tagore himself has written a historical novel, too: *Bauthakuranir Haat* (1883).

[8]Quoted in Mallick, 'Modern Historical Writing in Bengali', in Philips 1961: 450.

[9]Quoted in Kedar Nath Mukherjee 1982: 81. For the dialectic of unity and diversity, see Tagore's review of Abdul Karim's history of Muslim rule in India (1898): 'Grantha-samalocana', in *Rabindra Rachanavali*, XIII, 484–7; cf. Partha Chatterjee 1993: 112.

[10]The text written in Bengali (*Bharatbarsher Itihaser Dhara*, 1912) was translated into English by Jadunath Sarkar and published in *The Modern Review* 14 (Aug. 1913), 113–18, 231–36.

is made clear in the article 'A Vision of India's History',[11] in which Tagore dealt with the integration of Aryan and non-Aryan races in India.

It is Tagore's handling of Gandhi's critique of modern civilization which is particularly instructive with regard to a differentiated understanding of Indian tradition and western modernity. Tagore sought to transcend the 'mechanical repetitiveness' typical as much of the western as of the Indian way of life. If India was subjected to the 'rule of things as they have always been', the West was then subjected to the 'rule of things forever on the march'. Both remained, in their respective ways, slaves of the 'rule of things' and did not reach human autonomy, which, according to Tagore, required the dominance of the inner over the outer life.[12]

The essay 'Nationalism in India' is based on a series of lectures delivered by Tagore during a journey across the U.S.A. from September 1916 to January 1917. The reflections are directed against any form of nationalism that restricts. Tagore rejects the path of western civilization as a solution to the problems of India, all the more since it contradicted its own premises and betrayed its claims to historicity.

Nationalism in India (1917)

Tagore begins by describing his idea of the primacy of the Social over the Political. India, in particular, had always been confronted with the problem of the coexistence of different races. If, in the West, unfavourable natural conditions had given culture a 'character of political and commercial aggressivity' (77), adjustment between the races was the historical mission of India. 'In finding the solution of our problem we shall have helped to solve the world problem as well. What India has been, the whole world is now.' (78) Even at the global level, the issue was whether compassion and helpfulness or struggle and self-interest gained the upper hand:

I have no hesitation in saying that those who are gifted with the moral power of love and vision of spiritual unity, who have the least feeling of enmity against aliens, and the sympathetic insight to place themselves in the position of others, will be the fittest to take their permanent place in the age that is lying before us, and those who are constantly developing their instincts for fight and intolerance of aliens will be eliminated. For this is the problem before us, and we have to prove our humanity by solving it through the help of our higher nature. [...]

The educated Indian at present is trying to absorb some lessons from history contrary to the lessons of our ancestors. The East, in fact, is attempting to take unto itself a history, which is not the outcome of its own living. Japan, for example, thinks she is getting powerful through adopting western methods but, after she has exhausted her inheritance, only the borrowed weapons of civilisation will remain to her. She will not have developed herself from within.

Europe has her past. Europe's strength therefore lies in her history. We in India must make up

---

[11]*The Vishva Bharati Quarterly* (April 1923), 5–31. This is a revised version of the essay of 1912 (see above), picking up some ideas of Tagore's brother Dwijendranath. Creativity is seen here, in deviation from some ideologues of Aryanism, as a specifically Dravidian heritage.

[12]Cf. Suresh Sharma, 'Swaraj and the Quest for Freedom—Rabindranath Tagore's Critique of Gandhi's Non-Cooperation', *Thesis Eleven* 39 (1994), 93–104, here 98. See also Tagore's essays: 'The East and the West' (1891); 'Civilization and Progress' (1924), in 1980: 42–59.

our minds that we cannot borrow other people's history, and that if we stifle our own we are committing suicide. When you borrow things that do not belong to your life, they only serve to crush your life. And therefore I believe that it does India no good to compete with western civilisation in its own field. But we shall be more than compensated if, in spite of the insults heaped upon us, we follow our own destiny.

There are lessons which impart information or train our minds for intellectual pursuits. These are simple and can be acquired and used with advantage. But there are others which affect our deeper nature and change our direction of life. Before we accept them and pay their value by selling our own inheritance, we must pause and think deeply. In man's history there come ages of fireworks which dazzle us by their force and movement. They laugh not only at our modest household lamps but also at the eternal stars. But let us not for that provocation be precipitate in our desire to dismiss our lamps. Let us patiently bear our present insult and realise that these fireworks have splendour but not permanence, because of the extreme explosiveness which is the cause of their power, and also of their exhaustion. They are spending a fatal quantity of energy and substance compared to their gain and production. [...]

The mistake that we make is in thinking that man's channel of greatness is only one—the one which has made itself painfully evident for the time being by its depth of insolence. We must know for certain that there is a future before us and that future is waiting for those who are rich in moral ideals and not in mere things. And it is the privilege of man to work for fruits that are beyond his immediate reach, and to adjust his life not in slavish conformity to the examples of some present success or even to his own prudent past, limited in its aspiration, but to an infinite future bearing in its heart the ideals of our highest expectations.

We must recognise that it is providential that the West has come to India. And yet someone must show the East to the West, and convince the West that the East has her contribution to make to the history of civilisation. India is no beggar of the West. And yet even though the West may think she is, I am not for thrusting off western civilisation and becoming segregated in our independence. Let us have a deep association. If Providence wants England to be the channel of that communication, of that deeper association, I am willing to accept it with all humility. I have great faith in human nature, and I think the West will find its true mission. I speak bitterly of western civilisation when I am conscious that it is betraying its trust and thwarting its own purpose. The West must not make herself a curse to the world by using her power for her own selfish needs but, by teaching the ignorant and helping the weak, she should save herself from the worst danger that the strong is liable to incur by making the feeble acquire power enough to resist her intrusion. And also she must not make her materialism to be the final thing, but must realise that she is doing a service in freeing the spiritual being from the tyranny of matter.

I am not against one nation in particular, but against the general idea of all nations. What is the Nation? It is the aspect of a whole people as an organised power. This organisation incessantly keeps up the insistence of the population on becoming strong and efficient. But this strenuous effort after strength and efficiency drains man's energy from his higher nature where he is self-sacrificing and creative. For thereby man's power of sacrifice is diverted from his ultimate object, which is moral, to the maintenance of this organisation, which is mechanical. Yet in this he feels all the satisfaction of moral exaltation and therefore becomes supremely dangerous to humanity.

He feels relieved of the urging of his conscience when he can transfer his responsibility to this machine which is the creation of his intellect and not of his complete moral personality. By this device the people which loves freedom perpetuates slavery in a large portion of the world with the comfortable feeling of pride in having done its duty; men who are naturally just can be cruelly unjust both in their act and their thought, accompanied by a feeling that they are helping the world to receive its deserts; men who are honest can blindly go on robbing others of their human rights for self-aggrandisement, all the while abusing the deprived for not deserving better treatment. We have seen in our everyday life even small organisations of business and profession produce callousness of feeling in men who are not naturally bad, and we can well imagine what a moral havoc it is causing in a world where whole peoples are furiously organising themselves for gaining wealth and power.

Nationalism is a great menace. It is the particular thing which for years has been at the bottom of India's troubles. And inasmuch as we have been ruled and dominated by a nation that is strictly political in its attitude, we have tried to develop within ourselves, despite our inheritance from the past, a belief in our eventual political destiny. [...] The thing we in India have to think of is this: to remove those social customs and ideals which have generated a want of self-respect and a complete dependence on those above us—a state of affairs which has been brought about entirely by the domination in India of the caste system and the blind and lazy habit of relying upon the authority of traditions that are incongruous anachronisms in the present age. [...]

Therefore in her caste regulations India recognised differences, but not the mutability which is the law of life. In trying to avoid collisions she set up boundaries of immovable walls, thus giving to her numerous races the negative benefit of peace and order but not the positive opportunity of expansion and movement. She accepted nature where it produces diversity, but ignored it where it uses that diversity for its world game of infinite permutations and combinations. She treated life in all truth where it is manifold, but insulted it where it is ever moving. Therefore Life departed from her social system and in its place she is worshipping with all ceremony the magnificent cage of countless compartments that she has manufactured.

The same thing happened where she tried to ward off the collisions of trade interests. She associated different trades and professions with different castes. This had the effect of allaying for good the interminable jealousy and hatred of competition—the competition which breeds cruelty and makes the atmosphere thick with lies and deception. In this also India laid all her emphasis upon the law of heredity, ignoring the law of mutation, and thus gradually reduced arts into crafts and genius into skill. [...]

The general opinion of the majority of the present day nationalists in India is that we have come to a final completeness in our social and spiritual ideals, the task of the constructive work of society having been done several thousand years before we were born, and that now we are free to employ all our activities in the political direction. We never dream of blaming our social inadequacy as the origin of our present helplessness, for we have accepted as the creed of our nationalism that this social system has been perfected for all time to come by our ancestors, who had the superhuman vision of all eternity and supernatural power for making infinite provision for future ages. Therefore, for all our miseries and shortcomings, we hold responsible the historical surprises that burst upon us from outside. This is the reason why we think that our one task is to build a political miracle of freedom upon the quicksand of social slavery. In fact we want to dam up the true course of our own historical stream, and only borrow power from the sources of other peoples' history.

Those of us in India who have come under the delusion that mere political freedom will make us free have accepted their lessons from the West as the gospel truth and lost their faith in humanity. We must remember that whatever weakness we cherish in our society will become the source of danger in politics. The same inertia which leads us to our idolatry of dead forms in social institutions will create in our politics prison-houses with immovable walls. The narrowness of sympathy which makes it possible for us to impose upon a considerable portion of humanity the galling yoke of inferiority will assert itself in our politics in creating the tyranny of injustice. When our nationalists talk about ideals they forget that the basis of nationalism is wanting. The very people who are upholding these ideals are themselves the most conservative in their social practice. [...]

But the present-day commercial civilisation of man is not only taking too much time and space but killing time and space. Its movements are violent; its noise is discordantly loud. It is carrying its own damnation because it is trampling into distortion the humanity upon which it stands. It is strenuously turning out money at the cost of happiness. Man is reducing himself to his minimum in order to be able to make amplest room for his organisations. He is deriding his human sentiments into shame because they are apt to stand in the way of his machines. [...]

This commercialism with its barbarity of ugly decorations is a terrible menace to all humanity, because it is setting up the ideal of power over that of perfection. It is making the cult of self-seeking exult in its naked shamelessness. Our nerves are more delicate than our muscles. Things that are the most precious in us are helpless as babes when we take away from them the careful protection which they claim from us for their very preciousness. Therefore, when the callous rudeness of power runs amuck in the broad way of humanity it scares away by its grossness the ideals which we have cherished with the martyrdom of centuries.

The temptation which is fatal for the strong is still more so for the weak. And I do not welcome it in our Indian life, even though it be sent by the Lord of the Immortals. Let our life be simple in its outer aspect and rich in its inner gain. Let our civilisation take its firm stand upon its basis of social co-operation and not upon that of economic exploitation and conflict. How to do it in the teeth of the drainage of our life blood by the economic dragons is the task set before the thinkers of all oriental nations who have faith in the human soul. It is a sign of laziness and impotency to accept conditions imposed upon us by others who have other ideals than ours. We should actively try to adapt the world powers to guide our history to its own perfect end.

[From: Tagore, *Nationalism* (Calcutta: Rupa & Co., 1992), 77–99, here 79, 83–8, 90, 93–4, 98–9.][13]

[13]First edition: *Nationalism* (London: Macmillan, 1917). Further reading: Sachin Sen 1947; Hay 1970; Arabinda Poddar, 'Rabindranath Tagore: Beyond Nationalism', in idem 1977: 168–95; T. P. Mukherjee, 'Rabindranath Tagore's Political Writings', in Moore 1979: 172–90; Tapati Dasgupta, 1993; Nandy 1994.

AUROBINDO GHOSE (1872–1950) conceived, on the basis of his interpretation of the Upanishads, a theory of cosmic and human history in which a spiritual age and divine life in this world represent the ultimate aim.

> *Aurobindo (Arabinda Akryod Ghose) was born in Calcutta. His Anglophile father, a physician associated with the Brahmo Samaj, sent his sons to a boarding school in Darjeeling, in order to keep them away from Indian culture. In 1879, they were sent for further education to England. Aurobindo spent the next fourteen years in Manchester, London, and Cambridge where he learnt European languages and belonged to a nationalist Indian student association. In 1893, he returned to India and joined the services of the Maharaja of Baroda, after he had been disqualified in the examination for the civil service because of a failed riding test. While he worked as a professor of English (from 1900 on), he began to acquire a knowledge of Bengali and Sanskrit.[14] In 1903, he moved to Calcutta, where he participated in the swadeshi movement and the boycott of governmental institutions. Together with Bipin Chandra Pal, he edited, from 1906 on, the magazine Bande Mataram, in which the demand for swaraj was openly raised. In connection with a bomb attack, Aurobindo was arrested in 1908 but discharged one year later. His political activities ended abruptly in 1910 when Aurobindo, facing new detention, fled to the French enclave of Pondicherry. Secluded in his Ashram, which emerged after the first difficult years at Pondicherry, Aurobindo dedicated himself, during the next few decades, to meditation and the teaching of integral Yoga.*

During his years in England Aurobindo developed an interest in history and the image of a glorious Indian past later had a decisive influence on his political commitment in India. Stimulated by the writings of Bankimchandra and Vivekananda, Aurobindo believed in India's universal mission of Aryanization.[15]

This is the idea on which his play *Bhavani Mandir* is based. As in Bankimchandra's novel *Anandamath*, a group of sannyasis is at the centre of events. The antagonism between different forces (*shakti*), indigenous and alien can be solved only through the extinction of the foreigners. Like Bankimchandra, Aurobindo invokes 'the mother as mother of strength, she is pure Shakti'. He says, very much in the sense of Vivekananda, 'The deeper we look, the more we are convinced that the one which is necessary, which we all have to yearn for, is strength, physical strength, intellectual strength, moral strength, but above all spiritual strength, which is an inexhaustible and unperishable source of all other (forms of strength).'[16]

Even nationalism was shakti guided by God.[17] In the idea of a political Vedanta, independent statehood and personal salvation, swaraj and moksha, were closely associated with each other. The nexus between swaraj and the principles of dharma constituted the essential difference between the soul of Asia (India in particular) and that of Europe.[18] As his last political will,

---

[14]Aurobindo gives testimony of this in Aurobindo 1953.

[15]Cf. Aurobindo, *The Doctrine of Passive Resistance*, 2nd ed. (Pondicherry 1952). For Aurobindo's assessment of Bankimchandra, see his *Bankim Chandra Chatterjee* (Pondicherry 1894).

[16]Quoted in Klimkeit 1971: 121. The motherland 'is a powerful shakti'. Ibid.

[17]'The Life of Nationalism', in Aurobindo 1965: 33–9.

[18]Cf. the contributions to *Bande Mataram*, 1907–8; Klimkeit 1971: 134.

Aurobindo declared unconditional fidelity to the nation: 'Our ideal is *swaraj* or absolute autonomy, free of foreign control. We claim the right of every nation, in accordance with its own ideals, to lead its own life out of its own forces.'[19]

During his imprisonment in 1909, while reflecting on his former life Aurobindo began to believe that he was personally guided by Krishna.[20] After the retreat to the Ashram, he kept away from politics and turned to an individual search for salvation. He increasingly felt inspired by the cosmic force which determined the fate of the world.

The Human Cycle (published in 1949) is based on a series of contributions to the philosophical monthly *Arya* under the title 'The Psychology of Social Development', written between the years 1916 and 1918. For the book edition, the texts have been revised.

The Advent and Progress of the Spiritual Age (1918–49)

Aurobindo starts by describing the attempt of modern science 'to base upon physical data even its study of Soul and Mind' (1). Turning away from this tendency, he relates to the five-stages theory of civilization (symbolic, typal, conventional, individualist, and subjective) of the German historian Karl Lamprecht. This was 'a first psychological theory of history', even if Lamprecht 'was not able to carry it very far or probe very deep'. Aurobindo, while reconstructing the stages of the Indian spiritual evolution, makes some qualifying remarks about the freedom achieved in the individualistic age: 'A partial and external freedom, still betrayed by the conventional age that preceded it into the idea that the Truth can be found in outsides, dreaming vainly that perfection can be determined by machinery, but still a necessary passage to the subjective period of humanity through which man has to circle back towards the recovery of his deeper self and a new upward line or a new revolving cycle of civilisation' (10). After having dealt with individualism and the subjective age, Aurobindo concludes with an outlook on the 'spiritual age'.

If a subjective age, the last sector of a social cycle, is to find its outlet and fruition in a spiritualised society and the emergence of mankind on a higher evolutionary level, it is not enough that certain ideas favourable to that turn of human life should take hold of the general mind of the race, permeate the ordinary motives of its thought, art, ethics, political ideals, social effort, or even get well into its inner way of thinking and feeling. It is not enough even that the idea of the kingdom of God on earth, a reign of spirituality, freedom and unity, a real and inner equality and harmony—and not merely an outward and mechanical equalisation and association—should become definitely an ideal of life; it is not enough that this ideal should be actively held as possible, desirable, to be sought and striven after, it is not enough even that it should come forward as a governing preoccupation of the human mind. [...]

For the way that humanity deals with an ideal is to be satisfied with it as an aspiration which is for the most part left only as an aspiration, accepted only as a partial influence. The ideal is not allowed to mould the whole life, but only more or less to colour it; it is often used even as a

[19]Quoted in Klimkeit 1971: 129. In *The Foundations of Indian Culture*, self-rule is related also to *moksha*.
[20]Klimkeit relates this to Aurobindo's experience of pietistic Christianity during his stay in England. Klimkeit 1971: 128.

cover and a plea for things that are diametrically opposed to its real spirit. Institutions are created which are supposed, but too lightly supposed to embody that spirit and the fact that the ideal is held, the fact that men live under its institutions is treated as sufficient. The holding of an ideal becomes almost an excuse for not living according to the ideal; the existence of its institutions is sufficient to abrogate the need of insisting on the spirit that made the institutions. But spirituality is in its very nature a thing subjective and not mechanical; it is nothing if it is not lived inwardly and if the outward life does not flow out of this inward living. [...]

Here we have to enlarge and to deepen the pragmatic principle that truth is what we create, and in this sense first, that it is what we create within us, in other words, what we become. Undoubtedly, spiritual truth exists eternally beyond, independent of us in the heavens of the Spirit; but it is of no avail for humanity here, it does not become truth of earth, truth of life until it is lived. The divine perfection is always there above us; but for man to become divine in consciousness and act and to live inwardly and outwardly the divine life is what is meant by spirituality; all lesser meanings given to the word are inadequate fumblings or impostures.

This, as the subjective religions recognise, can only be brought about by an individual change in each human life. The collective soul is there only as a great half-subconscient source of the individual existence; if it is to take on a definite psychological form or a new kind of collective life, that can only come by the shaping growth of its individuals. As will be the spirit and life of the individuals constituting it, so will be the realised spirit of the collectivity and the true power of its life. A society that lives not by its men but by its institutions is not a collective soul, but a machine; its life becomes a mechanical product and ceases to be a living growth. Therefore the coming of a spiritual age must be preceded by the appearance of an increasing number of individuals who are no longer satisfied with the normal intellectual, vital and physical existence of man, but perceive that a greater evolution is the real goal of humanity and attempt to effect it in themselves, to lead others to it and to make it the recognised goal of the race. In proportion as they succeed and to the degree to which they carry this evolution, the yet unrealised potentiality which they represent will become an actual possibility of the future.

A great access of spirituality in the past has ordinarily had for its result the coming of a new religion of a special type and its endeavour to impose itself upon mankind as a new universal order. This, however, was always not only a premature but a wrong crystallisation which prevented rather than helped any deep and serious achievement. The aim of a spiritual age of mankind must indeed be one with the essential aim of subjective religions, a new birth, a new consciousness, an upward evolution of the human being, a descent of the Spirit into our members, a spiritual reorganisation of our life; but if it limits itself by the old familiar apparatus and the imperfect means of a religious movement, it is likely to register another failure. A religious movement brings usually a wave of spiritual excitement and aspiration that communicates itself to a large number of individuals and there is as a result a temporary uplifting and an effective formation, partly spiritual, partly ethical, partly dogmatic in its nature. [...]

The ambition of a particular religious belief and form to universalise and impose itself is contrary to the variety of human nature and to at least one essential character of the Spirit. For the nature of the Spirit is a spacious inner freedom and a large unity into which each man must be allowed to grow according to his own nature. Again—and this is yet another source of inevitable failure—the usual tendency of these credal religions is of turn towards an after-world and to make the regeneration of the earthly life a secondary motive; this tendency grows in proportion as the original hope of a present universal regeneration of mankind becomes more and more feeble. Therefore, while many new spiritual waves with their strong special motives and disciplines must necessarily be the forerunners of a spiritual age, yet their claims must be subordinated in the general mind of the race and of its spiritual leaders to the recognition that all motives and disciplines are valid and yet none entirely valid since they are means and not the one thing to be done. The one thing essential must take precedence, the conversion of whole life of the human being to the lead of the Spirit. The ascent of man into heaven is not the key, but rather his ascent here into the Spirit and the descent also of the Spirit into his normal humanity and the transformation of this earthly nature. For that and not some post-mortem salvation is the real new birth for which humanity waits as the crowning movement of its long obscure and painful course.

Therefore the individuals who will most help the future of humanity in the new age will be those who will recognise a spiritual evolution as the destiny and therefore the great need of the human being. Even as the animal man has been largely converted into a mentalised and at the top a highly mentalised humanity, so too now or in the future an evolution or conversion—it does not greatly matter which figure we use or what theory we adopt to support it—of the present type of humanity into a spiritualised humanity is the need of the race and surely the intention of Nature; that evolution or conversion will be their ideal and endeavour. They will be comparatively indifferent to particular belief and form and leave men to resort to the beliefs and forms to which they are naturally drawn. They will only hold as essential the faith in this spiritual conversion, the attempt to live it out and whatever knowledge—the form of opinion into which it is thrown does not so much matter—can be converted into this living.

They will especially not make the mistake of thinking that this change can be effected by machinery and outward institutions; they will know and never forget that it has to be lived out by each man inwardly or it can never be made a reality for the kind. They will adopt in its heart of meaning the inward view of the East which bids man seek the secret of his destiny and salvation within; but also they will accept, though with a different turn given to it the importance which the West rightly attaches to life and to the making the best we know and can attain the general rule of all life. They will not make society a shadowy background to a few luminous spiritual figures or a rigidly fenced and earth-bound root for the growth of a comparatively rare and sterile flower of ascetic spirituality. They will not accept the theory that the many must necessarily remain for ever on the lower ranges of life and only a few climb into the free air and the light, but will start from the standpoint of the great spirits who have striven to regenerate the life of the earth and held that faith in spite of all previous failures. [...]

For before the decisive change can be made the stumbling intellectual reason has to be converted into precise and luminous intuitive, until that again can rise into higher ranges to overmind and supermind or gnosis. The uncertain and stumbling mental will has to rise towards the sure intuitive and into a higher divine and gnostic will, the psychic sweetness, fire and light of the soul behind the heart, *hrdaye guhayam*, has to alchemise our crude emotions and the hard egoisms and clamant desires of our vital nature. All our other members have to pass through a similar conversion under the compelling force and light from above. The leaders of the spiritual march will start from and use the knowledge and the means that past effort has developed in this direction, but they will not take them as they are without any deep necessary change or limit themselves by what is now known or cleave only to fixed and stereotyped systems or given groupings of results, but will follow the method of the Spirit in Nature. A constant rediscovery and new formulation and larger synthesis in the mind, a mighty remoulding in its deeper parts because of a greater enlarging Truth not discovered or not well fixed before, is that Spirit's way with our past achievement when he moves to the greatness of the future.

This endeavour will be a supreme and difficult labour even for the individual, but much more for the race. It may well be that, once started, it may not advance rapidly even to its first decisive stage; it may be that it will take long centuries of effort to come into some kind of permanent birth. But that is not altogether inevitable, for the principle of such changes in Nature seems to be a long obscure preparation followed by a swift gathering up and precipitation of the elements into the new birth, a rapid conversion, a transformation that in its luminous moment figures like a miracle. Even when the first decisive change is reached, it is certain that all humanity will not be able to rise to that level. There cannot fail to be a division into those who are able to live on the spiritual level and those who are only able to live in the light that descends from it into the mental level. And below these too there might still be a great mass influenced from above but not yet ready for the light. But even that would be a transformation and a beginning far beyond anything yet attained. This hierarchy would not mean as in our present vital living an egoistic domination of the undeveloped by the more developed, but a guidance of the younger by the elder brothers of the race and a constant working to lift them up to greater spiritual level and wider horizons. And for the leaders too this ascent to the first spiritual levels would not be the end of the divine march, a culmination that left nothing more to be achieved on earth. For there would be still yet higher levels within the supramental realm, as the old Vedic poets knew when they spoke of the spiritual life as a constant ascent,

> brahmanas tva satakrata
> ud vamsam iva yemire.
> yat sanoh sanum aruhad
> bhuri aspasta kartvam,

'The priests of the word climb thee like a ladder, O hundred-powered. As one ascends from peak to peak, there is made clear the much that has still to be done.'

But once the foundation has been secured, the rest develops by a progressive self-unfolding and the soul is sure of its way. As again it is phrased by the ancient Vedic singers,

> abhyavasthah pra jayante
> pra vavrer vavris ciketa.
> upasthe matur vi caste.

'State is born upon state; covering after covering becomes conscious of knowledge; in the lap of the Mother the soul sees.'

This at least is the highest hope, the possible destiny that opens out before the human view, and it is a possibility which the progress of the human mind seems on the way to redevelop. If the light that is being born increases, if the number of individuals who seek to realise the possibility in themselves and in the world grows large and they get nearer the right way, then the Spirit who is here in man, now a concealed divinity, a developing light and power, will descend more fully as the Avatar of a yet unseen and unguessed Godhead from above into the soul of mankind and into the great individualities in whom the light and power are the strongest. There will then be fulfilled the change that will prepare the transition of human life from its present limits into those larger and purer horizons; the earthly evolution will have taken its great impetus upward and accomplished the revealing step in a divine progression of which the birth of thinking and aspiring man from the animal nature was only an obscure preparation and a far-off promise.

> [From: Sri Aurobindo, *The Human Cycle* (together with *Ideal of Human Unity* and *War and Self-Determination*) (Pondicherry: Sri Aurobindo Ashram, 1962), 1–254, here 247–54.][21]

The art historian ANANDA KENTISH COOMARASWAMY (1877–1947)[22] counterposed the idea of traditionality and *philosophia perennis* to the western concept of history, oriented towards change and progress.

> *Coomaraswamy, born in Colombo, the son of an English mother and a renowned lawyer of Singhalese-Tamilian origin, passed the major part of his youth in England. After a study of geology in London, he went to Ceylon for some years in order to explore its mineral resources. Here he began to take an interest in traditional culture and to defend it against the challenges of westernization. During his visits to India, Coomaraswamy became acquainted with the swadeshi movement and Tagore's poetry. While his initiative to found a National Museum of Indian Arts met with failure due to a lack of support, he succeeded in establishing, on the basis of the objects he collected himself, an Indian section at the Boston Museum of Fine Arts. From 1917, Coomaraswamy lived in America, serving as a curator of the museum collection and working on Indian arts and philosophy.*

In accordance with the Swadeshi Art Movement,[23] Coomaraswamy's interest in the arts was at first related to the Indian struggle for autonomy. Like the nationalist historians in the realm of political history, Coomaraswamy rejected western allegations about Greek influence on early Indian arts as exaggerated. In regard to the Buddhist Gandhara art, he stated: 'The Buddha image

[21]Original edition: Pondicherry: Sri Aurobindo Ashram, 1949. Further reading: Vishwanath Prasad Varma 1960; D. P. Chattopadhyaya 1976; Grace E. Cairns, 'Aurobindo's Conception of the Nature and Meaning of History', in Mahadevan and Cairns 1977: 1–20; V. Madhusudan Reddy 1966; idem, 1984.

[22]See, R. W. Lipsey, *Signature and Significance. A Study of the Life and Writings of A. K. Coomaraswamy* (Diss. New York 1974); idem, *Coomaraswamy: His Life and Work* (Princeton 1977).

[23]See Partha Mitter, 'The Doctrine of Swadeshi Art: Art and Nationalism in Bengal', *The Vishwa Bharati Quarterly* 49 (1987), 82ff.; idem, 1994.

was Hellenistic in depiction but Indian in conception.' The image of the sitting Yogi was 'specially Indian, being foreign to Western psychology'.[24] In search of a unifying principle of the Indian nation, however, he did not refer to 'racial unity' or the common language, but to 'geographical unity' and a 'common historic evolution or culture'. He defined Indian identity with reference not to origin but to common aims or purposes. In this respect, the distant British rulers were alien in a way incomparable to the alienness of the Muslim rulers of India who had settled here.[25]

Coomaraswamy increasingly distanced himself from the quest for historicization in the modern sense and emphasized the fact that, traditionally, politics in India was not shaped by the 'interested' but by the 'disinterested'.[26] The later development of Coomaraswamy was influenced by the writings of William Morris, who discovered in the Indian crafts the lost quality of the arts of the European Middle Ages, and by the thought of René Guénon.[27] It is to the latter that Coomaraswamy's concept of tradition can be traced. In *Spiritual Authority and Temporal Power in the Indian Theory of Government* (1978), Coomaraswamy explicitly tied political rule to the sphere of the eternal divine law and truth (dharma, satya).[28] In *Time and Eternity* (1947), he directed his comparative interest to time concepts in Hinduism and Buddhism, classical Greece, Islam, and Christianity.

In his early collection of essays, *The Dance of Shiva*, Coomaraswamy sought to describe the specific rhythm of Indian philosophy, 'this deep slow breath of thought'.[29] The title of his essay 'What has India Contributed to Human Welfare?' suggests a comparison with Max Müller's lectures on India's contribution to history. Unlike Müller, however, Coomaraswamy rejects any allusion to include India into the temporal perspective of the West. He views the contribution of India with regard not to universal stages of evolution but to the presence of the eternal.

What has India Contributed to Human Welfare? (1915)

Each race contributes something essential to the world's civilization in the course of its own self-expression and self-realization. The character built up in solving its own problems, in the experience of its own misfortunes, is itself a gift which each offers to the world. The essential contribution of India, then, is simply her Indianness; her great humiliation would be to substitute or to have substituted for this own character (svabhava) a cosmopolitan veneer, for then indeed she must come before the world empty-handed.

If now we ask what is most distinctive in this essential contribution, we must first make it clear that there cannot be anything absolutely unique in the experience of any race. Its peculiarities will be chiefly a matter of selection and emphasis, certainly not a difference in specific humanity. If we regard the world as a family of nations, then we shall best understand the position of India which has passed through many experiences and solved many problems which younger races

---

[24]Coomaraswamy, 'The Influence of Greek on Indian Art', in idem., 1981 [1909]: 91–6, quoted in Ratnabali Chattopadhyay, 'The Alternative Vision', *Calcutta Historical Journal* 11 (1986–7), 42–68, here 56. The reception of Indian arts was lastingly influenced by Coomaraswamy's writings.

[25]'Indian Nationality', in idem 1981: 7–13.

[26]'Young India', in idem, 1918: 153–71, here 156.

[27]René Guénon, 1924, 1929, 1968.

[28]Cf. Roger Lipsey, 'Spiritual Authority and Temporal Power in the South Asian Theory of Government', in idem, *Daedalus. Lectures Commemorating the Birth Centenary of A. K. Coomaraswamy* (Dharwad 1980), 81–100.

[29]*The Dance of Shiva*, quoted in Iyengar 1985: 586.

have hardly yet recognized. The heart and essence of the Indian experience is to be found in a constant intuition of the unity of all life, and the instinctive and ineradicable conviction that the recognition of this unity is the highest good and the uttermost freedom. All that India can offer to the world proceeds from her philosophy. This philosophy is not, indeed, unknown to others—it is equally the gospel of Jesus and of Blake, Lao Tze, and Rumi—but nowhere else has it been made the essential basis of sociology and education.

Every race must solve its own problems, and those of its own day. I do not suggest that the ancient Indian solutions of the special Indian problems, though its lessons may be many and valuable, can be directly applied to modern conditions. What I do suggest is that the Hindus grasped more firmly than others the fundamental meaning and purpose of life, and more deliberately than others organized society with a view to the attainment of the fruit of life; and this organization was designed, not for the advantage of a single class, but, to use a modern formula, to take from each according to his capacity, and to give to each according to his needs. How far the *rishis* succeeded in this aim may be a matter of opinion. We must not judge of Indian society, especially Indian society in its present moment of decay, as if it actually realized the Brahmanical social ideals; yet even with all its imperfections Hindu society as it survives will appear to many to be superior to any form of social organization attained on a large scale anywhere else, and infinitely superior to the social order which we know as 'modern civilization'. But even if it were impossible to maintain this view—and a majority of Europeans and of English-educated Indians certainly believe to the contrary—what nevertheless remains as the most conspicuous special character of the Indian culture, and its greatest significance for the modern world, is the evidence of a constant effort to understand the meaning and the ultimate purpose of life, and a purposive organization of society in harmony with that order and with a view to the attainment of the purpose. The Brahmanical idea is an Indian 'City of the gods'—as *devanagari*, the name of the Sanskrit script, suggests. The building of that city anew is the constant task of civilization; and though the details of our plans may change, and the contours of our building, we may learn from India to build on the foundations of the religion of Eternity.

Where the Indian mind differs most from the average mind of modern Europe is in its view of the value of philosophy. In Europe and America the study of philosophy is regarded as an end in itself, and as such it seems of but little importance to the ordinary man. In India, on the contrary, philosophy is not regarded primarily as a mental gymnastic, but rather, and with deep religious conviction, as our salvation (*moksha*) from the ignorance (*avidya*) which forever hides from our eyes the vision of reality. Philosophy is the key to the map of life, by which are set forth the meaning of life and the means of attaining its goal. It is no wonder, then, that the Indians have pursued the study of philosophy with enthusiasm, for these are matters that concern all. [...]

How, then could the Brahmans tolerate the practical diversity of life, how provide for the fact that a majority of individuals are guided by selfish aims, how could they deal with the problem of evil? They had found the Religion of Eternity (*Nirguna Vidya*); what of the Religion of Time (*Saguna Vidya*)? [...]

We can now examine the Brahmanical theory a little more closely. An essential factor is to be recognized in the dogma of the rhythmic character of the world-process. This rhythm is determined by the great antithesis of Subject and Object, Self and non-Self, Will and Matter, Unity and Diversity, Love and Hate, and all other 'Pairs'. The interplay of these opposites constitutes the whole of sensational and registrateable existence, the Eternal Becoming (*samsara*), which is characterized by birth and death, evolution and involution, descent and ascent, *srishti* and *samhara*.[30] Every individual life—mineral, vegetable, animal, human, or personal god—has a beginning and an end, and this creation and destruction, appearance and disappearance, are of the essence of the world-process and equally originate in the past, the present, and the future.

According to this view, then, every individual ego (*jivatman*), or separate expression of the general Will to Life (*ichchha, trishna*), must be regarded as having reached a certain stage of its own cycle (*gati*). The same is true of the collective life of a nation, a planet, or a cosmic system. It is further considered that the turning point of this curve is reached in man, and hence the immeasurable value which Hindus (and Buddhists) attach to birth in human form. Before the turning point is reached—to use the language of Christian theology—the natural man prevails; after it is passed, regenerate man. The turning point is not to be regarded as sudden, for the two conditions interpenetrate, and the change of psychological centre of gravity may occupy a succession of lives; or if the turning seems to be a sudden event, it is only in the sense that the fall of a ripe fruit appears, sudden.

According to their position on the great curve, that is to say, according to their spiritual age, we can recognize three prominent types of men. There is first the mob, of those who are preoccupied with the thought of I and Mine, whose objective is self-assertion, but are restrained on the one hand by fear of retaliation and of legal or after-death punishment, and on the other by the beginnings of love of family and love of country. These, in the main, are the 'Devourers' of Blake, the 'Slaves' of Nietzsche. Next there is a smaller, but still larger number of thoughtful and good men whose behaviour is largely determined by a sense of duty, but whose inner life is still the field of conflict between the old Adam and the new man. Men of this type are actuated on the one hand by the love of power and fame, and ambition more or less noble, and on the other by the disinterested love of mankind. But this type is rarely pan-human, and its outlook is often simultaneously unselfish and narrow. In times of great stress, the men of this type reveal their true nature, showing to what extent they have advanced more or less than has appeared. But all these, who have but begun to taste of freedom, must still be guided by rules. Finally, there is the much smaller number of great men—heroes, saviours, saints and avatars—who have definitely passed the period of greatest stress and have attained peace, or at least have attained to occasional and unmistakable vision of life as a whole. These are the 'Prolific' of Blake, the 'Masters' of Nietzsche, the true Brahmans in their own right, and partake of the nature of the Superman and the Bodhisattva. Their activity is determined by their love and wisdom, and not by rules. In the world, but not of it, they are the flower of humanity, our leaders and teachers.

[From: Coomaraswamy, 'What has India Contributed to Human Welfare?', in *The Dance of Shiva. Fourteen Indian Essays. On Indian Art and Culture* (Reprint, New Delhi: Sagar Publications, 1991), 3–21, here 3–5, 10, 13–15.][31]

---

[30]*srishti*: creation; *samhara*: destruction.

[31]Reprint with kind permission by Sagar Publications, New Delhi. First published in *Athenaeum* (London 1915). Further reading: Kenneth R. Stunkel, 'The Meeting of East and West in Coomaraswamy and Radhakrishnan', *Philosophy East and West* 23 (1973), 517–24.

The most influential defender of Indian traditions and, at the same time, their unremitting innovator in the encounter with the modern West was MOHANDAS KARAMCHAND GANDHI (1869–1948). His principles of thinking and acting were in stark conflict with orthodox or revivalist readings of Indian culture and with the western concept of history. Nevertheless, he made his 'experiments with truth'[32] a force of political self-assertion and social change.

> *Gandhi was born in Porbandar (Gujarat), the son of a family of the Bania caste (Vaishya). His father, Kaba Gandhi, served the prince of Porbandar and the prince of Rajkot as Dewan (prime minister), and his mother gave the family the character of deep vaishnavite piety. The young Gandhi received his education first in Gujarati and later in English. Contrary to the tradition of his caste (travel overseas conflicted with the established rules), he went to London, where he studied law from 1888 to 1891. In 1893, he went to South Africa for an Indian association of lawyers. He stayed on till 1914 and became the political leader of the Indian immigrants, also making his first experiments with the method of non-violent resistance. Back in India (1915), Gandhi soon became a protagonist in the fight against British colonial rule. From 1919, he organized campaigns of civil disobedience and satyagraha, and several times he was imprisoned. With the approaching of Independence, it became evident that his ideas of swaraj and economic self-sufficiency were hardly compatible with those of the majority in the INC. In 1948, Gandhi, who had always favoured understanding between Hindus and Muslims, was murdered by Nathuram Godse, a follower of Savarkar.*

Gandhi, unlike other leaders of the Independence movement, such as Tilak and Nehru, undertook no attempt to engage in historical investigations and the intention to link India to world history was strikingly absent from his thinking. Yet, he did not conceive a systematic alternative to the Western idea of history either. Gandhi's scattered remarks about history evolved mostly from practical situations and while confronting current needs. What appears as a sign of inconsistency[33] to some represents the specific logic of his thinking and acting to others.[34] It is also through word-coining (often using Sanskrit neologisms such as satyagraha) and symbolizations (such as the *chakra*) that the principles and perspectives of his actions are expressed.[35]

An early attempt at giving a foundation to his political thinking was undertaken by Gandhi in *Hind Swaraj*. In this comparative analysis of western and Indian civilization, Gandhi denied the former any evolutionary priority. He defended tradition against modernity, in the reflection on the double significance of swaraj (self-rule and self-control),[36] and also tried, in a general sense and historical perspective, to strengthen the power of inner as against outer history.

[32]Gandhi has described his life history under the title: An *Autobiography or the Story of My Experiments with Truth* (1927).

[33]See for instance M. G. Gupta 1991, specifically 83ff.

[34]For Gandhi's attempt to find in Indian tradition answers to modern challenges, see D. N. Pathak, 'Gandhiji: Tradition and Change: A study in modernisation', in S. C. Biwas 1968: 150–7.

[35]See for instance, 'The Use and Scope of Truth-Force', in *Essential Writings* 1993: 301ff. Originally under the title 'The Theory and Practice of Passive Resistance', *Indian Opinion* (Dec. 1914).

[36]For the two sides of *swaraj* and the distinction between eternal *atman* and spatio-temporal *dehin* in Gandhi's concept of Self according to the *Bhagavadgita*, see Parel 1997: pp. XLIX–XLIXI.

Hind Swaraj can be read as a programme for the reorganization of Indian society after colonialism, even though it never had this status for the independence movement as a whole. G. K. Gokhale expressed his disapproval, Nehru continued to claim later took a critical stance. Marxists like S. A. Dange and M. N. Roy mostly reacted with criticism, as did Ambedkar. Gandhi himself continued to claim *Hind Swaraj* to be his 'seed text' until 1945.[37] The political impact of Gandhi was mainly through his particular kind of reconciliation between differences and opposites (Partha Chatterjee 1996: 155–6). Thus, his rejection of the modern concept of history, according to Gyan Prakash, came as the 'reinterpretation of the premodern as the nonmodern'.[38]

In the eyes of the INC-establishment, Gandhi's task was completed with the achievement of Independence. His social and political ideas were soon overtaken by India's politics of modernization, apart from a few concessions in the Constitution, such as the village panchayat. The concepts presented in *Hind Swaraj* and experimented with during the various campaigns, however, are still stimulating elements of current politics at the grass-roots level.[39] Repercussions on India also come from Gandhi's worldwide reception in the alternative movements (Kantowsky 1986: 169–85).

Hind Swaraj—Indian Self Rule (1909)

In the form of a dialogue[40] *between a reader and the editor of a newspaper, Gandhi begins with an analysis of the historical situation and moves on to the description of western civilization, where 'bodily welfare' had become the aim of life. He gives numerous instances of how life in modern Europe changed because of manual work with the replacement of production by machines. All this was celebrated as civilization and progress, even if it meant a loss in morality and religion. Gandhi is convinced: 'This civilization is such that one has only to be patient and it will be self-destroyed. According to the teaching of Mahomed, this would be considered a Satanic Civilization. Hinduism calls it the Black Age.' (21) This 'civilization only in name' is contrasted by Gandhi with his description of traditional Indian civilization.*

[37]Cf. Suresh Sharma, 'Hind Swaraj as a Statement of Tradition in the Modern World', in Dalmia and Stietencron 1995: 283–93, here 284. See the extracts from the Gandhi-Nehru correspondence in Parel 1997: 149–56.

[38]'It was by rescuing of the premodern from its assigned space as history, from its designation as colonialism's self-confirming other and by inserting it in the same time as the modern that Gandhi was able to formulate his concept of the nonmodern.' Gyan Prakash, 'Introduction', in idem 1995: 7. Partha Chatterjee places Gandhi's critique of western civilization in the context of the evolution of Indian nationalism and (taking up a concept of Gramsci) interprets it as the incorporation of a part of the antithesis into the thesis: 1996: 51 passim. Cf. also C. Heesterman 1985, who views the conflict between the renouncer and the politician personified in Gandhi.

[39]Tagore initiated an important debate about the principles formulated here, as he saw a dependence on the machine even in the simple manual work favoured by Gandhi. For the debate on 'mechanical repetitiveness', see Sharma, 'Swaraj and the Quest for Freedom—Rabindranath Tagore's Critique of Gandhi's Non-Cooperation', *Thesis Eleven* 39 (1994), 93–104, here, 97.

[40]This was, according to Gandhi's remark on the Gujarati text, the best method for dealing with difficult subjects. Moreover, it is derived from the actual dialogues with friends and political activists (among whom V. D. Savarkar) during the stay in London. See Gandhi's 'Preface to the English Translation'.

What is True Civilization?

READER: You have denounced railways, lawyers, and doctors. I can see that you will discard all machinery. What, then, is civilization ?

EDITOR: The answer to that question is not difficult. I believe that the civilization India has evolved is not to be beaten in the world. Nothing can equal the seeds sown by our ancestors. Rome went, Greece shared the same fate; the might of the Pharaohs was broken; Japan has become westernized; of China nothing can be said, but India is still, somehow or other, sound at the foundation. The people of Europe learn their lessons from the writings of the men of Greece or Rome, which exist no longer in their former glory. In trying to learn from them, the Europeans imagine that they will avoid the mistakes of Greece and Rome. Such is their pitiable condition. In the midst of all this India remains immovable and that is her glory. It is a charge against India that her people are so uncivilized, ignorant and stolid, that it is not possible to induce them to adopt any changes. It is a charge really against our merit. What we have tested and found true on the anvil of experience, we dare not change. Many thrust their advice upon India, and she remains steady. This is her beauty: it is the sheet-anchor of our hope.

Civilization is that mode of conduct which points out to man the path of duty. Performance of duty and observance of morality are convertible terms. To observe morality is to attain mastery over our mind and our passions. So doing, we know ourselves. The Gujarati equivalent for civilization means 'good conduct'.[41]

If this definition be correct, then India, as so many writers have shown, has nothing to learn from anybody else, and this is as it should be. We notice that the mind is a restless bird; the more it gets the more it wants, and still remains unsatisfied. The more we indulge our passions, the more unbridled they become. Our ancestors, therefore, set a limit to our indulgences. They saw that happiness was largely a mental condition. A man is not necessarily happy because he is rich, or unhappy because he is poor. The rich are often seen to be unhappy, the poor to be happy. Millions will always remain poor. Observing all this, our ancestors dissuaded us from luxuries and pleasures. We have managed with the same kind of plough as existed thousands of years ago. We have retained the same kind of cottages that we had in former times and our indigenous education remains the same as before. We have had no system of life-corroding competition. Each followed his own occupation or trade and charged a regulation wage. It was not that we did not know how to invent machinery, but our forefathers knew that, if we set our hearts after such things, we would become slaves and lose our moral fibre. They, therefore, after due deliberation decided that we should only do what we could with our hands and feet. They saw that our real happiness and health consisted in a proper use of our hands and feet. They further reasoned that large cities were a snare and a useless encumbrance and that people would not be happy in them, that there would be gangs of thieves and robbers, prostitution and vice flourishing in them and that poor men would be robbed by rich men. They were, therefore, satisfied with small villages. They saw that kings and their swords were inferior to the sword of ethics, and they, therefore, held the sovereigns of the earth to be inferior to the Rishis and the

[41]This is the meaning of *su*, that is, good, *dharo* [way of life]. (CWMG)

Fakirs.[42] A nation with a constitution like this is fitter to teach others than to learn from others. This nation had courts, lawyers and doctors, but they were all within bounds. Everybody knew that these professions were not particularly superior; moreover, these vakils and vaids[43] did not rob people; they were considered people's dependants, not their masters. Justice was tolerably fair. The ordinary rule was to avoid courts. There were no touts to lure people into them. This evil, too, was noticeable only in and around capitals. The common people lived independently and followed their agricultural occupation. They enjoyed true Home Rule.

And where this cursed modern civilization has not reached, India remains as it was before. The inhabitants of that part of India will very properly laugh at your new-fangled notions. The English do not rule over them, nor will you ever rule over them. Those in whose name we speak we do not know, nor do they know us. I would certainly advise you and those like you who love the motherland to go into the interior that has yet been not polluted by the railways and to live there for six months; you might then be patriotic and speak of Home Rule. Now you see what I consider to be real civilization. Those who want to change conditions such as I have described are enemies of the country and are sinners. [...]

How can India become free?

READER: I appreciate your views about civilization. I will have to think over them. I cannot take them in all at once. What, then, holding the views you do, would you suggest for freeing India?

EDITOR: I do not expect my views to be accepted all of a sudden. My duty is to place them before readers like yourself. Time can be trusted to do the rest.[44] We have already examined the conditions for freeing India, but we have done so indirectly; we will now do so directly. It is a world-known maxim that the removal of the cause of a disease results in the removal of the disease itself. Similarly if the cause of India's slavery be removed, India can become free.

READER: If Indian civilization is, as you say, the best of all, how do you account for India's slavery?

EDITOR: This civilization is unquestionably the best, but it is to be observed that all civilizations have been on their trial. That civilization which is permanent outlives it. Because the sons of India were found wanting, its civilization has been placed in jeopardy. But its strength is to be seen in its ability to survive the shock. [...]

Passive Resistance

READER: Is there any historical evidence as to the success of what you have called soul-force or truth-force? No instance seems to have happened of any nation having risen through soul-force. I still think that the evil-doers will not cease doing evil without physical punishment.

EDITOR: The poet Tulsidas has said: 'Of religion, pity, or love, is the root, as egotism of the

---

[42]Rishis and Fakirs: sages and ascetics. (CWMG)

[43]Vakils and vaids: lawyers and doctors. (CWMG)

[44]The original has: 'Time will show whether they find them acceptable or not.' (CWMG)

body.[45] Therefore, we should not abandon pity so long as we are alive.' This appears to me to be a scientific truth. I believe in it as much as I believe in two and two being four. The force of love is the same as the force of the soul or truth. We have evidence of its working at every step. The universe would disappear without the existence of that force. But you ask for historical evidence. It is, therefore, necessary to know what history means. The Gujarati equivalent means: 'It so happened.' If that is the meaning of history, it is possible to give copious evidence. But, if it means the doings of kings and emperors, there can be no evidence of soul-force or passive resistance in such history. You cannot expect silver-ore in a tin-mine. History, as we know it, is a record of the wars of the world, and so there is a proverb among Englishmen that a nation which has no history, that is, no wars, is a happy nation. How kings played, how they became enemies of one another, how they murdered one another, is found accurately recorded in history, and if this were all that had happened in the world, it would have been ended long ago. [...]

Hundreds of nations live in peace. History does not and cannot take note of this fact. History is really a record of every interruption of the even working of the force of love or of the soul. Two brothers quarrel; one of them repents and re-awakens the love that was lying dormant in him;[46] the two again begin to live in peace; nobody takes note of this. But if the two brothers, through the intervention of solicitors or some other reason take up arms or go to law—which is another form of the exhibition of brute force,—their doings would be immediately noticed in the Press, they would be the talk of their neighbours and would probably go down to history. And what is true of families and communities is true of nations. There is no reason to believe that there is one law for families and another for nations. History, then, is a record of an interruption of the course of nature. Soul-force, being natural, is not noted in history.

READER: According to what you say, it is plain that instances of this kind of passive resistance are not to be found in history. It is necessary to understand this passive resistance more fully. It will be better, therefore, if you enlarge upon it.

EDITOR: Passive resistance is a method of securing rights by personal suffering; it is the reverse of resistance by arms.[47] When I refuse to do a thing that is repugnant to my conscience, I use soul-force. For instance, the Government of the day has passed a law which is applicable to me. I do not like it. If, by using violence, I force the Government to repeal the law, I am employing what may be termed body-force. If I do not obey the law and accept the penalty for its breach, I use soul-force. It involves sacrifice of self. Everybody admits that sacrifice of self is infinitely superior to sacrifice of others. [...]

Machinery

READER: When you speak of driving out western civilization, I suppose you will also say that we want no machinery.

[45]For the translation 'sin' instead of 'body', cf. the note to the Tulsidas quotation in Parel (ed.), *Hind Swaraj*, 88.
[46]The original has: 'One of them practises satyagraha against the other.' (CWMG)
[47]The original has: 'Satyagraha is referred to in English as passive resistance. The term denotes the method of ....' (CWMG)

EDITOR: By raising this question you have opened the wound I have received. When I read Mr. Dutt's *Economic History of India*, I wept; and as I think of it again my heart sickens. It is machinery that has impoverished India. It is difficult to measure the harm that Manchester has done to us. It is due to Manchester that Indian handicraft has all but disappeared.

But I make a mistake. How can Manchester be blamed? We wore Manchester cloth and this is why Manchester wove it. I was delighted when I read about the bravery of Bengal.[48] There were no cloth-mills in that Presidency. They were, therefore, able to restore the original hand-weaving occupation. It is true, Bengal encourages the mill-industry of Bombay. If Bengal had proclaimed a boycott of *all* machine-made goods, it would have been much better.

Machinery has begun to desolate Europe. Ruination is now knocking at the Indian[49] gates. Machinery is the chief symbol of modern civilization; it represents a great sin. [...]

READER: Are the mills, then, to be closed down?

EDITOR: That is difficult. It is no easy task to do away with a thing that is established. We, therefore, say that the non-beginning of a thing is supreme wisdom.

[From: Gandhi, 'Hind Swaraj', in *The Collected Works of Mahatma Gandhi* (New Delhi: Publications Division, Ministry of Information and Broadcasting, Government of India, 1958–84), Vol. X, 6–68, here 36–9, 47, 57–8.][50]

[48]The reference, obviously, is to the Swadeshi Movement. (CWMG)

[49]For the erroneous version 'English gates' in the English translation, see the note in Parel (ed.), *Hind Swaraj*, 107–8.

[50]*Hind Swaraj* was written by Gandhi during his voyage from England to South Africa in 1909. The text (in Gujarati) appeared first in two sequels on 11 and 18 December 1909 as a contribution to *Indian Opinion*; Gandhi himself wrote a free English translation of it, which was published as a book under the title *Indian Home Rule* at Johannesburg/South Africa in 1910. *Hind Swaraj* was immediately banned by the British authorities in Bombay. Numerous editions and reprints have appeared, the first Indian edition of the English text was published in Madras in 1919, the first Hindi version in 1921. In America it appeared in 1924 under the title *Sermon on the Sea*, edited by H. T. Mazumdar. A new edition with introduction and commentary has been published recently by Anthony J. Parel, along with some of the other important texts by Gandhi on the same subject, among these the letters to H. S. L. Polak and Lord Ampthill, in which Gandhi expressed his critique of western civilization in a condensed form: Parel 1997. In the appendix of *Hind Swaraj*, Gandhi mentions some of the authors who have influenced his ideas and whose books he recommends to the readers. Among these are the works of Tolstoi, Thoreau and Ruskin as well as the writings of Naoroji and R. C. Dutt. Further reading: Raghavan N. Iyer, 'Gandhi's Interpretation of History', *Gandhi Marg* 6, No. 4 (1962), 319–27; Rudolph and Rudolph 1983 [1967]; Balkrishna Govind Gokhale, 'Gandhi and History', *History and Theory* 11 (1972), 214–25; special issue of *Gandhi Marg* (1973), with the texts of a Symposium on *Hind Swaraj*; Nageshwar 1985; Jürgen Lütt, 'Mahatma Gandhis Kritik an der modernen Zivilisation', *Saeculum* 37 (1986), 96–112; K. Raghavendra Rao, 'Communication against Communication: The Gandhian Critique of Modern Civilization in *Hind Swaraj*', in Parekh and Pantham 1987: 266–76; Ashis Nandy, 'From outside the imperium. Gandhi's Critique of the West', in idem.: 1987: 127–62; Partha Chatterjee, 'Gandhi and the Critique of Civil Society', *Subaltern Studies* 3 (1989), 153–95; Parekh 1989; Paranjape 1993.

After Colonialism: Historical Thinking in Contemporary South Asia

4.1 Objectivity, Prejudice, and the Call for Indian Frameworks of Interpretation

The change in political conditions after Independence was reflected in the realm of historical culture: in the establishment of new institutions of research and teaching[1] as well as in some comprehensive projects of historiography, such as the eleven volumes of *The History and Culture of the Indian People* (1951–77)[2] and the six volumes of *The Cultural Heritage of India* (1956–86).[3] Mohammad Habib's 'Presidential Address' at the first session of the Indian History Congress after Independence can also be regarded as a document of the turning point of 1947.[4]

One of the characteristics of the new development was the researchers' growing awareness

[1]Most important for the advancement of historical studies was the foundation of the Indian Council of Historical Research (ICHR) in New Delhi and the many new universities with their departments of history. Looking at Indian reality from a general perspective, it has been observed, however: 'No other new country has been able to begin its independent career with such an inheritance of institutions.' Shils 1961: 45 For an overview of research institutions, see Sahay 1987. A few remarks about the access to sources and documents are found in N. Gerald Barrier, 'India: Recent Writing on the History of British India', in Iggers and Parker 1979: 387–402.

[2]Edited by R. C. Majumdar and published by Bharatiya Vidya Bhavan, Bombay.

[3]First published in three volumes in 1937 by the Sri Ramakrishna Birth Centenary Publication Committee (Calcutta). The rewriting of history, in fact, had started well before Independence.

[4]In his speech, the historian of Aligarh Muslim University urged 'that our historical vision will and must undergo a complete change with reference to all our past'. Independence also meant freeing oneself from the 'spirit of constraint' connected with the fact of foreign rule: *Proceedings of the 10th Session of the Indian History Congress* (Bombay 1947), 9–21, here 18, 20. For an overview of the trends in Indian historiography in the period of transition, see Satish Chandra, 'Main Trends in Historical Sciences in India: 1900–70', in idem 1996: 57–82.

of the nexus between historical knowledge and the quest for political orientation. In the accounts of the past the historiography of an epoch was regarded as a political factor,[5] and historians also reflected on the embeddedness of their own work in social and political contexts of the present. In an attempt to sum up the main tendencies of modern Indian historiography, it has been said: 'Since the days of Sir R. G. Bhandarkar political history of ancient India has made great advance. It has gradually progressed from the state of noble innocence to that of consciousness and then to the states of self-consciousness and critical self-consciousness.' History was not only 'conscious of itself, aware of its aims and scope'; it also became 'conscious of its own growth and development'.[6]

The increasing self-reflexivity became perceptible in the growing number of introductions to the history and theory of historiography.[7] In these manuals, however, as also in overviews of recent historical research, the efforts to critically examine historical thinking in post-colonial India and give it a new foundation were rarely mentioned; they referred mainly to the successful application of standards established in the West.[8] This was true even in those cases where attention was drawn to India-specific problems of research, as was done by Nilakanta Sastri and Ramanna in their *Historical Method in Relation to Indian History*[9] or by Pratap Chandra in his methodological reflections regarding the history of philosophy (Pratap Chandra 1977: 104–23). The establishment of an India-centred historiography, admittedly, had to overcome specific difficulties, beginning with the lack of non-official, that is, non-colonial, sources for some parts of modern history.[10] The realization of an Indian viewpoint in history was attempted mainly by archaeologists, who also played an important role in the issue of the disputed holy sites of the Hindus.[11]

The fact that special efforts were necessary to get rid of the colonial views and premises has been made evident in various attempts at stocktaking of historical research in India. The two approaches presented here were developed in the context of specific strategies.[12] The first attempt was to identify and criticize certain residues of colonialism in contemporary historical imagination. The critique was based, however, on universal standards of research. The proponents of the second approach, with their demonstrative interest in Indian frameworks of interpretation, questioned the very validity of some of the established standards. Nevertheless, they did refer to them in part,

[5]See, e.g., Bipan Chandra et al. 1987, and Sumit Sarkar 1983.
[6]Shankar Goyal, 'Political History: The Loss of Innocence', in Pande 1992: 290–9, here 291, 292.
[7]For the histories of modern Indian historiography, see Michael Gottlob, 'Writing the History of Modern Indian Historiography: A Review Article', *Storia della Storiografia* 27 (1995), 125–46.
[8]See, e.g., Tarasankar Banerjee 1987; Correia-Afonso 1979: 10–81. See also Khandelwal 1968.
[9]Nilakanta Sastri and Ramanna 1956. In the chapter 'Development of Indian Historiography', there are only three Indians among the twenty historians presented, namely R. G. Bhandarkar, G. S. Sardesai, and Jadunath Sarkar.
[10]Pandey, 'Encounters and Calamities: The History of a North Indian Qasba in the Nineteenth Century', *Subaltern Studies* 3 (1984), 231–70, here 231ff.
[11]For the development of archaeological research in post-colonial India, see the survey by Shrimali 1996.
[12]See the contributions to the conferences *Problems of Historical Writing* (India International Centre 1963) and *Problems of Indian Historiography* (Indian History and Culture Society 1978).

while denouncing the first approach as being politically motivated.[13] Romila Thapar[14] upholds the tradition of Indian historiography which, since the days of R. G. Bhandarkar, reflected on its theoretical foundations and practical contexts. She reinforces the analytical potential of methodical research against the politically motivated construction of myths and legends, without denying the link between the interest in the past and issues of politics. Her public comments on the instrumentalization of historical knowledge have exposed her to attacks from political opponents, for instance during the 'textbook controversy' in the years 1977 to 1979. In recent times she has again taken a stand against the tendencies to communalize the interpretation of Indian history.[15]

Thapar's main field of research is the history of ancient India (Thapar 1961, 1984). This includes the early forms of Indian historical thinking, which had often been misunderstood by western researchers. Thapar tries to reconstruct them from their inner logic.[16] In the following text, she questions certain stereotypes which go back to the time of colonial rule but still determine the image of the Indian past and sometimes give rise to political disputes.[17]

The Past and Prejudice (1975)

It is generally conceded that the history of the colonial period in India, of the last two centuries, is an unavoidable preface to an understanding of the present; it has a direct connection with the present. But I shall try in these lectures to suggest that even the more ancient part of the history of our country is relevant to the present. This can perhaps best be done by first discussing

[13]That these questions are still open to debate is also shown by Ruchi Banthiya, who argues against the 'politics of imperialist knowledge' and the 'legacy of academic colonialism' and postulates the 'formulation of indigenous concepts'. Banthiya 1994: 148–9. Alien concepts of historicity and also post-modern categories are criticized here as being non-authentic.

[14]Romila Thapar, born in 1931, studied at Panjab University and the University of London; she taught at the School of Oriental and African Studies (London, 1959–61), in Kurukshetra (1961–3), at Delhi University (1963–70); from 1970 to 1993, she was Professor of Ancient Indian History at the Centre for Historical Studies, Jawaharlal Nehru University, New Delhi. She also taught at the Universities of California, Bejing and Pennsylvania. In 1983, she was General President of the Indian History Congress; in 1989, she delivered the Radhakrishnan Lectures at the University of Oxford. Further reading: 'Interpretations of Indian History. Interview with Geeti Sen', *Perceiving India. Insight and Inquiry. India International Centre Quarterly* (Spring-Summer 1993), 115–35; Indira Viswanathan Peterson, 'Romila Thapar', in Boyd 1999: 1177–8.

[15]Thapar 1969; idem, 'Syndicated Moksha', *Seminar* 313 (Sept. 1985), 14–22; 'Communalism and History', based on a talk given by Romila Thapar at Khandala Workshop organized by Vikas Adhyayan Kendra: *www.mnet.fr/aiindex/ch2.html.*

[16]For the revaluation of the puranas and epics as historical sources, see 'The Tradition of Historical Writing in Early India', 'Origin Myths and the Early Indian Historical Tradition', 'Genealogy as a Source of Social History'; all in *Ancient Indian Social History* (1978), 268–93, 294–325, 326–60; 'Society and Historical Consciousness: The Itihasa-purana Tradition', in *Interpreting Early India* (1992), 137–73; *Time as a Metaphor of History* (1996).

[17]Sometimes the dispute turns polemic. For the critique of the 'leftist conspiracy' and the 'subversion of scholarship' in connection with the issue of the 'Aryan Invasion', see Talageri 1993; Rajaram 1995. Rajaram is attacking in particular Romila Thapar and other JNU historians: ibid., 199ff.

the image of the past which has so far been generally projected: an image which on occasion has led to deeply-rooted prejudices in the minds of both Indians and others. I shall then indicate the kind of evidence and interpretation, which is forcing historians to reconsider this image.

It is still a popular belief that the Indians were an a-historical people and kept no records of their history. The ancient Indians did keep records of those aspects which they felt were significant and worth preserving. It is true that most of these records do not deal with political events and activities. They are more in the nature of genealogies, legends and monastic chronicles—all legitimate constituents of a historical tradition but not, unfortunately, very useful as a description of contemporary happenings. This latter type of record developed in the period after about AD 500. Court chronicles and historical biographies of considerable authenticity were maintained by the Turkish and Mughal courts and the tradition remained alive until recent times. So, when the Europeans arrived in India and began to look for histories of India, they found ample evidence on the period after about AD 1000. But the earlier centuries remained historically blurred. Even the factual records of this early period—the inscriptions—were written largely in the *Brahmi* script, which could no longer be read by Indians. Consequently, the discovery of the Indian past was initiated under the auspices of the new ruler, the British. A major contradiction in our understanding of the entire Indian past is that this understanding derives largely from the interpretations of Indian history made in the last two hundred years.

There is a qualitative change between the traditional writing of history and history as we know it today. The modern writing of history was influenced in its manner of handling the evidence by two factors. One was the intellectual influence of the scientific revolution, which resulted in an emphasis on a systematic uncovering of the past and on checking the authenticity of historical facts. The other was the impact on the motivation of history by the new ideology of nationalism, with its stress on the notion of a common language, culture, and history of a group. Indeed, historical studies the world over have assumed special significance in proving the background of nationalism.

Thus nationalism in Europe had led in the eighteenth century to a new look at the European past. It was not however in that spirit that those who settled and colonised Asia and Africa, sought familiarity with the history of these regions. With the transformation of trading connections into colonial relations, the need to know the history of the colonies was based not merely on an intellectual curiosity but also on the exigencies of administration. If the norms, traditions and behaviour patterns of a colony were to be understood, then research into the history of the colony would have to be carried out.

The search for or discovery of the Indian past resulted in a number of interpretations of the past. These were notions which were constantly repeated since they were first enunciated and which have become stereotypes of Indian history and culture. Even though today they are being questioned, they are still widespread. Some of these stereotypes are related to the needs of imperialism, for economic imperialism had its counterpart in cultural domination. Historical writing coming from this source aimed at explaining the past in a manner which facilitated imperial rule. Others arose, in contrast, from Indian national sentiments opposed to the nature of imperial rule, and seeking justification in the reading of the past. The ideology of Indian nationalism found not only political expression, but influenced every aspect of intellectual life—philosophy, literature, the arts and history—in the early twentieth century.

The relationship with historians was especially close. The national movement itself had picked up facets from the reconstruction of the Indian past. Those historians who were sensitive to the stirrings of nationalism also responded to these facets. Because of the cultural domination implicit in imperialism, nationalism of the anti-colonial variety had to incorporate a programme of cultural nationalism as well, in order to regenerate the indigenous culture. The intellectual content of nationalism arose out of the need for Indians to react to the experience of colonialism, industrialisation and economic backwardness. Paucity of evidence also assisted in the creation of the stereotypes. Some of the recent questioning has been necessitated by greater and improved evidence. The more persistent of the stereotypes have dominated not only historical interpretation but have become the foundation of modern political ideologies.

That Indian society has always been an unchanging society, based on a caste structure, which in turn made it oppressive and averse to any change, or alternatively, that it was an idyllic society characterized by harmony and an absence of social tension—a utopian society; these beliefs are still with us. The first of these notions encouraged the development of the theory of Oriental Despotism. This had been popular in Europe for long and was revived in the nineteenth century with reference to the past of Asia. Yet another stereotype was the sharp distinction between the nature of Oriental and Occidental culture; where the Oriental was described as spiritual and unconnected with material culture, the Occidental was branded as obsessed by material values. In the words of Vivekananda: 'To the Oriental the world of Spirit is as real as to the Occidental is the world of senses. In the spiritual, the Oriental finds everything he wants or hopes for; in it he finds all that makes life real to him.'[18]

The dichotomy between Oriental and Occidental was not the only one which came to dominate Indian historical thinking. Two other dichotomies were introduced which have served political, rather than historical, purposes. The Aryan–non-Aryan distinction was based on a supposed racial difference. The myth of two separate nations was developed to explain away, and sometimes even to justify, cases of tension between Hindus and Muslims. What is most striking about all these stereotypes is that they do not occur as facts in the cultural tradition of pre-British India.

The notion of an Aryan *race* is alien to the Indian tradition. There are frequent references in early literature to the *aryas*, either in the sense of the more honoured persons of society or else, as distinct from the *mleccha* and the *an-arya*. The criteria of difference are primarily language and the observance of the *varnasramadharma*, that is, the organisation of society on the basis of caste and the prescription of the four stages in the life of a man. In the very early texts additional differences are recognised as those of appearance, and religious worship. But, very soon after, the criteria of language and culture alone remained. The Aryans are seen as a separate cultural group but not as a distinct race. This is also borne out in the early sources where there are references to the *aryavarta*, the land of the *aryas*. The definition of the *aryavarta* varies in each

[18]Swami Vivekananda, 'My Master' (1896), in *Complete Works* (1989), IV, 155.

group of sources in accordance with the culture which the source represents and the geographical location of its nuclear area.

The later Vedic texts speak of *aryavarta* as essentially the Ganga Yamuna Doab and its fringes. Lands beyond this are generally listed as *mleccha-desa*. Thus we are told that Magadha and Ainga (Patna, Gaya, Monghyr and Bhagalpur districts in Bihar) are inhabited by the *sankirna-jatis* (mixed castes) and are unfit for the *arya*. In Jaina sources however, these regions are listed as a part of the *aryavarta*, as also in the Buddhist sources where the location of *aryavarta* is distinctly to the east of the Doab, in the modern Rajmahal area. By the time of Manu, *aryavarta* was defined more or less as northern India, north of the Vindhyas.[19] Race is not the criterion and obviously could not be, for the concept of race both in the scientific and the popular sense is a product of modern Europe.

Again, Indians in the pre-eighteenth century never claimed that they were more spiritual than other peoples, or that the Indian way of life was concerned solely with things spiritual. The ideal of the earlier texts that the best life on earth is a balance between *dharma, artha* and *kama*, shows a healthy unconcern for any obsession with either the spiritual or the material. As for the static, unchanging quality of Indian society, this is also contrary to what is said in Indian sources. There are frequent references to changes in society some of which are approved and others deplored. Hindu, Buddhist and Islamic cosmology state that society is perpetually undergoing change. From an initial utopian condition, society has not only changed but deteriorated. Ultimately however, it will move towards the return of the utopia, be it a fresh *Satyayuga* or a final Judgment Day. From where then did these stereotypes emerge and why did they receive the sanction of recent times? For an answer one has to look at the intellectual and political background of the last two centuries in India and Europe.

It is worth noticing that the colonial period of other Asian countries also reflects similar stereotypes in the historical interpretation of the past. The search for a superior race, the claim to spirituality and the description of an unchanging utopian past, are all concepts in the history of other Asian cultures and have been projected during recent decades.

[From: Thapar, *The Past and Prejudice* (New Delhi: National Book Trust, 1975), 2–8.][20]

Academic history in South Asia, with its methodological procedures, its search for practical orientation, and its conceptualizations of temporal change, did not differ very much from that of the West. During the 1970s, however, the quest for a specifically Indian approach to history intensified. Some historians, who organized themselves into the Indian History and Culture Society (IHCS), opposed the alleged Marxist tendencies within the Indian History Congress

---

[19]*Baudhayana*, 1. 2. 13 among others lists Magdha and Anga as being unfit for aryas. The Jaina *Bhagavatisutra* and the Buddhist *Mahavagga*, V. 12.13 and *Divyavadana*, 22 place the *aryavarta* to the east. Manu, 11. 21–3. (RT)

[20]The extract is taken from the first of three lectures delivered by Thapar in All India Radio (*Sardar Patel Memorial Lectures*, 1972) and later published as a book. In a somewhat different form, the same problem is dealt with in: 'Ideology and the Interpretation of Early Indian History', in *Interpreting Early India* (1992), 1–22. For the treatment of ancient Indian history in the context of Indian nationalism, see also: 'Imagined Religious Communities? Ancient History and the Modern Search for a Hindu Identiy', in *Interpreting Early India*, 60–88.

and other associations and institutions and demanded a critical revision of concepts and frameworks of interpretation. In 1978, D. Devahuti[21] and her colleagues organized a conference on problems of Indian historiography in which they offered the IHCS as a forum for what they called 'the third alternative in the present state of affairs'. The state of historiography in modern India, it was said, could be compared to that of a permanent civil war. There was one group of historians (imperialists, Marxists, including some pseudo-secularists and Muslim-communalists) who slandered the Indian tradition in their works, whereas the other group (nationalists and Hindu-communalists) romanticized it.[22] The advocates of the 'third alternative' looked for a new path which led towards an objective treatment of history, without denying the subjective elements in it.[23]

Problems of Indian Historiography (1979)

The Indian History and Culture Society has been formed at a time when it has become necessary to ask some basic questions about the study and writing of history in our country. A forum is needed for a dialogue among like-minded as well as contending historians so that a consensus can be reached, no doubt to give rise to conflict and then a further consensus, in a continuing process. [...]

For the study of Indian history in general, we are very much in need of Indian frameworks of reference because the general becomes intelligible only through the specific, the universal through the unique. Abstractions are intimately connected with actualities and must flow from them. Moreover, one view of actuality may differ from another in time and space and lead to a different set of abstractions, even in the matter of universal institutions. Thus, not only would the medieval European approach to family and kingship be found to be different from the modern European, but the latter would be unlike the modern American, Chinese or Indian. While different historical approaches are valid for their own time and place, they will ring true to us, if they do, in part or in whole, or not at all, only if we comprehend them in terms of our own reality and our own past experience. We have to be our own 'messiahs', to feel, to understand, to interpret our own history, and to appreciate the validity or otherwise of the 'revelations' of others, of their frames of reference in other words, in our context of time and place.

To comprehend history we have to keep on observing the remains and reading our sources till we are able to see those objects in use and those people in action. The essential matter of history is not what happened, but what people thought and said about it. The essential matter of Indian history is what the Indian people, ordinary or special, thought and said about events and ideas. It is that self-definition which represents the Indian feel for, attitude towards, and use of history

[21]Devahuti studied in Lahore, Delhi, and London and taught at universities in Malaya and Australia and at Delhi University. Among her publications are: 1983 and 1965; with regard to historical thinking in India: 'Writing History. An Indian View', *Manthan* (Sept. 1978), 53–5.

[22]Devahuti 1979: XVIII. For the political controversies over historiography in post-colonial India, see the next Section.

[23]In the preface of the volume comprising the papers of the successive conference on 'Bias in Indian Historiography', Devahuti once again reiterated the IHCS' intention 'to arrive at new and viable frames of reference for the reinterpretation of Indian history through the identification of its unique, i.e. specific features.' Devahuti 1980: I.

even if it be the rejection of history as real, i.e., of ultimate significance, and therefore its transmutation into myths and symbols. By understanding the process of how they made history, the philosophers, the kings, the social reformers, the artists, the artisans, the tillers, shall we be able to discern their attitude to history. This will supply us with Indian frameworks possibly dissimilar to each other owing to factors of space, time and external influences. It may indeed be that some of these are analogous to frameworks worked out by other civilizations. The important thing is that we would have cognised them as Indian assumptions. Comparisons with others would no doubt provide us with a more meaningful understanding of Indian frameworks.

To discuss these and related questions the Indian History and Culture Society organised a seminar in March 1978 on the theme, *Indian History Writing* for which it proposed the framework discussed below.

I. The Problem of Identification: We need to know the past in order to discover our identity. The resultant rootedness has the potential of universality necessary for an objective view of history. It has so far been common, in fact fashionable, to use comparative and alien frameworks for the study of Indian history causing in the process great harm to the student as well as the subject. We need to form and use Indian frames of reference on the basis of the facts of Indian history. Indeed the different frames will coincide in their interpretation of facts up to a point, but beyond that they would diverge in proportion to the difference in their underlying assumptions. [...]

II. Conflict and Consensus: The urges, both for conflict and consensus, are present in human beings. We need to examine the place of each as the motivating factor in individual action and societal progression. The spirit of consensus requires concession as far as possible; that of conflict, resistance as far as possible. [...] We need to examine, at what time, in which fields, Indian society opted for conflict or consensus. [...]

III. Ancient Terms and Modern Connotations: The connotation of terms, specially if they have conceptual content often alters radically with the passage of time. The phenomenon is explicable in terms of the changing historical situation. The confusion becomes worse confounded when the terms are translated in a foreign language. Apart from the problems of language and culture-differentiation, the deliberate prejudices, if any, of the translator further vitiate the situation.

The interpretation of ancient and medieval Indian concepts and institutions, and thus of Indian history in general, has suffered greatly on this account in the last hundred years or so. It is imperative that we try to understand the meaning of such terms in the context of their time and place with the help of original sources. In fact, we should try to give up inadequate English equivalents in order to get a true feel of the meaning of such terms which only comes from using them. Some such terms are: *Dharma, Danda, Rashtra, Samanta, Zamindar, Vakil*, etc.[24]

IV. Classification of Period (Periodization) and Classifiction of Regions: Indian historiography has seen various illogical classifications with regard to periods and regions. Emphatic on the diversities and lukewarm on the compositeness of Indian culture, British writers gave the categories

---

[24]*Danda*: punishment; *Rashtra*: country, nation; *Samanta*: system of local or regional rule in Rajasthan; *Zamindar*: landed proprietor; *Vakil*: lawyer.

North and South India which we continue to foster. They also compartmentalised Indian history into three periods and devised the inconsistent and historically incorrect nomenclature, Hindu, Muslim and British for that purpose. Since then we have renamed the periods as Ancient, Medieval, and Modern after the European model. The terms, once again, are value-laden in their connotation. The whole question needs re-examination. Neither period nor region should be regarded as fixed categories. Their classification should be determined by factors such as the nature of historical enquiry, methodological criteria, a dominant historical situation, etc. In this connection, we may also take into consideration the distinction between Past, i.e. Oral Tradition, and History, and the importance of the former in the Indian context.

V. Approaches to Indian History: The various standpoints from which Indian history has been viewed: the imperialist or nationalist, i.e. in terms of narrow foreign or native self-interest; communalist or marxist, i.e. in terms of religious or economic factors; genealogical or ethnic, i.e. in terms of dynastic or linguistic domination; insular, through neglect of, or over-emphasis on regions, movements etc.; romantic or cynical, i. e., oblivious either of the dark or the bright aspects of a given situation, and so forth. There is need for a scientific, as well as indivisible, approach to history which would treat facts with respect and not use them to serve causes.

[From: Devahuti (ed.), *Problems of Indian Historiography* with a Message by the Indian Prime Minister Morarji Desai (Delhi: D. K. Publications, 1979), pp. IX–XIV.][25]

4.2 UNITY AND DIVERSITY, PARTICULARITY AND UNIVERSALITY

4.2.1 *World History, National History, Regional History*

Western conceptualizations of world history, which allowed only for a subordinate role of the South Asian peoples and cultures, had been under dispute since the end of the nineteenth century. A new world historical consciousness found expression in India in the philosophical sketches of Vivekananda, in the critiques of modern civilization by Tagore and Gandhi, and in the political strategies of M. N. Roy and Nehru.[26] At the beginning of the twentieth century, Durgadas Lahiri envisaged a history of the world in thirty volumes.[27] At the same time, the sociologist and economist Benoy Kumar Sarkar (1887–1949) developed the theory of an asynchronous evolution of 'Eur-America' and India/Asia which, starting from the Renaissance, would culminate in a world society (Sarkar 1922).

The work of the diplomat and historian (Sardar) KAVALAM MADHAVA PANIKKAR (1895–1963)[28]

[25]Reprint with kind permission by B. R. Publishing Corporation, New Delhi. The papers presented at the third session of the IHCS (Ahmedabad 1980) are incorporated in Devahuti 1982. A periodical published by the IHCS is: *Souvenir* (1978ff).

[26]Cf. *Glimpses of World History*, which has been described as 'world history from the prison'. See David Kopf, 'A Look at Nehru's World History from the Dark Side of Modernity', *Journal of World History* 2 (1991), 47–63.

[27]Cf. A. R. Mallick, 'Modern Historical Writing in Bengali,' in Philips 1961: 446–60, here 451.

[28]Panikkar, born in Kavalam (Kerala), was a student of Madras Christian College and Oxford University. After a short period of teaching at Aligarh Muslim University and the University of Calcutta, he served as editor of the *Hindustan Times* in Delhi. Some time later, he became Secretary to the Chancellor of the Chamber

can be seen as a step towards a historiographical concretization of world history from an Indian perspective. Panikkar strove to break away from dynastic history, still widespread among Indian historians at that time, and to pave the way for a new Indian historiography. Distancing himself from the school of thought of the 'national apologetics', he was mainly interested in the tendencies of social progress and development.[29] Panikkar was invited by UNESCO and the International Commission for a History of the Scientific and Cultural Development of Mankind to write the last volume of the *History of Mankind* (Vol. 6, 1966), together with Caroline F. Ware and J. M. Romein.

Asia and Western Dominance, which was written mainly during Panikkar's diplomatic mission in Peking, was the outcome of twenty-five years of work.[30] The 'Survey of the Vasco da Gama Epoch of Asian History' was welcomed both in the East and in the West and was translated into several languages.[31] A controversial issue was the assessment of Christian missionary activity among the Asian peoples.[32] Also criticized was the fact that the West Asian countries were largely overlooked in the account.

Asia and Western Dominance (1953)

The 450 years which began with the arrival of Vasco da Gama in Calicut (in 1498), and ended with the withdrawal of British forces from India in 1947 and of the European navies from China in 1949, constitute a clearly marked epoch of history. It may have passed through many stages, undergone different developments, appeared in different periods under different leadership, but as a whole it had certain well-marked characteristics which differentiated it as a separate epoch in history. Its motivations underwent changes; one major strand in the original idea, that of a crusade against Islam and a strategic outflanking of Muslim power, disappeared after the menace to Western Europe from the growth of Islamic imperialism ended with the Battle of Lepanto. The original desire for the monopoly of the spice trade changed in a hundred years to the import into Europe of textiles, tea and other goods, which again changed after the Industrial Revolution in Britain into an urge to find markets for European manufactured goods and finally for investment of capital. Originally confined to trade, European interests became in the nineteenth century predominantly political over many years. The leadership of European peoples in this period also underwent change. From Portugal the supremacy in trade was wrested by the Dutch. In the middle of the

---

of Princes and subsequently served various Indian princes as foreign minister. After Independence Panikkar continued his diplomatic and political career in the Nehru administration and served as Indian ambassador in different countries and continents. Finally, he took office as Vice-Chancellor of the University of Jammu and Kashmir and the University of Mysore.

[29] See Panikkar's numerous publications: 1947, 1950, 1955, 1961, 1963 and 1964.

[30] Panikkar had already given an idea of the fundamental geo-political issue in his essay 'India and the Indian Ocean—An Essay on the Influence of Sea Power on Indian History' (1945).

[31] It was also owing to the free-flowing prose that Panikkar's work made a lasting impact on his readers. In almost all the Indian histories of historiography, Panikkar figures as one of the most important and influential historiographers of modern India.

[32] Although Panikkar was not a communalist, a certain amount of 'Hindu bias' has been noted in his writings. Cf. Tarasankar Banerjee, 'Sardar K. M. Panikkar', in Sibapada Sen 1973, 329–51, here 349.

eighteenth century Britain and France contested for it for a short time. Since then, the authority of Britain was never seriously challenged till the beginning of the Second World War.

In spite of these changes and developments, it is none the less true that the da Gama epoch presents a singular unity in its fundamental aspects. These may be briefly stated as the dominance of maritime power over the landmasses of Asia; the imposition of a commercial economy over communities whose economic life in the past had been based not on international trade, but mainly on agricultural production and internal trade; and thirdly the domination of the peoples of Europe, who held the mastery of the seas, over the affairs of Asia. It was an age of maritime power, of authority based on the control of the seas. Till the beginning of the present century, for a period of 400 years from the time of Vasco da Gama, sea-power, capable of deciding Oceanic policies, did not exist outside the Atlantic. The control of the Atlantic thus meant the mastery of the Indian Ocean and ultimately of the Pacific. During the first hundred years the Iberian powers had the mastery of the Atlantic, but from the time of dispersal of Philip of Spain's Armada, that supremacy began gradually to diminish and was inherited by other European Powers. The essential feature, that of the control of the Asian seas, remained

The imposition of a commercial economy on the peoples of Asia and the gradual revolution in almost every aspect of life that it brought about are among the principal themes of this study and they do not require any discussion here. All that need be said is that from the beginning of the period to its end they constituted the dominant features of Europe's relations with Asia. Even when the motive of weakening Islam was proclaimed as a major objective, it is significant to note, as Albuquerque said in his speech to his soldiers at Malacca, that it was by excluding the Moors from the spice trade that the Portuguese hoped to sap the strength of Islam. Trade, enforced by a naval supremacy, was the simple policy of the Portuguese. The creation of a world market in spices as a result of the immense quantities which began to be shipped to Europe led to a change in the economy of the coastal and island regions which produced these commodities, but it did not seriously affect the bigger land powers, at least in the time of the Portuguese. However, with the arrival of the Dutch and the British the position began slowly to change. The British trade with India was not to any large extent in spices, but in cotton textiles, luxury goods, indigo and saltpetre, necessary for the manufacture of gunpowder. The demand for these goods was so great that during the course of the eighteenth century India's economy became to a large extent dependent on her seaborne trade. The shift of economic and political power from the inland areas to the coast, and the growth and rise to power of a commercial class in alliance with the foreign mercantile interests, are major developments both in Indian and Chinese history after European trade became nationally important. Through all the changes, from the first monopoly · in spice trade to the large-scale export of capital in the three decades preceding the First World War, the dominance of a commercial economy on the life of Asian people is what gives the epoch its distinctive colouration.

The third feature, the political domination of European peoples over almost the entire territory of Asia, which was a spectacular development and naturally attracted the most attention, was but the result of the first two factors. The control of the sea made it possible for the European nations to bring their strengths to bear on any point in Asia, especially after the economic and political strength of the great empires had been undermined by the European monopoly of maritime trade. Political domination brought in its train a doctrine of racialism and a feeling of European solidarity as against the Asians; and in the consideration of the relations between Asia and the West these two factors gain a significance which they did not possess in the earlier periods.

There is a further feature which gives unity to this period and that is the attempt made during the time by European nations to Christianize Asia. It would, however, be a mistake to think that this was an essential characteristic of Europe's relations with the East. The Portuguese during the age of discovery were undoubtedly animated by the spirit of the great Crusades: but that was essentially an anti-Islamic spirit and did not seriously include the problem of evangelization. It was only during the great upsurge in the Catholic world known in history as the counter-reformation that the spirit of evangelization began to take Asia into its sphere. St Francis Xavier was the embodiment of that spirit and for a short period, following his example, there was a great movement to convert the heathen in Asia. It was not the Jesuits in Peking who represented that spirit but the evangelists in Japan. But this was a temporary phase. After the arrival of the Dutch and the English and the decline of Portuguese power in the East there was but little missionary activity anywhere in Asia for over a century. Actually the Protestant sects began to feel interest in evangelization only by the end of the eighteenth century and their missionary activities in India and China, which became so prominent a feature of European relations with Asia, were connected with Western political supremacy in Asia and synchronized with it.

These features give to the epoch its special character and stamp it as the reflection in history of a great movement. It may be objected that though the European political authority over Asian countries has ceased the chapter of their relations is not closed: that Europe continues to have even closer connections than before in many spheres of Asian activity: that trade between Asia and Europe is much larger today than it was before. Undoubtedly all that and much more is true. But the essential difference is that the basis of relationship has undergone a complete change. If economic relations are closer they are on the basis of reciprocity and as determined by the national interests of both parties and not imposed by Europe. The political relations between the Asian and European nations are as between independent countries. Asia and Europe confront each other and many vitally important historical results may flow from this new confrontation. But it is no longer the relationship of the da Gama epoch, for a revolutionary and qualitative change intervenes between the new era which has now opened and the epoch that preceded it. [...]

The final failure of the European effort to conquer and hold Asia is an example of the limitation of sea-power and has lessons which no one can overlook. Hilaire Belloc, discussing the failure of the Crusades in Palestine, claimed that it 'is an illustration of something which you find running through all military history, to wit, that dependence on sea-power in military affairs is a lure leading to ultimate disappointment. In the final and decisive main duels of history the party which begins with high sea-power is defeated by the land power; whether that sea-power be called Carthage or Athens or the Phoenician fleet of the Great King, it loses in the long run and the land power wins'. Ultimately in Asia also, the landmasses asserted themselves against the power based on the sea, and the withdrawal of European power from Asia is in effect a reassertion of the power of land empires shaking themselves free from the shackles of maritime mercantilism.

Some European writers have been inclined to view the European expansion as the effect of a civilization on the march. Sir George Sansom, for example, observes: 'It (the invasion of the Asian world) was the expression, the inevitable expression of a civilization on the march. It marked a new phase in the development of human society.'[33] Professor Tawney, on the other hand, sees in the early European invasions of Asia only the hand of the grasping merchants of Antwerp.

Actually the early European expansion in Asian waters was neither 'a civilization on the march' as Sansom would have us believe, nor a puppet show managed by clever merchants from behind the scenes. It was, as we shall try to establish, an attempt to get round the overwhelming land power of Islam in the Middle East, supplemented by an urge to break through the 'prison of the Mediterranean' to which European energies were confined. By the nineteenth century, Europe, with its social, economic and political structure reorganized by the tremendous industrial and revolutionary upheavals of the end of the eighteenth century, represented indeed a civilization on the march. It challenged the basis of Asian societies; it imposed its will on them and brought about social and political changes in Asia which are of fundamental importance. But to see in the commercial adventurism of the first three centuries of European contact the grand conception of an epic conflict between the East and the West is perhaps reading into past events the meaning of what happened much later.

Though this epoch, because of its importance, has been the subject of many valuable studies, so far they have been concerned mainly with special areas. No study of the relations of Europe with non-Islamic Asia as a whole has yet been attempted. On the purely historical side there are many works of great value dealing with each country separately and ignoring the basic unity of the problem, which was to a large extent obscured by the position of the British Empire in India which a distinguished Foreign Secretary of that Government once described as neither the Far East, nor the Middle East, but INDIA. The British position in India was thus isolated from the rest of the problem, rendering a correct perspective of Asia difficult if not impossible.

The present attempt, therefore, is to restore that perspective, which was well understood and fully realized in the seventeenth and eighteenth centuries. Also it may be added as a final word that this is perhaps the first attempt by an Asian student to see and understand European activities in Asia for 450 years.

[From: Panikkar, *Asia and Western Dominance. A Survey of the Vasco Da Gama Epoch of Asian History 1498–1945* (London 1953), 13–7.][34]

[33]Sansom, *The Western World and Japan* (1950). (KMP)

[34]Reprinted with permission of Harper Collins Publishers Ltd., London, copyright Panikkar 1953. Further reading: Barun De, 'Sardar K. M. Panikkar', *Bengal Past and Present* (Jan.-June 1964); Tarasankar Banerjee 1977; K. K. N. Kurup, 'Sardar K. M. Panikkar (1895–1963)', *Journal of Indian History* 60 (1982), 347–63; Jayati Chaturvedi, 'KM Pannikar', in Ramesh Chandra Sharma et al. 1991: 114–43.

REGIONAL HISTORIOGRAPHY,[35] as, for instance, the histories of the Marathas,[36] the Bengalis,[37] or the Tamils, is not a by-product or sequel of national history. Chronologically, it preceded the modern historiography of India. It was on the regional level that the demand for autonomy and independence from colonial rule found its first expression. Sometimes, the claim to regional identity competed or even conflicted with the centripetal tendencies of Indian nationalism.[38] But regional history today does not necessarily include a propensity to regionalism. It aims first and foremost at a better understanding of and respect for the patterns and rhythms specific to the various parts of the subcontinent.[39]

Moreover, the use of the regional languages as mediums of historical research and representation is encouraged, considering the dominance of English and Hindi. This is also seen as a way to popularize history and as an enlargement of the source material beyond the texts of the elite. In 1972, the Indian Council of Historical Research launched a programme, in the course of which over a hundred historical monographies have been translated into various Indian languages.[40]

It is, in particular, in the South of India that the claim to regional traditions was and is articulated, against the reduction of Indian history to merely that of the Gangetic plain. The history of the South stood in the shadow of the 'more national' history of the North for a long time. After the pioneering works of S. Krishnaswamy Iyengar (1871–1953),[41] it was, above all, the Tamil historian K. A. NILAKANTA SASTRI (1892–1975)[42] who took up the cause of throwing light on the history of South India through research and writing. Nilakanta resisted the temptation to play off the Dravidian element against that of the Aryans.[43] Instead of proposing a separate

---

[35]For a survey of historiography in regional languages, see De Souza and Kulkarni 1972; Tarasankar Banerjee 1987. For the relationship between regional and national identity, see P. C. Chatterji 1989; Singh and Mohan 1994; Bhawani Singh, 1993.

[36]The most prominent representative of modern historiography in Marathi is Govind Sakharam Sardesai (1865–1959). Among his works is *The New History of the Marathas* 1946–8 (abridged English version of the eight-volume Marathi work *Marath Riyasat*, 1932). For other historians from Maharashtra, see V. D. Dighe, 'Modern Historical Writing in Marathi', in: Philips 1961: 473–80.

[37]For Bengali historiography, see A. R. Mallick, 'Modern Historical Writing in Bengali', in Philips 1961: 446–60; Prabodhchandra Sen 1995.

[38]The problem of regionalist tendencies is analysed, within the general debate on communalism and nationalism, in S. Srinivasa Iyengar's speech on the occasion of the 41st Session of the INC; reprinted in Ramachandrasekhara Rao 1969: 57–9.

[39]The reconstruction of their historical development often also requires different periodizations.

[40]Cf. Barun De, 'Problems of the Study of Indian History, 6.

[41]See for instance *Beginnings of South Indian History* (1918); *Contributions of South India to Indian Culture* (1928).

[42]Nilakanta Sastri grew up in an orthodox Brahman family in Kallidaikurichi in the Tirunelveli district. After his studies in Madras, he taught as Professor for history in Tirunelveli and at Benares Hindu University (1918–20). Subsequently he served as Principal of the Sri Meenakshi College in Chidambaram, which later became the Annamalai University. From 1929 to 1946, he taught at the University of Madras; from there he moved to Mysore as Professor of Indology. Finally, Nilakanta assumed the directorship of the UNESCO-supported Institute of Traditional Culture in Madras.

[43]Some critics even accused him of pro-Sanskritic tendencies. Cf. Subrahmanian, *Tamilian Historiography*, 146.

identity of the Dravidians, he aimed at presenting the importance of the South for Indian history as a whole, thus integrating the regional with the national.[44]

A History of South India (1947)

Our aim in this book is to present a brief general survey of the ancient history of South India to the middle of the seventeenth century AD. Then began a new epoch with the downfall of the empire of Vijayanagar, its partition between the sultanates of Bijapur and Golconda, and the establishment of the English East India Company at several points on the coast of peninsular India. We mean by South India all the land lying south of the Vindhyas—Dakshina (the Deccan) in the widest sense of the term. Our knowledge of the history of this region has been greatly advanced during the last sixty years by many important discoveries, archaeological and literary. Much of this new source material lies embedded in the inaccessible periodical reports of the different branches of the Archaeological Survey of India, and of the more important 'Indian states', such as Hyderabad, Mysore and Travancore. Scholars, none too many, have addressed themselves to the task of interpreting the data and have written learned monographs mostly confined to particular dynasties, areas, or topics; these are very helpful as far as they go, but by their very nature cannot give a general idea of the main lines of movement in the history of politics and culture. Sir R. G. Bhandarkar's *Early History of the Dekkan* (1895) is the nearest approach to a general history; but that brilliant sketch is now outdated and does not deal with the history of the extreme South. Dr S. K. Aiyangar wrote several papers and books elucidating many aspects, but they fall far short of being a regular history of the country. P. T. Srinivasa Iyengar's *History of the Tamils* (1929) deals only with the early history of the extreme South.

In general histories of India, the part of the country with which we are concerned figures in a small way. Vincent Smith rightly observed: 'Hitherto most historians of ancient India have written as if the South did not exist', and explained this neglect of the South in two ways. 'The historian of India', he said, 'is bound by the nature of things to direct his attention primarily to the North, and is able to give only a secondary place to the story of the Deccan plateau and the far South'. Again, 'the northern record is far less imperfect than that of the peninsula. Very little is known definitely concerning the southern kingdoms before AD 600, whereas the history of Hindustan may be carried back twelve centuries earlier. The extreme deficiency of really ancient records concerning the peninsula leaves an immense gap in the history of India which cannot be filled.' Scanty as our information is on the earliest phase of the history of the South, the situation is not so hopeless as Smith depicts it and this will become clear as we proceed.

On any view the history of South India is an integral and not the least interesting part of the history of India. The Deccan is one of the oldest inhabited regions of the world and its prehistoric archaeology and contacts with neighbouring lands, so far as they are traceable, constitute an important chapter in the history of the world's civilizations. All over India the foundations of Indian culture were laid by the fusion of Indo-Aryan and pre-Aryan elements in varying conditions

---

[44]Among Nilakanta's main publications are: *The Cholas* (1935–7), *Foreign Notices of South India* (1939), *Further Sources of Vijayanagar History* (1946), *Advanced History of India* (1970), *Historical Method in Relation to Indian History* (1956).

and proportions; and in the languages, literatures and institutions of the South there has survived much more of pre-Aryan India than anywhere else. The Marathas of the western Deccan are the southernmost of the Indo-Aryan-speaking peoples of India and all the country to the east and south of them speaks languages that fall into a single group, the Dravidian, of which Tamil is the oldest surviving literary idiom. And the earliest strata of Tamil literature take us back at least to the early centuries of the Christian era. A picture of politics and society drawn on the basis of this early literature must be interesting in itself and go some way to help unravel problems of early culture contacts between Aryan and pre-Aryan. The rise of Hindu kingdoms in the eastern lands across the Bay of Bengal is but an expansion and continuation of the process by which South India and Ceylon were colonized and aryanized; and beyond doubt the Deccan and the far South formed the advanced base from which this transmarine movement started in the early centuries before and after the Christian era: in Indonesia and Indo-China emigrants from India met the same problems as in India south of the Vindhyas and solved them in more or less the same manner. A detailed study of the many interesting analogies between the results of these early culture-contacts in these different lands has not yet been attempted and lies beyond the scope of this book; but we should do well to remember that the history of India has been too long studied more or less exclusively in isolation and from the continental point of view, little regard being paid to the maritime side of the story. The Satavahanas were described as 'lords of the three oceans' and promoted overseas colonization and trade. Under them Buddhist art attained the superb forms of beauty and elegance preserved to this day in the cave-temples of western India and the survivals from the stupas of Amaravati, Goli, Nagarjunikonda and other places in the Krishna valley; and the tradition was continued long after the Satavahanas by their successors both in the eastern and western Deccan. The latter half of Satavahana rule in the Deccan coincides with the age of the literature of the Sangam in Tamil and of active trade between India and the Roman empire in the west, and there is good reason to believe that the plastic arts of the Deccan in this period and the succeeding one owed something to Graeco-Roman models and artists.

[From: Nilakanta Sastri, A History of South India. From Prehistoric Times to the Fall of Vijayanagar, 4th ed. (Madras: Oxford UP, 1975 [1955, 1947]), 1–3.][45]

4.2.2 Communalism and Secularism

The issue of the survival and the role of cultural heritage presents one of the main challenges to historical thinking in post-colonial India—in the face of the accelerated modernization of society, as much as in view of the continuing tensions between religious and ethnic communities.[46]

[45]Further reading: Prof. K. A. Nilakanta Sastri Felicitation Volume (1971); G. Subbiah, 'K. A. Nilakanta Sastri (1892–1975)', Journal of Indian History 60 (1982), 331–46. The Tamil tradition of historiography is well documented in Subrahmanian 1988.

[46]For this fundamental problematic in the various communalisms of Hindus, Muslims and Sikhs, see T. N. Madan 1997.

While secularism was established as one of the basic principles of the Indian state, the Constitution also refers to the religious ties of the people. The opposition party Jana Sangh, in particular, demanded better safeguard of Hindu traditions.[47]

The issue of communalism and secularism also had its impact on the major historiographical projects in post-colonial India.[48] Special importance for the self-image of contemporary India was attached to the memory of the freedom struggle, similar to a foundation myth of the Republic. At the first session of the Indian Historical Records Commission (IHRC) after the end of colonial rule, a decision was taken to prepare an 'authentic and comprehensive history of the different phases of the Indian struggle for independence'.[49] A board of editors, headed by R. C. Majumdar, had already begun collecting material and approved Majumdar's draft for the first volume when, towards the end of 1955, the board was dissolved. Subsequently, Tara Chand was commissioned for the task.[50]

Even later, there were attempts to exercise a political influence on the writing of history. The Janata Government, in office during the years 1977 to 1980, contemplated the exclusion of some textbooks, written by renowned historians, from their use in schools—an idea which

[47]See the Jana Sangh's 'Resolution on Indianisation' (Kanpur 1952), in Balraj Madhok, *Indianisation? (What, Why and How)*, (Delhi: S. Chand & Co., 1971), 98–9. For the debate on communalism and secularism, see V. K. Sinha (ed.), *Secularism in India* (Bombay: Lalvani Publication House, 1968); Ashis Nandy, 'An anti-secularist manifesto', *Seminar* 314 (October 1985), 14–24; Achin Vanaik, *Communalism Contested: Religion, Modernity and Secularisation* (Delhi: Vistaar, 1997). For communalism and historiography, see Romila Thapar, 'Communalism and the Historical Legacy: Some Facets', in K. N. Panikkar (ed.), *Communalism in India: History, Politics and Culture* (New Delhi: Manohar, 1991), 17–33; Gyanendra Pandey, 'Nationalism, Communalism, and the Struggle over History', in Mehdi Arslan and Janaki Rajan (eds), *Communalism in India: Challenge and Response* (New Delhi: Manohar, 1994), 50–60; Thapar et al., *Selected Writings on Communalism* (New Delhi: People's Publishing House, 1994); Asghar Ali Engineer, *Communalism in India: A Historical and Empirical Study* (New Delhi: Vikas, 1995); K. N. Panikkar, *Communal Threat, Secular Challenge* (Madras: Earthworm Books, 1997); Rajeev Bhargava, 'History, Nation and Community: Reflections on Nationalist Historiography of India and Pakistan', *EPW* 22 January 2000, 193–200.

[48]An early example is the account of the Mutiny, written on the occasion of its centenary in 1957. In Surendra Nath Sen's *Eighteen Fifty-Seven* (1957), the common interests of Hindus and Muslims during the events are emphasized. The same applies to Sasi Bhusan Chaudhuri 1957. R. C. Majumdar, in contrast, negated the national character of the uprising and highlighted its local and reactionary elements. In the Preface of *The Sepoy Mutiny until the Revolt of 1857* (1963), Majumdar described the difficulties he faced in bringing to bear his interpretation. For the controversy that arose over this point, see S. B. Chaudhuri 1965.

[49]Janab Humayun Kabir, then Minister for Scientific Research and Cultural Affairs, in the Preface of Tara Chand 1961: p. VII.

[50]See Tara Chand 1961. The book is guided by the intention to present Indian history in its continuity and to show Indians as united in their resistance to colonial rule. For his secular views, which seemed to be a guarantee that the past would be represented in a politically correct way, see also the other writings by Tara Chand 1936 and 1966. The interference of the Government is commented on by Majumdar in an appendix to his own version of the *History of the Freedom Movement in India*, I (2nd ed., Calcutta 1971), 445–57.

was dropped in the face of nation-wide protests.[51] Another public debate on textbooks arose at the beginning of the 1990s, about the representation of Indian history since Independence.[52] After the last change of government (1998), textbooks and some state-financed research projects were once again the objects of politically motivated intervention.[53] The struggle over the interpretation of history and the conclusions to be drawn from it intensified over the years. In the communalization of the past, some have gone so far as to subject it to nothing short of an ethnic-religious cleansing: the misdeeds of the Muslims were given particular emphasis and their achievements were called into question.[54] In these accounts, Muslim invaders provided the perfect foil for the heroes of Hindu resistance (Sita Ram Goel 1984). The medium of communalist tendencies is popular literature rather than scientific research, often in the form of illustrated booklets where the lines between myth and history are blurred.[55] Some textbooks used in the schools and colleges run by the RSS organisation Vidya Bharti ('Indian Wisdom') are

[51]Only the new textbook on Ancient India, written by R. S. Sharma (New Delhi 1977), was definitely withdrawn in 1978; in the case of other books the distribution was curtailed. Sharma reacted to the critique expressed by members of the Arya Samaj in Sharma 1978. Under attack were also Romila Thapar, Harbans Mukhia, Bipan Chandra and their book *Communalism and the Writing of Indian History* (1969). For the 'textbook controversy', see Vijay Chandra Prasad Chaudhary 1977; L. I. and S. H. Rudolph, 'Rethinking Secularism: Genesis and Implications of the Textbook Controversy, 1977–9', *Pacific Affairs* 56 (1983), 15–37.

[52]For the historians' difficulties in dealing with the recent past, and in particular the circumstances of Partition, see Gyanendra Pandey, 'Partition and Politics of History', in Madhusree Dutta, Flavia Agnes, and Neera Adarkar (eds), *The Nation, the State: Indian Identity* (Calcutta: Samya, 1996), 1–26; Mushirul Hasan, 'Memories of a Fragmented Nation: Rewriting the Histories of India's Partition', in Katja Fülberg-Stolberg, Petra Heidrich and Ellioner Schöne (eds), *Dissociation and Appropriation: Responses to Globalisation in Asia and Africa* (Berlin: Das Arabische Buch, 1999), 167–84.

[53]See the report on the January 2001 meeting of the IHC by Suhrid Sankar Chattopadhyay in *Frontline* (2/2001: www.the-hindu.com/fline/fl1802/18020840.htm). A comprehensive reckoning with the 'eminent historians', who had been entrusted by the Congress-led Governments with important historiographical projects and who had allegedly used the Indian Council of Historical Research (ICHR) for political purposes and for their personal enrichment, has been presented recently in Shourie 1998. According to Shourie, the secular historians have betrayed the Hindu position in the Ayodhya conflict.

[54]P. N. Oak, president of an 'Institute for Rewriting Indian History', denounced *Some Blunders of Indian Historical Research* (1966) and demanded to do away with the falsifications of Indian history after more than a thousand years of foreign rule. Among the 'blunders', he counted not only disrooted facts ('Indian Monuments Credited to Alien Muslims', such on the Taj Mahal and other masterpieces of Indian architecture, 'Hindu Origin of Prophet Mohammed'), but also the omitting of entire chapters of history, such as the Indian Kshatrya empire from Bali to the Baltic. It is questionable if western authors like Elst (1992) or Gautier (1996) try to legitimate Hindu nationalist revisionism and thus compensate the European's bad conscience with regard to colonialism by referring to a common anti-Islamism.

[55]Cf. K. N. Panikkar, 'Introduction' in idem 1991: 13. The screen adaptations of the great Hindu epics and their serialized presentation in the national TV programme have also been seen as a concession to the nostalgia for the mythic past. Krishna Kumar, 'Hindu Revivalism and Education', in Panikkar 1991: 173–95, here 194. However, there have also been film versions of the Bible and of Muslim heroes like Tipu Sultan. For the representation of history in television and cinema, see Geeta Kapur, 'Mythic Material in Indian Cinema', *Journal of Arts and Ideas* (Jan.–April 1987).

particularly doctrinal in character. They claim to teach the 'Hindu View of History'[56] and correct the 'distorted history' provided by professional historians.[57]

The dispute about the interpretation of Indian history reached its culmination in the Ram-Janmabhumi campaign and the destruction of the Babri Masjid in Ayodhya in December 1992. During the nineteenth century, the town, venerated as the birthplace of the god Rama and visited by many pilgrims, had become one of the central stages of the Hindu-Muslim conflict.[58] In recent years, the Vishva Hindu Parishad (VHP), in particular, has propagated the view that the mosque stood at the site of a Rama temple, which had been destroyed by Muslims. Throughout the country, activists agitated for the demolition of the mosque and the construction of temple.

In 1990, at the request of the Indian government, the anti-communalist All-India Babri Masjid Action Committee (AIBMAC), as well as the VHP, presented documents in order to and substantiate their respective standpoints.[59] Part of the AIBMAC's documentation was the statement of twenty-five historians of Jawaharlal Nehru University in New Delhi, extracts of which are reproduced in the following. The focus is on the assessment of Ayodhya as the birthplace of Rama and on the question of whether the Ayodhya of today is identical with that of the Ramayana.[60]

The Political Abuse of History (1989)

Behind the present Babri masjid–Ramajanmabhumi controversy lie issues of faith, power and politics. Each individual has a right to his or her belief and faith. But when beliefs claim the legitimacy of history, then the historian has to attempt a demarcation between the limits of belief and historical evidence. When communal forces make claims to 'historical evidence' for the purposes of communal politics, then the historian has to intervene.

Historical evidence is presented here not as a polemic or as a solution to the Ramajanmabhumi–Babri masjid conflict, for this conflict is not a matter of historical records alone. The conflict emerges from the widespread communalization of Indian politics. Nevertheless it is necessary to review the historical evidence to the extent it is brought into play in the communalization of society.

I. Is Ayodhya the birthplace of Rama? This question raises a related one: Is present day Ayodhya the Ayodhya of Ramayana?

[56]See the list of Hindi publications in Pandey, 'The Appeal of Hindu History', in Dalmia and Stietencron 1995, 369–88, here 372. Ibid., 373. See also the sample in B. D. Chattopadhyaya, 'Cultural Plurality, Contending Memories and Concerns of Comparative History: Historiography and Pedagogy in Contemporary India', forthcoming in Rüsen et al.

[57]Panikkar 1991: 14. See also: National Steering Committee on Textbook Evaluation, *Recommendations and Report*, 2 parts (typescript) (New Delhi: National Council of Educational Research Training, n.d. [1993]).

[58]The Somnath temple, too, has played an important role. See Peter van der Veer, 'Ayodhya and Somnath: Eternal Shrines, Contested Histories', *Social Research* 59 (1992), 85–111.

[59]Some of the documents are reprinted in the special edition of *Internationales Asienforum* 25 (1994), 345–74.

[60]For the historical context of the issue, see Peter van der Veer 1996: 159, and the entire chapter on 'Conceptions of Time', 142–64.

The events of the story of Rama, originally told in the Rama-Katha which is no longer available to us, were rewritten in the form of a long epic poem, the Ramayana, by Valmiki. Since this is a poem and much of it could have been fictional, including characters and places, historians cannot accept the personalities, the events or the locations as historically authentic unless there is other supporting evidence from sources regarded as more reliable by historians. Very often historical evidence contradicts popular beliefs. According to Valmiki Ramayana, Rama, the King of Ayodhya, was born in the Treta Yuga, that is thousands of years before the Kali Yuga which is supposed to begin in 3102 BC.

(i) There is no archaeological evidence to show that at this early time the region around present day Ayodhya was inhabited. The earliest possible date for settlements at the site are of about the eighth century BC. The archaeological remains indicated a fairly simple material life, more primitive than that is described in the Valmiki Ramayana.

(ii) In the Ramayana, there are frequent references to palaces and buildings on a large scale in an urban setting. Such descriptions of an urban complex are not sustained by the archaeological evidence of the eighth century BC.

(iii) There is also a controversy over the location of Ayodhya. Early Buddhist texts refer to Shravasti and Saketa, not Ayodhya, as the major cities of Koshala. Jaina texts also refer to Saketa as the capital of Koshala. There are very few references to an Ayodhya, but this is said to be located on the Ganges, not on river Saryu which is the site of present day Ayodhya.

(iv) The town of Saketa was renamed Ayodhya by a Gupta king. Skanda Gupta in the late fifth century AD moved his residence to Saketa and called it Ayodhya. He assumed the title Vikramaditya, which he used on his gold coins. Thus what may have been the fictional Ayodhya of the epic poem was identified with Saketa quite late. This does not necessarily suggest that the Gupta king was a bhakta of Rama. In bestowing the name of Ayodhya on Saket he was trying to gain prestige for himself by drawing on the tradition of the Suryavamsi kings,[61] a line to which Rama is said to have belonged.

(v) After the seventh century, textual references to Ayodhya are categorical. The Puranas, dating to the first millennium AD and the early second millennium AD follow the Ramayana and refer to Ayodhya as the capital of Koshala. (Vishnudharmottara Mahapurana, 1.240.2)

(vi) In a way, the local tradition of Ayodhya recognizes the ambiguous history of its origin. The story is that Ayodhya was lost after the Treta Yuga and was rediscovered by Vikramaditya. While searching for the lost Ayodhya, Vikramaditya met Prayaga, the king of tirthas, who knew about Ayodhya and showed him where it was. Vikramaditya marked the place but could not find it later. Then he met a yogi who told him that he should let a cow and a calf roam. When the calf came across the janmabhumi milk would flow from its udder. The king followed the yogi's advice. When at a certain point the calf's udders began to flow, the king decided that this was the site of the ancient Ayodhya.

This myth of 're-discovery' of Ayodhya, this claim to an ancient sacred lineage, is an effort to impart to a city a specific religious sanctity which it lacked. But even in the myths the process of identification of the sites appears uncertain and arbitrary.

[61]Suryavamshi kings: rulers of the solar dynasty.

If present day Ayodhya was known as Saket before the fifth century, then the Ayodhya of Valmiki's Ramayana was fictional. If so, the identification of Rama janmabhumi in Ayodhya today becomes a matter of faith, not of historical evidence.

The historical uncertainty regarding the possible location of the Rama janmabhumi contrasts with the historical certainty of the birthplace of the Buddha. Two centuries after the death of the Buddha, Asoka Maurya put up an inscription at the village of Lumbini to commemorate it as the Buddha's birthplace. However, even in this case, the inscription merely refers to the village near which he was born and does not even attempt to indicate the precise birthplace.

II. Ayodhya has been a sacred centre of many religions, not of the Rama cult alone. Its rise as a major centre of Rama worship is, in fact, relatively recent.

(i) Inscriptions from the fifth to the eighth centuries AD and even later refer to people from Ayodhya but none of them refer to its being a place associated with the worship of Rama. (*Epigraphica Indica*, 10. p. 72; 15. p. 143; 1. p. 14)

(ii) Hsuan Tsang writes of Ayodhya as a major centre of Buddhism with many monasteries and stupas and few non-Buddhists. For Buddhists Ayodhya is a sacred place where Buddha is believed to have stayed for some time.

(iii) Ayodhya has been an important centre of Jain pilgrimage. To the Jains it is the birthplace of the first and fourth Jaina Tirthamkaras. An interesting archaeological find of the fourth–third century BC is a Jaina figure in grey terracotta, being amongst the earliest Jaina figures found so far.

(iv) The texts of the eleventh century AD refer to the Gopataru tirtha at Ayodhya, but not to any links with the janmabhumi of Rama.

The cult of Rama seems to have become popular from the thirteenth century. It gains ground with the gradual rise of the Ramanandi sect and the composition of the Rama story in Hindi. Even in the fifteenth and sixteenth centuries Ramanandis had not settled in Ayodhya on a significant scale. Shaivism was more important than the cult of Rama. Only from the eighteenth century do we find the Ramanandi sadhus settling on a large scale. It was in the subsequent ceuturies that they built most of their temples in Ayodhya.

III. So far no historical evidence has been unearthed to support the claim that the Babri mosque has been constructed on the land that had been earlier occupied by a temple.

(i) Except for the verses in Persian inscribed on the two sides of the mosque door, there is no other primary evidence to suggest that a mosque had been erected there on Babur's behalf. Mrs. Beveridge, who was the first to translate Babur Nama, gives the text and the translation of these above verses in an appendix to the memoirs. The crucial passage reads as follows: 'By the command of the Emperor Babur, whose justice is an edifice reaching up to the very height of the heavens, the good hearted Mir Baqi built the alighting place of angels. *Bawad [Buwad] khair baqi* (may this goodness last for ever)'. (*Babur Nama*, translated by A. F. Beveridge, 1922, II, pp. LXXVII ff.)

The inscription only claims that one Mir Baqi, a noble of Babur, had erected the mosque.

Nowhere does either of the inscriptions mention that the mosque had been erected on the site of a temple. Nor is there any reference in Babur's memoirs to the destruction of any temple in Ayodhya.

(ii) The *Ain-i-Akbari*[62] refers to Ayodhya as 'the residence of Ramachandra who in the Treta age combined in his own person both spiritual supremacy and kingly office'. But nowhere is there any mention of the erection of the mosque by the grandfather of the author's patron on the site of the temple of Rama.

(iii) It is interesting that Tulsidas, the great devotee of Rama, a contemporary of Akbar and an inhabitant of the region, is upset at the rise of the mleccha but makes no mention of the demolition of a temple at the site of Rama janmabhumi.

(iv) It is in the nineteenth century that the story circulates and enters official records. These records were then cited by others as valid historical evidence on the issue. [...]

To British officials who saw India as a land of mutually hostile religious communities, such stories may appear self-validating. Historians, however, have to carefully consider the authenticity of each historical statement and the records on which they are based. While there is no evidence about the Babri mosque having been built on the site of a temple, the mosque according to the medieval sources, was not of much religious and cultural significance for the Muslims. The assumption that Muslim rulers were invariably and naturally opposed to the sacred place of Hindus is not always borne out by historical evidence. [...]

This is not to suggest that there were no conflicts between Hindus and Muslims, but in neither case were they homogeneous communities. There was hostility between factions and groups within a community, as there was amity across communities. The above review of historical evidence suggests that the claims made by Hindu and Muslim communal groups can find no sanction from history. As a sacred centre the character of Ayodhya has been changing over the centuries. It has been linked to the history of many religions. Different communities have vested it with their own sacred meaning. The city cannot be claimed by any one community as its exclusive sacred preserve. The appropriation of history is a continual process in any society. But in a multi-religious society like ours, appropriations which draw exclusively on communal identities engender endless communal conflicts. And attempts to undo the past can only have dangerous consequences. It is appropriate, therefore, that a political solution is urgently found: 'Rama janmabhumi–Babri Masjid' area be demarcated and declared a national monument.

[From: Sarvepalli Gopal et al., *The Political Abuse of History* (New Delhi: Centre for Historical Studies, Jawaharlal Nehru University, 1989).][63]

---

[62]*Ain-i-Akbari*: contemporary account by Abu l-Fazl about the administration of the Mughal empire (last part of *Akbar-nama*, sixteenth century).

[63]The text was reprinted in various Indian newspapers; also in Mishra and Singh 1991: 177–84. Further reading: Neeladri Bhattacharya, 'Myth, History, and the Politics of Ramjanmabhuni', in Sarvepalli Gopal 1991: 122–40; Susan Bayly, Susan Bayly, 'Hijacking History: Fundamentalism in the Third World Today', in *Ritual, State and History in South Asia. Essays in Honour of J. C. Heesterman*, ed. A. W. van den Hoek, D. H. A. Kolff and M. S. Oort (Leiden etc.: Brill, 1992), 417–32; Peter van der Veer, 'History and Culture in Hindu Nationalism', ibid., 717–732. For the earlier history of Hindu-Muslim relations: Christopher A. Bayly, 'The Pre-History of

On the part of the Vishva Hindu Parishad, the debate is conducted pointedly as one over the correct use of the sources. The VHP based its evidence on archaeological remains and literary sources and enclosed numerous documents. It reacted to the AIBMAC documentation with a 'Rejoinder', presented to the Government in January 1991.[64] 'Evidence' and 'Rejoinder' are summarized in a press release that is reprinted here in a slightly abridged version.

Summary of the Ram Janmabhoomi Evidence (1991)

1. Sacredness of the site: The Ram Janmabhoomi site has been a sacred site for crores of Hindus since time immemorial, and was kept alive as a focus of Ram devotion even in the face of the forcible Muslim occupation of the site during more than four centuries. Why this is a sacred site, is beyond the limits of the dispute, firstly because the Government of India had asked us for evidence for the pre-existence of the Mandir on the Babri Masjid site, no more, no less; and secondly because we do not have to prove and justify the sacredness of our sacred sites, anymore than the Muslims have ever been asked to prove that, against all available indications, the Kaaba was built by Abraham.

Many dozens of Sanskrit texts from the first millennium BC and the first millennium AD attest the veneration for Ram, and put to rest recent allegations that the Ram cult became popular only in the last few centuries. There is multiple archaeological and iconometrical evidence for Ram worship since at least the 5th century AD.

2. Archaeological evidence for the temple: Archaeological excavations have brought to light the remains of an 11th century building on the disputed site. This was already clear from the first brief report of the excavations led by Prof. B.B. Lal in 1975–80 (though motivated 'eminent historians' have tried first to conceal and later to deny this pertinent fact), but recently more details have been made public, especially the rows of pillar-bases, aligned with the pillars of the present structure. Datable pottery remains indicate that the building was in use till at least the late 15th century. Nothing points to a period of disuse between this building's demolition and the Masjid's erection. But the 'robber's trench' around the pillar-bases indicates that the materials of the demolished building had been taken for use in a new building, probably the Masjid.

That the pre-existing building was a Mandir, is coherent with all the evidence so far, and requires no special assumptions or ad hoc hypotheses. More importantly, it is positively indicated by the 14 black pillars of schistose used in the Masjid. Documentary evidence from the 18th century as well as common sense dictate that, in conformity with a general pattern, these were materials of the demolished temple incorporated in the Masjid built over it. The disfigured

---

"Communalism"? Religious Conflict in India, 1700–1860', MAS 19 (1985): 177–203; Sanjay Subrahmanyam, 'Before the Leviathan: Sectarian Violence and the State in Pre-Colonial India', in Basu and Subrahmanyam 1996: 44–80; Brajadulal Chattopadhyaya 1998. For the relationship between Self and Other in a wider perspective, see Gyanendra Pandey 1993. For the role of history between the interest in change and the ideological creation of boundaries, see David Ludden, 'History outside Civilisation and the Mobility of South Asia', *South Asia*, XVII, 1 (1994), 1–23.

[64]'Rejoinder to the AIBMAC Documents', in: *History versus Casuistry*, 35–69.

sculptures on the black pillars all belong to Hindu religious iconography. Some of the motifs are common to different traditions, including Buddhist and Shaiva, but some are specifically Vaishnava.

All indications converge easily, without any artificial theoretical assumptions, on the hypothesis that a Vaishnava temple stood on the Janmabhoomi site until it was forcibly replaced with the Masjid. That it was specifically a Ram temple, is indicated by a wealth of documentary evidence.

3. Documentary evidence for the temple tradition: There are plenty of authentic documents available that unanimously prove two things: everyone agreed, and no one ever doubted, that the site on which the Babri Masjid was built, was taken from the Hindus; and the Hindu devotees kept coming back to the site for worship. Some sources suggest that in some periods the Hindus even used the Masjid itself. At any rate they set up a Ram chabootra just outside the Masjid, and in the 18th century they also built a make-do Janmasthan temple just nearby.

Among the most remarkable of the Muslim testimonies, we may mention the Chahal *Nasaih*, written by Aurangzeb's granddaughter around 1700, in which she exhorts Muslims to assert their presence in the 'places of worship of the Hindus situated at Mathura, Banaras and Awadh etc., in which the Kafirs have great faith—the birthplace of Kanhaiya, the place of Rasoi Sita, the place of Hanuman ... were all destroyed for the strength of Islam, and at all these places mosques have been constructed'.[65] Ten other testimonies of local Muslims confirm that the Babri Masjid had replaced the Ram Janmasthan temple. That Hindus kept coming for worship as nearby the site as possible, and that they kept claiming the site, is attested by a number of these same sources, as well as by a Faizabad Qazi in 1735.

Among the European records, the most remarkable is probably Josef Tieffenthaler's (1767), who describes in detail how Hindus kept on worshipping in the Masjid courtyard, with a big celebration on Ram Navami day,[66] and how everyone believed that the pre-existent Ram Mandir had been forcibly replaced with the Masjid, though opinions differed on whether this had been done by Babar or Aurangzeb. All the British surveyors, archaeologists and Gazetteer-writers, as well as the District Judge of Faizabad in 1886, saw no reason at all to doubt the unanimous local tradition that the Masjid had been built on the forcibly demolished temple marking Ram's birthplace.

Revenue records show that the disputed site has always been known as Janmasthan. Recent attempts to manipulate these records cannot change that, just like recent attempts to conceal or even obliterate pieces of testimony by local Muslims cannot change the facts to which these uncalculating witnesses testified.

4. Evidence must be coherent: All these authentic testimonies of various kinds converge, without exception, on the following scenario. A Ram Mandir standing on the now disputed site since the 11th century was demolished and replaced by a Muslim ruler, probably Babar or his aide Mir Baqi, who flaunted the victory over Paganism by using and displaying some of the temple

[65]Kafir: non-Muslim; Rasoi Sita: Sita's kitchen.
[66]Ram Navami: Rama's birthday.

pillars in his Masjid. But because the place was so sacred to them, the Hindus kept on trying to continue the worship on the site, or as close as possible.

This scenario, which is confirmed by all the available evidence of every kind, is moreover in perfect consonance with well-attested behaviour patterns of people in general (who built castles or temples on elevated and central places), of Muslim rulers (who destroyed thousands of temples to replace them with mosques, and often visibly displayed the iconoclastic origin of their Masjid), and of Hindu devotees (who in many cases kept on revering the desecrated site).

5. The AIBMAC non-evidence: In contrast to our own collection of coherent testimony for one precise scenario, our AIBMAC friends have just given a pile of papers, without adding even an attempt to show the coherence [...]. One example out of a dozen: while disputing the belief that Ram was born on the Janmabhoomi site, they do not build up coherent evidence that he was born at a specific other site. Instead, they give 'evidence' that Ram was born in Nepal, in Panjab, in Afghanistan, in Egypt, in Varanasi, in Ayodhya on a different site, in an unknowable other place, or not at all. So, each of these 8 'evidences' is contradicted by 7 other pieces of 'evidence' in the AIBMAC's own pile. [...]

6. The rebuttal: In our rejoinder, we have dealt with all the AIBMAC documents relevant to the historical question, but the AIBMAC has not replied to our own evidence. [...] Since they have not challenged our evidence, not even in this round of Government-sponsored scholarly contest, they must be considered as having accepted our evidence.

7. This debate is now closed: Since our AIBMAC friends have not disproven nor even denied the validity of the evidence we have given, the way we have demonstrated the utter inadequacy of their bulky but incoherent and irrelevant documentation, our evidence stands. It should now count as a proven proposition, i.e. supported by all the evidence available, not disproven and not even challenged, that the Babri Masjid was built on a Hindu sacred place, forcibly replacing a Mandir.

All the Babri polemists and secularist intellectuals who were so cocksure in lambasting us for clinging on to 'myths', spreading 'distortions' and denying 'history', now have to face the fact that it is we who have given conclusive evidence, while they have merely given politically motivated opinions and swearwords, apart from erudite considerations on issues beside the point. From now on (as until a few years ago), the established historical opinion is that the Babri Masjid has forcibly replaced a Ram Mandir built on a specially sacred Hindu site.

In our opinion, any Government decisions should from now on honour this established position of historical science, without giving in to further distraction manouevres such as calls for 'non-partisan' arbitration. Since our evidence has not even been challenged by the AIBMAC, there is no need for any arbitration. The historical facts themselves are the only competent and non-partisan arbitrator, and they have spoken through the authentic and unchallenged testimonies which we have collected and submitted to the Government.

8. Our request: Since it is now firmly established, and no longer being competently challenged, that the disputed site was one of the Hindu sacred places, we would like to ask our Muslim friends and fellow-countrymen the following questions:

1) In the Middle Ages, theologians and conquerors told you it was alright to destroy and occupy other communities' sacred places. Now in this age of secularism, do you still insist on continuing this occupation, or do you opt for 'equal respect for all religions'? We are not occupying your Kaaba or Al-Aqsa mosque, so is it not time you renounce the occupation of our most sacred places?

2) The last few years, motivated politicians and anti-Hindu propagandists, both communalist and communist, have concocted the theory that there was no temple at this site, that the Masjid was innocently built on empty land. Given the pretentious titles they flaunted, like 'protectors of Islam' and 'eminent historians', we can understand that you were misled into believing their made-up story. But now, scientific research has firmly established that this theory was indeed a concoction, and that the Masjid was built on a Hindu sacred site. Even the AIBMAC has not challenged the evidence which re-establishes that the Masjid has replaced a Hindu temple by force. In view of the renewed certainty that this Masjid was wilfully located on a Hindu sacred site in order to disturb and humiliate the religious practices of your Hindu fellow-countrymen, do you still insist on resuming the occupation of our Ram Janmabhoomi site, or do you agree to leave this Hindu sacred site to the Hindus ?

[From: Vishva Hindu Parishad, 'Summary of the Ram Janmabhoomi Evidence' (New Delhi, released to the press on 10 January 1991).][67]

4.2.3 Muslim History in India and Pakistan

SAYYID ABUL HASAN ALI NADWI (1914–2000), called 'Alî Miyân, is regarded as one of the most famous Muslim historiographers of independent India. His dozens of works, which include numerous treatises about Muslim India, biographies about mystics and scholars (the series *Saviours of Islamic Spirit*), travelogues, and, above all, the internationally known *The influence of rise and fall of Muslims on the world* (Arabic edition 1950) are translated in various European and Islam languages. They reveal the tension between national integration and Islamism in secular India.

---

[67]The complete version of the 'Evidence for Ramjanmabhoomi Mandir' (as well as the 'Summary') is found in *History Versus Casuistry: Evidence of The Ramajanmabhoomi Mandir Presented by the Vishva Hindu Parishad to the Government of India in December–January 1990–91* (New Delhi: Voice of India, 1991), 1–34; also in Mishra and Singh 1991, 185–218; and in *Internationales Asienforum* 25 (1994), 358–63. The archaeological findings by B. B. Lal, which caused a great sensation, is dealt with in the report of the four historians R. S. Sharma, M. Athar Ali, D. N. Jha and Suraj Bhan (*Ramjanmabhumi—Baburi Masjid. A Historians' Report to the Nation* (New Delhi 1991). The Government has reacted to the documentations and to the events of 1992 by presenting white papers on the issue. Since then the debate on Ayodhya and on the political use of history has gone on. See for instance D. Mandal, *Ayodhya. Archaeology After Demolition* (Orient Longman, 1993); Gyanendra Pandey, 'Modes of History Writing: New Hindu History of Ayodhya', *EPW* (18 June 1994), 1523–28.

Nadwi was an integrating figure of the colourful Islamic public in India, and has written an extensive autobiography.[68]

Nadwi regarded himself as historian and social theoretician: 'The truth is that historiography is based on facts. It is so realistic and sensitive, that one can manipulate it not even for any concessions, as historical proofs, references, figures and other information are necessary. History therefore does not cease to challenge even the greatest thinker, founder of religion and intellectual' (Abul Hasan Ali Nadwi: *Asr-e hâdir men dîn kî tafhîm o tashrîh*, Lucknow: Publishing House, 1980, 107).

His scientific efforts were directed towards the redefining of the independent position of Islamic scholars, not only in India but in the entire Islamic world. This effort was based on his specific Indian-Muslim experience of diaspora as well as his positive attitude to mysticism, which enjoys immense popularity in South Asia. In this, he has followed the footsteps of his father—S. 'Abd al-Hayy (1869–1923)—, himself chairman of the council of Islamic scholars for a long time, who, through his historical works, mainly in the Arabic language attempted to convey the achievements of Indian Muslims to the Arabic world. Consequently, Nadwi also started, very early, to criticize the Arabic Wahhabiya and accuse it of totalitarianism. Probably due to his specific Indian experience, Nadwi rejected every form of Muslim or Islamist legitimation of state and government, as demanded by Muhammad Iqbal and Sayyid Abul A'la Maududi.

His view of history, in contrast to the rather defeatist one of Maududi, displays Muslim achievements in South Asia, including those of one of his ancestors from Rai Bareli—particularly the leaders of the mystic association called Tariqa Muhammadiya. His writings are, however, dominated by the idea of the axiomatic supremacy of Muslims in India, a view which he reiterates even in the foreword of a work by his father, translated by him from Arabic to Urdu in the 1970s. In it Nadwi attempts to articulate the specific experience of Indian Islam as against that of non-Indian Muslims and the views of Hindu communalists. In addition he contrasts, under the aspect of development processes, the Muslim presence in India from British colonialism. Islam had led every conquered territory to the peaks of civilization, because the Muslims had not exploited the country like the Europeans but had cultivated and nurtured it. This applied also to India, which had been stagnant, passive, and decadent before the advent of Islam,—here Nadwi appears to take up widespread essentialist arguments of the European historiography of the nineteenth century, as he also cites Christian authors and western philosophers as authorities for his ideas. Muslims had given, according to Nadwi, an excellent gift to this desolate land, namely the belief in a pure and unmixed monotheism, in human dignity, and in equality; and a

---

[68] Abûl Hasan comes from an Alidian family, which emigrated to South Asia after the fall of Baghdad. His ancestors settled in Rai Bareli not far from Lucknow and founded a place of pilgrimage there. After attending various Islamic schools in India—primarily in Lucknow and Delhi—Abûl Hasan went on pilgrimage to Mecca and became there, too, a famous member of the Islamic public. Since 1961, he managed the internationally renowned theology school Nadwat al-'Ulamâ', founded at Kanpur in 1893 (since 1894 in Lucknow), and belonged to the leading representatives of traditional erudition and Islamic mysticism (Naqshbandi Order). Nadwi's influence stretched from Indian political circles—he was, for instance, the Chairman of the All-India Muslim Personal Law Board—to internationalist Islamic forums, like the Islamic World League, of which he was a founder member.

social system without discrimination of caste and class. Islam represented an exquisite culture. The champions of these achievements were Islamic scholars and mystics. Nadwi's main works were published (in various languages) in the Academy of Islamic Research & Publications, Lucknow: Nadwat al-'Ulama.

India During Muslim Rule (1977)

To whichever country the Muslim took the torch of Islam, it witnessed a great revolution exhibiting a tremendous upsurge in the people in numerous spheres of social and political life. The touch of Islam unfolded the hidden potentialities of each country, lying dormant for thousands of years, in a variety of brilliant colours of light and shade. Taking a leap from the obscurity of dark ages, each one of these countries took its rightful place in the comity of nations and made valuable contributions towards enriching human knowledge and culture. And what is more, all these lands also adopted these newcomers as their beloved sons and daughters.

No country conquered by the Muslims was ever treated by them as a milch cow or a beast of burden. Nor they ever acted as parasites of a conquered land: they never contrived to transfer the riches of the country they held in hand to the land from which they had hailed like the nations of the West. Rather, they diffused the most valuable treasure they had with them—the wealth of faith in One God and prophethood—and dispersed their conviction in virtues of human dignity and equality, their administrative skill and practical genius and their refined taste of arts and culture among the people of their adopted land. In every sphere of life, social or intellectual, in manners and customs, in arts and culture they inevitably impressed their mark. The forces they set in motion had always had profound and lasting effect upon society and culture, arts and literature of the land conquered by them. They established peace and order, planned and set up new cities, developed agriculture and commerce, promoted fine arts and architecture, set up educational institutions and cultivated new branches of learning not known to those countries. The lands they conquered were actually reborn, with a renewed zest and vigour, in a new and brighter world. [...]

The spectacle India presented was not different from other countries before the advent of Islam. Isolated from the rest of the world, the country was cut off by the sea in the south and east and the great chain of Himalayas in the North-West. The world had only a hazy idea of the land and its inhabitants. It was considered to be an extensive and fertile land, irrigated by innumerable rivers, great and small, whose people were devoted to philosophic ideals of *Vedanta*, practised penance and self-mortification and delved into the problems of mathematics and astrology.

The world had been able to peep into this closed land only occasionally through the windows opened by an ambitious conqueror like Alexander or a traveller like Alberuni. India had preserved its culture and social structure without any noticeable change for more than a thousand years with the result that stagnation and decay had set in almost in every field of life. Its artisans and entrepreneurs were not engaged, like those in the adjoining lands, in introducing new stratum in the old and static Indian culture, arts and literature, nor were there any visible signs of change in the development of its resources, mode of agriculture, commerce and industry or other fields of creative endeavour. At last the Muslims entered this ancient land and entrusted to its care the most precious gifts they had—the gift of belief in pure and unalloyed monotheism, human dignity and equality, a social system free from distinctions of caste and class, an exquisite culture refined and enriched by the consummate intellectual and creative genius of different peoples and a clean and effective system of administration evolved and perfected by a long and varied experience. In fine, it was a whiff of fresh air which rejuvenated and integrated different streams of thought and sciences, arts and culture and gave birth to a tremendous pulsation of the people in many spheres of social, intellectual, and political life of the country.

It was in this country that the valour of the Turks, perseverance of the Mongols and the stately pride of the Afghans mingled with the Islamic ideals of justice and compassion. The venturesome characteristics of the dauntless and chivalrous people coming to India from abroad blended with the mild and pacific disposition of the dwellers of this great land. The spirit of adventure, knowing no fear and defying every danger, came to terms with the soul of serenity, mild and soft, which knew no other language save that of love and harmony, through the integrative and moderating influence of Islam. And the culture thus coming into being by this happy accord of ideas and ideals could justifiably be called Indo-Islamic; its administrative set-up was a union of Turkish, Indian, and Islamic systems, generally known as the Moghul system of administration; and its design of construction as Indo-Islamic architecture. [...]

Indian Islam, thus, constituted a world in itself: a world within the world of Islam with its own distinctive administrative pattern, cultural attainment, and thought content. The achievement of Islam in India was not limited to one of its greatest and enduring conquests; for, it also made, in this land, important contributions to every branch of the classical Arab tradition, introduced a new stratum into the Islamic culture, struck upon new ideas in arts and literature, and created a distinctive style of architecture.

It was but necessary to take stock of these achievements of the Indian Islam, if only to shed light on the valuable gifts it has bequeathed to humanity. It was all the more necessary to make an assessment of the cultural synthesis, the atmosphere of amity and cooperative endeavour ushered in the country by the genius of Islam in order to strengthen the hands of the people aspiring to revive the spirit of harmony between different sections of the Indian people. This task could have, however, been accomplished only by a steady and untiring historian who had waded through the vast literature produced during the course of centuries with the avidity of a legatee looking forward to the lost treasure inherited by him.

[From: Ali Nadwi, 'Introduction', in Syed Abdul Hai, *India during Muslim Rule*, transl. by Mohiuddin Ahmad (Lucknow 1977), 2–3, 5–7, 9–10.]

Fundamental reflections on the role of history in Pakistan are found in K. M. Ishaque, 'Role of history in the growth of national consciousness', *Journal of the Pakistan Historical Society* 17 (1969), 25–39; D. R. Abdallah, 'Tharik ki ahmiyyat Iqbal ki nazr men', *Journal of the Pakistan Historical Society* 17 (1977), Part IV, Special Issue Allamah Centenary, 1–21.

For questions of the organization of historical research in Pakistan, which, after Partition, had to work largely without the material remaining in the Indian Archives, see Khurshid Kamal Aziz, *Some Problems of Research in Modern History*, (Rawalpindi 1969); idem, *The Pakistani Historian*, (Delhi 1994). Even in Pakistan the history of the freedom fight functions as the foundational legend of the new state: M. Husain (ed.), *A History of the Freedom Movement* (Karachi 1957). Like Savarkar, who had attempted to claim the revolt in 1857 as the first war for liberation, in Pakistan, too, the Independence movement was traced back to earlier forms of resistance like the struggle of Tipu Sultan.

ISHTIAQ HUSSAIN QURESHI (1903–81) was one of the leading Muslim nationalist historians, who supported the cause of independent Pakistan, without, however, over-emphasizing the significance of Islam.[69] Qureshi strove to support his position by including the Indus culture into the Pakistan theory. In the foreword of a book on the history of Pakistan he wrote:

This small book is intended to serve the purpose of a textbook at the undergraduate level. It will be found to be of interest to the general reader as well. The question may be raised: Is it possible to write the history of Pakistan at all? Can it be disentangled sufficiently from the history of India to stand by itself? The answer is that for certain periods the history of Pakistan can be narrated almost independently and for other periods the areas constituting Pakistan were drawn into the whirlpool of regional history so strongly that what happened here had only a local significance and this also could not be fully understood without reference to greater happenings involving larger areas. Sometimes the dominant role in our history was played by events outside the subcontinent, especially in Central Asia and the Iranian plateau.

So far as India is concerned, its events have not always been the dominant factor in our history. For long periods we have been the arbiters of India's historical destiny. This fact needs recognition. And if it is recognized, no eyebrows will be raised on the title of this book, even though sometimes the most significant drama may have been played outside our boundaries. Sometimes movements have taken birth or received their inspiration in Pakistan, though they worked themselves out in India as well. Numerous examples could be given of this phenomenon. When the novelty of some of the ideas put forward in this book wears off, there will be less reluctance to accept its approach to history in placing the emphasis on Pakistan and Pakistanis.

It is true that Pakistan is new, but the land and its people are not new. They have existed, by whatever names they might have been known before the present country of Pakistan came into existence. This land and these people have a history which sometimes flows by itself and sometimes it commingles its waters with other streams. This stream, however, was not lost and when it again found a new channel, it may have lost its pristine characteristics but it could assert its own new found entity as a resurrection, not a new birth.[70]

Qureshi can be regarded as a representative of the colourful Islamic public, with occasionally strong contradictions. He attempted, like many other Islamic modernists and the so-called

---

[69]Qureshi came from the old-established elite of society and studied history and Persian in the University of Delhi. He acquired a Ph.D. in Cambridge (1939). St Stephens College, Delhi (1928–39), University of Delhi (1940–7), Punjab (1948–9), Columbia (1955–60), Director of the Islamic Research Institute (1960–2), Karachi University (1961–71), Cambridge (1972–3), Rector of the University of Karachi, President of the Pakistan Historical Conference (twice) and Pakistan Political Science Conference, founder of the Muqtadira Qaumi Zuban (1979), Deputy Minister of Education, Minister of Education were the positions he held in his professional life. He was an active member of the Kalifat movement, Member of the National Pakistan Movement in Cambridge under the leadership of Chaudhri Rahmat Ali. He was awarded the 'Star of Pakistan' for his achievements.

[70]Introductory note in Dani 1967.

fundamentalists, to link the Islamic tradition and modern achievements, which according to him, are not guaranteed in the political development of Pakistan. He criticizes, similarly to Maududi, both the limited intelligence of the technocrats and the narrow-mindedness of the orthodox scholars.

Lost Opportunities (1979)

When I expressed the idea that Islam was waiting for an opportunity to prove not only its relevance, but also its efficacy, I had our demand for Pakistan in mind, for I was a member of the Pakistan National Movement founded by Chaudhri Rahmat Ali. At that time our optimism was matched only by our enthusiasm. We knew that it was not easy to establish Pakistan, but we were naïve enough to think that once established, it would develop in accordance with our dreams. This optimism never came under the shadow of even a passing cloud of doubt, because we were a band of enthusiastic and ardent believers in the good sense of our people, firmly holding the view that their loyalty to Islam was so strong that it would easily surmount all the difficulties in the way of implementing a revolutionary programme of nothing short of reconstructing the pattern of a decadent life. We were too naïve to understand the stupendous nature of the task that we wanted to assign to Pakistan, if it ever came to be established. [...]

Were we mistaken in our assessment of the enthusiasm of our people for Islam? The eagerness with which the idea of Pakistan was greeted by them would belie such a suspicion. However, it would be correct to say that their emotional loyalty to Islam was not matched by a true understanding of its tenets and goals. That is the reason why the technique of subverting Islam in the name of Islam has recently proved so successful. Those who are busy morning and evening in consciously destroying Islam and all that it stands for swear all the time by its name. The people are ignorant, gullible and confused. Besides, there is a world of difference between deep-seated intelligent adherence to religion and superficial sentimental religiosity. Of the latter there is a surfeit among the Muslims of the subcontinent; of the former much too little. The truly intelligent believer cannot be fraudulently converted into an instrument for the destruction of Islam, whereas the ignorant sentimentalist can unwillingly become a party to digging the grave of what he professes to love. [...]

The urge for freedom is deeply implanted in every human heart and we had stifled it for about two centuries without having extinguished it. The desire for Pakistan was natural; it was stronger because it was the logical culmination of our history of more than a millennium. But what was not natural was our impervious indifference towards the problem of our backwardness. It is true that the backlog of poverty and ignorance cannot be removed by mere enthusiasm, but then a resurgent spirit is the only guarantee that the effort will be made in earnest. As a people we laid no store by the cultivation of the spirit. We thought that independence would be enough; in fact it could pay the right dividends only if it were considered to be a removal of shackles on the desire and capacity to strive for higher goals. With the acquisition of that spirit, the shortages in intellectual vision and technical know-how would have been short-lived. [...]

We had been in danger of losing ourselves in the milieu of the subcontinent which had absorbed militarily equally virile immigrants into its social and religious system. Only Islam saved us from that fate, because it gave us a sense of uniqueness. We were anxious to save our faith which was more precious to us than our lives and so long as we strove to save it, it saved our existence and entity. This struggle continued when we were merely small trading communities settled on the coast; it did not abate when we were rulers, because our efforts to reconcile the local population and establish friendly contacts with them exposed us to the danger of assimilating their ideas and beliefs; it became more imperative when we became one of the subject races of the subcontinent. Every time we came out with flying colours and became so used to fighting the challenge that the constant endeavour looked almost effortless except in periods of great stress. Hence the decision to demand Pakistan and to work for it seemed only natural. And when Pakistan was established, it seemed equally natural to serve it with sincerity and devotion. And then, slowly and surely, our loyalty came to be undermined; our enthusiasm flagged; we lost interest in defending our integrity. [...]

We kept the old educational system alive and did not have the wisdom to adapt it to our needs. Even such good qualities as the old system had possessed were permitted to decay. Standards deteriorated, discipline was decried by some students and their political mentors, teachers ceased to look upon their profession as a vocation, with disastrous effects upon the students. Religious education was added as an afterthought, a mere unimportant appendage to a programme that did not harmonise with it, and even as such, it seldom went beyond teaching the rules and rites of prayers and fasting. What is the use of teaching a child how to pray and prepare for it, if his loyalty has not been canvassed so that he begins to attach importance to prayer and, for that matter, to the Faith itself? In this manner we turned generations of students into victims of a deep schizophrenia, living in two worlds, the world of belief and the world of actual life. It is strange that the results have been less disastrous than could have been expected. It was not unexpected when the *elite* schools produced sceptics and unbelievers, because most of them had consciously set this objective before themselves. The unexpected outcome is that some, because of the wholesome influence of a few homes, escaped contamination. Those who turned away from Islam were at least saved the tortures of schizophrenia into which most of those who went through the ordinary schools have come to suffer. How could our government and educational planners be so blind as not to see the disastrous consequences of their sins of omission and commission? [...]

But any attempt to abolish the supremacy of a foreign language is resisted by all vested interests, so that the positions of power and prestige may remain the preserve of the few already entrenched there. These few think that a superficial veneer of Anglo-Indian mannerisms is the height of culture and perpetuate ludicrous vanity and shallowness through their cock-eyed thinking. The products of the system are tragically inferior to the educated classes of other countries and accept their inferiority by an uncritical acceptance of any rubbish that might be current in the lands that they worship and adore. All this would, perhaps, have led only to material inferiority as it invariably does, had its corrosive effects not destroyed the soul of this class as a whole. That is the real reason of the decay of our nationalism, our pride, and our loyalty. It has destroyed the sense of identification with the people among the *elite*, resulting in a contempt for those outside their magic circle. [...]

It will be easily recognised that all this is the very negation of Islam, which can never prosper in such an environment. The real leadership has passed into the hands of a class that not only does not understand Islam, but is allergic to it, because it sees in its democratic principles an end of its undeserved dominance, whose nefarious influence has destroyed democracy. [...]

These lines must not be misconstrued as a plea for cultural isolation or cutting ourselves off from scientific and technological progress. We have to keep a window open on every side from which the light of scientific progress may be coming, but this is quite different from opening the floodgates of trivialities and irrelevant cultural and moral notions coming from decadent or immoral societies. We have done just the reverse: of the scientific advancement and intellectual efforts of the West we have imported precious little; of the superficialities and evils, which do not fail to trouble even some of the best minds of the countries of their origin and which we adopt so gleefully, there is no limit. [...]

We have a selfish schizophrenic *elite* and a gullible population. Between the two the cause of Islamic reconstruction seems to be lost. It is not only the cause of Islam that is in jeopardy. Because of the follies of the ruling elite the Muslim states are threatened with disruption and subjugation. If we want to build a brave new world for ourselves, we have to build a new capable ruling *elite*. The real service to Islam today lies in bringing up children, unaided by the state, if need be, not only as true Muslims but simultaneously as brilliant experts in all walks of life, capable of thinking for themselves and holding their own against their counterparts in other lands.

[From: Qureshi, 'Lost Opportunities: The Musing of a Student of History', in Khurshid Ahmad and Zafar Ishaq Ansari (eds), *Islamic Perspectives. Studies in Honour of Mawlana Sayyid Abul A'la Mawdudi* (London: The Islamic Foundation, 1979), 57–73, here 57–61, 65–7, 73.][71]

4.3 TRADITION AND MODERNITY, CONTINUITY AND CHANGE

The extent to which the political and social language in contemporary South Asia is infiltrated with ideas of modernization and development is evident in official documents and party manifestos as well as social science research and theory.[72] While sociologists and economists were increasingly interested in the phenomena of change, historians turned to issues of society and economy.[73] The numerous histories of science and technology also testify to the urge to innovate and mordernize.[74]

[71]Reprint with kind permission by The Islamic Foundation, Markfield, Leicestershire, UK. Further reading: Daniela Bredi, 'Historiography and national identity: The Pakistan case', in: *The East and the Meaning of History* (1994), 303–18; Satish Chandra, 'History Writing in Pakistan and the Two-Nation Theory', in idem 1997: 43–56.

[72]See Appadorai 1973; Bhagwati and Desai 1970. For the main trends in social theory, see the overview in Pantham 1995.

[73]An overview of the research in social and economic history is given in the contributions to R. S. Sharma 1986.

[74]See Qaisar 1982; Irfan Habib and Dhruv Raina, 'Copernicus, Columbus, Colonialism, and the Role of Science in Nineteenth-Century India', *Social Scientist* 190–1 (1989), 51–66; Dhruv Raina and Irfan Habib, 'The unfolding of an engagement: "The Dawn" on science, technical education, and industrialization: India, 1896–1912', *Studies in History* 9 n.s. (1993). For the close link between politics, scientific research, and economic planning, particularly during the era of Nehru, see the survey of V. V. Krishna, 'A Portrait of the Scientific Community in India: Historical Growth and Contemporary Problems', in Gaillard, Krishna, and Waast 1997: 236–80.

The processes of socio-economic development are generally accompanied by and interdependent with a change of culture and mentality. This problem was frequently dealt with in the framework of comparative analysis, especially in the wake of the works of Max Weber and Louis Dumont.[75] The Latin American theory of the 'development of underdevelopment' resulting from structures of colonial exploitation (dependency theory),[76] had an Indian counterpart in the 'Mode-of-Production Debate' during the 1970s.[77] The idea of a dissociation of non-European societies and economics from the development in the West has been elaborated by in Alvares 1991.

Development economics, in a wider historical dimension, has been discussed by Deepak Lal (1983, 1988, 1989). The economist Amartya Sen, who hails from Calcutta and taught at the Delhi School of Economics for some time, and who was awarded the Nobel Prize in 1998, has thrown new light on the problem of social inequality.[78]

The 'Directive Principles of State Policy' of the Indian Constitution express the general opening up of the horizon of expectations and partly imply a radical breakaway from the traditional social order.[79] They oblige the state 'to promote the welfare of the people by securing and protecting as effectively as it may a social order in which justice, social, economic and political, shall inform all the institutions of the national life' (Art. 38).[80] In 1953, the first Five-Year Plan for economic

[75]Weber 1958; idem, 1964; Dumont 1970; and idem 1975, therein: 'Le problème de l'histoire', 35–64; idem 1970a. An example of the debates on western modernity and Indian tradition is Loomis and Loomis 1969. For the reception of the work of Max Weber in India, see Detlef Kantowsky, 'Max Weber on India and Indian Interpretations of Weber', Contributions to Indian Sociology (N. S.) 16 (1982), 141–74; idem 1986a. For the issues of development in a comparative perspective as well as cultural implications of social change, see R. Murray Thomas, 'Hindu Theory of Development', in idem 1988: 29–73; Subrata K. Mitra 1999.

[76]See Andre Gunder Frank, 'The Development of Underdevelopment', Monthly Review 18 (September 1966), who has also dealt with India and its history: 'Reflections on Green, Red and White Revolutions in India', Critique and Anti-critique: Essays on Dependence and Reformism (London: Macmillan, 1984); idem, ReOrient: Global Economy in the Asian Age (New Delhi; Vistaar Publications, 1998).

[77]Most articles contributing to this debate were published in Economic Political Weekly. The debate is documented in Patnaik 1990. See also Bagchi 1982; Apter 1987.

[78]See Sen 1973 and 1984. In collaboration with Jean Drèze, Sen has given an overview of economic development in post-colonial India finishing with the policies of liberalization in the 1990s: (1995). See also Sen and Drèze 1996. Sen has also dealt with the history of the cultural encounter between India and the West: 'Indian Traditions and the Western Imagination', Daedalus 126 (1997), 1–26. At the 61st session of the Indian History Congress in Calcutta in January 2001, he held the inauguration lecture, talking about the connection between epistemological questions and the political perspectives of scientific research: 'History and the enterprise of knowledge', in: Frontline, 20 Jan.–2 Feb. 2001 (www.the-hindu.com/fline/fl1802/18020860.htm).

[79]In view of the Directive Principles, it has been stated: 'The Indian Constitution extended the Brahmo social reform program of the nineteenth century to every Indian citizen.' By the abolition of Untouchability, 'centuries of caste discrimination [...] were declared illegal, although in practice caste institutions and attitudes appear to be extraordinarily resilient'. David Kopf [et al.], Comparative History of Civilizations in Asia, II, 759.

[80]Sources of Indian Tradition, II, 337.

development was presented by the National Planning Commission.[81] Here, the concept of 'development' was specially explained.

The Problem of Development (1953)

The urge to economic and social change under present conditions comes from the fact of poverty and of inequalities in income, wealth, and opportunity. The elimination of poverty cannot, obviously, be achieved merely by redistributing existing inequalities. Nor can a programme aiming only at raising production remove existing ineqalities. The two have to be considered together; only a simultaneous advance along both these lines can create the conditions in which the community can put forth its best efforts for promoting development. The problem, therefore, is not one of merely rechannelling economic activity within the existing socio-economic framework; that framework has itself to be remoulded so as to enable it to accommodate progressively those fundamental urges which express themselves in the demands for the right to work, the right to adequate income, the right to education, and to a measure of insurance against old age, sickness, and other disabilities. The Directive Principles of State Policy enunciated in Articles 36 to 51 of the Constitution make it clear that for the attainment of these ends, ownership and control of the material resources of the country should be so distributed as best to subserve the common good, and that the operation of the economic system should not result in the concentration of wealth and economic power in the hands of a few. It is in this larger perspective that the task of planning has to be envisaged.

[...] Persistent effort must be made to give a new sense of direction and purpose to the community. It is important also to ensure that in the process of development, the force of growth from within be not stifled by attempts abruptly to superimpose preconceived patterns of life and activity. The strengthening of these inner forces and the creation of new institutions must proceed side by side so as to facilitate rapid advance through a process of interaction. The modern world is changing so rapidly that it is not enough to think in terms of slow changes and marginal adjustments, a minor shake-up here and a little cementing elsewhere. An underdeveloped country which has suffered long from the effects of cramped development desires inevitably to progress rapidly and in many directions; the aim of planning must be to make this possible. Political independence provides the needed opportunity. It is therefore natural that improvement in economic and social conditions through the acceptance of more progressive ideas and through suitable institutional changes is regarded as the practical test for judging the adequacy of the new political system.

The rapid advances in science and technology over the last few decades have opened out new possibilities in the direction of abolition of want and the restoration of man to a new sense of dignity, but they also carry potentialities of harm and danger. Our knowledge of the socio-economic changes which utilisation of these techniques calls for is neither complete nor certain. In the nature of the case, the problem does not admit of a generalised solution. Conditions vary as between countries, and each country has to evolve a solution in the light not only of

[81]In the 42nd Amendment of the Constitution (1976), India has been explicitly declared a state with a 'socialistic pattern of society'.

contemporary conditions but also of its traditions and culture. In planning for a transformation along the right lines, there are many pitfalls to be avoided, and it is of the utmost importance to strike the appropriate balance between various considerations so as to secure the optimum pattern and rate of progress. Parallels from past history or from contemporary conditions in other countries are useful up to a point, but they cannot provide a complete answer. A nation, like an individual, has to work out its inner potentialities by a process of experimentation. All that can be said is that there is need, on the one hand, for clarity in regard to basic values and, on the other, for readiness to adapt practical solutions to the concrete problems arising in the process of transition to a different economic and social order.

[From: Government of India, Planning Commission, *The First Five Year Plan* (New Delhi 1953), 8–9.]

Sociologists and anthropologists have often regarded traditional Indian society as ahistorical. On the other hand, those involved in ethnographical fieldwork had better access to the heterogeneity of local traditions than the historians, who worked mainly with the text material of the elite.[82] This helped them gain insight into specific processes of change which had always been a part of South Asian reality.

MYSORE NARASIMHACHAR SRINIVAS,[83] in his investigations into phenomena of social change in India, has thrown light on typical forms of mobility, which he has summarized and systematized under the term 'Sanskritization'. Two aspects are to be distinguished with regard to Sanskritization. First, it was a process of integration of heterogenous cultural traditions in India through the dissemination of Brahmanic teaching. In this way, common values were conveyed to all people in India, thus creating a sense of unity: 'The spread of Sanskritic rites, and the increasing Sanskritization of non-Sanskritic rites, tend to weld the hundreds of sub-castes, sects, and tribes all over India into a single community.'[84] Second, Srinivas' interest was directed at the phenomena

[82]Cf. Satish Saberwal on 'ingrained' and 'external ideologies': 'Societal Designs in History, here 440. About the conceptual relation of these studies both to the issue of Orientalism and that of communalism, see (with special reference to Louis Dumont) Peter van der Veer, 'The Foreign Hand. Orientalist Discourse in Sociology and Communalism', in Breckenridge and Peter van der Veer 1993: 23–44. Kunal Chakrabarti, too, discusses the fact 'that the question of fundamental unity or fundamental diversity in the religious spectrum is simply the result of the method of studying religion': 'Anthropological Models of Cultural Interaction and the Study of Religious Process', *Studies in History* 8:1, n.s. (1992), 123–49, here 147.

[83]Srinivas (1916–99) studied sociology at the University of Bombay. At the beginning of the 1940s he carried out fieldwork in Karnataka, the results of which were presented in *The Coorgs: A Socio-Ethnic Study* (1944). In 1945, he went to Oxford, where he studied Social Anthropology with A. R. Radcliffe-Brown and E. E. Evans-Pritchard. Subsequently, he taught 'Indian Sociology' at Oxford. In 1951, Srinivas became Professor of Sociology at the newly founded University of Baroda. Continuing his field studies in the South Indian village of Rampura, his main interest shifted to the issues of social change. In 1959, Srinivas was appointed Professor at the University of Delhi, with the task of establishing the new Department of Sociology, which became the Centre of Advanced Studies in 1971. One year later, Srinivas moved to Bangalore, where he was among the founders of the Institute for Social and Economic Change.

[84]Srinivas 1952, quoted in Chakrabarti, 'Anthropological Models', 125. See also Srinivas 1992. Such processes of social integration had already been analysed by other authors. Thus Alfred Lyall (1882) and H. H.

of change in the social stratification connected with the upward mobility of individual castes within the hierarchy due to the emulation of certain Brahmanic practices. The reform policy and advancing secularization during colonial rule were in complex interaction with the processes of Sanskritization and, directly or indirectly, accelerated and intensified them.

A weakness of the concept has been the disregard for macro-concepts and the lack of proper distinction between endogenous and exogenous causes of social change.[85] Furthermore, according to some of the critics, the increasing use of the term Sanskritization, identifying it almost with that of modernization, signified a loss in historical specificity.

The discovery of the effects of Sanskritization contributed to the politicization of the concept of caste as expressed in the debates about protective discrimination towards backward classes. Srinivas also tried to reflect the investigator's personal interest as a constitutive factor of social analysis. 'The sociologist who is engaged in the study of his own society is likely to be influenced by his social position. [...] But this need not always be a source of error—it might even be a source of insight.'[86] Since the formerly privileged were urged to concessions, it was understandable 'if some Indian sociologists become hostile to all change' while others become enthusiasts of development.[87]

A Note on Sanskritization and Westernization (1956)

The structural basis of Hindu society is caste, and it is not possible to understand Sanskritization without reference to the structural framework in which it occurs. Speaking generally, the castes occupying the top positions in the hierarchy are more Sanskritized than castes in the lower and middle legions of the hierarchy and this has been responsible for the Sanskritization of the lower castes as well as the outlying tribes. The lower castes always seem to have tried to take over the customs and way of life of the higher castes. The theoretical existence of a ban on their adoption of Brahmanical customs and rites was not very effective, and this is clear when we consider the fact that many non-Brahminical castes practise many Brahminical customs and rites. A more effective barrier to the lower castes' taking over of the customs and rites of the higher castes was the hostile attitude of the locally dominant caste, or of the king of the region. In their case there was physical force which could be used to keep the lower groups in check.

The point which is really interesting to note is that in spite of the existence of certain obstacles, Brahminical customs and way of life did manage to spread not only among all Hindus but also among some outlying tribes. This is to some extent due to the fact that Hindu society is a stratified one, in which there are innumerable small groups each of which tries to pass for a higher group. And the best way of staking a claim to a higher position is to adopt the customs and way of life of a higher caste. As this process was common to all the castes except the highest, it meant that

---

Risley (1891) had formulated the idea of 'Sanskritization' and discovered the capacity for synthetization as a specific feature of Indian tradition. Cf. Sabyasachi Bhattacharya, 'Paradigms Lost: Notes on Social History in India', *EPW* XVII (April 1982), 690–6, here 695; Ramakrishna Mukherjee, 'Trends in Indian Sociology' (*Current Sociology* 25, 1977).

[85]Cf. Saberwal, 'Societal Designs in History', 437; Bhattacharya, 'Paradigms Lost', 695.

[86]Srinivas, 'Some Thoughts on the Study of One's Own Society', in idem 1972: 155–71, here 161.

[87]Ibid., 166.

the Brahminical customs and way of life spread among all Hindus. It is possible that the very ban on the lower castes' adoption of the Brahminical way of life had an exactly opposite effect.

Though, over a long period of time, Brahminical rites and customs spread among the lower castes, in the short run the locally dominant caste was imitated by the rest. And the locally dominant caste was frequently not Brahmin. It could be said that in the case of the numerous castes occupying the lowest levels, Brahminical customs reached them in a chain reaction. That is, each group took from the one higher to it, and in turn gave to the group below. Sometimes, however, as in the case of the smiths of South India, a caste tried to jump over all its structural neighbours, and claimed equality with the Brahmins. The hostility which the smiths have attracted is perhaps due to their collective social megalomania. [...]

The idea of hierarchy is omnipresent in the caste system; not only do the various castes form a hierarchy, but the occupations practised by them, the various items of their diet, and the customs they observe all form separate hierarchies. Thus, practising an occupation such as butchery, tanning, herding swine or handling toddy, puts a caste in a low position. Eating pork or beef is more defiling than eating fish or mutton. Castes which offer blood-sacrifices to deities are lower than castes making only offerings of fruit and flower. The entire way of life of the top castes seeps down the hierarchy. And as mentioned earlier, the language, cooking, clothing, jewellery, and way of life of the Brahmins spread eventually to the entire society.

Two 'legal fictions' seem to have helped the spread of Sanskritization among the low castes. Firstly, the ban against the non-twice born castes' performance of Vedic ritual was circumvented by restricting the ban only to the chanting of mantras from the Vedas. That is, the ritual acts were separated from the accompanying mantras and this separation facilitated the spread of Brahminic ritual among all Hindu castes, frequently including Untouchables. Thus several Vedic rites, including the rite of the gift of the virgin (*kanyadan*), are performed at the marriage of many non-Brahminical castes in Mysore State. And secondly, a Brahmin priest officiates at these weddings. He does not chant Vedic mantras, however, but instead, the *mangalashtaka stotras* which are post-Vedic verses in Sanskrit. The substitution of these verses for Vedic mantras is the second 'legal fiction'.

[...] Sanskritization means not only the adoption of new customs and habits, but also exposure to new ideas and values which have found frequent expression in the vast body of Sanskrit literature, sacred as well as secular. *Karma, dharma, papa, maya, samsara,* and *moksha* are examples of some of the most common Sanskritic theological ideas, and when a people become Sanskritized these words occur frequently in their talk. These ideas reach the common people through Sanskritic myths and stories. The institution of *harikatha*[88] helps in spreading Sanskrit stories and ideas among the illiterate. In a *harikatha* the priest reads and explains a religious story to his audience. Each story takes a few weeks to complete, the audience meeting for a few hours every evening in a temple. *Harikathas* may be held at any time, but festivals such as Dasara, Ramanavami, Shivaratri, and Ganesh Chaturthi[89] are considered especially suitable for listening to *harikathas.*

---

[88]harikatha: histories of gods, sung by bards.

[89]Dasara: festival in honour of the mother goddess Devi; Ramanavami: birthday of the god Rama; Shivaratri: festival in honour of the god Shiva; Ganesh Chaturthi: birthday of the god Ganesh.

The faithful believe that such listening leads to the acquisition of spiritual merit. It is one of the traditionally approved ways of spending one's time. [...]

No analysis of modern Indian social life would be complete without a consideration of Westernization and the interaction between it and Sanskritization. In the nineteenth century, the British found in India institutions such as slavery, human sacrifice, suttee, thuggery, and in certain parts of the country, female infanticide. They used all the power at their disposal to fight these institutions which they considered barbarous. There were also many other institutions which they did not approve of, but which, for various reasons, they did not try to abolish directly.

The fact that the country was overrun by aliens who looked down upon many features of the life of the natives, some of which they regarded as plainly barbarous, threw the Indian leaders on the defensive. Reformist movements such as the Brahmo Samaj were aimed at ridding Hinduism of its numerous 'evils'. The present was so bleak that the past became golden. The Arya Samaj, another reformist movement within Hinduism, emphasized a wish to return to Vedic Hinduism, which was unlike contemporary Hinduism. The discovery of Sanskrit by Western scholars, and the systematic piecing together of India's past by Western or Western-inspired scholarship, gave Indians a much-needed confidence in their relations with the West. Tributes to the greatness of ancient Indian culture by Western scholars such as Max Muller were gratefully received by Indian leaders.[90] It was not uncommon for educated Indians to make extravagant claims for their own culture, and to run down the West as materialistic and unspiritual. [...]

The net result of the Westernization of the Brahmins was that they interposed themselves between the British and the rest of the native population. The result was a new and secular caste system superimposed on the traditional system, in which the British, the New Kshatriyas, stood at the top, while the Brahmins occupied the second position, and the others stood at the base of the pyramid. The Brahmins looked up to the British, and the rest of the people looked up to both the Brahmins and the British. The fact that some of the values and customs of the British were opposed to some Brahminical values made the situation confusing. However, such a contradiction has always been implicit, though not in such a pronounced manner, in the caste system. Kshatriya and Brahminical values have always been opposed to some extent, and in spite of the theoretical superiority of the Brahmin to all the other castes, the Kshatriya, by virtue of the political (and through it the economic) power at his disposal, has throughout exercised a dominant position. The superimposition of the British on the caste system only sharpened the contrast.

The position of the Brahmin in the new hierarchy was crucial. He became the filter through which Westernization reached the rest of Hindu society in Mysore. This probably helped Westernization as the other castes were used to imitating the ways of the Brahmins. But while the Westernization of the Brahmins enabled the entire Hindu society to Westernize, the Brahmins themselves found some aspects of Westernization, such as the British diet, dress, and freedom from pollution, difficult to accept.

[From: Srinivas, 'A Note on Sanskritization and Westernization', in *Caste in Modern India and Other Essays* (Bombay: Asia Publishing House, 1962), 42–62, here 44–52.][91]

[90]See for instance the appendices in Mahatma Gandhi's *Hind Swaraj*. (MNS)
[91]The essay appeared first in *The Far Eastern Quarterly* 15 (1956), 481–96. More essays by Srinivas on

With the attainment of political independence and the advancement of industrialization, India had joined, according to western views, the mainstream of development and found its connection to world history. However, it remained difficult to reconcile universalist concepts with the specific social and cultural features of India. This was particularly evident in the case of the Marxists among Indian historians,[92] who tried to understand why class struggles in India took forms other than those in the West.[93]

DAMODAR DHARMANAND KOSAMBI (1907–66)[94] was the exponent of a Marxist school of historical research in India. His use of Marxist concepts was undogmatic, however, and he sought to keep in mind the peculiar features of Indian history which deviated from the general model of social evolution. He combined sound theory with empirical research, thus gaining a great reputation, which stretched well beyond Marxist circles. His work has been characterized as a shift in paradigm of the historical discipline in India.[95]

It is, above all, the *Introduction to the Study of Indian History* (1956) which is regarded as a milestone in the evolution of Indian historical research. Here, dialectical materialism is presented by Kosambi as the 'underlying philosophy' of his approach, warning, at the same time, against too schematic an application of it to Indian history, since this could lead to untenable conclusions.[96] He rejected Marx's statement that Indian history was only a series of conquests by foreign powers.

---

aspects of social mobility are in Srinivas 1972. Among these 'Tagore Lectures', delivered at the invitation of the Association for Asian Studies in Berkely in 1963, are: 'Sanskritization', 'Westernization', 'Secularization'. Further reading: Harold A. Gould, 'Sanskritization and Westernization: A Dynamic View', *Economic Weekly* 13, No. 25, 24 June 1961, 945–50; J. F. Staal, 'Sanskrit and Sanskritization', *JAS* 22 (1962), 261–75; Singer 1972; Shah et al. 1996; Satish Deshpande, 'M. N. Srinivas on sociology and social change in India: Extracts from an interview', *Contributions to Indian Sociology* 34 (2000), 105–17.

[92]For M. N. Roy, see above. S. A. Dange had argued against the idea of a specifically Indian evolution and maintained the validity of the laws of Historical Materialism for India. In his *India. From Primitive Communism to Slavery* (1949), Dange applied the current Soviet reading of Historical Materialism to the history of early India. This, however, led to criticism even among Marxists, who pointed to the lack of empirical evidence for slavery in India. See the review by D. D. Kosambi, 'Marxism and Ancient Indian Culture', *Annals of the Bhandarkar Oriental Research Institute* 29 (1949), 271–7. The existence of a slave economy in ancient India was assumed also by E. M. S. Namboodiripad, leader of the Communist Party of India (Marxist): *The National Question in Kerala* (1952). See also his article 'Marx, the Asiatic Mode and the Study of Indian History', in *Selected Writings* (1982).

[93]For the theoretical discussion, see Habib 1987 and 1995; Rudra 1980.

[94]Kosambi was born in Kostben (Goa), the son of a Buddhist scholar. After his study of Mathematics at Harvard University (USA), he taught at Benares Hindu University, Aligarh Muslim University, Fergusson College (Pune) and the Tata Institute of Fundamental Research. Kosambi established his reputation as a historian when he applied methods of statistics to numismatic research. His wide horizon of interests included Pre- and Protohistory and Archaeology as well as Sanskrit poetry (see for instance *The Satakatrayam of Bhartrihari with the commentary of Ramarsi*, ed. by Kosambi in collaboration with Pandit K. V. Krishnamoorty Sharma, *Anandasrama Sanskrit Series* No. 127 [Poona 1947]). Even without an academic appointment as a historian, Kosambi exerted a considerable influence on historical research in India.

[95]Cf. Romila Thapar, 'The Contribution of D. D. Kosambi to Indology', in Thapar1992: 89–113, here 90.

[96]Cf. Kosambi's criticism of S. A. Dange's thesis about slavery in early India.

If one took the relations of production to be more important than the life of the rulers, one had to recognize that India's reality was not without historical evolution. Kosambi called for a clarification as to 'what is meant by the Asiatic mode of production never clearly defined by Marx' (Kosambi 1956: 10).

In his popular book *Culture and Civilization of Ancient India*, Kosambi emphasized the continuity of Indian culture through all political changes as an important element of its historicity.[97] Some of the specific problems of the modern historian in reconstructing ancient Indian civilization are described in the following extract.

The Difficulties Facing the Historian (1964)

What has been said so far might lend colour to the theory sometimes expressed that India was never a nation, that Indian culture and civilisation is a by-product of foreign conquest, whether Muslim or British. If this were so, the only Indian history worth writing would be the history of and by the conquerors. The textbooks that the foreigner has left behind him naturally heighten this impression. But when Alexander of Macedon was drawn to the East by the fabulous wealth and magic name of India, England and France were barely coming into the Iron Age. The discovery of America was due to the search for new trade routes to India; a reminder of this is seen in the name 'Indians' given to the American aborigines. The Arabs, when they were intellectually the most progressive and active people in the world, took their treatises on medicine and a good deal of their mathematics from Indian sources. Asian culture and civilisation have China and India as their two primary sources. Cotton textiles (even words like 'calico', 'chintz', 'dungaree', 'pyjamas', 'sash' and 'gingham' are of Indian origin) and sugar are India's specific contribution to everyday life, just as paper, tea, porcelain, silk are China's.

The mere variety that India offers is not enough to characterise the ancient civilisation of the country. Africa or the single province of Yunnan in China offer as much diversity. But the great African culture of Egypt has not the continuity that we find in India over the last three thousand years or more. Egyptian and Mesopotamian culture as we trace them back from today does not go beyond the Arabic. Also there is no Yunnanese civilisation as such. China's development amounts to the predominance of the Han people over the rest with an early, stable imperial system. The many other nationalities of China did not make comparable contributions of their own. The Incas and Aztecs vanished soon after the Spanish Conquest. The culture of Mexico, Peru, and Latin America in general is European, not indigenous. The Romans left their mark on world culture through direct conquest of the Mediterranean basin. The continuity was preserved mainly in those areas where the Latin language and culture was carried forward by the Catholic Church. In contrast, Indian religious philosophy was welcomed in Japan and China without the force of Indian arms, even though almost no Indians visited or traded with those lands. Indonesia, Viet Nam, Thailand, Burma, Ceylon certainly owe a great deal of their cultural history to Indian influence without Indian occupation. The continuity of Indian culture in its own country is perhaps its most important feature. How Indian culture influenced other countries is a matter for other books. Our task here is to trace its origins and the main character of its development in India.

---

[97]Kosambi shares the evident interest in continuity with many other progressive thinkers and politicians in modern India, reaching from the early reformers till Nehru. Cf. Nehru, *The Discovery of India*, 71.

At the very outset we are faced with what appears to be an insuperable difficulty. India has virtually no historical records worth the name. Chinese imperial annals, county records, the work of early historians like Ssu-ma Chien, inscriptions on graves and oracle-bones enable the history of China to be traced with some certainty from about 1400 BC. Rome and Greece offer less antiquity, but far better historical literature. Even the Egyptian, Babylonian, Assyrian, and Sumerian records have been read. In India there is only vague popular tradition, with very little documentation above the level of myth and legend. We cannot reconstruct anything like a complete list of kings. Sometimes whole dynasties have been forgotten. What little is left is so nebulous that virtually no dates can be determined for any Indian personality till the Muslim period. It is very difficult to say over how much territory a great king actually ruled. There are no court annals in existence, with a partial exception for Kashmir and Camba.[98] Similarly for great names in Indian literature. The works survive, but the author's date is rarely known. With luck, it may be possible to determine roughly the century to which the writing belonged; often it can only be said that the writer existed. Sometimes even that is doubtful; many a work known by a particular author's name could not possibly have been written by any one person.

This has led otherwise intelligent scholars to state that India has no history. Certainly, no ancient Indian history is possible with the detailed accuracy of a history of Rome or Greece. But what is history? If history means only the succession of outstanding megalomaniac names and imposing battles, Indian history would be difficult to write. If, however, it is more important to know whether a given people had the plough or not than to know the name of their king, then India has a history. For this work, I shall adopt the following definition: *History is the presentation in chronological order of successive changes in the means and relations of production.* This definition has the advantage that history can be written as distinct from a series of historical episodes. Culture must then be understood also in the sense of the ethnographer, to describe the essential ways of life of the whole people. [...]

Man does not live by bread alone, but we have not yet developed a human breed that can live without bread, or at least some form of food. Strictly speaking, unleavened bread is a late neolithic discovery, a considerable advance in the preparation and preservation of food. 'Give us this day our daily bread' still forms part of the Christian's daily prayer, though Christian theology places the world of the spirit above all material considerations. The basis of any formal culture must lie in the availability of a food supply beyond that needed to support the actual food-producer. To build the imposing ziggurat temples of Mesopotamia, the Great Wall of China, the pyramids of Egypt, or modern skyscrapers, there must have been a correspondingly imposing surplus of food at the time. Surplus production depends upon the technique and instruments used—'the means of production', to adopt a convenient though badly abused term. The method by which surplus— not only surplus food but all other produce—passes into the hands of the ultimate user is determined by—and in turn determines—the form of society, the 'relations of production'. The negligible surplus of primitive food-gatherers is often divided and shared out by the women of the gathering group. With further development, the apportioning is the function of the patriarch, tribal chief, head of the clan; often through family units. When the surplus is large and concentrated, a great

[98]Camba: state in the Himalaya.

temple or the Pharaoh may decide upon its gathering and distribution, through priestly guilds or the nobility. Production and exchange in a slave society remain in the hands of those who own the slaves, but this class may again have developed out of former priests, nobles, or clan chiefs now performing new functions. The feudal baron controlling serfs is the main agent under feudalism. His counterpart, the trader and financier, must deal also with the craftsmen's guilds. The trader class may transform itself through manufacture to usher in the capitalist age in which man's labour becomes a commodity, too, while his person remains free. In all this, form and content may differ. Britain has the complete range of feudal nobility, lords and knights—though no serfs now remain as primary producers. For all that, English society is fully bourgeois, the first and most important development of the full modern bourgeoisie. Edward VII may have been crowned on the wooden chair of Edward the Confessor in the latter's Abbey; but the England over which these two kings reigned had meanwhile changed beyond all recognition. The last great modern bourgeoisie, namely those of Germany and Japan, even strengthened certain feudal forms while demolishing feudalism under cover of absolute loyalty to the emperor.

Our position has also to be very far from a mechanical determinism, particularly in dealing with India, where form is given the utmost importance while content is ignored. Economic determinism will not do. It is not inevitable, nor even true, that a given amount of wealth will lead to a given type of development. The complete historical process through which the social form has been reached is also of prime importance. [...] At every stage the survival of previous forms and the ideology of the top classes exert tremendous force—whether by tradition or revolt against tradition—upon any social movement. Language itself was formed out of the process of exchange, new goods, fresh ideas, and corresponding new words all going together.

Any important advance in the means of production immediately leads to a great increase in population, which necessarily means different relations of production. The chief who can regulate single-handed the affairs of a hundred people could not do this for a hundred thousand people without assistance. This would imply the creation of a nobility or a council of elders. The district with only two primitive hamlets needs no government; the same district with 20,000 large villages must have one and can support it. So, we have a peculiar zigzag process, particularly in India. A new stage of production manifests itself in formal change of some sort; when the production is primitive, the change is often religious. The new form, if it does increase production, is acclaimed and becomes set. However, this must also lead to a decided increase of population. If the superstructure cannot be adjusted during growth, then there is eventual conflict. Sometimes the old form is broken by a revolution in the guise of a reformation. Sometimes the class that gains by preserving the older form wins, in which case there is stagnation, degeneracy, or atrophy. The early maturity and peculiar helplessness of Indian society against later foreign invasions bears testimony to this general scheme.

[From: Kosambi, *The Culture and Civilization of Ancient India in Historical Outline* (Reprint, New Delhi: Vikas Publishing House, 1991), 8–12.][99]

[99]Other works by Kosambi: *Myth and Reality* (Bombay 1962); *Exasperating Essays: Exercises in the Dialectical Method* (Pune 1957); *D. D. Kosambi on History and Society: Problems of Interpretation*, ed. A. J. Syed (Bombay 1985) (therein: 'Caste and Class in India'; 'What Constitutes Indian History'; and a critical review of R. C. Majumdar's

After Kosambi had questioned Marx's concept of the Asiatic mode of production and brought out forms of feudalism in Indian history,[100] RAM SHARAN SHARMA[101] continued these investigations and elaborated on the concept, theoretically as well as empirically.

Sharma has furthered the cause of important debates among historians by confronting theoretical concepts with new results of source research. He also 'achieved a certain notoriety amongst Indian nationalists and Hindu chauvinists because of his ability to confound cherished myths with hard evidence, and his effective demonstration that the "golden age" of the Guptas was in fact a period of economic decay.' (O'Leary 1989: 324–5) Moreover, rejecting the idea of an unhistorical India, Sharma has shown that there did exist a consciousness of social change in ancient India.[102]

In his book *Indian Feudalism: c. AD 300–1200* (1965), Sharma revealed how, from the Gupta period on, land donations were made to Brahmans and to temples, thus gradually creating a new class of landowners. This was accompanied by various phenomena of decentralization of power, decline of trade, and the growing dependence and impoverishment of farmers.

In the essay from which the following extract is taken, the process of feudalization is seen as the turning-point between antiquity and the Middle Ages. This can be considered an alternative to the periodization based on dynasties or invaders.

Problem of Transition from Ancient to Medieval in Indian History (1974)

When, why and how the ancient period ends and the medieval period begins in India is very difficult to say. The advent of the Muslims in India is generally seen as marking the end of the

---

The History and Culture of the Indian People); D. D. Kosambi. *'Combined Methods in Indology' and Other Essays*, compiled, edited and introduced by B. D. Chattopadhyaya (Delhi: Oxford University Press, 2001). Further reading on Kosambi: D. N. Jha, 'D. D. Kosambi', in Sen 1973, 121–32; R. S. Sharma and V. Jha (eds), *Indian Society: Historical Probings in Memory of D. D. Kosambi* (New Delhi: People's Publishing House, 1974); Rekha Pande, 'D. D. Kosambi', in Boyd 1999, 662–3.

[100]According to Ashok Rudra 1988: 87, this is a result of the Stalinist revision of Marxism. In fact, already the Russian historian (I. M. Reisner 1932) had spoken about Indian Feudalism instead of the Asiatic Mode of Production. However, he, too, saw India characterized by stagnation, so that actually only the name changed, not the concept. Cf. O'Leary 1989: 318.

[101]R. S. Sharma (born in a village in Bihar in 1920) had done his Ph.D. with A. L. Basham on a study of *Shudras in Ancient India* (1958). He taught at the universities of Patna and Delhi and was president of the Indian Council of Historical Research until 1977. At the end of the 1970s, a textbook on Ancient India written by him was attacked by conservatives and communalists. For the 'textbook controversy', see above, Section 4.2.2. A bibliography of Sharma's works is to be found in D. N. Jha (ed.), *Society and Ideology in India: Essays in Honour of Professor R. S. Sharma* (New Delhi 1996).

[102]For the use of the *kaliyuga* concept in the Puranas as an interpretation of social tensions accompanying the process of feudalization, see Sharma, 'The Kali Age: A Period of Social Crisis', in S. N. Mukherjee 1982: 186–203. See also Sharma's essay 'Historiography of the Ancient Indian Social Order', in Philips 1961: 102–14, also in Sharma 1966: 1–18, and in idem, 1983: 3–22. Sharma has also dealt with problems of historiography in relation to current politics: 'Ideological Basis of Research on Ancient Indian Polity up to 1930', *Patna University Journal* 8 (March-June 1954), 81–90; *Communal History and Rama's Ayodhya*, 2nd ed. (New Delhi: People's Publishing House, 1992).

ancient period, and textbooks on ancient Indian history by eminent scholars such as R. D. Banerji, R. C. Majumdar, K. A. Nilakanta Sastri, and R. S. Tripathi carry the narrative roughly up to AD 1206. This position is based on the British scheme of dividing Indian history into Hindu, Muslim and British periods and is broadly accepted by the Indian History Congress, which brings the section on ancient India to AD 1206. But ancient India should not be confused with Hindu India and medieval India with Muslim India. If the establishment of the Muslim rule marks the beginning of medieval India, Turkey, Egypt, Iraq, Iran, Pakistan, Indonesia, etc., will have to be placed in the medieval period and Hindu Nepal in the ancient period. And then what happens to the onset of the medieval age in those countries where the Muslims did not appear as a political force?

Difference in the language of source materials from the 13th century may be adduced as another ground for such a periodization: for political history the Persian sources become more important than the Sanskrit sources. But in all periods—ancient, medieval, modern and contemporary—we notice radically different languages not only in different countries but even in a single country. In the vast subcontinent of India variation in source materials embodied in different languages is all the more marked. If the languages of the sources for modern history are taken into account, we will have to think of more than two dozen periods of modern Indian history at one and the same time. After all, language is the form in which modes of life are expressed; it cannot be considered identical with life.

What criteria, then, have to be adopted in demarcating one period of Indian history from another? Will it be correct to fix the watershed between the ancient and the medieval on the ground of political and dynastic history alone? On the basis of dynastic history several dates such as 646, 712, 750, 916, 985, 1174, 1206 and 1325 have been proposed, but none of these signifies an overall change from the ancient to the medieval. Processes of transition in polity, society, economy and culture take long to fructify and cannot be contained in a single fixed date. We have to find out whether these processes converge on some point.

H. C. Raychaudhuri's *Political History of Ancient India* ends with the fall of the Gupta empire, but he does not assign any reasons for bringing the ancient period to an end in the sixth century. It may be argued that after the fall of the Gupta empire the political unification of India under one head remained in abeyance for centuries. But this fact does not in itself provide sufficient ground for marking the end of the ancient period. The forcible imposition of the Maurya and Gupta rule over the greater part of our country did not make either the ancient period an age of lasting unification or the medieval period an age of permanent disintegration. Notwithstanding the seeming political unity under the Mauryas and the Guptas, there are basic differences between the two ages.[103] The Gupta period saw a strong feudalization of the state apparatus which is not to be found in Maurya times. The process was set in motion by the practice of making grants of lands to the brahmanas from the first century AD onwards. Although Asoka's charters are spread all over the country they do not speak of any land grants. The earliest epigraphic land grants belong to the first century BC. But these do not transfer administrative power to the beneficiary, which is done for the first time in the grants made to the Buddhist priests by the Satavahana

---

[103]The Mauryas governed 321–185 BC, the Guptas AD 320–535.

ruler Gautamiputra Satakarni in the second century AD. The land granted to them is described as *apravesyam* (not to be entered by royal troops), *anavamarsyam* (not to be molested by government officials) and *arastrasamvinayikam* (not to be interfered with by the district police).[104]

From the middle of the fourth century AD such grants in favour of the brahmanas become frequent. Their two significant features are the transfer of all sources of revenue and the surrender of the police and administrative functions. The grants of the second century AD surrender royal control only over salt, which implies that the king retains certain other sources of revenue. But in Berar the Vakataka princes give up their control over almost all sources of revenue including pasturage, hides and charcoal, mines for the purchase of salt, forced labour and all hidden treasures and deposits.[105] More important, the donor abandons his right to govern the people inhabiting the donated villages. In the Gupta period there are at least six grants of villages made by the big feudatories to the brahmanas in which the residents including cultivators and artisans are expressly asked by their respective rulers not only to pay their customary taxes to the donees but also to obey their commands. In two other land grants royal commands are issued to the government officials employed as *sarvadhyaksa* and also to regular soldiers and umbrella bearers asking them to leave the brahmanas undisturbed.[106] All this is good evidence of the transfer of the administrative power of the state. In the inscriptions of the fifth century AD the ruler generally retains the right to punish the thieves, which is one of the main bases of the state power, but in later times he empowers the beneficiaries to punish all offences against family property, person, etc. Thus the landed beneficiaries are given both powers of taxation and coercion, leading to the disintegration of the central authority. [...]

The rise of the quasi-feudal mode of production modified the varna-divided society. We notice a pronounced tendency to lump together the vaisyas and sudras in literature from the Gupta period. It seems that in the older settled brahmanical areas the vaisyas, who were hitherto mainly freemen possessing land, lost a good deal of their land rights to the feudal lords. On the cther hand the sudras, who were landless labourers, were granted some land and rose in social status. Further, the decline of trade and towns diverted both sudra artisans and vaisya merchants to cultivation. In this manner the vaisyas and sudras approximated to each other. [...]

Undoubtedly the establishment of the Muslim Turkish rule introduced certain significant changes in the social, economic and political organization of the country. But most features such as feudal state organization, reversion to closed economy, proliferation of castes, regional identity in art, script and language, *puja, bhakti* and tantra, which develop in medieval times and continue later, can be traced back to the sixth and seventh centuries. It would then appear that in these two centuries ancient India was coming to an end, and medieval India was taking shape. In these days of specialization no single scholar can identify with equal confidence the mainstreams in the history of society economy, polity, language, script and religion. The attempt to take a total view

---

[104]D. C. Sircar, *Select Inscriptions Bearing on Indian History and Civilization*, I, 2nd ed. (Calcutta University, 1965), 198–9. (RSS)

[105]Ibid., 432–4. (RSS)

[106]'Politico-Legal Aspects of the Caste System', *JBRS* 39, 3 (1953), 325. (RSS) *sarvadhyaksa*: chief minister or administrator.

of historical trends and to locate their converging point may be considered presumptuous. But the problem has to be faced, and the concept and content of medievalism have to be clarified and its origins understood not in relation to one aspect of Indian life but to all its aspects and to life as a whole.

[From: Sharma, 'Problem of Transition from Ancient to Medieval in Indian History', *IHR* 1 (1974), 1–9, here 1–2, 5–6, 9.][107]

4.4 Critique of the Western Concept of History and Development: The Dignity of Non-Modern Peoples

The increase in theoretical awareness within the discipline of history is reflected not only in the debates on fundamental principles of research, but also in global perspectives of historiography and in comparative interpretations.[108] It is accompanied, stimulated, and provoked by reflections on history outside the academic discourse: in related disciplines, philosophy, literature, religion, etc.[109]

The disappointment of expectations regarding economic development and social modernization in post-colonial South Asia led to a reconsideration of indigenous traditions and the specificity of South Asia's own historical experience.[110] The early attempts in India to combine Gandhi's swaraj and Jayaprakash Narayan's *sarvodaya* with Marxist theory (and in

[107]Cf. also R. S. Sharma, 'Methods and Problems of the Study of Feudalism in Early Medieval India', *IHR* 1 (1974), 81–5; 'How Feudal was Indian Feudalism?', *JPS* 12 (1985), 19–43, and the other contributions to this special issue (*Feudalism and Non-European Societies*) of *JPS*, ed. by T. J. Byres and Harbans Mukhia. For the debate on feudalism, see Dietmar Rothermund, 'Feudalism in India', in idem 1970: 165–78; Mukhia 1999.

[108]See for instance Balkrishna Govind Gokhale, '"THUS IT HAS BEEN". The Indian View of History', in idem 1961: 1–23; Webster 1971 and Samartha 1959. The works of Nirad Chaudhuri (1951 and 1966), also contain comprehensive interpretations of Indian history.

[109]A survey of the trends in Indian philosophy of history is provided in the volume by Mahadevan and Cairns 1977; therein: Kalidas Bhattacharyya, 'The Meaning and Significance of Social Revolution and of the Idea of Progress in Hegelian, Marxian, and Indian Philosophies of History', 61–92; Balkrishna Govind Gokhale, 'Toward a Pattern of Indian History', 169–85. See also Buddha Prakash, 'The Hindu Philosophy of History', *Journal of the History of Ideas* 16 (1955), 494–505; idem 1963; Pande 1989; Mohanty 1992; idem, 'Philosophy of History and its Presuppositions', in idem 1993, ed. by Purushottama Bilimoria 303–12. For a comparative philosophy of history, see Mall 1995. Worth mentioning is also P. R. Sarkar and his Progressive Utilisation Theory (PROUT); Johan Galtung refers to it as an Indian type of Macrohistory: Johan Galtung, 'World/Global/ Universal History and the Present Historiography', *Storia della Storiografia* 35 (1999), 141–61. For Sarkar see Shyam Sunder, 'Shri P. R. Sarkar on History', *PROUT. A Weekly Journal of Proutistic Views & Neo-Humanistic Analysis*, 18–24 December 1993, 8–11. An outstanding example of the linkage between historical investigation and literature is Amitav Ghosh 1992. For the dealing with Indian history in the English-language novel, see Crane 1992.

[110]Significant in this context is the interest in cyclical or typological approaches of western authors like Oswald Spengler and Arnold Toynbee, who seem to come close to Indian traditions of thinking. See, for instance, Lohia 1955; Lalwani 1974.

particular some concepts of Autonio Gramsci) were taken up again later.[111] The marginalization and depoliticization of large sections of the population, as well as the emergence of non-state actors and non-territorial crystallizations since the mid-1970s, led to a search for alternatives, which are inspired by the idea of Gandhian socialism and a '*swaraj* mode of development'.[112] Central to the critique of modernization as being a continuation of colonialism is the notion of a genuine, authentic approach to one's own history.

NIRMAL VERMA[113] is one of the Indian intellectuals whose assessment of western thinking and its current phenomena of crisis has resulted in a rejection of the modern conception of history as such. If about his creative writing it has been said: 'Memory is the seed of his narrative' (Sham Lal); Verma himself relates this finding to his personal experience of history: 'Disillusioned with history, one returns to memory, that process of subterranean recollection, which is all what literature is about. For writing is nothing but re-collecting the remnants of human-past.' In his essays, this relation becomes more specific: The crux of the problem is 'the nature of damage which a traditional culture like India's has suffered as a result of colonial intervention' and the 'legitimacy for its existence even in its ravaged state'.[114]

In the essay reproduced in extracts here, the writer, who had witnessed in Europe the violent end of the Prague Spring (1968), finishes with the western concept of history. It is a concept of enslavement and colonization which, under British rule, 'could be imposed, by force or by seduction, on Indian life, but had no place in its spirit' (see below). Verma holds the Bengal reformers of the nineteenth century, and the historicization of Indian consiousness promoted by them, as responsible for the erroneous development which has resulted in the current situation. It is under the direct impression of the Emergency, inflicted by Indira Gandhi (1975–7), that the following pages have been written.

The Past: A Self-Contemplation (1976)

Verma emphasizes Indian tradition in its uniqueness, in contrast to the western perception of tradition: 'I do not perceive tradition so much as beliefs and superstitions, but more as an

[111]See the overview by Rajni Kothari, 'Contributions to Theory', in 1986. A 'Marxist Hind Swaraj' was also conceived: cf. Pantham 1995: 91. See also Lohia 1963.

[112]See for instance Kothari 1976, 1988a, and 1988b. Kothari has contributed to institutionalizing the discourse on alternatives and to the foundation of the grass-roots organization 'Lokayan' ('People's Dialogue'). Cf. Pantham 1995: 164–5.

[113]Nirmal Verma, born in Shimla in 1929, studied history in Delhi and was a member of the Communist Party of India until 1956. From 1959 to 1968 he lived in Prague, where he worked at the Orientalist Institute and translated Czech literature into Hindi. After returning to India (1972), he did research at the Indian Institute of Advanced Studies in Shimla on 'mythic consciousness' in literature. He lives in Delhi and, with his short stories and novels, is one of the acclaimed Hindi authors. Among his most recent writings are: *Dark Dispatches* (1993); *A Rag Called Happiness* (1994); see also 'India and Europe. The Self and the Other', in: *Perceiving India. Insight and Inquiry. India International Centre Quarterly*, Spring-Summer (New Delhi 1993), 137–63; *Aadi, ant, aur arambh*, (New Delhi: Rajkamal Prakashan, 2001).

[114]Nirmal Verma, 'Preface', in *Word and Memory* (Bikaner 1989).

intangible rhythm that determines the flow, current, and movement of a nation. As the flowing current encompasses the purity of the origins as well as the final transformation at the end—a national tradition includes the past and the present in its pulsation.' What Indians call tradition is, according to Verma, 'nothing but the awareness of the continuity of this flow in our inner self.' (7–8) This Indian form of culture is, however, completely different from that of the cultural flow of the West, as western culture arose from 'a broken consciousness, in which man sees himself totally separated from nature, the universe and his fellow creature, and has to experience that this separation and division cannot be bridged by religious beliefs or tradition'. European culture is an attempt to bridge the 'chasm between individual consciousness and religious beliefs' by secular means (8–9). This characterization of modern western culture leads to the following observations:

In contrast to that, there is no such division in the Indian consciousness. This fact is noteworthy, because it veils an important aspect of the Indian culture. Here no line is drawn between the religious insights and the worldly (secular) experiences. Man discovered the sense of his worldly activities by means of religious symbols; on the other hand his rituals were linked to his daily routine. In other words, Indian culture was based on a closed, unbroken, and complete consciousness. It flowed uninterrupted in time, but history was not necessary for it to flow. It was not intimidated by history like the Western man, for it did not regard history as an 'instrument of change'. The development of the Indian mind is not characterized by an individual consciousness of history but by the many veins of those myths, symbols and rites, which do not deny history, but include its waves in its basic flow.

At this point it is important that in the specific meaning, which in the European context we have for 'history' as the different turning points of life, India has no history. In spite of external changes the basic flow of the Indian life did not undergo any major change. The way in which we always looked at reality, the way we have associated ourselves with time and nature, our attitude towards death, from which one can construe our view of life—all these have not changed basically, even if in the course of time the external reality has changed. [...]

If the Indian consciousness has remained relatively untouched by the changes, it does not mean that history has not exercised its incessant pressure on it. On the one hand the dark mythical roots of our consciousness which had remained unhurt were run over by the water of history and on the other hand we had to also make a compromise with the constantly changing historical reality at the practical level. In fact, the Indian 'character' was formed between these two extremes: accepting history on the practical level and totally ignoring its pressure on the mental level—in this dualistic process we have succeeded in creating an unusual balance; because only in this balance we could retain alive our basic identity. Before the arrival of the British, there was never the danger that we had to pay the price of life with giving up this identity.

During the course of the past twenty-five years in Independence, we could imagine to a certain extent the disastrous consequences, which the challenges of the British Raj in India implicated. In India the English rule was not only a symbol of imperial power. This power also represented values that were totally different. These values were (and are even today) contained in a way of life which was directly linked to a developed industrialized social order, the goal of which was to conquer nature. Unnecessary to say that the European states, before enslaving the African and Asian cultures, they had begun to enslave nature herself.

In the quarter of the nineteenth century, that we now call the 'Bengali Renaissance' the above-mentioned subject came under a long discussion, and this discussion did not limit itself to Bengal. Surprisingly we have forgotten this debate to a great extent, even if we now grapple more or less with the same issues, raised by our forefathers about a century ago. The British Raj forced the Indian intellectuals to inward contemplation for the first time. They were challenged to decide (and in the course of the discussion the two alternatives had become very clear), whether the path of progress and development was identical to the one presented to them by the English rulers as an ideal: the Western democratic institutions, the English educational system, English manners and behavioural patterns, the spreading of a civilization founded on industry and banks. This was the path along which modernization was possible and its most important condition was that we somehow could adapt ourselves to the 'image' of the European man and become 'historical'. The other alternative was the exact opposite of this. One could even state that it was a path on which we could have reduced to absurdity the wrong alternatives presented to us by the English. It was a matter neither of imitating the West nor of remaining shackled to the past—the very consideration of such an alternative was a mistake.

The basic issue was as to how we could consciously bring together the origins of our culture and way of life, in order to confront on our own conditions the challenge posed by the West. The dispute between the representatives of modernity and those of restoration in the nineteenth century, which is mentioned in our history books, was in reality a false one, a pseudo-dispute. The actual conflict was one between two lifestyles. With the help of English rule the Western civilization wanted to force the ideals of Man, History and Future upon a stream of life, that did not require these ideals at all, which could admittedly be imposed on the Indian lifestyle either by force or by enticement, but had no place in its spirit.

Raja Rammohan Roy and the liberal intellectuals of his generation understood this conflict very well, but the path they chose to resolve it was a wrong one. It led us in a direction from whose consequences we have to suffer now. In the face of the 'development-oriented' ideals of the Western civilization, these intellectuals perceived themselves to be inferior. In order to break free from this inferiority complex, they attempted to revive the greatness of the entire Indian past. They wanted to prove to the foreign rulers that the glory of the ancient culture could easily find a place beside the modern European values. But simultaneously they were fascinated by these 'modern European values', they regarded them as symbols of a higher civilization and wanted to prove themselves to be attractive and 'respectable'. On the one hand, the intellectuals of the Bengal Renaissance spoke in favour of the Vedas and the Upanishads; on the other hand, they declared their belief in the theories of John Stuart Mill and wanted to apply them to their own social order. On the one hand, they were proud of their own past, on the other they wanted to exchange this pride for European values and build the future of their country on them.

This movement of Indian intellectuals of the nineteenth century is usually called a 'movement of harmonization'. It was a superficial harmonization, admittedly, but at the same time it was misleading and destructive. The roots of the circle of persons, whom we describe today as the Western-educated, modern 'elite', are linked directly with this 'harmonizing': a circle of people, which praises the Indian tradition on the one hand and on the other copies the West in its entire way of life. Certainly, one refers to Marx and Mao now instead of John Stuart Mill, but the argument that was stated in the nineteenth century remains essentially the same.

A colonial mentality has been at work behind this dispute right from the beginning—in the nineteenth century not any more or any less than now. This mentality springs from a deep inferiority complex and a distrust of one's own national and regional identity. As a result, we felt a need to revive our past, as though it was a dead object, separated from and external to us, where the past of a nation in reality remains linked to its flow of life. It is not to be presented like a piece of jewel in the entirety of the Indian consciousness but is an element of life, not a burden that is loaded on one. It is a living symbol, which is one with the movement of the river and creates the future not according to the formulas of history but in harmony with the stream of life.

And this brings me to the other aspect of this colonial mentality, the blind belief in the inevitability of history. By making history to be the only criterion, the English rulers had attempted to establish their authority, their civilization that was oriented towards development, and even their superiority in the area of culture and thought. This claim to superiority by the English was in reality a part of the entire European thought in the nineteenth century (including even the ideas of Marx). Based on this criterion Europe was in the center of the civilization, the Asian and African cultures were regarded as symbols of a form of life that was 'oriented towards the past, retarded, overtaken in terms of history'. The mission and the claim of this civilization was to eradicate these declining cultures, in order that they could realize their progress keeping in step with history. In a certain sense this argument recognized only Europe and Christianity as synonyms for development and human freedom. [...]

It would be strange to argue that if any powerful country destroys the religious beliefs and customs and the life style of a nation we approve this in the name of history and progress as a just and necessary law, and we had to mould our entire future to a historical milieu that is not ours and which was forced upon us by the West. What a great irony it is that just like the Western-educated intellectuals of the nineteenth century today the Marxists have become fatalists of history. They, who have felled all the gods, finally have been brought to their knees before the God of history.

In reality the roots of the present Indian 'elite' (whether it be associated with political right or left wing) were already present in the intellectuals of the nineteenth century when they accepted a simplified, misleading equation like 'history = Europe = progress' using the pretext of combating the so-called 'challenge by the West' and steered the entire life flow of their country towards a future, which was nothing but self-deception. By practising that self-deception for the last hundred years we sowed the seeds of our current misery. A future, however beautiful it may be, cannot be created by deforming the present. [...]

I think we have reached a point, where we should reassess the decisions made by our forefathers in the nineteenth century. Because whatever we are today, is the result of these decisions. We are on the path, which was selected by them in the face of challenges from the English. Each nation, when it has reached a crucial point, re-examines its past, identity and culture. Exactly those questions, or questions of exactly this sort were asked by the Russian writers and intellectuals in the nineteenth century. A couple of years ago even in a small country like Czechoslovakia the entire nation in the hour of emergency held on to its tradition and attempted to conquer the darkness of the present in its light. This was the hour of contemplation.

In the hour of contemplation one has to bear the silence so that in the days to come the truth can find its expression in words.

[From: Verma, 'Die Vergangenheit: Eine Selbstbesinnung', in *Das Fällen des Banyanbaumes*, ed. by Lothar Lutze (New Delhi: Embassy of the Federal Republic of Germany, 1980), 5–21, here 10–15, 16–17, 20–1. From the German version of Lothar Lutze, translated by Nalini Adinarayanan.][115]

ASHIS NANDY,[116] in his numerous works on politics, society, and culture in modern India, embarks frequently on a fundamental critique of the western concept of history and rejects it, from the perspective of the victims of colonialism, as having caused specific forms of man-made suffering. Nandy arrives at his conclusions about history (and scientific history in particular) from the assessment of research results in two fields, which appear unconnected at first sight: political psychology and the cultures of science.[117] Starting from a general interest in the 'cultural psychology of Indian politics'[118] and the 'psychological biography of the modern nation-state in India' (Nandy 1994: IX), he has, in many separate investigations, traced the emergence of a modern consciousness and its impact on Indian society. With his reflections on central political concepts in modern India, such as secularism, nationalism, modernity, development, and Nandy has time and again intervened in public debates.[119]

Nandy's place in contemporary Indian thinking has been best indicated by himself in the ironical dedication of one of his books to V. D. Savarkar, D. D. Kosambi, and Nirad C. Chaudhuri, three intellectuals 'who symbolize the hundred-and-fifty-year-old attempt, to re-engineer the Indian'. His intention is, so he writes in the preface of the same volume, 'to develop a critique of the dominant, quasi-global consciousness that now frames the culture of commonsense for

[115]Reprint with kind permission by Embassy of the Federal Republic of Germany, New Delhi. The essay appeared originally in Hindi under the title 'Atita: eka atma-manthana', in: *Sabda aur smriti* (Delhi 1976).

[116]Ashis Nandy (born in 1937) is Senior Fellow and Director at the Centre for the Study of Developing Societies in Delhi, which was founded by Rajni Kothari. He is President of the Committee for Cultural Choices and Global Futures and an active member of the Civil Rights and Peace Movement. Nandy was Woodrow Wilson Fellow at the Wilson Center, Washington, Charles Wallace Fellow at the University of Hull and Fellow at the Institute for Advanced Studies in Humanities, University of Edinburgh. In 1994 he was the first to hold the UNESCO Chair at the Center for European Studies in the University of Trier (Germany).

[117]For the latter subject, see Nandy's book on J. C. Bose and Srinivasa Ramanujan (1980a), a description of the difficulties inherent in being a modern scientist and, at the same time, belonging to the Indian culture.

[118]Nandy 1980b: VII. Therein essays on the struggle against *sati* in the nineteenth century, on political cultures in India, and on the assassination of Mahatma Gandhi.

[119]Cf. for instance 'An Anti-Secularist Manifesto', *Seminar*, 314 (Oct. 1985), 14–24; 'Secularism', *Seminar*, 394 (June 1992), 29–30; 'The Politics of Secularism and the Recovery of Religious Tolerance', in Veena Das 1990: 69–93; 'The Idea of Development: The Experience of Modern Psychology as a Cautionary Tale and as Allegory', in Mallmann and Nudler 1986: 248–59. Nandy traces those semantic changes which the colonial discourse has brought about and which continue to determine the political culture, e.g. the definition of identity as a nation instead of earlier forms of association and dissociation.

all debates on public issues in modern India' (Nandy 1995: VII). Seeing himself as a 'child of modern India', Nandy searches for a 'language of social criticism' which is not alien to that majority of Indians 'who have been increasingly empowered by an open political process, however imperfect that openness.' (Ibid., IX)

In *The Intimate Enemy: Loss and Recovery of Self under Colonialism* (1983), Nandy turns to the ideological use of history in the context of colonialism. Here he analyses how the Europeans modelled their rule on the relationship of man and woman or on the human life cycles, thus characterizing it as natural and durable. The contrasting of child and adult, which helped legitimize colonial rule as a process of education, is an issue taken up in the essay 'Reconstructing Childhood: A Critique of the Ideology of Adulthood' (Nandy 1987). The essays of this volume investigate the dialectic between outer and inner forces, which only seemingly correspond to the real and the unreal world. They bring the argumentation of *The Intimate Enemy* to a tentative conclusion. In these essays, Nandy also seeks to rediscover 'nonmodern visions of a good society' ('Preface', XVIII) and to activate their subversive force.[120]

Towards a Third World Utopia (1978–87)

Theories of salvation do not save. At best, they reshape our social consciousness. Utopias, too, being ideas about the end-products of salvation, cannot hope to do more. They, too, can only promise a sharper awareness and critique of existing cultures and institutionalized suffering— the surplus suffering which is born, not of the human condition, but of faulty social institutions and goals.

In this sense, all utopias and visions of the future are a language. Whether majestic, tame, or down-to-earth, they are an attempt to communicate with the present in terms of the myths and allegories of the future. When such visions are vindictive, they are a warning to us; when they are benign or forgiving towards the present, they can be an encouragement. Like history, which exists ultimately in the minds of the historian and his believing readers and is thus a means of communication, utopian or futurist thinking is another aspect of—and a comment upon—the existent, another means of making peace with or challenging man-made suffering in the present, another ethic apportioning responsibility for this suffering and guiding the struggle against it on the plane of contemporary consciousness.[121]

Thus, no utopia can be without an implicit or explicit theory of suffering. This is especially so in the peripheries of the world, euphemistically called the third world. The concept of the third world is not a cultural category; it is a political and economic category born of poverty, exploitation, indignity and self-contempt. The concept is inextricably linked with the efforts of a large number of people trying to survive, over generations, quasi-extreme situations.[122] A

---

[120]The volume also contains essays on the traditions of technology and science as well as Gandhi's critique of western civilization.

[121]Such utopianism is of course very different from the ones Karl Popper or Robert Nozick have in mind. See Karl Popper, 'Utopia and Violence', in *Conjectures and Refutations: The Growth of Scientific Knowledge* (London: Routledge and Kegan Paul, 1978), 355–63; and Robert Nozick, *Anarchy, State and Utopia* (Oxford: Basil Blackwell, 1974), Part III. (AN)

[122]I have in mind the extremes Bruno Bettelheim describes in his 'Individual and Mass Behaviour in Extreme Situations' (1943), in *Surviving and Other Essays* (New York: Alfred Knopf, 1979), 4–83. (AN)

third-world utopia—the South's concept of a decent society, as Barrington Moore might call it—must recognize this basic reality.[123] To have a meaningful life in the minds of men, such a utopia must start with the issue of man-made suffering which has given the third world both its name and its uniqueness. This essay is an inter-civilizational perspective on oppression, with a less articulate psychology of survival and salvation as its appendage. It is guided by the belief that the only way the third world can transcend the sloganeering of its well-wishers is, first, by becoming a collective representation of the victims of man-made suffering everywhere in the world and in all past times; second, by internalizing or owning up the outside forces of oppression and, then, coping with them as inner vectors, and third, by recognizing the oppressed or marginalized selves of the first and the second worlds as civilizational allies in the battle against institutionalized suffering.[124] [...]

The experience of suffering of some third world societies has added a new dimension to utopianism by sensing and resisting the oppression which comes as 'history'. By history as oppression I mean not only the limits which our past always seems to impose on our visions of the future, but also the use of a linear, progressive, cumulative, deterministic concept of history—often carved out of humanistic ideologies—to suppress alternative world-views, alternative utopias and even alternative self-concepts. The peripheries of the world often feel that they are victimized not merely by partial, biased or ethnocentric history, but by the idea of history itself.

One can give a psychopathological interpretation of such scepticism towards history, often inextricably linked with painful, fearsome memories of man-made suffering. Defiance of history may look like a primitive denial of history and, to the extent the present is fully shaped by history in the modern perception, denial of contemporary realities. But, even from a strictly clinical point of view, there can be reasons for and creative uses of ahistoricity. What Alexander and Margarete Mitscherlich say about those with a history of inflicting suffering also applies to those who have a history of being victims: 'A very considerable expenditure of psychic energy is necessary to maintain this separation of acceptable and unacceptable memories; and what is used in the defence of a self anxious to protect itself against bitter qualms of conscience and doubts about its worth is unavailable for mastering the present.'[125]

The burden of history is the burden of such memories and anti-memories. Some cultures prefer to live with it and painfully excavate the anti-memories and integrate them as part of the present consciousness. Some cultures prefer to handle the same problem at the mythopoetic level. Instead of excavating for the so-called real past, they excavate for other meanings of the present,

---

[123]Barrington Moore, Jr., 'The Society Nobody Wants: A Look beyond Marxism and Liberalism', in Kurt H. Wolf and Barrington Moore, Jr. (eds), *The Critical Spirit: Essays in Honour of Herbert Marcuse* (Boston Beacon, 1968), 401–18. (AN)

[124]Though this is not relevant to the issues I discuss in this essay, the three processes seem to hint at the cultural-anthropological, the depth-psychological, and the Christian-theological concerns with oppression respectively. (AN)

[125]Alexander Mitscherlich and Margarete Mitscherlich, 'The Inability to Mourn', in Robert J. Lifton and Eric Olson (eds), *Explorations in Psychohistory: The Wellfleet Papers* (New York: Simon and Schuster, 1974), 257–70, here 262. (AN)

as revealed in traditions and myths about an ever-present but open past. The anti-memories at that level become less passionate and they allow greater play and lesser defensive rigidity.

What seems an ahistorical and even anti-historical attitude in many non-modern cultures is often actually an attempt on the part of these cultures to incorporate their historical experiences into their shared traditions as categories of thinking, rather than as objective chronicles of the past.[126] In these cultures, the mystical and consciousness-expanding modes are alternative pathways to experiences which in other societies are sought through a linear concept of a 'real' history. In the modern context these modes can sometimes become what Robert J. Lifton calls 'romantic totalism'—a post-Cartesian absolutism which seeks to replace history with experience.[127] But that is not a fate which is written into the origins of these modes. If the predicament is the totalism and not the romance, the *history* of civilizations after Christopher Columbus and Vasco da Gama also shows that that totalism can also come from a history which seeks to replace experience. Especially so when, after the advent of the idea of scientific history, history has begun to share in the near-monopoly science has already established in the area of human certitude. Albert Camus once drew a line between the makers of history and the victims of history. The job of the writer, he said, was to write about the victims. For the silent majority of the world, the makers of history also live in history and the defiance of history begins not so much with an alternative history as with the denial of history as an acreage of human certitude.

In their scepticism of history, the ahistorical cultures have an ally in certain recessive orientations to the past in the Western culture, which have re-emerged in recent decades in some forms of structuralism and psychoanalysis, in attempts to view history either as semiotics or as a 'screen memory' with its own rules of dream-work. As we well know, the dynamics of history, according to these disciplines, is not in an unalterable past moving towards an inexorable future; it is in the ways of thinking and in the choices of present times.[128]

The rejection of history to protect self-esteem and ensure survival is often a response to the structure of cognition history presumes. The more scientific a history, the more oppressive it tends to be in the experimental laboratory called the third world. It is scientific history which has allowed the idea of social intervention to be cannibalized by the ideal of social engineering at the peripheries of the world. For the moderns, history has always been the unfolding of a theory of progress, a serialized expression of a telos which, by definition, cannot be shared by communities on the lower rungs of the ladder of history. Even the histories of oppression and

[126]See a fuller discussion of these themes with reference to Gandhi's world-view in Nandy, 'The Intimate Enemy. (AN)

[127]Robert J. Lifton, *Boundaries Psychological Man in Revolution* (New York: Simon and Schuster, 1969), 106–6. On a different plane, Alvin Gouldner has drawn attention to the close links between utopianism and ahistoricity. See his *The Dialectic of Ideology and Technology: The Origins, Grammar and Future of Ideology* (London: Macmillan, 1976), 88–9. (AN)

[128]I need hardly add that within the modern idea of history, too, this view has survived as a latent—and, one is tempted to add, unconscious—strain. From Karl Marx to Benedetto Croce and from R. G. Collingwood to Michael Oakeshott, philosophers of history have often moved close to an approach to history which is compatible with traditional orientations to past times. (AN)

the historical theories of liberation postulate stages of growth which, instead of widening the victims' options, reduce them. No wonder that till now the main function of these theories has been to ensure the centrality of the cultural and intellectual experiences of a few societies, so that all dissent can be monitored and framed in the idiom of domination.

The ethnocentrism of the anthropologist can be corrected; he is segregated from his subject only socially and, some day, his subjects can talk back. The ethnocentrism towards the past mostly goes unchallenged. The dead do not rebel, nor can they speak out. So the subjecthood of the subjects of history is absolute, and the demand for a real or scientific history is the demand for a continuity between subjecthood in history and subjection in the present. The corollary to the refusal to accept the primacy of history is the refusal to chain the future to the past. This refusal is a special attitude to human potentialities, an alternative form of utopianism that has survived till now as a language alien to, and subversive of, every theory which in the name of liberation circumscribes and makes predictable the spirit of human rebelliousness.

> [From: Nandy, 'Towards a Third World Utopia', in idem, *Traditions, Tyranny, and Utopias* (Delhi: Oxford UP, 1992), 20–55, here 20–1, 46–9.][129]

4.5 Subalternity and Agency, Fragmentation and Globalization

The *Subaltern Studies. Writings on South Asian History and Society* were founded by Ranajit Guha.[130] They represent one of the most ambitious series of historical studies in and on South Asia with a reception and influence reaching far beyond this region. What unites the contributors

---

[129]The essay 'Towards a Third World Utopia' was written at the end of the 1970s as a contribution to 'Alternative Visions of Desirable Societies', a study group of the Centre de Estudios Economicos y Sociales del Tercier Mundo, the World Future Studies Federation, and the United Nations University (see also 'Evaluating Utopias', in the same volume, 1–19). It first appeared in *Alternatives*, 1978–9, 4(3), and was reprinted in revised and in abridged versions. Further publications by Nandy relating to history and colonialism: 'Cultural Frames for Social Transformation: A Credo', *Alternatives* 12 (1987), 113–23; Sardar, Nandy, and Davies, 1993; 'History's Forgotten Doubles', *History and Theory* 34 (1995), 44–66. For Nandy's intellectual biography and various aspects of his work, see the interview with Vinay Lal in *Emergences* 7–8 (1995–6), Special Issue, *Plural Worlds, Multiple Selves: Ashis Nandy and the Post-Columbian Future*, 3–76 (in the same issue, more essays on and by Nandy); Vinay Lal 2000. For the critique of the concept of development in an intercultural perspective, see Apffel-Marglin and Marglin 1996.

[130]Ranajit Guha has edited the first six volumes of *Subaltern Studies*. Born in the village of Siddhakati in East Bengal, 1922, he studied history at the University of Calcutta and was active in the Communist Party of India, which he left in 1956, after the uprising in Hungary. From 1959 to 1980, he lived mainly in England and taught at the School of African and Asian Studies, University of Sussex. In 1980, Guha joined the School of Pacific Studies at Australian National University in Canberra, as Senior Research Fellow. For more details, see the biographical note by Shahid Amin and Gautam Bhadra and the bibliography of his works in *Subaltern Studies* 8 (1994), 222–228; Dipesh Chakrabarty, 'Ranajit Guha' in Boyd 1999: 494–5. Guha developed his approach to Indian history while dealing with forms of peasant protest. Among his Guha writings are: 1982 and 1983. For the latter as a 'forerunner of Subaltern Studies', in which the 'unifying principles of the School are acknowledged to be found', see Ramakrishna Mukherjee, 'Illusion and Reality', *Sociological Bulletin* 37 (1988), 127–39.

is not so much a common theoretical position, but the shared mistrust of the modern 'elitist' historiography of India and the lasting impact of colonialism on it.[131]

The *Subaltern Studies* represent an attempt to overcome the limitations of British and Indian nationalist concepts alike. They establish an emancipatory perspective by claiming agency for those who are marginalized in elite history. This has led to a lively debate testifying to the good response, as much as evidencing the need of clarification of some of the basic assumptions and strategies. The postulated 'autonomous terrain' of the subaltern consciousness and the identity of the subalterns as a distinct group of suppressed have been questioned by various critics, some of whom point out a lack of empirical evidence. According to Darshan Perusek, the mere stating of insurgency is banal if the question of impact and telos is not raised.[132] Marxist commentators such as Ramakrishna Mukherjee criticize the concept as being itself elitistic or an idealistic distortion of Marxist assumptions. According to Mukherjee, Guha's method is a form of Weberianism.[133] Sumit Sarkar does not perceive any continuation of the project of liberation from domination in the more recent volumes of *Subaltern Studies*.[134]

The *Subaltern Studies* often comprise both historiography and reflections on it, as is evident from Guha's contributions[135] and those of Partha Chatterjee, Gyanendra Pandey, and Dipesh Chakrabarty.[136] The following text by Guha is the inaugural statement of the series.

On Some Aspects of the Historiography of Colonial India (1982)

1. The historiography of Indian nationalism has for a long time been dominated by elitism— colonialist elitism and bourgeois-nationalist elitism.[137] Both originated as the ideological product

[131]Partha Chatterjee, who contributes to the clarification of the project, nevertheless admits the lack of a common theoretical position among the collaborators which goes beyond the discontent about the present state of historiography. See 'Peasants, Politics, and Historiography: A Response', *Social Scientist*, no. 120 (May 1983), 58–65, here 58.

[132]Darshan Perusek, 'Subaltern Consciousness and Historiography of Indian Rebellion of 1857', *EPW* (11 September 1993), 1935–6.

[133]Cf. Mukherjee, 'Illusion and Reality', 137ff.

[134]Sarkar, 1998: 42ff. See also in greater detail idem, 'The Decline of the Subaltern in *Subaltern Studies*', in idem 1998: 82–108; for the post-modern critique of history in general, see idem, 'Post-modernism and the Writing of History', *Studies in History* 15: 2, n.s. (1999), 293–322.

[135]Guha has also worked on the history of Indian historiography (1988).

[136]Gyanendra Pandey, 'Encounters and Calamities: The History of a North Indian Qasba in the Nineteenth Century', *Subaltern Studies* 3 (1984), 231–70; Dipesh Chakrabarty 1989. At regular intervals, there were attempts at a theoretical revision of the project: Gayatri Chakravorty Spivak, 'Subaltern Studies: Deconstructing Historiography', *Subaltern Studies* 4 (1985), 330–63; Dipesh Chakrabarty, 'Invitation to a Dialogue', *Subaltern Studies* 4 (1985), 364–76; Veena Das, 'Subaltern as Perspective', *Subaltern Studies* 6 (1989), 310–24. For the emphasis on the fragmentary and the constructive in the new historiography see Gyanendra Pandey, 'In Defence of the Fragment: Writing about Hindu-Muslim Riots in India Today', *Representations* 37 (1992), 27–55; Amin 1995 and Singer 1997.

[137]The term 'elite' has been used in this statement to signify dominant *groups*, foreign as well as indigenous. The *dominant foreign* groups included all the non-Indian, that is, mainly British officials of the colonial state and

of British rule in India, but have survived the transfer of power and been assimilated to neo-colonialist and neo-nationalist forms of discourse in Britain and India respectively. Elitist historiography of the colonialist or neo-colonialist type counts British writers and institutions among its principal protagonists, but has its imitators in India and other countries too. Elitist historiography of the nationalist or neo-nationalist type is primarily an Indian practice but not without imitators in the ranks of liberal historians in Britain and elsewhere.

2. Both these varieties of elitism share the prejudice that the making of the Indian nation and the development of the consciousness—nationalism—which informed this process, were exclusively or predominantly elite achievements. In the colonialist and neo-colonialist historiographies these achievements are credited to British colonial rulers, administrators, policies, institutions and culture; in the nationalist and neo-nationalist writings—to Indian elite personalities, institutions, activities and ideas.

3. The first of these two historiographies defines Indian nationalism primarily as a function of stimulus and response. Based on a narrowly behaviouristic approach this represents nationalism as the sum of the activities and ideas by which the Indian elite responded to the institutions, opportunities, resources, etc. generated by colonialism. There are several versions of this historiography, but the central modality common to them is to describe Indian nationalism as a sort of 'learning process' through which the native elite became involved in politics by trying to negotiate the maze of institutions and the corresponding cultural complex introduced by the colonial authorities in order to govern the country. What made the elite go through this process was, according to this historiography, no lofty idealism addressed to the general good of the nation but simply the expectation of rewards in the form of a share in the wealth, power and

foreign industrialists, merchants, financiers, planters, landlords, and missionaries. The *dominant indigenous* groups included classes and interests operating at two levels. At the *all-India level* they included the biggest feudal magnates, the most important representatives of the industrial and mercantile bourgeoisie, and native recruits to the uppermost levels of the bureaucracy. At the *regional and local levels* they represented such classes and other elements as were either members of the dominant all-India groups included in the previous category *or* if belonging to social strata hierarchically inferior to those of the dominant all-India groups still *acted in the interests of the latter and not in conformity to interests corresponding truly to their own social being.* Taken as a whole and in the abstract, this last category of the elite was *heterogeneous* in its composition and thanks to the uneven character of regional economic and social developments, *differed from area to area.* The same class or element which was dominant in one area according to the definition given above, could be among the dominated in another. This could and did create many ambiguities and contradictions in attitudes and alliances, especially among the lowest strata of the rural gentry, impoverished landlords, rich peasants, and upper-middle peasants all of whom belonged, *ideally speaking,* to the category of 'people' or 'subaltern classes', as defined below. It is the task of research to investigate, identify, and measure the *specific* nature and degree of the *deviation* of these elements from the ideal and situate it historically. The terms 'people' and 'subaltern classes' have been used as synonymous throughout this note. The social groups and elements included in this category represent *the demographic difference between the total Indian population and all those whom we have described as the 'elite'.* Some of these classes and groups such as the lesser rural gentry, impoverished landlords, rich peasants, and upper-middle peasants who 'naturally' ranked among the 'people' and the 'subaltern', could under certain circumstances act for the 'elite', and therefore be classified as such in some local or regional situations—an ambiguity which it is up to the historian to sort out on the basis of a close and judicious reading of his evidence.

prestige created by and associated with colonial rule; and it was the drive for such rewards with all its concomitant play of collaboration and competition between the ruling power and the native elite as well as between various elements among the latter themselves, which, we are told, was what constituted Indian nationalism.

4. The general orientation of the other kind of elitist historiography is to represent Indian nationalism as primarily an idealist venture in which the indigenous elite led the people from subjugation to freedom. There are several versions of this historiography which differ from each other in the degree of their emphasis on the role of individual leaders or elite organizations and institutions as the main or motivating force in this venture. However, the modality common to them all is to uphold Indian nationalism as a phenomenal expression of.the goodness of the native elite with the antagonistic aspect of their relation to the colonial regime made, against all evidence, to look larger than its collaborationist aspect, their role as promoters of the cause of the people than that as exploiters and oppressors, their altruism and self-abnegation than their scramble for the modicum of power and privilege granted by the rulers in order to make sure of their support for the Raj. The history of Indian nationalism is thus written up as a sort of spiritual biography of the Indian elite.

5. Elitist historiography is of course not without its uses. It helps us to know more about the structure of the colonial state, the operation of its various organs in certain historical circumstances, the nature of the alignment of classes which sustained it; some aspects of the ideology of the elite as the dominant ideology of the period; about the contradictions between the two elites and the complexities of their mutual oppositions and coalitions; about the role of some of the more important British and Indian personalities and elite organizations. Above all it helps us to understand the ideological character of historiography itself.

6. What, however, historical writing of this kind cannot do is to explain Indian nationalism for us. For it fails to acknowledge, far less interpret, the contribution made by the people *on their own*, that is, *independently of the elite* to the making and development of this nationalism. In this particular respect the poverty of this historiography is demonstrated beyond doubt by its failure to understand and assess the mass articulation of this nationalism except, negatively, as a law and order problem, and positively, if at all, either as a response to the charisma of certain elite leaders or in the currently more fashionable terms of vertical mobilization by the manipulation of factions. The involvement of the Indian people in vast numbers, sometimes in hundreds of thousands or even millions, in nationalist activities and ideas is thus represented as a diversion from a supposedly 'real' political process, that is, the grinding away of the wheels of the state apparatus and of elite institutions geared to it, or it is simply credited, as an act of ideological appropriation, to the influence and initiative of the elite themselves. The bankruptcy of this historiography is clearly exposed when it is called upon to explain such phenomena as the anti-Rowlatt upsurge of 1919[138] and the Quit India movement of 1942[139]—to name only two of

---

[138]Against the Rowlatt-Bill (censorship, preventive custody, special courts), resistance was organized in a *satyagraha* campaign that was called off by Gandhi after the outbreak of violence.

[139]INC-campaign for immediate independence of India, in order to organize resistance against the Japanese approaching India from Burma.

numerous instances of popular initiative asserting itself in the course of nationalist campaigns in defiance or absence of elite control. How can such one-sided and blinkered historiography help us to understand the profound displacements, well below the surface of elite politics, which made Chauri-Chaura[140] or the militant demonstrations of solidarity with the RIN mutineers possible?

7. This inadequacy of elitist historiography follows directly from the narrow and partial view of politics to which it is committed by virtue of its class outlook. In all writings of this kind the parameters of Indian politics are assumed to be or enunciated as exclusively or primarily those of the institutions introduced by the British for the government of the country and the corresponding sets of laws, policies, attitudes and other elements of the superstructure. Inevitably, therefore, a historiography hamstrung by such a definition can do no more than to equate politics with the aggregation of activities and ideas of those who were directly involved in operating these institutions, that is, the colonial rulers and their *eleves*—the dominant groups in native society—to the extent that their mutual transactions were thought to be all there was to Indian nationalism, the domain of the latter is regarded as coincident with that of politics.

8. What clearly is left out of this un-historical historiography is the *politics of the people*. For parallel to the domain of elite politics there existed throughout the colonial period another domain of Indian politics in which the principal actors were not the dominant groups of the indigenous society or the colonial authorities but the subaltern classes and groups constituting the mass of the labouring population and the intermediate strata in town and country—that is, the people. This was an *autonomous* domain, for it neither originated from elite politics nor did its existence depend on the latter. It was traditional only in so far as its roots could be traced back to pre-colonial times, but it was by no means archaic in the sense of being outmoded. Far from being destroyed or rendered virtually ineffective, as was elite politics of the traditional type by the intrusion of colonialism, it continued to operate vigorously in spite of the latter, adjusting itself to the conditions prevailing under the Raj and in many respects developing entirely new strains in both form and content. As modern as indigenous elite politics, it was distinguished by its relatively greater depth in time as well as in structure.

9. One of the more important features of this politics related precisely to those aspects of mobilization which are so little explained by elitist historiography. Mobilization in the domain of elite politics was achieved vertically whereas in that of subaltern politics this was achieved horizontally. The instrumentation of the former was characterized by a relatively greater reliance on the colonial adaptations of British parliamentary institutions and the residua of semi-feudal political institutions of the pre-colonial period; that of the latter relied rather more on the traditional organization of kinship and territoriality or on class associations depending on the level of the consciousness of the people involved. Elite mobilization tended to be relatively more legalistic and constitutionalist in orientation, subaltern mobilization relatively more violent. The former was, on the whole, more cautious and controlled, the latter more spontaneous. Popular mobilization in the colonial period was realized in its most comprehensive form in

[140]In the North-Indian village of Chauri Chaura, a campaign of protest in 1921 led to violent attacks on policemen, who were burnt in the police station.

peasant uprisings. However, in many historic instances involving large masses of the working people and petty bourgeoisie in the urban areas too the figure of mobilization derived directly from the paradigm of peasant insurgency.

10. The ideology operative in this domain, taken as a whole, reflected the diversity of its social composition with the outlook of its leading elements dominating that of the others at any particular time and within any particular event. However, in spite of such diversity one of its invariant features was a notion of resistance to elite domination. This followed from the subalternity common to all the social constituents of this domain and as such distinguished it sharply from that of elite politics. This ideological element was of course not uniform in quality or density in all instances. In the best of cases it enhanced the concreteness, focus and tension of subaltern political action. However, there were occasions when its emphasis on sectional interests disequilibrated popular movements in such a way as to create economistic diversions and sectarian splits, and generally to undermine horizontal alliances.

11. Yet another set of the distinctive features of this politics derived from the conditions of exploitation to which the subaltern classes were subjected in varying degrees as well as from its relation to the productive labour of the majority of its protagonists, that is, workers and peasants, and to the manual and intellectual labour respectively of the non-industrial urban poor and the lower sections of the petty bourgeoisie. The experience of exploitation and labour endowed this politics with many idioms, norms and values which put it in a category apart from elite politics.

12. These and other distinctive features (the list is by no means exhaustive) of the politics of the people did not of course appear always in the pure state described in the last three paragraphs. The impact of living contradictions modified them in the course of their actualization in history. However, with all such modifications they still helped to demarcate the domain of subaltern politics from that of elite politics. The co-existence of these two domains or streams, which can be sensed by intuition and proved by demonstration as well, was the index of an important historical truth that is, the *failure of the Indian bourgeoisie to speak for the nation*. There were vast areas in the life and consciousness of the people which were never integrated into their hegemony. The *structural dichotomy* that arose from this is a datum of Indian history of the colonial period, which no one who sets out to interpret it can ignore without falling into error.

13. Such dichotomy did not, however, mean that these two domains were hermetically sealed off from each other and there was no contact between them. On the contrary, there was a great deal of overlap arising precisely from the effort made from time to time by the more advanced elements among the indigenous elite, especially the bourgeoisie, to integrate them. Such effort when linked to struggles which had more or less clearly defined anti-imperialist objectives and were consistently waged, produced some splendid results. Linked, on other occasions, to movements which either had no firm anti-imperialist objectives at all or had lost them in the course of their development and deviated into legalist, constitutionalist or some other kind of compromise with the colonial government, they produced some spectacular retreats and nasty reversions in the form of sectarian strife. In either case the braiding together of the two strands of elite and subaltern politics led invariably to explosive situations indicating that the masses mobilized by the elite to fight for their own objectives managed to break away from their control and put the characteristic imprint of popular politics on campaigns initiated by the upper classes.

14. However, the initiatives which originated from the domain of subaltern politics were not, on their part, powerful enough to develop the nationalist movement into a full-fledged struggle for national liberation. The working class was still not sufficiently mature in the objective conditions of its social being and in its consciousness as a class-for-itself, nor was it firmly allied yet with the peasantry. As a result it could do nothing to take over and complete the mission which the bourgeoisie had failed to realize. The outcome of it all was that the numerous peasant uprisings of the period, some of them massive in scope and rich in anti-colonialist consciousness, waited in vain for a leadership to raise them above localism and generalize them into a nationwide anti-imperialist campaign. In the event, much of the sectional struggle of workers, peasants and the urban petty bourgeoisie either got entangled in economism or, wherever politicized, remained, for want of revolutionary leadership, far too fragmented to form effectively into anything like a national liberation movement.

15. It is the study of this *historic failure of the nation to come to its own*, a failure due to the inadequacy of the bourgeoisie as well as of the working class to lead it into a decisive victory over colonialism and a bourgeois-democratic revolution of either the classic nineteenth-century type under the hegemony of the bourgeosie or a more modern type under the hegemony of workers and peasants, that is, a 'new democracy'—*it is the study of this failure which constitutes the central problematic of the historiography of colonial India*. There is no one given way of investigating this problematic. Let a hundred flowers blossom and we don't mind even the weeds. Indeed we believe that in the practice of historiography even the elitists have a part to play if only by way of teaching by negative examples. But we are also convinced that elitist historiography should be resolutely fought by developing an alternative discourse based on the rejection of the spurious and un-historical monism characteristic of its view of Indian nationalism and on the recognition of the co-existence and interaction of the elite and subaltern domains of politics.

16. We are sure that we are not alone in our concern about the present state of the political historiography of colonial India and in seeking a way out. The elitism of modern Indian historiography is an oppressive fact resented by many others, students, teachers and writers like ourselves. They may not all subscribe to what has been said above on this subject in exactly the way in which we have said it. However, we have no doubt that many other historiographical points of view and practices are likely to converge close to where we stand. Our purpose in making our own views known is to promote such a convergence. We claim no more than to try and indicate an orientation and hope to demonstrate in practice that this is feasible. In any discussion which may ensue we expect to learn a great deal not only from the agreement of those who think like us but also from the criticism of those who don't.

[From: Guha, 'On Some Aspects of the Historiography of Colonial India',
Subaltern Studies 1 (1982), 1–8.][141]

[141] A selection from the first set of volumes has been published under the title: *Selected Subaltern Studies*, Foreword E. Said, Preface R. Guha (New York 1988). Further reading: Rosalind O'Hanlon and David Washbrook, 'After Orientalism: Culture, Criticism, and Politics in the Third World', *Comparative Studies in Society and History* 34 (January 1992), 141–67; Gyan Prakash, 'Can the Subaltern Ride? A Reply to O'Hanlon and Washbrook',

The role of women in Indian history was included in the agenda by a few nationalist historians as early as the 1930s. But it was only with the shift to issues of social history that the realm of feminine experience and the changes in gender relations became relevant to historians. Not only did the participation of women in the historical process become a topic of research, but also the peculiarity of this participation in comparison to that of men.[142] The increasing interest in women as historical actors since the 1970s has given rise to new approaches in historiography, from which gradually emerged feminist and gender history in South Asia. This process was stimulated further by the more recent turn to cultural studies, leading to the rediscovery of forgotten, invisible or neglected areas of human experience.[143] Like the *Subaltern Studies*, the investigations into women's history, too, are in a double confrontation with colonial and indigenous structures of power. And not only traditionalists even modernizers could occasionally be carriers of patriarchal ideologies.[144]

In the following text, reproduced in extracts, Uma Chakravarti[145] describes specific limitations in the initial occupation with the history of women in India, as it is represented by the work of A. S. Altekar.[146]

Comparative Studies in Society and History 34 (January 1992), 168–84; Ramachandra Guha, 'Subaltern and Bhadralok Studies', *EPW* 30 (19 August 1995), 2056–8; Dipesh Chakrabarty, 'Radical Histories and Question of Enlightenment Rationalism: Some Recent Critiques of Subaltern Studies', *EPW* 30 (8 April 1995), 751–9; K. Sivaramakrishnan, 'Situating the Subaltern: History and Anthropology in the Subaltern Studies Project', *Journal of Historical Sociology* 8 (1995), 395–429; Mohantry 1998; Richard M. Eaton, '(Re)imag(in)ing Other²ness: A Post-mortem for the Postmodern in India', *Journal of World History* 11 (2000), 57–78; Jacques Pouchepadass, 'Les *Subaltern Studies* ou la critique postcoloniale de la modernité', *L'Homme* 156 (2000), 161–86.

[142]Cf. J. Krishnamurti 1989: VIII. This volume contains a collection of earlier works on the situation of women during colonialism (articles from *Indian Social and Economic History Review*), revealing also certain methodological problems in connection with the 'invisibility' of women in earlier history.

[143]The emergence of the historiographical self-representation of women in India is traced by Tanika Sarkar 'Women's Histories and Feminist Writings in India: A Review and a Caution' (Plenary Session Address, Seventh Berkshire Conference, Chapel Hill, North Carolina, June 1996).

[144]A compilation of important contributions to women's history in India with a look at the actual complexity of cultural processes is presented by Sangari and Vaid 1989. Thanks to the critical revision of the history of the discipline itself, the earlier self-testimonies of women, which had been encouraged by the reform movements in the nineteenth century, now are reconsidered as expressions of historical consciousness. See Meenakshi Mukherjee, 'The Unperceived Self: A Study of Five Nineteenth-Century Autobiographies', in Chanana 1988. A survey of the movement for women's rights in modern India is given by Radha Kumar (1993).

[145]Uma Chakravarti taught at Miranda House College for Women, Delhi University. Among her publications are: 'The Sita Who Refused the Fire Ordeal', *Manushi*, No. 8 (1981); 'Whatever Happened to the Vedic Dasi? Orientalism, Nationalism, and a Script for the Past', in Sangari and Vaid 1989: 27–87; 'Conceptualizing Brahmanical Patriarchy in Early India: Gender, Class, and State', *EPW* (3 April 1993); idem 1998.

[146]The page numbers in the text relate to Altekar 1987 [1938].

Towards a New Understanding of Gender Relations in
Early Indian History (1988)

The best known and most internally coherent nationalist work on women is Altekar's study on the position of women in Hindu civilization. His work is based primarily on Brahmanical sources and outlines the position of women from earliest times right up to the mid-fifties of this century when the Hindu Code Bill[147] was under consideration. Altekar's work represents the best that is available to us by way of women's studies in history but it also shows up very sharply the limitations of the traditional approach. Although the work unravels in detail the entire body of opinion of the law-makers on such areas as the education of women, marriage and divorce, the position of the widow, women in public life, proprietary rights of women, and the general position of women in society it is steeped in the nationalist understanding of the women's question. Further his overwhelming concern is with women in the context of the family and one almost gets the feeling that the status of women needs to be raised in order to ensure the healthy development of the future race of India. In this he was reflecting the opinion of nationalist writers from the second half of the nineteenth century who placed tremendous importance on the physical regeneration of the Hindus. [...]

Altekar's own genuine commitment to reforming women's status led him to sometimes making quaint statements which he intended as positive and progressive. Thus he suggests that although 'Women have low fighting value they have potential military value. By giving birth to sons they contribute indirectly to the fighting strength and efficiency of their community.' (3) Further, Altekar's programme for women, despite his apparent liberality and sympathy for them, was to view women primarily as stock-breeders of a strong race. This view is particularly noticeable in his suggestions about women's education. In Altekar's programme of reform women were to be educated enough but in doing so one had to ensure that no undue strain was placed upon them. He expressed his fears thus: 'As things stand today girls have to pass the *same* examinations as boys and to learn house-keeping at home as well, all the while having less physical strength than their brothers. This certainly puts too much strain upon them and is *injurious to the future well being of the race*' (28, italics UC).

Establishing the high status of women was the means by which 'Hindu' civilization could be vindicated. This was the finished version of the nationalist answer to James Mill's denigration of Hindu civilization published a century ago; the locus of the barbarity of Hindu civilization in James Mill's work (A *History of British India*) had lain in the abject condition of Hindu women. By reversing the picture Altekar was attempting to lay Mill's ghost aside. But it was easier to provide a general picture than to deal with a variety of customs oppressing women that still obtained in the early twentieth century. Altekar was thus forced to provide explanations for existing biases against women. [...]

Altekar is particularly weak in his attempts at relating the status of women at a given point of time with social organization as a whole. Thus early Vedic society which did not as yet have noticeable concentration of power, or a well developed institution of kingship, is the context for Altekar's unnecessary explanation for the absence of queens. Since Altekar is convinced

[147]The Hindu Code Bill reformed and standardized the traditional 'personal law' of the Hindus in 1955–6.

about the high status of women in the Vedic period he feels he has to account for why we do not hear of women as queens. Thus he is constrained to suggest that, 'Aryans were gradually establishing their rule in a foreign country surrounded on all sides by an indigenous hostile population that considerably outnumbered them. Under such circumstances queens ruling in their own rights or as regents were *naturally unknown*' (339, italics UC). Similarly Altekar has a facile explanation for why women did not own property. According to him, 'Landed property could be owned only by one who had the power to defend it against actual or potential rivals and enemies. Women were obviously unable to do this and so could hold no property.' (339)

In his inability to see women within a specific social organization and recognizing patriarchal subordination of women Altekar was not unique. Like others he was reflecting a deeply internalized belief in biological determinism and therefore in the physical inferiority of women. Very occasionally however Altekar shows flashes of insight into the socio-economic context within which women's subordination was achieved. For example in his analysis of the causes for the 'fall' of the status of the Aryan women Altekar suggests a connection with the subjugation of the Sudras as a whole. He argues that the Aryan conquest of the indigenous population and its loose incorporation as members of a separate *varna* had given rise to a huge population of semi-servile status. In such a situation Aryan women ceased to be producing members of society and thus lost the esteem of society. But even as he makes this broadly contextual explanation Altekar is insensitive to the crucial distinction between the participation of women as producers and participation in terms of *controlling production*. Thereafter Altekar's semi-historical insight is unfortunately lost and popular prejudice takes over. Like the ancient Brahmanical law-givers he appears to have a horror of Sudra women. [...]

The possibility that the Sudra woman, whom he regards as a threat, could have contributed to a more dynamic and active kind of womanhood for Hindu society would not even occur to Altekar because his focus is on Aryan women (regarded then as the progenitors of the upper caste women of Hindu society) and in his racist view Sudra women counted for nothing. The most important consequence of Altekar's limited repertoire of biological and psychological explanations was that the logic of the distorted social relations between men and women is completely obscured. The kind of explanations offered by Altekar might appear to be astoundingly trivial to us today but it is important to remember that, by and large, nationalist historians were content to restrict historical explanations to cultural factors while writing about ancient India. This was in contrast to their focus on economic and social factors while discussing British rule in India.

In summing up nationalist historiography on women in early India we might draw attention to the fact that the Altekarian paradigm, though limiting and biased, continues to nevertheless influence and even dominate historical writing. In essence what emerges from the mass of detail he accumulated is the construction of a picture of the idyllic condition of women in the Vedic age. It is a picture which now pervades the collective consciousness of the upper castes in India and has virtually crippled the emergence of a more analytically rigorous study of gender relations in ancient India. There is thus an urgent need to move forward and rewrite history, a history that does justice to women by examining social processes, and the structures they create, thus crucially shaping and conditioning the relations between men and women. Just as Altekar displaced Mill in his work, it is time we realized that despite Altekar's substantial contribution we must lay his ghost aside and begin afresh.

[From: Chakravarti, 'Beyond the Altekarian Paradigm: Towards a New Understanding of Gender Relations in Early Indian History', *Social Scientist* 16 (1988), 44–52, here 48–52.][148]

ENVIRONMENTAL HISTORY, like other new branches of historical research in India, at first followed patterns established in the West. In identifying its themes, it was largely influenced by the works about the American colonization and by the approach of French historians to the phenomena of 'longue durée'.[149] Ramachandra Guha,[150] who has contributed substantially towards outlining the agenda of environmental history in India, lists important fields of research: social conflicts over natural resources, indigenous conservation systems, the change of attitudes to nature, and the comparison of concepts of nature in various cultures and religions.[151]

Guha also endeavours to reconstruct the specific Indian tradition of ecological thinking. The evolution of environmental awareness and ecological research in India has to be seen in connection with modern history as a whole. In general, it can be stated that the environmental debate 'is an argument in the cities about what is happening in the countryside'. If today's environmentalists refer to Gandhi's critique of industrial society, one must not forget that for a long time there was an 'overwhelming consensus in favour of resource-intensive industrialisation, a strategy which accepted as axiomatic the subordination of the village to the city, of the community to the nation, and of nature to man'.[152]

The ecological movements criticize the continuity of the current developmental policy (or, at least, certain forms of Government planning) with that of the colonial power. In eco-imperialism the domination of nature is linked to the oppression of societies that are close to nature; this is especially felt today by the tribal population living in remote areas. In the exploitation of resources and the construction of dams, modern economic interests are in sharp contrast with traditional ways of life.[153]

[148]Further reading: Uma Chakravarti and Kumkum Roy, 'In Search of Our Past: A Review of the Limitations and Possibilities of the Historiography of Women in Early India', *EPW* (30 April 1988), WS 2–10; Meenakshi Mukherjee, 'Story, history, and her story', *Studies in History* 9 (1993), 71–85; Aloka Parasher, 'Women in Nationalist Historiography: The Case of Altekar', in Kasturi and Mazumdar 1994: 16–27; Nita Kumar 1994: Indira Chowdhury 1998. Detailed information about sources, bibliographies, state of research, etc., is found in the 'Bibliographic Essay' by Geraldine Forbes (1996), 255–81.

[149]Ramachandra Guha, 'Writing Environmental History in India', *Studies in History* 9 (1993), 119–29.

[150]Ramachandra Guha has worked mainly on social history; he is Fellow at the Nehru Memorial Museum and Library in New Delhi and Fellow at the Centre for Studies in Social Sciences, Calcutta.

[151]Cf. Ramachandra Guha, 'Forestry and Social Protest in British Kumaun, c. 1893–1921', *Subaltern Studies* 4 (1985), 54–100.

[152]Ramachandra Guha, 'The Prehistory of Indian Environmentalism: Intellectual Traditions', *EPW* (4–11 January 1992), 57–64, here 57, 63. For the systematic elaboration of Gandhi's economic ideas, see Kumarappa 1938, 1948, and 1948. Another pioneer of ecological thinking in India is Radhakamal Mukerjee (1942).

[153]Here again, one has to insist on the plurality of the claims to historicity, which is too easily overlooked or even suppressed in the nationalist discourse (see above, Sections 2.2 and 4.2.1). An instructive example is

The first comprehensive environmental history of India is the work by Ramachandra Guha and the ecologist Madhav Gadgil: *This Fissured Land*.[154] The following extract is taken from the concluding chapter.

Cultures in Conflict (1993)

Sidestepping for the most part the question of the extent to which the colonization of India actually enabled the European 'miracle', we have tried to document the other side of the coin, namely the impact it had *within* the subcontinent. British imperialism could not wipe out the population of India—ironically, it set in motion a process of demographic expansion—but it did certainly disrupt, perhaps irrevocably, the ecological and cultural fabric of its society. And after it formally left Indian shores, the tasks it had left unfinished were enthusiastically taken up by the incoming nationalist elites, whose unswerving commitment to a resource-intensive pattern of industrialization has only intensified the processes of ecological and social disturbance initiated by the British.

From an ecological perspective, the clash of pre-industrial and industrial cultures in India may be represented in terms of the closure and creation of niches. In India, as elsewhere, the British usurped the ecological niches occupied by the hunter-gatherers, many of whom also practised shifting cultivation, and diminished substantially the niche space occupied by food producers, by alienating them from access to non-cultivated lands. The resource processors and transporters of European civilization had by the nineteenth century a tremendously greater access to resources, largely because of their technological ability to tap additional sources of energy and materials. They out-competed and usurped the niche space of Indian handicraft workers and artisans, as well as of itinerant traders. This tremendous shrinkage of the niche space available to the Indian population was only marginally compensated by new niches which opened up to collaborators of the British, in the usurpation and transport of resources, as their clerks and trading partners.

The literate castes of pre-British India, involved in priesthood and administration, filled the clerical jobs, with merchants and shopkeepers in the role of trading partners. These groups prospered as time went by, and moved into the modern resource-processing industry. But the others—hunter-gatherers, peasants, artisans, and pastoral and non-pastoral nomads—had all to squeeze into the already diminishing niche space for food production. And they, we have seen, suffered great impoverishment.

While the British ruled India, they discouraged Indians from taking up resource-processing and transport on the basis of modern technology and with access to fossil fuel and other modern energy sources. With time, however, this resistance was broken down, and India began to industrialize. The emerging Indian capitalist class, in fact, provided financial support to the national movement, aware that in an independent country they would face less competition. Following Independence, industrialists were able to steer the course of development on a path

the Jharkhand tribes' struggle for regional autonomy. See Javeed Alam, 'The Category of "Non-Historic Nations" and Tribal Identity in Jharkhand', in P. C. Chatterji 1989: 153–64. For the historical consciousness of the tribal population (Adivasi), see Hira Lal Shukla 1988; Suresh Sharma 1994. See also the hints for further reading in Section 2.2 (Ambedkar, Dalit).

[154]Madhav Gadgil is Professor of Ecological Sciences at the Indian Institute of Science in Bangalore.

beneficial to them, namely as an all-out state-subsidized effort to intensify the use of resources such as land, water, vegetation, minerals, and energy. [...]

In India the ongoing struggle between the peasant and industrial modes of resource use has come in two stages: colonial and post-colonial. It has left in its wake a fissured land, ecologically and socially fragmented beyond belief and, to some observers, beyond repair. Where do we go from here? There seems no realistic hope of emulating European or New World modes of industrial development. There is no longer a 'frontier' available with which to easily dispose of our population. Nor are there readily available substitutes for energy or construction material, enabling us to prevent our forest resources getting depleted. On both these counts the Western world has pre-empted the two-thirds of humanity which is lumped under the label 'Third World'. Through most of the Third World, the transition from the peasant to the industrial mode is very incomplete and, indeed, likely to remain incomplete for a very long time to come.

Not surprisingly, the Indian environmental debate has taken an altogether different track from its Western counterpart. Western environmentalists, contemplating the arrival of the 'post-industrial' economy and for the most part unaware of the damage its industrial economy is doing to other parts of the globe, are moving towards a 'post-materialist' perspective in which the forest is not central to economic production but rather to the enhancement of the 'quality of life'. In India, by contrast, the debate around the forest, and the environment debate more generally, is firmly rooted in questions of production and use. The issues in contention include the relative claims of the industrial and agrarian sector over natural resources (and within each, the claims of large versus small units), the uses of nature for subsistence or for profit, the respective proprietary claims of individuals, communities, and the state, and finally the role of natural resource management in an alternative development strategy.

[From: Gadgil and Guha, *This Fissured Land* (Delhi: Oxford UP, 1993), 242–5.][155]

[155]Further reading: Gadgil and Guha 1995; Arnold and Guha 1995; Grove, Damodaran, and Sangwan 1998.

Glossary

Adivasi:	indigenous inhabitants, tribal people.
Advaita:	philosophical system of Monism (see Vedanta), expounded by Shankara (ca. 788–820 AD).
ahimsa:	non-violence.
Aligarh-movement:	movement of Muslim intellectuals, related to the educational institutions at Aligarh founded by S. A. Khan.
Arya Samaj:	Hindu reform movement, founded in 1875 by Dayanand Sarasvati.
aryavarta:	'land of Aryans'.
Avatar:	incarnation of a deity.
Banya:	caste of businessmen (Vaishya).
bhadralok:	elite castes or educated middle class in Bengal.
bhakti:	form of devotion in Hinduism, personal worship of a god, often organized in groups of the followers of poets or holy men.
bhat:	genealogist.
Brahmacharya, Brahmachari:	celibacy, celibate; student of a Guru.
Brahmo Samaj:	Hindu reform movement, founded in 1828 by Rammohun Roy.
Carita:	biographical account.
charkha:	spinning wheel, symbol of self-reliance during the freedom fight.
Chitpavan:	Brahman caste which had migrated from the Malabar coast to the Dekkhan; particularly influential in Maharashtra.
compradors:	class of people who have become rich by trading with the British.
Dalit:	'broken men', Marathi word chosen by the 'Untouchables' in order to avoid euphemistic terms like Gandhi's 'Harijan' (children of God) or the 'Scheduled Castes' of the Constitution.

dar-al harb (or *Jihad*):	house of war and irreligiosity.
dar-al Islam:	house of Islam, land where Islam dominates and is practised.
darshan:	sight of a divine image of a god or holy person.
Deoband:	town with an important *madrasa* or Dar al-'Ulum (school of Koranic theology) founded by Abid Hussayn in 1867.
dharma:	duty, ethic, religion, eternal law.
Dharmashastra:	text describing the duties of Hindus.
Diwali:	'festival of lights', New Year according to the Vikrami era, return of Lord Rama to Ayodhya.
Diwan:	official of the finance or tax authority (Diwani) in the Mughal administration.
Doab:	'land between two rivers', e. g. the area of Ganges and Yamuna.
dubash-do bhasha:	bi-lingual; Indian manager, often in the service of a European administrator or merchant.
Hindu Mahasabha:	Great Assembly of the Hindus, founded in 1919.
Hindutva:	Hindudom, Hinduness: political movement for the national self-assertion of Hindus.
jama'at:	group, party.
Jana Sangh:	political party, founded in 1951 by S. P. Mookerji (former Hindu Mahasabha president), political wing of the RSS.
Janata Party:	party coalition formed in 1977, in opposition to Indira Gandhi and her Emergency Rule; in power 1977 to 1979 with Morarji Desai as Prime Minister.
jati:	'descendence'; one of the Indian terms for 'caste'; social group defined by descendence and endogamy, also by profession, region, race etc.
jihad:	holy war, striving for religious perfection (against the lower instincts), war of Muslims against non-Muslims.
Kali:	goddess, one of Shiva's wives, incarnation of *shakti* (energy)
kalpa:	world age, one day in the life of Lord Brahma, 1000 *mahayugas* of 4.320.000 years each.
karmayoga:	yoga practised through and inside action; selfless action as fulfillment of *dharma*.
Kayasta:	high caste in Bengal which used to serve the princes as writers.
Kulin:	high caste of Bengali Brahmans.
Lunar:	the 28 or 29 days between two occurrences of new moon.
madrasa:	school attached to a mosque, offering instruction in Islamic law, theology, etc.
Mahakavya:	'Great poem', a poetical narrative of heroic character and exploits.
mahayuga:	complete cycle (4.320.000 years) of Kritayuga (Satyayuga), Tretayuga, Dvaparayuga, Kaliyuga.
mandir:	temple.
Manu:	mythical first human being; god-king; author of *Manava Dharmashastra* or *Manusmriti* (codification of Brahmanical law, first to second centuries AD).
mantra:	verbal formula with supposed magic power.
masjid:	mosque.
math:	Hindu monastery.
maya:	illusion.
Maulana:	title of an Islamic scholar.
mela:	fair at a pilgrimage centre.
mleccha:	impure, foreigner, barbarian.
moksha:	redemption.
moulvie, maulawi:	Islamic priest or scholar (below the level of a *Maulana*).

Nagari-Script, Devanagari:	'city of the gods', characters used in Sanskrit and some modern Indian languages.
namaz:	the five daily prayers of Muslims.
Nawab:	deputy or viceroy of the Mughal emperors, sometimes almost independent rulers; later honorary title in the Muslim elite.
Nayar:	warrior caste in Kerala.
niyoga:	ancient Hindu custom permitting widows to give birth to children.
Nizam:	regent, ruler.
Panchayat:	'council of five'; traditional system of Indian village administration.
Pandit:	Hindu scholar, priest.
papa:	sin.
Parishad:	council.
Permanent Settlement Act, 1793:	fixing of the land tax in Bengal by Lord Cornwallis.
puja:	worship, offerings made to a deity.
Puranas:	sacred texts, myths of the old times, written down during the first millennium AD.
Raj, Raja:	rule, king.
Rajput:	warrior caste in Northern India.
Ramanuja:	one of the great teachers of Vishnuism in South India, 11th/12th century; interpreted the monism of the Vedanta assuming the existence of a personal god.
Ramjanmabhumi:	'birthplace of Rama' in Ayodhya.
rashtra:	land, administrative unit, nation.
rishi:	seer, inspired sage.
sadhu:	religious mendicant, wandering ascetic, renouncer.
samaj:	society, association.
samsara:	chain of rebirths, transmigration of souls.
sanatana dharma:	eternal *dharma*, traditional Hindu religiousity as different from the constructions of neo-Hindu reformers.
Sangam:	Tamil academy in Madurai.
Sangh:	association.
sannyasi:	ascetic, renouncer, last stage of the Hindu life cycle.
sarvodaya:	'welfare for all'; Gandhian form of socialism.
sati:	virtuous woman; a woman who sacrifices her life on the pile of her dead husband.
satya:	truth.
satyagraha:	adherence to truth, truth force.
sipahi, Sepoy:	soldier; Indian soldiers in the service of the East India Company.
Shaivite:	devotee of Lord Shiva.
shakti:	female power, energy.
Shastra, Shastri:	Hindu religious or secular treatise; scholar of Hindu scriptures.
Satakarni:	ruler of the Satavahana dynasty.
Satavahana:	dynasty of the Andhra empire (northern Dekkhan) from the first century BC to the end of the second century AD.
Sayyid:	descendant of the Prophet Muhammad.
shruti:	'that what has been heard', revealed texts.
Shudra:	peasant class, fourth in the *varna* system.

smriti, manusmriti:	discourse on the traditional Hindu code of behaviour (different from revelation: *shruti*)
subahdar:	Governor in the Mughal administration.
Sutra:	manual, compendium.
swadeshi:	belonging to (or produced in) one's own country.
swadharma:	one's own duty, moral.
Swami:	Hindu monk.
swaraj:	self rule, self control.
ulama:	Islamic scholars, experts of Islamic law (*sharia*).
umma:	totality of the Muslims.
Upanishads:	philosophical writings dealing above all with the concepts of Brahman and Atman (their unity) as well as with the theory of Karma; 800 till 500 BC.
Urdu:	language of the army; combined Persian and Hindi (written in Arabic script), developed into a language of high culture under Muslim rule.
Vaishnavite:	devotee of Lord Vishnu.
Vaishya:	one of the four *varnas* (merchants).
vakil:	advocate.
varna:	'colour'; old Aryan system of classification (*varnashramadharma*) distinguishing the four levels of Brahmans, Kshatriyas, Vaishyas, and Shudras.
Veda:	'Wisdom'; collection of the earliest religious wisdom of the Indians, consisting of the four parts of Rigveda, Samaveda, Yajurveda, Atharvaveda; oldest parts ca. 1500 BC.
Vedanta:	'completion of the Veda'; one of the six philosophical systems in Ancient India; search for the identity of the individual and world soul, the unity of Atman and Brahman, the 'non-duality' (advaita); mainly based on the Upanishads and the *Bhagavadgita*; the most important teacher of the V. was Shankara (AD 788–820)
Vyasa:	title of the authors or editors of the monumental literary works in Ancient India, e.g. the *Mahabharata*.
yuga:	measure of time, one period in the world age (*kalpa*).
Zamindar:	land owner, tenant, tax collector.

Abbreviations

BJP	Bharatiya Janata Party (Indian People's Party)
CSSH	*Comparative Studies in Society and History*
EPW	*Economic and Political Weekly*
H.	Muslim era, beginning with the year of Muhammad's flight (Hijra) to Medina, AD 622
IESHR	*Indian Economic and Social History Review*
IHR	*Indian Historical Review*
IIAS	Indian Institute of Advanced Studies, Shimla
INC	Indian National Congress
JAS	*Journal of Asian Studies*
MAS	*Modern Asian Studies*
RSS	Rashtriya Swayamsevak Sangh (National Volunteer Corps)
Sources of Indian Tradition	Wm. Theodore de Bary, in collab. with Stephen Hay and J. H. Qureshi (eds): *Sources of Indian Tradition.* 2 Vols, ed. and rev. by Ainslie T. Embree. 2nd edn New York: Columbia UP, 1988 [1958].
UP	University Press
VHP	Vishva Hindu Parishad (World Council of Hindus)

Bibliography

I have tried to include as many positions as possible on the current debate on historical thinking in South Asia. The limitation to titles in European languages is regretted; it points to the necessity of a reappraisal of historical writing in South Asian languages. Information about first and later editions of the texts presented in this volume, as well as hints for further reading, are given in the notes of the respective section.

BIBLIOGRAPHIES

Abidi, Sartaj A. and Sharma, Suresh K. (1974). *Fifty Years of Indian Historical Writings: Index to Articles in Journal of Indian History*, Vols 1–50 (1921–72), New Delhi: Prakashan.

Case, Margaret H. (1968). *South Asian History 1750–1950: A Guide to Periodicals, Dissertations and Newspapers*, Princeton: Princeton UP ('Historiography and Oriental Studies', 312–22).

Gupta, Brijen K. and Kharbas, Datta S. *India* (World Bibliographical Series, Vol. 26). Oxford, Santa Barbara: Clio Press, n. d. ('Historians and Historiography', 33–5).

Kulke, Hermann, Leue, Horst-Joachim, Lütt, Jürgen and Rothermund, Dietmar (1982). *Indische Geschichte vom Altertum bis zur Gegenwart: Literaturbericht über neuere Veröffentlichungen*, Historische Zeitschrift, Special Issue 10, München: Oldenbourg ('Historiography', 110–15; 'Images of History and Source Critique', 172–9).

Lal, Vinay (1996). *South Asian Cultural Studies: A Bibliography*, New Delhi: Manohar.

Patterson, Maureen L. P. (ed.) (1981). *South Asian Civilizations: A Bibliographical Synthesis*, Chicago: University of Chicago Press.

DICTIONARIES, ANTHOLOGIES, INTRODUCTIONS

Agrawal, R. S. (1983). *Important Guidelines on Research Methodology (Specially for Research in History)*, Delhi: B. R. Publishing Corporation.

Baxter, Craig and Rahman, Syedur (1989). *Historical Dictionary of Bangladesh* (Asian Historical Dictionaries, No. 2), Metuchen/N. J.: The Scarecrow Press.

Bhattacharya, Sachidananda (1994). *A Dictionary of Indian History*, New Delhi: Cosmo Publications.

Boia, Lucian, Nore, Ellen, Hitchins, Keith, and Iggers, Georg G. (eds) (1991). *Great Historians of the Modern Age: An International Dictionary*, New York: Greenwood Press. (Section on India, 351–67)

Boyd, Kelly (ed.) (1999). *Encyclopedia of Historians and Historical Writings*, London/Chicago: Fitzroy Dearborn Publishers.

Burki, Shahid Javed (1991). *Historical Dictionary of Pakistan* (Asian Historical Dictionaries, No. 3, ed. Jon Woronoff). Metuchen/N. J.: The Scarecrow Press.

Chande, M. B. (1995). *A Concise Encyclopaedia of Indian History*, New Delhi: Atlantic Publishers and Distributors.

Chaudhary, K. P. (1975). *The Effective Teaching of History in India*, New Delhi: NCERT.

Embree, Ainslie T. (ed.) (1988). *Encyclopedia of Asian History*, 4 Vols, New York: Scribner/London: Macmillan (for the Asia Society).

Guide to the Sources of Asian History. Vols 3.1 and 3.2 (India), 1987, 1992, International Council on Archives, New Delhi: National Archives of India.

Iggers, Georg G. and Parker, Harold T. (eds) (1979). *International Handbook of Historical Studies: Contemporary Research and Theory*, Westport: Greenwood Press.

Khandelwal, R. L. (ed.) (1968). *Research Methodology: A Symposium*, Vallabh Vidyanagar (Gujarat).

Kochhar, S. K. (1984). *Teaching of History*, revised and enlarged ed., New Delhi: Sterling.

Kosambi, Damodar Dharmanand (1956). *An Introduction to the Study of Indian History*. Bombay: Popular Prakashan.

Kurian, George Thomas (1976). *Historical and Cultural Dictionary of India*. (Historical and Cultural Dictionaries of Asia, No. 8). Metuchen/N. J.: Scarecrow Press.

Majumdar, R. K. and Srivastva, A. N. (1988). *Historiography (Method of History)*, 3rd ed., New Delhi: Surjeet Book Depot.

Mansingh, Surjit (1996). *Historical Dictionary of India* (Asian Historical Dictionaries, No. 20, ed. Jon Woronoff), Lanham, Md./London: The Scarecrow Press.

Mehra, Parshotam (1985). *A Dictionary of Modern Indian History 1707–1947*, Delhi: Oxford UP.

Metcalf, Thomas R. (ed.) (1990). *Modern India: An Interpretive Anthology*, New Delhi: Sterling Publishers.

Nilakanta Sastri, K. A. and Ramanna, H. S. (1956). *Historical Method in Relation to Indian History*, Madras: Viswanathan.

Sahay, Prem Nath (1987). *Historical and Indological Institutions in India: A Brief Survey*, Delhi: S.S. Publishers.

Samarasinghe, S. W. R. de A. and Samarasinghe, Vidyamali (1998). *Historical Dictionary of Sri Lanka* (Asian/Oceanian Historical Dictionaries, No. 26). Lanham, Md., London: The Scarecrow Press.

Satya Murty, K. (1995). *Handbook of Research Methodology in History*, New Delhi: Sterling.

Sheik Ali, B. (1978). *History: Its Theory and Method*, Madras: Macmillan India.

Sills, David L. (ed.) (1968–79). *International Encyclopedia of the Social Sciences*, New York: Macmillan.

Sources of Indian Tradition (1988), 2 Vols, ed. Wm. Theodore de Bary, in collab. with Stephen Hay and J. H. Qureshi, 2nd revised ed. by Ainslie T. Embree, New York: Columbia UP; 1st pub. 1958.

Subrahmanian, N. (1978). *Historiography*, Madurai: Koodal Publishers (1st pub. 1973) (5th ed. as: *Historiography and Historical Methods*, Udumalpet 1993).

_____ (1980). *Historical Research: Methodology*, Madurai.

Vajreswari, R. (1966). *A Handbook for History Teachers*, Bombay: Allied Publishers.

Woolf, Daniel R. (ed.) (1998). *A Global Encyclopedia of Historical Writing*, New York/London: Garland Pub.

Sources

Adhikary, G. (ed.) (1971). *Documents of the Communist Party of India*, I, Delhi.

Ahmad, A. and Grunebaum, G. E. von (eds) (1970). *Muslim Self-Statement in India and Pakistan, 1857–1968*, Wiesbaden: Harrassowitz.

Ahmad, Jamil-ud-Din (ed.) (1960). *Speeches and Writings of Mr. Jinnah*, Lahore.

Aiyar, K. V. Subrahmanya (1941). 'Methods of Historical Research', in *Three Lectures* (Kannada Research Lectures Series No. 2), Dharwar, 1–38.

Alvarez, Claude (1991). *Decolonizing History: Technology and Culture in India, China and the West 1492 to the Present Day*, Mapusa: The Other India Bookstore; 1st pub. as *Homo Faber: Technology and Culture in India, China and the West 1500 to the Present Day* in 1979 by Allied Publishers, New Delhi)

Ambedkar, Bhimrao Ramji (1948). *The Untouchables: Who Were They and Why They Became Untouchables?*, New Delhi.

_____ (1987). *Dr. Babasaheb Ambedkar: Writings and Speeches*, Bombay: Government of Maharashtra.

_____ (1990). *The Annihilation of Caste*, ed. Mulk Raj Anand, New Delhi: Arnold Publishers.

Appadorai, A. (ed.) (1973). *Documents on Political Thought in Modern India*, Delhi: Oxford UP.

Arnold, David and Guha, Ramachandra (eds) (1995). *Nature, Culture, Imperialism: Essays on the Environmental History of South Asia*, Oxford: Oxford UP.

Aurobindo (1947). *Bankim, Tilak, Dayananda*, 2nd ed., Pondicherry: Sri Aurobindo Ashram.

_____ (1950). *The Ideal of Human Unity*, 2nd ed., Pondicherry: Sri Aurobindo Ashram.

_____ (1952). *The Renaissance in India*, 4th ed., Pondicherry: Sri Aurobindo Ashram.

_____ (1953). *The Foundations of Indian Culture*, New York: Sri Aurobindo Library.

_____ (1964). *Evolution*, 6th ed., Pondicherry: Sri Aurobindo Ashram.

_____ (1965). *On Nationalism, First Series*, Pondicherry: Sri Aurobindo Ashram.

Bagchi, Amiya Kumar (1982). *The Political Economy of Underdevelopment*, Cambridge: Cambridge UP.

Bhagwati, J. N. and Desai, P. (1970). *India: Planning for Industrialization: Industrialization and Trade Policies Since 1951*, London, New York: Oxford UP.

Bhandarkar, Ramkrishna Gopal (1933). *Collected Works of Sir R. G. Bhandarkar*, eds Narayana Bapuji Utgikar and Vasudev Gopal Paranjpe, Poona: Bhandarkar Oriental Research Institute.

_____ (1985). *Early History of the Dekkan: Down to the Mahomedan Conquest*, 2nd ed., New Delhi: Asian Educational Services; 1st pub. 1895.

Bunsen, C. C. J. (ed.) (1854). *Outlines of the Philosophy of Universal History*, 2 Vols, London: Longman, Brown, Green, and Longmans.

Chakravarti, Uma (1998). *Rewriting History: The Life and Times of Pandita Ramabai*, New Delhi: Kali for Women.

Chand, Tara (1936). *Influence of Islam on Indian Culture*, Allahabad: Indian Press.

_____ (1961). *History of the Freedom Movement in India*, 4 Vols, New Delhi: Ministry of Information and Broadcasting, Publications Division.

_____ (1966). *Material and Ideological Factors in Indian History*, Allahabad: University of Allahabad.

Chandra, Bipan, Mukherjee, Mridula, Mukherjee, Aditya, Panikkar, K. N., and Sucheta, Mahajan (1987). *India's Struggle for Independence1857–1947*, New Delhi: Penguin.

Chatterjee, Bankimchandra (1965–9). *Bankim Rachanavali*, 2 Vols, ed. Jogesh Chandra Bagal, Calcutta: Sahitya Samsad.

Chatterji, Mohini Mohan (1927). *History as a Science*, London.

Chaudhuri, Nirad C. (1951). *Autobiography of an Unknown Indian*, London: Macmillan.

_____ (1966). *The Continent of Circe*, Bombay.

Chaudhuri, Sasi Bhusan (1957). *Civil Rebellion in the Indian Mutinies, 1857–1859*, Calcutta.

Coomaraswamy, A. K. (1981). *Essays in National Idealism*, New Delhi; 1st pub. 1909.

Dange, Shripad Amrit (1949). *India: From Primitive Communism to Slavery: A Marxist Study of Ancient History in Outline*, New Delhi: People's Publishing House.

Dange, Shripad Amrit (1974). *Selected Writings*, Bombay: Lok Vangmaya Griha.

Devahuti, D. (1965). *India and Ancient Malaya*, Singapore: Eastern UP.

_____ (1983). *Harsha: A Political Study*, 2nd ed., Delhi: Oxford UP.

Dumont, Louis (1970). *Homo hierarchicus: An Essay on the Caste System*, translated by Mark Sainsbury, Chicago: University of Chicago Press.

_____ (1971). *Religion, Politics and History in India: Collected Papers in Indian Sociology*, The Hague, Paris: Mouton.

_____ (1975). *La civilisation indienne et nous*, Paris: Librairie Armand Colin.

Dutt, Romesh Chunder (1963). *Early Hindu Civilization BC 200 To 320*, 4th ed., Calcutta; first published as *History of Civilization in Ancient India*, London 1888.

Elliot, Henry M. (1849). 'Original Preface', in idem and John Dowson (eds) (1867). *The History of India as Told by its own Historians*, I, London, pp. XV–XXVII.

Gadgil, D. R. (1971). The Industrial Evolution of India in Recent Times 1860–1939, 5th ed., Bombay: Oxford UP; 1st ed. 1924.

Gadgil, Madhav and Guha, Ramachandra (1995). *Ecology and Equity: The Use and Abuse of Nature in Contemporary India*, Delhi: Penguin.

Gandhi, Mohandas Karamchand (1958–). *The Collected Works of Mahatma Gandhi*, 90 Vols, New Delhi: Publications Division. (Quoted: CWMG)

_____ (1993). *The Essential Writings of Mahatma Gandhi*, ed. Raghavan Iyer, Delhi: Oxford UP.

Ghosh, Amitav (1992). *In an Antique Land*, Delhi: Ravi Dayal Publisher.

Goel, Sita Ram (1984). *Heroic Hindu Resistance to Muslim Invaders (636 AD to 1206)*, New Delhi: Voice of India.

Grove, Richard H., Damodaran, Vinita, and Sangwan, Satpal (eds) (1998). *Nature and the Orient: The Environmental History of South and Southeast Asia*, Delhi: Oxford UP.

Grover, Verinder (ed.) (1990). *B. G. Tilak* (Political Thinkers of Modern India, IV), New Delhi: Deep & Deep Publications.

_____ (ed.) (1990). *M. G. Ranade* (Political Thinkers of Modern India, III), New Delhi: Deep & Deep Publications.

_____ (ed.) (1992). *Raja Rammohun Roy* (Political Thinkers of Modern India, I), New Delhi: Deep & Deep Publications.

_____ (ed.) (1993). *Dadabhai Naoroji* (Political Thinkers of Modern India, XII), New Delhi: Deep & Deep Publications.

_____ (ed.) (1993). *V. D. Savarkar* (Political Thinkers of Modern India, XIV), New Delhi: Deep & Deep Publications.

Guénon, René (1924). *Orient et Occident*, Paris: Payot.

_____ (1929). *La métaphysique orientale*, Paris.

_____ (1968). *Étude sur l'Hindouisme*, Paris.

Guha, Ranajit (1982). *A Rule of Property for Bengal: An Essay on the Idea of Permanent Settlement*, 2nd ed., New Delhi: Orient Longman; 1st edn, Paris: Mouton, 1963.

_____ (1983). *Elementary Aspects of Peasant Insurgency in Colonial India*, Delhi: Oxford UP.

Hai, Maulana Hakim Syed Abdul (1977). *India during Muslim Rule*, Lucknow: Academy of Islamic Research and Publications.

Hegel, Georg Wilhelm Friedrich (1970). *Vorlesungen über die Philosophie der Geschichte* (Theorie Werkausgabe, XII), Frankfurt/M.: Suhrkamp; English: *Lectures on the Philosophy of History*, translated by J. Sibree, Buffalo: Prometheus Books, 1991.

Jayaswal, K. P. (1990). *History of India 150 AD to 350 AD*, Delhi: Low Price Publications; 1st ed. Lahore: Motilal Banarsi Das, 1933.

Jeffrey, Robin (ed.) (1990). *India, Rebellion to Republic: Selected Writings, 1857–1990*, New Delhi: Sterling Publishers.

Jones, William (1807). *Works*, ed. Anna Maria Jones, with a Life of the Author by Lord Teignmouth, 13 Vols, London: Stockdale and Walker.

Kane, Pandurang Vaman (1968). *History of Dharmashastra: Ancient and Mediaeval Religious and Civil Law in India*, 5 Vols, Poona: Bhandarkar Research Institute.

Khan, Sayyid Ahmad (1972). *Sir Sayyid Ahmad Khan's History of the Bijnor Rebellion*, translated by Hafeez Malik and Morris Dembo, East Lansing: Michigan State University.

_____ (1972). *Writings and Speeches of Sir Syed Ahmad Khan*, ed. Shan Muhammad, Bombay: Nachiketa.

Kothari, Rajni (1976). *Democratic Polity and Social Change*, Bombay: Allied.

_____ (1988a). *Transformation and Survival: In Search of a Humane World*, Delhi: Ajanta.

_____ (1988b). *Rethinking Development: In Search of Humane Alternatives*, Delhi: Ajanta.

Kumarappa, J. C. (1938). *Why the Village Movement?*, 2nd ed., Rajahmundry: Hindusthan Publishing Corporation.

_____ (1948). *The Economy of Permanence*, 2nd ed., Wardha: All India Village Industries Association.

_____ (1948). *The Gandhian Economy and Other Essays*, Wardha: All India Village Industries Association.

Kumar, Radha (1993). *The History of Doing*, New Delhi: Kali for Women.

Lal, Deepak (1983). *The Poverty of 'Development Economics'*, London: Institute of Economic Affairs.

———— (1988). *Cultural Stability and Economic Stagnation: India c1500 BC–AD 1980*, Oxford: Clarendon Press.

———— (1989). *Aspects of Indian Labour*, Oxford: Clarendon Press.

Lohia, Ram Manohar (1955). *Wheel of History*, Hyderabad: Navahind Prakashan.

———— (1963). *Marx, Gandhi and Socialism*, Hyderabad: Navahind Prakashan.

Lutze, Lothar (1980). *Das Fällen des Banyanbaumes*, New Delhi: Embassy of the Federal Republic of Germany.

Lyall, Alfred C. (1882). *Asiatic Studies, Religious and Social*, London: John Murray.

———— (1910). *The Rise and Expansion of the British Dominion in India*, 5th ed., London: John Murray; 1st pub. 1893.

Macaulay, Thomas Babington (1935). *Speeches by Lord Macaulay, with His Minute on Indian Education*, ed. G. M. Young, London: Oxford UP.

Madhok, Balraj (1971). *Indianisation? (What, Why and How)*, Delhi: S. Chand & Co.

Maine, Henry Sumner (1875). *The Effects of Observation of India on Modern European Thought*, London.

Majumdar, Jatindra Kumar (ed.) (1983). *Raja Rammohan Roy and Progressive Movements in India: A Selection from Records, 1775–1845*, Calcutta: Brahmo Mission Press; 1st pub. 1941.

Majumdar, Romesh Chandra (1927). *Ancient Indian Colonies in the Far East*, Lahore: The Punjab Sanskrit Book Depot.

———— (1960). *Glimpses of Bengal in the Nineteenth Century*, Calcutta.

———— (1963). *The Sepoy Mutiny until the Revolt of 1857*, revised edition, Calcutta: Firma K. L. Mukhopadhyay; 1st pub. 1957.

———— (1971). *History of the Freedom Movement in India*, 3 Vols, 2nd ed., Calcutta; 1st pub. 1961–2.

———— (ed.) (1951–77). *History and Culture of the Indian People*, 11 Vols, Bombay: Bharatiya Vidya Bhavan.

Mallmann, Carlos and Nudler, Oscar (eds) (1986). *Human Development in its Social Context: A Collective Exploration*, London.

Marshall, Peter J. (ed.) (1970). *The British Discovery of Hinduism in the Eighteenth Century*, Cambridge: Cambridge UP.

Marshman, John Clark (1844). *Outline of the History of Bengal, compiled for the use of youths in India*, 5th ed., Serampore.

———— (1867). *The History of India from the Earliest Period to the Close of Lord Dalhousie's Administration*, London: Longman's, Green.

Marx, Karl (1970). *Das Kapital: Kritik der politischen Oekonomie*, I (Marx-Engels-Werke, Vol. 23), Berlin; 1st pub. Hamburg 1867; English: *Capital I*, Moscow: Progress Publishers, 1977.

———— and Engels, Friedrich (1960). *The First Indian War of Independence 1857–1859*, Moscow: Foreign Language Publishing House.

Maududi, Abu'l-ala (1946). *Tahrik-e zdi-ye hind war musalman* (Freedom Movement in India and the Muslims); reprint Lahore 1966.

———— (1955). *Islamic Law and Constitution*, Karachi, Jamaat-e-Islami Publications.

Mies, Maria and Shiva, Vandana (1993). *Ecofeminism*, Halifax: Fernwood/London: Zed Books.

Mill, James (1820). *The History of British India*, 3 Vols, 2nd ed., London: Baldwin, Cradock and Joy; 1st pub. 1817. (Quoted: HBI)

———— (1840). *The History of British India*, 10 Vols, ed. Horace Hayman Wilson (London: James Madden & Co. Quoted: HBI, 4th ed.)

———— (1931). *James and John Stuart Mill on Education*, ed. by F. A. Cavenagh, Cambridge: Cambridge UP.

Mishra, Vinay Chandra and Singh, Parmanand (eds) (1991). *Ram Janmabhoomi Babri Masjid: Historical Documents, Legal Opinions and Judgements*, Delhi: The Bar Council of India Trust.

Mitra, Rajendralal (1875–80). *The Antiquities of Orissa*, 2 Vols, Calcutta: Wyman & Co.

Mookerji, Radha Kumud (1912). *Indian Shipping: A History of the Sea-Borne Trade and Maritime Activity of the Indians from the Earliest Times*, Bombay, London, New York: Longmans, Green and Co.

———— (1914). *The Fundamental Unity of India*, London, New York: Longmans, Green and Co.

Mookerji, Radha Kumud (1921). *Nationalism in Hindu Culture*, London: Theosophical Publishing House.

Mukerjee, Radhakamal (1942). *Social Ecology*, London: Longmans, Green and Company.

Mukherjee, H. (1959). *The Emancipation of Historical Research*, Calcutta.

Mukherji, D. P. (1945). *On Indian History*, Bombay.

_____ (1948). *Modern Indian Culture*, Bombay.

Mukherji, Hiren (1946). *India's Struggle for Freedom*, Bombay.

Müller, Max (1864). *Lectures on the Science of Language*, London: Longmans, Green.

_____ (1873). *Introduction to the Science of Religion*, London: Longmans, Green.

_____ (1977). *Comparative Mythology*, New York: Arno Press.

Naoroji, Dadabhai (1887). *Essays, Speeches, Addresses, and Writings*, ed. C. L. Parekh, Bombay: Caxton.

Nehru, Jawaharlal (1989). *The Discovery of India*, New Delhi: Jawaharlal Nehru Memorial Fund.

Nilakanta Sastri, K. A. (1955). *The Cholas*, 2 Vols, 2nd ed., rev., Madras: University of Madras; 1st ed. 1935–7.

_____ (1939). *Foreign Notices of South India from Megasthenes to Ma Huan*, Madras: University of Madras.

_____ (with N. Venkataramanayya) (1946). *Further Sources of Vijayanagar History*, Madras: University of Madras.

Norma, Dorothy (ed.) (1965). *Nehru—The First Sixty Years*, 2 Vols, New Delhi: Asia Publishing House.

O'Malley, L. S. S. (ed.) (1951). *Modern India and the West: A Study of the Interaction of their Civilizations*. London, New York, Toronto: Oxford UP.

Panikkar, K. M. (1947). *A Survey of Indian History*, Bombay: Asia Publishing House.

_____ (1961). *Hindu Society at Crossroads*, London: Asia Pub. House.

_____ (1955). *Geographical Factors in Indian History*, Bombay: Bharatiya Vidya Bhavan.

_____ (1961). *The Determining Periods of Indian History*, Bombay: Bharatiya Vidya Bhavan.

_____ (1963). *The Foundations of New India*, London: Allen & Unwin.

_____ (1964). *Essential Features of India Culture*, Bombay: Bharatiya Vidya Bhavan.

Parel, Anthony J. (ed.) (1997). *Hind Swaraj and Other Writings*, Cambridge: Cambridge UP.

Patnaik, Utsa (ed.) (1990). *Agrarian Relations and Accumulation: The 'Mode of Production' Debate in India*, Bombay: Oxford UP.

Philips, C. H. (ed.) (1962). *The Evolution of India and Pakistan 1858–1974*, Selected Documents. London, New York, Toronto: Oxford UP.

Prakash, Indra (1938). *A Review of the History and Work of the Hindu Mahasabha and the Hindu Sanghatan Movement*, New Delhi.

Prasad, Shiva (1873). *History of Hindustan*, II, Allahabad.

Purani, A. B. (1959). *Evening Talks with Sri Aurobindo*, Pondicherry: Sri Aurobindo Ashram Trust.

Qaisar, Ahsan Jan (1982). *The Indian Response to European Technology and Culture* (AD 1498–1707), Delhi: Oxford UP.

Ranade, Mahadev Govind (1906). *Essays on Indian Economics*, Madras: Natesan; 3rd ed. Madras: G. A. Natesan, 1920; also: Bombay: Thacker and Co., 1896.

_____ (1902). *Religious and Social Reform: A Collection of Essays and Speeches by Mahadeva Govind Ranade*, ed. M. B. Kolaskar, Bombay: Narayan.

_____ (1915). *The Miscellaneous Writings*, ed. Ramabai Ranade, Poona: Ramabai Ranade (New Delhi : Sahitya Akademi, 1992).

Rao, R. V. Ramachandrasekhara (ed.) (1969). *Indian Unity: A Symposium*, New Delhi: Publications Division, Government of India.

Ray, N. R. (ed.) (1980–1984). *Sources of the History of India*, 4 Vols, Calcutta: Institute of Historical Studies.

Redfield, Robert (1962). *The Little Community, and Peasant Society and Culture*, Chicago: University of Chicago Press.

Reisner, Igor Mikhailovich (1932). *Essays on the Class Struggle in India*.

Richards, Glyn (ed.) (1985). *A Source-Book of Modern Hinduism*, London: Curzon Press.

Risley, Herbert Hope (1891). *The Tribes and Castes of Bengal*, 2 Vols, Calcutta: The Bengal Secretariat Press.

Roy, Manabendra Nath (1964). *Memoirs*, Bombay: Allied Publishers.

_____ (1983). *Fascism: Its Philosophy, Professions and Practices*, Calcutta.

296   Historical Thinking in South Asia

Roy, Manabendra Nath (1987). *Selected Works of M. N. Roy*, ed. Sibnarayan Ray, Delhi: Oxford UP.

Roy, Rammohun (1906). *The English Works of Raja Rammohun Roy*, ed. Jogendra Chunder Ghose, Allahabad: The Panini Office.

_____ (1945–58). *The English Works of Rammohan Roy*, 6 Vols, ed. Kalidas Nag and Debajyoti Burman, Calcutta: Sadharan Brahmo Samaj.

_____ (1999). *The Essential Writings of Raja Rammohun Roy*, ed. Bruce Carlisle Robertson, Delhi: Oxford UP.

Sarkar, Jadunath (1988). *Fall of the Mughal Empire*, 4 Vols, 4th ed., New Delhi: Orient Longman; 1st pub. 1932.

Sarkar, Sumit (1983). *Modern India 1885–1947*, Madras: Macmillan.

Savarkar, Vinayak Damodar (1946). *Joseph Mazzini* (Atmacharitra Ani Raikaran), Pune: Vheenus Book Stall.

Schlözer, August Ludwig (1797). *Kritisch-historische NebenStunden*, Göttingen: Vandenhoeck und Ruprecht.

Sen, Amartya (1973). *On Economic Inequality*, New Delhi: Oxford UP.

_____ (1984). *Resources, Values and Development*, Oxford: Blackwell/Cambridge: Harvard UP.

_____ and Drèze, Jean (1995) *India: Economic Development and Social Opportunity*, Delhi: Oxford UP.

_____ and Drèze, Jean (eds) (1996). *Indian Development: Selected Regional Perspectives*, Delhi: Oxford UP.

Sen, Siba Pada (ed.) (1978–80). *Sources of the History of India*, 3 Vols, Calcutta: Institute of Historical Studies.

Sharma, Ram Sharan (1965). *Indian Feudalism: c300–1200 AD*, Calcutta: Calcutta UP.

_____ (1977). *Ancient India*, New Delhi: Eurasia Publishing House.

Shiva, Vandana (1988). *Staying Alive: Women, Ecology and Survival in India*, New Delhi: Kali for Women.

Sircar, D. C. (ed.) (1966). *Land System and Feudalism in Ancient India*, Calcutta: Calcutta UP.

Srinivas, M. N. (1952). *Religion and Society Among the Coorgs*, Oxford: Clarendon Press.

_____ (1972). *Social Change in Modern India*, Hyderabad: Orient Longman; 1st pub. Berkeley: University of California Press, 1966.

_____ (1989). *The Cohesive Role of Sanskritization and Other Essays*, Delhi: Oxford UP.

Stewart, Charles (1813). *The History of Bengal*, London.

Tagore, Rabindranath (1939–65). *Rabindra Rachanavali*, Calcutta: Vishva Bharati.

_____ (1980). *Lectures and Addresses*, selected from the Speeches of the Poet by Anthony X. Soares, Delhi: Macmillan.

Thapar, Romila (1961). *Ashoka and the Decline of the Mauryas*, London: Oxford UP.

_____ (1984). *From Lineage to State: Social Formations in the mid-First Millenium B. C. in the Ganga Valley*, Delhi: Oxford UP.

Tilak, B. G. (1893). *Orion or Researches into the Antiquity of the Vedas*, Bombay: Mrs. Rádhábdi Atmarám Sagoon.

_____ (1903). *The Arctic Home in the Vedas*, Poona: Kesari.

_____ (1919). *His Writings and Speeches*, enlarged ed., Madras; 3rd ed., Madras: Ganesh & Co., 1922.

Valangkar, G. P. (1888). *Vinanti Patra*, Bombay.

Verma, Nirmal (1989). *Word and Memory*, Bikaner: Vagdevi Prakashan.

Vidyasagar, Iswar Chandra (1848). *Banglar Itihasa* (History of Bengal).

Vivekananda (1989). *The Complete Works of Swami Vivekananda*, Calcutta: Advaita Ashrama. (Quoted: *CW*)

Weber, Max (1958). *The Religion of India*, Glencoe, Ill.: Free Press.

_____ (1963). *The Sociology of Religion*, Boston: Beacon Press.

STUDIES ON HISTORICAL THINKING IN MODERN SOUTH ASIA

Adam, Ian and Tiffin, Helen (eds) (1991). *Past—The Last Post: Theorizing Post-Colonialism and Post-Modernism*, New York: Harvester Wheatsheaf.

Ahmad, Aijaz (1991). 'Between Orientalism and Historicism: Anthropological Knowledge of India', *Studies in History* 7, 135–63.

_____ (1994). *In Theory: Classes, Nations, Literatures*, Delhi: Oxford UP.

Ahmad, Aziz (1967). *Islamic Modernism in India and Pakistan*, Oxford: Oxford UP.

Ahmed, Rafiuddin (1981). *The Bengal Muslims, 1871–1906: A Quest for Identity*, Delhi: Oxford UP.

Amin, Shahid (1995). *Event, Metaphor, Memory: Chauri Chaura 1922–1992*, Delhi: Oxford UP.

Anand, Sugam (1991). *Modern Indian Historiography: From Pillai to Azad*, Agra: MG Publishers.

Anderson, Benedict (1991). *Imagined Communities: Reflections on the Origin and Spread of Nationalism*, revised and enlarged ed., London/New York; 1st pub. 1983.

Aonshuman, Ashok (1992). *Nation Building in a Colonial Society: The Historiographical Responses, 1900–1930*, Patna: Janaki Prakashan.

Apffel-Marglin, Frédérique and Marglin, Stephen A. (eds) (1996). *Decolonizing Knowledge: From Development to Dialogue*, Oxford: Clarendon Press.

Apter, David E. (1987). *Rethinking Development: Modernization, Dependency, and Postmodern Politics*, New Delhi: Sage.

Assmann, Jan (1999). *Das kulturelle Gedächtnis*, 2nd ed., München: Beck.

Asthana, Pratima (1992). *The Indian View of History*, Agra: MG Publishers.

Aziz, Khurshid Kamal (1969). *Some Problems of Research in Modern History*, Rawalpindi.

Bajaj, Satish K. (1998). *Recent Trends in Historiography*, New Delhi: Anmol Publications.

Ballhatchet, Kenneth (1984). 'The Rewriting of South Asian History by South Asian Historians after 1947', *Asian Affairs* (London) XV, 27–38.

Balslev, Anindita Niyogi (1986). 'Reflections on Time in Indian Philosophy: With Comments on So-Called Cyclic Time', in *Time, Science, and Society in China and the West: The Study of Time*, eds J. T. Fraser, N. Lawrence, and F. C. Haber Amherst: University of Massachusetts Press, 104–12.

Banerjee, Tarasankar (1977). *S. K. M. Panikkar: The Profile of a Historian: A Study in Modern Historiography*, Calcutta: Ratna Prakashan.

———— (ed.) (1987). *Historiography in Modern Indian Language 1800–1947*, Calcutta: Naya Prokash.

———— (ed.) (1987). *Indian Historical Research Since Independence*, Calcutta: Naya Prokash.

Banthiya, Ruchi (1994). *From Historicity to Postmodernity: A Case of South Asia*, Jaipur, New Delhi: Rawat Publications.

Barlingay, S. S. (1984). L'historie, l'être historique et l'historiographie', in *Histoire et diversité des cultures: Etudes préparés pour L'UNESCO*, Paris, 193–213.

Basham, A. L. (1959). 'Der indische Subkontinent in historischer Perspektive', *Saeculum* 10, 196–207.

Basu, Kaushik and Subrahmanyam, Sanjay (eds) (1996). *Unravelling the Nation: Sectarian Conflict and India's Secular Identity*, New Delhi: Penguin.

Bayly, C. A. (1979). 'English Language Historiography on British Expansion and Indian Reactions since 1940', in *Reappraisals in Overseas History*, eds P. C. Emmer and H. L. Wesseling, Leiden: Brill, 21–53.

———— (1996). *Empire and Information: Intelligence Gathering and Social Communication in India, 1780–1870*, Cambridge: Cambridge UP.

Berger, Peter L., Berger, Brigitte, and Kellner, Hansfried (1975). *Das Unbehagen in der Modernität*, Frankfurt/M. (English: *The Homeless Mind: Modernization and Consciousness*, New York: Vintage Books, 1973)

Bhalla, Alok and Chandra, Sudhir (eds) (1993). *Indian Responses to Colonialism in the 19th Century*, New Delhi: Sterling.

Bharati, Agehananda (1970). 'The Hindu Renaissance and its Apologetic Patterns', *Journal of Asian Studies* 29, 267–87.

Bhargava, Rajeev (2000). 'History, Nation and Community: Reflections on Nationalist Historiography of India and Pakistan', *Economic and Political Weekly*, 22 Jan, 193–200.

Bhattacharya, Sabyasachi (1982). 'Paradigms Lost: Notes on Social History in India', *Economic and Political Weekly* XVII, April, 690–6.

———— (1983). 'History from Below', *Social Scientist* 119, April, 3–20.

———— and Thapar, Romila (eds) (1986). *Situating Indian History: For Sarvepalli Gopal*, New Delhi: Oxford UP.

Bhattacharyya, N. N. (1996). *Indian Religious Historiography*, Vol. 1, New Delhi: Munshiram Manoharlal.

Biwas, S. C. (ed.) (1968). *Gandhi: Theory and Practice: Social Impact and Contemporary Relevance: Proceedings of a Seminar*, Shimla.

Borden, Carla M. (ed.) (1989). *Contemporary India: Essays on the Uses of Tradition*, Delhi: Oxford UP.

Borsa, Giorgio (1994). 'L'India moderna nella storiografia britannica e in quella nazionalista indiana', in idem, *Europa e Asia tra modernità e tradizione*, Milano: FrancoAngeli, 97–133.

Borsa, Giorgio and Beonio-Brocchieri, P. (eds) (1984). *Garibaldi, Mazzini e il Risorgimento nel Risveglio dell'Asia e dell'Africa*, Milano: FrancoAngeli.

Breckenridge, Carol A. and Veer, Peter van der (eds) (1993). *Orientalism and the Postcolonial Predicament: Perspectives on South Asia*, Philadelphia: University of Pennsylvania Press.

Brown, Donald E. (1988). *Hierarchy, History, and Human Nature*, Tucson: University of Arizona Press.

Carrère d'Encausse, Hélène and Schramm, Stuart R. (1989). *Marxism and Asia*, London: Allen Lane.

Carrier, James G. (ed.) (1995). *Occidentalism: Images of the West*, Oxford: Clarendon Press.

Chakrabarti, Dilip K. (1997). *Colonial Indology: Socio-Politics of the Indian Past*, New Delhi: Munshiram Manoharlal.

Chakrabarti, Kunal (1992). 'Anthropological Models of Cultural Interaction and the Study of Religious Process', *Studies in History* 8:1, n.s., 123–49.

Chakrabarty, Dipesh (1989). *Rethinking Working-Class History: Bengal 1890–1940*, Delhi: Oxford UP.

―――― (1991). 'History as Critique and Critique(s) of History', *Economic and Political Weekly*, 14 September, 2162–6.

―――― (1992). 'Post-Coloniality and the Artifice of History: Who Speaks for the "Indian" Pasts?', *Representations* 37, Winter, 1–26.

―――― (2000). *Provincializing Europe: Postcolonial Thought and Historical Difference*, Princeton: Princeton UP.

Chakravarty, Amiya (1952). *Nehru Looks at History*, New York.

Chambers, Ian and Curti, Lidia (eds) (1996). *The Post-Colonial Question: Common Skies, Divided Horizons*, London/New York: Routledge.

Chanana, Karuna (ed.) (1988). *Socialisation, Education and Women: Explorations in Gender Identity*, New Delhi: Orient Longman.

Chandra, Bipan (1966). *The Rise and Growth of Economic Nationalism in India: Economic Policies of Indian National Leadership, 1880–1905*, New Delhi: People's Publishing House.

―――― (1984). *Communalism in Modern India*, New Delhi: Vikas.

―――― (1986). 'Nationalist Historians' Interpretations of the Indian National Movement', in Bhattacharya and Thapar 1986, 194–238.

―――― (1993). *Essays on Indian Nationalism*, New Delhi: Har-Anand Publications.

Chandra, Pratap (1977). *The Hindu Mind*, Shimla: Indian Institute of Advanced Study.

Chandra, Satish (1996). *Historiography, Religion and the State in Medieval India*, New Delhi: Har-Anand Publications.

Chandra, Sudhir (1992). *The Oppressive Present: Literature and Social Consciousness in Colonial India*, Delhi: Oxford UP.

Chatterjee, Bhabatosh (ed.) (1994). *Bankimchandra Chatterjee: Essays in Perspective*, New Delhi: Sahitya Akademi.

Chatterjee, Partha (1994). 'Claims on the Past: The Genealogy of Modern Historiography in Bengal'. *Subaltern Studies* VIII (Essays in Honour of Ranajit Guha), Delhi: Oxford UP, 1–49.

―――― (1995). *The Nation and its Fragments: Colonial and Postcolonial Histories*, Delhi: Oxford UP; 1st pub. Princeton 1993.

―――― (1996). *Nationalist Thought and the Colonial World: A Derivative Discourse?*, Delhi; 1st pub. London: Zed Books, 1986.

Chatterji, Joya (1995). *Bengal Divided: Hindu Communalism and Partition 1932–1947*, New Delhi: Foundation Books/Cambridge UP.

Chatterji, P. C. (ed.) (1989). *Self-Images, Identity and Nationality*, Shimla: Indian Institute of Advanced Study/ Allied Publishers.

Chattopadhyaya, Brajadulal (1998). *Representing the Other? Sanskrit Sources and the Muslims*, Delhi: Manohar.

―――― 'Cultural Plurality, Contending Memories and Concerns of Comparative History: Historiography and Pedagogy in Contemporary India', forthcoming in *Historical Cultures*, ed. Jörn Rüsen, Michael Gottlob, and Achim Mittag, New York/Oxford: Berghahn Books.

Chattopadhyaya, D. P. (1976). *History, Society, and Polity: Integral Sociology of Sri Aurobindo*, Madras: Macmillan.

Chaudhary, Vijay Chandra Prasad (1977). *Secularism Versus Communalism: An Anatomy of the National Debate on Five Controversial History Books*, Patna: Navdhara Samiti.

Chaudhuri, Nirad C. (1974). *Scholar Extraordinary: The Life of Friedrich Max Müller*, Delhi: Orient Paperbacks.

Chaudhuri, Sashi Bhusan (1965). *Theories of the Indian Mutiny (1857–59): A Study of the Views of an Eminent Historian on the Subject*, Calcutta: World Press.

_____ (1979). *English Historical Writings on the Indian Mutiny: 1857–59*, Calcutta: World Press.

Chowdhury, Indira (1998). *The Frail Hero and Virile History: Gender and the Politics of Culture in Colonial Bengal*, Delhi/New York: Oxford UP.

Cohn, Bernhard S. (1987). *An Anthropologist among the Historians and Other Essays*, Delhi: Oxford UP.

_____ (1998). 'The Past in the Present: India as Museum of Mankind', *History and Anthropology* 11:1, 1–38.

_____ (1997). *Colonialism and its Forms of Knowledge: The British in India*, Delhi: Oxford UP.

Copland, Ian (1998). 'Indian Historiography—Colonial Period', in Woolf 1998, 458–61.

Correia-Afonso, John (ed.) (1979). *Historical Research in India*, New Delhi: Munshiram Manoharlal.

Crane, Ralph J. (1992). *Inventing India: A History of India in English-Language Fiction*, London: Macmillan/New York: St. Martin's Press.

Crane, Robert I. (ed.) (1970). *Transition in South Asia: Problems of Modernization*, Durham, N. C.: Duke University.

Crook, Nigel (1996). *The Transmission of Knowledge in South Asia: Essays on Education, Religion, History and Politics*, Delhi: Oxford UP.

Dalmia, Vasudha (1997). *The Nationalization of Hindu Traditions: Bharatendu Harishchandra and Nineteenth-century Banaras*, Delhi: Oxford UP.

_____ and Stietencron, Heinrich von (eds) (1995). *Representing Hinduism: The Construction of Religious Traditions and National Identity*, New Delhi: Sage.

Das, Veena (ed.) (1990). *Mirrors of Violence: Communities, Riots and Survivors in South Asia*, Delhi: Oxford UP.

Dasgupta, K. K. (1976). *Indian Historiography and Rajendralal Mitra*, Calcutta.

Dasgupta, Tapati (1993). *Social Thought of Rabindranath Tagore: A Historical Analysis*, New Delhi: Abhinav Publications.

Datta, Bhagavat (1954). *Western Indologists: A Study in Motives*, Delhi: Itihas Prakashana-Mandal.

De Souza, J. P. and Kulkarni, C. M. (eds) (1972). *Historiography in Indian Languages* (Dr. G. M. Moraes Felicitation Volume), Delhi: Oriental Publishers.

De, Barun (1977). 'A Historiographical Critique of Renaissance Analogues for Nineteenth Century India', in idem (ed.), *Perspectives in Social Sciences*, I (Historical Dimensions), Calcutta: Oxford UP, 178–218.

_____ (1989). 'Problems of the Study of Indian History. With Particular Reference to Interpretations of the 18th Century', *Proceedings of the Indian History Congress, 49th Session*, Dharwad, 1–56.

Desai, A. R. (1946). *Social Background of Indian Nationalism*, Bombay: Popular Prakashan, Oxford University Press 1948

Devahuti, D. (ed.) (1979). *Problems of Indian Historiography*, Delhi: D. K. Publications.

_____ (ed.) (1980). *Bias in Indian Historiography*, Delhi: D. K. Publications.

_____ (ed.) (1982). *Historical and Political Perspectives*, New Delhi: Books and Books.

Devaraja, N. K. (1975). *Hinduism and the Modern Age*, New Delhi: Islam and Modern Age Society.

Dhillon, Pradeep Ajit (1994). *Multiple Identities: A Phenomenology of Multicultural Communication*, Frankfurt/M.: P. Lang.

Diouf, Mamadou (ed.) (1999). *L'historiographie indienne en débat: Colonialisme, nationalisme et sociétés postcoloniales*, Paris/Amsterdam: Éditions Karthala/South-South Exchange Programme for Research on History of Development, SEPHIS.

Dirks, Nicholas B. (ed.) (1992). *Colonialism and Culture*, Ann Arbor: The University of Michigan Press.

Elst, Koenraad (1992). *Negationism in India: Concealing the Record of Islam*, New Delhi: Voice of India.

Embree, Ainslie T. (1988). *India's Search for National Identity*, 2nd ed., Delhi: Chanakya Publications.

_____ and Gluck, Carol (eds) (1997). *Asia in Western and World History: A Guide for Teaching*, Armonk, London.

Fabian, Johannes (1983). *Time and the Other: How Anthropology Makes its Object*, New York: Columbia UP.

Forbes, Geraldine (1996). *Women in Modern India* (The New Cambridge History of India, IV.2), Cambridge UP.

Frykenberg, Robert Eric (1996). *History and Belief: The Foundations of Historical Understanding*, Cambridge: Erdmans Publishing Company.

Fuchs, Eckhardt and Stuchtey, Benedikt (eds) (2002). *Across Cultural Borders: Historiography in a Global Perspective*, Lanham, Oxford: Rowman & Littlefield.

Fuchs, Martin (1999). *Kampf um Differenz: Repräsentation, Subjektivität und soziale Bewegungen: Das Beispiel Indien*, Frankfurt/M.: Suhrkamp.

Gadgil, Madhav (1985). 'Towards an Ecological History of India', *Economic and Political Weekly*, Special Issue, 1909–38.

Gaillard, Jacques, Krishna, V. V., Waast, Roland (eds) (1997). *Scientific Communities in the Developing World*, New Delhi: Sage.

Ganguly, B. N. (1965). *Dadabhai Naoroji and the Drain Theory*, Bombay: Asia Publishing House.

Gardet, Louis et al. (1976). *Cultures and Time*, Paris: UNESCO Press.

Gautier, François (1996). *Rewriting Indian History*, New Delhi: Vikas Publishing House.

Ghosh, J. C. (1948). *Bengali Literature*, London: Oxford UP.

Ghoshal, U. N. (1957). *Studies in Indian History and Culture*, revised ed. Calcutta: Orient Longmans; first published as: *The Beginnings of Indian Historiography and Other Essays*, Calcutta 1944.

Goel, Dharmendra (1967). *Philosophy of History*, Delhi.

———— (ed.) (1989). *Philosophy and Social Change*, Delhi: Ajanta Publications.

Gokhale, Balkrishna Govind (1961). *Indian Thought through the Ages: A Study of Some Dominant Concepts*, New York: Asia Pub. House.

———— (1977). 'Toward a Pattern of Indian History', in T. M. P. Mahadevan and Grace E. Cairns (eds), *Contemporary Indian Philosophers of History*, Calcutta: The World Press, 169–85.

Gopal, Sarvepalli (ed.) (1991). *Anatomy of a Confrontation: The Babri Masjid—Ramjanmabhumi Issue*, Delhi: Penguin.

Gordon, David C. (1971). *Self-Determination and History in the Third World*, Princeton/N.J.: Princeton UP.

Gordon, Leonard A. (1974). *Bengal: The Nationalist Movement 1876–1940*, Delhi: Manohar.

Gottlob, Michael (1995). 'Writing the History of Modern Indian Historiography: A Review Article'. *Storia della Storiografia* 27, 125–46.

———— (1997). 'Indische Geschichtswissenschaft und Kolonialismus', in Wolfgang Küttler, Jörn Rüsen, and Ernst Schulin (eds), *Geschichtsdiskurs*, Vol. IV (Krisenbewußtsein, Katastrophenerfahrungen und Innovationen 1880–1945), Frankfurt/M.: Fischer, 314–38.

Goyal, Shankar (1992). 'Political History: The Loss of Innocence', in G. C. Pande 1992, 290–9.

Green, William A. and Deasey Jnr., John P. (1985). 'Unifying Themes in the History of British India, 1757–1857: An Historiographical Analysis', *Albion* 17, 15–45.

Grewal, Jagtar Singh (1970). *Muslim Rule in India: The Assessment of British Historians*, Calcutta: Oxford UP.

———— (1975). *Medieval India: History and Historians*, Amritsar: Guru Nanak University.

Guha, Ranajit (1988). *An Indian Historiography of India: A Nineteenth-Century Agenda and its Implications*, Calcutta: K. P. Bagchi.

———— (1998). *Dominance without Hegemony: History and Power in Colonial India*, Delhi: Oxford UP.

Gunawardana, R. A. L. H. (1995). *Historiography in a Time of Ethnic Conflict: Construction of the Past in Contemporary Sri Lanka*, Colombo: Social Scientists' Association.

Gunderson, Warren (1970). *The World of the Babu: Rajendralal Mitra and Cultural Change in Modern India*, Ph.D. Diss., University of Chicago.

———— (1975). 'The Fate of Religion in Modern India: The Cases of Rammohan Ray and Debendranath Tagore', *Studies on Bengal* (East Lansing), 125–42.

Gungwu, Wang (1968–79). 'South and Southeast Asian Historiography', in Sills 1968–79, 420–8.

Gupta, Atulchandra (ed.) (1958). *Studies in the Bengal Renaissance: In Commemoration of the Birth Centenary of Bipinchandra Pal*, Calcutta.

Gupta, M. G. (1991). *Gandhism Redefined*, Agra: MG Publishers.

Habib, Irfan (1987). *Interpreting Indian History*, Shillong: North-Eastern University Publications.

———— (1995). *Essays in Indian History: Towards a Marxist Perception*, New Delhi: Tulika.

Halbfass, Wilhelm (1990). *India and Europe: An Essay in Philosophical Understanding*, Delhi: Motilal Banarsidass.

Hasan, Mushirul (ed.) (1981). *Communal and Pan-Islamic Trends in Colonial India*, Delhi: Manohar.

Hay, Stephen (1970). *Asian Ideas of East and West: Tagore and His Critics in Japan, China and India*, Cambridge/Mass.

Heehs, Peter (1994). 'Myth, History, and Theory', *History and Theory* 33, 1–19.

Heehs, Peter (1998). *Nationalism, Terrorism, Communalism: Essays in Modern Indian History*, Delhi: Oxford UP.

Heesterman, Jan C. (1985). *The Inner Conflict of Tradition: Essays in Indian Ritual, Kingship, and Society*, Chicago: University of Chicago Press.

Histoire et diversité des cultures: Etudes préparés pour L'UNESCO, Paris 1984.

Hobsbawm, Eric and Ranger, Terence (eds) (1983). *The Invention of Tradition*, Cambridge: Cambridge UP.

Inamdar, N. R. (ed.) (1983). *Political Thought and Leadership of Lokmanya Tilak*, New Delhi: Concept Publishing Company.

Inden, Ronald (1986). 'Orientalist Construction of India', *Modern Asian Studies* 20:3, 401–46.

_____ (1990). *Imagining India*, Oxford: Blackwell.

Irschick, Eugene F. (1986). *Tamil Revivalism in the 1930s*, Madras: Cre-A.

_____ (1994). *Dialogue and History: Constructing South India, 1795–1895*, Berkeley: University of California Press.

Iyengar, K. R. Srinivasa (1985). *Indian Writing in English*, 5th ed., New Delhi: Sterling; 1st pub. 1962.

Jeganathan, Pradeep and Ismail, Qadri (eds) (1995). *Unmaking the Nation: The Politics of Identity and History in Modern Sri Lanka*, Colombo: Social Scientists' Association.

Jones, Kenneth W. (1976). *Arya Dharm: Hindu Consciousness in 19th Century, Punjab*, Berkeley, Los Angeles, London: University of California Press.

_____ (1989). *Socio-Religious Reform Movements in British India* (The New Cambridge History of India, III.1), Cambridge.

Jordens, J. T. F. (1978). *Dayanand Saraswati: His Life and Ideas*, Delhi: Oxford UP.

_____ (1998). 'Dayanand Sarasvati's Concept of the Vedic Golden Age', in idem, *Dayananda Sarasvati: Essays on His Life and Ideas*, Delhi: Manohar, 64–76.

_____ (1998). *Dayananda Sarasvati: Essays on His Life and Ideas*, Delhi: Manohar.

Joshi, P. C. and Damodaran, K. (eds) (1975). *Marx Comes to India*, Delhi: Manohar.

Joshi, V. C. (ed.) (1975). *Rammohun Roy and the Process of Modernization in India*, Delhi: Vikas.

Juergensmeyer, Mark (1993). *The New Cold War? Religious Nationalism Confronts the Secular State*, Berkeley: University of California Press.

Kakar, Sudhir (1978). *The Inner World: A Psycho-analytic Study of Childhood and Society in India*, Delhi: Oxford UP.

Kantowsky, Detlef (1986). *Indien: Gesellschaft und Entwicklung*, Frankfurt/M.: Suhrkamp.

_____ (ed.) (1986a). *Recent Research on Max Weber's Studies on Hinduism*, München.

Kasturi, Leela and Mazumdar, Vina (eds) (1994). *Women and Indian Nationalism*, New Delhi: Vikas.

Kaviraj, Sudipta (1995). *The Unhappy Consciousness: Bankimchandra Chattopadhyay and the Formation of Nationalist Discourse in India*, Delhi: Oxford UP.

Kedourie, Elie (ed.) (1970). *Nationalism in Asia and Africa*, London.

Kejariwal, O. P. (1988). *The Asiatic Society of Bengal and the Discovery of India's Past 1784–1838*, Delhi: Oxford UP.

Khan, Shafa'at Ahmad (1939). *History and Historians of British India*, London/Allahabad: Kitabistan.

Klimkeit, Hans-Joachim (1971). *Anti-religiöse Bewegungen im modernen Südindien: Eine religionssoziologische Untersuchung zur Säkularisierungsfrage*, Bonn: Roehrscheid.

_____ (1981). *Der politische Hinduismus: Indische Denker zwischen religiöser Reform und politischem Erwachen*, Wiesbaden: Harrassowitz.

Kopf, David (1969). *British Orientalism and the Bengal Renaissance: The Dynamics of Indian Modernization, 1773–1835*, Berkeley, Los Angeles: University of California Press.

_____ (1979). *The Brahmo Samaj and the Shaping of the Modern Indian Mind*, Princeton: Princeton UP.

Kopf, David (with Farmer, Edward L. et al.) (1977). *Comprehensive History of Civilizations in Asia*, Reading, Mass.: Addison-Wesley Pub. Co.

Kothari, Rajni (1986). 'Contributions to Theory', in *A Survey of Research in Political Science, IV: Political Thought*, New Delhi: Indian Council of Social Science Research/Allied Publishers.

Krishnamurti, J. (ed.) (1989). *Women in Colonial India: Essays on Survival, Work and the State*, Delhi.

Kulkarni, S. G. (1982). 'Imperialism of Categories: Colonial Man in Search of a Cultural Identity', in B. Narsing Rao and Kadir Zaman (eds), *Modern Thought and Contemporary Literary Trends: A Felicitation Volume*, Hyderabad: Committee on Modern Thought and Contemporary Literary Trends, 33–44.

Kumar, Nita (ed.) (1994). *Women as Subjects: South Asian Histories*, New Delhi: Stree.

Kumar, Ravinder (ed.) (1984). *Philosophical Theory and Social Reality*, New Delhi: Allied Publishers.

Kurian, K. Mathew (ed.) (1975). *India—State and Society: A Marxian Approach*, Bombay: Orient Longman.

Küttler, Wolfgang, Rüsen, Jörn, and Schulin, Ernst (eds) (1997). *Geschichtsdiskurs*, III (Die Epoche der Historisierung), Frankfurt/M.: Fischer.

Lal, Vinay (ed.) (2000). *Dissenting Knowledges, Open Futures: The Multiple Selves and Strange Destinations of Ashis Nandy*, Delhi: Oxford UP.

Lalwani, Kastur Chand (1974). *Philosophy of Indian History*, Vol. 1 (The Burden of the Past), Calcutta: Minerva Associates.

Lannoy, Richard (1971). *The Speaking Tree: A Study of Indian Culture and Society*, London, Oxford, New York: Oxford UP.

Lelyveld, David (1996). *Aligarh's First Generation: Muslim Solidarity in British India*, Delhi: Oxford UP.

Leopold, Joan (1974). 'British Applications of the Aryan Theory of Race to India, 1850–1870', *English Historical Review* 89, 578–603.

Lohuizen de Leeuw, J. E. van (1970). 'India and its Cultural Empire', in *Orientalism and History*, ed. Denis Sinor, Bloomington: Indiana UP, 35–67; 1st pub. 1954.

Loomba, Ania and Kaul, Suvir (eds) (1994). *On India: Writing History, Culture, Post-Coloniality*, Oxford Literary Review, Special Issue 16.

Loomis, C. P. and Loomis, Z. K. (eds) (1969). *Socio-Economic Change and the Religious Factor in India: An Indian Symposium of Views on Max Weber*, New Delhi: Affiliated East-West Press.

Lorenzen, D. (1982). 'Imperialism and the Historiography of Ancient India', in *India—History and Thought: Essays in Honour of A. L. Basham*, ed. S. N. Mukherjee, Calcutta: Subarnarekha, 84–102.

Ludden, David (ed.) (1996). *Making India Hindu*, Delhi: Oxford UP.

Lütt, Jürgen (1970). *Hindu-Nationalismus in Uttar Pradesh*, Stuttgart: Klett.

MacKenzie, John M. (1995). *Orientalism: History, Theory and the Arts*, Manchester, New York: Manchester UP.

Madan, T. N. (1997). *Modern Myths, Locked Minds: Secularism and Fundamentalism in India*, Delhi: Oxford UP.

Mahadevan, T. M. P. and Cairns, Grace E. (eds) (1977). *Contemporary Indian Philosophy of History*, Calcutta: World Press.

Majeed, Javed (1992). *Ungoverned Imaginings: James Mill's* The History of British India *and Orientalism*, Oxford: Clarendon Press.

Majumdar, Romesh Chandra (1961). 'Nationalist Historians', in Philips 1961, 416–28.

——— (1970). *Historiography in Modern India*, London: Asia Publishing House.

Malik, Jamal (1994). 'The Making of a Council: The Nadwat al-Ulama', *Zeitung der Deutschen Morgenländischen Gesellschaft*, 144:1, 60–91.

——— (1997). *Islamische Gelehrtenkultur in Nordindien: Entwicklungsgeschichte und Tendenzen am Beispiel Lucknow*, Leiden: Brill.

Mall, Ram Adhar (1995). *Philosophie im Vergleich der Kulturen*, Darmstadt: Wissenschaftliche Buchgesellschaft.

Mani, Lata (1989). 'Contentious Traditions: The Debate on *Sati* in Colonial India', in Sangari and Vaid 1989, 88–126.

Marshall, Peter J. (1999). 'India: Since 1750', in Boyd 1999, 580–2.

——— and Williams, Glyndwr (1982). *The Great Map of Mankind: Perception of New Worlds in the Age of Enlightenment*, London: Dent.

Masselos, Jim (1998). 'Indian Historiography—Postcolonial', in Woolf 1998, 461–3.

Mathur, Laxman Prasad (1987). *Historiography and Historians of Modern India*, New Delhi: Inter-India Publications.

Matthes, Joachim (ed.) (1992). *Zwischen den Kulturen? Die Sozialwissenschaften vor dem Problem des Kulturvergleichs*, Soziale Welt, Special Issue 8), Göttingen.

Metcalf, Thomas R. (1995). *Ideologies of the Raj* (The New Cambridge History of India, III.4), New Delhi.

Mies, Maria (1969). 'Das indische Dilemma: Neo-Hinduismus, Modernismus und die Probleme der wirtschaftlichen Entwicklung', *Kölner Zeitschrift für Soziologie und Sozialpsychologie*, Special Issue 13, 163–81.

Miller, Robert J. (1966). 'Button, Button ... Great Tradition, Little Tradition, Whose Tradition?', *Anthropological Quarterly* 39, 26–42.

Mitra, Subrata K. (1999). *Culture and Rationality: The Politics of Social Change in Post-colonial India*, New Delhi: Sage.

———— and Lewis, R. Alison (eds) (1996). *Subnational Movements in South Asia*, Oxford: Westview Press.

Mittal, S. C. (1995–8). *India Distorted: A Study of British Historians on India*, 3 Vols, New Delhi: MD Publications.

Mitter, Partha (1994). *Art and Nationalism in Colonial India, 1850–1922*, Cambridge: Cambridge UP.

Mohantry, Satya P. (1998). *Literary Theory and the Claims of History: Postmodernism, Objectivity, Multicultural Politics*, Delhi: Oxford UP.

Mohanty, Jitendra Nath (1992). *Reason and Tradition in Indian Thought: An Essay on the Nature of Indian Philosophical Thinking.* Oxford: Clarendon Press.

———— (1993). *Essays on Indian Philosophy, Traditional and Modern*, ed. Purushottama Bilimoria, Delhi: Oxford UP.

Mookerjee, Ajit (1988). *Kali: The Feminine Force*, New York: Destiny Books.

Moore, Robin J. (ed.) (1979). *Tradition and Politics in South Asia*, New Delhi: Vikas Publishing House.

Morearty, John (1975). 'The Two-Edged Word: The Treacherousness of Symbolic Transformation: Rammohan Roy, Debendranath, Vivekananda and "The Indian Golden Age"', *Studies on Bengal* (East Lansing), 85–105.

Morris, Morris David (1969). *Indian Economy in the Nineteenth Century: A Symposium*, Delhi: Indian Economic and Social History Association.

Mukherjee, Kedar Nath (1982). *Political Philosophy of Rabindranath Tagore*, New Delhi: S. Chand & Co.

Mukherjee, Meenakshi (1985). *Realism and Reality: The Novel and Society in India*, Delhi: Oxford UP.

Mukherjee, Rudrangshu (1988–9). 'Recent Trends in the Writing of Modern Indian History', *Calcutta Historical Journal* 13, 138–56.

Mukherjee, S. N. (1968). *Sir William Jones: A Study in Eighteenth-Century British Attitudes to India*, Cambridge: Cambridge UP.

———— (ed.) (1982). *India, History and Thought: Essays in Honour of A. L. Basham*, Calcutta: Subarnarekha.

———— (1996). *Citizen Historian: Explorations in Historiography*, New Delhi: Manohar.

Mukhia, Harbans (ed.) (1999). *The Feudalism Debate*, New Delhi: Manohar.

Mukhopadhyay, Amal Kumar (ed.) (1979). *The Bengali Intellectual Tradition from Rammohun Ray to Dinendranath Sen*, Calcutta: K. P. Bagchi & Company.

Mukhopadhyay, Subodh Kumar (1981). *Evolution of Historiography in Modern India, 1900–60: A Study of the Writing of Indian History by her Own Historians*, Calcutta, New Delhi: K. P. Bagchi.

Mundadan, A. M. (1971). 'Hindu and Christian Views of History', in Webster 1971, 67–94.

Murshid, Tazeen M. (1997). 'State, Nation, Identity: The Quest for Legitimacy in Bangladesh', *South Asia*, 20:2, 1–34.

Nakamura, Hajime (1964). *Ways of Thinking of Eastern Peoples: India, China, Tibet, Japan*, ed. Philip Wiener, Honolulu: University Press of Hawai.

Nandy, Ashis (1980a). *Alternative Sciences: Creativity and Authenticity in Two Indian Scientists*, New Delhi: Oxford UP.

———— (1980b). *At the Edge of Psychology: Essays in Politics and Culture* Delhi: Oxford UP; reprint 1990.

———— (1983). *The Intimate Enemy: Loss and Recovery of Self under Colonialism*, Delhi: Oxford UP.

———— (1987). *Traditions, Tyranny, and Utopias: Essays in the Politics of Awareness*, Delhi: Oxford UP.

———— (1994). *The Illegitimacy of Nationalism: Rabindranath Tagore and the Politics of Self*, Delhi: Oxford UP.

———— (1995). 'History's Forgotten Doubles', *History and Theory*', Theme Issue 34: World Historians and their Critics, ed. Philip Pomper, Richard H. Elphick, and Richard T. Vann, 44–66.

Nandy, Ashis, Sardar, Zia, and Davies, Merryl Wyn (1993). *Barbaric Others: Manifesto on Western Racism*, London: Pluto Press.

Nandy, Ashis, Trivedy, Shikha, Mayaram, Shail, and Yagnik, Achyut (1995). *Creating a Nationality: The Ramjanmabhumi Movement and Fear of the Self*, Delhi: Oxford UP.

Nikam, N. A. (1977). *Philosophy of Indian Culture: A Metaphysic of the Idea of History*, in Mahadevan and Cairns 1977, 265–77.

Oak, P. N. (1966). *Some Blunders of Indian Historical Research*, Delhi: Raj Art Press.

Oberoi, Harjot (1981). *Literature and Society: An Approach to the Novels of Bhai Vir Singh*, M. Phil. Dissertation, Jawaharlal Nehru University, New Delhi.

Oddie, Geoffrey A. (1994). '"Orientalism" and British Protestant Missionary Constructions of India in the Nineteenth Century', *South Asia* 17:2, 27–42.

O'Hanlon, Rosalind (1985). *Caste, Conflict and Ideology: Mahatma Jotirao Phule and Low Caste Protest in Nineteenth-Century Western India*, Cambridge: Cambridge UP.

O'Leary, Brendan (1989). *The Asiatic Mode of Production: Oriental Despotism, Historical Materialism and Indian History*, Oxford: Blackwell.

Omvedt, Gail (1995). *Dalit Visions: The Anti-Caste Movement and the Construction of an Indian Identity*, Hyderabad: Orient Longman.

Oommen, T. K. (ed.) (1997). *Citizenship and National Identity: From Colonialism to Globalism*, New Delhi: Sage.

Pande, Govind Chandra (1989). *The Meaning and Process of Culture: As Philosophy of History*, Allahabad: Raka Prakashan.

_____ (ed.) (1992). *Political History in a Changing World*, Jodhpur: Kusumanjali Prakashan.

Pandey, Gyanendra (1990). *The Construction of Communalism in Colonial North India*, Delhi: Oxford UP.

_____ (ed.) (1993). *Hindus and Others: The Question of Identity in India Today*, New Delhi: Penguin.

Pandian, Jacob (1995). *The Making of India and Indian Traditions*, Englewood Cliffs/N. J.: Prentice Hall.

Panikkar, K. N. (ed.) (1986). 'The Intellectual History of Colonial India: Some Historiographical and Conceptual Questions', in Bhattacharya and Thapar 1986, 403–33.

_____ (ed.) (1990). *Culture and Consciousness in Modern India: A Historical Perspective*, New Delhi: People's Publishing House.

_____ (ed.) (1991). *Communalism in India. History, Politics and Culture*, New Delhi: Manohar.

_____ (ed.) (1994). 'In Defence of 'Old' History', *Economic and Political Weekly*, 1 October, 2595–7.

_____ (ed.) (1995). 'Search for Alternatives: Meaning of the Past in Colonial India', in idem, *Culture, Ideology, Hegemony: Intellectuals and Social Consciousness in Colonial India*, New Delhi: Tulika, 108–22.

Panikkar, R. K. (1976). 'Time and History in the Tradition of India: Kala and Karma', in Gardet et al. 1976, 63–88.

Pantham, Thomas (1995). *Political Theories and Social Reconstruction: A Critical Survey of the Literature on India*, New Delhi: Sage.

_____ and Deutsch, Kenneth L. (eds) (1986). *Political Thought in Modern India*, New Delhi: Sage.

Paranjape, Makarand (1993). *Decolonization and Development: Hind Svaraj Revisioned*, New Delhi: Sage.

Parekh, Bhikhu (1989). *Colonialism, Tradition and Reform: An Analysis of Gandhi's Political Discourse*, New Delhi: Sage.

_____ and Pantham, Thomas (eds) (1987). *Political Discourse: Explorations in Indian and Western Political Thought*, New Delhi: Sage.

Parthasarathy, Malini (1993). 'Soft Hindutva and Nationalism', *Seminar* 411, 19–22.

Pawar, Kiran (1985). *Sir Jadu Nath Sarkar: A Profile in Historiography*, New Delhi: Books & Books.

Philips, Cyril Henry (ed.) (1961). *Historians of India, Pakistan, and Ceylon* (Historical Writing on the Peoples of Asia), London/New York/Toronto: Oxford UP.

Poddar, Arabinda (1977). *Renaissance in Bengal: Search for Identity*, Shimla: Indian Institute of Advanced Study.

Prakash, Buddha (1963). *The Modern Approach to History*, Delhi.

Prakash, Gyan (1990). 'Writing Post-Orientalist Histories of the Third World: Perspectives from Indian Historiography', *Comparative Studies in Society and History* 32, 383–408.

Prakash, Gyan (1992). 'Post-colonial Criticism and Indian Historiography', *Social Text* 31/32.

―――― (ed.) (1995). *After Colonialism: Imperial Histories and Postcolonial Displacements*, Princeton/N.J.

Prasad, Hari Shankar (ed.) (1992). *Time in Indian Philosophy: A Collection of Essays*, Delhi: Sri Satguru Publications.

Prasad, Nageshwar (ed.) (1985). *Hind Swaraj: A Fresh Look*, New Delhi: Gandhi Peace Foundation.

Problems of Historical Writing In India (Proceedings of the Seminar held at the India International Centre), New Delhi, 21–25 January 1963.

Rajaram, Navaratna S. (1995). *The Politics of History: Aryan Invasion Theory and the Subversion of Scholarship*, New Delhi: Voice of India.

Randeria, Shalini (1994). 'Hindu-Nationalismus: Aspekte eines Mehrheits-Ethnizismus', in Reinhart Kößler and Tilman Schiel (eds), *Nationalstaat und Ethnizität*, Frankfurt/M.: IKO-Verlag für Interkulturelle Kommunikation, 75–110.

Rao, M. S. A. (1979). *Social Movements and Social Transformation*, Delhi: Macmillan.

Ravindran, T. K. (1980). *Nehru's Idea of History*, New Delhi: Light & Life Publications.

Ray, Sibnarayan (1967). 'India: After Independence (Contemporary Indian Historiography)', *Journal of Contemporary History* 2, 125–40.

Reddy, V. Madhusudan (1966). *Sri Aurobindo's Philosophy of Evolution*, Hyderabad: Institute of Human Study.

Reddy, V. Madhusudan (1984). *Meta-History: The Unfoldment and Fulfilment of Human Destiny*, Hyderabad: Aurodarshan Trust.

Rothermund, Dietmar (1970). *The Phases of Indian Nationalism and Other Essays*, Bombay: Nachiketa Publications.

―――― (1975). 'Indiens Verhältnis zu seiner Geschichte', *Indo-Asia*, Heft 1, 41–50.

―――― (1989). 'Der Traditionalismus als Forschungsgegenstand für Historiker und Orientalisten', *Saeculum* 40, 142–8.

Rudolph, Lloyd I. and Hoeber-Rudolph, Susanne (1967). *The Modernity of Tradition: Political Development in India*, Chicago: University of Chicago Press.

Rudra, Ashok (1988). *Non-Eurocentric Marxism and Indian Society*, Calcutta: People's Book Society.

Rule, Pauline (1977). *The Pursuit of Progress: A Study of the Intellectual Development of Romesh Chunder Dutt, 1848–1888*, Calcutta: Editions Indian.

Rüsen, Jörn, Gottlob, Michael and Mittag, Achim (eds). *Historical Cultures*, New York/Oxford: Berghahn Books; forthcoming.

Saberwal, Satish (1986). 'Societal Designs in History: The West and India', in Bhattacharya and Thapar 1986, 434–63.

Said, Edward W. (1991). *Orientalism: Western Conceptions of the Orient*, London: Penguin Books; 1st pub. Routledge & Kegan Paul 1978.

Samartha, S. J. (1959). *The Hindu View of History, Classical and Modern*, Bangalore.

Sangari, Kumkum and Vaid, Sudesh (eds) (1989). *Recasting Women: Essays in Colonial History*, New Delhi: Kali for Women.

Sarkar, Sumit (1991). 'Many Worlds: The Construction of History in Modern India'. *Storia della storiografia* 19, 61–72.

―――― (1997). *Writing Social History*, Delhi: Oxford UP.

Saxena, N. C. (1981). 'Historiography of Communalism in India', in Hasan 1981, 165–77.

Schulin, Ernst (1958). *Die weltgeschichtliche Erfassung des Orients bei Hegel und Ranke*, Göttingen: Vandenhoeck und Ruprecht.

Schwartz, Michael B. (1989). 'Indian Untouchable Texts of Resistance: Symbolic Domination and Historical Knowledge', in Seneviratne 1989, 131–41.

Schwarz, Henry (1997). *Writing Cultural History in Colonial and Postcolonial India*, Philadelphia: University of Pennsylvania Press.

Sen, Asok (1977). *Iswar Chandra Vidyasagar and His Elusive Milestones*, Calcutta: Riddhi-India.

Sen, Prabodhchandra (1995). *Bengal: A Historiographical Quest*, Calcutta: K. P. Bagchi & Co.

Sen, Sachin (1947). *The Political Thought of Tagore*, Calcutta: General Printers & Publishers.

Sen, Siba Pada (ed.) (1973). *Historians and Historiography in Modern India*, Calcutta: Institute of Historical Studies.

Sen, Siba Pada (ed.) (1975). *History in Modern Indian Literature*, Calcutta: Institute of Historical Studies.

———— (ed.) (1977). *Historical Writings on the Nationalist Movement in India*, Calcutta: Institute of Historical Studies.

———— (ed.) (1979). *Historical Biography in Indian Literature*, Calcutta: Institute of Historical Studies.

Sen, Snigdha (1992). *The Historiography of the Indian Revolt of 1857*, Calcutta: Punthi-Pustak.

Seneviratne, H. L. (ed.) (1989). *Identity, Consciousness and the Past: The South Asian Scene*, Social Analysis: Journal of Cultural and Social Practice, Special Issue 25.

Seth, Sanjay (1995). *Marxist Theory and Nationalist Politics: The Case of Colonial India*, New Delhi: Sage Publications.

Shah, A. M., Baviskar, B. S., and Ramaswamy, E. A. (eds) (1996). *Social Structure and Change, I: Theory and Method-Evaluation of the Work of M. N. Srinivas*, New Delhi: Sage.

Sharma, A. (1974). 'The Notion of Cyclical Time in Hinduism', *Contributions to Asian Studies* 5, 26–35.

Sharma, B. S. (1965). *The Political Philosophy of M. N. Roy*, Delhi: National Pub. House.

———— (1966). *Light on Early Indian Society and Economy*, Bombay: Manaktala.

Sharma, Ram Sharan (1978). *In Defence of 'Ancient India'*, New Delhi: People's Publishing House.

———— (1983). *Perspectives in Social and Economic History of Early India*, New Delhi: Munshiram Manoharlal.

———— (ed.) (1986). *Survey of Research in Economic and Social History of India*, Delhi: Indian Council of Social Science Research.

———— (1992). *Communal History and Rama's Ayodhya*, 2nd ed., New Delhi: People's Publishing House.

———— (1996). *Aspects of Political Ideas and Institutions in Ancient India*, 4th revised ed., Delhi: Motilal Banarsidass.

Sharma, Ramesh Chandra, Singh, Atul Kumar, Anand, Sugam, Chaturvedi, Gyaneshwar, and Chaturvedi, Jayati (1991). *Historiography and Historians in India since Independence*, Agra: MG Publishers.

Sharma, Suresh (1994). *Tribal Identity and the Modern World*, New Delhi: Sage Publications.

———— (1995). 'Das Ende der Geschichte und das Credo der Moderne', in *Entwicklung mit menschlichem Antlitz: Die Dritte und die Erste Welt im Dialog*, ed. Klaus M. Leisinger and Vittorio Hösle, München: Beck, 56–70.

———— (1995). 'Savarkar's Quest for a Modern Hindu Consolidation', *Studies in Humanities and Social Sciences* 2, 189–215.

Sheth, D. L. 'Politics of Historical Sense Generation: The Case of India', forthcoming in *Historical Cultures*, ed. Jörn Rüsen, Michael Gottlob, and Achim Mittag, New York/Oxford: Berghahn Books.

Shils, Edward Albert (1961). *The Intellectual Between Tradition and Modernity: The Indian Situation*, Den Haag: Mouton.

Shourie, Arun (1998). *Eminent Historians: Their Technology, Their Line, Their Fraud*, Noida: ASA.

Shrimali, K. M. (ed.) (1996). *Indian Archaeology Since Independence*, Delhi.

Shukla, Hira Lal (1988). *Tribal History: A New Interpretation*, Delhi: B. R. Publishing Corporation.

Singer, Milton (1972). *When a Great Tradition Modernizes: An Anthropological Approach to Indian Civilization*, London: Pall Mall Press.

Singer, Wendy (1997). *Creating Histories: Oral Narratives and the Politics of History-making*, Delhi: Oxford UP.

Singh, Bhawani (1993). *Regionalism and Politics of Separatism in India*, Jaipur: Printwell.

Singh, Fauja (ed.) (1978). *Historians and Historiography of the Sikhs*, New Delhi.

Singh, M. P. and Mohan, Chandra (eds) (1994). *Regionalism and National Identity: Interdisciplinary Perspectives: Canada—India*, Delhi: Pragati.

Sinha, Mrinalini (1995). *Colonial Masculinity, the 'Manly Englishman' and the 'Effeminate Bengali' in the Late Nineteenth Century*, Manchester: Manchester UP.

Sinha, Ramesh Chandra Prasad (1978). *The Indian Autobiographies in English*, New Delhi: S. Chand.

Someswarananda (1986). *Vivekananda's Concept of History*, Calcutta: Dilip Chattopadhyay Samata Prokasani.

Sontheimer, Günther D. and Kulke, Hermann (eds) (1989). *Hinduism Reconsidered*, New Delhi: Manohar.

Srivastava, S. K. (1989). *Sir Jadunath Sarkar: The Historian at Work*, Delhi: Anamika Prakashan.

Stokes, Eric (1959). *The English Utilitarians and India*, Oxford: Clarendon Press.

Subrahmanian, N. (1988). *Tamilian Historiography*, Madurai: Ennes Publications.

———— (1989). *The Meaning of Indian History*, Madurai: Ennes.

Syed, A. (1984). *Pakistan: Islam, Politics and National Security*, Lahore.

Talageri, Shrikant G. (1993). *The Aryan Invasion Theory: A Reappraisal*, Delhi: Voice of India.

Thapar, Romila, Mukhia, Harbans, and Chandra, Bipan (1969). *Communalism and the Writing of Indian History*, Delhi: People's Publishing House.

Thapar, Romila (1978). *Ancient Indian Social History: Some Interpretations*, Hyderabad: Orient Longman.

_____ (1992). *Interpreting Early India*, New Delhi: Oxford UP.

_____ (ed.) (1995). *Recent Perspectives of Early Indian History*, Bombay: Popular Prakashan.

_____ (1996). *Time as a Metaphor of History: Early India*, Delhi: Oxford UP.

_____ 'The Search for a Historical Tradition: Early India', forthcoming in *Historical Cultures*, ed. Jörn Rüsen, Michael Gottlob, and Achim Mittag, New York/Oxford: Berghahn Books.

The East and the Meaning of History, Roma: Università Di Roma 'La Sapienza'/Bardi Editore, 1994.

Thomas, R. Murray (ed.) (1988). *Oriental Theories of Human Development: Scriptural and Popular Beliefs from Hinduism, Buddhism, Confucianism, Shinto, and Islam*, New York: P. Lang.

Tikekar, Shripad Ramachandra (1964). *On Historiography: A Study of Methods of Historical Research and Narration of Sir Jadunath Sarkar, G. S. Sardesai and P. K. Gode*, Bombay.

Tripathi, Amales (1973). *Vidyasagar: The Traditional Moderniser*, Calcutta: Orient Longman.

Trivedi, Harish and Mukherjee, Meenakshi (eds) (1996). *Interrogating Post-colonialism: Theory, Text and Context*, Shimla: Indian Institute of Advanced Study.

Troll, Christian W. (1978–9). *Sayyid Ahmad Khan: A Reinterpretation of Muslim Theology*, Oxford.

_____ (1982). *Islam in India: Studies and Commentaries*, Vol. 1, Delhi: Vikas.

Tucker, Richard (1977). *Ranade and the Roots of Indian Nationalism*, Bombay: Popular Prakashan.

Varma, Vishwanath Prasad (1960). *The Political Philosophy of Sri Aurobindo*, Bombay: Asia.

_____ (1967). *Modern Indian Political Thought*, 3rd ed., Agra.

Veer, Peter van der (1996). *Religious Nationalism: Hindus and Muslims in India*, Delhi: Oxford UP.

Viswanathan, Gauri (1989). *Masks of Conquest: Literary Study and British Rule in India*, New York: Columbia UP.

Warder, Antony Kennedy (1972). *An Introduction to Indian Historiography*, Bombay: Popular Prakashan.

Webster, John C. B. (ed.) (1971). *History and Contemporary India*, London: Asia Publishing House.

Wolf, Eric R. (1982). *Europe and the People without History*, Berkeley: University of California Press.

Wolff, Otto (1957). *Indiens Beitrag zum neuen Menschenbild*, Hamburg: Rowohlt.

Yapp, M. and Taylor, D. (ed.) (1977). *Political Identity in South Asia*, London.

Young, Richard Fox (1981). *Resistant Hinduism: Sanskrit Sources on Anti-Christian Apologetics in Early Nineteenth-Century India*, Vienna: Indological Institute, University of Vienna.

Young, Robert (1990). *White Mythologies: Writing History and the West*, London: Routledge.

Zelliot, Eleanor (1996). *From Untouchable to Dalit: Essays on the Ambedkar Movement*, New Delhi: Manohar.

Subject Index

The subject index lists general terms and concepts of historical thinking (no geographical indications, historical events, or works which are less relevant in this context). Supplementing the systematic (as well as chronological) arrangement of source material it helps pursue multiple research interests in the field of historical culture.

agency 2–3, 17–18, 20, 30–31, 33, 35, 36n, 41–2, 44, 46, 56, 62, 64, 67, 72n, 76n, 82–6, 139, 144n, 152–3, 272–3

ahistorical 3, 8–9, 11n, 32, 43, 74, 77, 81, 84, 91, 139, 252, 270–71

alienation 3, 22, 32, 42, 56, 59n, 62n, 66, 80, 114, 283

amnesia, forgetting, oblivion 2, 28, 34, 49n, 72n, 111, 143, 191–2, 258, 266, 279

arts, aesthetics 7, 15, 37n, 59, 66, 92, 94–5, 99, 101, 123, 130, 134–5, 197, 200, 207–8, 232

authenticity 2, 24, 30, 66n, 67, 70, 80, 93, 98, 142n, 219–20, 233, 236, 238, 240–41, 264

backwardness 8, 10, 12–13, 33, 39n, 46, 52, 54, 69n, 76–7, 182, 188, 191, 193–4, 221, 247

caste 41–3, 55n, 58, 61n, 65, 74, 78, 119–23, 143, 167–9, 175, 180, 200, 221, 244–5, 253–5

categories 19, 21, 23, 41n, 44n, 49, 55, 66–7, 71, 78, 80–81n, 82, 107, 125–6, 141n, 153, 219, 224–5, 269, 271

change 2–3, 10, 17, 19, 22–3, 29, 31–2, 38, 43–7, 50–55, 57–60, 63n, 64, 73–7, 79–80, 83, 87, 108n, 109, 114, 116, 120n, 124, 163, 167, 171–2, 178, 189–91, 195–7, 199, 204–7, 210–11, 213–14, 217, 220–21, 226–9, 238–9n, 244, 249–53, 258–61, 265–6; unchangeable, unchanging 47, 55, 114, 221–2

civilization 2, 4–9, 12, 28–9, 35, 38, 50n, 52, 58–9, 61, 68, 81n, 83, 93, 96–102, 114, 133, 135–7, 143, 155, 161–3, 177–8, 183, 190, 197–9, 201, 203, 208–9, 211–16, 224–5, 229, 231, 243, 257, 266–7, 270–71; civilizing mission 17n, 38, 48, 70n, 194

colonialism 1, 3, 9, 11–12, 29, 32, 38–9, 41, 44–50, 64, 66, 70n, 71, 73, 76–7, 80, 82–7, 104, 107, 125, 176, 183, 190, 212, 218–19, 234n, 243, 264, 268–70, 273–8; anti-colonial 39, 41, 51, 56, 82, 84, 141; postcolonial 1, 3, 64–5, 67, 74, 79, 81n, 83, 85–6, 104, 107; precolonial 1, 23n, 75

colonize, colonization 3, 8, 38, 41n, 76, 80–82, 86, 95, 128, 141n, 232, 264, 283; de-colonization 41n, 74, 82, 85n

classification 9n, 12, 55n, 58, 71n, 224–5, 274n

communalism 40, 57n, 69–72, 139–40, 147, 150, 156, 165, 219, 223, 232–5, 242–3, 252n

comparison, comparative history 6,

Author Index

This index lists authors both of source texts and secondary works of historical thinking in modern South Asia thus including historical research and writing and the reflection on it.